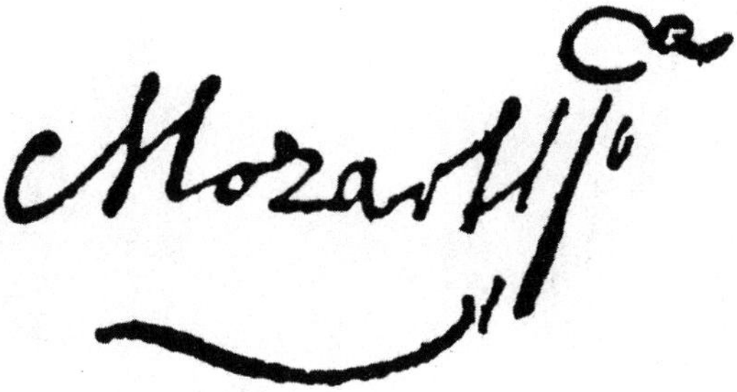
Mozart

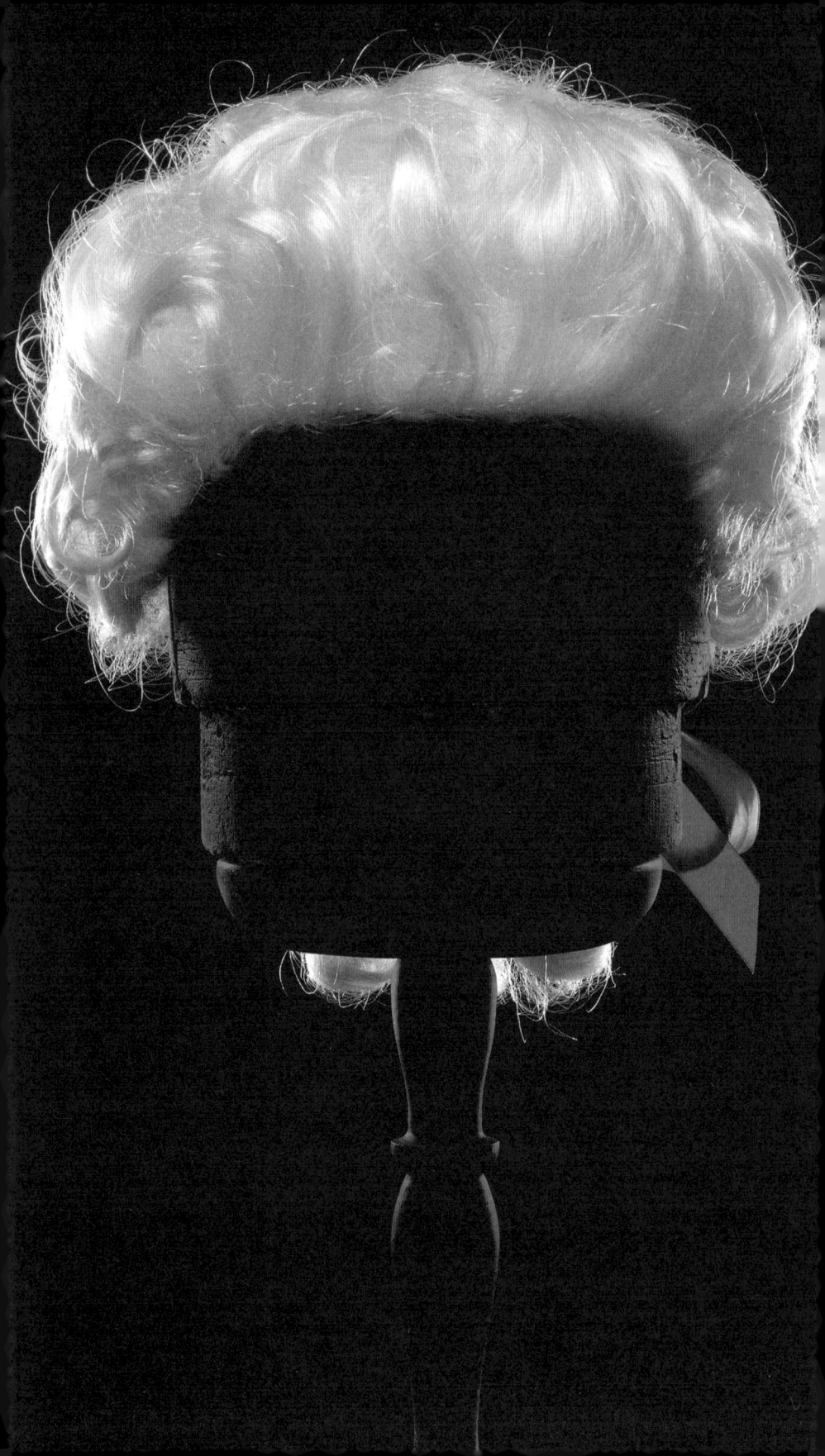

SEVEN
Mozart
LIBRETTOS

A Verse Translation by

J. D. McCLATCHY

W. W. NORTON & COMPANY

NEW YORK · LONDON

Photographs by Geoff Spear

For information about permission to reproduce selections from this book,
write to Permissions, W. W. Norton & Company, Inc.,
500 Fifth Avenue, New York, NY 10110

For information about special discounts for bulk purchases, please contact
W. W. Norton Special Sales at specialsales@wwnorton.com or 800-233-4830

Manufacturing by RR Donnelley, Harrisonburg, VA
Book design by Mark Melnick
Production manager: Anna Oler

Library of Congress Cataloging-in-Publication Data

Mozart, Wolfgang Amadeus, 1756–1791.
[Operas. Librettos. Polyglot. Selections.]
Seven Mozart librettos / a verse translation by J. D. McClatchy.
p. cm.
ISBN 978-0-393-06609-8 (hardcover)
1. Operas—Librettos. I. McClatchy, J. D., 1945– trl II. Title.
III. Title: 7 Mozart librettos. IV. Title: Mozart librettos.
ML49.M83O64 2011
782.1'0268—dc22
2010033400

W. W. Norton & Company, Inc.
500 Fifth Avenue, New York, N.Y. 10110
www.wwnorton.com

W. W. Norton & Company Ltd.
Castle House, 75/76 Wells Street, London W1T 3QT

1 2 3 4 5 6 7 8 9 0

For Peter Gelb

Contents

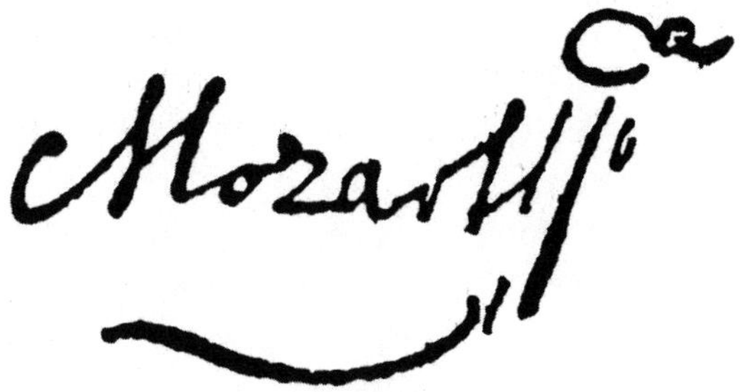
Mozart

⁓ Introduction ⁓

"OPERA COMES TO ME BEFORE EVERYTHING ELSE,"
Mozart once said. He wrote his first opera, *Apollo et Hyacinthus*,
in 1767, at the age of eleven, a "school drama" for the Salzburg
Gymnasium, with a libretto by a priest who taught there. Other
operas followed regularly in subsequent years—comedies and
dramas, *Singspiel* or *dramma per musica*, ten in all, with staid,
uninspiring librettos. The commissions came, the performances
went. His apprenticeship lasted just over a decade, until *Idomeneo* in 1781, an astonishing advance and his first triumph in the
opera house. He had just ten more years to live, and in that
decade he wrote seven of the most enduring operas in the history
of music. But why is Mozart's name on the cover of this book, and
not the five librettists who wrote the texts for these seven operas?
That only one of them—Lorenzo Da Ponte—achieved a lasting
fame is unimportant. The reason is that Mozart himself was the
dramatist of his operas. With the exception of *La Clemenza di
Tito* (which was revised to his specifications), Mozart himself
chose the librettos he wished to set, and worked closely with his
librettists to create an effective drama. Above all, it was his music
that shaped our sense of both plot and character. But this is not
a book about his music. It is a book of translations, intended to
give the reader a sense of what Mozart was working with, the
better to appreciate his astonishing achievement.

Translations of opera librettos these days are generally of
three kinds. First, and most ubiquitous, are supertitles. These

are meant to be telegraphic, to give an *impression* of what is being sung on stage. Concision is more crucial than accuracy. There is no depth or nuance, and the drama itself is sometimes jeopardized by information being given before it should. Hence the anger of a singer when an audience laughs before her joke has been delivered—because it had been read on the titles screen before she had a chance to make it. Some opera houses, in the interests of purity, project the entire libretto (plus translations, sometimes multiple), which often keeps the audiences glued to a text and not the stage. However necessary they have become in performance, titles remain a rather crude technology.

The other two kinds are printed, not projected. The most familiar is the standard booklet sold in opera shops or found in CD packages. In it the libretto is rendered into prose, fluent but flat, sometimes lineated but often not. The point is to give the reader a full sense of the text, of its characters and story, but not of the textures of the language in which the original is cast—textures crucial both to the composer's musical decisions and to the tone of the opera as it unfolds. There are, in addition, singing translations—and over the years, many of them have been made for the Mozart operas. These, of course, are more faithful to the rhymes and repetitions of the original, but the necessity of adapting the English to the score's notes and stresses too often results in a translation that can be nearly as incomprehensible as any other foreign language. *To yonder palace, dear Prince, we now must go, / Our hearts there forever to overflow.*

For this book I have tried to follow the original texts with both fidelity and imagination. Though the texts of each of these operas have stretches of prose, whether recitative or spoken dialogue, at the heart of each are arias and exchanges written in verse. The language at these points tightens into a stylized emotion—urgent or funny, quizzical or torn, tender or outraged—where Mozart crafted the most intimate portraits of his characters. Verse is the language of the heart talking to itself, and to its beloved. Verse has the advantage of both moving an emotion ahead and holding it back, of linking its stages of development by both reflection and anticipation. So, unlike most other translators, I have put into English verse what is verse in the original. I have followed the original's patterns of rhythm, rhyme, and imagery. (Naturally, there are places where this was—or seemed to me— impossible to duplicate exactly, and I was forced to stray into a more suitable solution. I have inevitably taken liberties, but they are rare, and in service to clarity and color.) The advantage of this edition is that the librettos in their original German or Italian are *en face*, so that the reader can see or study how passages were first put together. This is especially true for quick, interlocking exchanges of rhymed dialogue. But I didn't want merely a mirroring. A verse scheme can be rendered dull by its very fidelity. I tried too for a verse that, while celebrating its own self-consciousness, is something that people might actually think or say. The balance between the stylish and the natural is a precarious one, but that was the aim throughout. Only in this way can the effect of the text be felt. We see the text Mozart and his librettist shaped, what opportunities and challenges it presented the composer. Having the translations try to match the dexterity of the original also gives a clearer insight into the inner lives of characters—which is where Mozart lavished his art.

This book has an eerie symmetry. It begins and ends the same way, with an *opera seria* and a *Singspiel*. The two grandly serious operas, the early *Idomeneo* and the late *La Clemenza di Tito*, show an absolute mastery of the form, with a sure dramatic hand marshalling the allegories of power and mercy. The two comedies, though the later *Magic Flute* is obviously superior to the earlier *Abduction from the Seraglio*, again demonstrate Mozart's instinct to exploit his material for delicious theatrical effect, and also to show in the frivolous an unexpected depth. But between these two bookends are the three operas he wrote with Lorenzo Da Ponte, a collaboration now rightly considered to have been the greatest in opera history and the glory of Mozart's art.

There is a considerable variety to these texts, and though the voice of a single translator may iron out the wrinkles of individuality, I have tried to respond to each as a world of its own making. The *opera seria* librettos of Giovanni Battista Varesco (*Idomeneo*) and Caterino Mazzolà (*La Clemenza di Tito*) have considerable tension in their dramas of situation, while the florid arias that close each scene may have a more stately tone. At these moments, the opera stops while a character considers his place in its moral fable. Accordingly, the language of the translations will be more formal. The texts by Gottlieb Stephanie the Younger and Emanuel Schikaneder for the two *Singspiels* (*The Abduction from the Seraglio* and *The Magic Flute*, respectively) are, of course, broadly sketched. Comedy, even in opera, demands speed, crisis, a glimpsed tenderness, and a happy ending. Characters are usually—and appropriately—two-dimensional types. The librettos for both *The Abduction from the Seraglio* and *The Magic Flute* have been disparaged by high-minded critics (though never by audiences), yet each provides moments of surprising intensity, and *The Magic Flute* offers sublime astonishments.

The three librettos by Lorenzo Da Ponte—*The Marriage of Figaro, Don Giovanni*, and *Così Fan Tutte*—are by far the most celebrated, and the standards by which we finally judge Mozart as an opera composer. But they are also the reason why we count Da Ponte—along with Pietro Metastasio, Felice Romani, Arrigo Boito, and Hugo von Hofmannsthal—as one of the true poets of the opera theater. His texts fizz and sparkle where they need to, are introspective or ironic or melancholy when they must be. As does Mozart's music, their tone shifts quickly, often unexpectedly, the better to give a human complexity to the drama. In *Figaro*, for instance, the Countess's aria, "Dove sono," as famous an aria as exists in the whole repertory, is a poignant pause. Slowly she broods on what she has lost, what hopes her marriage has crushed. And yet, through the apparently resigned sadness there pulses both an anger at and a passion for the man she loathes and loves at once:

> Where are they now, the vanished days,
> The moments of pleasure's afterglow?
> Where are the vows, the murmured praise
> Spoken by that liar so long ago?
> Why, if sweetness turns to regret,
> If every hope becomes a grief,
> Why is it still I cannot forget
> The love that vies with disbelief?
> If only my waiting, my long endurance,
> The patience that true love imparts,
> Could bring the slightest reassurance
> Of changing his ungrateful heart!

A few scenes after this searing look into a woman's heart, Figaro delivers a cynical retort:

> Open wide your eyes,
> Avoid a sad surprise,
> Look out for women, men,
> See them as they are.
> Goddesses, so called!
> One day you will awaken,
> Rudely stunned and shaken
> By the whole canard.
> Enchantingly they sing
> A song that nags and mocks.
> A siren song they sing
> To drive us onto rocks.
> Owls can hypnotize
> And mice are easily caught.
> Comets tantalize,

Then blind us on the spot.
Roses boast of thorns,
One hears of vixens who charm,
Smiling cows with horns
And doves who do real harm,
Nymphs of voluptuous deceit,
Angels who hover to cheat,
First sigh to us, then lie,
Have no love left to buy,
Or pity by now to spare.
The rest I need not share.
Every man can testify.

And, correspondingly, this aria contains Figaro's attraction to what he is warning against. (What the verse cannot do is reproduce the horn call of cuckoldry that sounds at the aria's end—another layer of irony.) The libretto that holds two such contrasting emotional states in equilibrium is a challenge to the translator because his work lacks music's ability to distinguish and blend scenes. Set pieces succeed each other with little of the exposition we feel entitled to, and yet the score supplies a continuity that creates shape, momentum, and shading.

It must also be admitted that any translation is a shadow. English lacks some of German's grandeur and almost all of Italian's sonic beauty and ease of rhyming (one reason why it is the ideal tongue for operatic setting). But English has an unsurpassed range and expressivity, and an ability to capture an emotion at various exposures. Still, when confronted by a libretto, it must struggle with an especially difficult medium. The opera libretto is a literary genre of its own. It does not have the expansiveness of a play, or the subtlety of a poem. Its aim is simultaneously to create a compelling dramatic vehicle for the stage and vivid musical opportunities for the composer. The form can discourage psychological nuance and philosophical depth. The text has to be understood when delivered by operatic voices that often distort words in the interests of pure sound; and it has to be heard over a large orchestra, which can either accompany or compete. It is all about entrances and exits, and the language of the libretto seems constantly to be one of greetings and farewells. Yet with all these restricting conditions, the libretto is where every opera begins; its words elicit the music, and together they create a theatrical illusion of breathtaking proportions and heartbreaking effect. It starts with words, and I hope these new translations will give the reader a better sense of what first drew Mozart to them.

One problem with the existing translations of Mozart's operas is that, for all their earnestness or cleverness, often they don't really give you what the characters are actually saying in the original, or they distort the tone of delivery. Take the opening lines of *Don Giovanni*, with the Don's manservant Leporello impatiently waiting out in the dark while his master is enjoying a lady's favors inside. The Italian goes this way, in a kind of shivering staccato that emphasizes each syllable:

> Notte e giorno faticar
> per chi nulla sa gradir,
> piova e vento sopportar,
> mangiar male e mal dormir . . .

One of the more literal translations now in print translates this as

> I work hard day and night,
> And he never thanks me.
> I endure winds and rain,
> Poor food and little sleep.

Granted, that is the gist of Leporello's complaint, but hardly gives the flavor of his witty, if whiny, sense of life's unfairness. Even the amateur can hear in the original the tetrameter line with its *abab* rhyme scheme, and pick up the sense of parallel pairs of terms (*notte e giorno* [night and day], *piova e vento* [rain and wind]). When W. H. Auden and Chester Kallman translated the opera in 1957, they wisely took a freer hand, and observed the Italian's pattern of images and rhymes in a fluent English verse:

> On the go from morn till night,
> Running errands, never free,
> Hardly time to snatch a bite;
> This is not the life for me.

One appreciates the slang ("on the go," "snatch a bite") that adds color to the moment and allows the singer to elicit a smile from the audience. But, presumably in an effort to add some background and prepare for what is to come, the second and fourth lines here are entirely made up; and the problem is not that Leporello eats hurriedly, but that he eats badly. My own version tries to keep the verse scheme of the original as well as accurately carry over into English everything the Italian is saying, while still trying to brush up the character's grumbling personality:

> Always working, night and day,
> And not a word of gratitude.
> Wind and rain, come what may,
> Never a nap, and rotten food.

Let me offer another example. Some years ago I was asked to translate *The Magic Flute* for a new artist's book. When that edition appeared and came to the attention of stage director Julie Taymor, who was then directing a new production of the opera at the Metropolitan Opera, she asked if I would adapt my translation for the supertitles to be used on seatback screens. And when they proved successful, the Met then asked if I would create a singing translation in a shortened adaptation for holiday presentation. In the opera house and on television and DVD, that version has had a success of its own, and the English—along with Taymor's brilliant stage pictures, and performances of the highest caliber—have brought many new viewers, particularly young ones, into the magical world Mozart created. While I was working on these various versions, I was continually struck by the need to use English verse in a way to capture the charm of the German (Mozart's native language but one he used only for comic operas) but also to be convincing as human speech. This is true not only in the famous set pieces but in the give-and-take between characters. Looking back over older translations was sometimes dismaying. The standard English singing translation, used for years at the Met and elsewhere, was made by Ruth and Thomas Martin in 1941. At a point early in Act I, the birdcatcher Papageno has had a padlock put on his mouth when the Three Ladies caught him telling lies. Papageno turns to his new friend, the prince Tamino, and tries to get his help. Here is their exchange—and the moment of his release:

PAPAGENO: *(points sadly to the padlock on his mouth)*
Hm! hm! hm! hm! hm! hm! hm! hm!

TAMINO:
The poor young lad must surely suffer,
He tries to talk, but all in vain!

PAPAGENO:
Hm! hm! hm! hm! hm! hm! hm! hm!

TAMINO:
I can no help or comfort offer.
I wish I could relieve your pain.
(Enter the Three Ladies.)

FIRST LADY:
The Queen forgives you graciously.
(removes the padlock)
From punishment you shall be free.

PAPAGENO:

Oh, what joy again to chatter!

SECOND LADY:

Be truthful, and you will fare better!

PAPAGENO:

No lie shall ever come from me.

THE THREE LADIES:

This padlock shall your warning be!

In their 1955 translation, Auden and Kallman, having changed the order of scenes and fussily manipulated the opera's tone and ambitions, had Tamino say to Papageno instead:

His wits, by lack of words unwitty,
Express what he is sentenced to:
By words I can express my pity,
But that is all my words can do.

Neither version satisfies, either as verse or as speech. My Tamino first observes from a distance:

The poor man's punishment is plain.
His tongue is under lock and key.

Then he addresses his padlocked friend:

I sympathize but can't explain,
And have no power to set you free.

When the First Lady returns to remove the padlock, the scene continues:

FIRST LADY:

The Queen has heard your mumbled plea
And bids us lift her stern decree.

(She removes the padlock.)

PAPAGENO:

At last! Again! A chatterbox!

SECOND LADY:

Another lie, and double locks!

PAPAGENO:

I'll never tell another lie!

THE THREE LADIES:

This lock should warn you not to try!

Verse will always draw attention to itself, but it needs first of all to draw a reader into the scene and the character, and in ways that may astonish but must always convince. What sounds smart and chiseled in one era may sound stiff and contrived in the next. My own versions, which admire the classical restraint and technical virtuosity of the original texts, strive to appeal to contemporary ears, but to a pair that is familiar with the poet's task and with the great tradition of memorable verse. I want the reader to hear the verse, but listen to the drama.

If the seven operas gathered here have one thing in common, it is that each in its own way deals with the trials of love. The operas dramatize many kinds of love, of course—noble and base, romantic and paternal, frustrated and fulfilled. But in each opera, the central conflict is how to achieve true love. *True* can mean honest or lasting, strong or pure. The trials of love and their resolution go to the heart of Mozart's fascination with opera, and seem to have been close to the core of his being. One of the first biographies written of Mozart, by Franz Xaver Niemetschek, was published in 1798, just seven years after the composer's death. It is short, worshipful, and inaccurate. But it was written by a man who had met Mozart and many of his friends, and had the approval of his widow. That lends it a kind of intimacy that later, more authoritative volumes sometimes lack. In any case, Niemetschek's portrait of Mozart as a child is revealing. Many of the traits that dominated his personality as an adult are fully on display in the boy. When Mozart and his sister Nannerl, for instance, were paraded by their father as child prodigies before the courts of Europe and made to play, Niemetschek noted that even then the boy showed "his contempt for all praise from the nobility and a certain diffidence about playing to them, if they were not, at the same time, knowledgeable people. When compelled to do so nevertheless, he would play nothing but trivial pieces, dances, etc.—unimportant trifles. But when experts were present he was all fire and enthusiasm." Even as a six-year-old he knew his own worth, although that precocious self-awareness was shadowed always by a loneliness from which he sought constant relief but that seems to have haunted him to the end. How else could he feel, a child in a miniature court costume and wig, seated on a Queen's lap, surrounded by fat, powdered fawners?

This is why one detail in Niemetschek's account of Mozart's earliest years stands out. The boy and his older sister—the only two out of the family's seven children who survived—were from the start drilled in music by their cold, ambitious father. Harmony and song were in his ear before language—"music was the first word and idea which he comprehended." That, of course, we would expect. But when he was not at his lessons, when he and his sister were allowed to be with their friends and the adults were off with their own business, it was another matter. The assiduous, petulant little genius gave way to an individual altogether more vulnerable. "He entered into his childish playing," writes Niemetschek, "with a wholeheartedness which made him forget everything else, and love for those around him or for any who occupied themselves with him was his driving force; he asked all with whom he came in contact whether they loved him, and burst into tears if they jokingly denied it." How quickly the confidence at the keyboard collapses. The account continues: "In fact, even as a child and later as a boy he concentrated entirely on people and things of interest to him, and showed them the utter sincerity and warmth of feeling of which his gentle nature was capable. This trait in his character was typical of him when he grew up, and was often his undoing."

His undoing, presumably, because he did not pay close enough attention later to those who took advantage of him. But would it be fair to say that, at least insofar as his mature operas are concerned, this fascination with how people responded to him, this need to be loved, those tears in anticipation of rejection, also made him a great opera composer? Whatever it was—a deep, abiding sense of isolation and loneliness is what I suspect—it allowed him as a musician to respond to the characters and plots of librettos in a way that drove shafts of darkness through effervescent moments, that made uncertainty and disguise seem like necessary ordeals. He wanted to be loved, but stood apart, concentrated but aloof, capable of tears but listening to other people as notated voices in a score he was constantly revising.

Unfortunately, we have only scattered accounts of how Mozart actually worked on his operas. There are reports by singers and contemporaries; there are letters. If only we had detailed reports of his working relationship with Da Ponte, of the back-and-forth as their operas developed! But they were neighbors in Vienna while they collaborated, and there was no need for correspondence. Still, we have a vivid picture of how Mozart worked with one of his earlier librettists, Gottlieb Stephanie the Younger, a popular Viennese playwright. He and Mozart had never met, and Mozart's father acted as their intermediary. The letters Mozart wrote to his father about his progress on the opera's composition are a rare look inside his methods. It is 1781. The opera is *The Abduction from the Seraglio*, a comedy set in a Turkish harem and filled with intrigue and pratfalls. Even at the age of twenty-five, Mozart was a seasoned theatrical composer, and knew a good deal about the abilities of singers and the expectations of audiences. He knew too that comedy made special demands on the pace of things. *The Abduction* originally opened with a monologue by Belmonte, but Mozart insists that Stephanie make it into "a little arietta." Then follows the one little song embedded in the original text—Osmin's early "Wer ein Liebchen hat gefunden" ("If you find yourself a sweetheart")—and he insists that it be made into a duet for Belmonte and Osmin. One can see him tightening the plot thereby. He also wants to take advantage of the bass singing Osmin, Ludwig Fischer.

Not only does he shape the drama, but from the beginning he is aware of music's instinct to depict and amplify the individual characters.

> In composing the aria I made Fischer's beautiful deep tones really glisten . . . The passage *Therefore, by the beard of the Prophet*, etc., is, to be sure, in the same tempo but with quick notes—and as his anger increases more and more, the allegro assai—which comes just when one thinks the aria is over—will produce an excellent Effect because it is in a different tempo and in a different key. A person who gets into such a violent rage transgresses every order, moderation, and limit; he no longer knows himself.—In the same way the Music must no longer know itself . . . Now about Bellmont's aria in A Major. "Oh how anxious, oh how passionate!" do you know how I expressed it?—even expressing the loving, throbbing heart?—with two violins playing in octaves . . . And it was written entirely for Adamberger's voice; one can see the trembling—faltering—one can see his heaving breast—which is expressed by a crescendo—one can hear the whispering and

the sighing—which is expressed by the first violins with mutes and one flute playing unisono.

He tells his father how he changed the text when he thought a word unsuitable, or how the trio at the end of Act I has to move with exceptional speed: "at the end it will become very noisy— and that's really what you need for the end of an act—the noisier, the better;—the shorter, the better—so the audience won't cool off in its applause." He tells his father he has finished Act I, and parts of Act II, but that work has come to a temporary halt. "I can't do anything else right now, because the whole story is being reworked—and it is done at my insistence." This is when he conceives the extraordinary finale for Act II, and demands that Stephanie revise the text.

> Stephani has more work right now than he can handle; so I'll have to be patient a bit;—everyone is down on Stephani—it's possible that to me, too, he is only nice to my face—but he is doing the libretto for me—and he is doing it the way I want it—exactly—and, by god, I can't ask for anything more!

In another letter he complains to his father about badly written, ineptly rhymed librettos, and of how the effect of an opera can be ruined by an inferior text: "It is so much better if a good composer, who understands something about the stage and can make a suggestion here and there, is able to team up with an intelligent Poet and create a true Phoenix." "A suggestion here and there" is hardly the way Mozart worked with his poets. He implies that he bullied Stephanie—behavior that was never necessary with the brilliant Da Ponte. But with each of his librettists, he took the upper hand in creating the text (how it is built, how it moves), interpreting the characters (what they think and feel, how they react), and attending to the audience's reactions.

He loved going to the theater, and was friendly with several of Vienna's leading actors. But when writing an opera, Mozart didn't go about it the way most playwrights would. He would begin with the ensembles, move then to trios and duets, then arias, and last the recitatives, accompanied or simple. That may be because he wanted to suit the arias to the specific voices of the singers who would first undertake the roles, but it also points to his fascination with the interplay of characters, his conviction that people may be revealed by what they say to themselves, but are more likely understood when we see them with others. In any case, in conceiving of a drama, he moved from the complicated to the casual. He liked to write backwards, from the end of an act towards its start. He wanted to figure out first the rushing cascade of voices as they overlap and contradict. (It could be maintained that concerted ensembles are "realistic" in the extreme because they dramatize the way, in groups, each individual thinks his own thoughts while entertaining those of the others.) It might be fair to say he preferred *mixed emotions.*

When he was at his desk, his musical unconscious seemed to run ahead of his pen. This may be why he had musical ideas about scenes for his operas even before he had the text. There is a well-known forgery of a letter by Mozart, one in which he describes himself at work. It first surfaced in 1815, just twenty-five years after his death, and could have been a concoction based on a true account. Its style does not sound like the real Mozart, who in his letters is spirited, spontaneous, and unself-conscious. Still, I like this forgery, because it comes close to what we know from elsewhere of Mozart's character. In this "letter," as in his life, he can seem remarkably self-effacing when we know that in fact he was possessed of a supreme self-confidence.

> When I am, as it were, completely myself, entirely alone, and of good cheer—say, traveling in a carriage, or walking after a good meal, or during the night when I cannot sleep—it is on such occasions that my ideas flow best and most abundantly. *Whence* and *how* they come, I know not; nor can I force them. Those ideas that please me I retain in memory, and

am accustomed, as I have been told, to hum them to myself. If I continue in this way it soon occurs to me how I may turn this or that morsel to account, so as to make a good dish of it, that is to say, agreeably to the rules of counterpoint, to the peculiarities of various instruments, etc.

All this fires my soul, and, provided I am not disturbed, my subject enlarges itself, becomes methodized and defined, and the whole, though it be long, stands almost complete and finished in my mind, so that I can survey it, like a fine picture or a beautiful statue, at a glance . . .

When I proceed to write down my ideas, I take out of the bag of my memory, if I may use that phrase, what has been previously collected into it in the way I have mentioned. For this reason, the committing to paper is done quickly enough, for everything is, as I said before, already finished, and it rarely differs on paper from what it was in my imagination. At this occupation I can, therefore, suffer myself to be disturbed; for, whatever may be going on around me, I write, and even talk, but only of fowls and geese, or of Gretel or Bärbel, or some such matters. But why my productions take from my hand that particular form and style that makes them *Mozartish*, and different from the works of other composers, is probably owing to the same cause which renders my nose so large, so aquiline, or, in short, makes it Mozart's, and different from those of other people, for I really do not study or aim at any originality.

Mozart never met most of his librettists. Some were distant, some were dead. But he had known Emanuel Schikaneder, the librettist for *The Magic Flute*, for some years before they collaborated. In 1780, Schikaneder and his wife befriended the Mozart family in Salzburg, and a few years later even produced a revival of *The Abduction from the Seraglio* in Vienna. Mozart admired dedicated and talented professionals, and Schikaneder was certainly that, a theater man to his toes. Their work together on *The Magic Flute* was a happy inspiration. And of course Mozart knew

Da Ponte. They seem to have met at a crowded party in Vienna in 1783. Mozart was itching to write something new, an *opera buffa*, or even—as he once wrote in a letter—something that combined *opera seria* and *opera buffa*, a hybrid that could take advantage of both genres. Da Ponte, meanwhile, was busy with other commissions, but each soon enough saw in the other a professional rigor and inventiveness to be admired. Their sensibilities were parallel, building on complementary strengths and a common aim. In his preface to the printed libretto of *The Marriage of Figaro*, Da Ponte described what their purpose was in all three operas: "the variety of the development of this drama . . . to paint faithfully and in full color the diverse passions that are aroused, and to realize our special purpose, which was to offer a new type of spectacle."

Da Ponte was born Emanuele Conegliano in 1749 to a Jewish family in the village of Ceneda in the Veneto region of Italy. (He was given, as was then customary, the local bishop's name when the family converted.) As a young man he was a compulsive lover of women, an ordained priest, and a skillful poet. (He specialized in sparkling rhymes of a kind Mozart was not particularly fond of—until he realized how deft Da Ponte's were.) Scandal drove him out of Venice and he fled to Austria, arriving finally in Vienna in 1783, with a letter of introduction to Antonio Salieri. He was soon appointed by Emperor Joseph II as the Court Poet (a post once held by the greatest of an earlier generation of librettists, Pietro Metastasio), responsible for providing librettos for the imperial theater. He devised librettos for Gluck, Antonio Salieri, Vicente Martín y Soler, and several other composers . . . and for Mozart, who was a little skeptical at first. "He promised to write something New," he wrote to his father, "but who knows whether he will keep his word—or even wants to!—You know, these Italian gentlemen, they are very nice to your face!"

The "something New" that Da Ponte soon gave to Mozart, the "new kind of spectacle," were texts with plots and characters of a truly human dimension—complex, troubling, funny when they needed to be, ironic at other times, heartbreaking, exuberant, and joyous. There had never been librettos like this, and these would change the way audiences thought of the libretto's capabilities. (In the theater world too, things were changing; the taste for high-flown tragedy was fading because of the work of Pierre de Marivaux in France and Carlo Goldoni in Italy, with their interest in the lives and conflicts of the emerging middle classes.) Mozart responded to Da Ponte's texts by making them his own—that is, by reworking them so that the dramatic and musical shapes coincided, by plumbing the depths of character in his arrangements and orchestration, by shading traditional roles with unexpected color and nuance. In the words of music critic David Cairns, "For the first time music has found the means of embodying the interplay of living people, the feelings and passions and thoughts of rounded human beings, servants and masters, as they arise in response to life, each speaking in their own characteristic idiom, all inhabiting an actual world, enchanted yet recognizable, companionable but full of danger." This has something to do as well with the fact that *The Marriage of Figaro* and *Don Giovanni*, along with *The Magic Flute*, are the first operas in history to have been continuously staged, all over the world, in every conceivable venue, ever since their first performances.

What is emerging, then, from the strictures of tragedy and the fluster of comedy is tragicomedy with high ambitions and popular appeal. The new form that Mozart had in mind, and that Da Ponte helped him realize, transcended prescribed expectations. In *Così Fan Tutte*, for instance, he gives the heroine, Fiordiligi, a show-stopping aria in each of the opera's two acts. The first, "Come scoglio" ("Like a rocky fortress"), has all the serious bravura of an aria in the best tradition of *opera seria*. But in the next act, her "Per pietà" ("Have pity on me") is something altogether different, pliant, varied, infinitely touching, its vocal leaps the cry of passion, the portrait of a woman afraid of a forbidden love. Musically, one can hear the statuesque tragic form cracking from inside, a more human character emerging from the stiff convention. Yet at the same time, it is convincing dramaturgy. Fiordiligi's strength of character makes her subsequent weakness more touching in its conflicted vulnerability.

Even as Mozart explored a new depth in the psychology of operatic characters, and orchestrated that psychology in remarkable ways (with woodwinds—the instruments closer to the sound of the voice than any others—playing an unprecedented role), so too did he give a new prominence to women in his operas. (They were prominent too in his life. The three people he was probably closest to were his mother, who died in Paris with just her son at her bedside; his only sibling, his sister Nannerl; and his wife, Constanze, to whom he was passionately devoted.) To be sure, from Monteverdi to Handel there were strong heroines on stage. Mozart gave us human ones, complex, elusive, intimate, surprising. In *Figaro*, there are Susanna and the Countess, the one down-to-earth, the other ghostly, and both of them learning from each other, exchanging identities. In *Don Giovanni*, Donna Anna and Donna Elvira, antitypes joined in grief, one noble, the other vindictive. In *Così*, the sisters Fiordiligi and Dorabella, who at first seem as interchangeable as twins but are revealed to be very different women indeed, one reluctantly seduced, the other gladly. In his earlier operas as well, there are extraordinary women—Ilia and Electra in *Idomeneo*, Constanza in *The Abduction*, each revealed, or rather developed, so carefully that none is what she had seemed at the start. And in *The Magic Flute*, Pamina is perhaps Mozart's most touching heroine—nearly driven to suicide by her fate but strong enough in the end to lead the hero by the hand through the trials their love is subjected to. Like the quizzical, tremulous child in Niemetschek's biography of Mozart, the composer was fascinated by friends in a small group in front of him, as he sat at the piano. What fascinated him is how they reacted to him and to each other. As an adult, he may have wanted to watch them in extremes—at the limits to which their feelings are driven. He was clearly drawn to women because of their ability to experience and to understand their feelings better than men.

What we think of as the end of his life he no doubt thought of as its middle, the peak of his powers. In Mozart's last four years—a time beset with depression and financial anxiety—he wrote his three last symphonies, concertos for piano and clarinet, string quartets and quintets, the sublime motet *Ave Verum*, much incidental music and several arrangements, songs and dances, the uncompleted *Requiem*, along with *Così Fan Tutte*, *The Magic Flute*, and *La Clemenza di Tito*. That he wrote those last two operas back to back, and within three months, shows how his dramatic imagination worked, riding easily between the strictures of *opera seria*, to which he gave a new humanity and richness, and the exuberance of *Zauberoper*, comic opera based on magic spectacle, to which he gave a new urgency. At the heart of both operas is a wise ruler—Titus and Sarastro—a figure who restores order from chaos, who counters intrigue and darkness to create a new city governed by youth and love and guided by reason. It is hard not to think he was drawn to these stories because they drew on his deepest fantasies about the power of music itself.

Mozart lived for scarcely two months after *The Magic Flute* was first performed. In November, he fell ill, fearing he had somehow been poisoned. For fifteen days, during his final struggle with acute rheumatic fever, his body swelled and he was wracked by spells of vomiting, until his sufferings ended on December 5. The afternoon before he died, two of the cast members of *The Magic Flute* visited him and helped him work on the *Requiem*—until Mozart broke down in tears, unable to go on. Later that night, he lapsed into a delirium. *The Magic Flute*, into which he had poured so much life, was his refuge in death. With almost his last words, whispered to his wife, he imagined he was back in the theater, a part of the audience at a performance of his opera.

His sister-in-law, Josepha Hofer, was singing the Queen of the Night's great aria. Candles were blazing. The Queen's anger was surging. "Listen!" Mozart murmured. "Hofer is taking her top F. Now, how strongly she takes and holds the B flat. 'Hört . . . Hört! der Mutter Schwur!'" *Hear, vengeful gods, a mother's curse!* It should be noted that he was thinking of both his notes and the words, of both music and drama. It is at once the opera's darkest and its most virtuosic moment. All of Mozart's canny and humane understanding of the motives of his characters and the abilities of his singers is concentrated in this breathtakingly brilliant aria. In a sense, then, in his last moments Mozart was listening to the power of his own music as drama. And throughout all his operas, his music is an immortal blending of passion with serene detachment, driving always towards a gloriously ascendant freedom.

An impulse to freedom was the keynote to Mozart's life. Of course one hears that in the music; the very earliest compositions are marked by febrile changes of mood within the conventional forms. And nearly all his dealings with others were dominated by his urge to be free of any authority or control other than that of his own desire to write music. In *The Magic Flute*, the final freedom is love itself. Some of its characters—the Queen and Monostatos—are blinded by their passions and destroyed by their anarchic instincts. In this, they are like characters in other of his operas: Electra and Osmin and, on a grander scale, Don Giovanni. Papageno, like Pedrillo and Leporello, is content with mere appetite and habit. But the *Flute*'s young lovers, Tamino and Pamina, give up their freedom for love's sake, and in doing so discover a still greater freedom, encouraged by reason and goodness. No doubt Constanza and Belmonte, Ilia and Idamantes, Servilia and Annius are similar pairs. We would like to think that the Count and Countess in *Figaro*, Masetto and Zerlina in *Don Giovanni*, and the lovers in *Così* will achieve the harmony they try to promise themselves, but the musical undertones encourage our suspicions. The lucky ones patiently make their

own happiness, but it is important to remember that Mozart lav-
ishes the sympathy of his musical attention on all his characters,
regardless of their moral bearings. Tamino and Pamina discover
that love's dependence, one on the other, husband on wife, lover
on beloved, frees them of repressive jealousies and ungenerous
feelings. In joining together, they are free to be themselves, and
something more than themselves. *The Magic Flute* poignantly
dramatizes their trial the better to celebrate their victory. But
then, each of these operas has been a trial—separation, deceit,
appetite, corruption, and the temptations of power—their pro-
tagonists must endure. Each is transformed in the process. In
those who fail and in those who triumph, in those who cannot
change and in those who do, we are meant to find an image of
what is possible for ourselves.

Like most books, this one can be read in silence, from start to
finish. But I would expect the reader to move around in it, from
opera to opera as needs be. And perhaps the best way to read
each opera is with a recording of it playing. Only then is the
full drama of the libretto revealed. In Mozart's music—radiant,
sovereign, tender—we can hear the heart's own yearnings and
struggles. We can hear the rare balance of the comic and the
solemn, the melancholy and romantic and mysterious—which
is, finally, the laughter in the soul.

A Note on the Translations

SOME DETAILS IN THIS BOOK DESERVE A WORD OF explanation. A word, first, about the titles I have used for each opera. When they are named after their heroes, the choice is made for one. And English-speaking readers have taken easily to *The Magic Flute*, *The Marriage of Figaro*, and *The Abduction from the Seraglio*. (Indeed, the idea of updating it to, say, *The Kidnapping from the Harem* grates on the ear.) But for two of the operas I have kept the original Italian title: *Così Fan Tutte*, because there is no good English translation of the phrase. *Thus Are They All* or *Women Are Like That* sound fussy and unfamiliar. Likewise with *La Clemenza di Tito*, because any straightforward translation—*The Clemency of Titus*—sounds wooden. Operagoers are used to these titles in the original, and with good reason.

In nearly all the arias of all these operas, there are phrases that are repeated for musical reasons. I have not repeated them here, because they are not a part of the original text. The printed format of arias is often a matter of choice—one long blocky stanza or three with a similar rhyme scheme?—and I have followed my instincts.

For each text I have used the version in the most recent vocal score published by Bärenreiter. In *Idomeneo*, I have dipped into the score's appendix and have included the two alternative scenes that can open Act II, and also added Idamantes' aria in Act III, Scene 9, Electra's aria in Act III, Scene 10, and Idomeneus's aria in the very last scene of the opera. For *Don Giovanni* I have followed the original score of the 1787 Prague premiere, but added Don Ottavio's aria "Dalla sua pace" (Act I, Scene 14) and Donna Elvira's aria "In quali eccessi . . . Mi tradì quell'alma ingrate" (Act II, Scene 10a), both of which Mozart inserted for the Vienna production the following year.

For the sake of concision and consistency, recitatives in the Italian librettos have been set as the prose they are rather than in *settenari*, the seven-syllable artificial "lines" traditionally employed. A vertical line in the margin indicates passages that are sung simultaneously. In the original-language librettos used here, provided by the Salzburg Mozarteum, certain words and names are, for scholarly reasons, spelled in a way that differs from what is traditional (as "Guilelmo" and "Guglielmo" in *Così Fan Tutte*, or "Manostatos" for "Monostatos" in *Die Zauberflöte*). In my translations, I have persisted with the familiar spellings.

The translation of *The Magic Flute* has been expanded from a version that first appeared in a book illustrated by Davide Pizzagoni and published by Abbeville Press in 2000. Quotations from Mozart's letters—with all their stylistic idiosyncrasies—are taken from *Mozart's Letters, Mozart's Life: Selected Letters*, edited and translated by Robert Spaethling (New York: W. W. Norton, 2000). Quotations from Franz Xaver Niemetschek are from *Mozart: The First Biography*, translated by Helen Mautner (New York: Berghahn Books, 2007).

÷ Acknowledgments ÷

THIS BOOK WAS ROBERT WEIL'S IDEA, AND OWES everything to his encouragement, patience, and intelligence. His crew backstage at Norton—Sue Carlson, Mark Melnick, Michael Ochs, Anna Oler, Nancy Palmquist, Don Rifkin, Elizabeth Riley, Jeff Shreve—set and lit this production with a rare elegance. The original language librettos are based on the critical edition of the librettos prepared by the Digital Mozart Edition, a project of the Internationale Stiftung Mozarteum, Salzburg, and the Packard Humanities Institute, Los Altos, California. The editorial work was accomplished by Iacopo Cividini (Italian librettos) and by Anja Morgenstern and Till Reininghaus (German librettos). Dr. Ulrich Leisinger at the Mozarteum deserves a hand for his invaluable role in supplying and greatly facilitating the use of the original texts. I'm grateful for other kinds of help as well to Susan Bianconi, Mario Corradi, Paul Cremo, Dennis Giauque, Patrick Merla, Michael Panayos, Jeffrey Posternak, Craig Rutenberg, Geoff Spear, Julie Taymor, and The Bogliasco Foundation. Many years ago, the late David Stivender taught me lessons about opera I have never forgotten and remain indebted to. The person I most love having in the seat next to mine at any opera is Chip Kidd.

I

Idomeneo

IDOMENEO

•

Dramma per musica, 1781

Libretto by Giovanni Battista Varesco

The Characters
Idomeneus, King of Crete
Idamantes, his son
Ilia, Trojan princess, daughter of Priam
Electra, princess and daughter of Agamemnon, King of Argos
Arbaces, confidant of the King
High Priest of Neptune
The Voice of the Oracle of Neptune
Two Cretan Women
Two Trojans

Chorus, priests, Trojan prisoners,
men and women of Crete, Argive sailors

Setting: Cydonia, capital of Crete

OF ALL HIS OPERAS, MOZART IS SAID TO HAVE MOST loved *Idomeneo*. Many years after his death, his widow remembered the time when she and Mozart were visiting his father Leopold in Salzburg. Joined by Mozart's sister Nannerl, the four of them sang through the great quartet from Act III, and Mozart "was so overcome that he burst into tears and quit the chamber, and it was some time before I could console him." That Mozart and his father were singing together—and presumably singing the roles of the son Idamantes and his father Idomeneus, joined in suffering—is an irony worth noting. Leopold Mozart had dominated his son's life in ways that can almost seem brutal, and the several strong father figures in Mozart's operas, right up to Titus and Sarastro in the last year of the composer's life, demonstrate a wise benevolence that it is difficult to imagine Mozart found in his own father. In the original French text that was adapted to become *Idomeneo*'s libretto, the King has fallen in love with Ilia, is stricken mad by the gods, and kills his own son. When he recovers and realizes what he has done, he attempts suicide but is prevented by Ilia who declares that she alone must die. The emphasis in Mozart's libretto is on a kind father wracked by the vow he has made to an unjust god. "O my son, my dear son! Forgive me," pleads the King. The figure of a grief-stricken, repentant, generous, and warm father . . . what were Mozart's feelings as he created this character? Those feelings must have been equally strong when he set Idamantes' words to his father: "Now I understand that your agitation was not anger, but fatherly love."

Clearly Mozart's preference for this opera owed everything to the exceptional circumstances of its making. He was working with the best orchestra in Europe; his writing for chorus was grander and more extensive than anything he later wrote for the opera house; the theater was equipped with the finest stage machinery for spectacular theatrical effects, and he worked closely with the set designer Lorenzo Quaglio and the ballet master Le Grand; he knew and trusted his cast, even while aware of some short-comings. And he was working in a style—the Metastasian *opera seria*—that drew out his strongest gifts as a dramatic composer. Mozart already knew the story of Idomeneus, having encountered it during his 1778 stay in Paris when he pored over texts looking for a libretto. The influence of French opera can be felt in the textures of *Idomeneo*, especially in its dance music and extended choruses. But at heart it is an *opera seria*, a genre that stressed classical decorum and aristocratic history. The action of these operas turned on grand themes which embroil personal lives and state affairs, romantic love and rational duty. Individual scenes are animated by unanticipated conflicts at the end of which a major character sings an extended, sometimes show-stopping aria that probes the emotional ramifications of what has just happened. For all its noble surprises, elegant structure, and powerfully restrained emotions, modern audiences have found the form static. In 1879, for instance, the famous Viennese music critic Eduard Hanslick wrote of *Idomeneo*: "First comes the libretto! That is the source of all mischief. The book of *Idomeneo* is in bad taste, empty, wearisome, and all in the indescribably antiquated garb proper to the mythological opera of gods and heroes." This view now seems as outdated as the *opera seria* seemed to Hanslick. Besides, Mozart streamlined the genre's dramatic build and effects. First, he could take advantage of the reforms to the genre already initiated by librettist Ranieri Calzabigi and composer Christoph Willibald Gluck with their insistence on a more natural, less virtuosic and self-conscious style of performance. Ornamentation gave way to intensity. And the results in *Idomeneo* are vividly dramatic, with entrances and exits carefully calculated, while an underlying menace suffuses the whole plot.

The backdrop of *Idomeneo* is a war that has left both winners and losers in despair. A princess is in chains, a hero is destitute. The opera's conflicts are played out privately, without much direct confrontation, so that the action is as much inward and psychological as it is between open enemies and allies. The first, and ultimately most dire, of these conflicts is between the human world and the divine. It is Neptune's will that Idomeneus must obey, Neptune's anger he must placate. It is Neptune's sea-thundering power that renders the King helpless, and Neptune's wrath—embodied in the monster that devastates the island—that must be confronted. The second conflict, played out in the King's heart and in his tortured silence, is between Idomeneus and his son Idamantes. A parent forced to sacrifice his own child is a grave psychic image that echoes down from Abraham's dilemma in the Bible. The third conflict centers on Idamantes and the two women who love him—the two princesses, both victims of the recent war, one trapped in her memories, the other in her arrogance.

The way these men and women are characterized musically is the reason *Idomeneo* is considered the first work of Mozart's maturity. Electra's simmering jealousy rising to a manic rage that outdoes even the Queen of the Night's is but one example. Arbaces' steady hand, Idamantes' confusion and resolve, Ilia's strength of will, the King's tortured response to his impossible choice, the hollow voice of the great god, and the chorus rejoicing or tremulous—each is a remarkably dramatic portrait, and they are combined in ensembles of genuine power. The singer who first undertook the role of Idomeneus, Anton Raaff, complained to Mozart about his part in the Act III quartet. Mozart was insistent that he sing what was written; he told Raaff that he would adjust any singer's individual arias, but that the ensembles were the composer's moment to layer and deepen the story's emotions. Mozart reported that Raaff returned a few days later and admitted he had been wrong. That may as well have been the experience of critics down the ages. The more often one hears this opera, the cannier its construction seems, the grander its cumulative effect is.

THE STORY

ACT I

In the royal palace in Cydonia, the capital of Crete, the captive princess Ilia is alone in her rooms. The recently ended Trojan War has ruined her homeland and killed her family. The Greek fleet too seems ruined, and King Idomeneus dead, but the King's son, Idamantes, has rescued her and her love for him is what truly enslaves her. She worries, though, about the rival for his affection, Electra, the princess of Argos, and her heart is torn by conflicting emotions. Idamantes arrives to say that his father's ships have been sighted near the coast, and that he himself promises to be a generous victor. His love for Ilia assures that; no matter what his people may think of his loving an enemy, he says he only wants to bring consolation to the Trojans. The prisoners are led in and Idamantes has their chains removed, as the chorus sings his praises. Electra enters, jealously accusing Idamantes of protecting Greece's enemies. Arbaces, the King's counselor, hurries in with the sad news that the King has, in fact, drowned. To herself, Electra broods on the possibility of a despised Trojan princess soon sharing the throne with the prince, and she vows vengeance.

Meanwhile, on a rugged seacoast with the wreckage of ships scattered on shore, dazed sailors are begging the gods for mercy. Neptune appears and motions for the waves to subside, and when

Idomeneus—who has indeed survived—sees the god and begs for his help, Neptune plunges back into the sea. The King paces the beach in contemplation, knowing that in exchange for his survival he has vowed to sacrifice to the gods the first person he encounters, a pledge he now deeply regrets. He sees a man approaching and realizes that must be his victim. It turns out to be Idamantes, searching for his father, whom he finally sees but does not recognize. Idamantes is happy to help the shipwrecked man, Idomeneus is grieved to realize it is his son. Finally Idamantes recognizes his father and they embrace. But Idomeneus, in horror, backs away, and Idamantes, mystified and sorrowful, leaves.

The Cretan troops sing of their joy in returning home; their wives too rejoice and there is general dancing to celebrate Neptune's power.

ACT II

In the palace, Idomeneus reveals to Arbaces the vow he has made and the encounter he has had with his son. Arbaces suggests that Idamantes be sent far away and that they try to find some other way to placate Neptune. Let him, in fact, have Idamantes accompany Electra back to her native Argos. Idomeneus agrees, and Arbaces swears his loyalty to the King. Elsewhere, Ilia begs Idamantes to forget her and marry Electra, but he would rather face death than lose her. She goes to the King to thank him for his generosity, and Idomeneus pledges his love and help to her. She feels reborn a happy woman. When she leaves, the King wonders if his son has been acting rashly, but even more he sinks under the weight of his impending fate. Electra comes to thank the King for putting her in Idamantes' charge, and as he departs she vows to extinguish the flame that burns in the prince's heart for Ilia, and to rekindle it for herself.

In the ship-lined harbor, Electra rejoices that she will be

returning to her homeland, especially in the company of the
man she longs for, and the chorus wishes for a pleasant voyage. Idomeneus and Idamantes join her, and though Idamantes
bids his father farewell he whispers to himself that his heart will
remain behind. Idomeneus grieves as well, because he knows the
real reason his son is being sent away. As Electra and Idamantes are about to embark, a violent storm erupts, a ship catches
fire, and a huge monster appears above the waves. As the crowd
panics, Idomeneus alone knows the cause and calls out to the
god to punish him and not an innocent man. The crowd flees
the monster.

ACT III

In the royal garden Ilia sits alone, dreaming of her beloved, and
suddenly he enters and confesses to her that his soul is troubled.
His father avoids him for no reason, and Ilia herself is distant.
She tries to console him, and admits her heart is filled with both
love and fear. The love is for Idamantes, and she tells him, "If
you wish to die, grief will have already killed me before you can."
The lovers pledge themselves to each other. The King enters and
discovers them embracing. Electra is with him and seethes. Idamantes asks how he has offended his father, and Idomeneus tells
him that Neptune has turned his anger on him. The King cannot
tell him why and urges him to seek a safe haven in another land.
Ilia asks Electra to comfort her after this grievous news, but is
rebuffed. Idamantes resolves to leave, Ilia says she will follow
him whatever happens, Idomeneus worries about his son's fate,
and Electra awaits her vengeance. Arbaces enters to tell them a
crowd has gathered outside the palace, the High Priest of Neptune at their head, demanding to speak with the King. As the
others leave, Arbaces expresses his concern for his homeland.
Heaven seems deaf to its sorrows, and to its King's dilemma.

In the great square before the palace, the King takes his place on the throne used for public audiences. Before him, the High Priest tells him of what destruction the monster has wrought on their city. The people are in despair, and the sacrificial victim must be delivered up. Idomeneus tells the crowd that the victim is Idamantes, and that he is being forced to kill his own son. He leaves in distress as the crowd realizes the horror of the situation.

The people and priests have gathered at the Temple of Neptune, preparing the ceremony of sacrifice. Idomeneus arrives with his retinue. He and the priests pray that the anger of the gods will abate and peace be restored to Crete. Arbaces suddenly rushes in with news: Prince Idamantes, running to meet the monster, struggled with it and killed the savage thing, saving the land. Idamantes is led in in a white robe, surrounded by guards and priests, prepared to lay down his life. He now realizes that his father had been acting out of love. Idomeneus still cannot raise the knife, despite Idamantes' courage. He urges his father on: "Though you lose a son, you gain a hundred gods as friends. Your people are now your sons." He asks too that he protect Ilia. After a tearful farewell, Idomeneus is about to strike when Ilia suddenly appears and prevents the blow. Instead she offers herself as the sacrifice, telling the King that heaven wishes Greece rid of its enemies, not its sons. A mighty roar is heard. The statue of Neptune is shaken, and a deep voice pronounces a verdict: "Idomeneus shall no longer be King. Idamantes shall reign, and Ilia be his bride." Idomeneus is relieved, and Electra, in a poisonous fury, runs off. The King now proclaims peace, and yields the throne to his son, urging his people to obey him. As Idamantes is crowned, the people rejoice.

THE BACKGROUND

The opera's full title is *Idomeneo, Rè di Creta ossia Ilia e Idamante* (*Idomeneus, King of Crete, or Ilia and Idamantes*).

Mozart was twenty-four and already an experienced opera composer when he received a commission from the Bavarian Elector Karl Theodor in Munich for a new *opera seria* to celebrate the 1781 carnival season there. The court too chose Giovanni Battista Varesco (1735–1805), a court chaplain in Salzburg, as librettist, and directed that he use as his model an older libretto from 1712 with the same story in the French *tragédie lyrique* style, by Antoine Danchet. Mozart found Varesco's work to be confused and wordy, and he worked feverishly to reshape the text. Mozart's father acted as intermediary between the two men, and no doubt tried to temper his son's impatience. On November 13, 1780, for instance, Mozart writes: "The 2nd Duetto is going to be omitted altogether—and it will be more to the advantage of the opera than to its disadvantage; for if you read the scene over again, you will see that if we put an Aria or Duetto in there the scene will become bland and uninspired—and very awkward for all the others onstage who just have to stand there; apart from that, it would make the noble struggle between Ilia and Idamante too long and thereby diminish its effect." Many letters review his progress, adjusting the score to the singers' abilities, cutting and reshaping the text for the sake of both dramatic intensity and musical invention. He changed individual words and syllables, as well as whole scenes. When Varesco would send him new versions of things and they did not satisfy Mozart, the composer rejected them and demanded more work. Even during rehearsals extensive cuts were made. When the Oracle's speech was shortened, Mozart wrote simply, "Varesco need know nothing of this—it will be printed just as he wrote it."

The Elector attended a rehearsal and was pleased, though, as Mozart reports it, his praise was condescending: "He once again gave me his friendliest approbation and said, laughing: *Who should think that such great things can come out of such a small head.*" The premiere took place at the Cuvilliés-Theater on January 29, 1781. Idomeneo was sung by Anton Raaff, whose tenor voice was reputedly one of the most beautiful of the day but past its prime. Idamantes, a soprano castrato part, was sung by Vincenzo dal Prato. (Of them both, Mozart wrote, "They are the most Wretched actors ever to appear on a stage.") Dorothea Wendling was Ilia, her sister Elisabeth Wendling was Electra, Domenico de' Panzacchi was Arbaces, and Giovanni Valesi the High Priest. Christian Cannabich led the orchestra. Years after Mozart's death, his widow said that the time he had spent in Munich working on *Idomeneo* was the happiest in his entire life. After the first three performances in Munich, there was only one other performance in Mozart's lifetime, in 1786. The *opera seria* style fell out of favor, and this opera along with it, though connoisseurs always cherished it.

Atto primo

Appartamenti d'Ilia nel palazzo reale.
In fondo al prospetto una galleria.

Scena 1

ILIA SOLA.

Recitativo

ILIA: Quando avran fine ormai l'aspre sventure mie? ... Ilia infelice, di tempesta crudel misero avanzo, del genitor e de' germani priva, del barbaro nemico misto col sangue il sangue vittime generose, a qual sorte più rea ti riserbano i numi? ... Pur vendicaste voi di Priamo e di Troia i danni e l'onte: perì la flotta argiva, e Idomeneo pasto forse sarà d'orca vorace ... Ma che mi giova—oh ciel! –, se al primo aspetto di quel prode Idamante, che all'onde mi rapì, l'odio deposi, e pria fu schiavo il cor che m'accorgessi d'essere prigioniera! Ah, qual contrasto—oh dio!— d'opposti affetti mi destate nel sen, odio ed amore! ... Vendetta deggio a chi mi diè la vita, gratitudine a chi vita mi rende ... Oh Ilia, oh genitor, oh prence, oh sorte! Oh vita sventurata, oh dolce morte! Ma che? M'ama Idamante? ... Ah no, l'ingrato per Elettra sospira, e quell'Elettra, meschina principessa, esule d'Argo, d'Oreste alle sciagure a queste arene fuggitiva, raminga, è mia rivale. Quanti mi siete intorno carnefici spietati? ... Orsù,

⎯⎯⎯⎯ :· Act I ·: ⎯⎯⎯⎯

*The apartments of Ilia in the royal palace;
in the background a gallery.*

Scene 1

ILIA, ALONE.

Recitative

ILIA: When will my bitter misfortunes be over? Miserable Ilia! Wretched survivor of a raging tempest, bereft of father and brothers, pitiful victims whose noble blood is mixed with that of the barbarous enemy—what harsher fate have the gods prepared for you? . . . Have the ruin and shame of Priam and Troy, ye gods, not been your revenge? The Greek fleet has perished, and Idomeneus is likely the prey of a voracious sea monster . . . But what comfort is it to me, oh heavens, if at the first sight of valiant Idamantes who rescued me from the waves, I put aside my hatred, and my heart was enslaved before I realized I was a prisoner. Oh God, what a conflict of conflicting emotions, hate and love, have you set at odds in my heart! I owe vengeance to him who gave me life, gratitude to him who saved my life . . . Oh Ilia! Oh Father! Oh Prince! Oh my destiny! Oh unfortunate life! Oh sweet death! What then? What if Idamantes loves me? But no, selfishly he loves Electra, and Electra, unhappy princess exiled from Argos who fled to these shores to escape the misfortunes of Orestes, she is my rival. How many of you surround me now,

sbranate, vendetta, gelosia, odio ed amore, sbranate, sì, quest'infelice core!

N° 1 Aria

ILIA:
Padre, germani, addio!
Voi foste, io vi perdei.
Grecia, cagion tu sei,
e un greco adorerò?

D'ingrata al sangue mio
so che la colpa avrei,
ma quel sembiante—oh dei! –
odiare ancor non so.

Recitativo

ILIA: Ecco, Idamante—ahimè!—sen vien. Misero core, tu palpiti e paventi. Deh, cessate per poco, o miei tormenti!

Scena 2

IDAMANTE, ILIA. SEGUITO D'IDAMANTE.

Recitativo

IDAMANTE: *(al seguito)* Radunate i troiani, ite, e la corte sia pronta questo giorno a celebrar. *(a Ilia)* Di dolce speme a un raggio scema il mio duol. Minerva, della Grecia protettrice, involò al furor dell'onde il padre mio. In mar di qui non lunge comparser le sue navi. Indaga, Arbace, il sito che a noi toglie l'augusto aspetto.

ILIA: *(con ironia)* Non temer: difesa da Minerva è la Grecia, e tutta ormai scoppiò sovra i troian l'ira de' numi.

IDAMANTE: Del fato de' troian più non dolerti: farà il figlio per

you bloodthirsty tormentors? Come then, attack—vengeance, jealousy, hatred, and love, tear apart this unhappy heart!

Aria

ILIA:
Father, brothers, now farewell!
You are no more. You are lost to me.
Greece has caused this catastrophe,
And shall I now adore a Greek?

If against my own kin I rebelled
I know how guilty I would be.
But, dear God, the face I see—
I cannot hate the man I seek.

Recitative

ILIA: Alas, Idamantes is coming. My poor heart, how it flutters and is afraid. Will my anguish never cease for a moment?

Scene 2

IDAMANTES AND ILIA; THE RETINUE OF IDAMANTES.

Recitative

IDAMANTES: *(to his retinue)* Go, assemble the Trojans, and let the Court prepare to celebrate this day. *(to Ilia)* My grief subsides with one ray of sweet hope. Minerva, protectress of Greece, saved my father from the sea's fury. His ships have been sighted not far from here. Arbaces is searching for the site that hides his royal countenance from us.

ILIA: *(with irony)* Fear not. Greece is protected by Minerva, and all the wrath of the gods has fallen on the Trojans.

IDAMANTES: Grieve no more over the fate of the Trojans. The

lor quanto farebbe il genitor e ogn'altro vincitor generoso. Ecco, abbian fine, principessa, i lor guai: rendo lor libertade, e ormai fra noi sol prigioniero fia, sol fia chi porte che tua beltà legò care ritorte.

ILIA: Signor, che ascolto? Non saziaro ancora d'implacabili dei l'odio, lo sdegno, d'Ilio le gloriose or diroccate mura, ah, non più mura, ma vasto e piano suol? A eterno pianto dannate son le nostre egre pupille?

IDAMANTE: Venere noi punì, di noi trionfa. Quanto il mio genitor—ahi rimembranza!—soffrì de' flutti in sen? Agamennone, vittima in Argo alfin, a caro prezzo comprò que' suoi trofei, e non contenta di tante stragi ancor la dea nemica che fe'? Il mio cor trafisse, Ilia, co' tuoi bei lumi più possenti de' suoi, e in me vendica adesso i danni tuoi.

ILIA: Che dici?

IDAMANTE: Sì, di Citerea il figlio incogniti tormenti stillommi in petto. A te pianto e scompiglio Marte portò, cercò vendetta Amore in me de' mali tuoi, quei vaghi rai, quei tuoi vezzi adoprò … Ma all'amor mio d'ira e rossor tu avvampi?

ILIA: In questi accenti mal soffro un temerario ardir. Deh, pensa, pensa, Idamante,—oh dio!—il padre tuo qual è, qual era il mio.

son will do for them what his father would, and any generous victor. See, princess, their woes have come to an end. I restore their liberty. Among us now there will be only one prisoner, only one, the man bound by your beauty's dear chains.

ILIA: What are you saying, my lord? Has not the hatred of the implacable gods been satiated by the glorious walls of Troy, now in ruins, brought down to a deserted rubble? Are we a people condemned to eternal tears?

IDAMANTES: Venus punished us, and triumphs over us. How much my father—oh, the memory!—suffered in the waves! Agamemnon in the end was a victim in Argos, and all his trophies came at a dear price. Not content with all that destruction, what did the menacing goddess do next? She let your beautiful eyes, Ilia, more powerful even than her own, pierce my heart, and now avenges her losses through me.

ILIA: What are you saying?

IDAMANTES: Yes, the son of Cytheraea has infected my heart. To you Mars brought confusion and tears. Cupid has sought to avenge your sufferings in me, using your eyes, your enchantments. But you turn red. Are you ashamed of my love?

ILIA: The audacity of your words pains me. Oh God! Think who your father is, Idamantes, and who was mine.

N° 2 Aria

IDAMANTE:

Non ho colpa e mi condanni,
idol mio, perché t'adoro.
Colpa è vostra, o dei tiranni,
e di pena afflitto io moro
d'un error che mio non è.

Se tu il brami, al tuo impero
aprirommi questo seno.
Ne' tuoi lumi il leggo, è vero,
ma mel dica il labbro almeno,
e non chiedo altra mercé.

Recitativo

ILIA: *(vede condurre i prigionieri)* Ecco il misero resto de' troiani, da nemico furor salvi.

IDAMANTE: Or quei ceppi io romperò, vo' consolarli adesso. (*da sé*) (Ahi! Perché tanto far non so a me stesso?)

Scena 3

IDAMANTE, ILIA. TROIANI PRIGIONIERI,
UOMINI E DONNE CRETESI.

IDAMANTE: Scingete le catene, (*Si levano a' prigionieri le catene, li quali dimostrano gratitudine.*) ed oggi il mondo, o fedele Sidon suddita nostra, vegga due gloriosi popoli in dolce nodo avvinti e stretti di perfetta amistà. Elena armò la Grecia e l'Asia, ed ora disarma e riunisce ed Asia e Grecia eroina novella, principessa più amabile e più bella.

Aria

IDAMANTES:
I am innocent, yet you blame me,
My idol, because I adore you.
The tyrannous gods defame me
And now I die, my pain renewed
By a mistake that is not mine.

If you wish, at your command
I will plunge this knife in my breast.
I see your eyes now on my hand.
If your lips but make the request,
That will be the final sign.

Recitative

ILIA: *(watching the prisoners led in)* Here are the pitiful few Trojans who escaped their enemy's butchery.

IDAMANTES: I will break their chains. I want only to console them now. *(to himself)* (Ah, why am I unable to do as much for myself?)

Scene 3

IDAMANTES AND ILIA. TROJAN PRISONERS, AND
CRETAN MEN AND WOMEN.

IDAMANTES: Unlock their chains, *(As the prisoners have their chains removed, they show their gratitude.)* and let the world see today, O loyal subjects of Cydonia, our two glorious peoples bound by the ties of true friendship. Helen brought Asia and Greece to war, and now a new heroine, a princess more lovely and kind, brings peace to Asia and Greece, together again.

N° 3 Coro

TUTTI:
Godiam la pace,
trionfi Amore:
ora ogni core
giubilerà.

DUE CRETESI:
Grazie a chi estinse
face di guerra:
or sì la terra
riposo avrà.

TUTTI:
Godiam la pace,
trionfi Amore:
ora ogni core
giubilerà.

DUE TROIANI:
A voi dobbiamo,
pietosi numi,
e a quei bei lumi
la libertà.

TUTTI:
Godiam la pace,
trionfi Amore:
ora ogni core
giubilerà.

Chorus

CHORUS:

Let peace be ours
And love impart
To every heart
Joy evermore.

TWO CRETANS:

Let him be praised
Who brought us peace.
The land released
From horrid wars.

CHORUS:

Let peace be ours
And love impart
To every heart
Joy evermore.

TWO TROJANS:

O merciful gods,
To you we owe the sight,
And to her eyes so bright,
Of freedom's shore.

CHORUS:

Let peace be ours
And love impart
To every heart
Joy evermore.

Scena 4

ELETTRA E DETTI.

Recitativo

ELETTRA: *(agitata da gelosia)* Prence, signor, tutta la Grecia oltraggi: tu proteggi il nemico.

IDAMANTE: Veder basti alla Grecia vinto il nemico. Opra di me più degna a mirar s'apparecchi, o principessa: vegga il vinto felice. *(Vede venire Arbace.)* Arbace viene.

Scena 5

ARBACE E DETTI. (ARBACE È MESTO.)

IDAMANTE: *(timoroso)* Ma quel pianto ch'annunzia?

ARBACE: Mio signore, de' mali il più terribil...

IDAMANTE: *(ansioso)* Più non vive il genitor?

ARBACE: Non vive: quel che Marte far non poté finor, fece Nettuno, l'inesorabil nume, e degl'eroi il più degno—ora il riseppi—presso a straniera sponda affogato morì.

IDAMANTE: Ilia, de' viventi eccoti il più meschin. Or sì dal cielo soddisfatta sarai... Barbaro fato!... Corrasi al lido... Ahimè! Son disperato! *(Parte.)*

ILIA: Dell'Asia i danni ancora troppo risento, eppur d'un grand'eroe al nome, al caso, il cor parmi commosso, e negargli i sospir, ah no, non posso. *(Parte sospirando.)*

Scene 4

ELECTRA, AND THOSE BEFORE.

Recitative

ELECTRA: *(aroused by jealousy)* Prince, my lord, you insult all of Greece by protecting our enemy.

IDAMANTES: It is enough that Greece has seen its enemy vanquished. Now, princess, it should see an action worthier of me. Let it see the defeated made happy. *(He sees Arbaces approaching.)* Arbaces is coming.

Scene 5

ARBACES, AND THOSE BEFORE. (ARBACES IS DOWNCAST.)

IDAMANTES: *(fearful)* But what does this sad look portend?

ARBACES: My lord, most terrible news . . .

IDAMANTES: *(anxious)* My father is no longer alive?

ARBACES: No longer alive. What Mars could not so far do, Neptune, the implacable god, has done. And the worthiest of heroes, I was just told, has drowned near a foreign shore.

IDAMANTES: Ilia, here now before you stands the most miserable of human beings. Now you will be satisfied by heaven's will . . . barbarous fate! . . . I must hurry to the shore! . . . Alas, I am in despair! *(He leaves.)*

ILIA: The trials of Asia still eat at me, yet at the very name, at the fate of a great hero my heart is moved. I cannot—ah, no—deny him my sighs. *(She leaves sighing.)*

Scena 6

ELETTRA SOLA.

ELETTRA: Estinto è Idomeneo? ... Tutto a' miei danni, tutto congiura il ciel. Può a suo talento Idamante disporre d'un impero e del cor, e a me non resta ombra di speme? ... A mio dispetto—ahi lassa!—vedrò, vedrà la Grecia a suo gran scorno una schiava troiana di quel soglio e del talamo a parte ... Invano, Elettra, ami l'ingrato ... E soffre una figlia d'un re—ch'ha re vassalli—ch'una vil schiava aspiri al grand'acquisto? ... Oh sdegno! Oh smanie! Oh duol! ... Più non resisto.

N° 4 Aria

ELETTRA:
Tutte nel cor vi sento,
furie del crudo averno,
lunge a sì gran tormento
amor, mercé, pietà.

Chi mi rubò quel core,
quel che tradito ha il mio,
provi dal mio furore
vendetta e crudeltà.
(Parte.)

Scene 6

ELECTRA, ALONE.

ELECTRA: Idomeneus is dead? Heaven conspires to have every-thing add to my misfortune. Can Idamantes at a whim throw away an empire and his heart, and leave no shadow of hope for me? His contempt of me! Yet I will see—and to its shame Greece will see—a Trojan slave share his throne and his bed . . . In vain, Electra, you love this ingrate . . . Shall the daughter of a king, who has kings as vassals, allow a cowardly slave to aspire to these great honors? Oh wrath! Oh frenzy! Oh sorrow! . . . I can bear it no more.

Aria

ELECTRA:
In my heart I feel you all,
You furies from bitter hell.
Far from torment's gall
Be pity and mercy and love.

Let her who stole his heart,
Let him who betrayed mine
Feel my vengeance start,
The rage they should be fearful of.
(She leaves.)

Spiagge del mare ancora agitato, attorniate da dirupi.
Rottami di navi sul lido.

Scena 7

N° 5 Coro

CORO VICINO:
Pietà, numi, pietà!
Aiuto, o giusti numi!
A noi volgete i lumi ...

CORO LONTANO:
Pietà, numi, pietà!
Il ciel, il mare, il vento
ci opprimon di spavento ...

CORO VICINO:
Pietà, numi, pietà!
In braccio a cruda morte
ci spinge l'empia sorte ...

CORO VICINO, CORO LONTANO:
Pietà, numi, pietà!

Scena 8

Pantomima

NETTUNO COMPARISCE SUL MARE. FA CENNO A' VENTI DI
RITIRARSI ALLE LORO SPELONCHE. IL MARE A POCO A
POCO SI CALMA. IDOMENEO, VEDENDO IL DIO DEL MARE,
IMPLORA LA SUA POTENZA. NETTUNO RIGUARDANDOLO
CON OCCHIO TORVO E MINACCEVOLE SI TUFFA
NELL'ONDE E SPARISCE.

A seacoast with tumultuous waves, surrounded by crags.
The wreckage of ships on the beach.

Scene 7

Chorus

NEARBY CHORUS:
Have pity, gods, pity!
O just gods, help us,
Turn your gaze on us ...

DISTANT CHORUS:
Have pity, gods, pity!
The sea, the wind, the sky
Oppress and terrify ...

NEARBY CHORUS:
Have pity, gods, pity!
Fate demands our last breath
Be strangled by the hand of death ...

BOTH CHORUSES:
Have pity, gods, pity!

Scene 8

Pantomime

NEPTUNE APPEARS ON THE SEA. HE MOTIONS FOR THE
WINDS TO RETURN TO THEIR CAVES. GRADUALLY THE SEA
GROWS CALM. IDOMENEUS, SEEING THE GOD OF THE SEA,
BEGS FOR HIS HELP. NEPTUNE, REGARDING HIM WITH
A GRIM AND THREATENING SCOWL, PLUNGES INTO THE
WAVES AND VANISHES.

Scena 9

IDOMENEO CON SEGUITO.

Recitativo

IDOMENEO: *(al suo seguito)* Eccoci salvi alfin. O voi, di Marte e di Nettuno all'ire, alle vittorie, ai stenti fidi seguaci miei, lasciatemi per poco qui solo respirar e al ciel natio confidar il passato affanno mio.

(Il seguito si ritira ed Idomeneo solo s'inoltra sul lido contemplando.)

IDOMENEO: Tranquillo è il mar, aura soave spira di dolce calma, e le cerulee sponde il biondo dio indora. Ovunque io miro, tutto di pace in sen riposa e gode. Io sol, io sol su queste aride spiagge, d'affanno e da disagio estenuato, quella calma, o Nettuno, in me non provo che al tuo regno impetrai. In mezzo a flutti e scogli dall'ira tua sedotto, a te lo scampo dal naufragio chiedei, e in olocausto il primo de' mortali, che qui intorno infelice s'aggiri, all'are tue pien di terror promisi. All'empio voto eccomi in salvo, sì, ma non in pace … Ma son pur quelle—oh dio!—le care mura dove la prima io trassi aura vitale? … Lungi da sì gran tempo, ah, con qual core ora vi rivedrò, se, appena in seno da voi accolto, un misero innocente dovrò svenar! … Oh voto insano, atroce! Giuramento crudel! Ah, qual de' numi mi serba ancor in vita, o qual di voi mi porge almen aita?

Scene 9

IDOMENEUS, WITH HIS RETINUE.

Recitative

IDOMENEUS: *(to his retinue)* We are saved at last. You who have been with me in victories and hardships and endured the wrath of both Mars and Neptune, leave me here alone for a while to catch my breath, and to confide to my native skies the grief I feel.

(His followers withdraw and Idomeneus, alone, paces the beach in contemplation.)

IDOMENEUS: The sea is tranquil, a gentle breeze blows sweetly, and the golden-haired god makes the sand by the blue sea glisten. Wherever I look, everything is peaceful and pleasant. I alone, on these barren shores, exhausted by anguish and weakness, I alone do not feel within myself that calm, O Neptune, which I asked from your realm. Amid waves and rocks, cowering from your wrath, I prayed that you keep me from shipwreck. Terrified, I pledged as an offering on your altar the life of the first poor mortal I encountered. Because of that rash vow I have been saved, but am not at peace . . . But, O God, are these the dear walls of the city where I first drew breath? . . . Having been gone so long, how my heart longs to see you again, even if I will barely be home before I must sacrifice a poor innocent! What an insane and hateful vow! Cruel oath! Ah, which of the gods looks out for my life? Which of them will help me now?

N° 6 Aria

IDOMENEO:
Vedrommi intorno
l'ombra dolente
che notte e giorno:
"sono innocente"
m'accennerà.

Nel sen trafitto,
nel corpo esangue
il mio delitto,
lo sparso sangue
m'additerà.

Qual spavento!
Qual dolore!
Di tormento
questo core
quante volte morirà!
(Vede un uomo che s'avvicina.)

Recitativo

IDOMENEO: Cieli! Che veggo? Ecco, la sventurata vittima—
ahimè!—s'appressa ... Ah, qual dolore mostra quel ciglio! Mi si
gela il sangue ... Fremo d'orror ... E vi fia grata, o numi, legittima
vi sembra ostia umana innocente? ... E queste mani le ministre
saran? ... Mani esecrande! Barbari, ingiusti numi! Are nefande!

Scena 10

IDAMANTE, IDOMENEO IN DISPARTE.

IDAMANTE: Spiagge romite e voi scoscese rupi, testimoni al mio
duol siate e cortesi di questo vostro albergo a un agitato cor ...
Quanto spiegate di mia sorte il rigor, solinghi orrori! ... Vedo fra
quegli avanzi di fracassate navi su quel lido sconosciuto guerrier

Aria

IDOMENEUS:
Before me I shall see
His mournful shade,
Night and day by me,
Come to upbraid—
"I am innocent."

On his wounded breast,
On his corpse so wan,
The blood will confess
What I have done—
My crime now evident.

Oh the horror of it all!
What sorrow and pain!
How long will it befall
My heart to remain
In endless torment!
(He sees a man approaching.)

Recitative

IDOMENEUS: Heavens! What do I see? Behold, the unfortunate victim, alas, is coming . . . Must these hands be the instruments of his death? . . . Hateful hands! Savage, unjust gods! Abominable altars!

Scene 10

IDOMENEUS, AND IDAMANTES IN THE DISTANCE.

IDAMANTES: Solitary shores and rugged cliffs, bear witness to my sorrow, and kindly shelter an anguished heart . . . How exactly in your lonely terror you reflect my own harsh fate! . . . I can make out, among the ruin of ships here, an unknown war-

... Voglio ascoltarlo, vo' confortarlo e voglio in letizia cangiar quel suo cordoglio. *(S'appressa e parla a Idomeneo.)* Sgombra, o guerrier, qual tu ti sia, il timore: eccoti pronto a tuo soccorso quello che in questo clima offrir tel può.

IDOMENEO: *(da sé)* (Più il guardo, più mi strugge il dolor.) *(a Idamante)* De' giorni miei il resto a te dovrò. Tu quale avrai premio da me?

IDAMANTE: Premio al mio cor sarà l'esser pago d'averti sollevato, difeso: ahi, troppo, amico, dalle miserie mie instrutto io fui a intenerirmi alle miserie altrui!

IDOMENEO: *(da sé)* (Qual voce, qual pietà il mio sen trafigge!) *(a Idamante)* Misero tu? Che dici? ... Ti son conte le tue sventure appien?

IDAMANTE: Dell'amor mio—cielo!—il più caro oggetto in quegli abissi spinto giace l'eroe Idomeneo estinto. Ma tu sospiri e piangi? T'è noto Idomeneo?

IDOMENEO: Uom più di questo deplorabil non v'è, non v'è chi plachi il fato suo austero.

IDAMANTE: Che favelli? Vive egli ancor? *(da sé)* (Oh dei! Torno a sperar.) *(a Idomeneo)* Ah, dimmi, amico, dimmi: dov'è? Dove quel dolce aspetto vita mi renderà?

IDOMENEO: Ma d'onde nasce questa che per lui nutri tenerezza d'amor?

IDAMANTE: *(con enfasi)* Ah, ch'egli è il padre ...

rior . . . I will listen to him, comfort him, and turn his grief into gladness. *(He approaches and speaks to Idomeneus.)* Whoever you are, soldier, do not be afraid. Here, ready to help you, is someone who has the power in this land to do so.

IDOMENEUS: *(to himself)* (The more I look at him, the more sorrow I feel.) *(to Idamantes)* I owe you the rest of my life. What reward would you have of me?

IDAMANTES: My heart will be rewarded by knowing I have rescued and comforted you. Ah, my friend, miseries of my own have well taught me to sympathize with those of others.

IDOMENEUS: *(to himself)* (His voice, his pity pierces my heart!) *(to Idamantes)* You miserable? What are you saying? Do you really know the extent of your miseries?

IDAMANTES: The dearest object of my love, alas, the hero Idomeneus, lies dead in these depths. You too sigh and weep. Did you know Idomeneus?

IDOMENEUS: No man is more to be pitied than he, and nothing can ease his harsh fate.

IDAMANTES: What do you mean! Is he still alive? *(to himself)* (Oh gods! Hope returns.) *(to Idomeneus)* Tell me, friend, tell me where he is. Where is that kind face whose look will give me back my life?

IDOMENEUS: Where does it come from, this tender love for him you nourish?

IDAMANTES: *(emphatically)* Oh, because he is my father . . .

IDOMENEO: *(interrompendolo impaziente)* Oh dio! Parla: di chi è egli il padre?

IDAMANTE: *(con voce fiacca)* È il padre mio!

IDOMENEO: *(da sé)* (Spietatissimi dei! ...)

IDAMANTE: Meco compiangi del padre mio il destin? ...

IDOMENEO: *(dolente)* Ah figlio! ...

IDAMANTE: *(tutto giulivo)* Ah padre! Ah numi! Dove son io? ... Oh, qual trasporto! ... Soffri, genitor adorato, che al tuo seno ... *(Vuole abbracciarlo.)* e che un amplesso ... *(Il padre si ritira turbato.)* Ahimè! Perché ti sdegni? ... Disperato mi fuggi? ... Ah dove, ah dove?

IDOMENEO: Non mi seguir, tel vieto: meglio per te saria il non avermi veduto or qui. Paventa il rivedermi. *(Parte in fretta.)*

IDAMANTE: Ah, qual gelido orror m'ingombra i sensi! ... Lo vedo appena, il riconosco, e a' miei teneri accenti in un balen s'invola. Misero! In che l'offesi e come mai quel sdegno io meritai, quelle minacce? ... Vo' seguirlo e veder—oh sorte dura!—qual mi sovrasti ancor più rea sventura.

N° 7 Aria

IDAMANTE:
Il padre adorato
ritrovo, e lo perdo:
mi fugge sdegnato
fremendo d'orror.

IDOMENEUS: *(interrupting him impatiently)* Oh God! Speak—whose father is he?

IDAMANTES: *(in a weary voice)* He is my father!

IDOMENEUS: *(to himself)* (Most pitiless gods!)

IDAMANTES: You mourn my father's fate with me?

IDOMENEUS: *(sadly)* Ah son! . . .

IDAMANTES: *(full of joy)* Father! . . . Oh gods! Where am I? . . . How happy! . . . Dearest father, let me embrace . . . *(He goes to embrace him.)* . . . my arms around you . . . *(His father steps back in agitation.)* Alas! Why do you pull away from me? Will you run from me in despair? . . . And where to? Where?

IDOMENEUS: Do not follow me. I forbid it. It would have been better if you had never seen me at all. Beware of seeing me again! *(He leaves hurriedly.)*

IDAMANTES: Oh, what an icy terror grips me! . . . Hardly do I see and recognize him than, at the sound of my tender voice, he flees. Poor man! How did I offend him that I earned his anger and those threats? . . . I will follow him to see, oh hard fate, what further misfortunes may await me.

Aria

IDAMANTES:
My dear father I find
Only to lose him again.
He flees me, anger-blind,
Trembling with fright.

Morire credei
di gioia e d'amore,
or—barbari dei! —
m'uccide il dolor.
(Parte addolorato.)

Fine dell'atto primo.

I thought I would die
Of joy and love for him.
But now, ye gods on high,
Sorrow is my plight.
(He leaves sorrowfully.)

End of Act 1.

Intermezzo

IL MARE È TUTTO TRANQUILLO. SBARCANO LE TRUPPE
CRETESI ARRIVATE CON IDOMENEO. I GUERRIERI
CANTANO IL SEGUENTE CORO IN ONORE DI NETTUNO. LE
DONNE CRETESI ACCORRONO AD ABBRACCIARE I LORO
FELICEMENTE ARRIVATI E SFOGANO LA VICENDEVOLE
GIOIA CON UN BALLO GENERALE CHE TERMINA COL CORO.
MARCIA GUERRIERA DURANTE LO SBARCO.

N° 8 Marcia

N° 8a Ballo delle donne cretesi

N° 9 Coro

CORO DI GUERRIERI SBARCATI:
Nettuno s'onori,
quel nome risuoni,
quel nume s'adori,
sovrano del mar.
Con danze e con suoni
convien festeggiar.

PARTE DEL CORO:
Da lunge ei mira
di Giove l'ira,
e in un baleno
va all'Eghe in seno,
da regal sede
tosto provvede,
fa i generosi
destrier squamosi
ratto accoppiar.

Intermezzo

THE SEA IS ALL CALM. THE CRETAN TROOPS THAT
ARRIVED WITH IDOMENEUS DISEMBARK. THE SOLDIERS
SING THE FOLLOWING CHORUS IN HONOR OF NEPTUNE.
HAPPY THEY HAVE LANDED, THE CRETAN WOMEN RUSH UP
TO EMBRACE THEIR MEN, AND BOTH EXPRESS THEIR JOY
IN SEEING EACH OTHER WITH A GENERAL DANCE WHICH
ENDS WITH A CHORUS. WARLIKE MUSIC SOUNDS WHILE
THEY DISEMBARK.

March

Dance of the Cretan Women

Chorus

CHORUS OF DISEMBARKED SOLDIERS:
May Neptune be honored,
Let his name resound,
Let our prayers be heard
By the sovereign of the sea!
With dances and with song
Come celebrate joyously.

PART OF CHORUS:
From afar he sees
Jove is displeased,
And speeds without rest
To the Aegean crest.
From his royal throne
His wishes are known.
Then his scaly steeds
Are harnessed indeed,
So impatient to run.

Dall'onde fuore
suonan sonore
tritoni araldi
robusti e baldi
buccine intorno.
Già ride il giorno,
ché il gran tridente
il mar furente
seppe domar.

TUTTI:
Nettuno s'onori,
quel nome risuoni,
quel nume s'adori,
sovrano del mar.
Con danze e con suoni
convien festeggiar.

PARTE DEL CORO:
Su conca d'oro,
regio decoro,
spira Nettuno.
Scherza Portuno
ancor bambino
col suo delfino,
con Anfitrite.
Or noi di Dite
fe' trionfar.

Nereidi amabili,
ninfe adorabili,
che alla gran dea
con Galatea
corteggio fate,

From out of the waves,
Muscled and brave,
The heralds of the sea
Sound so sonorously
Their trumpets all around.
Daylight now abounds,
Since the mighty trident
Made the ocean relent,
Its raging storms undone.

CHORUS:
May Neptune be honored,
Let his name resound,
Let our prayers be heard
By the sovereign of the sea!
With dances and with song
Come celebrate joyously.

PART OF CHORUS:
On his conch of gold,
Emblem of his control,
Mighty Neptune blows.
Portumnus to and fro,
A child still, dashes,
With a dolphin splashes
And with Amphitrite.
Fierce Hades' might
We triumph over now.

Nereids so lithe,
Nymphs so blithe,
Who with Galatea fair
Are the court beyond compare
Of the goddess so great,

deh, ringraziate
per noi quei numi
che i nostri lumi
fero asciugar.

TUTTI:
Nettuno s'onori,
quel nome risuoni,
quel nume s'adori,
sovrano del mar.
Con danze e con suoni
convien festeggiar.

Or suonin le trombe:
solenne ecatombe
andiam preparar.

Fine dell'intermezzo.

Our thanks now relate
To the gods who dried
Our tears, and pacified
The ocean's feverish brow.

CHORUS:
May Neptune be honored,
Let his name resound,
Let our prayers be heard
By the sovereign of the sea!
With dances and with song
Come celebrate joyously.

Let the trumpets blare,
And our solemn sacrifice
Let us now prepare.

End of the Intermezzo.

Atto secondo

Appartamenti reali.

Scena 1
IDOMENEO, ARBACE.

N° 10a *Recitativo ed aria*
Recitativo

IDOMENEO: Siam soli. Odimi, Arbace, e il grand'arcano in sen racchiudi. Assai per lungo uso m'è nota tua fedeltà.

ARBACE: Di fedeltà il vassallo merto non ha: virtù non è il dover. Ecco la vita, il sangue...

IDOMENEO: Un consiglio or mi fa d'uopo. Ascolta: tu sai quanto a' troiani fu il brando mio fatal.

ARBACE: Tutto m'è noto.

IDOMENEO: Gonfio di tante imprese al varco alfin m'attese il fier Nettuno.

ARBACE: E so che a' danni tuoi ad Eolo unito e a Giove il suo regno sconvolse...

Act II

The royal chambers

Scene 1

IDOMENEUS AND ARBACES.

Recitative and Aria
Recitative

IDOMENEUS: We are alone. Listen to me, Arbaces, and guard this secret in your heart. You have always been loyal to me.

ARBACES: Loyalty in a subject is to be expected. Virtue is no mere duty. I owe you my life, my blood ...

IDOMENEUS: I need your advice about a matter. It's this. You know how fatal my sword was to the Trojans.

ARBACES: I know very well.

IDOMENEUS: Overproud of my exploits, I found dreaded Neptune lying in wait for me ...

ARBACES: And I know how, together with Aeolus and Jove, he turned his realm into a turmoil, to spite you ...

IDOMENEO: Sì, che m'estorse in voto umana vittima.

ARBACE: Di chi?

IDOMENEO: Del primo che sulla spiaggia incauto a me s'appressi.

ARBACE: Or dimmi: chi primo tu incontrasti?

IDOMENEO: Inorridisci: il mio figlio ...

ARBACE: Idamante! ... *(perdendosi d'animo)* Io vengo meno! ... *(raccoltosi)* Ti vide? ... Il conoscesti?

IDOMENEO: Mi vide e a offrirmi ogni sollievo accorse, credendomi stranier e il morto padre piangendo. Al lungo ragionar l'un l'altro conobbe alfin—ahi conoscenza! ...

ARBACE: A lui il suo destin svelasti?

IDOMENEO: No, che da orror confuso io m'involai, disperato il lasciai.

ARBACE: Povero padre! Idamante infelice!

IDOMENEO: Dammi, Arbace, il consiglio: salvami, per pietà, salvami il figlio!

ARBACE: *(pensa, poi risolve)* Trovisi in altro clima altro soggiorno.

IDOMENEO: Dura necessità! ... Ma dove mai, dove ad occhio immortal potrà celarsi?

IDOMENEUS: Yes. So much so that he forced me to promise a human sacrifice.

ARBACES: Who?

IDOMENEUS: The first person whom I happened to meet on the shore.

ARBACES: And so, whom did you meet first?

IDOMENEUS: You will be horrified. My son.

ARBACES: Idamantes! *(overcome)* . . . I feel faint . . . *(recovering himself)* He saw you? You acknowledged him?

IDOMENEUS: He saw me, and even rushed to help me, believing me a stranger, and weeping for his dead father. But after we spoke at length, each knew the other. Oh, what knowledge . . .

ARBACES: Did you reveal his fate to him?

IDOMENEUS: No, in horror and confusion I fled, and left him there desperate.

ARBACES: Poor father! Unhappy Idamantes!

IDOMENEUS: Give me your advice, Arbaces. Save me, for pity's sake, save my son.

ARBACES: *(who ponders and then decides)* He must find another place to live, another country.

IDOMENEUS: Harsh necessity! . . . But where, where could he hide himself from a god's eye?

ARBACE: Purché al popol si celi. Per altra via intanto Nettun si placherà, qualch'altro nume di lui cura n'avrà.

IDOMENEO: Ben dici, è vero … *(Vede venire Ilia.)* Ilia s'appressa, ahimè! … *(Resta un poco pensoso e poi decide.)* In Argo ei vada e sul paterno soglio rimetta Elettra … Or vanne a lei e al figlio, fa' che sian pronti, il tutto sollecito disponi. Custodisci l'arcano, a te mi fido. A te dovranno, o caro, o fido Arbace, la vita il figlio e il genitor la pace.

Aria

ARBACE:
Se il tuo duol, se il mio disio
sen volassero del pari
a ubbidirti qual son io,
saria il duol pronto a fuggir.

Quali al trono sian compagni,
chi l'ambisce or veda e impari:
stia lontan o non si lagni
se non trova che martir.
(Parte.)

Scena 1 [alternativo]

ILIA, IDAMANTE.

N° 10b Scena con rondò

Recitativo

ILIA: Non più. Tutto ascoltai, tutto compresi. D'Elettra e d'Idamante noti sono gli amori. Al caro impegno omai mancar non dei: va', scordati di me, donati a lei.

ARBACES: Only human eyes. Meanwhile, Neptune will be placated in some other way. Another god will watch over your son.

IDOMENEUS: A good plan, it is true . . . *(He sees Ilia approaching.)* Ilia is coming, alas! . . . *(He stays thinking for a little and then makes up his mind.)* Let him go to Argos, and take Electra back to her native land . . . Go to her and to my son, have them prepare. Quickly make all the arrangements. Not a word to anyone. I trust you. To you, my dear, faithful Arbaces, my son will owe his life, and his father his peace of mind.

Aria

ARBACES:
If your sorrow and my desire,
Were now one and the same,
Your grief would quickly expire,
As obedient to you as I am.

Let him who covets the throne
Learn who guards the King.
Let him beware, or not bemoan
If he finds that he is damned.
(He leaves.)

Scene 1 (alternative)

ILIA AND IDAMANTES.

Scene with Rondo

Recitative

ILIA: No more. I have heard everything, and understand it all. The love between Electra and Idamantes is known to all, and you must not now break your word. Go, forget me and give yourself to her.

IDAMANTE: Ch'io mi scordi di te? Che a lei mi doni puoi consigliarmi? E puoi voler che in vita ...

ILIA: Non congiurar, mia vita, contro la mia costanza. Il colpo atroce mi distrugge abbastanza.

IDAMANTE: Ah no, sarebbe il viver mio di morte assai peggior! Fosti il mio primo amore, e l'ultimo sarai. Venga la morte—intrepido l'attendo! —, ma ch'io possa struggermi ad altra face, ad altr'oggetto donar gl'affetti miei? Come tentarlo? Ah, di dolor morrei!

Rondò

Non temer, amato bene,
per te sempre il cor sarà.
Più non reggo a tante pene,
l'alma mia mancando va.
Tu sospiri? Oh duol funesto!
Pensa almen che istante è questo!
Non mi posso—oh dio!—spiegar.
Stelle barbare, spietate!
Perché mai tanto rigor?

Alme belle che vedete
le mie pene in tal momento,
dite voi s'egual tormento
può soffrir un fido cor,
dite voi s'egual tormento
può soffrir un fido cor.
(Parte.)

IDAMANTES: Forget you? You ask that I give myself to her? Do you then think I could live?

ILIA: Do not argue, my love, against my determination. This dreadful blow is difficult enough to endure.

IDAMANTES: Ah no, such a life would be worse than death itself. You were my first love, and will be my last. Let death come. I wait for it fearlessly. But how could I gaze on another's face, how could I give my heart to anyone else? Oh, I would die of sorrow.

Rondo

Never fear, beloved one,
My heart is always yours.
To agony I must succumb.
My soul has no recourse.
You sigh? Oh, horrid pain!
Think what now I face.
Oh God, I cannot explain.
Never fear, beloved one,
My heart is always yours.

Stars so cruel and pitiless,
Why this fate that you enforce?
Kind souls can see my distress
And ask, at this awful moment,
If ever such relentless torment
Has caused a man such remorse.
(He leaves.)

Scena 2

IDOMENEO, ILIA.

Recitativo

ILIA: Se mai pomposo apparse sull'argivo orizzonte il Dio di Delo, eccolo in questo giorno, o sire, in cui l'augusta tua presenza i tuoi diletti sudditi torna in vita e lor pupille, che ti piansero estinto, or rasserena.

IDOMENEO: Principessa gentil, il bel sereno anche alle tue pupille ormai ritorni, il lungo duol dilegua.

ILIA: Io piansi, è vero, e invano l'are tue, o glauca dea, bagnai. Ecuba genitrice, ah, tu lo sai! Piansi in veder l'antico Priamo genitor dell'armi sotto al grave incarco, al suo partir, al tristo avviso di sua morte, e piansi poi al vedere nel tempio il ferro, il fuoco, la patria distrutta e me rapita in questa acerba età, fra nemici e tempeste, prigioniera sotto un polo stranier...

IDOMENEO: Assai soffristi ... ma ogni trista memoria or si sbandisca.

ILIA: Poiché il tuo amabil figlio libertà mi donò, di grazie e onori mi ricolmò, tutta de' tuoi la gioia in me raccolta io sento. Eccomi, accetta l'omaggio ed in tributo il mio non più infelice, ma avventurato cor al figlio, al genitor grato e divoto. Signor, s'umile è il don, sincero è il voto.

IDOMENEO: Idamante mio figlio, allorché libertà ti diè, non fu che interprete felice del paterno voler. S'ei mi prevenne, quanto ei fece a tuo pro tutto io confermo. Di me, de' miei tesori, Ilia, disponi, e mia cura sarà dartene chiare prove dell'amicizia mia.

Scene 2

IDOMENEUS AND ILIA.

Recitative

ILIA: If ever the god of Delos has appeared in his magnificence on the Argive horizon, it is today, sire, the day your august presence restores your rejoicing subjects to life, and clears their eyes, which tears for your death had clouded.

IDOMENEUS: Gentle princess, may calm return to your eyes as well, and may your long suffering cease.

ILIA: I wept, it is true, and in vain bathed your altar with tears, O gray-eyed goddess, for my mother, Hecuba. You know I did! I wept at the news of my old father Priam's death, under the sad burden of war. I wept to see swords and fire in the temple, to see my homeland destroyed and myself abducted at a tender age, amid enemies and tempests, a prisoner in exile . . .

IDOMENEUS: You have suffered greatly . . . But let your sad memories now vanish.

ILIA: Because your generous son has granted me my freedom and bestowed favor and honors on me as well, I feel inside all the joy of your people. I bow before you. Accept my homage, and in tribute my heart, no longer unhappy, but blessed, thankful and devoted to both son and father. Sire, though the gift be humble, the pledge is sincere.

IDOMENEUS: My son, Idamantes, in granting you your freedom, acted as the interpreter of his father's will. If he anticipated me in the good he did you, I confirm it all. I and all I own, Ilia, are at your disposal, and I shall strive to give you certain proof of my friendship.

ILIA: Son certa, e un dubbio in me colpa saria. Propizie stelle! Qual benigno influsso la sorte mia cangiò? Dove temei strazio e morte incontrar, lieta rinasco: colgo dove credei avverso il tutto dell'amare mie pene il dolce frutto.

N° 11 Aria

ILIA:
Se il padre perdei,
la patria, il riposo,
(a Idomeneo)
tu padre mi sei,
soggiorno amoroso
è Creta per me.

Or più non rammento
l'angosce, gl'affanni:
or gioia e contento,
compenso a' miei danni,
il cielo mi diè.
(Parte.)

Scena 3
IDOMENEO SOLO.

Recitativo

IDOMENEO: Qual mi conturba i sensi equivoca favella? ... Ne' suoi casi qual mostra a un tratto intempestiva gioia la frigia principessa? ... Quei ch'esprime teneri sentimenti per il prence sarebber forse—ahimè! ...—sentimenti d'amor, gioia di speme? ... Non m'inganno: reciproco è l'amore. Troppo, Idamante, a scior quelle catene sollecito tu fosti ... Ecco il delitto che in te punisce il ciel ... Sì sì, a Nettuno il figlio, il padre ed Ilia tre vittime saran sull'ara istessa, da egual dolor afflitte, una dal ferro e due dal duol trafitte.

ILIA: I am sure of it, and to doubt it would be wrong. Propitious stars! What benign influence has changed my destiny? Where I feared torture and death, I am reborn a happy woman. Where I thought everything hostile to me, I reap now the sweet fruit of my bitter pain.

Aria

ILIA:
Though my past was taken from me,
You are now my native land,
(to Idomeneus)
My father, my tranquillity.
Crete, by your benevolent hand,
Is now my blessed haven.

My mind is no longer fraught
With anxieties and with grief.
Now contentment, as it ought,
Is heaven's gift and relief.
At last I feel strengthened.
(She leaves.)

Scene 3
IDOMENEUS, ALONE.

Recitative

IDOMENEUS: How her ambiguous words trouble my mind! . . . Why, in her situation, does the Phrygian princess suddenly show such unexpected joy? . . . Her tender sentiments for the prince, could they perhaps be . . . alas! . . . feelings of love, the joy of hope? . . . I am not mistaken. Their love is mutual. Idamantes, you were too hasty in loosening those chains . . . That is the crime for which heaven now punishes you . . . Yes, yes, Neptune will have three victims punished on his altar—one killed by a sword, and two by sorrow.

N° *12a/b Aria*

IDOMENEO:

Fuor del mar ho un mar in seno,
che del primo è più funesto,
e Nettuno ancor in questo
mai non cessa minacciar.

Fiero nume! Dimmi almeno:
se al naufragio è sì vicino
il mio cor, qual rio destino
or gli vieta il naufragar?

Recitativo

IDOMENEO: Frettolosa e giuliva Elettra vien. S'ascolti.

Scena 4

IDOMENEO, ELETTRA.

ELETTRA: Sire, da Arbace intesi quanto la tua clemenza s'interessa per me. Già all'infinito giunser le grazie tue, l'obbligo mio. Or, tua mercé, verdeggia in me la speme di vedere ben tosto depresso de' ribelli il folle orgoglio. E come a tanto amore corrisponder potrò?

IDOMENEO: Di tua difesa ha l'impegno Idamante, a lui men vado: farò che adempia or or l'intento mio, il suo dover, e appaghi il tuo disio.
(Parte.)

ELETTRA: Chi mai del mio provò piacer più dolce?

Aria

IDOMENEUS:

Far from the sea, my breast heaves
With storms more deadly still.
Neptune will not cease until,
Even here, he punishes me.

Relentless god! Tell me why,
My heart broken by the waves,
I am denied the watery grave
A final wreck would grant to me.

Recitative

IDOMENEUS: Electra is hurrying here, joy in her step. I shall hear what she says.

Scene 4

IDOMENEUS AND ELECTRA.

ELECTRA: Sire, I have learned from Arbaces how bountiful you have been on my behalf. Your kindness and my debt to it reach beyond reckoning. Now, thanks to you, I have hope that the foolish pride of the rebels will soon be crushed. How can I repay such generosity?

IDOMENEUS: Idamantes is charged with defending you. I am going to him now, and shall see to it that my intentions and his duty are carried out, and that he fulfills your wishes.
(He leaves.)

ELECTRA: Whose pleasure has ever been sweeter than mine?

Scena 5

ELETTRA SOLA.

ELETTRA: Parto, e l'unico oggetto ch'amo ed adoro—oh dei!—meco sen vien. Ah, troppo, troppo angusto è il mio cor a tanta gioia! Lunge della rivale farò ben io con vezzi e con lusinghe che quel foco, che pria spegnere non potei, a quei lumi s'estingua e avvampi ai miei.

N° 13 Aria

ELETTRA:
Idol mio, se ritroso
altra amante a me ti rende,
non m'offende
rigoroso,
più m'alletta austero amor.

Scaccerà vicino ardore
dal tuo sen l'ardor lontano:
più la mano
può d'amore
s'è vicin l'amante cor.

(S'ode da lontano armoniosa marcia.)

N° 14 Marcia

ELETTRA: Odo da lunge armonioso suono che mi chiama all'imbarco ... Orsù, si vada. *(Parte in fretta.)*

(Si sente sempre più vicina la marcia a misura che si muta la scena.)

Scene 5

ELECTRA, ALONE.

ELECTRA: I am leaving, and the one man I love and adore, O gods, is coming with me? Ah, my heart cannot hold all its happiness! Far from my rival, I shall use my charms and endearments to extinguish, as I never could before, the flame that burns in him for her eyes, and rekindle it for mine.

Aria

ELECTRA:
My idol, though I win
Your love from her
You long have reassured,
And though to my chagrin,
A difficult love is best.

Passion at hand will drive
A distant love away.
That heart holds sway
That artfully connives
To comfort its conquest.

(A harmonious march is heard in the distance.)

March

ELECTRA: I hear from afar the sweet music that summons me to board the ship. It is time to go. *(She hurries off.)*

(The march is heard coming nearer, as the scene is changed.)

Porto di Sidone con bastimenti lungo le spiagge.

Scena 6

ELETTRA, TRUPPA D'ARGIVI, DI CRETESI E DI MARINARI.

Recitativo

ELETTRA: Sidonie sponde, o voi per me di pianto e duol, d'amor nemico crudo ricetto, or ch'astro più clemente a voi mi toglie, io vi perdono, e in pace al lieto partir mio alfin vi lascio e do l'estremo addio.

N° 15 Coro

CORO:
Placido è il mar, andiamo:
tutto ci rassicura.
Felice avrem ventura:
su su, partiamo or or.

ELETTRA:
Soavi Zeffiri,
soli spirate,
del freddo Borea
l'ira calmate,
d'aura piacevole
cortesi siate,
se da voi spargesi
per tutto amor.

CORO:
Placido è il mar, andiamo:
tutto ci rassicura.
Felice avrem ventura:
su su, partiamo or or.

The harbor of Cydonia with ships along the shoreline.

Scene 6

ELECTRA, ARGIVE AND CRETAN TROOPS, AND SAILORS.

Recitative

ELECTRA: The shores of Cydonia! Once you cruelly sheltered my tears, my sorrow, my hateful love, but now that a more auspicious star takes me away, I pardon you. Now that I can at last leave in peace, I bid you farewell!

Chorus

CHORUS:
The sea is calm, let us depart.
The signs predict a fine outcome.
Our voyage will be a happy one.
Come, let us leave at once.

ELECTRA:
Gentle Zephyrs,
Sweetly blow,
Calm the anger
Of cold Boreas so.
As you please,
Let your breeze
Waft to and fro,
Love in the air
Scattered everywhere.

CHORUS:
The sea is calm, let us depart.
The signs predict a fine outcome.
Our voyage will be a happy one.
Come, let us leave at once.

Scena 7

IDOMENEO, IDAMANTE, ELETTRA.

SEGUITO DEL RE.

Recitativo

IDOMENEO: Vattene, prence.

IDAMANTE: Oh ciel!

IDOMENEO: Troppo t'arresti. Parti, e non dubbia fama di mille eroiche imprese il tuo ritorno prevenga. Di regnare se l'arte apprender vuoi, ora incomincia a renderti de' miseri il sostegno, del padre e di te stesso ognor più degno.

N° 16 Terzetto

IDAMANTE:
Pria di partir—oh dio! –
soffri che un bacio imprima
sulla paterna man.

ELETTRA:
Soffri che un grato addio
sul labbro il cor esprima:
addio, degno sovran!

IDOMENEO: *(a Elettra)*
Vanne, sarai felice.
(a Idamante)
Figlio, tua sorte è questa.

ELETTRA, IDAMANTE, IDOMENEO:
Seconda i voti, o ciel!

Scene 7

IDOMENEUS, IDAMANTES, AND ELECTRA.
THE KING'S RETINUE.

Recitative

IDOMENEUS: Go now, prince.

IDAMANTES: Oh heavens!

IDOMENEUS: You delay too long. Go, and may the bright fame of a thousand heroic deeds herald your return. If you would learn how to rule, begin now by making yourself the champion of the downtrodden, and become ever more worthy of your father and yourself.

Trio

IDAMANTES:
Before I leave, oh god!
Let me bend to kiss
Your hand in gratitude.

ELECTRA:
Before I leave, dear sire,
Let me first express
My deepest gratitude.

IDOMENEUS: *(to Electra)*
Go, you will be happy.
(to Idamantes)
My son, this is your destiny.

ELECTRA, IDAMANTES, AND IDOMENEUS: Grant what we pray, O heaven!

ELETTRA: Quanto sperar mi lice!

IDAMANTE: Vado ... *(da sé)* (e il mio cor qui resta.)

IDOMENEO: Addio!

IDAMANTE: Addio!

ELETTRA: Addio!

IDAMANTE, IDOMENEO: *(ognuno da sé)* (Destin crudel!)

IDAMANTE: *(da sé)* (Oh Ilia!)

IDOMENEO: *(da sé)* (Oh figlio!)

IDAMANTE: Oh padre! Oh partenza!

ELETTRA: Oh dei! Che sarà?

ELETTRA, IDAMANTE, IDOMENEO:
Deh, cessi il scompiglio!
Del ciel la clemenza
sua man porgerà.
(Vanno verso le navi.)

(Mentre vanno ad imbarcarsi sorge improvvisa tempesta. Il popolo canta il seguente coro.)

ELECTRA: How great are my hopes!

IDAMANTES: I go! *(to himself)* (But my heart remains here.)

IDOMENEUS: Farewell!

IDAMANTES: Farewell!

ELECTRA: Farewell!

IDAMANTES AND IDOMENEUS: *(each to himself)* (What a cruel fate!)

IDAMANTES: *(to himself)* (Oh, Ilia!)

IDOMENEUS: *(to himself)* (Oh, son!)

IDAMANTES: Oh, father! I must leave you now!

ELECTRA: Oh, gods! What will happen now?

ELECTRA, IDAMANTES, AND IDOMENEUS:
May all this confusion come to rest.
May the mercy of heaven itself
Stretch forth its hand to bless.
(They proceed towards the ships.)

(As they are about to embark, a sudden storm breaks out.)

N° 17 *Coro*

CORO:

Qual nuovo terrore!
Qual rauco muggito!
De' numi il furore
ha il mar infierito.
Nettuno, mercé!

(Incalza la tempesta, il mare si gonfia, il cielo tuona e lampeggia, e i fre-
quenti fulmini incendiano le navi. Un mostro formidabile s'appresenta
fuori dell'onde. Il popolo canta il seguente coro.)

CORO:

Qual odio, qual'ira
Nettuno ci mostra!
Se il cielo s'adira,
qual colpa è la nostra?
Il reo qual è?

Recitativo

IDOMENEO: Eccoti in me—barbaro nume!—il reo: io solo errai,
me sol punisci, e cada sopra di me il tuo sdegno. La mia morte
ti sazi alfin; ma se altra aver pretendi vittima al fallo mio, una
innocente darti io non posso, e se pur tu la vuoi, ingiusto sei:
pretenderla non puoi.

(La tempesta continua. I cretesi spaventati fuggono e nel seguente coro
col canto e con pantomime esprimono il loro terrore, ciò che tutto forma
un'azione analoga e chiude l'atto col solito divertimento.)

Chorus

CHORUS:

Terror rages forth again!
What an unbearable roar!
Their fury the gods now send.
The sea is swallowing the shore.
Neptune, we beg your mercy!

(The storm grows worse, the sea heaves, the sky thunders and flashes, and lightning sets the ships on fire. A huge monster appears above the waves.)

CHORUS:

What anger and what hatred
Neptune shows to us!
What have we done to dread
The tempest he lets loose?
Which one among us is guilty?

Recitative

IDOMENEUS: It is I, vengeful god! I am the guilty one! I alone have sinned. I alone must be punished. Let your wrath fall on me. Let my death satisfy you. But if you demand another victim for my sin, I cannot give you an innocent man. If that is what you demand, you are an evil god and cannot be served.

(The storm rages on. The frightened Cretans flee and in the following chorus their song and mime express their terror, so that it all creates an appropriate ending, closing it with the expected divertimento.)

N° 18 Coro

CORO:

Corriamo, fuggiamo
quel mostro spietato!
Corriamo, fuggiamo,
ah, preda già siamo!
Chi, perfido fato,
più crudo è di te?

Fine dell'atto secondo.

Chorus

CHORUS:
Let us run, let us flee!
The ravenous monster, run!
It is already too late.
What a horrifying fate!
Death for everyone!

End of Act II.

Atto terzo

Giardino reale.

Scena 1
ILIA SOLA.

Recitativo

ILIA: Solitudini amiche, aure amorose, piante fiorite e fiori vaghi, udite d'una infelice amante i lamenti che a voi lassa confido. Quanto il tacer presso al mio vincitore, quanto il finger ti costa, afflitto core!

N° 19 Aria

ILIA:
Zeffiretti lusinghieri,
deh, volate al mio tesoro
e gli dite ch'io l'adoro,
che mi serbi il cor fedel.

E voi piante e fior sinceri
che ora innaffia il pianto amaro,
dite a lui che amor più raro
mai vedeste sotto al ciel.

Act III

The royal garden.

Scene 1

ILIA, ALONE.

Recitative

ILIA: Solitude my friend, and loving breezes, trees in bloom and flowers so fair, hear the lament of an unhappy lover that I whisper now to you. How much it hurts my afflicted heart to be silent and pretend, when it is so close to its conqueror!

Aria

ILIA:
Sweet, caressing breezes, fly,
Fly to my one true love.
Tell him what I dream of,
That he keep his heart for me.

And you, delicious flowers
My tears now water so,
Tell him that you scarcely know
A lover who pines more tenderly.

Recitativo

ILIA: Ei stesso vien … Oh dei! … Mi spiego o taccio? … Resto … parto … o m'ascondo? … Ah, risolver non posso! Ah, mi confondo!

Scena 2

ILIA, IDAMANTE.

Recitativo

IDAMANTE: Principessa, a' tuoi sguardi se offrirmi ardisco ancor, più non mi guida un temerario affetto: altro or non cerco che appagarti e morir.

ILIA: Morir? Tu, prence?

IDAMANTE: Più teco io resto, più di te m'accendo e s'aggrava mia colpa. A che il castigo più a lungo differir?

ILIA: Ma qual cagione morte a cercar t'induce?

IDAMANTE: Il genitore, pien di smania e furore, torvo mi guarda e fugge, e il motivo mi cela. Da tue catene avvinto, il tuo rigore a nuovi guai m'espone. Un fiero mostro fa dappertutto orrida strage. Or questo a combatter si vada e vincerlo si tenti, o finisca la morte i miei tormenti.

ILIA: Calma, o prence, un trasporto sì funesto: rammenta che tu sei d'un grand'impero l'unica speme.

IDAMANTE: Privo del tuo amore, privo, Ilia, di te, nulla mi cale.

ILIA: Misera me! … Deh, serba i giorni tuoi.

Recitative

ILIA: He's coming here himself . . . Oh gods! . . . Shall I speak to him or be silent? . . . Shall I stay . . . no, leave . . . or should I hide? . . . Ah, I cannot decide! Oh, what confusion!

Scene 2

ILIA AND IDAMANTES.

Recitative

IDAMANTES: Princess, if I dare appear before you again, it is because passion no longer impels me. I desire nothing but to serve your pleasure, or die.

ILIA: Die? You, Prince?

IDAMANTES: The more I stay near you, the more I burn for you, and the greater my guilt grows. Why postpone my punishment any longer?

ILIA: But what is the reason you seek death?

IDAMANTES: My father, restless and angry, scowls and avoids me without telling me why. Now that I am ensnared by you, your harshness only adds to my woe. A terrifying monster wreaks death and chaos everywhere. I am determined now to find and destroy it, or let death end my torment.

ILIA: Dear Prince, calm your tortured mind. Remember that you are the only hope of a great empire.

IDAMANTES: Without you and your love, Ilia, I care about nothing.

ILIA: Woe is me! . . . You must live!

IDAMANTE: Il mio fato crudel seguir degg'io.

ILIA: Vivi... Ilia tel chiede.

IDAMANTE: Oh dei! Che ascolto? Principessa adorata!...

ILIA: Il cor turbato a te mal custodì la debolezza mia: pur troppo amore e tema indivisi ho nel sen.

IDAMANTE: Odo? O sol quel che brama finge l'udito, oppure il grand'ardore m'agita i sensi e il cor lusinga oppresso un dolce sogno?

ILIA: Ah! Perché pria non arsi che scoprir la mia fiamma? Mille io sento rimorsi all'alma! Il sacro mio dovere, la mia gloria, la patria, il sangue de' miei ancor fumante, oh, quanto al core rimproverano il mio ribelle amore!... Ma alfin che fo? Giacché in periglio estremo ti vedo, o caro, e trarti sola io posso, odimi, io tel ridico: t'amo, t'adoro, e se morir tu vuoi, pria che m'uccida il duol morir non puoi.

N° 20a Duetto

IDAMANTE:
S'io non moro a questi accenti,
non è ver che amor uccida,
che la gioia opprima un cor.

ILIA:
Non più duol, non più lamenti:
io ti son costante e fida,
tu sei il solo mio tesor.

IDAMANTE: Tu sarai...

ILIA: ... qual tu mi vuoi.

IDAMANTES: I must follow my cruel destiny.

ILIA: Live . . . Ilia implores you.

IDAMANTES: Oh gods! What do I hear? My beloved Princess!

ILIA: My troubled heart can no longer hide my weakness from you. My breast shelters both love and fear.

IDAMANTES: What are you saying? Or am I only hearing what I long to hear? Does my passion so excite my senses that a sweet dream teases my dejected heart?

ILIA: Oh, I should have perished rather than reveal my passion. My soul feels a thousand pangs of remorse. My sacred duty, my honor, my homeland, the spilled blood of my family, all reproach my heart for its rebellious love! . . . But what can I do? I see you, my dearest, in danger, and only I can save you. Let me tell you again—I love you, I adore you, and if you wish to die, grief will have already killed me before you can.

Duet

IDAMANTES:
I have not died of what you say.
It is not true that love can kill
Or too much joy destroy a heart.

ILIA:
Lament and sorrow hold no sway.
I have been constant, and always will.
Let nothing ever keep us apart.

IDAMANTES: You will be . . .

ILIA: Whatever you wish.

IDAMANTE: La mia sposa …

ILIA: Lo sposo mio sarai tu?

ILIA, IDAMANTE:
Lo dica Amor.
Ah! Il gioir sorpassa in noi
il sofferto affanno rio:
tutto vince il nostro ardor!

Scena 3
IDOMENEO, ELETTRA E DETTI.

Recitativo
IDOMENEO: *(da sé)* (Cieli! Che vedo?)

ILIA: *(a Idamante)* Ah, siam scoperti, o caro!

IDAMANTE: *(a Ilia)* Non temer, idol mio!

ELETTRA: *(da sé)* (Ecco l'ingrato.)

IDOMENEO: *(da sé)* (Io ben m'apposi al ver. Ah crudo fato!)

IDAMANTE: Signor, già più non oso padre chiamarti: a un sud-dito infelice, deh, questa almen concedi unica grazia.

IDOMENEO: Parla.

ELETTRA: *(da sé)* (Che dirà?)

IDAMANTE: In che t'offesi mai? Perché mi fuggi? … M'odi e aborrisci?

ILIA: *(da sé)* (Io tremo.)

IDAMANTES: My wife . . .

ILIA: You will be my husband!

ILIA AND IDAMANTES:
Let our love be proclaimed!
Ah, now every joy is so much more
Than any suffering once endured.
Nothing defeats what love imparts.

Scene 3
IDOMENEUS, ELECTRA, AND THOSE BEFORE.

Recitative
IDOMENEUS: *(to himself)* (Heavens! What is this?)

ILIA: *(to Idamantes)* We are discovered, my darling.

IDAMANTES: *(to Ilia)* Have no fear, my treasure.

ELECTRA: *(to herself)* (Look at that ungrateful man.)

IDOMENEUS: *(to himself)* (It is as I suspected. Ah, cruel fate!)

IDAMANTES: Sire—I dare no longer call you father—grant one favor to your unhappy subject.

IDOMENEUS: Speak.

ELECTRA: *(to herself)* (What will he say?)

IDAMANTES: What did I do to offend you? Why do you avoid me, hate me, turn from me?

ILIA: *(to herself)* (I am trembling.)

ELETTRA: *(da sé)* (Io tel direi.)

IDOMENEO: Figlio, contro di me Nettuno irato gelommi il cor. Ogni tua tenerezza l'affanno mio raddoppia, il tuo dolore tutto sul cor mi piomba, e rimirarti senza ribrezzo e orror non posso.

ILIA: *(da sé)* (Oh dio!)

IDAMANTE: Forse per colpa mia Nettun sdegnossi? Ma la colpa qual è?

IDOMENEO: Ah, placarlo potessi senza di te!

ELETTRA: *(da sé)* (Ah, potessi i torti miei or vendicar!)

IDOMENEO: *(a Idamante)* Parti, te lo comando: fuggi il paterno lido e cerca altrove sicuro asilo.

ILIA: *(a Elettra)* Ahimè! … Pietosa principessa, ah, mi conforta!

ELETTRA: Ch'io ti conforti? E come? … *(da sé)* (Ancor m'insulta l'indegna.)

IDAMANTE: Dunque io me n'andrò! … Ma dove? … Oh Ilia! … Oh genitor!

ILIA: *(risoluta)* O seguirti o morir, mio ben, vogl'io.

IDAMANTE: Deh, resta, o cara, e vivi in pace … Addio!

ELECTRA: *(to herself)* (I can tell what it is.)

IDOMENEUS: My son, Neptune in his anger has frozen my heart against you. Your tenderness is salt in my wound. Your sorrow is a burden only on me. I cannot look at you and not shudder with horror.

ILIA: *(to herself)* (Oh god!)

IDAMANTES: Perhaps Neptune is angry because of something I did. What have I done wrong?

IDOMENEUS: Oh, if only I could placate his wrath without involving you!

ELECTRA: *(to herself)* (If only I could avenge my wrongs now!)

IDOMENEUS: *(to Idamantes)* Go, I command you. Flee your native land and seek safe haven elsewhere.

ILIA: *(to Electra)* Alas! Compassionate princess, comfort me!

ELECTRA: Comfort you? How would I do that? *(to herself)* (That shameless woman insults me yet again.)

IDAMANTES: So I must leave for good! . . . But where? . . . Oh Ilia! Oh father!

ILIA: *(with resolve)* I will follow you or die, beloved.

IDAMANTES: No, stay here, my dearest, and live in peace. Farewell!

N° 21 Quartetto

IDAMANTE:
Andrò ramingo e solo,
morte cercando altrove
finché la incontrerò.

ILIA:
M'avrai compagna al duolo
dove sarai, e dove
tu moia io morirò.

IDAMANTE: Ah no ...

IDOMENEO:
Nettun spietato!
Chi per pietà m'uccide?

ELETTRA: *(da sé)* (Quando vendetta avrò?)

ILIA, IDAMANTE: *(a Idomeneo)* Serena il ciglio irato.

ILIA, IDAMANTE, IDOMENEO: Ah, il cor mi si divide!

ILIA, ELETTRA, IDAMANTE, IDOMENEO:
Soffrir più non si può.
Peggio è di morte
sì gran dolore:
più fiera sorte,
pena maggiore
nessun provò!

IDAMANTE: Andrò ramingo e solo.
(Idamante parte addolorato.)

Quartet

IDAMANTES:
I will wander away, alone,
Searching for death elsewhere.
I will encounter it at last.

ILIA:
Your grief will be my own.
Whatever happens I will share.
To death I will hold fast.

IDAMANTES: Ah, no . . .

IDOMENEUS:
Neptune, pitiless as the sea!
Who will kill me, for pity's sake?

ELECTRA: *(to herself)* (When will vengeance be mine?)

ILIA AND IDAMANTES: *(to Idomeneus)* Calm your anger, we plead.

ILIA, IDAMANTES, AND IDOMENEUS: Oh, my poor heart will break!

ILIA, IDAMANTES, IDOMENEUS, AND ELECTRA:
Suffer even more?
A sorrow so great
Is worse than death.
A harsher fate,
Fiercer punishment,
Who has ever borne?

IDAMANTES: I will wander away, alone.
(He leaves sorrowfully.)

Scena 4

ARBACE, IDOMENEO, ILIA, ELETTRA.

Recitativo

ARBACE: Sire, alla reggia tua immensa turba di popolo affollato ad alta voce parlar ti chiede.

ILIA: *(da sé)* (A qualche nuovo affanno preparati, mio cor.)

IDOMENEO: *(da sé)* (Perduto è il figlio.)

ARBACE: Del dio de' mari il sommo sacerdote la guida.

IDOMENEO: *(da sé)* (Ahi, troppo disperato è il caso! ...) *(ad Arbace)* Intesi, Arbace ...

ELETTRA: *(da sé)* (Qual nuovo disastro!)

ILIA: *(da sé)* (Il popol sollevato ...)

IDOMENEO: Or vado ad ascoltarla. *(Parte confuso.)*

ELETTRA: Ti seguirò. *(Parte.)*

ILIA: Voglio seguirti anch'io. *(Parte.)*

Scena 5

ARBACE SOLO.

Recitativo

ARBACE: Sventurata Sidon! In te quai miro di morte, stragi e orror lugubri aspetti? Ah, Sidon più non sei, sei la città del pianto, e questa reggia quella del duol! ... Dunque è per noi

Scene 4

ARBACES, IDOMENEUS, ILIA, AND ELECTRA.

Recitative

ARBACES: Sire, a huge crowd has gathered at the palace, demanding to speak with you.

ILIA: *(to herself)* (Prepare yourself, my heart, for some new sorrow.)

IDOMENEUS: *(to himself)* (My son is lost.)

ARBACES: The High Priest of Neptune is at their lead.

IDOMENEUS: *(to himself)* (The situation is desperate!) *(to Arbaces)* I understand, Arbaces ...

ELECTRA: *(to herself)* (What new disaster?)

ILIA: *(to herself)* (The people in arms ...)

IDOMENEUS: I will go and hear them. *(He leaves in distress.)*

ELECTRA: I will follow! *(She leaves.)*

ILIA: I, too, must follow them. *(She leaves.)*

Scene 5

ARBACES, ALONE.

Recitative

ARBACES: Poor, unhappy Cydonia! What a vision of death, destruction, and horror do I foresee! Ah, you are longer Cydonia, but the city of tears and this palace one of sorrow. Does heaven

dal cielo sbandita ogni pietà? ... Chi sa? ... Io spero ancora che qualche nume amico si plachi a tanto sangue: un nume solo basta tutti a piegar ... alla clemenza il rigor cederà ... ma ancor non scorgo qual ci miri pietoso ... Ah, sordo è il cielo! Ah, Creta tutta io vedo finir sua gloria sotto alte rovine! No, sue miserie pria non avran fine.

N° 22 Aria

ARBACE:
Se colà ne' fati è scritto,
Creta—oh dei! –, s'è rea, or cada.
Paghi il fio del suo delitto;
ma salvate il prence, il re.

Deh, d'un sol vi plachi il sangue!
Ecco il mio, se il mio v'aggrada,
e il bel regno che già langue
– giusti dei!—abbia mercé.
(*Parte.*)

*Gran piazza abbellita di statue avanti al palazzo
di cui si vede da un lato il frontespizio.*

Scena 6

ARRIVA IDOMENEO ACCOMPAGNATO D'ARBACE E DAL
SEGUITO REALE. IL RE SCORTATO D'ARBACE SI SIEDE
SOPRA IL TRONO DESTINATO ALLE PUBBLICHE UDIENZE.
GRAN SACERDOTE E QUANTITÀ DI POPOLO.

N° 23 Recitativo

GRAN SACERDOTE: Volgi intorno lo sguardo, o sire, e vedi qual strage orrenda nel tuo nobil regno fa il crudo mostro. Ah, mira allagate di sangue quelle pubbliche vie! Ad ogni passo vedrai chi geme e l'alma gonfio d'atro velen dal corpo esala. Mille e mille in

forbid us any pity? Who can know? I still hope that a kind god will be sated by all this blood. One god is enough to make the difference. Severity will yield to clemency . . . But I cannot yet glimpse the one who might regard us with pity. Heaven is deaf! I see all of Crete with her glory buried deep in ruins! No, her woes will not be over before this happens.

Aria

ARBACES:
If the fates have thus decreed
That Crete is guilty and must fall,
Then let it suffer and bleed
But spare our prince, the King.

Let the blood of one man appease.
Here is mine, if that will do.
But on this fair kingdom, please,
Have mercy. It is weakening.
(He leaves.)

The great square, adorned with statues, in front of the palace whose façade can be seen at one side.

Scene 6

IDOMENEUS ARRIVES ACCOMPANIED BY ARBACES AND THE ROYAL RETINUE. THE KING, ESCORTED BY ARBACES, TAKES HIS PLACE ON THE THRONE USED FOR PUBLIC AUDIENCES. THE HIGH PRIEST AND A NUMBER OF PEOPLE.

Recitative

HIGH PRIEST: Look around you, sire, and see what horrible devastation the savage monster has wrought in your realm. Behold the streets running with blood, someone groaning in every doorway, the soul leaving another body swollen with black

quell'ampio e sozzo ventre pria sepolti che morti perire io stesso vidi. Sempre di sangue lorde son quelle fauci e son sempre più ingorde. Da te solo dipende il ripiego, da morte trar tu puoi il resto del tuo popolo ch'esclama sbigottito e da te l'aiuto implora, e indugi ancor? ... Al tempio, sire, al tempio! Qual è, dov'è la vittima? ... A Nettuno rendi quello ch'è suo ...

IDOMENEO: Non più. Sacro ministro e voi popoli, udite: la vittima è Idamante, e or or vedrete—ah numi! Con qual ciglio?— svenar il genitor il proprio figlio. *(Parte turbato.)*

N° 24 Coro

CORO:
Oh voto tremendo!
Spettacolo orrendo!
Già regna la morte,
d'abisso le porte
spalanca crudel.

GRAN SACERDOTE:
Oh cielo clemente!
Il figlio è innocente,
il voto è inumano:
arresta la mano
del padre fedel!

CORO:
Oh voto tremendo!
Spettacolo orrendo!
Già regna la morte,
d'abisso le porte
spalanca crudel.
(Partono tutti dolenti.)

poison. I myself have seen thousands perish, buried before they were dead in its immense belly. Its jaws are dipping with blood and greedy for more. On you alone the outcome depends. Only you can save the rest of your people from death. They cry out in despair to you, begging you to help, and yet still you delay . . . To the temple, sire, to the temple! Who is the victim and where is he? . . . Render to Neptune what is his.

IDOMENEUS: No more. Holy priest and you, my people, listen. The victim is Idamantes, and soon you will see—oh gods!—the look on a father's face as he executes his own son. *(He leaves in distress.)*

Chorus

CHORUS:
Oh terrible vow!
Horrendous sight!
Death reigns now
And opens in fright
The door to the abyss.

HIGH PRIEST:
Heaven most clement!
The son is innocent,
The vow merciless.
Stay the hand
Of a father so pious.

CHORUS:
Oh terrible vow!
Horrendous sight!
Death reigns now
And opens in fright
The door to the abyss.
(They all leave in sorrow.)

Veduta esteriore del magnifico tempio di Nettuno con vastissimo atrio che la circonda, attraverso del quale si scopre in lontano spiaggia di mare.

Scena 7

L'ATRIO E LE GALLERIE DEL TEMPIO SONO RIPIENE D'UNA MOLTITUDINE DI POPOLO, LI SACERDOTI PREPARANO LE COSE APPARTENENTI AL SACRIFICIO.

N° 25 *Marcia*

ARRIVA IDOMENEO ACCOMPAGNATO DI NUMEROSO E FASTOSO SEGUITO.

N° 26 *Cavatina con coro*

IDOMENEO:
Accogli, o re del mar, i nostri voti:
placa lo sdegno tuo, il tuo rigor!

SACERDOTI:
Accogli, o re del mar, i nostri voti:
placa lo sdegno tuo, il tuo rigor!

IDOMENEO:
Tornino a lor spelonche gl'Euri, i Noti,
torni Zeffiro al mar, cessi il furor!
Il pentimento e il cor de' tuoi devoti
accetta e a noi concedi il tuo favor!

SACERDOTI:
Accogli, o re del mar, i nostri voti:
placa lo sdegno tuo, il tuo rigor!

*The exterior view of the magnificent Temple of Neptune,
surrounded by an immense portico beyond which the distant
sea can be viewed.*

Scene 7

THE PORTICO AND ARCADES OF THE TEMPLE ARE FILLED
WITH A MULTITUDE OF PEOPLE; PRIESTS ARE PREPARING
THE CEREMONY OF SACRIFICE.

March

IDOMENEUS ARRIVES ACCOMPANIED BY A LARGE AND
SPLENDID RETINUE.

Cavatina with Chorus

IDOMENEUS:

Accept our vows, O King of the Sea.
Abate your anger and severity.

PRIESTS:

Accept our vows, O King of the Sea.
Abate your anger and severity.

IDOMENEUS:

Let the violent winds return to their caves.
Let their fury cease, and calm winds return.
Accept the repentance which you crave.
Grant us the peace for which we yearn.

PRIESTS:

Accept our vows, O King of the Sea.
Abate your anger and severity.

CORO: *(entro le scene)*
Stupenda vittoria!
Eterna è tua gloria:
trionfa, o signor!

Recitativo
IDOMENEO: Qual risuona qui intorno applauso di vittoria?

Scena 8

ARBACE FRETTOLOSO E DETTI.

Recitativo
ARBACE: Sire, il prence, Idamante l'eroe, di morte in traccia
disperato correndo il trionfo trovò. Sull'empio mostro scagliossi
furibondo, il vinse e uccise. Eccoci salvi alfin.

IDOMENEO: Ahimè! Nettuno di nuovo sdegno acceso sarà contro
di noi... Or or, Arbace, con tuo dolor vedrai che Idamante trovò
quel che cercava e di morte egli stesso il trionfo sarà.

ARBACE: *(vede condurre Idamante.)* Che vedo?... Oh numi!

Scena 9

IDAMANTE IN VESTE BIANCA CON GHIRLANDA DI FIORI
IN CAPO, CIRCONDATO DA GUARDIE E DA SACERDOTI.
MOLTITUDINE DI MESTO POPOLO E SUDDETTI.

N° 27 Recitativo
IDAMANTE: Padre, mio caro padre, ah dolce nome! Eccomi a'
piedi tuoi: in questo estremo periodo fatal, su questa destra, che
il varco al sangue tuo nelle mie vene aprir dovrà, gl'ultimi baci
accetta. Ora comprendo che il tuo turbamento sdegno non era

CHORUS: *(behind the scene)*
A mighty victory!
All hail your glory!
Triumph, majesty!

Recitative

IDOMENEUS: What are these shouts of victory that echo all around?

Scene 8

ARBACES IN HASTE, AND THOSE BEFORE.

Recitative

ARBACES: Sire, our young hero, Prince Idamantes, running desperately to meet his death, has triumphed instead. He threw himself furiously at the savage monster, struggled with it, and killed it. We are saved at last.

IDOMENEUS: Alas! Neptune's wrath will only flare up again at us . . . Soon to your sorrow, Arbaces, you will see that Idamantes has found what he was seeking. He himself will be death's victim.

ARBACES: *(seeing Idamantes being led in)* What is this I see? . . . Oh gods!

Scene 9

IDAMANTES IN A WHITE ROBE, HIS HEAD GARLANDED WITH FLOWERS, SURROUNDED BY GUARDS AND PRIESTS. A CROWD OF PEOPLE IN MOURNING, AND THOSE BEFORE.

Recitative

IDAMANTES: Father—my dear father, ah sweet name! I present myself to you. At this dire moment, let me kiss one last time your right hand, which must make your blood flow from my veins. Now I understand that your agitation was not anger, but fatherly

già, ma amor paterno. O mille volte e mille fortunato Idamante, se chi vita ti diè vita ti toglie, e togliendola a te la rende al cielo, e dal cielo la sua in cambio impetra, ed impetra costante a' suoi la pace e de' numi l'amor sacro e verace!

IDOMENEO: Oh figlio! Oh caro figlio! Perdona: il crudo uffizio in me scelta non è, pena è del fato ... Barbaro, iniquo fato! ... Ah no, non posso contro un figlio innocente alzar l'aspra bipenne ... da ogni fibra già sen fuggon le forze, e gl'occhi miei torbida notte ingombra ... Oh figlio! ...

IDAMANTE: *(languente, poi risoluto)* Oh padre! ... Ah, non t'arresti inutile pietà, né vana ti lusinghi tenerezza d'amor! Deh, vibra un colpo che ambi tolga d'affanno!

IDOMENEO: Ah, che natura mel contrasta e ripugna!

IDAMANTE: Ceda natura al suo autor: di Giove questo è l'alto voler. Rammenta il tuo dover. Se un figlio perdi, cento avrai numi amici. Figli tuoi i tuoi popoli sono. Ma se in mia vece brami chi t'ubbidisca ed ami, chi ti sia accanto e di tue cure il peso teco ne porti, Ilia ti raccomando. Deh, un figlio tu esaudisci che moribondo supplica e consiglia: s'ella sposa non m'è, deh, siati figlia!

N° 27a Aria

IDAMANTE:
No, la morte io non pavento,
se alla patria, al genitore
frutta, o numi, il vostro amore
e di pace il bel seren.

Agli Elisi andrò contento,
e riposo avrà quest'alma,
se in lasciare la mia salma
vita e pace avrà il mio ben.

love. A thousand times fortunate is Idamantes if he who gave him life now takes it and returns it to heaven, receiving in turn his own life from heaven, a lasting peace for his people, and the sacred and true love of the gods.

IDOMENEUS: O my son, my dear son! Forgive me. This horrifying task is not my choice, but the punishment of fate . . . A barbarous, unjust fate! . . . No, I cannot raise the brutal axe against my innocent son . . . strength drains from every fiber of my being, and darkness clouds my eyes . . . Oh son! . . .

IDAMANTES: *(faint, then resolute)* Oh father! . . . Do not let a futile pity stop you, nor the useless tenderness of love delude you. Strike the blow that will release us both from our sorrow.

IDOMENEUS: Ah, Nature abhors this, and stops my hand.

IDAMANTES: Let Nature yield to who created her. This is the will of Jove. Remember your duty. Though you lose a son, you gain a hundred gods as friends. Your people are now your sons. But if in my stead you desire someone to obey and love you, to stand by your side and help bear the burden of your cares, I commend Ilia to you. Listen to your son, who pleads with you on the brink of death. If she cannot be my wife, let her be your daughter.

Aria

IDAMANTES:
No, it is not death I fear,
If your love, ye gods, allows
The serenity of peace now
For my father and my country.

I will go to the Elysian Fields
And my soul will be at rest.
If you grant one last request—
Grant my beloved tranquility.

Recitativo

IDAMANTE: Ma che più tardi? Eccomi pronto, adempi il sacri‐
fizio, il voto.

IDOMENEO: Oh, qual mi sento in ogni vena insolito vigor? ... Or
risoluto son ... l'ultimo amplesso ricevi ... e mori.

IDAMANTE: Oh padre! ...

IDOMENEO: Oh figlio! ...

IDAMANTE, IDOMENEO: Oh dio! ...

IDAMANTE: *(da sé)* (Oh Ilia ... ahimè! ...) *(a Idomeneo)* Vivi felice.

IDAMANTE, IDOMENEO: Addio!

(Nell'atto di ferire sopravviene Ilia ed impedisce il colpo.)

•

Scena 10

ILIA FRETTOLOSA, ELETTRA E DETTI.

Recitativo

ILIA: *(corre a ritenere il braccio d'Idomeneo.)* Ferma, o sire, che fai?

IDOMENEO: La vittima io sveno che promisi a Nettuno.

IDAMANTE: Ilia, t'accheta ...

GRAN SACERDOTE: *(a Ilia)* Deh, non turbar il sacrifizio ...

Recitative

IDAMANTES: But why delay any longer? I am ready. Make the sacrifice, fulfill your vow.

IDOMENEUS: What is this strange strength I suddenly feel in every nerve? . . . I am resolved now . . . Receive my last embrace . . . and die.

IDAMANTES: Oh father! . . .

IDOMENEUS: Oh son! . . .

IDAMANTES AND IDOMENEUS: Oh God!. . .

IDAMANTES: *(to himself)* (Oh Ilia . . . Alas! . . .) *(to Idomeneus)* May you live happily.

IDAMANTES AND IDOMENEUS: Farewell.

(As Idomeneus is about to strike, Ilia suddenly appears and prevents the blow.)

Scene 10

ILIA, HURRIEDLY; ELECTRA, AND THOSE BEFORE.

Recitative

ILIA: *(rushing to stay Idomeneus's arm)* Stop, sire! What are you doing?

IDOMENEUS: I must kill the victim promised to Neptune.

IDAMANTES: Ilia, be silent . . .

HIGH PRIEST: *(to Ilia)* Do not interrupt the sacrifice . . .

ILIA: Invano quella scure altro petto tenta ferir. Eccoti, sire, il mio: la vittima io son.

ELETTRA: *(da sé)* (Oh, qual contrasto!)

ILIA: *(a Idomeneo)* Innocente è Idamante, è figlio tuo, e del regno è la speme. Tiranni i dei non son, fallaci siete interpreti voi tutti del divino voler. Vuol sgombra il cielo de' nemici la Grecia, e non de' figli. Benché innocente anch'io, benché ora amica, di Priamo son figlia e frigia io nacqui, per natura nemica al greco nome. Orsù, mi svena. *(s'inginocchia avanti al Gran Sacerdote.)*

(S'ode gran strepito sotterraneo, la statua di Nettuno si scuote; Il Gran Sacerdote si trova avanti l'ara in estasi. Tutti rimangono attoniti ed immobili per lo spavento. Una voce profonda e grave pronunzia la seguente sentenza del cielo.)

N° 28a La Voce

LA VOCE: Idomeneo cessi esser re ... lo sia Idamante ... ed Ilia a lui sia sposa.

N° 29 Recitativo

IDOMENEO: Oh ciel pietoso!

IDAMANTE: Ilia ...

ILIA: Idamante, udisti?

ARBACE: Oh gioia, oh amor, oh numi!

ELETTRA: Oh smania, oh furie! Oh disperata Elettra! Vedrò Idamante alla rivale in braccio, e dall'uno e dall'altra mostrarmi a dito? ... Ah no, il germano Oreste ne' cupi abissi io vo' seguir.

ILIA: In vain will that axe strike anyone else's breast. Here is mine, sire. I am your victim.

ELECTRA: *(to herself)* (What a turn of events!)

ILIA: *(to Idomeneus)* Idamantes is innocent. He is your son, and the hope of the kingdom. The gods are not tyrants. You have all read wrongly the divine will. Heaven wishes Greece rid of its enemies, not of its children. I too am innocent, and now your friend, but I am Priam's daughter and born a Phrygian, so by nature an enemy to Greece. Come, kill me. *(She kneels before the High Priest.)*

(A loud noise is heard from underground. The statue of Neptune is shaken. The High Priest stands before the altar in ecstasy. Everyone remains trans-fixed and stunned by fear. A deep voice pronounces the following judgment from heaven.)

The Voice

THE VOICE: Idomeneus shall no longer be king. Idamantes shall reign, and Ilia be his bride.

Recitative

IDOMENEUS: Oh merciful heaven!

IDAMANTES: Ilia . . .

ILIA: Idamantes, did you hear?

ARBACES: What joy! Oh love! Oh gods!

ELECTRA: Oh frenzy! Oh furies! Oh Electra's despair! . . . Will I see Idamantes in my rival's arms, and have each of them point at me? No, I would prefer to follow my brother Orestes into the

Ombra infelice! Lo spirto mio accogli: or or compagna m'avrai
là nell'inferno a' sempiterni guai, al pianto eterno.

N° 29a Aria

ELETTRA:
D'Oreste, d'Aiace
ho in seno i tormenti;
d'Aletto la face
già morte mi dà.

Squarciatemi il core,
ceraste, serpenti,
o un ferro il dolore
in me finirà.
(Parte infuriata.)

Scena ultima

IDOMENEO, IDAMANTE, ILIA, ARBACE. SEGUITO
D'IDOMENEO, D'IDAMANTE E D'ILIA; POPOLO.

N° 30 Recitativo

IDOMENEO: Popoli, a voi l'ultima legge impone Idomeneo qual
re. Pace v'annunzio. Compiuto è il sacrifizio e sciolto il voto. Nettuno e tutti i numi a questo regno amici son. Resta che al cenno
loro Idomeneo ora ubbidisca. Oh, quanto, o sommi dei, quanto
m'è grato il cenno! Eccovi un re, un altro me stesso: a Idamante
mio figlio, al caro figlio cedo il soglio di Creta e tutto insieme il
sovrano poter. I suoi comandi rispettate, eseguite ubbidienti,
come i miei eseguiste e rispettaste, onde grato io vi son: questa
è la legge. Eccovi la real sposa. Mirate in questa bella coppia un
don del cielo serbato a voi. Quanto a sperar vi lice! Oh Creta
fortunata! Oh me felice!

deep abyss. Unhappy ghost! Receive my spirit, and soon in hell you will have me at your side, in eternal woe, in endless weeping.

Aria

ELECTRA:
By the fate of Orestes and Ajax,
And Alecto's burning torch,
My breast is already wracked.
They lead me on to death.

Vipers and serpents, here,
Poison the rest of my heart.
Let a jagged rock be my bier,
A blade take my last breath!
(She runs off, engorged with fury.)

Final Scene

IDOMENEUS, IDAMANTES, ILIA, AND ARBACES. THE RETINUES OF IDOMENEUS, IDAMANTES, AND ILIA; THE PEOPLE.

Recitative

IDOMENEUS: My people, Idomeneus now gives you his final command as your king. I proclaim peace. The sacrifice is completed, the vow fulfilled. Neptune and all the gods now look favorably on our land. It remains only for Idomeneus to obey their wishes. O mighty gods, how welcome your wishes are. Here is your new king, my other self. To Idamantes, my dearest son, I give over the throne of Crete, together with all my sovereign power. Respect his commands, follow them obediently, as you once did mine. You have my gratitude, and now my word. Here is the royal bride. Behold in this handsome couple the gift bestowed on you by heaven. Here are all your hopes! Oh fortunate Crete! What happiness this is for me!

N° 30a Aria

IDOMENEO:

Torna la pace al core,
torna lo spento ardore,
fiorisce in me l'età.
Tal la stagion di Flora
l'albero annoso infiora,
nuovo vigor gli dà.

*Segue l'incoronazione d'Idamante che s'eseguisce in pantomima, il coro
che si canta durante l'incoronazione, ed il ballo.*

N° 31 Coro

CORO:

Scenda Amor, scenda Imeneo
e Giunone ai regi sposi.
D'alma pace ormai gli posi
la dea pronuba nel sen!

N° 32 Ballet

Fine del dramma.

Aria

IDOMENEUS:

Peace returns now to my heart.
The exhausted love returns.
Vigor rises in me once more.
Just as in spring there start
New leaves on old trees, we learn
Youth comes where age was before.

(The coronation of Idamantes follows, which is performed in mime, and a chorus sung during the ceremony and the dancing.)

Chorus

CHORUS:

May Cupid, Hymen, and Juno
Descend to this royal pair.
May the goddess of marriage bear
Them years of peace, we implore.

Ballet

End of the Opera.

2

The Abduction

from the

Seraglio

THE ABDUCTION FROM THE SERAGLIO

·

Singspiel, 1782

**Libretto by Christoph Friedrich Bretzner,
adapted by Gottlieb Stephanie the Younger**

The Characters

Constanza, a Spanish lady, beloved of Belmonte

Blanche, Constanza's maid

Belmonte, a Spanish nobleman

Pedrillo, Belmonte's valet

Osmin, overseer of the Pasha's country estate

Pasha Selim

A mute, a slave of Osmin's

Klaas, a mate of Pedrillo's

Chorus of Janissaries

Setting: The Pasha's country estate

THERE ARE SOME ASTUTE COMMENTATORS WHO would insist that the chief characteristic of Mozart's music is its restlessness. It is a note he struck in his professional life, and in his view of opera itself. Not long before composing *The Abduction from the Seraglio*, he had secured his independence from the Archbishop of Salzburg's patronage and set himself up in Vienna as a freelance pianist and composer; he had taken up—in ways that caused some scandal—with the nineteen-year-old Constanze Weber, whom he would marry a year later, over his father's objections. And though he felt "there shouldn't be anything frivolous in an opera Seria . . . [nor] anything serious in an opera Buffa," his restless sense of what each form might include changed the way opera was written.

The Abduction is filled with contradictions. For an opera with so much spoken dialogue in it, the music itself is unusually rich and difficult. From the overture on, "Turkish" effects in the score give it an exotic appeal, contrasting with the urgent music for Belmonte and the noble music for Constanza. (That the heroine shared a name with Mozart's beloved must have pleased him.) The comedy of the first half of the opera gives way to something altogether darker. In the Act II finale, what had been a passing remark in the original text Mozart transformed into a quartet that explores romantic fidelity with an astonishing complexity. And when, towards the end of the final act, both Belmonte and Constanza contemplate their imminent deaths at the hands of the Pasha, the comic opera has become what it shouldn't: *serious*. This is even more true of Mozart's other mature *Singspiel*, but *The Magic Flute*'s romance is by nature more capacious than comedy.

Italian and, to a lesser extent, French opera held sway in Vienna, until Emperor Joseph II, for his own political reasons, encouraged the creation of more German theater and opera. From this grew the commission for Mozart, who was enthusiastic about the idea of a national art: "Every nation has its own opera, so why not Germany? Isn't German as singable a language as French or English?" And by chance he had recently been working on an opera, *Zaïde*, which dealt with the rescue of a beloved from Turkish pirates (though in this case the captive is a man, and his valiant rescuer a woman). The Ottoman subject would also have appealed to the Emperor, who had opposed the Turks and a few years later joined with Russia in a disastrous attack on Turkish forces—a campaign that must have had its roots in the advance of the Turks a hundred years earlier to the very gates of Vienna. But at the same time, the figure of Pasha Selim is of an enlightened ruler, and that too may have pleased the Emperor, or at least those bowing deeply around him.

The characters in *The Abduction* will be familiar as types from other Mozart operas. Osmin turns up again in the even nastier Monostatos in *The Magic Flute*, just as Constanza seems to prefigure Pamina. But there are also pairings of note within the opera itself. Osmin and Selim are mirror images of each other. Both men are angry, but Selim's anger is restrained and justified, while Osmin's is blustery and brutal. Selim wisely restores order, and Osmin just storms out. The pairs of lovers are a studied contrast as well. Constanza is so wrapped up in her melancholy that she seems its servant; she is remote, a noble abstraction, as pale and unchanging as a statue. But her maid Blanche, on the other hand, is clever, practical, spirited, a match for any man who approaches her. Belmonte is the distracted romantic, intent on how things *should* be but rather vague on how to bring that about. All these characters mirror each other in a way that gives more solidity and dimension to a slight comedy than it might have had.

On the page, the difference between spoken dialogue and sung material is not as stark as it is on stage. The bulk of spoken dialogue in *The Abduction* made it harder for Mozart to make the opera more substantial. It is music, after all, that finally shapes the emotions dramatized, which is why he tried to expand the musical sections of the libretto and rearrange the story so that the finale of Act II assumed greater weight. To that point, the opera has been much concerned with a leering sensuality and cruelty—a standard Western conception at the time of the Muslim world—and what has been parodied in the figure of Osmin becomes, by the time of this finale, an element in the unconscious of both Belmonte and Pedrillo. At the very moment when they have conquered their fear of Osmin and succeeded in reaching their sweethearts, the men realize that their real fears were not of a huge ogre but of the black dwarf in their hearts—their own suspicions of the women's hearts. The fears they have defied now return as "a secret anxiety." At the moment of escape they are captives of their own doubts. When Constanza can finally dry her tears, they start again. "You have no faith in me?" she asks her beloved. The men, the valiant rescuers, are humbled and beg forgiveness . . . which they are granted. They all conclude:

> Well, now that is behind us!
> Long live love!
> Let love be all we desire.
> Let nothing stoke the fire
> Of a jealousy that might blind us.

But can the question, having once been asked, be truly dismissed? The quartet's final words echo comedy's sense of reconciliation, but they leave an overtone that lurks and will be fully exploited, not in Act III but in *Così Fan Tutte*.

The dark suspicions of the lovers contrast with the apparent nobility and generosity of Pasha Selim at the opera's end. That the part is only a speaking one makes him seem less a victim of his own strong emotions, which in any case arise from frustration rather than meanness. His reasonable explanation contrasts too with Constanza's fierce resolve to resist him, expressed in her powerful aria "Marten aller Arten" ("Tortures most surely await"). The music silences him. (He says he will resort to cunning instead of force, but that element of the plot was dropped, and the moment remains a loose thread.) The true force in the opera is its heroine's steadfastness. In that, she resembles several of Mozart's other leading ladies. His men may pout or swagger, boast or threaten, praise or curse. His women think and feel.

THE STORY

ACT I

Outside the palace of Pasha Selim, Belmonte pines for his beloved Constanza, who has been kidnapped by Turkish pirates and kept by the Pasha as his intended. Belmonte has come to rescue her, and is wondering how he might scale the palace walls when he sees Osmin, the overseer of the Pasha's estate, come out to pick figs—by using a ladder. Osmin is singing a song about how to keep women faithful, and pays no mind to Belmonte's persistent questions. He finally gets the annoyed Osmin's attention, and asks if he may speak with Pedrillo, who now works as a gardener for the Pasha and, until he too was kidnapped along with Constanza and her maid Blanche, was Belmonte's manservant. The very mention of the name fills Osmin with fury and he and Belmonte start trading insults, until Osmin shoves him aside.

As Belmonte leaves, Pedrillo arrives. Osmin means to catch him if he sneaks into the women's quarters, but feels he enjoys the Pasha's favor and is wary. When Pedrillo offers him a truce, Osmin scorns him as a conniving dandy and warns him that he will put an end to Pedrillo's plotting. The more Pedrillo protests he is innocent, the fiercer the punishment Osmin promises.

Osmin storms off, and Belmonte approaches and reveals himself. He wants above all to know if Constanza is still alive. Assured by Pedrillo that she is well, he is distressed to hear that Pasha Selim—enlightened enough not to force himself on her—is ardently wooing her. Has she remained faithful to me, he demands to know. Pedrillo assures him again, but wonders if his own sweetheart, Blanche, has succumbed to Osmin's advances. Belmonte has a plan. He has a ship waiting nearby to take them off, and all he needs is a way to get to the women. But the Pasha is approaching, and Pedrillo tells him to stand to one side so that he may see his beloved. When he does, his heart leaps. Janissaries singing his praises escort the Pasha, who arrives on a pleasure boat with Constanza. He grandly asks for her love, and she confesses her love for another. She is grateful for the Pasha's generosity, but—she will not lie—she is bound to Belmonte. Pasha Selim gives her until tomorrow to change her mind. Pedrillo approaches, wishing to introduce the Pasha to a new young architect offering his services. It is, of course, Belmonte, who is hired on. But before they can enter the palace, Osmin returns to bluster and threaten them. Each side shouts at the other, but finally Belmonte and Pedrillo force Osmin aside and enter the palace.

ACT II

In the palace garden, Blanche is pouting and complaining to Osmin about her treatment. He reminds her that the Pasha gave her to him as his slave. She reminds him that she is a freeborn Englishwoman and nobody's slave. In fact, she tells him that all men are slaves to women, and that she intends to liberate all the harem women with her bold ideas. Osmin swears to punish her but is secretly afraid of her spirited personality. When she threatens to scratch his eyes out, he timidly backs away. Blanche notices that Constanza is walking nearby, lost in her melancholy thoughts. Blanche tries to console, and even encourage her, but Constanza despairs—and suddenly the Pasha enters. He reminds her that tomorrow she must decide whether or not to marry him, but she is resolute. She will endure any suffering, but never change her heart's affections. As she storms out, Selim marvels at her courage, and decides that, where his pleas have failed, perhaps his cunning may succeed.

Pedrillo and Blanche meet secretly so that he can tell her that Belmonte intends to rescue them all, and is in the palace disguised as the Pasha's new architect. He explains that Belmonte will come to Constanza's window with a ladder at midnight, and that he himself will come to Blanche's, and that Osmin will be asleep—having carefully been given a sleeping potion.

She rushes off to tell Constanza. Pedrillo resolves to stifle his fears and help with the plan, and when Osmin appears he tricks him into drinking the forbidden wine. They swill and toast, Osmin gets drunker and drunker, and Pedrillo finally leads him off to bed.

Belmonte arrives to start the rescue. Constanza is at her window, enthralled at the sight of him. They sing to one another of their love, while Pedrillo and Blanche reassure one another as well. The men decide, at the last minute, to check with the women that they have remained faithful during their captivity, and the very imputation angers the women. The men beg for forgiveness, and all swear themselves again to love.

ACT III

It is midnight, in the square before the Pasha's palace. The ladders are ready, everything is prepared, hearts are aflutter.

Belmonte prays that Love will see them all through the coming trial. Pedrillo, instead, sings a ballad to pass the time. Constanza climbs down the ladder and she and Belmonte escape. Pedrillo then climbs through Blanche's window, when Osmin, still half asleep, unexpectedly appears with a mute who mimes for him that something is wrong. He staggers around, but slumps against the ladder and falls back to sleep. As Pedrillo and Blanche start down the ladder, they spot Osmin and climb back up, Osmin now pursuing them. The uproar draws the palace guards, who think Osmin is trying to break into the palace, and Pedrillo taunts him. But other guards now lead in Belmonte and Constanza, who have been captured and beg for their release. But Osmin now gloats that he has them all in his power at last.

The commotion has roused the Pasha. Osmin explains the treachery of the captives, who throw themselves on his mercy. As he begs for his life, Belmonte reveals that he is a Spanish nobleman, and that his surname is Lostados. The Pasha is startled. That was the archenemy who had once stripped him of all his standing and wealth. Now he has his enemy's son in his hands, and he goes off to decide his fate.

Belmonte and Constanza resign themselves to death and reaffirm their love. Pedrillo and Blanche too face the worst. The Pasha returns, and says that he must not repeat the dastardly behavior of Belmonte's father, and that he has decided to free the captives. As Osmin sputters, the Pasha silences him. "If you cannot conquer by kindness, then better not fight at all." The four lovers praise Pasha Selim's goodness.

THE BACKGROUND

In a letter to his father dated August 1, 1781, Mozart wrote excitedly: "Well, the day before yesterday Stephanie the Younger brought me a libretto with the intent that I set it to music. I must tell you frankly that, unpleasant as he can be at times to other people, about which I really know nothing, he is a good friend to me.—The libretto is good. The subject is Turkish and the play is entitled: *Bellmont* [actually *Belmont*] *und Konstanze* [actually *Constanze*] oder *die verführung aus dem Serail*." (He mistakenly wrote *Verführung*, or seduction, rather than *Entführung*, or abduction.) Mozart knows his singers and has already started composing. "Time is short, that's true; the performance is to take place in mid-September;—yet—the circumstances associated with its first performance and, generally speaking, all the other prospects have lifted my spirits so high that I'm now hurrying to my desk with greatest eagerness and remain seated there with the greatest joy in my heart."

Gottlieb Stephanie (1741–1800) had been appointed by Joseph II as director of the National Singspiel, the company that performed German operas, and Stephanie commissioned the opera to be performed for the visit to Vienna of the Russian Grand Duke Paul Petrovich and his wife. (That visit was cancelled, but the opera proceeded.) Mozart urged that the original libretto by Christoph Friedrich Bretzner (1748–1807) be expanded. The part of Osmin was made more conspicuous, arias were added for the women and for Belmonte, and the Act II finale was added. Mozart's father complained about the quality of the verse, but Mozart defended it as exactly suited to the characters and situations: "It agrees so completely with the musical ideas that had been wandering around my head, even before I had seen the text, so I couldn't help liking it;—and I'm willing to bet that when it is performed, nothing will be found inadequate." The score was finally completed in April, and the work was premiered at the Burgtheater in Vienna, on July 16, 1782. Catarina Cavalieri sang Constanza, and Valentin Adamberger sang Belmonte. The virtuosic bass Ludwig Fischer was Osmin, Johann Ernst Dauer was Pedrillo, and Therese Teyber was Blanche. The opera was a success, despite mistakes that infuriated Mozart. The score was considered advanced, and prompted Joseph II's famous remark: "Far too beautiful for our ears, my dear Mozart, and a monstrous quantity of notes." The fame of the opera, however, spread quickly and helped carry Mozart's renown beyond Austria. At a production in Bonn the year following the premiere, it has been said that Beethoven assisted in the musical preparations.

Erster Aufzug

Platz vor dem Palast des Bassa am Ufer des Meers.

Erster Auftritt

BELMONTE ALLEIN.

N° 1 Aria

BELMONTE:
Hier soll ich dich denn sehen,
Konstanze! dich mein Glück!
Lass Himmel es geschehen!
Gib mir die Ruh zurück!
Ich duldete der Leiden,
O Liebe! allzu viel!
Schenk mir dafür nun Freuden
Und bringe mich ans Ziel.

BELMONTE: Aber wie soll ich in den Palast kommen? – wie sie sehen? – wie sprechen?

Zweiter Auftritt

BELMONTE, OSMIN (MIT EINER LEITER, WELCHE ER AN EINEN BAUM VOR DER TÜRE DES PALASTS LEHNT, HINAUF STEIGT UND FEIGEN ABNIMMT).

Act I

The square in front of the Pasha's palace at the seaside.

First Scene

BELMONTE, ALONE.

Aria

BELMONTE:
Here is where I am to see you.
Constanza! My idol! My shrine!
Oh heaven, let it all be true!
Restore my peace of mind.
The torment I have endured!
O love, release me, I pray.
What I have, only love can cure.
Help me, no more delay!

BELMONTE: *(speaking)* But how can I get into the palace? How can I see her, speak to her?

Second Scene

BELMONTE, OSMIN (WITH A LADDER WHICH HE LEANS AGAINST A TREE IN FRONT OF THE PALACE, THEN CLIMBS AND PICKS FIGS).

N° 2 *Lied und Duett*

OSMIN:

Wer ein Liebchen hat gefunden,
Die es treu und redlich meint,
Lohn es ihr durch tausend Küsse,
Mach ihr all das Leben süße,
Sei ihr Tröster, sei ihr Freund.
Trallalera, trallalera!

BELMONTE: Vielleicht, dass ich durch diesen Alten etwas erfahre. – He, Freund! ist das nicht das Landhaus des Bassa Selim?

OSMIN: *(singt wie zuvor während der Arbeit)*

Doch sie treu sich zu erhalten,
Schließ' er Liebchen sorglich ein:
Denn die losen Dinger haschen
Jeden Schmetterling und naschen
gar zu gern von fremdem Wein.
Trallalera, trallalera!

BELMONTE: He, Alter, he! hört ihr nicht? – Ist hier des Bassa Selim Palast? –

OSMIN: *(sieht ihn an, dreht sich herum und singt wie zuvor)*

Sonderlich beim Mondenscheine,
Freunde, nehmt sie wohl in Acht!
Oft lauscht da ein junges Herrchen,
Kirrt und lockt das kleine Närrchen,
Und dann, Treue, gute Nacht!
Trallalera, trallalera!

BELMONTE:

Verwünscht seist du samt deinem Liede!
Ich bin dein Singen nun schon müde;
So hör doch nur ein einzig Wort!

Song and Duet

OSMIN:
If you find yourself a sweetheart
Who is faithful all the time,
Shower her with kisses,
Show her what real bliss is,
A friend at dawn and dinnertime.
Tral-la-le-ra, tral-la-le-ra.

BELMONTE: *(speaking)* Perhaps I can find out something from this old man. Hey there, friend, isn't this the estate of Pasha Selim?

OSMIN: *(singing as before, while working)*
If you want to keep her true,
Then carefully lock her up.
They grab whatever flutters by,
Follow every butterfly,
Drink from any stranger's cup.
Tral-la-le-ra, tral-la-le-ra.

BELMONTE: *(speaking)* Hey, old man, psst! Didn't you hear me? Is this Pasha Selim's house?

OSMIN: *(noticing him, but turning back and singing as before)*
You must pay close attention
When the moon is shining bright.
Young men may be lurking,
Their flattery may be working,
And, sweetheart, oh, goodnight!
Tral-la-le-ra, tral-la-le-ra.

BELMONTE:
The devil take you and your ditty.
Your singing has worn me out.
Stop and listen to what I say!

OSMIN:

Was Henker lasst ihr euch gelüsten,
Euch zu ereifern, euch zu brüsten?
Was wollt ihr? Hurtig! ich muss fort.

BELMONTE: Ist das des Bassa Selim Haus?

OSMIN: He? –

BELMONTE: Ist das des Bassa Selim Haus?

OSMIN: Das ist des Bassa Selim Haus. *(will fort)*

BELMONTE: So wartet doch – –

OSMIN: Ich kann nicht weilen.

BELMONTE: Ein Wort –

OSMIN: Geschwind! denn ich muss eilen.

BELMONTE: Seid ihr in seinen Diensten, Freund?

OSMIN: He? –

BELMONTE: Seid ihr in seinen Diensten, Freund?

OSMIN: He?

BELMONTE: Seid ihr in seinen Diensten, Freund? –

OSMIN: Ich bin in seinen Diensten, Freund.

OSMIN:
The devil take your blasted self-pity.
How dare you stamp and shout?
What do you want? I'm on my way.

BELMONTE: Is that the house of Pasha Selim?

OSMIN: Eh?

BELMONTE: Is that the house of Pasha Selim?

OSMIN: That is the house of Pasha Selim.
(starts to leave)

BELMONTE: Wait a minute—

OSMIN: I cannot stay.

BELMONTE: Just a word—

OSMIN: Quick about it, I am in a hurry.

BELMONTE: Are you in his employ, friend?

OSMIN: Eh?

BELMONTE: Are you in his employ, friend?

OSMIN: Eh?

BELMONTE: Do. You. Work. For. Him?

OSMIN: I am in his employ, friend.

BELMONTE:

Wie kann ich den Pedrill wohl sprechen,
Der hier in seinen Diensten steht?

OSMIN:

Den Schurken? – der den Hals soll brechen? –
Seht selber zu, wenn's anders geht. *(will fort)*

BELMONTE: *(für sich)* Was für ein alter grober Bengel!

OSMIN: *(ihn betrachtend, auch für sich)* Das ist just so ein Galgen-
schwengel.

BELMONTE: *(zu ihm)* Ihr irrt, es ist ein braver Mann.

OSMIN: So brav, dass man ihn spießen kann.

BELMONTE: Ihr müsst ihn wahrlich nicht recht kennen.

OSMIN: Recht gut. Ich ließ' ihn heut verbrennen.

BELMONTE: Es ist fürwahr ein guter Tropf!

OSMIN: Auf einen Pfahl gehört sein Kopf!
(will fort)

BELMONTE: So bleibet doch!

OSMIN: Was wollt ihr noch?

BELMONTE: Ich möchte gerne . . .

OSMIN: *(spöttisch)*
So hübsch von ferne
Ums Haus rumschleichen

BELMONTE:

Is it possible to speak with Pedrillo,
Who is a servant here as well?

OSMIN:

That scoundrel?—I'll break his neck!
Find him yourself! Farewell! *(turning to leave)*

BELMONTE: *(to himself)* What a rude ruffian he is!

OSMIN: *(inspecting him, also to himself)* The same sort of buzzard!

BELMONTE: *(to Osmin)* You are wrong. He is an honest man.

OSMIN: So honest I will kill him if I can.

BELMONTE: You must not know him very well.

OSMIN: Well enough to burn him like a caramel.

BELMONTE: He is a man whom everyone likes.

OSMIN: His head would look best on a pike.
(He starts to leave.)

BELMONTE: Stay a second!

OSMIN: What else do you want?

BELMONTE: I would like to . . .

OSMIN: *(mockingly)*
You would like to
Creep around the house,

und Mädchen stehlen? –
Fort, euresgleichen
Braucht man hier nicht.

BELMONTE:
Ihr seid besessen!
Sprecht voller Galle
Mir so vermessen
Ins Angesicht!

OSMIN: Nur nicht in Eifer!

BELMONTE: Schont euren Geifer.

OSMIN: Ich kenn euch schon.

BELMONTE: Lasst euer Drohn.

OSMIN: Schert euch zum Teufel –

BELMONTE: Es bleibt kein Zweifel –

OSMIN:
Ihr kriegt, ich schwöre,
Sonst ohne Gnade
Die Bastonade:
Noch habt ihr Zeit.
(stößt ihn fort)

BELMONTE:
Ihr seid von Sinnen!
Welch ein Betragen
Auf meine Fragen!
Seid doch gescheid.
(ab)

Quiet as a mouse,
And steal the girls!
We don't need your kind of churl.

BELMONTE:
You are mad, I say!
So disrespectful,
Utterly rejectful,
The kind of insults you hurl!

OSMIN: Oh, do calm down!

BELMONTE: Spare me the venom.

OSMIN: I know your type.

BELMONTE: You only growl and gripe.

OSMIN: To the devil with you!

BELMONTE: No doubt now at all!

OSMIN:
You'll get, I swear
For all your bravado,
The bastinado!
Yes, there's time for that!
(pushes him away)

BELMONTE:
Out of your mind!
What a callous suggestion
For my casual question.
This started out as a chat.
(He leaves.)

Dritter Auftritt

OSMIN, HERNACH PEDRILLO.

Dialog

OSMIN: *(allein)* Könnt ich mir doch noch so einen Schurken auf die Nase setzen wie den Pedrillo, so einen Gaudieb, der Tag und Nacht nichts tut, als nach meinen Weibern herumzuschleichen und zu schnobern, ob's nichts für seinen Schnabel setzt. Aber ich laure ihm sicher auf den Dienst; und wohl bekomm dir die Prügelsuppe, wenn ich dich einmal beim Kanthaken kriege! – Hätt er sich nur beim Bassa nicht so eingeschmeichelt, er sollte den Strick längst um den Hals haben.

PEDRILLO: Nun, wie stehts, Osmin? Ist der Bassa noch nicht zurück?

OSMIN: Sieh darnach, wenn du's wissen willst.

PEDRILLO: Schon wieder Sturm im Kalender? – Hast du das Gericht Feigen für mich gepflückt?

OSMIN: Gift für dich, verwünschter Schmarotzer!

PEDRILLO: Was in aller Welt ich dir nun getan haben muss, dass du beständig mit mir zankst. Lass uns doch einmal Friede machen.

OSMIN: Friede mit dir? mit so einem schleichenden spitzbübischen Passauf, der nur spioniert, wie er mir eins versetzen kann? Erdrosseln möcht ich dich! –

PEDRILLO: Aber sag nur, warum? warum?

OSMIN: Warum? – weil ich dich nicht leiden kann.

Third Scene

OSMIN, THEN PEDRILLO.

Spoken Dialogue

OSMIN: *(alone)* I can't afford another Pedrillo, that layabout who spends all his time sniffing around my women to find one to nibble on. I'll lie in wait for him—and I hope you enjoy the thrashing when I catch you! If he hadn't wheedled himself into the Pasha's favor, I'd have throttled him by now.

PEDRILLO: Well, how are things, Osmin? Is the Pasha back yet?

OSMIN: Go look for yourself, if you want to know.

PEDRILLO: Stormy weather again, I see. Come on, let's make peace.

OSMIN: Poison rather! You sniveling parasite!

PEDRILLO: What in the world could I have done that makes you take against me so? Let's call a truce for once.

OSMIN: A truce, with you? With a creeping, rascally little runt who is always looking for ways to make a fool of me? I would rather strangle you!—

PEDRILLO: But tell me, why? Why?

OSMIN: Why?—Because I loathe you.

N° 3 Aria

OSMIN:

Solche hergelaufne Laffen,
Die nur nach den Weibern gaffen,
Mag ich vor den Teufel nicht.
Denn ihr ganzes Tun und Lassen
Ist, uns auf den Dienst zu passen,
Doch mich trügt kein solch Gesicht.
Eure Tücken, eure Ränke,
Eure Finten, eure Schwänke,
Sind mir ganz bekannt.
Mich zu hintergehen,
Müsst ihr früh aufstehen,
Ich hab auch Verstand.
Drum, beim Barte des Propheten!
Ich studiere Tag und Nacht,
Ruh nicht, bis ich dich seh töten,
Nimm dich, wie du willst, in Acht.

PEDRILLO: Was bist du für ein grausamer Kerl, – und ich hab dir nichts getan. – –

OSMIN:

Du hast ein Galgengesicht. Das ist genug.
Erst geköpft, dann gehangen,
Dann gespießt auf heißen Stangen,
Dann verbrannt, dann gebunden
Und getaucht, zuletzt geschunden.
(geht ins Haus)

Aria

OSMIN:

You dandies, so sham and so shady,
Whose talent is ogling a lady,
You can all go to hell in a cart!
All that is ever on your mind
Is not getting off your behind.
You could never trick me. I'm smart!
Dirty tricks and lazy dreams,
Waggish pranks and wanton schemes,
I know all your conniving ways.
I can sleep with one eye open.
Just in case you might be hoping
I won't notice your little forays.
So, by the Prophet's own beard,
I am watching you day and night!
I will catch you, don't you fear,
Take what precautions you might.

PEDRILLO: *(speaking)* What a nasty man you are—and I have
done absolutely nothing—

OSMIN: *(speaking)*
You look like a buzzard. That is enough. *(singing)*
First beheaded, then hung like a hound,
What's left can be put on a skewer.
Then burned, and bound, and drowned—
A thoroughly dead wrongdoer!
(He goes into the house.)

Vierter Auftritt

PEDRILLO, HERNACH BELMONTE.

Dialog

PEDRILLO: *(allein)* Geh nur, verwünschter Aufpasser, es ist noch nicht aller Tage Abend. Wer weiß, wer den andern überlistet; und dir misstrauischem, gehässigem Menschenfeinde eine Grube zu graben, sollte ein wahres Fest für mich sein.

BELMONTE: Pedrillo, guter Pedrillo!

PEDRILLO: Ach mein bester Herr! Ist's möglich? Sind Sie's wirklich? Bravo, Madam Fortuna, bravo! das heißt doch Wort gehalten! Schon verzweifelte ich, ob einer meiner Briefe Sie getroffen hätte.

BELMONTE: Sag, guter Pedrillo, lebt meine Konstanze noch?

PEDRILLO: Lebt, und noch, hoff ich, für Sie. Seit dem schrecklichen Tage, an welchem das Glück uns einen so hässlichen Streich spielte und unser Schiff von den Seeräubern erobern ließ, haben wir mancherlei Drangsal erfahren. Glücklicherweise traf sich's noch, dass der Bassa Selim uns alle drei kaufte: Ihre Konstanze nämlich, meine Blonde und mich. Er ließ uns sogleich hier auf sein Landhaus bringen. Donna Konstanze ward seine auserwählte Geliebte. –

BELMONTE: Ah! was sagst du?

PEDRILLO: Nu, nur nicht so hitzig! Sie ist noch nicht in die schlimmsten Hände gefallen. Der Bassa ist ein Renegat und hat noch so viel Delikatesse, keine seiner Weiber zu seiner Liebe zu zwingen. Und soviel ich weiß, spielt er noch immer den unerhörten Liebhaber.

Fourth Scene

PEDRILLO, THEN BELMONTE.

Spoken Dialogue

PEDRILLO: *(alone)* Get out of here, you tattletale! The game isn't over yet. Who knows which of us will win. I'd be happy to show you to your grave, you suspicious, scurvy old misanthrope!

BELMONTE: Pedrillo, my good man Pedrillo!

PEDRILLO: Ah, my dear master! Is it possible? Is it really you? Bravo, Lady Luck, bravo! True to your word. I wasn't sure if any of my letters had reached you.

BELMONTE: Tell me, good Pedrillo, is my Constanza still alive?

PEDRILLO: She is, and, I hope, still lives for you. Ever since that awful day when luck played a bad joke on us and let our ship be captured by pirates, we have endured so many misfortunes. It was a blessing that Pasha Selim bought all three of us, your Constanza, my Blanche, and me. He had us taken at once to his house. Donna Constanza has become his favorite—

BELMONTE: What are you saying?

PEDRILLO: Now, now, hold on! She has not yet fallen into the worst hands. The Pasha is forward-looking, and sensitive enough never to force any of his women to love him. As far as I know, he is still playing the unrequited lover.

BELMONTE: Is it possible? Is Constanza still faithful?

BELMONTE: Wär es möglich? Wär Konstanze noch treu?

PEDRILLO: Sicher noch, lieber Herr! Aber wie's mit meinem Blondchen steht, weiß der Himmel! Das arme Ding schmachtet bei einem alten hässlichen Kerl, dem sie der Bassa geschenkt hat. Und vielleicht - ach, ich darf gar nicht dran denken! -

BELMONTE: Doch nicht der alte Kerl, der soeben ins Haus ging?

PEDRILLO: Eben der.

BELMONTE: Und dies ist der Liebling des Bassa?

PEDRILLO: Liebling, Spion und Ausbund aller Spitzbuben, der mich mit den Augen vergiften möchte, wenn's möglich wäre.

BELMONTE: O guter Pedrillo! was sagst du?

PEDRILLO: Nur nicht gleich verzagt! Unter uns gesagt: Ich hab auch einen Stein im Brette beim Bassa. Durch mein bisschen Geschick in der Gärtnerei hab ich seine Gunst weggekriegt, und dadurch hab ich so ziemlich Freiheit, die tausend andere nicht haben würden. Da sonst jede Mannsperson sich entfernen muss, wenn eine seiner Weiber in Garten kommt, kann ich bleiben. Sie reden sogar mit mir und er sagt nichts darüber. Freilich mault der alte Osmin, besonders wenn mein Blondchen ihrer Gebieterin folgen muss.

BELMONTE: Ist's möglich? Du hast sie gesprochen? - O sag, sag! Liebt sie mich noch?

PEDRILLO: Hm! dass Sie daran zweifeln! Ich dächte, Sie kennten die gute Konstanze mehr als zu gut, hätten Proben genug ihrer Liebe. - Doch damit dürfen wir uns gar nicht aufhalten. Hier ist bloß die Frage, wie's anzufangen ist, hier wegzukommen?

PEDRILLO: I'm certain of it, dear master! But how things stand with my little Blanche, heaven only knows! The poor thing languishes in the home of an ugly old man to whom the Pasha has given her, and maybe—no, I can't let myself think about that.

BELMONTE: Not the old fool who just went into the house?

PEDRILLO: The same.

BELMONTE: And the Pasha dotes on him?

PEDRILLO: Dotes! A spy and the most roguish of rascals. He would poison me with a glance if he could.

BELMONTE: Good Pedrillo, what are you getting at?

PEDRILLO: Don't give up hope! Just between us, I am also in favor with the Pasha. My small skill at gardening has caught his eye, and I am more at liberty than many others would be. Any other man would have to leave if one of the Pasha's women came into the garden, but I can stay. The ladies even speak to me—and the Pasha doesn't notice. True, old Osmin scowls if my little Blanche must accompany her mistress.

BELMONTE: Is it possible? Have you spoken to her? Tell me, tell me—does she still love me?

PEDRILLO: Hmm. Can you doubt it? I thought you knew your darling Constanza well enough, and had countless proofs of her love. But let's not waste any more time with this. The question now is, how do we get away from here?

BELMONTE: O, da hab ich für alles gesorgt! Ich hab hier ein Schiff in einiger Entfernung vom Hafen, das uns auf den ersten Wink einnimmt, und –

PEDRILLO: Ah, sachte, sachte! Erst müssen wir die Mädels haben, ehe wir zu Schiffe gehen. Und das geht nicht so husch, husch, wie Sie meinen.

BELMONTE: O lieber, guter Pedrillo, mach nur, dass ich sie sehen, dass ich sie sprechen kann! Das Herz schlägt mir vor Angst und Freude! –

PEDRILLO: Pfiffig müssen wir das Ding anfangen und rasch müssen wir's ausführen, damit wir den alten Aufpasser über-tölpeln. Bleiben Sie hier in der Nähe. Jetzt wird der Bassa bald von einer Lustfahrt auf dem Wasser zurückkommen. Ich will Sie ihm als einen geschickten Baumeister vorstellen: Denn Bauen und Gärtnerei sind seine Steckenpferde. Aber lieber, goldner Herr, halten Sie sich in Schranken; Konstanze ist bei ihm –

BELMONTE: Konstanze bei ihm? Was sagst du? Ich soll sie sehen?

PEDRILLO: Gemach, gemach ums Himmels willen, lieber Herr! Sonst stolpern wir. – Ah, ich glaube, dort seh ich sie schon ange-fahren kommen. Gehn Sie nur auf die Seite, wenn er kommt. Ich will ihm entgegengehen. *(geht ab)*

BELMONTE: Oh, I have thought of everything! I have a ship here, lying at anchor a little offshore. At my signal, it will take us on board, and—

PEDRILLO: Easy, easy! Before we hop on board, we have to have the girls with us, and that's not as simple as you suppose.

BELMONTE: Oh, good, sweet Pedrillo, just arrange for me to see her, to speak with her! My heart is racing with anxiety and joy!—

PEDRILLO: This thing has to be planned carefully and carried out swiftly, so that we can trick the old fool. Stay close by. The Pasha will soon return from a pleasure trip on the water. I will introduce you to him as a famous architect, since buildings and gardens are his obsessions. But, sir, wonderful master, you must keep yourself under control. Constanza will be with him—

BELMONTE: Constanza with him? What are you saying? I will see her?

PEDRILLO: Gently, gently, dear master, for heaven's sake! Otherwise we may stumble.—Ah, I think I already see them on their way here. When he arrives, just keep to the side. Stay right here, and I will go greet them. *(He goes off.)*

Fünfter Auftritt
BELMONTE ALLEIN.

N° 4 Recitativo ed Aria

Recitativo

BELMONTE: Konstanze! dich wieder zu sehen! – dich! –

Aria

O wie ängstlich, o wie feurig
Klopft mein liebevolles Herz!
Und des Wiedersehens Zähre,
Lohnt der Trennung bangen Schmerz.
Schon zittr' ich und wanke,
Schon zag ich und schwanke,
Es hebt sich die schwellende Brust.
Ist das ihr Lispeln?
Es wird mir so bange;
War das ihr Seufzen?
Es glüht mir die Wange;
Täuscht mich die Liebe,
War es ein Traum?

PEDRILLO: *(kömmt hurtig gelaufen)* Geschwind, geschwind auf die Seite und versteckt! Der Bassa kömmt.

(Belmonte versteckt sich.)

Fifth Scene
BELMONTE, ALONE.

Recitative and Aria

Recitative

BELMONTE: Constanza! Just to see you again! You!—

Aria

How fearfully, wildly, it beats,
The loving heart in my breast!
Let the tears I shed when we meet
Make up for all the rest.
I feel myself tremble and quiver.
I he-hesitate, then shiver.
My little heart swells and heaves.
Is that her whispering?
I can't get it out of my head.
Is that her sighing?
My cheeks are turning red.
Does love deceive me?
Is it all a dream?

PEDRILLO: *(running in, speaking)* Quickly, quickly, stand to the side and hide! The Pasha is coming.

(Belmonte hides himself.)

Sechster Auftritt

N° 5a Marcia

DER BASSA SELIM UND KONSTANZE KOMMEN IN EINEM
LUSTSCHIFFE ANGEFAHREN, VOR WELCHEM EIN
ANDERES SCHIFF MIT JANITSCHARENMUSIK VORAUS
LANDET. DIE JANITSCHAREN STELLEN SICH AM UFER
IN ORDNUNG, STIMMEN FOLGENDEN CHOR AN UND
ENTFERNEN SICH DANN.

N° 5b Chor der Janitscharen

TUTTI:

Singt dem großen Bassa Lieder,
Töne, feuriger Gesang;
Und vom Ufer halle wider
Unsrer Lieder Jubelklang!

SOLO:

Weht ihm entgegen,
kühlende Winde,
Ebne dich sanfter,
Wallende Flut!

Singt ihm entgegen,
Fliegende Chöre,
Singt ihm der Liebe
Freuden ins Herz!

TUTTI:

Singt dem großen Bassa Lieder
Töne, feuriger Gesang;
Und vom Ufer halle wider
Unsrer Lieder Jubelklang!

(Janitscharen ab)

Sixth Scene

March

PASHA SELIM AND CONSTANZA ARRIVE ON A PLEASURE
BOAT, PRECEDED BY ANOTHER BOAT CARRYING JANISSARY
MUSICIANS. THE JANISSARIES LINE UP IN RANKS ON
SHORE, SING THE FOLLOWING CHORUS, THEN DEPART.

Chorus of the Janissaries

CHORUS:

Sing to mighty Pasha Selim,
Sing a fiery song.
Let our voices roundly hail him.
To him our praises belong.

SOLOISTS:

Cooling breezes,
Fan his brow.
Gentle waters,
Smooth his way.

Fluting birds,
Sing of how
Love is in
His heart to stay.

CHORUS:

Sing to mighty Pasha Selim,
Sing a fiery song.
Let our voices roundly hail him.
To him our praises belong.

(The Janissaries leave.)

Siebenter Auftritt

SELIM, KONSTANZE.

Dialog

SELIM: Immer noch traurig, geliebte Konstanze? immer in Tränen? – Sieh, dieser schöne Abend, diese reizende Gegend, diese bezaubernde Musik, meine zärtliche Liebe für dich. – Sag, kann nichts von allem dich endlich beruhigen, endlich dein Herz rühren? – Sieh, ich könnte befehlen, könnte grausam mit dir verfahren, dich zwingen – *(Konstanze seufzt.)* Aber nein, Konstanze, dir selbst will ich dein Herz zu danken haben – dir selbst –

KONSTANZE: Großmütiger Mann! o dass ich es könnte! dass ich's erwidern könnte – aber –

SELIM: Sag, Konstanze, sag, was hält dich zurück?

KONSTANZE: Du wirst mich hassen.

SELIM: Nein, ich schwöre dir's. Du weißt, wie sehr ich dich liebe, wie viel Freiheit ich dir vor allen meinen Weibern gestatte; dich wie meine Einzige schätze –

KONSTANZE: O so verzeih!

N° 6 Aria

KONSTANZE:
Ach, ich liebte, war so glücklich,
Kannte nicht der Liebe Schmerz!
Schwur ihm Treue, dem Geliebten,
Gab dahin mein ganzes Herz:

Seventh Scene

SELIM AND CONSTANZA.

Spoken Dialogue

SELIM: Still so sad, beloved Constanza? Still in tears?—Look, such a lovely evening, these exquisite grounds, the enchanting music, my tender love for you—tell me, can none of this finally calm you, finally move your heart?—See here, I could command you, I could be cruel and compel you—*(Constanza sighs.)* But no, Constanza, I want to thank you for your heart because you gave it—you yourself—

CONSTANZA: Most generous of men! Oh, if only I could! If only I could respond—but—

SELIM: Tell me, Constanza, what are you holding back?

CONSTANZA: You will hate me.

SELIM: No, I swear to you. You know how I love you, how much freedom I allow you compared to other women, how much I treasure you as my only—

CONSTANZA: Oh, then forgive me!

Aria

CONSTANZA:
Oh, I was in love, so filled with joy,
And never knew that love could pain.
I gave my heart to a handsome boy
And promised always to remain.

Doch wie schnell schwand meine Freude,
Trennung war mein banges Los;
Und nun schwimmt mein Aug in Tränen,
Kummer ruht in meinem Schoß.

(Während des Gesanges geht der Bassa unwillig hin und her.)

Dialog

KONSTANZE: Ach, ich sagt' es wohl, du würdest mich hassen. Aber verzeih, verzeih dem liebekranken Mädchen! – Du bist ja so großmütig, so gut. – Ich will dir dienen, deine Sklavin sein, bis ans Ende meines Lebens: Nur verlange nicht ein Herz von mir, das auf ewig versagt ist. –

SELIM: Ha, Undankbare! Was wagst du zu bitten?

KONSTANZE: Töte mich, Selim, töte mich! Nur zwinge mich nicht, meineidig zu werden. – Noch zuletzt, wie mich der Seeräuber aus den Armen meines Geliebten riss, schwur ich aufs Feierlichste –

SELIM: Halt ein! Nicht ein Wort! Reize meinen Zorn nicht noch mehr. Bedenke, dass du in meiner Gewalt bist –

KONSTANZE: Ich bin es: Aber du wirst dich ihrer nicht bedienen, ich kenne dein gutes, dein mitleidvolles Herz. Hätte ich's sonst wagen können, dir das meinige zu entdecken? –

SELIM: Wag es nicht, meine Güte zu missbrauchen –

KONSTANZE: Nur Aufschub gönne mir, Herr! nur Zeit, meinen Schmerz zu vergessen –

SELIM: Wie oft schon gewährt' ich dir diese Bitte –

How quickly my joy then disappeared.
Separation was my bitter fate.
Now my eyes are drowned in tears.
I eat from sorrow's empty plate.

(As she sings, the Pasha paces angrily back and forth.)

Spoken Dialogue

CONSTANZA: Oh, I told you that you would hate me. Forgive a silly, lovesick maiden!—You are so generous, so good—I will serve you, be your slave for as long as I live. Only do not ask for my heart, which can never be yours.

SELIM: How ungrateful you are! What do you dare to ask of me?

CONSTANZA: Kill me, Selim, kill me! Only do not force me to lie. At the moment the pirate snatched me from the arms of my beloved, I solemnly swore—

SELIM: Enough! Not another word! Do not provoke my answer any more. Remember, you are in my power—

CONSTANZA: I am, but you will not take advantage of it. I know you have a kind and compassionate heart. Would I ever have revealed my own heart if you hadn't?

SELIM: Do not presume to abuse my patience—

CONSTANZA: Just give me a little more time, my lord, a little time to forget my sorrow—

SELIM: I have given you time already—

KONSTANZE: Nur noch diesmal!

SELIM: Es sei! zum letzten Male! – Geh, Konstanze, geh! Besinne dich eines Bessern, und morgen –

KONSTANZE: *(im Abgehn)* Unglückliches Mädchen! O Belmonte, Belmonte!

Achter Auftritt
SELIM, PEDRILLO, BELMONTE.

Dialog

SELIM: Ihr Schmerz, ihre Tränen, ihre Standhaftigkeit bezaubern mein Herz immer mehr, machen mir ihre Liebe nur noch wünschenswerter. Ha! wer wollte gegen ein solches Herz Gewalt brauchen? – Nein, Konstanze, nein, auch Selim hat ein Herz, auch Selim kennt Liebe –

PEDRILLO: Herr! verzeih, dass ich es wage, dich in deinen Betrachtungen zu stören –

SELIM: Was willst du, Pedrillo?

PEDRILLO: Dieser junge Mann, der sich in Italien mit vielem Fleiß auf die Baukunst gelegt, hat von deiner Macht, von deinem Reichtum gehört und kommt her, dir als Baumeister seine Dienste anzubieten.

BELMONTE: Herr! könnte ich so glücklich sein, durch meine geringen Fähigkeiten deinen Beifall zu verdienen.

SELIM: Hm! Du gefällst mir. Ich will sehen, was du kannst. – *(zum Pedrillo)* Sorge für seinen Unterhalt. Morgen werde ich dich wieder rufen lassen. *(geht ab)*

CONSTANZA: Just a little more!

SELIM: So be it! For the last time!—Go, Constanza, go! Change your mind, and tomorrow—

CONSTANZA: (*as she goes*) Unhappy maiden! Oh Belmonte, Belmonte!

Eighth Scene
SELIM, PEDRILLO, AND BELMONTE.

Spoken Dialogue

SELIM: Her anguish, her tears, her steadfastness have bewitched my heart all the more. I want her love more than ever. Ha! Who would want to use force on such a creature?—No, Constanza, no, even Selim has feelings. Even Selim knows love—

PEDRILLO: Excellency, forgive my interrupting your reverie—

SELIM: What do you want, Pedrillo?

PEDRILLO: This young man, who has diligently studied architecture in Italy, has heard of your power and wealth, and has come to offer you his services as an architect.

BELMONTE: Excellency, if only I could win your favor through my small talents!

SELIM: Hmm. You interest me. I will see what you can do.—*(to Pedrillo)* See to his needs. Tomorrow I will summon you again. *(He leaves.)*

Neunter Auftritt

BELMONTE, PEDRILLO.

Dialog

PEDRILLO: Ha! Triumph, Triumph, Herr! der erste Schritt war getan.

BELMONTE: Ach lass mich zu mir selbst kommen! – Ich habe sie gesehen, hab das gute treue beste Mädchen gesehen! – O Konstanze, Konstanze! was könnt ich für dich tun, was für dich wagen?

PEDRILLO: Ha! gemach, gemach, bester Herr! Stimmen Sie den Ton ein bisschen herab; Verstellung wird uns weit bessere Dienste leisten. Wir sind nicht in unserm Vaterlande. Hier fragen sie den Henker darnach, ob's einen Kopf mehr oder weniger in der Welt gibt. Bastonade und Strick um Hals sind hier wie ein Morgenbrot.

BELMONTE: Ach, Pedrillo! wenn du die Liebe kenntest –

PEDRILLO: Hm! Als wenn's mit unsereinem gar nichts wäre. Ich habe so gut meine zärtlichen Stunden als andere Leute. Und denken Sie denn, dass mir's nicht auch im Bauche grimmt, wenn ich mein Blondchen von so einem alten Spitzbuben, wie der Osmin ist, bewacht sehen muss?

BELMONTE: O wenn es möglich wäre, sie zu sprechen –

PEDRILLO: Wir wollen sehen, was zu tun ist. Kommen Sie nur mit mir in Garten: Aber um alles in der Welt, vorsichtig und fein. Denn hier ist alles Aug und Ohr.

(Sie wollen in den Palast; Osmin kommt ihnen in der Tür entgegen und hält sie zurück.)

Ninth Scene

BELMONTE AND PEDRILLO.

Spoken Dialogue

PEDRILLO: Aha! Success, master, success! We've taken the first step.

BELMONTE: Ooph, I have to recover myself!—I have seen her, seen the sweetest, truest, bestest maiden!—Oh, Constanza, Constanza! What I wouldn't do for you, dare for you!

PEDRILLO: Gently, gently, dear master! Lower your voice a little. Pretending is better than proclaiming. We aren't in Italy, after all. Here they ask the executioner whether there's one less head in the world now. The bastinado and hangman's rope are as regular as breakfast in these parts.

BELMONTE:
Ah, Pedrillo, if only you knew what love is—

PEDRILLO: As if for people like me there were no such thing! I have just as many flirtations as the next man. And do you think it doesn't gall me when I see my little Blanche with that old scoundrel Osmin drooling after her?

BELMONTE: If only I could speak to her—

PEDRILLO: We'll see what can be done. Come with me to the garden, but for heaven's sake, be quiet about it. Everything here has eyes and ears.

(As they are about to enter the palace, Osmin comes out of the door and holds them back.)

Zehnter Auftritt

VORIGE, OSMIN.

OSMIN: Wohin?

PEDRILLO: Hinein!

OSMIN: *(zu Belmonte)* Was will das Gesicht? – Zurück mit dir, zurück!

PEDRILLO: Ha, gemach, Meister Grobian, gemach! er ist in des Bassa Diensten.

OSMIN: In des Henkers Diensten mag er sein! Er soll nicht herein!

PEDRILLO: Er soll aber herein!

OSMIN: Kommt mir nur einen Schritt über die Schwelle –

BELMONTE: Unverschämter! Hast du nicht mehr Achtung für einen Mann meines Standes?

OSMIN: Ei, ihr mögt mir vom Stande sein! – Fort, fort, oder ich will euch Beine machen.

PEDRILLO: Alter Dummkopf! Es ist ja der Baumeister, den der Bassa angenommen hat.

OSMIN: Meinethalben sei er Stockmeister: Nur komm er mir hier nicht zu nahe. Ich müsste nicht sehen, dass es so ein Kumpan deines Gelichters ist und dass das so eine abgeredte Karte ist, uns zu überlisten. Der Bassa ist weich wie Butter, mit dem könnt ihr machen, was ihr wollt: Aber ich habe eine feine Nase. Gaune-

Tenth Scene

THOSE BEFORE, AND OSMIN.

OSMIN: And where do you think you are going?

PEDRILLO: Inside!

OSMIN: *(to Belmonte)* And what does *he* want?—Back, I say, stand back!

PEDRILLO: Easy there, Mister Muscleman, easy! He is working for the Pasha.

OSMIN: He could be the hangman's assistant, for all I care. He is not coming in here!

PEDRILLO: But he *is* coming in!

OSMIN: Just try to take a step through this door—

BELMONTE: Insolent chap! Have you no respect for a man of my standing?

OSMIN: Think I care about your *standing!*—Get out of here or I'll stand on *you!*

PEDRILLO: You old dimwit! This is the architect whom the Pasha has hired.

OSMIN: I don't care what he calls himself, just don't let him come any closer. I wouldn't want to see another of your cronies, another of the little traps you try to lay for me. The Pasha is as soft as butter, you can do what you like with him. But I have a nose for nonsense. Deceit is the stock in trade for you oily for-

rei ist's um den ganzen Kram mit euch fremden Gesindel, und ihr abgefeimten Betrüger habt lange euer Plänchen angelegt, eure Pfiffe auszuführen: Aber wart ein bisschen! Osmin schläft nicht. Wär ich Bassa, ihr wärt längst gespießt. – Ja! schneid't nur Gesichter, lacht nur höhnisch in Bart hinein!

PEDRILLO: Ereifere dich nicht so, Alter. Es hilft dir doch nichts. Sieh, soeben werden wir hineinspazieren.

OSMIN: Ha! das will ich sehen!
(stellt sich vor die Türe)

PEDRILLO: Mach keine Umstände. –

BELMONTE: Weg, Niederträchtiger!

N° 7 Terzett

OSMIN:
Marsch! marsch! marsch! trollt euch fort!
Sonst soll die Bastonade
Euch gleich zu Diensten stehn.

BELMONTE, PEDRILLO:
Ei, ei! das wär ja schade,
Mit uns so umzugehn.

OSMIN: Kommt nur nicht näher.

BELMONTE, PEDRILLO: Weg von der Türe.

OSMIN: Sonst schlag ich drein.

BELMONTE, PEDRILLO: Wir gehn hinein.

(Sie drängen ihn von der Türe weg.)

eigners, and you crafty swindlers have long been hatching your little schemes. But just you wait! Osmin never sleeps. If I were Pasha, you'd have been sliced into pieces long ago.—Yes, yes, go ahead, make faces, laugh in your beards!

PEDRILLO: Don't get so riled up, old man. It won't help. As a matter of fact, we'll be going in right now.

OSMIN: Ha! We'll see about that!
(He stands astride the doorway.)

PEDRILLO: Don't make any fuss.

BELMONTE: Out of the way, you wretch!

Trio

OSMIN:
March! March! March!
Off you go
Or you'll feel my whip!

BELMONTE AND PEDRILLO:
Ouch! Ouch! Ouch!
There you go!
What about friendship!

OSMIN: Not one step more!

BELMONTE AND PEDRILLO: Away from the door!

OSMIN: You'd prefer a scar!

BELMONTE AND PEDRILLO: Just leave it ajar!

(They push him from the doorway.)

OSMIN: Marsch fort! Ich schlage drein!

BELMONTE, PEDRILLO: Platz fort! Wir gehn hinein.

(Sie stoßen ihn weg und gehn hinein.)

Ende des ersten Aufzugs

OSMIN: March away! I'll make you pay!

BELMONTE AND PEDRILLO: We're going in, whatever you say!

(They force him aside and enter.)

End of Act I

Zweiter Aufzug

Garten am Palast des Bassa Selim;
an der Seite Osmins Wohnung.

Erster Auftritt

OSMIN, BLONDE.

BLONDE: O des Zankens, Befehlens und Murrens wird auch kein Ende! Einmal für allemal: Das steht mir nicht an! Denkst du alter Murrkopf etwa eine türkische Sklavin vor dir zu haben, die bei deinen Befehlen zittert? O da irrst du dich sehr! Mit europäischen Mädchen springt man nicht so herum; denen begegnet man ganz anders.

N° 8 Aria

BLONDE:

Durch Zärtlichkeit und Schmeicheln,
Gefälligkeit und Scherzen
Erobert man die Herzen
Der guten Mädchen leicht:
Doch mürrisches Befehlen
Und Poltern, Zanken, Plagen
Macht, dass in wenig Tagen
So Lieb als Treu entweicht.

Act II

*The garden of the Pasha Selim's palace;
on one side, Osmin's quarters.*

First Scene

OSMIN AND BLANCHE.

BLANCHE: *(speaking)* There's no end to these squabbles and
scolding and summons! Once and for all, I won't stand for it!
Do you think, you old grouch, that you have a Turkish slave at
your feet, who trembles at your commands? You are very much
mistaken! European girls cannot be treated that way. They must
be approached very differently.

Aria

BLANCHE:
With pretty words and smiles,
With promises of rapture,
A man may hope to capture
A gentle maiden's heart.
But spitefulness and snarls,
Bluster and threatening displays
Ensure, in a matter of days,
Love will up and depart.

Dialog

OSMIN: Ei seht doch mal, was das Mädchen vorschreiben kann! Zärtlichkeit! Schmeicheln! – Es ist mir wie pure Zärtlichkeit! – Wer Teufel hat dir das Zeug in Kopf gesetzt? – Hier sind wir in der Türkei und da geht's aus einem andern Tone. Ich dein Herr, du meine Sklavin. Ich befehle, du musst gehorchen!

BLONDE: Deine Sklavin? ich deine Sklavin! – Ha! ein Mädchen eine Sklavin! Noch einmal sag mir das, noch einmal!

OSMIN: *(für sich)* Ich möchte toll werden, was das Mädchen für ein starrköpfiges Ding ist. *(laut)* Du hast doch wohl nicht vergessen, dass dich der Bassa mir zur Sklavin geschenkt hat?

BLONDE: Bassa hin, Bassa her! Mädchen sind keine Ware zum Verschenken! Ich bin eine Engländerin, zur Freiheit geboren, und trotz jedem, der mich zu etwas zwingen will!

OSMIN: *(beiseite)* Gift und Dolch über das Mädchen! – Beim Mahomet! sie macht mich rasend. – Und doch lieb ich die Spitzbübin, trotz ihres tollen Kopfes! *(laut)* Ich befehle dir augenblicklich, mich zu lieben.

BLONDE: Hahaha! Komm mir nur ein wenig näher, ich will dir fühlbare Beweise davon geben.

OSMIN: Tolles Ding! Weißt du, dass du mein bist und ich dich dafür züchtigen kann?

BLONDE: Wag's nicht, mich anzurühren, wenn dir deine Augen lieb sind.

OSMIN: Wie? du unterstehst dich –

Spoken Dialogue

OSMIN: Just look what the little lady recommends! Tenderness! Flattery!—I'll tenderize you, alright!—What devil put these ideas into your head? We are in Turkey here, and hum quite another tune. I am the master, you are the slave. I command, you obey.

BLANCHE: Your slave? Your slave!—Ha! A modern young woman be a slave! Just try saying that to me again!

OSMIN: *(to himself)* She'll drive me crazy! This girl is so pigheaded. *(aloud)* I hope you haven't forgotten that the Pasha gave you to me as my slave.

BLANCHE: Pasha this, Pasha that! Girls are not cattle. I am a freeborn Englishwoman, and I defy anyone who wants to force me to do anything.

OSMIN: *(aside)* A plague on this girl!—By Mohammed, she'll drive me mad!—Still, I love the little scamp, despite all her stubbornness. *(aloud)* I order you to love me this instant.

BLANCHE: Ha ha! Just come a little closer, and I'll give you a sample of my love.

OSMIN: Crazy girl! Don't you realize you are my property and I could punish you for saying that?

BLANCHE: Don't you dare lay a hand on me, unless you want your eyes poked out.

OSMIN: What? You have the impudence—

BLONDE: Da ist was zu unterstehen? Du bist der Unverschämte, der sich zu viel Freiheit herausnimmt. So ein altes hässliches Gesicht untersteht sich, einem Mädchen wie ich, jung, schön, zur Freude geboren, wie einer Magd zu befehlen! Wahrhaftig, das stünde mir an! Uns gehört das Regiment, ihr seid unsre Sklaven und glücklich, wenn ihr Verstand genug habt, euch die Ketten zu erleichtern.

OSMIN: Bei meinem Bart, sie ist toll! Hier, hier in der Türkei?

BLONDE: Türkei hin, Türkei her! Weib ist Weib, sie sei, wo sie wolle! Sind eure Weiber solche Närrinnen, sich von euch unterjochen zu lassen, desto schlimmer für sie. In Europa verstehen sie das Ding besser. Lass mich nur einmal Fuß hier gefasst haben, sie sollen bald anders werden.

OSMIN: Beim Allah! die wär imstande, uns allen die Weiber rebellisch zu machen. - Aber -

BLONDE: Aufs Bitten müsst ihr euch legen, wenn ihr etwas von uns erhalten wollt; besonders Liebhaber deines Gelichters.

OSMIN: Freilich, wenn ich Pedrillo wär, so ein Drahtpüppchen wie er, da wär ich vermutlich willkommen. Denn euer Mienenspiel hab ich lange weg.

BLONDE: Erraten, guter Alter, erraten! Das kannst du dir wohl einbilden, dass mir der niedliche Pedrillo lieber ist wie dein Blasbalggesicht. Also wenn du klug wärst -

OSMIN: Sollt ich dir die Freiheit geben, zu tun und zu mach'n, was du wolltest? He?

BLONDE: Besser würdest du immer dabei fahren: Denn so wirst du sicher betrogen.

BLANCHE: The impudence? You are shameless, trying to take liberties. An old, ugly dog has the nerve to boss around a pretty, young—*and free*—girl as if she were a servant! Utter nonsense! We are in charge here! You are our slaves and you're lucky if you have the sense to loosen your chains a bit.

OSMIN: By the Prophet's beard, she is crazy! Here, in Turkey?

BLANCHE: Turkey this, Turkey that! A woman is a woman, wherever she is. If the women here are silly enough to let themselves be under your fat thumbs, so much the worse for them. In Europe, we understand these things better. Just let me set up shop here and I'll soon change your women.

OSMIN: By Allah! She would turn all the women here into rebels—but—

BLANCHE: If you want anything, then you will have to beg for it—especially lovers of your sort.

OSMIN: Of course if I were a floppy puppet like Pedrillo, then I would be welcome. I've seen the way you two carry on.

BLANCHE: And quite right you are, old man. You can see that darling Pedrillo appeals to me more than your fat face does. If you had any sense—

OSMIN: You want me to give you the freedom to do as you please. Is that it?

BLANCHE: You would be wise to do so. It is better than being deceived.

OSMIN: Gift und Dolch! Nun reißt mir die Gedult! Den Augenblick hinein ins Haus! Und wo du's wagst –

BLONDE: Mach mich nicht zu lachen.

OSMIN: Ins Haus, sag ich!

BLONDE: Nicht von der Stelle!

OSMIN: Mach nicht, dass ich Gewalt brauche.

BLONDE: Gewalt werd ich mit Gewalt vertreiben. Meine Gebieterin hat mich hier in Garten bestellt. Sie ist die Geliebte des Bassa, sein Augapfel, sein Alles; und es kostet mir ein Wort, so hast du funfzig auf die Fußsohlen. Also geh –

OSMIN: *(für sich)* Das ist ein Satan. Ich muss nachgeben, so wahr ich ein Muselmann bin; sonst könnte ihre Drohung eintreffen.

N° 9 Duetto

OSMIN:
Ich gehe, doch rate ich dir,
den Schurken Pedrillo zu meiden.

BLONDE:
O pack dich, befiehl nicht mit mir,
Du weißt ja, ich kann es nicht leiden.

OSMIN: Versprich mir – – –

BLONDE: Was fällt dir da ein!

OSMIN: Zum Henker!

BLONDE: Fort, lass mich allein.

OSMIN: Blast you! I'm losing my patience! Into the house this minute! And if you dare—

BLANCHE: You make me laugh.

OSMIN: Into the house, I say!

BLANCHE: Not on your life.

OSMIN: Don't make me force you.

BLANCHE: I'll match force with force. My mistress has summoned me here to the garden. She is the Pasha's favorite, the apple of his eye, his everything. One word from me, and you would have fifty lashes on the soles of your feet. Out of my way—

OSMIN: *(to himself)* She is the very devil. As a true Muslim, I must give in. Otherwise, she might act on her threat!

Duet

OSMIN:
I am going, but you beware!
That Pedrillo—keep away from him.

BLANCHE:
Off now! That is my affair.
I won't stand your butting in.

OSMIN: Promise me—

BLANCHE: What's come over you!

OSMIN: Damnation!

BLANCHE: Go away now. Shoo!

OSMIN:

Wahrhaftig kein'n Schritt von der Stelle,
Bis du zu gehorchen mir schwörst.

BLONDE:

Nicht so viel, du armer Geselle,
Und wenn du der Großmogul wärst.

OSMIN:

O Engländer! seid ihr nicht Toren,
Ihr lasst euren Weibern den Willen;

BLONDE:

Ein Herz, so in Freiheit geboren,
Lässt niemals sich sklavisch behandeln,

OSMIN:

Wie ist man geplagt und geschoren,
Wenn solch eine Zucht man erhält!

BLONDE:

Bleibt, wenn schon die Freiheit verloren,
Noch stolz auf sie, lachet der Welt.

BLONDE: Nun troll dich.

OSMIN: So sprichst du mit mir?

BLONDE: Nicht anders.

OSMIN: Nun bleib ich erst hier.

BLONDE: *(stößt ihn fort)*
Ein andermal, itzt musst du gehen.

OSMIN:

I will not move another inch
Until you promise to obey me.

BLANCHE:

You think that I will flinch?
Not even Allah could tame me!

OSMIN:

You English are buffoons
To let your women run free.

BLANCHE:

A heart can never be enslaved
That was born to be truly free.

OSMIN:

Once they learn to call the tune
You must sing it endlessly.

BLANCHE:

If captured, it will be brave.
And laugh off a tyrant's decree.

BLANCHE: Off with you now!

OSMIN: You dare say that to me?

BLANCHE: That's what I said.

OSMIN: I won't budge, you'll see.

BLANCHE: *(pushing him away)*
One more time, out of here!

OSMIN: Wer hat solche Frechheit gesehen!

BLONDE: *(stellt sich, als wollte sie ihm die Augen auskratzen)*
Es ist um die Augen geschehen,
Wofern du noch länger verweilst.

OSMIN: *(furchtsam zurückweichend)*
Nur ruhig, ich will ja gern gehen,
Bevor du gar Schläge erteilst.
(geht ab)

Zweiter Auftritt
BLONDE, KONSTANZE.

BLONDE: Wie traurig das gute Mädchen daherkommt! Freilich tut's weh, den Geliebten zu verlieren und Sklavin zu sein. Es geht mir wohl auch nicht viel besser. Aber ich habe doch noch das Vergnügen, meinen Pedrillo manchmal zu sehen, ob's gleich auch mager und verstohlen genug geschehen muss: Doch wer kann wider den Strom schwimmen!

N° 10 Recitativo ed Aria
Recitativo
KONSTANZE: *(ohne Blondchen zu bemerken)*
Welcher Wechsel herrscht in meiner Seele
Seit dem Tag, da uns das Schicksal trannte!
O Belmont! hin sind die Freuden,
Die ich sonst an deiner Seite kannte!
Banger Sehnsuchts Leiden
Wohnen nun dafür in der beklemmten Brust.

OSMIN: Never, in all my career—

BLANCHE: *(pretending she wants to scratch out his eyes)*
I'll scratch your beady eyes out
If you stay a second longer.

OSMIN: *(timidly backing away)*
Temper! No need to shout.
I know which one is stronger.
(He goes off.)

Second Scene
BLANCHE AND CONSTANZA.

BLANCHE: *(speaking)* How sadly my mistress approaches! Truly
it hurts to lose your beloved and be a slave. It is not much better for me, but at least I have the joy of sometimes seeing my
Pedrillo. It's not often and the moments are stolen. But when
you are swimming upsteam . . .

Recitative and Aria
Recitative

CONSTANZA: *(without noticing Blanche)*
What upheavals grip my soul
Since that day Fate separated us!
Oh Belmonte! Gone are the joys
I once knew at your side.
The pangs of anxious yearning
Now oppress my suffering heart.

Aria

Traurigkeit ward mir zum Lose,
Weil ich dir entrissen bin.
Gleich der wurmzernagten Rose,
Gleich dem Gras im Wintermoose
Welkt mein banges Leben hin.
Selbst der Luft darf ich nicht sagen
Meiner Seele bittern Schmerz:
Denn, unwillig ihn zu tragen,
Haucht sie alle meine Klagen
Wieder in mein armes Herz.

Dialog

BLONDE: Ach mein bestes Fräulein! noch immer so traurig?

KONSTANZE: Kannst du fragen, die du meinen Kummer weißt?
– Wieder ein Abend und noch keine Nachricht, noch keine Hoffnung! – Und morgen – ach Gott! ich darf nicht daran denken.

BLONDE: Heitern Sie sich wenigstens ein bisschen auf. Sehn Sie,
wie schön der Abend ist, wie blühend uns alles entgegenlacht,
wie freudig uns die Vögel zu ihrem Gesang einladen! Verbannen
Sie die Grillen und fassen Sie Mut!

KONSTANZE: Wie glücklich bist du, Mädchen, bei deinem
Schicksal so gelassen zu sein! O dass ich es auch könnte!

BLONDE: Das steht nur bei Ihnen. Hoffen Sie –

KONSTANZE: Wo nicht der mindeste Schein von Hoffnung mehr
zu erblicken ist?

Aria

CONSTANZA:
Sorrow has become my fate
Because I was torn from you.
Like the rose that autumn awaits,
Like the grass under winter's weight,
My life is one death pursues.
I must not speak to the air
Of the suffering I have known.
A breeze could never bear
My grief, would send it elsewhere—
Back to my heart, as a moan.

Spoken Dialogue

BLANCHE: Ah, my dear lady! Still so sad?

CONSTANZA: Can you ask, you who knows my agony? Another evening and still no news, still no hope.—And tomorrow—oh God! I dare not think about it.

BLANCHE: Try to be a little more cheerful. Look how lovely the evening is, how everything blooms and smiles, how the birds bid us hear their singing. Put away your melancholy thoughts and take heart!

CONSTANZA: How lucky you are, friend, to be so calm about your fate. If only I could.

BLANCHE: That depends on you. Be hopeful—

CONSTANZA: Where not the slightest ray of hope can be seen?

BLONDE: Hören Sie nur: Ich verzage mein Lebtage nicht, es mag auch eine Sache noch so schlimm aussehen. Denn wer sich immer das Schlimmste vorstellt, ist auch wahrhaftig am schlimmsten dran.

KONSTANZE: Und wer sich immer mit Hoffnung schmeichelt und zuletzt betrogen sieht, hat alsdenn nichts mehr übrig als die Verzweiflung.

BLONDE: Jedes nach seiner Weise. Ich glaube bei der meinigen am besten zu fahren. Wie bald kann ihr Belmont mit Lösegeld erscheinen oder uns listigerweise entführen? Wären wir die ersten Frauenzimmer, die den türkischen Vielfraßen entkämen? – Dort seh ich den Bassa.

KONSTANZE: Lass uns ihm aus den Augen gehn.

BLONDE: Zu spät. Er hat Sie schon gesehen. Ich darf aber getrost aus dem Wege trollen, er schaffte mich ohnehin fort. *(im Weggehen)* Courage! wir kommen gewiss noch in unsre Heimat.

Dritter Auftritt

KONSTANZE, SELIM.

SELIM: Nun, Konstanze, denkst du meinem Begehren nach? Der Tag ist bald verstrichen, morgen musst du mich lieben, oder –

KONSTANZE: Muss? Welch albernes Begehren! Als ob man die Liebe anbefehlen könnte wie eine Tracht Schläge! – – Aber freilich wie ihr Türken zu Werke geht, lässt sich's auch allenfalls befehlen – Aber ihr seid würklich zu beklagen. Ihr kerkert die Gegenstände eurer Begierden ein und seid zufrieden, eure Lüste zu büßen.

BLANCHE: Listen to me. As long as I live I will never give up, no matter how hopeless things seem. She who always imagines the worst will find herself worse off.

CONSTANZA: And she who lets herself be deceived by hope finds nothing in the end but despair.

BLANCHE: An adage for everyone. I believe my way is best. How soon can Belmonte show up with the ransom money and cleverly rescue us? Would we be the first women to escape from a Turkish harem?—I see the Pasha coming.

CONSTANZA: Let us avoid being seen.

BLANCHE: Too late. He has already seen you. I had better leave now, because he would only send me away. *(as she goes)* Courage! We will soon be home again.

•

Third Scene
CONSTANZA AND SELIM.

SELIM: Now, Constanza, have you considered my request? The day is soon done, and tomorrow you must love me or—

CONSTANZA: Must? What an absurd demand! As if you could order someone to love, the way you can order someone to be beaten. Maybe you Turks can actually do that. Then you are to be pitied. You imprison what you fancy and then just indulge your desires.

SELIM: Und glaubst du etwan, unsre Weiber wären weniger glücklich als ihr in euren Ländern?

KONSTANZE: Die nichts bessers kennen!

SELIM: Auf diese Art wäre wohl keine Hoffnung, dass du je anders denken wirst.

KONSTANZE: Herr! Ich muss dir frei gestehn – – – denn was soll ich dich länger hinhalten, mich mit leerer Hoffnung schmeicheln, dass du dich durch mein Bitten erweichen ließest. – – Ich werde stets so denken wie itzt: Dich verehren, aber – – lieben? Nie.

SELIM: Und du zitterst nicht vor der Gewalt, die ich über dich habe?

KONSTANZE: Nicht im geringsten. Sterben ist alles, was ich zu erwarten habe, und je eher dies geschieht, je lieber wird es mir sein.

SELIM: Elende! Nein! Nicht sterben, aber Martern von allen Arten – – –

KONSTANZE: Auch die will ich ertragen; du schreckst mich nicht, ich erwarte alles.

N° 11 Aria

KONSTANZE:
Martern aller Arten
Mögen meiner warten,
Ich verlache Qual und Pein.
Nichts soll mich erschüttern,
Nur dann würd ich zittern,
Wenn ich untreu könnte sein.

SELIM: Do you really believe the women in our country are less happy than those in yours?

CONSTANZA: They don't know anything better.

SELIM: So there is no hope that you will change your mind.

CONSTANZA: My lord, I must confess to you—why put it off any longer, why deceive myself with the empty hope that you would listen to my pleas? I will always think as I do now. I will honor you, but love you—never.

SELIM: And you do not tremble before the power I have over you?

CONSTANZA: Not in the least. All that I have to look forward to is death, and the sooner it comes the better.

SELIM: Damn you! No, not death, but tortures past enduring—

CONSTANZA: I will endure them as well. You do not frighten me. I await anything.

Aria

CONSTANZA:
Tortures most surely await.
Let dawn bring on my fate.
I laugh at the rack and screw.
Nothing will ever shake me.
No fear will overtake me
While my loving heart stays true.

Lass dich bewegen,
Verschone mich!
Des Himmels Segen
Belohne dich!
Doch du bist entschlossen.
Willig, unverdrossen
Wähl ich jede Pein und Not.
Ordne nur, gebiete,
Lärme, tobe, wüte,
Zuletzt befreit mich doch der Tod.
(geht ab)

Vierter Auftritt
SELIM ALLEIN.

SELIM: Ist das ein Traum? Wo hat sie auf einmal den Mut her, sich so gegen mich zu betragen? Hat sie vielleicht Hoffnung, mir zu entkommen? Ha! das will ich verwehren! *(will fort)* Doch das ist's nicht, dann würde sie sich eher verstellen, mich einzuschläfern suchen. – – – Ja! es ist Verzweiflung! Mit Härte richt' ich nichts aus – mit Bitten auch nicht – – also, was Drohen und Bitten nicht vermögen, soll die List zuwege bringen. *(geht ab)*

Fünfter Auftritt
BLONDE ALLEIN.

BLONDE: Kein Bassa, keine Konstanze mehr da? Sind sie miteinander eins worden? – – Schwerlich, das gute Kind hängt zu sehr an ihrem Belmont! Ich bedaure sie von Grund meines Herzens. Sie ist zu empfindsam für ihre Lage. Freilich, hätt ich meinen Pedrillo nicht an der Seite, wer weiß, wie mir's ginge! Doch würd ich nicht so zärteln wie sie. Die Männer verdienen's wahrlich nicht, dass man ihrenthalben sich zu Tode grämt. – – Vielleicht würd ich muselmännisch denken.

If you love me, set me free.
Heaven will bless your mercy!
But if you will not spare me,
Then know you cannot scare me.
I will suffer any pain.
Give your order, but never doubt.
Rant and rage and shout!
Your threats are all in vain.
(She storms off.)

Fourth Scene
SELIM, ALONE.

SELIM: *(speaking)* Is this a dream? From where does she summon the courage to set on me like that? Does she hope she can escape? Ha, I will see about that! *(He starts to leave.)* No, that cannot be it. If that were true she would pretend to flatter me.—Yes, it must be despair! I will accomplish nothing by cruelty—or with begging. Where threats and pleas have failed, cunning may succeed. *(He leaves.)*

Fifth Scene
BLANCHE, ALONE.

BLANCHE: *(speaking)* No Pasha here, and no Constanza. Have they come to an agreement?—Hardly! That sweet thing is too devoted to her Belmonte. I pity her from the bottom of my heart. She is too sensitive for this situation. If I didn't have my Pedrillo nearby, I'm sure I don't know what I'd do. I wouldn't be as droopy as she is. Men don't deserve women who pine after them.—I would undoubtedly think like . . . a Muslim.

Sechster Auftritt
BLONDE, PEDRILLO.

Dialog

PEDRILLO: Bst, Bst! Blondchen! Ist der Weg rein?

BLONDE: Komm nur, komm! Der Bassa ist wieder zurück. Und meinem Alten habe ich eben den Kopf ein bisschen gewaschen. Was hast du denn?

PEDRILLO: O Neuigkeiten, Neuigkeiten, die dich entzücken werden.

BLONDE: Nun? hurtig heraus damit!

PEDRILLO: Erst, liebes Herzensblondchen, lass dir vor allen Dingen einen recht herzlichen Kuss geben: Du weißt ja, wie gestohlnes Gut schmeckt.

BLONDE: Pfui, pfui! Wenn das deine Neuigkeiten alle sind –

PEDRILLO: Närrchen, mach darum keinen Lärm: Der alte spitzbübische Osmin lauert uns sicher auf den Dienst.

BLONDE: Nun? und die Neuigkeiten? –

PEDRILLO: Sind, dass das Ende unsrer Sklaverei vor der Türe ist. – *(Er sieht sich sorgfältig um.)* Belmonte, Konstanzens Geliebter, ist angekommen. Und ich hab ihn unter dem Namen eines Baumeisters hier im Palast eingeführt.

BLONDE: Ah, was sagst du? Belmonte da?

PEDRILLO: Mit Leib und Seele!

Sixth Scene

BLANCHE AND PEDRILLO.

Spoken Dialogue

PEDRILLO: Psst, psst! Blanche! Is the way clear?

BLANCHE: Come on, come. The Pasha has gone, and I have just scared off the old man. So, what do you have?

PEDRILLO: News, news that will delight you.

BLANCHE: What? Out with it!

PEDRILLO: First, my darling Blanche, let me give you a big kiss. You know how sweet stolen kisses are.

BLANCHE: Phooey! If that's all your news—

PEDRILLO: Look here, you little fool, don't make a fuss. That old scoundrel Osmin is probably watching us.

BLANCHE: What is your news then?

PEDRILLO: The end of our days in slavery is at hand.— *(He looks around carefully.)* Constanza's beloved Belmonte has arrived, and I have gotten him into the palace as an architect.

BLANCHE: What are you saying? Belmonte is here?

PEDRILLO: Body and soul.

BLONDE: Ha! das muss Konstanze wissen! *(will fort)*

PEDRILLO: Hör nur, Blondchen, hör nur erst: Er hat ein Schiff hier in der Nähe in Bereitschaft und wir haben beschlossen, euch diese Nacht zu entführen.

BLONDE: O allerliebst, allerliebst! Herzens-Pedrillo! das verdient einen Kuss. Geschwind, geschwind zu Konstanzen! *(will fort)*

PEDRILLO: Halt nur, halt, und lass erst mit dir reden. Um Mitternacht kommt Belmonte mit einer Leiter zu Konstanzens Fenster und ich zu dem deinigen, und dann gehts heidi davon!

BLONDE: O vortrefflich! Aber Osmin?

PEDRILLO: Hier ist ein Schlaftrunk für den alten Schlaukopf, den misch ihm fein manierlich ins Getränke, verstehst du? Ich habe dort auch schon ein Fläschchen angefüllt. Geht's hier nicht, wird's dort wohl gehen.

BLONDE: Sorg nicht für mich! - Aber kann Konstanze ihren Geliebten nicht sprechen?

PEDRILLO: Sobald es vollends finster ist, kommt er hier in Garten. Nun geh und bereite Konstanzen vor. Ich will hier Belmonten erwarten. Leb wohl, Herzchen, leb wohl!

BLONDE: Leb wohl, guter Pedrillo! Ach, was werd ich für Freude anrichten!

BLANCHE: Ha! Constanza must know! *(She starts to leave.)*

PEDRILLO: Not so fast. First let me explain, Blanche. He has a ship at anchor nearby and we have decided to abduct you this very night.

BLANCHE: You genius! You savior! My darling Pedrillo! Indeed, you deserve a kiss. Hurry, though, I have to tell Constanza. *(She starts to leave.)*

PEDRILLO: Not so fast. First let me explain. At midnight Belmonte will come to Constanza's window with a ladder, and I will come to yours. And then we're off!

BLANCHE: Oh splendid! But Osmin . . .

PEDRILLO: Here is a sleeping potion for that old sourpuss. Mix it into his drink, understand? I also have a bottle already dosed. If one doesn't work, we'll use the other.

BLANCHE: Don't worry about me. But can't Constanza speak to her beloved?

PEDRILLO: As soon as it's completely dark, he'll come to the garden here. Now go tell Constanza. I will wait here for Belmonte. Farewell, my sweetheart, farewell!

BLANCHE: Farewell, dear Pedrillo! Oh, what happiness I will bring her!

N° 12 Aria

BLONDE:

Welche Wonne, welche Lust
Herrscht nunmehr in meiner Brust!
Ohne Aufschub will ich springen
Und ihr gleich die Nachricht bringen
Und mit Lachen und mit Scherzen
Ihrem schwachen, feigen Herzen
Freud und Jubel prophezeihn.

(geht fort)

Siebenter Auftritt
PEDRILLO ALLEIN.

PEDRILLO: Ah, dass es schon vorbei wäre! dass wir schon auf offner See wären, unsre Mädels im Arm und dies verwünschte Land im Rücken hätten! Doch sei's gewagt: Entweder itzt oder niemals. Wer zagt, verliert!

N° 13 Aria

PEDRILLO:

Frisch zum Kampfe! Frisch zum Streite!
Nur ein feiger Tropf verzagt.
Sollt ich zittern? Sollt ich zagen?
Nicht mein Leben mutig wagen?
Nein, ach nein, es sei gewagt!
Frisch zum Kampfe! Frisch zum Streite!
Nur ein feiger Tropf verzagt.

Aria

BLANCHE:

What joy, what delight!
My heart now feels so light!
I shall run immediately
And tell her she will be free.
I shall laugh and tease her
With news that will please her,
Her and her grieving heart.

(She hurries out.)

Seventh Scene

PEDRILLO ALONE.

PEDRILLO: *(speaking)* Oh, if only it were all over now! To be on the open sea, our girls in our arms and our backs to this cursed country! But this is the sticking point. Now or never! He who hesitates is lost!

Aria

PEDRILLO:

On to battle! On to strife!
Only a coward is afraid.
Will I tremble or run away?
No, I'll bravely risk my life!
Duty must be obeyed.
Only a coward is afraid.
On to battle! On to strife!

Achter Auftritt

PEDRILLO, OSMIN.

Dialog

OSMIN: Ha! Geht's hier so lustig zu? Es muss dir verteufelt wohl gehen.

PEDRILLO: Ei, wer wird so ein Kopfhänger sein, es kommt beim Henker da nichts bei heraus! Das haben die Pedrillos von jeher in ihrer Familie gehabt. Fröhlichkeit und Wein versüßt die härteste Sklaverei. Freilich könnt ihr armen Schlucker das nicht begreifen, dass es so ein herrlich Ding um ein Gläschen guten, alten Lustigmacher ist. Wahrhaftig, da hat euer Vater Mahomet einen verzweifelten Bock geschossen, dass er euch den Wein verboten hat. Wenn das verwünschte Gesetz nicht wäre, du müsstest ein Gläschen mit mir trinken, du möchtest wollen oder nicht. *(für sich)* Vielleicht beißt er an: Er trinkt ihn gar zu gerne.

OSMIN: Wein mit dir? Ja Gift –

PEDRILLO: Immer Gift und Dolch, und Dolch und Gift! Lass doch den alten Groll einmal fahren und sei vernünftig. Sieh einmal, ein Paar Flaschen Zypernwein! – Ah – *(Er zeigt ihm zwo Flaschen, wovon die eine größer als die andere ist.)* Die sollen mir trefflich schmecken!

OSMIN: *(für sich)* Wenn ich trauen dürfte?

PEDRILLO: Das ist ein Wein, das ist ein Wein!
(Er setzt sich nach türkischer Art auf die Erde und trinkt aus der kleinen Flasche.)

OSMIN: Kost einmal die große Flasche auch.

Eighth Scene

PEDRILLO AND OSMIN.

Spoken Dialogue

OSMIN: And what's so funny? Things going pretty well for you?

PEDRILLO: So we should be sad? No future in that. The Pedrillo clan has always had a cheerful side. Happiness and wine sweeten the cruelest slavery. Of course, you poor wretches can't understand the effects of a good glass of wine. Old Father Mohammad got it all wrong when he forbade you to drink wine. If it weren't for that silly law, you'd be having a glass right now with me, and it would depend on what you wanted. *(to himself)* Maybe he'll bite. He looks like he wants to.

OSMIN: Wine? With you? Poison!

PEDRILLO: Always poison and daggers, daggers and poison! Let go of your anger just once and be sensible. Look here, two bottles of Cyprian wine—Ah!—*(He shows him two bottles, one larger than the other.)* They'll taste delicious to me!

OSMIN: *(to himself)* If only I trusted him!

PEDRILLO: What a wine! What a wine!
(He sits on the ground in the Turkish manner and drinks from the smaller bottle.)

OSMIN: Now drink out of the big bottle too.

PEDRILLO: Denkst wohl gar, ich habe Gift hinein getan? Ha! lass dir keine grauen Haare wachsen. Es verlohnte sich der Mühe, dass ich deinetwegen zum Teufel führe. Da sieh, ob ich trinke. *(Er trinkt aus der großen Flasche ein wenig.)* Nun, hast du noch Bedenken? traust mir noch nicht? Pfui, Osmin! sollt'st dich schämen – Da nimm! *(Er gibt ihm die große Flasche.)* Oder willst du die kleine?

OSMIN: Nein, lass nur, lass nur! Aber wenn du mich verrätst. – *(sieht sich sorgfältig um)*

PEDRILLO: Als wenn wir einander nicht weiter brauchten. Immer frisch! Mahomet liegt längst auf'm Ohr und hat nötiger zu tun, als sich um deine Flasche Wein zu bekümmern.

N° 14 Duetto

PEDRILLO:
Vivat Bachus! Bachus lebe!
Bachus war ein braver Mann!

OSMIN:
Ob ich's wage? – Ob ich's trinke?
Ob's wohl Allah sehen kann?

PEDRILLO:
Was hilft das Zaudern? Hinunter, hinunter!
Nicht lange, nicht lange gefragt!

(Osmin trinkt.)

OSMIN:
Nun war's geschehen, Nun war's hinunter:
Das heiß ich, das heiß ich gewagt!

PEDRILLO: Do you think I've put poison in it? Ha! Don't get gray hair over it. It isn't worth the trouble going to the devil over you. Watch how I drink. *(He takes a small sip from the large bottle.)* Now, still have doubts? Still don't trust me? Oof, Osmin! You should be ashamed—Here, take it! *(He offers him the large bottle.)* Or would you rather have the smaller one?

OSMIN: No, give it here, give it! But if you are deceiving me—*(He looks around carefully.)*

PEDRILLO: As if we won't need each other later on. Go on! Mohammad has been asleep for a long time now and has other things on his mind than a bottle of wine.

Duet

PEDRILLO:
Viva Bacchus! To the god of wine!
Bacchus was a good old soul!

OSMIN:
Should I dare to take a sip of wine?
What if Allah is at a keyhole?

PEDRILLO:
Why hesitate? Drink it down!
Don't be all day about it.

(Osmin drinks.)

OSMIN:
Now I've swallowed, now it's down!
My courage—who can doubt it!

PEDRILLO, OSMIN:
Es leben die Mädchen, die Blonden, die Braunen,
Sie leben hoch!

PEDRILLO: Das schmeckt trefflich!

OSMIN: Das schmeckt herrlich!

PEDRILLO, OSMIN: Ah! das heiß ich Göttertrank!

OSMIN:
Vivat Bachus! Bachus lebe!
Bachus, der den Wein erfand!

Dialog

PEDRILLO: Wahrhaftig, das muss ich gestehen, es geht doch nichts über den Wein. Wein ist mir lieber als Geld und Mädchen. Bin ich verdrüsslich, mürrisch, launisch: Hurtig nehm ich meine Zuflucht zur Flasche, und kaum seh ich den ersten Boden: Weg ist all mein Verdruss! – Meine Flasche macht mir kein schiefes Gesicht wie mein Mädchen, wenn ihr der Kopf nicht auf dem rechten Flecke steht. Und schwatzt mir von Süßigkeit der Liebe und des Ehestands, was ihr wollt: Wein auf der Zunge geht über alles!

(Osmin fängt bereits an, die Wirkung des Weins und des Schlaftrunks zu spüren, und wird bis zu Ende des Auftritts immer schläfriger und träger; doch darf's der Schauspieler nicht übertreiben und muss nur immer halb träumend und schlaftrunken bleiben.)

OSMIN: Das ist wahr – Wein – Wein – ist ein schönes Getränke; und unser großer – Prophet mag mir's nicht übel nehmen – Gift und Dolch! Es ist doch eine hübsche Sache um den Wein! – Nicht – – Bruder Pedrillo?

PEDRILLO AND OSMIN:
Here's to the girls, blondes and brunettes!
Long may they live!

PEDRILLO: This is downright delicious!

OSMIN: Absolutely audacious!

PEDRILLO AND OSMIN: Ah, it is fit for the gods!

OSMIN:
Viva Bacchus! To the god of wine!
Bacchus first discovered this stuff!

Spoken Dialogue

PEDRILLO: Truthfully, I must confess, there is nothing better than wine! Wine is better than gold, better than girls. If I'm in a bad temper or grouchy or moody, then I grab a bottle, and by the time I can see the bottom of the first one, my annoyance is gone!—My bottle doesn't make faces, the way a girl does when something goes wrong. Talk to me all you want about sweet love, marriage . . . *anything*. Wine on the tongue is the best thing in the world!

(Osmin is already beginning to feel the effects of the wine and sleeping potion and until the end of this scene he grows more sluggish and sleepy. The actor should not exaggerate, but should remain half-dreaming and drugged with sleep.)

OSMIN: True enough—wine—wine—is a lovely drink, and our Great—Prophet should not think ill of me if—poison and daggers! Wine is such a wonderful thing!—isn't it ever—brother Pedrillo?

PEDRILLO: Richtig, Bruder Osmin, richtig!

OSMIN: Man wird gleich so - munter - *(Er nickt zuweilen.)* so vergnügt - so aufgeräumt - - Hast du nichts mehr, Bruder? *(Er langt auf eine lächerliche Art nach einer zwoten Flasche, die Pedrillo ihm reicht.)*

PEDRILLO: Hör du, Alter: Trink mir nicht zu viel; es kommt einem in Kopf.

OSMIN: Trag doch keine - Sorge, ich bin so - so - nüchtern wie möglich - Aber das ist wahr - *(Er fängt an, auf die Erde hin und her zu wanken.)* es schmeckt - - vortrefflich! -

PEDRILLO: *(für sich)* Es wirkt, Alter, es wirkt!

OSMIN: Aber verraten musst du mich nicht - Brüderchen - verraten - denn - wenn's Mahomet - - nein, nein - der Bassa wüsste - - denn siehst du - - liebes Blondchen - - ja oder nein! - -

PEDRILLO: *(für sich)* Nun wird's Zeit, ihn fortzuschaffen! *(laut)* Nun komm, Alter, komm, wir wollen schlafen gehn! *(Er hebt ihn auf.)*

OSMIN: Schlafen? - Schämst du dich nicht? - - Gift und Dolch! Wer wird denn so schläfrig sein - es ist ja kaum Morgen -

PEDRILLO: Hoho, die Sonne ist schon hinunter! - Komm, komm, dass uns der Bassa nicht überrascht!

OSMIN: *(im Abführen)* Ja, ja - - eine Flasche - guter - Bassa - geht über - - alles! - gute Nacht - - Brüderchen - gute Nacht. -

(Pedrillo führt ihn hinein, kommt aber gleich wieder zurück.)

PEDRILLO: Right, brother Osmin, right you are!

OSMIN: One gets so happy—right away—*(He nods several times.)* so jolly—so happy!—Do you have any more, brother? *(He reaches in a lurching way for the second bottle, which Pedrillo gives him.)*

PEDRILLO: Now listen, old man, don't drink too much. It goes to your head.

OSMIN: Don't you—worry, I am so—so—very sober—But it's true—*(He starts to stagger back and forth.)* it tastes—wonderful.

PEDRILLO: *(to himself)* It's working, old man, it's working!

OSMIN: But you must not betray me—little brother—betray— because—if Mohammad—no, no—the Pasha knew—then you see—dear Blanche—yes or no!

PEDRILLO: *(to himself)* Now is the time to make our escape. *(aloud)* Come now, old man, let's go get some sleep. *(He helps him up.)*

OSMIN: Sleep?—Shame on you!—Poison and daggers! Who could sleep now—it's not yet morning—

PEDRILLO: Ha! The sun has already set. Come, come, so the Pasha won't discover us.

OSMIN: *(while being led out)* Yes, yes—a bottle—good—Pasha—is better—everything!—Goodnight—little brother—goodnight.

(Pedrillo leads him inside, but comes out again immediately.)

Neunter Auftritt

PEDRILLO, HERNACH BELMONTE, KONSTANZE, BLONDE.

PEDRILLO: *(macht's Osmin nach)* Gute Nacht – Brüderchen – gute Nacht! Hahahaha, alter Eisenfresser! erwischt man dich so? Gift und Dolch! – Du hast deine Ladung! Nur fürcht ich, ist's noch zu zeitig am Tage. Bis Mitternacht sind noch drei Stunden und da könnt er leicht wieder ausgeschlafen haben. – – Ach! kommen Sie, kommen Sie, liebster Herr! Unser Argus ist blind. Ich hab ihn tüchtig zugedeckt.

BELMONTE: O dass wir glücklich wären! – Aber sag: Ist Konstanze noch nicht hier?

PEDRILLO: Eben kommt sie da den Gang herauf. Reden Sie alles mit ihr ab: Aber fassen Sie sich kurz, denn der Verräter schläft nicht immer.

(Während der Unterredung des Belmonte mit Konstanzen unterhält sich Pedrillo mit Blonden, der er durch Pantomime den ganzen Auftritt mit dem Osmin vormacht und jenen nachahmt; zuletzt unterrichtet er sie ebenfalls, dass er um Mitternacht mit einer Leiter unter ihr Fenster kommen wolle, um sie zu entführen.)

KONSTANZE, BELMONTE (EINANDER IM ARME).

KONSTANZE: O mein Belmonte!

BELMONTE: O Konstanze!

KONSTANZE: Ist's möglich? – Nach so viel Tagen der Angst, nach so viel ausgestandnen Leiden, dich wieder in meinen Armen –

BELMONTE: Oh, dieser Augenblick versüßt allen Kummer, macht mich all meinen Schmerz vergessen –

Ninth Scene

PEDRILLO, LATER BELMONTE, CONSTANZA, BLANCHE.

PEDRILLO: *(imitating Osmin)* Goodnight—little brother—goodnight! Ha-ha-ha, old braggart! So that's how one gets to you! Poison and daggers!—You have a load on, but I fear it's too soon. Three hours still until midnight and maybe he'll sleep it off. Come, come, dear master. Our Argus is blind. I have tucked him in.

BELMONTE: Oh, if only things go well! Tell me, is Constanza here yet?

PEDRILLO: She is just now coming up the walk. Work things out with her, but make it brief because that slug won't sleep forever.

(While Belmonte speaks with Constanza, Pedrillo talks quietly with Blanche, showing her through mime the whole scene with Osmin, imitating him; finally he tells her that at midnight he will be coming to her window with a ladder in order to abduct her.)

CONSTANZA AND BELMONTE (ARM IN ARM).

CONSTANZA: Oh my Belmonte!

BELMONTE: Oh Constanza!

CONSTANZA: Is it possible?—After so many days filled with anxiety, after enduring so much suffering, you are again in my arms—

BELMONTE: Oh, this moment sweetens all my grief, makes me forget all the pain—

KONSTANZE: Hier will ich an deinem Busen liegen und weinen!
– Ach, jetzt fühl ich's – die Freude hat auch ihre Tränen!

N° 15 Aria

BELMONTE:

Wenn der Freude Tränen fließen,
Lächelt Liebe dem Geliebten hold!
Von den Wangen sie zu küssen,
Ist der Liebe schönster, größter Sold.
Ach Konstanze! dich zu sehen,
Dich voll Wonne, voll Entzücken
An mein treues Herz zu drücken,
Lohnt fürwahr nicht Krösus' Pracht!
Dass wir uns niemals wiederfinden!
So dürfen wir nicht erst empfinden,
Welchen Schmerz die Trennung macht.

Dialog

BELMONTE: Ich hab hier ein Schiff in Bereitschaft; um Mitternacht, wenn alles schläft, komm ich an dein Fenster, und dann sei die Liebe unser Schutzengel!

KONSTANZE: Mit tausend Freuden! Was wollt ich nicht mit dir wagen? Ich erwarte dich –

PEDRILLO: Also, liebes Blondchen, pass ja hübsch auf, hörst du's?

BLONDE: Sorge für mich nicht. Das wär das erste Abenteuer, das ein Mädchen verschlafen hätte.

CONSTANZA: I want to lie here on your bosom and weep! Oh, now I feel—that joys also have their tears!

Aria

BELMONTE:
When tears of joy flow freely,
Love sweetly laughs at the sight.
To kiss them from her face may be
Love's greatest gift and right.
Oh, Constanza, just to see you,
So happy through and through,
To cherish a heart so true—
The wealth of Croesus counts less!
If we had not found each other,
We would have had to discover
Separation's bitterness.

Spoken Dialogue

BELMONTE: I have a ship in readiness here. At midnight, when everyone is asleep, I will be at your window, and may love be our guardian angel!

CONSTANZA: A thousand joys! What wouldn't I dare with you? I will be waiting—

PEDRILLO: Also, dear Blanche, keep a sharp eye out, do you hear?

BLANCHE: Don't worry about me. That would be the first adventure a maiden ever slept through.

PEDRILLO: Du wirst's schon merken, wenn du so was Gesungenes hörst, wie's so meine Art des Abends immer ist. Dann pass auf und dann mit einem Sprung ins Schiff! – Nur hübsch Mut gefasst und nicht verzagt: Wer alles zu verlieren hat, muss alles wagen!

KONSTANZE: Wenn es aber nur glücklich abläuft!

BELMONTE: Wir wollen's hoffen; die Liebe wird unsre Geleiterin sein.

N° 16 Quartetto

KONSTANZE: Ach Belmonte! ach mein Leben

BELMONTE: Ach Konstanze! ach mein Leben!

KONSTANZE:
Ist es möglich? Welch Entzücken!
Dich an meine Brust zu drücken
Nach so vieler Tage Leid.

BELMONTE:
Welche Wonne, dich zu finden!
Nun muss aller Kummer schwinden!
O wie ist mein Herz erfreut!

KONSTANZE: Sieh die Freudenträne fließen.

BELMONTE: Holde! lass hinweg sie küssen,

KONSTANZE: Dass es doch die letzte sei!

BELMONTE: Ja, noch heute wirst du frei.

PEDRILLO: You will know everything's ready when you hear someone singing—which is always my way in the evening. Be on guard, then jump into the ship!—Just keep your wits about you and your courage high. He who has everything to lose must risk all.

CONSTANZA: If only it all goes smoothly!

BELMONTE: We all hope for the best. Love will guard us on our way.

Quartet

CONSTANZA: Ah, Belmonte my love!

BELMONTE: Ah, Constanza my love!

CONSTANZA:
Is it possible? Joy unexpressed!
Let me press you to my breast
After so many days of grief.

BELMONTE:
Soon I will set you free.
All your sorrows will flee.
This is joy beyond belief.

CONSTANZA: See these tears of joy on my face.

BELMONTE: I shall kiss each one while we embrace.

CONSTANZA: May these be the last I shed.

BELMONTE: Yes, only freedom lies ahead.

PEDRILLO:

Also Blondchen hast's verstanden?
Alles ist zur Flucht vorhanden,
Um Schlag zwölfe sind wir da.

BLONDE:

Unbesorgt! es wird nichts fehlen,
Die Minuten werd ich zählen,
Wär der Augenblick schon da!

KONSTANZE, BLONDE, BELMONTE, PEDRILLO:

Endlich scheint die Hoffnungssonne
Hell durchs trübe Firmament!
Voll Entzücken, Freud und Wonne
Sehn wir unsrer Leiden End!

BELMONTE:

Doch ach! bei aller Lust
Empfindet meine Brust
Noch manch geheime Sorgen!

KONSTANZE:

Was ist es, Liebster, sprich,
Geschwind, erkläre dich,
O halt mir nichts verborgen!

BELMONTE: Man sagt: – man sagt: – du seist –
(sieht Konstanze stillschweigend furchtsam an)

KONSTANZE: Nun weiter?
(sieht den Belmonte stillschweigend furchtsam an)

PEDRILLO: *(zeigt, dass er wage gehenkt zu werden)*
Doch Blondchen, ach: die Leiter!
Bist du wohl so viel wert?

PEDRILLO:

Blanche, have you got it all straight?
The plans are set for our escape.
At the stroke of twelve we'll be there.

BLANCHE:

Never fear. No need to tell me again.
I'm counting the minutes until then.
If only midnight were already here!

CONSTANZA, BLANCHE, BELMONTE, AND PEDRILLO:

At last the hopeful rays of sun
Shine through the dark and clouded sky.
Delight unbounded and joy finespun
Put flight to the fears we now defy.

BELMONTE:

Still, with all this pleasure
Stored in my breast like treasure,
I feel too a secret anxiety.

CONSTANZA:

What is it, beloved, speak!
If there's a reason you feel weak,
Keep nothing hidden from me.

BELMONTE: They say—you are—
(He looks at Constanza anxiously and in silence.)

CONSTANZA: Well?
(She looks at Belmonte anxiously and in silence.)

PEDRILLO: *(showing his fear of being hanged)*
But Blanche, ah! The ladder!
Are you really worth all this?

BLONDE:
Hanns Narr! schnappt's bei dir über?
Ei! hättest du mir lieber
Die Frage umgekehrt.

PEDRILLO: Doch Herr Osmin – –

BLONDE: Lass hören –

KONSTANZE: Willst du dich nicht erklären? –

BELMONTE:
Ich will. Doch zürne nicht,
Wenn ich nach dem Gerücht,
So ich gehört, es wage,
Dich zitternd, bebend frage,
Ob du den Bassa liebst?

KONSTANZE: *(Sie weint.)* Oh! wie du mich betrübst!

PEDRILLO:
Hat nicht Osmin etwann,
Wie man fast glauben kann,
Sein Recht als Herr probieret
Und bei dir exerzieret?
Dann wär's ein schlechter Kauf!

BLONDE: *(gibt dem Pedrillo eine Ohrfeige)*
Da nimm die Antwort drauf.

PEDRILLO: *(hält sich die Wange)*
Nun bin ich aufgeklärt!

BLANCHE:
You think I've been untrue, you fool?
Why, maybe you should give
That question the opposite twist.

PEDRILLO: But there's Osmin, old Osmin—

BLANCHE: Let me hear you say it—

CONSTANZA: You should explain yourself—

BELMONTE:
I will. But don't be mad
When I dare to ask—
Trembling as I do—
If the rumor is true
That the Pasha loves you?

CONSTANZA: *(in tears)* Oh! How you grieve me!

PEDRILLO:
Has Osmin, as the story goes—
Leave out what I suppose—
Done what masters do
And had his way with you?
That would mean we're through.

BLANCHE: *(slapping Pedrillo's face)*
Here is my reply to you!

PEDRILLO: *(holding his cheek)*
Now I know the answer indeed!

BELMONTE: *(kniend)*
Konstanze! ach vergib!

BLONDE: *(geht zornig von Pedrillo)*
Du bist mich gar nicht wert.

KONSTANZE: *(seufzend sich von Belmonte wegwendend)*
Ob ich dir treu verblieb!

BLONDE: *(zu Konstanze)*
Der Schlingel fragt sich an,
Ob ich ihm treu geblieben?

KONSTANZE: *(zu Blonde)*
Dem Belmont sagte man,
Ich soll den Bassa lieben!

PEDRILLO: *(hält sich die Wange)*
Dass Blonde ehrlich sei,
Schwör ich bei allen Teufeln.

BELMONTE: *(zu Pedrillo)*
Konstanze ist mir treu,
Daran ist nicht zu zweifeln.

KONSTANZE, BLONDE:
Wenn unsrer Ehre wegen
Die Männer Argwohn hegen,
Verdächtig auf uns sehn,
Das ist nicht auszustehn.

BELMONTE, PEDRILLO:
Sobald sich Weiber kränken,
Dass wir sie untreu denken,
Dann sind sie wahrhaft treu,
Von allem Vorwurf frei.

BELMONTE: *(kneeling)*
Constanza, forgive me!

BLANCHE: *(flouncing angrily away from Pedrillo)*
You don't deserve me at all!

CONSTANZA: *(sighing, turning away from Belmonte)*
You have no faith in me?

BLANCHE: *(to Constanza)*
This rascal dares to ask
If I have ever failed him.

CONSTANZA: *(to Blanche)*
How can anyone dare ask
If I love Pasha Selim?

PEDRILLO: *(still rubbing his cheek)*
That Blanche is honorable
I swear by the devil's tail.

BELMONTE: *(to Pedrillo)*
Constanza has been true to me.
Let honesty prevail.

CONSTANZA AND BLANCHE:
If men trample upon, or
Will not respect our honor,
Or suspiciously narrow their eyes,
They are not to be recognized.

BELMONTE AND PEDRILLO:
As soon as women are upset
By talk they have things to regret,
Then isn't that the very clue
That they are blameless and true?

PEDRILLO:

Liebstes Blondchen! ach! verzeihe,
Sieh, ich bau auf deine Treue,
Mehr itzt als auf meinen Kopf!

BLONDE:

Nein, das kann ich dir nicht schenken,
Mich mit so was zu verdenken,
Mit dem alten dummen Tropf!

BELMONTE:

Ach Konstanze! ach mein Leben,
Könntest du mir doch vergeben,
Dass ich diese Frage tat?

KONSTANZE:

Belmont! wie du konntest glauben,
Dass man dir das Herz könnt rauben?
Das nur dir geschlagen hat!

BELMONTE: Ach verzeihe!

PEDRILLO: Ach verzeihe!

BELMONTE: Ich bereue!

PEDRILLO: Ich bereue!

KONSTANZE, BLONDE:

Ich verzeihe
Deiner Reue!

PEDRILLO:
Dearest Blanche, forgive me!
Your loyalty is far more trusty
Than this old noodle of mine!

BLANCHE:
No, forgive you I will not,
Not since you put in earshot
That I was had by that old swine.

BELMONTE:
Oh, Constanza! Oh, my life!
How can we end this strife
My stupid question started?

CONSTANZA:
Belmonte! Could you believe
That I would ever conceive
A deed after which we parted?

BELMONTE: Ah, forgive me!

PEDRILLO: Ah, forgive me!

BELMONTE: I am repentant!

PEDRILLO: I am repentant!

CONSTANZA AND BLANCHE:
I accept your remorse.

KONSTANZE, BLONDE, BELMONTE, PEDRILLO:
Wohl, es sei nun abgetan!
Es lebe die Liebe!
Nur sie sei uns teuer,
Nichts fache das Feuer
Der Eifersucht an.

(alle ab)

Ende des zweiten Aufzugs.

CONSTANZA, BLANCHE, BELMONTE, AND PEDRILLO:
Well, now that is behind us!
Long live love!
Let love be all we desire.
Let nothing stoke the fire
Of a jealousy that might blind us.

(They all leave.)

End of Act II

Dritter Aufzug

Platz vor dem Palaste des Bassa Selim; auf einer Seite der Palast des Bassa, gegenüber die Wohnung des Osmin, hinten Aussicht aufs Meer. Es ist Mitternacht.

Erster Auftritt
PEDRILLO, KLAAS (DER EINE LEITER BRINGT).

Dialog

PEDRILLO: Hier, lieber Klaas, hier leg sie indes nur nieder und hole die zwote vom Schiff. Aber nur hübsch leise, dass nicht viel Lärm gemacht wird: Es geht hier auf Tod und Leben.

KLAAS: Lass mich nur machen, ich versteh das Ding auch ein bisschen, wenn wir sie nur erst am Bord haben.

PEDRILLO: Ach, lieber Klaas! wenn wir mit unsrer Beute glücklich nach Spanien kommen: Ich glaube, Don Belmonte lässt dich in Gold einfassen.

KLAAS: Das möchte wohl ein bisschen zu warm aufs Fell gehn, doch das wird sich schon geben. Ich hole die Leiter. *(geht ab)*

PEDRILLO:
Ach! wenn ich sagen sollte, dass mirs Herz nicht klopfte, so sagt ich eine schreckliche Lüge. Die verzweifelten Türken verstehn

---

Act III

The square in front of Pasha Selim's palace; to one side, the Pasha's palace; opposite it, Osmin's quarters; in the rear, a view of the sea. It is midnight.

First Scene

PEDRILLO AND KLAAS (WHO IS BRINGING A LADDER).

Spoken Dialogue

PEDRILLO: Here, my good Klaas, put it down here and get the other one from the ship. Be quiet about it. I don't want any noise. It's a matter of life and death.

KLAAS: Leave it to me. I understand these things.—If only we had them safely on board!

PEDRILLO: Ah, dear Klaas, if we get safely to Spain, I am sure Don Belmonte will cast you in gold.

KLAAS: That might be too warm a coat to wear. But I could get used to it. I'll go get the ladder.
(He goes off.)

PEDRILLO: If I said my heart wasn't pounding, I'd be an awful liar. These Turks can't take a joke, and while the Pasha is an odd

nicht den mindesten Spaß; und ob der Bassa gleich ein Renegat ist, so ist er, wenn's aufs Kopfab ankommt, doch ein völli-
ger Türke. *(Klaas bringt die zwote Leiter.)* So, guter Klaas, und nun
lichte die Anker und spann alle Segel auf: Denn eh eine halbe
Stund vergeht, hast du deine völlige Ladung.

KLAAS: Bring sie nur hurtig und dann lass mich sorgen.
(geht ab)

Zweiter Auftritt
BELMONTE, PEDRILLO.

PEDRILLO: Ach! – ich muss Atem holen. – Es zieht mirs Herz
so eng zusammen, als wenn ichs größte Schelmstück vorhätte
– Ach, wo mein Herr auch bleibt! –

BELMONTE: *(ruft leise)* Pedrillo! Pedrillo!

PEDRILLO: Wie gerufen!

BELMONTE: Ist alles fertig gemacht?

PEDRILLO: Alles! Jetzt will ich ein wenig um den Palast herum
spionieren, wie's aussieht. Singen Sie indessen eins. Ich hab
das so alle Abende getan. Und wenn Sie da auch jemand gewahr
wird oder begegnet, denn alle Stunden macht hier eine Janit-
scharenwache die Runde, so hat's nichts zu bedeuten, sie sind
das von mir schon gewohnt. Es ist fast besser, als wenn man Sie
so stille hier fände.

BELMONTE: Lass mich nur machen und komm bald wieder.

(Pedrillo geht ab.)

duck, he is at heart, when it comes to beheadings, most definitely a Turk. *(Klaas returns with the second ladder.)* So, good Klaas, raise the anchor and hoist the sails. In half an hour you'll have a full cargo.

KLAAS: Get them on board and I'll take over. *(He leaves.)*

Second Scene
BELMONTE AND PEDRILLO.

PEDRILLO: Ah!—I have to catch my breath.—My heart is squeezed as tightly as if I were committing a terrible crime.—And where is my master?—

BELMONTE: *(calling softly)* Pedrillo! Pedrillo!

PEDRILLO: Just in time!

BELMONTE: Is everything ready?

PEDRILLO: Everything! Now I'll sneak around the palace to get the lay of the land. In the meantime, sing a little something. I used to do that every evening. So if you encounter anyone or someone spots you—the Janissaries make their rounds every hour—they won't think anything of it. They are used to me. It would be better, in fact, than their coming on you just standing here.

BELMONTE: I'll take care of it. Just hurry back.

(Pedrillo leaves.)

Dritter Auftritt

BELMONTE ALLEIN.

BELMONTE: O Konstanze, Konstanze! wie schlägt mir das Herz! Je näher der Augenblick kommt, desto ängstlicher zagt meine Seele. Ich fürchte und wünsche, bebe und hoffe. O Liebe, sei du meine Leiterin!

N° 17 Aria

BELMONTE:
Ich baue ganz auf deine Stärke,
Vertrau, o Liebe! deiner Macht!
Denn ach! was wurden nicht für Werke
Schon oft durch dich – zustand gebracht
Was aller Welt ohnmöglich scheint,
Wird durch die Liebe doch vereint.

Vierter Auftritt

BELMONTE UND PEDRILLO.

Dialog

PEDRILLO: Alles liegt auf dem Ohr, es ist alles so ruhig, so stille als den Tag nach der Sündflut.

BELMONTE: Nun, so lass uns sie befreien. Wo ist die Leiter?

PEDRILLO: Nicht so hitzig. Ich muss erst das Signal geben.

BELMONTE: Was hindert dich denn, es nicht zu tun? Mach fort.

PEDRILLO: *(sieht nach der Uhr)* Eben recht, Schlag zwölfe. Gehen Sie dort an die Ecke und geben Sie wohl Acht, dass wir nicht überrascht werden.

Third Scene

BELMONTE ALONE.

BELMONTE: *(speaking)* Oh Constanza, Constanza! How my heart is pounding! The nearer the moment comes, the more anxious is my soul. I fear and yearn, tremble and hope. Oh love, be my guide!

Aria

BELMONTE:
I believe in your influence,
O love, and trust your power!
The victories you have dispensed
Have brought us to this hour.
Whatever the world would deny
Love brings about if you try.

Fourth Scene

BELMONTE AND PEDRILLO.

Spoken Dialogue

PEDRILLO: Everyone is asleep. Everything is calm. It's as quiet as the day after the Great Flood.

BELMONTE: Well, let's free them then. Where is the ladder?

PEDRILLO: Not so fast. First I have to give the signal.

BELMONTE: What's stopping you? Hurry up!

PEDRILLO: *(looking at his watch)* Just right. The stroke of midnight. Go over to the corner there and make sure we aren't surprised.

BELMONTE: Zaudre nur nicht!

(geht ab)

PEDRILLO: *(indem er seine Mandoline hervorholt)* Es ist doch um die Herzhaftigkeit eine erzläppische Sache. Wer keine hat, schafft sich mit aller Mühe keine an! Was mein Herz schlägt! Mein Papa muss ein Erzpoltron gewesen sein. *(fängt an zu spielen)* Nun, so sei es denn gewagt! *(singt und akkompagniert sich)*

N° 18 Romance

PEDRILLO:
In Mohrenland gefangen war
Ein Mädel hübsch und fein;
Sah rot und weiß, war schwarz von Haar,
Seufzt Tag und Nacht und weinte gar,
Wollt gern erlöset sein.

Da kam aus fernen Land daher
Ein junger Rittersmann,
Den jammerte das Mädchen sehr,
"Jach", rief er, "wag ich Kopf und Ehr,
Wenn ich sie retten kann".

PEDRILLO: Noch geht alles gut, es rührt sich noch nichts.

BELMONTE: *(kommt hervor)* Mach ein Ende, Pedrillo.

PEDRILLO: An mir liegt es nicht, dass sie sich noch nicht zeigen. Entweder schlafen sie fester als jemals oder der Bassa ist bei der Hand. Wir wollen's weiter versuchen. Bleiben Sie nur auf Ihren Posten.

(Belmonte geht wieder fort.)

BELMONTE: Just don't delay any longer!
(He goes off.)

PEDRILLO: *(taking up his mandolin)* Courage is an odd thing. When you don't have it, you can't find it. How my heart is racing! My father must have been a real coward. *(begins to play)* Might as well risk it! *(sings and accompanies himself)*

Romance

PEDRILLO:
In the far-off kingdom of the Moors,
A maiden, so fair and fine, was jailed.
Her red lips so fair,
And so black her hair,
She wept all day and tried the doors
And longed to be freed from her travails.

Then to that distant, desert land
A young knight rode one day.
He spied her cell.
His pity swelled.
"I shall dare whatever they demand
To rescue this maiden straightway."

PEDRILLO: *(speaking)* Everything seems fine, nothing stirring yet.

BELMONTE: *(coming back, speaking)* Get it over with, Pedrillo.

PEDRILLO: *(speaking)* It's not my fault they haven't appeared yet. Either they are sleeping more soundly than ever, or the Pasha is close by. We'll try again. Back to your post.

(Belmonte goes off again.)

PEDRILLO:

Ich komm zu dir in finstrer Nacht,
Lass, Liebchen, husch mich ein!
Ich fürchte weder Schloss noch Wacht,
Holla! horch auf um Mitternacht
Sollst du erlöset sein.

Gesagt, getan; Glock zwölfe stand
Der tapfre Ritter da;
Sanft reicht sie ihm die weiche Hand,
Früh man die leere Zelle fand;
Fort war sie, hopsasa!

Dialog
(Pedrillo hustet einige Mal, Konstanze öffnet das Fenster.)

PEDRILLO: Sie macht auf, Herr! sie macht auf.

BELMONTE: Ich komme, ich komme!

KONSTANZE: *(oben am Fenster)* Belmonte!

BELMONTE: Konstanze! hier bin ich! Hurtig die Leiter!

(Pedrillo stellt die Leiter an Konstanzens Fenster, Belmonte steigt hinein, Pedrillo hält die Leiter.)

PEDRILLO: Was das für ein abscheuliches Spektakel macht. *(hält die Hand aufs Herz)* Es wird immer ärger, weil es nun Ernst wird. Wenn sie mich hier erwischten, wie schön würden sie mit mir abtrollen zum Kopfabschlagen, zum Spießen oder zum Hängen. Je nu! der Anfang ist einmal gemacht, itzt ist's nicht mehr aufzuhalten. Es geht nun schon einmal aufs Leben oder auf den Tod los.

PEDRILLO:

"I come to you in the dark of night.
Quickly, fair maiden, let me in!
I fear no lock.
A guard I'd mock!
Listen to me, sweet girl, by midnight
You will no longer be shut in."

Just as he vowed, at midnight's stroke,
The valiant knight was at her door.
He'd come as planned.
She gave her soft hand.
They searched the jail when dawn next broke
And it was empty. Brave conquistador!

Spoken Dialogue
(Pedrillo coughs several times, Constanza opens her window.)

PEDRILLO: She's opening the window, master! She's opening it!

BELMONTE: I'm coming, I'm coming!

CONSTANZA: *(at her window)* Belmonte!

BELMONTE: Constanza! I am here! Hurry with that ladder!

(Pedrillo leans the ladder against Constanza's window. Belmonte climbs up, while Pedrillo steadies the ladder.)

PEDRILLO: What a horrible racket that makes. *(He puts his hand over his heart.)* It's beating faster because things are getting worse. If they catch me here, they'd march me off to hang and quarter me, behead me. Well! Once you start, you can't stop short. Now it's a matter of life or death.

(Belmonte kommt mit Konstanzen unten zur Türe heraus.)

BELMONTE: Nun, holder Engel! nun hab ich dich wieder, ganz wieder. Nichts soll uns mehr trennen.

KONSTANZE: Wie ängstlich schlägt mein Herz! Kaum bin ich imstande, mich aufrecht zu halten: Wenn wir nur glücklich entkommen.

PEDRILLO: Nur fort! nicht geplaudert! Sonst könnt es freilich schiefgehen, wenn wir da lange Rat halten und seufzen. *(stößt Belmonten und Konstanzen fort)* Nur frisch nach dem Strande zu! Ich komme gleich nach.

(Belmonte und Konstanze ab)

PEDRILLO: Nun, Cupido, du mächtiger Herzensdieb, halte mir die Leiter und hülle mich samt meiner Gerätschaft in einen dicken Nebel ein! *(Er hat unter der Zeit die Leiter an Blondens Fenster gelegt und ist hinaufgestiegen.)* Blondchen, Blondchen! mach auf ums Himmels Willen, zaudre nicht! Es ist um Hals und Kragen zu tun.

(Es wird das Fenster geöffnet, er steigt hinein.)

Fünfter Auftritt

OSMIN UND EIN SCHWARZER STUMMER ÖFFNEN DIE TÜRE VON OSMINS HAUSE, WO PEDRILLO HINEINGESTIEGEN IST. OSMIN NOCH HALB SCHLAFTRUNKEN HAT EINE LATERNE. DER STUMME GIBT OSMIN DURCH ZEICHEN ZU VERSTEHEN, DASS ES NICHT RICHTIG SEI, DASS ER LEUTE GEHÖRT HABE USW.

OSMIN: Lärmen hörtest du? Was kann's denn geben? Vielleicht Schwärmer? Geh, spioniere, bringe mir Antwort.

(Belmonte comes out of the door below with Constanza.)

BELMONTE: Now, gracious angel, I have you back again, all mine. Nothing will ever part us again.

CONSTANZA: My heart has been beating so anxiously! I fear I shall faint at any moment. We must get away from here.

PEDRILLO: Quickly now! No chatter! Everything will go wrong if we stop to reminisce and sigh. *(He pushes Belmonte and Constanza along.)* Quickly now to the beach. I'll be right behind you.

(Belmonte and Constanza leave.)

PEDRILLO: Now, Cupid, you wily thief of hearts, hold my ladder steady and wrap me in a mist. *(He has been leaning the ladder against Blanche's window, and climbing up.)* Blanche, Blanche! Open up, for heaven's sake, hurry! Our necks are on the line.

(The window is opened and he climbs inside.)

Fifth Scene

OSMIN AND A BLACK MUTE OPEN THE DOOR OF OSMIN'S QUARTERS WHERE PEDRILLO HAS ENTERED. OSMIN, STILL HALF ASLEEP, HAS A LANTERN. THE MUTE LETS OSMIN KNOW, BY MIMING, THAT SOMETHING IS AMISS, THAT HE HAS HEARD PEOPLE ABOUT, ETC.

OSMIN: You heard noise? What can that be? A party crowd perhaps? Go, my spy, and bring me news.

(Der Stumme lauscht ein wenig herum. Endlich wird er die Leiter an Osmins Fenster gewahr, erschrickt und zeigt sie Osmin, der wie im Taumel mit der Laterne in der Hand an seine Haustüre gelehnt steht und nickt.)

OSMIN: Gift und Dolch! Was ist das? Wer kann ins Haus steigen? Das sind Diebe oder Mörder. *(Er tummelt sich herum; weil er aber noch halb schlaftrunken ist, stößt er sich hier und da etc.)* Hurtig, hole die Wache! Ich will unterdessen lauren.

(Der Stumme ab; Osmin setzt sich auf die Leiter mit der Laterne in der Hand und nickt ein. Pedrillo kömmt rückwärts wieder zum Fenster herausgestiegen und will die Leiter wieder herunter. Blonde oben am Fenster wird Osmin gewahr und ruft Pedrillo zu.)

BLONDE: O Himmel, Pedrillo! wir sind verloren.

(Pedrillo sieht sich um; und so wie er Osmin gewahr wird, stutzt er, besieht ihn und steigt wieder zum Fenster hinein.)

PEDRILLO: Ah! welcher Teufel hat sich wider uns verschworen.

OSMIN: *(auf der Leiter dem Pedrillo nach, ruft)* Blondchen! Blondchen!

PEDRILLO: *(im Hineinsteigen zu Blondchen)* Zurück, nur zurück!

OSMIN: *(steigt wieder zurück)* Wart, Spitzbube, du sollst mir nicht entkommen. Hilfe! Hilfe! Wache, hurtig, hier gibt's Räuber! Herbei, herbei!

(Pedrillo kommt mit Blonden unten zur Haustüre heraus, sieht schüchtern nach der Leiter und schleicht sich dann mit Blonden darunter weg.)

PEDRILLO, BLONDE: *(im Abgehen)* O Himmel steh uns bei! sonst sind wir verloren.

(The mute snoops around and finally discovers the ladder at Osmin's window. He is startled and shows his amazement to Osmin who, still groggy, is leaning on his door with the lantern in his hand and nodding.)

OSMIN: Poison and daggers! What is that? Who can have climbed into the house? It's either thieves or murderers. *(He rushes around but, because he is still half drunk, he keeps bumping into things.)* Hurry, summon the guard! I'll keep watch here.

(The mute exits. Osmin sits on the ladder with his lantern in hand and nods off. Pedrillo comes out of the window again backwards and starts down the ladder. Blanche, at the window, spots Osmin and calls to Pedrillo.)

BLANCHE: Heavens, Pedrillo! We are done for.

(Pedrillo looks around and, as soon as he sees Osmin, stops and starts climbing back up towards the window.)

PEDRILLO: Oh! The devil is in league against us.

OSMIN: *(calling out as he climbs the ladder after Pedrillo)* Blanche! Blanche!

PEDRILLO: *(climbing back inside, to Blanche)* Back, get back!

OSMIN: *(climbing back down)* Wait, you rascal, You won't get away with this! Help! Help! Guard, hurry, there are thieves! This way! This way!

(Pedrillo comes with Blanche out of the door below, looks furtively at the ladder, and starts to sneak away with Blanche.)

PEDRILLO AND BLANCHE: *(as they go)* May heaven watch over us . . . or we're doomed.

OSMIN: Zu Hilfe! zu Hilfe! geschwind! *(Er will nach.)*

WACHE: *(mit Fackeln, halten Osmin auf)* Halt, halt! Wohin?

OSMIN: Dorthin, dorthin.

WACHE: Wer bist du?

OSMIN: Nur nicht lange gefragt, sonst entkommen die Spitzbuben. Seht ihr denn nicht? Hier ist noch die Leiter.

WACHE: Das sehn wir: Kannst nicht du sie angelegt haben?

OSMIN: Gift und Dolch! Kennt ihr mich denn nicht? Ich bin Oberaufseher der Gärten beim Bassa. Wenn ihr noch lange fragt, so hilft euer Kommen nichts. *(Ein Teil der Wache bringt Pedrillo und Blonden zurück.)* Ah endlich! Gift und Dolch! Seh ich recht! Ihr beide? Warte, spitzbübischer Pedrillo, dein Kopf soll am längsten fest gestanden sein.

PEDRILLO: Brüderchen, Brüderchen! wirst doch Spaß verstehen? Ich wollt dir dein Weibchen nur ein wenig spazieren führen, weil du heute dazu nicht aufgelegt bist. Du weißt schon *(heimlich zu Osmin)* wegen des Zypernweins.

OSMIN: Schurke, glaubst du, mich zu betäuben? Hier verstehe ich keinen Spaß. Dein Kopf muss herunter, so wahr ich ein Muselmann bin.

PEDRILLO: Und hast du einen Nutzen dabei? Wenn ich meinen Kopf verliere, sitzt deiner um so viel fester?

(Ein anderer Teil der Wache auch mit Fackeln bringt Belmonte und Konstanze.)

OSMIN: Help! Help! Hurry! *(He starts to follow them.)*

GUARD: *(with a torch, stopping Osmin)* Stop! Wait! Which way?

OSMIN: That way, that way.

GUARD: Who are you?

OSMIN: Don't ask questions or that rascal will get away. Can't you see? Here is the ladder.

GUARD: We see that. But couldn't you have put it there yourself?

OSMIN: Poison and daggers! Don't you recognize me? I am the Overseer of the Pasha's Gardens. If you delay any longer, you may as well not have come at all. *(Other guards bring Pedrillo and Blanche back.)* At last. Poison and daggers! Am I seeing right? Both of you? Just you wait, you rascal Pedrillo, your head will roll.

PEDRILLO: My brother, little brother! Don't you get the joke? I just thought I'd take your little lady out for a walk today because you're under the weather. You know, *(whispering to Osmin)* because of the Cyprian wine.

OSMIN: Scoundrel! Do you think you can trick me? Oh, I understand your little "joke." And your head will roll for it, as I am a true Muslim!

PEDRILLO: What use would that be to you? If I were to lose my head, would yours rest any easier?

(Other guards, carrying torches, lead in Belmonte and Constanza.)

BELMONTE: *(widersetzt sich noch)* Schändliche, lasst mich los!

WACHE: Sachte, junger Herr! sachte! uns entkömmt man nicht so geschwinde.

OSMIN: Sieh da! die Gesellschaft wird immer stärker. Hat der Herr Baumeister auch wollen spazieren gehen? O ihr Spitzbuben! Hatte ich heute nicht recht, *(zu Belmonte)* dass ich dich nicht ins Haus lassen wollte? Nun wird der Bassa sehen, was für sauberes Gelichter er um sich hat.

BELMONTE: Das beiseite! Lass hören, ob mit euch ein vernünftig Wort zu sprechen ist? Hier ist ein Beutel mit Zechinen, er ist euer, und noch zweimal so viel; lasst mich los.

KONSTANZE: Lasst euch bewegen!

OSMIN: Ich glaube, ihr seid besessen? Euer Geld brauchen wir nicht, das bekommen wir ohnehin: Eure Köpfe wollen wir. *(zur Wache)* Schleppt sie fort zum Bassa!

KONSTANZE, BELMONTE: Habt doch Erbarmen! Lasst euch bewegen!

OSMIN: Um nichts in der Welt! Ich habe mir längst so einen Augenblick gewünschet. Fort, fort!

(Die Wache führt Belmont und Konstanzen fort samt Pedrillo und Blonden.)

BELMONTE: *(still resisting)* Villains, let me go!

GUARD: Easy there, young man, easy. No one escapes from us.

OSMIN: Well, well! The party is growing more crowded. Did the architect want to go for a walk as well? Oh you scoundrels! Wasn't I right today *(to Belmonte)* when I didn't want to let you into the house? Now the Pasha will see what kind of people he has surrounded himself with.

BELMONTE: Let that go! Let's see if a reasonable word can get through to you. Here is a pouch of gold coins. It is yours. And there will be twice as much if you let us go.

CONSTANZA: Let yourself be moved.

OSMIN: I am certain you must be crazy. We don't want your gold. We'll grab that in any case. What we want are your heads! *(to the guards)* Take them to the Pasha!

CONSTANZA AND BELMONTE: Have mercy! We beg you, help us!

OSMIN: Not for anything in the world! I have long wished for this very moment. Off with them! Quickly!

(The guards take Belmonte and Constanza away, along with Pedrillo and Blanche. Osmin stays on alone.)

N° 19 Aria

OSMIN ALLEIN.

OSMIN:

Oh, wie will ich triumphieren!
Wenn sie euch zum Richtplatz führen
Und die Hälse schnürren zu;
Hüpfen will ich, lachen, springen
Und ein Freudenliedchen singen,
Denn nun hab ich vor euch Ruh.
Schleicht nur säuberlich und leise
Ihr verdammten Harems-Mäuse,
Unser Ohr entdeckt euch schon.
Und eh ihr uns könnt entspringen,
Seht ihr euch in unsern Schlingen
Und erhaschet euren Lohn.

(geht ab)

Sechster Auftritt

Zimmer des Bassa.

SELIM MIT GEFOLGE; HERNACH OSMIN, BELMONTE, KONSTANZE UND WACHE.

Dialog

SELIM: *(zu einem Offiziere)* Geht, unterrichtet euch, was der Lärm im Palast bedeutet. Er hat uns im Schlaf aufgeschreckt, und lasst mir Osmin kommen.

(Der Offizier will abgehen, indem kommt Osmin zwar hastig, doch noch ein wenig schläfrig.)

OSMIN: Herr! - Verzeih, dass ich es so früh wage - deine Ruhe zu stören.

Aria

OSMIN, ALONE.

OSMIN:

Oh, my gloating will run amok
When you're on the chopping block,
And the executioner tightens the ropes!
I will hop and skip and dance,
Lost in a triumphal trance,
The fulfillment of all my hopes!
If you creep around in paradise,
Behaving like harem-mice,
My ear is bound to hear you.
And before you can escape
My trap is sure to dog-ear you—
A reward from the caliphate!

(He leaves.)

Sixth Scene

The Pasha's room.

SELIM WITH HIS ATTENDANTS, THEN OSMIN,
BELMONTE, CONSTANZA, AND THE GUARDS.

Spoken Dialogue

SELIM: *(to an officer)* Go, find out what all the fuss is in the palace.
It has awakened me. And bid Osmin come see me.

(Just as the officer is leaving, Osmin hastily enters, still a little groggy.)

OSMIN: Master! I beg your pardon for disturbing you so early.

SELIM: Was gibt's, Osmin, was gibt's? Was bedeutet der Aufruhr?

OSMIN: Herr, es ist die schändlichste Verräterei in deinem Palast –

SELIM: Verräterei?

OSMIN: Die niederträchtigen Christen-Sklaven entführen uns – die Weiber. Der große Baumeister, den du gestern auf Zureden des Verräters Pedrillo aufnahmst, hat deine – schöne Konstanze entführt.

SELIM: Konstanze? entführt? Ah, setzt ihnen nach!

OSMIN: Oh, 's ist schon dafür gesorgt! Meiner Wachsamkeit – hast du es zu danken, dass ich sie wieder beim Schopfe gekriegt habe. Auch mir selbst hatte der – spitzbübische Pedrillo eine gleiche Ehre zugedacht, und er hatte mein Blondchen schon beim Kopfe, um mit ihr – in alle Welt zu reisen. – Aber, Gift und Dolch! er soll mir's entgelten! – Sieh, da bringen sie sie!

(Belmonte und Konstanze werden von der Wache hereingeführt.)

SELIM: Ah, Verräter! ist's möglich? – Ha, du heuchlerische Sirene! War das der Aufschub, den du begehrtest? Missbrauchtest du so die Nachsicht, die ich dir gab, um mich zu hintergehen?

KONSTANZE: Ich bin strafbar in deinen Augen, Herr, es ist wahr: Aber es ist mein Geliebter, mein einziger Geliebter, dem lang schon dieses Herz gehört. O nur für ihn, nur um seinetwillen fleh' ich Aufschub. – O lass mich sterben! Gern, gern will ich den Tod erdulden: Aber schone nur sein Leben. –

SELIM: Und du wagst's Unverschämte, für ihn zu bitten?

SELIM: What is it, Osmin, out with it! What is this uproar all about?

OSMIN: Master, there is treachery loose in your palace—

SELIM: Treachery?

OSMIN: Those conniving Christian slaves are abducting—our women. The great architect you hired yesterday at Pedrillo's urging has abducted your beautiful Constanza.

SELIM: Constanza? Abducted? After them!

OSMIN: Already taken care of! Thanks to my vigilance, we have them by the short hairs. That dastardly Pedrillo tried to play the same trick on me. He had gotten hold of my Blanche and was ready to take her who-knows-where.—Poison and daggers! He'll pay for this!—Look, they are being brought in now!

(Belmonte and Constanza are brought in by the guards.)

SELIM: The traitor! Is it possible? You hypocritical siren! Is that why you begged for time? To use the leniency I granted you to conspire against me?

CONSTANZA: I am guilty in your eyes, my lord, that is true. But this is my beloved, my only beloved, to whom my heart has long been pledged. Only for him, only on his account, did I beg for time. Oh, let me die! Gladly, gladly will I suffer death, if only you spare his life.

SELIM: You shameless woman, you dare to beg for him?

KONSTANZE: Noch mehr: Für ihn zu sterben!

BELMONTE: Ha, Bassa! Noch nie erniedrigte ich mich zu bitten, noch nie hat dieses Knie sich vor einem Menschen gebeugt: Aber sieh, hier lieg ich zu deinen Füßen und flehe dein Mitleid an. Ich bin von einer großen spanischen Familie, man wird alles für mich zahlen. Lass dich bewegen, bestimme ein Lösegeld für mich und Konstanze so hoch du willst. Mein Name ist Lostados.

SELIM: *(staunend)* Was hör ich! Der Kommandant von Oran, ist dir der bekannt?

BELMONTE: Das ist mein Vater.

SELIM: Dein Vater? Welcher glückliche Tag! den Sohn meines ärgsten Feindes in meiner Macht zu haben! Kann was angenehmers sein! Wisse, Elender! dein Vater, dieser Barbar, ist Schuld, dass ich mein Vaterland verlassen musste. Sein unbiegsamer Geiz entriss mir eine Geliebte, die ich höher als mein Leben schätzte. Er brachte mich um Ehrenstellen, Vermögen, um alles. Kurz, er zernichtete mein ganzes Glück. Und dieses Mannes einzigen Sohn habe ich nun in meiner Gewalt! Sage er an meiner Stelle, was würde er tun?

BELMONTE: *(ganz niedergedrückt)* Mein Schicksal würde zu beklagen sein.

SELIM: Das soll es auch sein. Wie er mit mir verfahren ist, will ich mit dir verfahren. Folge mir, Osmin, ich will dir Befehle zu ihren Martern geben. *(zu der Wache)* Bewacht sie hier.

CONSTANZA: More than that—to die for him!

BELMONTE: Pasha! Never before have I begged anything from anyone. Never before has my knee bent before any man. But I kneel at your feet and beg your mercy. I am from a noble Spanish family. They will pay any ransom. Set as high a ransom on me and Constanza as you wish. My name is Lostados.

SELIM: *(stunned)* What is that you say? The commandant of Oran, do you know him?

BELMONTE: He is my father.

SELIM: Your father? What a lucky day! To have the son of my archenemy in my power! Can anything be more delicious? Know this, you wretch—your father, that barbarian, forced me to leave my native land. His greed tore from me my beloved, who meant more to me than the world. He stripped me of my standing, my wealth, everything. In a word, he destroyed my happiness. And now this man's only son is in my hands! Tell me, if he were in my place, what would he do?

BELMONTE: *(completely shattered)* My fate would be dire.

SELIM: And so it shall be. As he did to me I shall do to you. Follow me, Osmin. I will give you instructions for their torture. *(to the guards)* Watch over them here.

Siebenter Auftritt

BELMONTE UND KONSTANZE.

N° 20 Recitativo e Duetto

Recitativo

BELMONTE:

Welch ein Geschick! o Qual der Seele!

Hat sich denn alles wider mich verschworen!

Ach! Konstanze! durch mich bist du verloren!

Welch eine Pein!

KONSTANZE:

Lass, ach Geliebter! lass dich das nicht quälen!

Was ist der Tod? – Ein Übergang zur Ruh!

Und dann, an deiner Seite

Ist er Vorgeschmack der Seligkeit!

BELMONTE:

Engels Seele,

Welch holde Güte!

Du flößest Trost in mein erschüttert Herz.

Du linderst mir den Todesschmerz.

Und ach! ich reiße dich ins Grab!

Duetto

BELMONTE:

Meinetwegen sollst du sterben!

Ach Konstanze! kann ich's wagen,

Noch die Augen aufzuschlagen?

Ich bereite dir den Tod!

Seventh Scene

BELMONTE AND CONSTANZA.

Recitative and Duet
Recitative

BELMONTE:

What a fate! Oh, my anguished soul!
Have the stars conspired against me?
Oh, Constanza! I have hurt you immensely!
How it pains me!

CONSTANZA:

No, beloved! Why torment yourself?
What is death?—The path to peace!
And then, at your side,
A foretaste of eternal bliss.

BELMONTE:

Angel's soul!
How good you are!
You comfort my agitated heart,
And bid my demons depart,
And all I give you is a grave!

Duet

BELMONTE:

Because of me, you are to die!
Oh, Constanza! Do I still dare
To look upon a face so fair?
I am leading you to death!

KONSTANZE:

Belmont! du stirbst meinetwegen!
Ich nur zog dich ins Verderben,
Und ich soll nicht mit dir sterben?
Wonne ist mir dies Gebot!

KONSTANZE, BELMONTE:

Edle Seele! dir zu leben
War mein Wunsch und all mein Streben;
Ohne dich ist mir's nur Pein,
Länger auf der Welt zu sein.

BELMONTE: Ich will alles gerne leiden,

KONSTANZE: Ruhig sterb ich und mit Freuden,

KONSTANZE, BELMONTE: Weil ich dir zur Seite bin.

BELMONTE: Um dich Geliebte!

KONSTANZE: Um dich Geliebter!

KONSTANZE, BELMONTE:

Geb ich gern mein Leben hin!
O welche Seligkeit!
Mit dem/der Geliebten sterben,
Ist seliges Entzücken!
Mit wonnevollen Blicken
Verlässt man da die Welt.

CONSTANZA:
Belmonte! You are dying for me.
It is I who lured you to your death,
And shall I not draw my last breath
With yours? Let it be so, I pray!

CONSTANZA AND BELMONTE:
Noble soul, to live for you
Was the only wish I ever knew.
To live without you now
Is a thought I disavow.

BELMONTE: I will gladly suffer whatever comes . . .

CONSTANZA: I will die with joy and peace . . .

CONSTANZA AND BELMONTE: . . . Since I am at your side.

BELMONTE: With you, beloved!

CONSTANZA: With you, beloved!

CONSTANZA AND BELMONTE:
I give my life with no regret!
Oh, the blessed sacrifice!
To die beside your love
Is a blessed happiness!
To have all one could possess
And leave this world for one above!

Achter Auftritt

PEDRILLO UND BLONDE WERDEN VON EINEM ANDERN TEIL
DER WACHE HEREINGEFÜHRT, UND DIE VORIGEN.

Dialog

PEDRILLO: Ach Herr! wir sind hin! An Rettung ist nicht mehr
zu denken. Man macht schon alle Zubereitungen, um uns aus
der Welt zu schaffen. Es ist erschrecklich, was sie mit uns anfangen wollen! Ich, wie ich im Vorbeigehen gehört habe, soll in Öl
gesotten und dann gespießt werden. Das ist ein sauber Traktament! Ach! Blondchen! Blondchen! was werden sie wohl mit
dir anfangen?

BLONDE: Das gilt mir nun ganz gleich. Da es einmal gestorben
sein muss, ist mir alles recht.

PEDRILLO: Welche Standhaftigkeit! Ich bin doch von gutem
altchristlichen Geschlecht aus Spanien, aber so gleichgültig kann
ich beim Tode nicht sein! – Weiß der Teufel . . . Gott sei bei mir!
Wie kann mir auch itzt der Teufel auf die Zunge kommen?

Letzter Auftritt

DIE VORIGEN, BASSA SELIM, OSMIN
(VOLL FREUDEN) UND GEFOLGE.

SELIM: Nun, Sklave! elender Sklave! zitterst du? Erwartest du
dein Urteil?

BELMONTE: Ja, Bassa, mit so vieler Kaltblütigkeit als Hitze du
es aussprechen kannst. Kühle deine Rache an mir, tilge das
Unrecht, so mein Vater dir angetan. – Ich erwarte alles und tadle
dich nicht.

Eighth Scene

PEDRILLO AND BLANCHE, BROUGHT IN BY
OTHER GUARDS, AND THOSE BEFORE.

Spoken Dialogue

PEDRILLO: Well, master, here we are! There's no question of
escaping now. They're already making preparations to send
us out of this world. It's terrifying to think what they have in
store for us! I have heard it said that I am to be boiled in oil and
then stuck on a spit! That's some treatment! And Blanche! Poor
Blanche! What are they going to do to you?

BLANCHE: At this point, I don't care. We have to die, and I don't
care how.

PEDRILLO: What a brick! I am from old Christian stock in Spain,
but even I can't be so calm in the face of death! The devil knows—
oops! God bless me! How can I mention the devil at a time like
this?

Final Scene

THOSE BEFORE, PASHA SELIM, OSMIN
(FILLED WITH JOY), AND ATTENDANTS.

SELIM: Now then, slave! Miserable slave! Are you trembling?
Awaiting your judgment?

BELMONTE: Yes, Pasha, as coolly on my side as you delivered it
so heatedly. Wreak your revenge on me, atone the injustice my
father did to you. I await anything and do not blame you.

SELIM: Es muss also wohl deinem Geschlechte ganz eigen sein, Ungerechtigkeiten zu begehen, weil du das für so ausgemacht annimmst? Du betrügst dich. Ich habe deinen Vater viel zu sehr verabscheut, als dass ich je in seine Fußstapfen treten könnte. Nimm deine Freiheit, nimm Konstanzen, segle in dein Vaterland, sage deinem Vater, dass du in meiner Gewalt warst, dass ich dich freigelassen, um ihm sagen zu können, es wäre ein weit größer Vergnügen, eine erlittene Ungerechtigkeit durch Wohltaten zu vergelten, als Laster mit Lastern tilgen.

BELMONTE: Herr! . . . du setzest mich in Erstaunen . . .

SELIM: *(ihn verächtlich ansehend)* Das glaub ich. Zieh damit hin und werde du wenigstens menschlicher als dein Vater, so ist meine Handlung belohnt.

KONSTANZE: Herr! vergib! Ich schätzte bisher deine edle Seele, aber nun bewundre ich . . .

SELIM: Still! Ich wünsche für die Falschheit, so Sie an mir begangen, dass Sie es nie bereuen möchten, mein Herz ausge-schlagen zu haben. *(im Begriff abzugehen)*

PEDRILLO: *(tritt ihm in Weg und fällt ihm zu Füßen)* Herr! dürfen wir beide Unglückliche es auch wagen, um Gnade zu flehen? - - Ich war von Jugend auf ein treuer Diener meines Herrn . . .

OSMIN: Herr! beim Allah! lass dich ja nicht von dem verwünsch-ten Schmarotzer hintergehn! Keine Gnade! Er hat schon hundert Mal den Tod verdient.

SELIM: Er mag ihn also in seinem Vaterlande suchen. *(zur Wache)* Man begleite alle viere an das Schiff. *(gibt Belmonte ein Papier)* Hier ist euer Passport.

SELIM: Your family must like to perpetuate injustice because you seem to take it for granted. You are deceiving yourself. I loathed your father too much ever to follow in his footsteps. Take your freedom, take Constanza, sail to your homeland. And tell your father that you were in my power and that I set you free. It is a far greater pleasure to repay a grave injustice with kindness than to keep paying an eye for an eye.

BELMONTE: My lord, . . . you astound me . . .

SELIM: *(looking at him with disdain)* That I believe. Depart then, and if you are more merciful than your father, my action will be rewarded.

CONSTANZA: My lord, forgive me. Until now I cherished your noble soul . . . now I admire . . .

SELIM: Silence! I can only hope that, having deceived me, you never come to regret having rejected my heart. *(He starts to leave.)*

PEDRILLO: *(stepping in his way and falling at his feet)* My lord! May we two unfortunate souls also beg for mercy? Since my childhood I have been the faithful servant of my master . . .

OSMIN: Master! In Allah's name! Don't let yourself be deceived by this parasite! No mercy! He has earned his death a hundred times over.

SELIM: Then he will surely earn his death again in his fatherland. *(to the guard)* Take all four of them to their ship. *(He gives Belmonte a document.)* Here is your passport.

OSMIN: Wie! meine Blonde soll er auch mitnehmen?

SELIM: *(scherzhaft)* Alter! sind dir deine Augen nicht lieb? – Ich sorge besser für dich, als du denkst.

OSMIN: Gift und Dolch! Ich möchte bersten!

SELIM: Beruhige dich. Wen man durch Wohltun nicht für sich gewinnen kann, den muss man sich vom Halse schaffen.

N° 21a Vaudeville

BELMONTE:
Nie werd ich deine Huld verkennen,
Mein Dank bleibt ewig dir geweiht!
An jedem Ort, zu jeder Zeit
Werd ich dich groß und edel nennen.
Wer so viel Huld vergessen kann,
Den seh man mit Verachtung an.

KONSTANZE, BLONDE, BELMONTE, PEDRILLO, OSMIN:
Wer so viel Huld vergessen kann,
Den seh man mit Verachtung an.

KONSTANZE:
Nie werd ich im Genuss der Liebe
Vergessen, was der Dank gebeut;
Mein Herz der Liebe nun geweiht,
Hegt auch dem Dank geweihte Triebe.
Wer so viel Huld vergessen kann,
Den seh man mit Verachtung an.

KONSTANZE, BLONDE, BELMONTE, PEDRILLO, OSMIN:
Wer so viel Huld vergessen kann,
Den seh man mit Verachtung an.

OSMIN: What! And take my Blanche with him?

SELIM: *(jokingly)* Old man! What's happened to your eyes? I am looking out for you better than you realize.

OSMIN: Poison and daggers! I am going to . . . explode!

SELIM: Calm down. If you cannot conquer by kindness, then better not fight at all.

Vaudeville

BELMONTE:
Your kindness is that of a king,
A debt I can never repay.
Wherever I am, night or day,
Your praises I will sing.
The man who could forget your reign
Should be looked upon with disdain.

CONSTANZA, BLANCHE, BELMONTE, PEDRILLO, AND OSMIN:
The man who could forget your reign
Should be looked upon with disdain.

CONSTANZA:
Though you granted my love to me,
You have taught me a lesson too.
My heart was filled with fantasy.
Kindness and gratitude are what is true.
The man who could forget your reign
Should be looked upon with disdain.

CONSTANZA, BLANCHE, BELMONTE, PEDRILLO, AND OSMIN:
The man who could forget your reign
Should be looked upon with disdain.

PEDRILLO:

Wenn ich es je vergessen könnte,
Wie nah ich am Erdrosseln war
Und all der anderen Gefahr:
Ich lief, als ob der Kopf mir brennte.
Wer so viel Huld vergessen kann,
Den seh man mit Verachtung an.

KONSTANZE, BLONDE, BELMONTE, PEDRILLO, OSMIN:

Wer so viel Huld vergessen kann,
Den seh man mit Verachtung an.

BLONDE:

Herr Bassa, ich sag recht mit Freuden
Viel Dank für Kost und Lagerstroh,
Doch bin ich recht von Herzen froh,
Dass er mich lässt von hinnen scheiden.
(auf Osmin zeigend)
Denn seh er nur das Tier dort an,
Ob man so was ertragen kann.

OSMIN:

Verbrennen sollte man die Hunde,
Die uns so schändlich hintergehn.
Es ist nicht länger auszustehn,
Mir starrt die Zunge fast im Munde,
Um ihren Lohn zu ordnen an:
Erst geköpft, dann gehangen,
Dann gespießt auf heiße Stangen,
Dann verbrannt, dann gebunden
Und getaucht, zuletzt geschunden.
(läuft wütend ab)

PEDRILLO:

How could I ever, ever forget
How close I came to strangulation
And other forms of emasculation?
I ran until I was in a sweat.
The man who could forget your reign
Should be looked upon with disdain.

CONSTANZA, BLANCHE, BELMONTE, PEDRILLO, AND OSMIN:

The man who could forget your reign
Should be looked upon with disdain.

BLANCHE:

Sir Pasha, I can say straight off,
Thanks for the food and the straw.
Much as I'd like to trade old saws,
I am happy now to be casting off.
(pointing to Osmin)
Look at that ogre over there!
How can you bear his ugly stare?

OSMIN:

Those dogs should be burned to death.
Shamefully they deceived us all.
Treachery like theirs can only appall.
My anger almost stifles my breath.
As for their reward, let it be this—
First beheaded, then hung like hounds,
What's left can be put on skewers.
Then burned, and bound, and drowned—
Four thoroughly dead wrongdoers!
(He storms off.)

KONSTANZE, BLONDE, BELMONTE, PEDRILLO:

Nichts ist so hässlich als die Rache,
Hingegen menschlich gütig sein
Und ohne Eigennutz verzeihn,
Ist nur der großen Seelen Sache.

KONSTANZE:

Wer dieses nicht erkennen kann,
Den seh man mit Verachtung an.

KONSTANZE, BLONDE, BELMONTE, PEDRILLO:

Wer dieses nicht erkennen kann,
Den seh man mit Verachtung an.

N° 21b Chor der Janitscharen

TUTTI:

Bassa Selim lebe lange!
Ehre sei sein Eigentum!
Seine holde Scheitel prange
Voll vom Jubel, voll von Ruhm.

Ende des Singspiels.

CONSTANZA, BLANCHE, BELMONTE, AND PEDRILLO:
Vengeance is an ugly deed.
To be merciful and humane,
To pardon those at blame
Is how great souls proceed.

CONSTANZA:
The man who could forget his reign
Should be looked upon with disdain.

CONSTANZA, BLANCHE, BELMONTE, AND PEDRILLO:
The man who could forget his reign
Should be looked upon with disdain.

Chorus of the Janissaries

CHORUS:
Long live Pasha Selim!
Let all now honor his name!
Let all his people hail him.
May joy and peace embellish his fame.
Long live Pasha Selim!
Let all now honor his name!

End of the Opera.

∴ 3 ∴

The Marriage of Figaro

THE MARRIAGE OF FIGARO

•

Commedia per musica, 1786

Libretto by Lorenzo Da Ponte

The Characters
Count Almaviva, a Spanish nobleman
Countess Almaviva, his wife
Susanna, the Countess's chambermaid
Figaro, the Count's valet, betrothed to Susanna
Cherubino, the Count's page, godson of the Countess,
enamored of her, Susanna, Barbarina, etc.
Marcellina, Bartolo's housekeeper, former governess of the Countess
Don Bartolo, the Count's doctor, former guardian of the Countess
Don Basilio, music master, former teacher of the Countess
Antonio, the estate gardener, uncle of Susanna
Barbarina, daughter of Antonio, in love with Cherubino
Don Curzio, a notary

Chorus, village men and women, servants, etc.

Setting: the castle of Count Almaviva

WHEN MOZART WAS RUDELY DISMISSED FROM HIS service by Count Colloredo, the Archbishop of Salzburg, in 1781, on his way out the door he was kicked in the behind by the Archbishop's chief steward. Though he was relieved to have his independence, he never forgot the humiliation. As he wrote then to his father, "It is the heart that enobles man; and though I am not a count, I have probably more Honor in me than many a count; and whether I am dealing with a lackey or a count, if he insults me, he is a scoundrel." It is no wonder that Figaro's suavely menacing "Se vuol ballare" ("If you want to dance") was added to the score, even though it is not featured in the original play by Pierre-Augustin Caron de Beaumarchais (1732–1799). But *Figaro* is not an opera of political resentments. In fact, Da Ponte removed most of the political edge from Beaumarchais's play as he revised it into a libretto. In the play's third act, for instance, there is an extended prickly dialogue between Figaro and the Count, and it was cut; in the final acts, too, much of Figaro's philosophizing on the social classes and the nature of truth were cut. What Da Ponte concentrates on is the human comedy—one that can be read as a political allegory, but is better not. Human desires are political by nature, but power and intrigue and betrayal are best studied in the workings of the individual heart.

The opera is certainly, and in a crucial sense, about identity. Like *Oedipus the King* or *The Importance of Being Earnest*, it is first of all a work about the main character's literal identity. The startling discovery about his parents—timely too, since he was about to be forced to marry his own mother—changes his status in the world, and provides the wherewithal for him to marry his beloved. In a more metaphorical but no less real sense, the identity of the other characters is also explored to great comic effect. The servants, Figaro and Susanna, are more worldly and effective than their masters, the fluttery Countess and the self-absorbed Count. Cherubino is dressed up and presented as a girl. The Countess and her maid change dresses and identities to catch the Count in his own game. New identities, in other words, are slipped into like clothes. And what, after all, are anyone's origins? The Count's title did not ensure a natural grace or benevolence (his apparent kindness is mere calculation), just as the Countess's marriage does not ensure domestic happiness. The point of comedy is to make us look twice. The point of great comedy is to let us see things from both sides. Marriage, for instance, can be a necessity, or a convenience that allows looseness and insincerity, or sorrow and loneliness.

Love is another identity we assume, the heart's emotions just as staged and manipulated as any title or idea, and *Figaro* is a marvelous anatomy of love. Buzzing around, in all of love's poses, is young Cherubino, whose name means "little Cupid," the god who presides over everything here. At the opera's end, four couples are lined up on stage: Young Love, uncertain and hormonal, represented by Cherubino and Barbarina; Hidden Love, carried on in secret shame for so long that it has been forgotten even by the lovers themselves—this is Marcellina and old Bartolo; Romantic Love, in the newly married, confident, spirited, lusty Figaro and Susanna; and Chastened Love, a patchwork of compromises and desires, of betrayal and forgiveness and resignation, in the persons of the Count and Countess. Every variation on the theme is rung.

Modern audiences have sympathized most with the Countess, not least because she seems the noble victim but also because Mozart's music has opened her heart to us in a transfixing way. So plaintive and moving are her two arias (and her "Dove sono" could be the motto for the whole opera), so heart-stopping is her forgiveness of her philandering husband (twice she forgives him, in Acts I and IV), that we see her as the emotional center of the opera. But it is actually Susanna who is the opera's heart. Her love is clear-eyed, not above innocent deception, resilient, sensuous, and finally triumphant. One has the sense that she will be a happy woman; not so the Countess.

It cannot be an accident that Beaumarchais's father was a watchmaker. His play is a mechanical wonder, giddily spinning, every hairspring and ratchet wheel wound and balanced and meshed. And Da Ponte kept its jewel-machined precision intact, even while editing it. The action of the whole opera transpires over the course of a single day, from the servants getting ready for the morning tasks to the marriage-feast fireworks. The characters are closely intertwined even before the action begins. Figaro (who is betrothed to Susanna, whose uncle is Antonio, who is also Barbarina's father) turns out to be the son of Marcellina and Bartolo, who were once the tutor and guardian of Rosina, the Countess, whose godson Cherubino is in love with her, when not after the affections of Susanna and Barbarina ... And around it goes. This is one reason why the last act is so breathtaking, with all the characters moving around, under cover of darkness and two of them in disguise, others pretending to be seen or hidden. The audience is never confused but constantly surprised.

Even the stage props work to forward the plot. Both the play and the libretto specify just a few items on stage for the first scene—a mirror, a bonnet, a bell, and an armchair. That armchair becomes almost another character by the time the act is over, and when the Count describes finding Cherubino in Barbarina's room, under a table—while he lifts the sheet to discover him again in the chair—the work is a masterpiece of physical comedy. Likewise in Act II, the action takes place between a closet and a window, a closed space and an open one, just the right arenas for a contest about honesty and secrecy. All of this is mirrored in Act IV, with the garden itself and closet-like pavilions, the evening's darkness a match for the moral murkiness of everyone's motivations. Think too of all the pieces of paper— Cherubino's commission, Susanna's note, Cherubino's song, the marriage contract. Wit is verbal, and is Figaro's domain. Comedy is physical, and is *Figaro*'s delight.

By the end of the evening, one marriage is secured and another is saved, and clearly reconciliation is the opera's theme. It requires Figaro's constantly improvised cleverness, yes, but even more it requires that Susanna yield to what disgusts her and the Countess to participate in something that might degrade her. Their willingness to do what they must finally allows them to become what they wish.

THE STORY

ACT I

The story takes place in eighteenth-century Seville, on the grand estate of the Count and Countess Almaviva. Their servants Figaro (who, years earlier, had helped the young Count lure the young Rosina away from her guardian and marry him) and Susanna are busy with preparations for their own wedding. Figaro is measuring the room for their marriage bed, Susanna is trying on a bonnet. When he comments on how convenient the room is to their masters' quarters, Susanna informs him that, in fact, the Count has been making advances towards her, hinting that he wants to claim his *droit du seigneur*, his feudal right to deflower the bride of a servant before her wedding night. Though he had abolished the law when he married the Countess, he wants to make an exception of Susanna. Figaro is furious. He realizes that the Count's plan to take them both to London, where he has been appointed ambassador, is only a ploy to keep Susanna nearby. He vows his revenge.

Marcellina and Bartolo enter. She reminds him that she had lent money to Figaro on the condition that, if he could not repay her, he must marry her. She is determined to block Susanna's chances, and Bartolo—having once been outsmarted by Figaro—is eager to pay him back. Susanna returns and she and Marcellina trade veiled insults, until the older woman leaves in a huff.

Suddenly Cherubino rushes in. He fears the Count's anger because the day before, the Count, on his way to seduce the young maiden, had discovered him in Barbarina's room. Susanna reminds him that he actually pines for the Countess, and Cherubino shows her the lyrics of a song he has written for the Countess. While she reads it, he snatches a ribbon from her, one that ties the Countess's nightcap, and swoons over it, declaring himself in love with love.

The Count can be heard outside the door, and Cherubino quickly hides behind an armchair. Susanna tries to distract the Count, who begs her to meet him tonight in the garden. Next Don Basilio can be heard entering, and now the Count hides behind the armchair—into whose sheeted seat Cherubino has deftly slid. Basilio wants to encourage her to look favorably on the Count's ardor, and mocks young Cherubino's panting after the Countess. Hearing this, the Count leaps up and angrily recounts the tale of finding Cherubino in Barbarina's room—and in the process uncovers Cherubino himself. He is about to punish the lad, when he realizes that Cherubino has heard from his hiding place his seductive words to Susanna. So he hastily forgives the boy, and as a reward appoints him to a military unit about to leave for maneuvers.

Figaro and the villagers have returned to ask the Count to preside over the wedding. Cherubino is distraught, Susanna is bemused, and Figaro sends the lad off with a song about the muddy, bloody glory of the military life.

ACT II

The Countess is alone in her bedchamber, sighing to herself that the romance has gone from her marriage. When Susanna enters, the Countess urges her to tell of the Count's attempted seduction, and the two women lament the facts of modern marriage. When Figaro arrives, he takes a more cynical view of the situation, and devises a scheme to encourage the Count's rendezvous in the garden, but substitute Cherubino for Susanna. Figaro leaves laughing and Cherubino enters with a long face. The Countess bids him sing the song he has composed for her, and he does so, with a sweet urgency. But it is time to fit him with women's clothes. While they are doing so, they notice that his military commission lacks a proper seal. And as the ladies are trying to transform Cherubino into a girl, the Countess discovers the ribbon Cherubino had taken and used to bandage a cut. As the Countess ties up a new one, Cherubino nearly swoons with adoration and—but suddenly there is a knock at the door.

It is the Count. Demanding to know why his wife's room is locked, he is trying to get in as the ladies hide Cherubino in the dressing room and Susanna leaves by a door at the back. Once in the room and suspicious, the Count hears something knocked over in the dressing room and demands to know who is there. The Countess at first denies there is anything, but when pressed by her husband, tells him it is Susanna, trying on her wedding dress. The Count calls for her to come out. The Countess, standing on her honor, demands she stay in there. (By this time Susanna has returned, and can hear everything from her hiding place.) The Count decides to empty and lock the room, find the dressing room key, and open the door himself. As soon as he and the Countess leave, Susanna tells Cherubino to come out. They both realize the situation is dire, and Cherubino impulsively decides to jump out of the window and flee through the garden.

The Count and Countess return, and as he tries to pry open the dressing room door she begins to admit that it is Cherubino in there after all. Accusing his wife of infidelity, he yells at the door, demanding the boy come out. The door finally opens, and to everyone's astonishment, it is Susanna. The Count begs forgiveness from his wife. At this moment, Figaro appears with the wedding party—eager for the ceremony to keep the Count from acting on his impulse. The Count shows Figaro a letter, supposedly from Susanna inviting the Count to an evening tryst in the garden. Figaro denies any knowledge of it.

Suddenly Antonio the gardener, drunk and disheveled, enters to say a man has jumped from the Countess's window. Figaro cleverly pretends it was he who jumped, but Antonio then produces the military commission that had dropped from Cherubino's pocket. Again, Figaro devises an explanation, when suddenly Marcellina, Bartolo, and Basilio enter to demand that Figaro marry her in default of his repayment of the loan she had advanced him. The two sides argue, the Count says he will decide the question, and general confusion prevails.

ACT III

The Count is alone, brooding on the turn of events. Susanna, with the Countess's approval, comes to the Count pretending to borrow his bottle of smelling salts for the Countess. When the Count presses himself on her, she agrees to meet him in the garden. Still, the Count is suspicious of a plot against him, and vows his revenge on his wily servants. The crowd of petitioners arrives, and the decision goes against Figaro. Desperate to stall things, Figaro claims he needs his parents' permission to marry, and they have disappeared. But when Figaro bares a birthmark on his arm, Marcellina realizes he is her long-lost son, and that Bartolo is his father. Susanna enters and, seeing Figaro embracing Marcellina, accuses him of betraying her. Figaro explains her mistake. In the spirit of reconciliation, Bartolo agrees to marry Marcellina, and she tears up Figaro's promissory note.

Barbarina plans to dress Cherubino as a girl, when the villagers go to present flowers to the Countess, who meanwhile is again brooding on her own unhappiness, wondering where the vanished days of pleasure have fled. The Count is questioning Antonio, who says he will show the Count where Cherubino is.

The Countess and Susanna have decided to fool the Count into meeting Susanna in the garden, and they write him a romantic note, sealing it with a pin. The village girls arrive to pay homage to the Countess, when Antonio and the Count burst in and uncover Cherubino. Figaro tries to keep the arrangements going, even as he stumbles deeper into his improvised lies. Tensions rise as the wedding ceremonies proceed. The love note is secretly passed to the Count, who registers his delight, and then sticks himself with the pin. He calls out for the wedding feast to begin, while intrigue swirls under the surface.

ACT IV

Barbarina has come in search of the lost pin, and inadvertently spills the truth to Figaro, who now thinks his betrothed plans to betray him with the Count. Marcellina tries to console him, but he leaves in a vengeful rage while Marcellina laments the lot of women. Slowly, characters accumulate in the twilit garden. Barbarina is told to wait in an arbor; Bartolo and Basilio are told to hide and wait for Figaro's signal, and Figaro himself angrily blames his wife—and all women—for their deceitfulness.

Susanna and the Countess appear, each dressed in the other's clothes. Marcellina hides, as does Figaro, who then overhears Susanna sing of her love for the Count—without knowing that she is playing a game. Cherubino arrives and, thinking the Countess is Susanna, tries to embrace her. The Count chases him away, and begins to seduce Susanna, without realizing it is his own wife in disguise. Figaro sees them go off together, furious, and the two ladies now know both men are caught in their trap.

Figaro sees "the Countess" but suddenly realizes it is his beloved's voice. He pretends, to Susanna's fury, to pay court to the Countess, until she finally slaps him and he confesses he has known who she is. The Count approaches and thinks Figaro is involved with the Countess. In all the confusion—the others have now been summoned—the Count's indignation is at its height, when the Countess—the real Countess—appears and asks that he forgive everyone. Humbled, he does, and the wedding feast begins.

THE BACKGROUND

In his *Memoirs*, Lorenzo Da Ponte reports that it was Mozart who came to him with the idea of an opera based on the sensational new play *La folle journée, ou Le Mariage de Figaro*, by Beaumarchais, which Mozart had probably read in a German translation that, because of the play's enormous success, appeared almost at once. The play had been completed in 1778, but not performed until 1784 at the Comédie Française, the delay occasioned by royal censorship. Both the scandal and the play's brilliance made it instantly and widely known. Still, it is unusual for any opera to appear just two years after its source's first performance. Also unusual is the fact that it was written without having been commissioned.

It took Da Ponte six weeks to write the libretto. He reduced the number of characters, eliminated an act, cut the play's more overt political content, arranged it into "numbers," and translated it into sparkling Italian verse. The libretto then had to be approved by the emperor, Joseph II, before Mozart could begin work on it, which he did in the autumn of 1785. Mozart's father, Leopold, wrote to his daughter, Nannerl, about the assignment: "I know the piece. It is a most tiresome play . . . There will be a great deal of running about and discussing things before he gets the libretto exactly the way he wants it." It took Mozart fifty days to write this opera, and the composer's first biographer said Mozart had worked on no other opera with such intensity. "As soon as I wrote the words," Da Ponte said, "Mozart set them to music."

The composer closely supervised the (sometimes stormy) rehearsals, and conducted the premiere from the harpsichord. The opera opened at the Burgtheater in Vienna on May 1, 1786. The Count was sung by Stefano Mandini, and the Countess by Luisa Laschi. The Figaro was bass Francesco Benucci, a singer Mozart admired. (Listening to him sing the Act I finale during rehearsals, Mozart kept saying *sotto voce*, "Bravo! Bravo, Benucci!") Susanna was the English soprano Nancy Storace, Cheubino was Dorothea Bussani, Maria Mandini was Marcellina, twelve-year-old Anna Gottlieb was Barbarina. Both the roles of Bartolo and Antonio were sung by Francesco Bussani. Michael Kelly, the Irish tenor who wrote colorful accounts of Mozart and *Figaro*, sang both Basilio and Don Curzio.

The opera somewhat puzzled its first audience, but subsequent performances were ecstatically received. By the time it reached Prague a few months later, Mozart could write to a friend: "Here they talk about nothing but 'Figaro.' Nothing played, sung, or whistled but 'Figaro.' Nothing is drawing like 'Figaro.' Nothing, nothing but 'Figaro.'" Over the next few years, for performances in other cities, Mozart made changes, writing new arias for individual singers. The finale of Act II is generally considered one of the most perfect scenes in the history of opera, though the finale of Act III was said to be Mozart's favorite part of the opera. The nineteenth century's strong Romantic sensibility preferred *Don Giovanni*, but in the twentieth century *Figaro*'s genius—its intimacy, humanity, and sublime theatricality—triumphed.

Atto primo

*Camera non affatto ammobiliata,
una sedia d'appoggio in mezzo.*

Scena 1

FIGARO CON UNA MISURA IN MANO E SUSANNA
ALLO SPECCHIO CHE SI STA METTENDO UN CAPPELLINO
ORNATO DI FIORI.

N° 1 Duettino

FIGARO: *(misurando)*
Cinque … dieci … venti … trenta …
trentasei … quarantatré …

SUSANNA: *(fra sé stessa, specchiandosi)*
Ora sì ch'io son contenta:
sembra fatto inver per me.
(seguitando a guardarsi)
Guarda un po', mio caro Figaro,
guarda adesso il mio cappello.

FIGARO:
Sì, mio core, or è più bello:
sembra fatto inver per te.

Act I

A partially furnished room, an armchair in the center of it.

Scene 1

FIGARO WITH A RULER IN HAND,
AND SUSANNA AT A MIRROR, TRYING ON A HAT
DECORATED WITH FLOWERS.

Duet

FIGARO: *(measuring)*
Five . . . ten . . . twenty . . . thirty . . .
Thirty-six . . . forty-three . . .

SUSANNA: *(looking in the mirror)*
Yes, now I'm pleased with it.
It seems made just for me.
(She continues to gaze at herself.)
Take a look, my darling Figaro,
Look at my bonnet.

FIGARO:
Yes, dear heart, much prettier now.
Seems made just for you.

SUSANNA, FIGARO:
Ah, il mattino alle nozze vicino
quanto è dolce al mio/tuo tenero sposo
questo bel cappellino vezzoso
che Susanna ella stessa si fe'.

Recitativo
SUSANNA: Cosa stai misurando, caro il mio Figaretto?

FIGARO: Io guardo se quel letto che ci destina il Conte farà buona figura in questo loco.

SUSANNA: E in questa stanza? …

FIGARO: Certo, a noi la cede generoso il padrone.

SUSANNA: Io per me te la dono.

FIGARO: E la ragione?

SUSANNA: *(toccandosi la fronte)* La ragione l'ho qui.

FIGARO: *(facendo lo stesso)* Perché non puoi far che passi un po' qui?

SUSANNA: Perché non voglio. Sei tu mio servo o no?

FIGARO: Ma non capisco perché tanto ti spiace la più comoda stanza del palazzo.

SUSANNA: Perch'io son la Susanna, e tu sei pazzo.

FIGARO: Grazie, non tanti elogi! Guarda un poco se potriasi star meglio in altro loco.

SUSANNA AND FIGARO:
Here it is, our wedding day,
And your (my) adoring groom
Thinks the bonnet Susanna made
All by herself is charming.

Recitative

SUSANNA: What are you measuring there, my little Figarino?

FIGARO: I'm checking to see if the bed the Count is giving us will look right here.

SUSANNA: In this room?

FIGARO: Why not? A gift from our generous master!

SUSANNA: I don't like it one bit.

FIGARO: And why not?

SUSANNA: *(tapping her forehead)* My reasons are right here.

FIGARO: *(doing the same)* Could you pass them along right here?

SUSANNA: But I do not wish to! Are you, or are you not, my servant?

FIGARO: I don't understand why you're not happy with the most convenient room in the palace.

SUSANNA: Because I am Susanna and you are a fool.

FIGARO: Thanks. Don't overdo the compliments! Can you find a better spot somewhere else?

N° 2 Duettino

FIGARO:

Se a caso madama
la notte ti chiama,
din din; in due passi
da quella puoi gir.
Vien poi l'occasione
che vuolmi il padrone,
don don; in tre salti
lo vado a servir.

SUSANNA:

Così se il mattino
il caro Contino,
din din; e ti manda
tre miglia lontan.
Don don; a mia porta
il diavol lo porta,
ed ecco in tre salti ...

FIGARO: Susanna, pian pian.

SUSANNA: Ascolta ...

FIGARO: Fa' presto ...

SUSANNA:

Se udir brami il resto
discaccia i sospetti
che torto mi fan.

FIGARO:

Udir bramo il resto:
i dubbi, i sospetti
gelare mi fan.

Duet

FIGARO:

If at night my lady
Should ring for you—
Ding-ding—in a flash
You could answer her call.
And whenever my lord
May need some help—
Dong-dong—I'm there
In no time at all.

SUSANNA:

And suppose one morning
Your dear little master—
Ding-ding—should send you
On an errand miles away . . .
Dong-dong—wouldn't that devil
Just have his day!
Dong-dong—in no time at all . . .

FIGARO: Stop, Susanna, enough—

SUSANNA: Listen.

FIGARO: Hurry.

SUSANNA:

If you want the rest,
Put aside your suspicions
That do me such wrong.

FIGARO:

I must have the rest.
My doubts and suspicions
Have gone on too long.

Recitativo

SUSANNA: Or bene, ascolta e taci.

FIGARO: *(inquieto)* Parla, che c'è di nuovo?

SUSANNA: Il signor Conte, stanco di andar cacciando le straniere bellezze forestiere, vuole ancor nel castello ritentar la sua sorte, né già di sua consorte, bada bene, appetito gli viene ...

FIGARO: E di chi dunque?

SUSANNA: Della tua Susannetta.

FIGARO: *(con sorpresa)* Di te?

SUSANNA: Di me medesma; ed ha speranza che al nobil suo progetto utilissima sia tal vicinanza.

FIGARO: Bravo! Tiriamo avanti.

SUSANNA: Queste le grazie son, questa la cura ch'egli prende di te, della tua sposa.

FIGARO: Oh, guarda un po' che carità pelosa!

SUSANNA: Chetati, or viene il meglio: Don Basilio, mio maestro di canto e suo mezzano, nel darmi la lezione mi ripete ogni dì questa canzone.

FIGARO: Chi? Basilio? Oh birbante!

SUSANNA: E tu credevi che fosse la mia dote merto del tuo bel muso!

Recitative

SUSANNA: All right, then. Listen and be quiet.

FIGARO: *(uneasily)* So, what's been happening?

SUSANNA: The Count is tired of chasing pretty girls up and down the countryside, and wants to try his luck in his own palace, though it's not his wife, mind you, who whets his appetite.

FIGARO: Who is it, then?

SUSANNA: Your own little Susanna.

FIGARO: *(taken aback)* You!

SUSANNA: The very same. And he's counting on our being nearby to help his scheme.

FIGARO: Clever! Keep going.

SUSANNA: This is his thanks, this is why he's being so kind to you and your bride.

FIGARO: I see it all! Some gift indeed!

SUSANNA: Wait, here's the best part: This is the same tune Don Basilio, my singing teacher and his factotum, hums every day during my lesson.

FIGARO: Who? Basilio? That scoundrel!

SUSANNA: Did you think my dowry owes anything to your good looks?

FIGARO: Me n'era lusingato.

SUSANNA: Ei la destina per ottener da me certe mezz'ore ... che il diritto feudale ...

FIGARO: Come? Ne' feudi suoi non l'ha il Conte abolito?

SUSANNA: Ebben, ora è pentito, e par che tenti riscattarlo da me.

FIGARO: Bravo! Mi piace: che caro signor Conte! Ci vogliam divertir: trovato avete ... *(Si sente suonare un campanello.)* Chi suona? La Contessa.

SUSANNA: Addio, addio, Fi-Fi-Figaro bello ...

FIGARO: Coraggio, mio tesoro.

SUSANNA: E tu cervello.
(Parte.)

Scena 2

FIGARO SOLO.

FIGARO: *(passeggiando con foco per la camera e fregandosi le mani)*
Bravo, signor padrone! ... Ora incomincio a capir il mistero ... e a veder schietto tutto il vostro progetto: a Londra, è vero? Voi ministro, io corriero e la Susanna ... secreta ambasciatrice. Non sarà, non sarà. Figaro il dice.

N° 3 *Cavatina*

FIGARO:
Se vuol ballare, signor Contino,
il chitarrino le suonerò.
Se vuol venire nella mia scuola

FIGARO: I wanted to think so . . .

SUSANNA: He's using it to steal a half hour with me . . . his "privilege" as lord of the manor . . .

FIGARO: What! Didn't the Count abolish that old system?

SUSANNA: Yes, but he regrets it and wants to restore it in my case.

FIGARO: Oh, I like that! What a nobleman! He wants his fun? I'll give it to him—*(A bell rings.)* Who's ringing? Ah, the Countess.

SUSANNA: Goodbye, goodbye, my love!

FIGARO: Be strong, my treasure!

SUSANNA: And you—you keep your wits about you! *(She leaves.)*

Scene 2

FIGARO, ALONE.

FIGARO: *(pacing the room in a huff, rubbing his hands)* Bravo, my lord! Now I begin to understand all the fuss . . . and see what's behind your scheme. To London, eh? You as minister, I your lackey, and Susanna . . . your "private secretary." It won't happen! Figaro's on to you!

Cavatina

FIGARO:
If you want to dance, my noble lord,
It is I who will call the tune!
Sit for your lessons in my school

la capriola le insegnerò.
Saprò … ma piano … meglio ogni arcano
dissimulando scoprir potrò!
L'arte schermendo, l'arte adoprando,
di qua pungendo, di là scherzando,
tutte le macchine rovescerò.
Se vuol ballare, signor Contino,
il chitarrino le suonerò.
(Parte.)

Scena 3

BARTOLO E MARCELLINA CON UN
CONTRATTO IN MANO.

Recitativo

BARTOLO: Ed aspettaste il giorno fissato alle sue nozze per parlarmi di questo?

MARCELLINA: Io non mi perdo, dottor mio, di coraggio: per romper de' sponsali più avanzati di questo bastò spesso un pretesto, ed egli ha meco, oltre questo contratto, certi impegni … So io … Basta … conviene la Susanna atterrir, convien con arte impuntigliarla a rifiutare il Conte. Egli per vendicarsi prenderà il mio partito, e Figaro così fia mio marito.

BARTOLO: *(prende il contratto dalle mani di Marcellina)* Bene, io tutto farò: senza riserve tutto a me palesate. (Avrei pur gusto di dar per moglie la mia serva antica a chi mi fece un dì rapir l'amica.)

N° 4 Aria

BARTOLO:
La vendetta—oh, la vendetta! –
è un piacer serbato ai saggi:

And I'll teach you *my* rigadoon.
I know just how your secret now
Can best be made known to the world!
Act by stealth, but act as one must,
Here a parry, and there a thrust—
Oh, your quickstep will be over soon!
If you want to dance, my noble lord,
It is I who will call the tune!
(He leaves.)

Scene 3

BARTOLO AND MARCELLINA, WITH A
CONTRACT IN HER HAND.

Recitative

BARTOLO: And you wait until the very day of their wedding to tell me this?

MARCELLINA: All is not lost, good doctor. Breaking up a wedding match, even at the altar, can be done. Besides, apart from this contract, he has other obligations to me . . . I could . . . Well, never mind! For now, we must intimidate Susanna. We must make her reject the Count's advances. He'll want revenge, he'll take my side! And Figaro will be *my* husband!

BARTOLO: *(taking the contract from Marcellina)* Well, I will do everything I can. But I need all the details. (I would enjoy giving him my old servant for a wife, to make up for his having helped steal my beloved Rosina.)

Aria

BARTOLO:
Oh, vengeance! Sweet vengeance!
The thinking man's best pleasure.

obliar l'onte e gli oltraggi
è bassezza, è ognor viltà.
Coll'astuzia ... coll'arguzia ...
col giudizio ... col criterio ...
si potrebbe ... Il fatto è serio ...
ma, credete, si farà.
Se tutto il codice dovessi volgere,
se tutto l'indice dovessi leggere,
con un equivoco, con un sinonimo
qualche garbuglio si troverà.
Tutta Siviglia conosce Bartolo:
il birbo Figaro vostro sarà.
(Parte.)

Scena 4
MARCELLINA, POI SUSANNA CON CUFFIA DA DONNA,
UN NASTRO E UN ABITO DA DONNA.

Recitativo
MARCELLINA: Tutto ancor non ho perso: mi resta la speranza.
Ma Susanna si avanza: io vo' provarmi ... *(piano)* Fingiam di non
vederla ... *(forte)* E quella buona perla la vorrebbe sposar!

SUSANNA: *(da sè, resta indietro)* (Di me favella.)

MARCELLINA: Ma da Figaro alfine non può meglio sperarsi:
argent fait tout.

SUSANNA: (Che lingua! Manco male ch'ognun sa quanto vale.)

MARCELLINA: Brava! Questo è giudizio! Con quegl'occhi modesti, con quell'aria pietosa, e poi ...

To forget an insult is a measure
Of the common man's stupidity.
With obsession or discretion,
With my learning I'll confound him!
I'll get round him, I will hound him!
Oh, believe me, I will win!
I will read every law in the book,
Search the smallest cranny and nook,
Check every quibble, statute, or scribble,
Each therefore and howso and wherein.
I'll keep fishing till I get a nibble.
That rascally Figaro will give in!
(He leaves.)

Scene 4

MARCELLINA, THEN SUSANNA CARRYING A LADY'S
NIGHTCAP, RIBBON, AND DRESSING GOWN.

Recitative

MARCELLINA: All is not yet lost! I still have hope! But here comes Susanna. Time to begin. *(quietly)* I'll pretend not to notice her. *(aloud)* So that's the priceless jewel he intends to make his own!

SUSANNA: *(remaining in the background, to herself)* (She's speaking about me.)

MARCELLINA: From Figaro one can't expect anything better. You get what you pay for.

SUSANNA: (What a spiteful tongue! At least everyone knows what she's like.)

MARCELLINA: Excellent! Such discretion! And those modest glances, the air of piety, the . . .

SUSANNA: (Meglio è partir.)

MARCELLINA: (Che cara sposa!)
(Vanno tutte e due per partire e s'incontrano alla porta.)

N° 5 Duettino

MARCELLINA: *(facendo una riverenza)*
Via, resti servita,
madama brillante.

SUSANNA: *(facendo una riverenza)*
Non sono sì ardita,
madama piccante.

MARCELLINA: *(facendo una riverenza)* No, prima a lei tocca.

SUSANNA: *(facendo una riverenza)* No no, tocca a lei.

SUSANNA, MARCELLINA: *(facendo una riverenza)*
Io so i dover miei,
non fo inciviltà.

MARCELLINA: *(facendo una riverenza)* La sposa novella!

SUSANNA: *(facendo una riverenza)* La dama d'onore!

MARCELLINA: *(facendo una riverenza)* Del Conte la bella!

SUSANNA: *(facendo una riverenza)* Di Spagna l'amore!

MARCELLINA: I meriti!

SUSANNA: L'abito!

MARCELLINA: Il posto!

SUSANNA: (I had better go.)

MARCELLINA: (What a sweet young bride!)
(Both go to leave, and they meet at the door.)

Duet

MARCELLINA: *(curtsying)*
Resplendent lady,
Pray, after you.

SUSANNA: *(curtsying)*
Worthy madame,
That I cannot do.

MARCELLINA: *(curtsying)* No, it must be you.

SUSANNA: *(curtsying)* No, only after you.

SUSANNA AND MARCELLINA: *(curtsying)*
I know what is due.
I will not be rude.

MARCELLINA: *(curtsying)* The bride-to-be!

SUSANNA: *(curtsying)* The maid-of-honor!

MARCELLINA: *(curtsying)* Clearly the Count's favorite!

SUSANNA: *(curtsying)* The idol of all Spain!

MARCELLINA: Your virtues!

SUSANNA: Your trappings!

MARCELLINA: Your dignity!

SUSANNA: L'età!

MARCELLINA: *(infuriata)*
Perbacco, precipito,
se ancor resto qua.
(Parte infuriata.)

SUSANNA: *(minchionandola)*
Sibilla decrepita,
da rider mi fa.

Scena 5
SUSANNA E POI CHERUBINO.

Recitativo

SUSANNA: Va' là, vecchia pedante, dottoressa arrogante, perché hai letti due libri e seccata madama in gioventù …

CHERUBINO: *(esce in fretta.)* Susannetta, sei tu?

SUSANNA: Son io, cosa volete?

CHERUBINO: Ah, cor mio, che accidente!

SUSANNA: Cor vostro! Cosa avvenne?

CHERUBINO: Il Conte ieri, perché trovommi sol con Barbarina, il congedo mi diede. E se la Contessina, la mia bella comare grazia non m'intercede, io vado via, *(con ansietà)* io non ti vedo più, Susanna mia!

SUSANNA: Non vedete più me! Bravo! Ma dunque non più per la Contessa secretamente il vostro cor sospira?

SUSANNA: Your age!

MARCELLINA: *(in a rage)*
That *thing* dares to brag!
I will not stay here!
(Marcellina leaves in a huff.)

SUSANNA: *(mockingly)*
That decrepit old bag!
If she knew how they sneer!

Scene 5

SUSANNA, AND THEN CHERUBINO.

Recitative

SUSANNA: Go on then, you old fusspot! You arrogant know-it-all! So you've read a couple of books, And annoyed my mistress in her youth . . .

CHERUBINO: *(entering in a hurry)* My little Susanna, is that you?

SUSANNA: Just me. What is it?

CHERUBINO: Oh, my sweetheart, what a disaster!

SUSANNA: Your sweetheart! What's happened?

CHERUBINO: Yesterday the Count found me alone with Barbarina, and for that he dismissed me. If the Countess, my . . . my beautiful godmother, does not intercede for me, I am done for and . . . *(anxiously)* I'd never see you again—you, my Susanna!

SUSANNA: Never see me again! That's all well and good, but you won't be able to sigh secretly after the Countess herself!

CHERUBINO: Ah, che troppo rispetto ella m'ispira! Felice te, che puoi vederla quando vuoi, che la vesti il mattino, che la sera la spogli, che le metti gli spilloni, i merletti ... *(con un sospiro)* Ah, se in tuo loco ... Cos'hai lì? Dimmi un poco ...

SUSANNA: *(imitandolo)* Ah, il vago nastro e la notturna cuffia di comare sì bella.

CHERUBINO: *(toglie il nastro di mano a Susanna)* Deh, dammelo, sorella; dammelo, per pietà.

SUSANNA: *(vuol riprenderglielo)* Presto, quel nastro!

CHERUBINO: *(si mette a girare intorno la sedia)*
Oh caro, oh bello, oh fortunato nastro!
(Bacia e ribacia il nastro.)
Io non tel renderò che colla vita!

SUSANNA: *(seguita a corrergli dietro, ma poi si arresta come fosse stanca)*
Cos'è quest'insolenza?

CHERUBINO: Eh via, sta' cheta! In ricompensa poi questa mia canzonetta io ti vo' dare.

SUSANNA: E che ne debbo fare?

CHERUBINO: Leggila alla padrona, leggila tu medesma; leggila a Barbarina, a Marcellina; *(con trasporti di gioia)* leggila ad ogni donna del palazzo!

SUSANNA: Povero Cherubin, siete voi pazzo!

CHERUBINO: Oh, I . . . respect her so! Lucky you, who can see her whenever you wish, who dress her each morning, undress her each night, arrange her pins, her lace . . . *(sighing)* Oh, if only I could do that . . . What have you got there? Tell me . . .

SUSANNA: *(mimicking him)* Ah the pretty ribbon and nightcap of your . . . *beautiful* godmother . . .

CHERUBINO: *(He snatches the ribbon from her hand.)* Oh give it to me. Be a love, give it here, please.

SUSANNA: *(trying to take it back)* Give it back at once!

CHERUBINO: *(circling the chair)*
Oh beautiful, blessed ribbon!
(He kisses and rekisses the ribbon.)
I would rather give up my life!

SUSANNA: *(chasing him, then stopping as if tired)* How dare you—!

CHERUBINO: Oh do quiet down! In exchange I'll give you this little song of mine.

SUSANNA: What am I supposed to do with this?

CHERUBINO: Show it to your mistress, read it to yourself, to Barbarina, to Marcellina . . . *(in a transport of joy)* read it to every woman in the palace!

SUSANNA: Poor Cherubino, have you gone mad?

N° 6 Aria

CHERUBINO:

Non so più cosa son, cosa faccio,
or di foco, ora sono di ghiaccio,
ogni donna cangiar di colore,
ogni donna mi fa palpitar.
Solo ai nomi d'amor, di diletto,
mi si turba, mi s'altera il petto,
e a parlare mi sforza d'amore
un desio ch'io non posso spiegar.
Parlo d'amor vegliando,
parlo d'amor sognando,
all'acque, all'ombre, ai monti,
ai fiori, all'erbe, ai fonti,
all'eco, all'aria, ai venti
che il suon de' vani accenti
portano via con sé.
E se non ho chi m'oda,
parlo d'amor con me.

(Va per partire e vedendo il Conte di lontano, torna indietro impaurito e si nasconde dietro la sedia.)

Scena 6

CHERUBINO, SUSANNA E POI IL CONTE.

Recitativo

CHERUBINO: Ah, son perduto!

SUSANNA: *(cerca mascherar Cherubino.)* Che timor! Il Conte! Misera me!

IL CONTE: Susanna, tu mi sembri agitata e confusa.

Aria

CHERUBINO:

What is this feeling, this mysterious yearning,
One moment freezing, the next moment burning?
Each woman I see makes me turn pale,
Each woman I meet makes my heart pound.
The merest mention of love's sweet delight
Gives my trembling heart a delicious fright.
Love's fearsome power, or its least detail—
They threaten and tease me, thrill and confound!
I speak of love in my sleep,
I speak of love till I weep . . .
To the streams, to the shadows, to the mountains,
To the flowers, to the meadows, to the fountains,
To the echo, to the air, to the breeze
Which carries my exquisite disease,
Carries it off and away . . .
And if no one listens, well,
I talk about love to myself!

(As he is leaving, he sees the Count in the distance and hides himself behind the chair.)

Scene 6

CHERUBINO, SUSANNA, AND THEN THE COUNT.

Recitative

CHERUBINO: I'm done for!

SUSANNA: *(trying to conceal Cherubino)* What's the— . . . The Count! Oh God!

THE COUNT: Susanna, you seem upset and confused.

SUSANNA: Signor ... io chiedo scusa ... ma ... se mai ... qui sorpresa ... Per carità, partite!

IL CONTE: Un momento e ti lascio. *(Si mette a sedere sulla sedia e prende Susanna per la mano.)* Odi.

SUSANNA: *(si distacca con forza)* Non odo nulla.

IL CONTE: Due parole. Tu sai che ambasciatore a Londra il re mi dichiarò; di condur meco Figaro destinai ...

SUSANNA: *(timida)* Signor, se osassi ...

IL CONTE: *(sorge)* Parla, parla, mia cara, *(con tenerezza e tentando di riprenderle la mano)* e, con quel dritto ch'oggi prendi su me finché tu vivi, chiedi, imponi, prescrivi.

SUSANNA: *(con smania)* Lasciatemi, signor; dritti non prendo, non ne vo', non ne intendo ... Oh me infelice!

IL CONTE: Ah no, Susanna, io ti vo' far felice! *(come sopra)* Tu ben sai quanto io t'amo: a te Basilio tutto già disse; or senti, se per pochi momenti meco in giardin sull'imbrunir del giorno ... Ah, per questo favore io pagherei ...

BASILIO: *(dentro la scena)* È uscito poco fa.

IL CONTE: Chi parla?

SUSANNA: Oh dei!

IL CONTE: Esci, e alcun non entri.

SUSANNA: My lord, I . . . begging your pardon . . . but . . . suppose, well . . . someone saw us . . . I pray you, go.

THE COUNT: I'll leave in a minute. *(He sits down in the chair and takes Susanna's hand.)* Listen.

SUSANNA: *(drawing her hand forcibly away)* I won't listen!

THE COUNT: Two words only. You know that the King has appointed me ambassador to London, and I planned to take Figaro with me.

SUSANNA: *(timidly)* Sir, if I may . . .

THE COUNT: *(rising)* Speak up, my dear, *(tenderly trying again to take her hand)* and with that power you have over me today—and will have as long as you live—ask me anything, whatever you wish . . .

SUSANNA: *(angrily)* Let me go, my lord! I have no power, and want none, claim none . . . This is making me very uncomfortable!

THE COUNT: Now, now, Susanna, I only want you to be happy! *(as above)* You know how much I love you. Basilio has told you everything already. Now listen. If you will allow me just a few minutes in the garden this evening . . . For such a favor, I would pay . . .

BASILIO: *(outside the door)* He has just gone out.

THE COUNT: Who the devil is that?

SUSANNA: Oh heavens!

THE COUNT: Go, and see that no one comes in here.

SUSANNA: *(inquietissima)* Ch'io vi lasci qui solo?

BASILIO: *(dentro la scena)* Da madama ei sarà, vado a cercarlo.

IL CONTE: *(addita la sedia.)* Qui dietro mi porrò.

SUSANNA: Non vi celate.

IL CONTE: Taci e cerca ch'ei parta.
(Il Conte vuol nascondersi dietro il sedile. Susanna si frappone tra il paggio e lui, il Conte la spinge dolcemente. Ella rincula, intanto il paggio passa al davanti del sedile, si mette dentro in piedi, Susanna il ricopre colla vestaglia.)

SUSANNA: Ohimè! Che fate?

Scena 7

DETTI E BASILIO.

BASILIO: Susanna, il ciel vi salvi: avreste a caso veduto il Conte?

SUSANNA: E cosa deve far meco il Conte? Animo, uscite.

BASILIO: Aspettate, sentite, Figaro di lui cerca.

SUSANNA: (Oh cieli!) Ei cerca chi dopo voi più l'odia.

IL CONTE: (Veggiam come mi serve.)

BASILIO: Io non ho mai nella moral sentito ch'uno ch'ama la moglie odi il marito. Per dir che il Conte v'ama ...

SUSANNA: *(nervously)* And leave you here alone?

BASILIO: *(outside)* He will be with my lady. I shall go and find him.

THE COUNT: *(pointing to the armchair)* I'll just slip behind this.

SUSANNA: No! Don't hide there!

THE COUNT: Hush, and try to make him go away!
(The Count goes to hide behind the armchair. Susanna steps between him and the page boy. The Count pushes her gently to one side. As she draws back, the page slips around to the front of the chair and curls up in the seat. Susanna covers him with the dressing gown.)

SUSANNA: Good Lord, what's going on here?

Scene 7
THOSE BEFORE, AND BASILIO.

BASILIO: Susanna! Heaven be praised! Have you by chance seen his lordship?

SUSANNA: And what would his lordship be doing with me? Off with you!

BASILIO: A moment, please. Figaro is looking for him.

SUSANNA: (Good God!) Then he's looking for the one man who, after you, hates him most!

THE COUNT: (Now we'll see what he has to say for himself!)

BASILIO: I have never heard it said that he who loves the wife must also hate the husband. The Count loves you in ways . . .

SUSANNA: Sortite, vil ministro dell'altrui sfrenatezza: (*con risentimento*) io non ho d'uopo della vostra morale, del Conte, del suo amor ...

BASILIO: Non c'è alcun male. Ha ciascun i suoi gusti: io mi credea che preferir dovreste per amante, come fan tutte quante, un signor liberal, prudente e saggio a un giovinastro, a un paggio ...

SUSANNA: *(con ansietà)* A Cherubino!

BASILIO: A Cherubino! A Cherubin d'amore ch'oggi sul far del giorno passeggiava qui d'intorno, per entrar ...

SUSANNA: *(con forza)* Uom maligno, un'impostura è questa.

BASILIO: È un maligno con voi chi ha gli occhi in testa. E quella canzonetta? Ditemi in confidenza, io sono amico ed altrui nulla dico: è per voi, per madama ...

SUSANNA: *(mostra dello smarrimento.)* (Chi diavol gliel'ha detto?)

BASILIO: A proposito, figlia, istruitelo meglio: egli la guarda a tavola sì spesso e con tale immodestia, che se il Conte s'accorge ... che su tal punto, sapete, egli è una bestia.

SUSANNA: Scellerato! E perché andate voi tai menzogne spargendo?

BASILIO: Io? Che ingiustizia! Quel che compro io vendo. A quel che tutti dicono io non ci aggiungo un pelo.

IL CONTE: *(sortendo dal loco etc.)* Come, che dicon tutti?

SUSANNA: Out, you vile go-between for other men's lusts! Out! *(resentfully)* I have no time for your moralizing . . . or for the Count and his "love"!

BASILIO: I meant no offense! Each to his own taste. I would have thought you might prefer to take as a lover, like any other woman, a nobleman who is rich, sophisticated, discreet . . . instead of a mere youth, a page boy . . .

SUSANNA: *(anxiously)* Cherubino?

BASILIO: Yes, Cherubino, that lovestruck cherub who early today was prowling around here, trying to get in . . .

SUSANNA: *(vehemently)* You wicked man! That is a lie!

BASILIO: Is it wicked to have eyes in one's head? Take that little song of his . . . Tell me in confidence . . . as a friend . . . no one will know . . . Was it for you, or for her ladyship?

SUSANNA: *(her bewilderment showing)* (Who the devil told him about that?)

BASILIO: By the way, my child, it would be wise to warn the boy. He should watch himself at the dinner table . . . He looks at her ladyship so immodestly that if his lordship noticed . . . well, on that point he can be quite fierce.

SUSANNA: You snake! Why do you go about spreading such lies?

BASILIO: I? Such an injustice! I only sell what I buy, and add not a jot to what everyone is saying.

THE COUNT: *(emerging)* And what is everyone saying?

BASILIO: Oh bella!

SUSANNA: Oh cielo!

N° 7 Terzetto

IL CONTE: *(a Basilio)*
Cosa sento! Tosto andate
e scacciate il seduttor.

BASILIO:
In mal punto son qui giunto,
perdonate, o mio signor.

SUSANNA: *(quasi svenuta)*
Che ruina, me meschina,
son oppressa dal dolor.

IL CONTE, BASILIO: *(sostenendola)*
Ah, già svien la poverina!
Come, oddio, le batte il cor!

BASILIO: *(approssimandosi al sedile in atto di farla sedere)*
Pian pianin su questo seggio.

SUSANNA: Dove sono? *(rinviene)*
Cosa veggio!
(staccandosi da tutti e due)
Che insolenza, andate fuor.

BASILIO:
Siamo qui per aiutarvi,
è sicuro il vostro onor.

BASILIO: Oh my!

SUSANNA: Oh no!

Trio

THE COUNT: *(to Basilio)*
What is this I hear? Off with you!
Show that seducer the back door!

BASILIO:
I come at an inopportune time.
I humbly beg your pardon, my lord!

SUSANNA: *(nearly fainting)*
A catastrophe! I am ruined now!
How can I endure all this uproar?

THE COUNT AND BASILIO: *(supporting her)*
Ah, the poor creature is fainting!
Good Lord, can she take any more?

BASILIO: *(He helps her to the chair.)*
Gently, gently, let her rest here!

SUSANNA: *(coming to)*
Where am I? What is—oh dear!
(She pushes both away.)
How dare you! You—you predator!

BASILIO:
We are only helping you.
Your honor is as it was before.

IL CONTE: *(con malignità)*
Siamo qui per aiutarti,
non turbarti, o mio tesor.

BASILIO: *(al Conte)*
Ah, del paggio quel che ho detto
era solo un mio sospetto.

SUSANNA:
È un'insidia, una perfidia,
non credete all'impostor.

IL CONTE: Parta, parta, il damerino!

SUSANNA, BASILIO: Poverino!

IL CONTE: *(ironicamente)*
Poverino!
Ma da me sorpreso ancor.

SUSANNA: Come! Che!

BASILIO: Che! Come!

IL CONTE:
Da tua cugina
l'uscio ier trovai rinchiuso;
picchio, m'apre Barbarina
paurosa fuor dell'uso.
Io, dal muso insospettito,
guardo, cerco in ogni sito,
ed alzando pian pianino

THE COUNT: *(spitefully)*
We are only helping you.
Do not worry, my evermore!

BASILIO: *(to the Count)*
And what I said about that boy,
Well, that was mere speculation.

SUSANNA:
It's all jealousy and wickedness!
Don't believe his insinuations.

THE COUNT: Still, that young fop must go.

SUSANNA AND BASILIO: Poor boy!

THE COUNT: *(sarcastically)*
Poor boy!
There are more surprises in store!

SUSANNA: How?

BASILIO: Which?

THE COUNT:
At your cousin's house
The door yesterday was locked,
And, more timid than a tiny mouse,
Barbarina opened it when I knocked.
Suspicious of her flustered glance,
I decided to leave nothing to chance
And, lifting it as gently as I was able,

il tappeto al tavolino
vedo il paggio ...
(Imita il gesto colla vestaglia e scopre il paggio.)
(con sorpresa)
Ah! Cosa veggio!

SUSANNA: (con timore) Ah! Crude stelle!

BASILIO: (con riso) Ah! Meglio ancora!

IL CONTE:
Onestissima signora,
or capisco come va!

SUSANNA:
Accader non può di peggio;
giusti dei, che mai sarà!

BASILIO:
Così fan tutte le belle,
non c'è alcuna novità!

Recitativo

IL CONTE: Basilio, in traccia tosto di Figaro volate: *(Addita Cherubino che non si muove di loco.)* io vo' ch'ei veda ...

SUSANNA: *(con vivezza)* ... ed io che senta: andate.

IL CONTE: Restate: che baldanza! E quale scusa, se la colpa è evidente?

SUSANNA: Non ha d'uopo di scusa un'innocente.

I raised the cloth that draped a table.
And found a bird in the cage!
(He imitates his gesture with the dressing gown, and discovers Cherubino.)
(with surprise)
Why, once again, our little page!

SUSANNA: *(fearfully)* All is lost!

BASILIO: *(laughing)*
Ah, better still!

THE COUNT:
Ah, most virtuous of ladies!
At last I see how things are!

SUSANNA:
I am at the end of my wits!
Things have simply gone too far!

BASILIO:
Thus are they all, these women!
Each one of them a bête noire!

Recitative

THE COUNT: Basilio, go and find Figaro at once. *(pointing to Cherubino, who does not move)* I want him to see this . . .

SUSANNA: *(excitedly)* And I want him to hear me . . . Hurry!

THE COUNT: Wait. The brazenness! Pray, what excuse will you give him when your guilt is so obvious?

SUSANNA: An innocent woman has no need of excuses.

IL CONTE: Ma costui quando venne?

SUSANNA: Egli era meco quando voi qui giungeste, e mi chiedea d'impegnar la padrona a intercedergli grazia: il vostro arrivo in scompiglio lo pose ed allor in quel loco si nascose.

IL CONTE: Ma s'io stesso m'assisi quando in camera entrai!

CHERUBINO: *(timidamente)* Ed allor di dietro io mi celai.

IL CONTE: E quando io là mi posi?

CHERUBINO: Allor io pian mi volsi e qui m'ascosi.

IL CONTE: *(a Susanna)* Oh cielo! Dunque ha sentito quello ch'io ti dicea!

CHERUBINO: Feci per non sentir quanto potea.

IL CONTE: Oh perfidia!

BASILIO: Frenatevi: vien gente.

IL CONTE: *(lo tira giù del sedile.)* E voi restate qui, picciol serpente!

THE COUNT: And when did he come in here?

SUSANNA: He was with me when you arrived. He was begging me to have my mistress intercede for him. Your arrival threw him into a panic, and so he hid himself in there.

THE COUNT: But I sat down there myself when I came into this room.

CHERUBINO: *(timidly)* At that point I was behind it.

THE COUNT: And when I went round the back?

CHERUBINO: Then I slipped around and hid here.

THE COUNT: *(to Susanna)* Damnation! Then he heard everything I said to you?

CHERUBINO: I tried hard not to listen.

THE COUNT: Bloody hell!

BASILIO: Restrain yourselves! Someone is coming.

THE COUNT: *(dragging Cherubino out of the chair)* You stay right here, you little reptile!

Scena 8

FIGARO, CONTADINE E CONTADINI, I SUDDETI.

(Figaro con bianca veste in mano. Coro di contadine e di contadini vestiti di bianco che spargono fiori, raccolti in piccoli panieri, davanti il Conte e cantano il seguente.)

N° 8 Coro

CORO:
Giovani liete,
fiori spargete
davanti il nobile
nostro signor.
Il suo gran core
vi serba intatto
d'un più bel fiore
l'almo candor.

Recitativo

IL CONTE: *(a Figaro con sorpresa)* Cos'è questa commedia?

FIGARO: *(piano a Susanna)* (Eccoci in danza: secondami, cor mio.)

SUSANNA: (Non ci ho speranza.)

FIGARO: Signor, non isdegnate questo del nostro affetto meritato tributo: or che aboliste un diritto sì ingrato a chi ben ama ...

IL CONTE: Quel dritto or non v'è più; cosa si brama?

FIGARO: Della vostra saggezza il primo frutto oggi noi coglierem: le nostre nozze si son già stabilite; or a voi tocca costei, che un vostro dono illibata serbò, coprir di questa, simbolo d'onestà, candida vesta.

Scene 8

FIGARO, THE VILLAGERS, AND THE REST.

(Figaro enters, carrying a white veil, followed by villagers dressed in white and strewing flowers before the Count out of small baskets.)

Chorus

VILLAGERS:
Joyful youth,
Cast your blooms
Before our master,
Our noble lord.
His generous heart
Keeps honesty,
The fairer flower,
As its reward.

Recitative

THE COUNT: *(surprised, to Figaro)* What is this nonsense?

FIGARO: *(aside, to Susanna)* (Now the fun starts. Back me up, my pet.)

SUSANNA: (I'm not hopeful.)

FIGARO: My lord, do not disdain this humble token of our affection. It is well-deserved now that you have abolished a custom so hated by those in love . . .

THE COUNT: The custom has been abolished. What is it now?

FIGARO: Today we come to gather the first fruits of your generosity. Our wedding is already arranged. It falls to you to place this white veil on the head of this woman, as a symbol of the purity your deed has assured.

IL CONTE: (Diabolica astuzia! Ma fingere convien.) Son grato, amici, ad un senso sì onesto! Ma non merto per questo né tributi né lodi, e un dritto ingiusto ne' miei feudi abolendo a natura, al dover lor dritti io rendo.

TUTTI: Evviva, evviva, evviva!

SUSANNA: *(malignamente)* Che virtù!

FIGARO: Che giustizia!

IL CONTE: *(a Figaro e Susanna)* A voi prometto compier la cerimonia. Chiedo sol breve indugio: io voglio in faccia de' miei più fidi e con più ricca pompa rendervi appien felici. (Marcellina si trovi.) Andate, amici.
(I contadini ripetono il coro, spargono il resto de' fiori e partono.)

N° 9 Coro

CORO:
Giovani liete,
fiori spargete
davanti il nobile
nostro signor.
Il suo gran core
vi serba intatto
d'un più bel fiore
l'almo candor.

Recitativo

FIGARO: Evviva!

SUSANNA: Evviva!

BASILIO: Evviva!

THE COUNT: (The cunning devil! But I must pretend.) I am grateful, friends, for your honest feelings, but I deserve no tributes, no praise. It was an unjust custom, and abolishing it restores the natural order of things.

ALL: Three cheers!

SUSANNA: (maliciously) Such nobility!

FIGARO: Such justice!

THE COUNT: (to Figaro and Susanna) I promise to perform the ceremony, but ask for a moment's delay. I want to crown your happiness in the presence of all my loyal subjects and with all the proper pomp. (Marcellina must be found.) Leave me, friends. (The villagers repeat the chorus, scattering the remaining flowers.)

Chorus

VILLAGERS:
Joyful youth,
Cast your blooms
Before our master,
Our noble lord.
His generous heart
Keeps honesty,
The fairer flower,
As its reward.

Recitative

FIGARO: Hurrah!

SUSANNA: Hurrah!

BASILIO: Hur . . . rah.

FIGARO: *(a Cherubino)* E voi non applaudite?

SUSANNA: È afflitto—poveretto!—perché il padron lo scaccia dal castello.

FIGARO: Ah, in un giorno sì bello!

SUSANNA: In un giorno di nozze!

FIGARO: Quando ognuno v'ammira!

CHERUBINO: *(s'inginocchia.)* Perdono, mio signor ...

IL CONTE: Nol meritate.

SUSANNA: Egli è ancora fanciullo!

IL CONTE: Men di quel che tu credi.

CHERUBINO: È ver, mancai; ma dal mio labbro alfine ...

IL CONTE: *(lo alza.)* Ben ben, io vi perdono. Anzi farò di più: vacante è un posto d'uffizial nel reggimento mio; io scelgo voi, partite tosto, addio. *(Il Conte vuol partire, Susanna e Figaro l'arrestano.)*

SUSANNA, FIGARO: Ah, fin domani sol ...

IL CONTE: No, parta tosto.

CHERUBINO: *(con passione e sospirando)* A ubbidirvi, signor, son già disposto.

IL CONTE: Via, per l'ultima volta la Susanna abbracciate.
(Cherubino abbraccia la Susanna che rimane confusa.)
(Inaspettato è il colpo.)

FIGARO: *(to Cherubino)* You're not cheering?

SUSANNA: He is unhappy, poor boy, because the master is turning him out of the palace.

FIGARO: And on such a happy day!

SUSANNA: A wedding day!

FIGARO: Just when everyone has taken notice of you!

CHERUBINO: *(kneeling)* My lord, I beg your forgiveness . . .

THE COUNT: You do not deserve it.

SUSANNA: He is just a child.

THE COUNT: Less so than you think.

CHERUBINO: It is true I was wrong. But I will never reveal . . .

THE COUNT: *(bidding him rise)* Well, well, well. I forgive you. In fact, I will go further. There is a vacancy for an officer in my regiment, and I appoint you to fill it. You are to leave at once. Farewell. *(The Count starts to leave, but Susanna and Figaro stop him.)*

SUSANNA AND FIGARO: Oh, just until tomorrow . . .

THE COUNT: No, he leaves at once.

CHERUBINO: *(fervently, with a sigh)* I am prepared to obey your lordship's order.

THE COUNT: Come and kiss Susanna one last time.
(Cherubino kisses Susanna, who stands there confused.)
(That caught them by surprise.)

FIGARO: Ehi, capitano, a me pure la mano … *(piano a Cherubino)* (Io vo' parlarti pria che tu parta.) *(con finta gioia)* Addio, picciolo Cherubino: come cangia in un punto il tuo destino!

N° 10 Aria

FIGARO: *(a Cherubino)*
Non più andrai, farfallone amoroso,
notte e giorno d'intorno girando,
delle belle turbando il riposo,
narcisetto, adoncino d'amor.
Non più avrai questi bei pennacchini,
quel cappello leggero e galante,
quella chioma, quell'aria brillante,
quel vermiglio, donnesco color.
Tra guerrieri, poffarbacco!
Gran mustacchi, stretto sacco.
Schioppo in spalla, sciabla al fianco,
collo dritto, muso franco,
un gran casco o un gran turbante,
molto onor, poco contante,
ed invece del fandango
una marcia per il fango,
per montagne, per valloni,
con le nevi e i solleoni,
al concerto di tromboni,
di bombarde, di cannoni
che le palle in tutti i toni
all'orecchio fan fischiar.
Cherubino, alla vittoria,
alla gloria militar!
(Partono tutti alla militare.)

Fine dell'atto primo.

FIGARO: Hey, captain, give me your hand! *(aside to Cherubino)* (I must speak with you before you leave.) *(with pretended joy)* Goodbye, then, master Cherubino! How suddenly your fate has changed!

Aria

FIGARO: *(to Cherubino)*
No more now will you flutter by
To bother the ladies night and day,
You preening, lovesick butterfly!
Let those beauties enjoy their rest.
No more now the ruffles and frills,
That feathered hat, all flash and flare,
That wavy hair, that dashing air,
Those cheeks so pink and caressed.
Off to the wars, my young friend!
Long mustaches and socks to mend,
Musket to shoulder, saber in place,
Back like a ramrod, sneer on your face,
A helmet to wear, my fine legionnaire,
Honor to squander, not a cent to spare.
No fancy balls and minuets,
Now it's all marching and bayonets.
Mountains, marshes, one by one,
Chilled by snow, scorched by sun.
How shrill the bugle call,
How loud the cannonball,
Blunderbuss and caterwaul,
All muddy, bitter, and gory.
On to victory, Cherubino!
Here's to military glory!
(They all leave to the strains of a march.)

End of Act I.

Atto secondo

Camera ricca con alcova e tre porte.

Scena 1

N° 11 Cavatina

LA CONTESSA:
Porgi, amor, qualche ristoro
al mio duolo, a' miei sospir:
o mi rendi il mio tesoro
o mi lascia almen morir.

Recitativo

LA CONTESSA: Vieni, cara Susanna, finiscimi l'istoria.

SUSANNA: *(sorte dal gabinetto)* È già finita.

LA CONTESSA: Dunque volle sedurti?

SUSANNA: Oh, il signor Conte non fa tai complimenti colle donne mie pari: egli venne a contratto di danari.

LA CONTESSA: Ah, il crudel più non m'ama!

── :· Act II ·: ──

A richly appointed room with an alcove and three doors.

Scene 1

Cavatina

THE COUNTESS:
Grant me, Love, at last an end
To my sorrow, oh hear my sigh.
Bring back the light of my life,
Or have mercy and let me die!

Recitative

THE COUNTESS: Come then, my dear Susanna, finish your story.

SUSANNA: *(entering from the dressing room)* There is no more to tell.

THE COUNTESS: So he tried to seduce you?

SUSANNA: Oh, his lordship does not offer such compliments to a woman of my station. He came to offer me money.

THE COUNTESS: Ah, that cruel man no longer loves me!

SUSANNA: E come poi è geloso di voi?

LA CONTESSA: Come lo sono i moderni mariti: per sistema infedeli, per genio capricciosi e per orgoglio poi tutti gelosi. Ma se Figaro l'ama ... ei sol potria ...

FIGARO: *(cantando entro la scena)* La la la la la la la la la.

SUSANNA: Eccolo: vieni, amico. Madama impaziente ...

FIGARO: *(con ilare disinvoltura)* A voi non tocca stare in pena per questo. Alfin di che si tratta? Al signor Conte piace la sposa mia, indi secretamente recuperar vorria il diritto feudale. Possibile è la cosa, e naturale.

LA CONTESSA: Possibil!

SUSANNA: Natural!

FIGARO: Naturalissima. E se Susanna vuol possibilissima.

SUSANNA: Finiscila una volta.

FIGARO: Ho già finito. Quindi prese il partito di sceglier me corriero e la Susanna consigliera secreta d'ambasciata. E perch'ella ostinata ognor rifiuta il diploma d'onor ch'ei le destina, minaccia di protegger Marcellina. Questo è tutto l'affare.

SUSANNA: Ed hai coraggio di trattar scherzando un negozio sì serio?

FIGARO: Non vi basta che scherzando io ci pensi? Ecco il progetto: per Basilio un biglietto io gli fo capitar che l'avvertisca di

SUSANNA: Then why is he so jealous of you?

THE COUNTESS: That is the way of husbands nowadays—unfaithful on principle, fickle by nature, and jealous out of pride. But if Figaro loves you . . . he alone might . . .

FIGARO: *(singing offstage)* La la la . . .

SUSANNA: And here he is! Come in here, Madame is impatient.

FIGARO: *(with a cheerful nonchalance)* No need to be upset by any of this. After all, what does it amount to? The Count is attracted to my bride, and secretly wants to restore his feudal right. That all seems perfectly natural, and possible.

THE COUNTESS: Possible!

SUSANNA: Natural!

FIGARO: Very natural! And, if Susanna gives in, *very* possible.

SUSANNA: Have you finished?

FIGARO: Finished. But that's why he decided to take me to the embassy with him as his courier, and Susanna as his "private secretary." Because she has been so stubborn and refused this "honorable position," he is now threatening to advance Marcellina's cause. That's the whole story.

SUSANNA: And you have the nerve to make light of such a serious matter?

FIGARO: Aren't you glad I can joke about it? Here's my plan. I'll see that he gets a letter, passed on by Basilio, warning him

certo appuntamento *(alla Contessa)* che per l'ora del ballo a un amante voi deste ...

LA CONTESSA: Oh ciel! Che sento! Ad un uom sì geloso! ...

FIGARO: Ancora meglio. Così potrem più presto imbarazzarlo, confonderlo, imbrogliarlo, rovesciargli i progetti, empierlo di sospetti e porgli in testa che la moderna festa ch'ei di fare a me tenta altri a lui faccia; onde qua perda il tempo, ivi la traccia. Così, quasi ex abrupto e senza ch'abbia fatto per frastornarci alcun disegno, vien l'ora delle nozze, *(segnando la Contessa)* e in faccia a lei non fia ch'osi d'opporsi ai voti miei.

SUSANNA: È ver, ma in di lui vece s'opporrà Marcellina.

FIGARO: Aspetta: al Conte farai subito dir che verso sera attendati in giardino; il picciol Cherubino, per mio consiglio non ancora partito, da femmina vestito faremo che in tua vece ivi sen vada. Questa è l'unica strada onde monsù sorpreso da madama sia costretto a far poi quel che si brama.

LA CONTESSA: *(a Susanna)* Che ti par?

SUSANNA: Non c'è mal.

LA CONTESSA: Nel nostro caso ...

SUSANNA: Quand'egli è persuaso ... E dove è il tempo?

FIGARO: Ito è il Conte alla caccia e per qualch'ora non sarà di ritorno: *(sempre in atto di partire)* io vado e tosto Cherubino vi mando; lascio a voi la cura di vestirlo.

of a rendezvous *(to the Countess)* you have arranged with a lover during the ball.

THE COUNTESS: Heavens! What are you saying? Give *that* to a jealous man . . . ?

FIGARO: So much the better. It makes it that much easier to embarrass him, confuse him, entangle him, upset his plans, plague him with suspicions, and make him realize that two can play at this game. He'll waste the whole day looking for the culprit and not finding him, and meanwhile, before he can interfere, we'll have gotten married, *(gesturing to the Countess)* and in your presence. He will not dare oppose it.

SUSANNA: True enough, but instead Marcellina will object.

FIGARO: Wait. If your ladyship lets the Count know at once that towards evening you will be waiting for him in the garden, I'll fetch young Cherubino, whom I have advised not to leave just yet, and have him go in your place . . . dressed as a woman. This is the only way for his lordship to be caught by my lady, and made to do what we wish.

THE COUNTESS: *(to Susanna)* What do you think?

SUSANNA: Not bad.

THE COUNTESS: Given the circumstances . . .

SUSANNA: When he is convinced . . . But is there enough time?

FIGARO: The Count is out hunting and will be gone for some time. *(as he departs)* I'll go collar Cherubino. I'll leave it to you to dress him up.

LA CONTESSA: E poi? ...

FIGARO: E poi ... Se vuol ballare, signor Contino, il chitarrino le suonerò.
(Parte.)

Scena 2

LA CONTESSA, SUSANNA, POI CHERUBINO.

Recitativo

LA CONTESSA: Quanto duolmi, Susanna, che questo giovinotto abbia del Conte le stravaganze udite! Ah, tu non sai! ... Ma per qual causa mai da me stessa ei non venne? ... Dov'è la canzonetta?

SUSANNA: Eccola: appunto facciam che ce la canti. Zitto, vien gente. È desso: avanti, avanti, signor uffiziale.

CHERUBINO: Ah, non chiamarmi con nome sì fatale! Ei mi rammenta che abbandonar degg'io comare tanto buona ...

SUSANNA: ... e tanto bella!

CHERUBINO: *(sospirando)* Ah sì ... certo ...

SUSANNA: *(imitandolo)* Ah sì ... certo ... ipocritone! Via, presto, la canzone che stamane a me deste a madama cantate.

LA CONTESSA: Chi n'è l'autor?

SUSANNA: *(additando Cherubino)* Guardate, egli ha due braccia di rossor sulla faccia.

LA CONTESSA: Prendi la mia chitarra e l'accompagna.

THE COUNTESS: And then?

FIGARO: And then . . . "If you want to dance, my noble lord, / It is I who will call the tune . . ."
(He leaves.)

Scene 2

THE COUNTESS, SUSANNA, AND THEN CHERUBINO.

Recitative

THE COUNTESS: Susanna, it grieves me that this boy should have overheard the Count's indiscretions. Ah, if only you knew . . . Why did he not come straight to me? Where is his song?

SUSANNA: Here it is. We can make him sing it. Hush, someone's coming! It's him! Come in, come in, gallant officer!

CHERUBINO: Oh don't call me by that hateful title! It reminds me that I must leave my godmother, who is so good to me . . .

SUSANNA: And so beautiful!

CHERUBINO: *(sighing)* Oh, yes . . . she is . . .

SUSANNA: *(imitating him)* Oh, yes . . . she is . . . You hypocrite! Quickly now, sing the song you gave me this morning, the one for my lady.

THE COUNTESS: And who wrote this song?

SUSANNA: *(pointing at Cherubino)* Look, he's gone all red in the face!

THE COUNTESS: Fetch my guitar and accompany him.

CHERUBINO: Io sono sì tremante … ma se madama vuole …

SUSANNA: Lo vuole, sì, lo vuol … Manco parole.

N° 12 Arietta

(La Susanna fa il ritornello sul chitarrino.)

CHERUBINO:
Voi che sapete
che cosa è amor,
donne, vedete
s'io l'ho nel cor.
Quello ch'io provo
vi ridirò,
è per me nuovo,
capir nol so.
Sento un affetto
pien di desir,
ch'ora è diletto,
ch'ora è martir.
Gelo e poi sento
l'alma avvampar,
e in un momento
torno a gelar.
Ricerco un bene
fuori di me,
non so chi 'l tiene,
non so cos'è.
Sospiro e gemo
senza voler,
palpito e tremo
senza saper.
Non trovo pace
notte né dì,
ma pur mi piace
languir così.

CHERUBINO: I . . . I . . . am trembling . . . But if my lady wishes . . .

SUSANNA: She wishes, of course she *wishes* . . . No more stalling.

Aria

(Susanna plays the introduction on the guitar.)

CHERUBINO:

Dear ladies, you know
The part love can play.
Is it to love that I owe
My heart led astray?
All that I feel inside,
The tumult and change,
I long to confide.
It is thrilling and strange.
First, I'm all fright,
Then, walking on air.
First, sheer delight.
Then, mere despair.
One moment, ice,
One moment, fire.
In such a paradise
I am bound to expire.
I need only to find
A treasure, I swear,
Beyond my own mind.
Oh but how? And where?
Day in and day out
I groan and I sigh.
I mumble and pout
Without knowing why.
Night after night
No rest to be found.
Why does anguish excite
And joy so confound?

Voi che sapete
che cosa è amor,
donne, vedete
s'io l'ho nel cor.

Recitativo

LA CONTESSA: Bravo! Che bella voce! Io non sapea che cantaste sì bene.

SUSANNA: Oh, in verità egli fa tutto ben quello ch'ei fa. Presto, a noi, bel soldato: Figaro v'informò …

CHERUBINO: Tutto mi disse.

SUSANNA: Lasciatemi veder. Andrà benissimo: *(Si misura con Cherubino.)* siam d'uguale statura … *(Gli cava il manto.)* Giù quel manto.

LA CONTESSA: Che fai?

SUSANNA: Niente paura.

LA CONTESSA: E se qualcuno entrasse?

SUSANNA: Entri, che mal facciamo? *(Chiude la porta.)* La porta chiuderò. Ma come poi acconciargli i capelli?

LA CONTESSA: Una mia cuffia prendi nel gabinetto. Presto … *(Susanna va nel gabinetto a pigliar una cuffia. Cherubino si accosta alla Contessa e le lascia veder la patente che terrà in petto: la Contessa la prende, la apre e vede che manca il sigillo.)* Che carta è quella?

Dear ladies, you know
The part love can play.
Is it to love that I owe
My heart led astray?

Recitative

THE COUNTESS: Bravo! What a lovely voice! I had no idea you sang so well.

SUSANNA: Indeed, everything he does he does well. Come along now, soldier boy. Figaro has told you . . .

CHERUBINO: He told me everything.

SUSANNA: Let me see, then. This will do nicely. *(measuring Cherubino)* We are the same height . . . *(She takes off his coat.)* Off with your jacket!

THE COUNTESS: What are you doing?

SUSANNA: Nothing to worry about.

THE COUNTESS: But if someone should come in . . .

SUSANNA: Let them. What are we doing wrong? *(She closes the door.)* Still, I'll just lock this door. Now, what can I do about his hair?

THE COUNTESS: Take one of my nightcaps from the dressing room. Quickly now! *(As Susanna goes to the dressing room for the cap, Cherubino approaches the Countess and shows her the commission he has in his breast pocket. The Countess takes it, opens it, and notices that the seal is missing.)* What is this paper?

CHERUBINO: La patente.

LA CONTESSA: Che sollecita gente!

CHERUBINO: L'ebbi or or da Basilio.

LA CONTESSA: Dalla fretta obliato hanno il sigillo.

SUSANNA: *(entra.)* Il sigillo di che?

LA CONTESSA: Della patente.

SUSANNA: Cospetto! Che premura! Ecco la cuffia.

LA CONTESSA: Spicciati ... Va bene. Miserabili noi, se il Conte viene.

N° 13 Aria

SUSANNA: *(prende Cherubino e se lo fa inginocchiare davanti poco discosto dalla Contessa che siede)*
Venite, inginocchiatevi:
restate fermo lì.
(Lo pettina da un lato, poi lo prende pel mento e lo volge a suo piacere.)
Pian piano, or via, giratevi:
bravo, va ben così.
(Cherubino, mentre Susanna lo sta acconciando, guarda la Contessa teneramente.)
La faccia ora volgetemi:
olà, quegli occhi a me.
(Seguita ad acconciarlo e a porgli la cuffia.)
Drittissimo: guardatemi ...
Madama qui non è.
Più alto quel colletto ...
quel ciglio un po' più basso ...
le mani sotto il petto ...

CHERUBINO: My commission.

THE COUNTESS: These people are in a hurry!

CHERUBINO: I just received it from Basilio.

THE COUNTESS: In their haste, they have forgotten the seal.

SUSANNA: *(returning)* The seal on what?

THE COUNTESS: On his commission.

SUSANNA: My, my, what haste! Here is the cap.

THE COUNTESS: Hurry now! That's right! The worse for us if the Count should come in now!

Aria

SUSANNA: *(making Cherubino kneel down in front of her, not far from where the Countess is sitting)*
Come and kneel down here.
And mind you stay still.
(She takes him by the chin and turns his head this way and that.)
Slowly now, turn this way.
Yes, yes . . . ah, what skill!
(While Susanna is fussing with his hair, Cherubino looks tenderly at the Countess.)
Now turn the other way.
Keep your eyes on me!
(She continues arranging his hair and hands him the cap.)
Straight ahead! Look right here!
Not at her ladyship's knee!
Your collar a bit higher,
Your glance a little lower.
Hands folded in front . . .

Vedremo poscia il passo
quando sarete in piè.
(piano alla Contessa)
Mirate il bricconcello!
Mirate quanto è bello!
Che furba guardatura!
Che vezzo, che figura!
Se l'amano le femmine
han certo il lor perché.

Recitativo

LA CONTESSA: Quante buffonerie!

SUSANNA: Ma se ne sono io medesma gelosa … *(Prende pel mento Cherubino.)* Ehi, serpentello, volete tralasciar d'esser sì bello?

LA CONTESSA: Finiam le ragazzate: or quelle maniche oltre il gomito gli alza onde più agiatamente l'abito gli si adatti.

SUSANNA: *(eseguisce etc.)* Ecco.

LA CONTESSA: Più indietro … Così. *(scoprendo un nastro onde ha fasciato il braccio)* Che nastro è quello?

SUSANNA: È quel ch'esso involommi.

LA CONTESSA: E questo sangue?

CHERUBINO: Quel sangue … io non so come … poco pria sdrucciolando … in un sasso … la pelle io mi graffiai … e la piaga col nastro io mi fasciai.

SUSANNA: Mostrate: non è mal. Cospetto! Ha il braccio più candido del mio! Qualche ragazza …

Your pace a little slower
When you cross the room.
(aside, to the Countess)
Just look at that little rake!
A fine picture he'll make!
The sly look on his face,
Such a peacock, such grace!
It would be no surprise
If the women all swoon!

Recitative

THE COUNTESS: Enough of this nonsense!

SUSANNA: Enough to make me jealous myself! *(She takes Cherubino by the chin.)* You little monkey, how dare you be so handsome?

THE COUNTESS: No more of this silliness! Tuck those sleeves above the elbow and the dress will fit better.

SUSANNA: *(doing as she says)* There!

THE COUNTESS: Up a little more. Like this . . . *(discovering a ribbon around his arm)* What is this ribbon . . . ?

SUSANNA: It is the one he stole from me!

THE COUNTESS: And this blood?

CHERUBINO: Blood . . . I had no idea . . . I slipped . . . scraped myself on a rock, yes, and bandaged the cut with the ribbon.

SUSANNA: Show me. It's nothing. Why, his arm is whiter than mine! Like a girl's . . .

LA CONTESSA: E segui a far la pazza? Va' nel mio gabinetto e prendi un poco d'inglese taffettà ch'è sullo scrigno. *(Susanna parte in fretta. La Contessa guarda un poco il suo nastro: Cherubino inginocchiato la osserva attentamente.)* In quanto al nastro ... inver ... per il colore mi spiacea di privarmene ...

SUSANNA: *(entra e le dà il taffettà e le forbici.)* Tenete. E da legargli il braccio?

LA CONTESSA: Un altro nastro prendi insiem col mio vestito. *(Susanna parte per la porta ch'è in fondo e porta seco il mantello di Cherubino.)*

CHERUBINO: Ah, più presto m'avria quello guarito!

LA CONTESSA: Perché? Questo è migliore!

CHERUBINO: Allorché un nastro ... legò la chioma ... ovver toccò la pelle ... d'oggetto ...

LA CONTESSA: *(interrompendolo)* ... forestiero è buon per le ferite! Non è vero? Guardate qualità ch'io non sapea!

CHERUBINO: Madama scherza, ed io frattanto parto.

LA CONTESSA: Poverin! Che sventura!

CHERUBINO: Oh me infelice!

LA CONTESSA: *(con affanno e commozione)* Or piange ...

CHERUBINO: Oh ciel! Perché morir non lice! Forse vicino all'ultimo momento ... questa bocca oseria ...

THE COUNTESS: No end to your foolishness? Go to my dressing room and bring a piece of that English taffeta from on top of my jewel box. *(Susanna rushes off. The Countess gazes at the ribbon. Cherubino, kneeling, stares at her intently.)* As for this ribbon . . . I think . . . this shade . . . I would be loath to part with it . . .

SUSANNA: *(returning with the taffeta and scissors)* Hold this. How can I tie it to his arm?

THE COUNTESS: Take another ribbon when you bring my dress. *(Susanna leaves by the door at the back, taking Cherubino's cloak with her.)*

CHERUBINO: The other one would have healed my wound faster.

THE COUNTESS: Why is that? A new one is better.

CHERUBINO: But when a ribbon has bound the hair or touched the skin of a . . .

THE COUNTESS: *(interrupting him)* . . . of a stranger, it has the power to heal, no? A power I had never heard of.

CHERUBINO: My lady mocks, even as I am on the point of leaving.

THE COUNTESS: Poor boy, what a calamity!

CHERUBINO: I am so miserable!

THE COUNTESS: *(moved and distressed)* But you are weeping . . .

CHERUBINO: Oh God! If only I could die! Maybe with my last breath I could tell you . . .

LA CONTESSA: *(gli asciuga gli occhi col fazzoletto)* Siate saggio: cos'è questa follia? ... *(Si sente picchiare alla porta.)* Chi picchia alla mia porta?

IL CONTE: *(fuori della porta)* Perché chiusa?

LA CONTESSA: Il mio sposo: oh dei! Son morta! Voi qui senza mantello! In quello stato! Un ricevuto foglio ... la sua gran gelosia!

IL CONTE: *(con più forza)* Cosa indugiate?

LA CONTESSA: *(confusa)* Son sola ... anzi ... son sola ...

IL CONTE: E a chi parlate?

LA CONTESSA: A voi ... certo ... a voi stesso ...

CHERUBINO: Dopo quel ch'è successo, il suo furore ... non trovo altro consiglio!
(Entra nel gabinetto. Chiude: la Contessa prende la chiave.)

LA CONTESSA: Ah, mi difenda il cielo in tal periglio!

Scena 3
LA CONTESSA E IL CONTE DA CACCIATORE.

Recitativo

IL CONTE: Che novità! Non fu mai vostra usanza di rinchiudervi in stanza!

LA CONTESSA: È ver, ma io ... io stava qui mettendo ...

THE COUNTESS: *(drying his eyes with her handkerchief)* Now be sensible. You have no idea what you are saying. *(a knock at the door)* Who can be knocking at the door?

THE COUNT: *(on the other side of the door)* Why is this locked?

THE COUNTESS: My husband! Good Lord! I am done for! You here, and without your coat! Dressed like this! He will have read the letter! Oh, and he can be so jealous! . . .

THE COUNT: *(louder)* Why the delay?

THE COUNTESS: *(confused)* I am alone. All alone.

THE COUNT: But you were speaking with someone!

THE COUNTESS: To you, of course . . . you only.

CHERUBINO: After what's happened, he will be furious . . . I don't know what to do!
(He runs into the dressing room and locks the door. The Countess takes the key.)

THE COUNTESS: Heaven help me now!

Scene 3

THE COUNTESS AND THE COUNT DRESSED
IN HIS HUNTING GEAR.

Recitative

THE COUNT: What's the idea! You never used to lock yourself in your room!

THE COUNTESS: I know, but I . . . I was trying . . .

IL CONTE: Via, mettendo ...

LA CONTESSA: Certe robe ... Era meco la Susanna ... che in sua camera è andata.

IL CONTE: Ad ogni modo voi non siete tranquilla. Guardate questo foglio.

LA CONTESSA: (Numi! È il foglio che Figaro gli scrisse! ...)
(Cherubino fa cadere un tavolino e una sedia in gabinetto con molto strepito.)

IL CONTE: Cos'è codesto strepito? In gabinetto qualche cosa è caduto.

LA CONTESSA: Io non intesi niente.

IL CONTE: Convien che abbiate i gran pensieri in mente.

LA CONTESSA: Di che?

IL CONTE: Là v'è qualcuno.

LA CONTESSA: Chi volete che sia?

IL CONTE: Lo chiedo a voi. Io vengo in questo punto.

LA CONTESSA: Ah sì, Susanna ... appunto ...

IL CONTE: Che passò, mi diceste, alla sua stanza! ...

LA CONTESSA: Alla sua stanza o qui, non vidi bene ...

IL CONTE: Susanna! E donde viene che siete sì turbata?

THE COUNT: Go on. "Trying . . ."

THE COUNTESS: . . . trying on some clothes . . . Susanna was with me . . . but now she has gone to her room.

THE COUNT: In any case, you seem distracted. Look at this letter.

THE COUNTESS: (Oh dear! The letter Figaro wrote!)
(Cherubino knocks over a table and chair in the dressing room, with much racket.)

THE COUNT: What's that noise? Something's fallen over in your dressing room.

THE COUNTESS: I heard nothing.

THE COUNT: You must have a great deal else on your mind.

THE COUNTESS: Such as?

THE COUNT: Someone is in there.

THE COUNTESS: And who might that be?

THE COUNT: I am asking you. I only just came in.

THE COUNTESS: Oh yes, Susanna, of course.

THE COUNT: Who has gone, you just told me, to her room.

THE COUNTESS: To her room, or to that one, I failed to notice.

THE COUNT: But if it is Susanna, then why are you so upset?

LA CONTESSA: *(con un risolino sforzato)* Per la mia cameriera?

IL CONTE: Io non so nulla, ma turbata senz'altro.

LA CONTESSA: Ah, questa serva più che non turba me turba voi stesso.

IL CONTE: È vero, è vero: e lo vedrete adesso.
(La Susanna entra per la porta ond'è uscita e si ferma vedendo il Conte che dalla porta del gabinetto sta favellando.)

LA CONTESSA, SUSANNA ED IL CONTE.

N° 14 *Terzetto*

IL CONTE:
Susanna, or via, sortite,
sortite, io così vo'.

LA CONTESSA: *(al Conte affannata)*
Fermatevi … sentite …
sortire ella non può.

SUSANNA:
Cos'è codesta lite?
Il paggio dove andò?

IL CONTE: E chi vietarlo or osa?

LA CONTESSA:
Lo vieta l'onestà:
un abito da sposa
provando ella si sta.

THE COUNTESS: *(with a forced smile)* With my maid?

THE COUNT: I wouldn't know about that, but you are upset.

THE COUNTESS: That maid seems to be upsetting *you* more than me.

THE COUNT: Perfectly true, and now you'll see why.
(Susanna enters by the door through which she left, and stops when she sees the Count, who is speaking to the dressing room door.)

THE COUNTESS, SUSANNA, AND THE COUNT.

Trio

THE COUNT:
Susanna, come out of there,
Come out here right away!

THE COUNTESS: *(to the Count, in distress)*
Please stop . . . listen to me . . .
She cannot do as you say.

SUSANNA:
Is this quarrel about me?
Where is the page boy, pray?

THE COUNT: Who dares contradict me, and why?

THE COUNTESS:
Mere decency, I confess.
She is in there to try
On her wedding dress.

IL CONTE:
Chiarissima è la cosa:
l'amante qui sarà.

LA CONTESSA:
Bruttissima è la cosa:
chi sa cosa sarà?

SUSANNA:
Capisco qualche cosa:
veggiamo come va.

IL CONTE:
Dunque, parlate almeno,
Susanna, se qui siete . . .

LA CONTESSA:
Nemmen, nemmen, nemmeno;
io v'ordino: tacete.
(Susanna si nasconde entro l'alcova.)

IL CONTE, LA CONTESSA:
Consorte mia/mio, giudizio:
un scandalo, un disordine
schiviam per carità.

SUSANNA:
Oh cielo! Un precipizio,
un scandalo, un disordine
qui certo nascerà.

THE COUNT:
It is as plain as day.
There is a lover in there.

THE COUNTESS:
What more can I say?
Do you want me to swear?

SUSANNA:
Things are in disarray!
I should be elsewhere!

THE COUNT:
Susanna, you think you're clever?
I will not stand such cheek!

THE COUNTESS:
Never, never, never, never!
I command you not to speak!
(*Susanna hides herself in the alcove.*)

THE COUNT AND THE COUNTESS:
My lord (My lady), I am sure you see
This shambles, this scandal
Must come to an end.

SUSANNA:
Heavens! A catastrophe!
A shambles! A scandal!
Where will it all end?

Recitativo

IL CONTE: Dunque voi non aprite?

LA CONTESSA: E perché deggio le mie camere aprir?

IL CONTE: Ebben, lasciate. L'aprirem senza chiavi: ehi, gente ...

LA CONTESSA: Come? Porreste a repentaglio d'una dama l'onore?

IL CONTE: È vero, io sbaglio: posso senza rumore, senza scandalo alcun di nostra gente andar io stesso a prender l'occorrente. Attendete pur qui ... ma perché in tutto sia il mio dubbio distrutto anco le porte io prima chiuderò. *(Chiude a chiave la porta che conduce alle stanze delle cameriere.)*

LA CONTESSA: *(a parte)* Che imprudenza!

IL CONTE: Voi la condiscendenza di venir meco avrete. *(con affettata ilarità)* Madama, eccovi il braccio, andiamo.

LA CONTESSA: *(con ribrezzo)* Andiamo.

IL CONTE: *(accenna il gabinetto)* Susanna starà qui finché torniamo. *(Partono.)*

Recitative

THE COUNT: So, you will not open this door?

THE COUNTESS: Must I be made to open my own room?

THE COUNT: Very well then, do as you please. We'll open it without a key . . . You there!

THE COUNTESS: What! You would dare jeopardize a lady's honor?

THE COUNT: Ah, my mistake! I can do it without a fuss, without shocking the servants. I shall go and bring the tools for the job myself. You wait here . . . But, to quiet my own suspicions, I shall first lock the other doors. *(He locks the door leading to the servants' quarters.)*

THE COUNTESS: *(aside)* The impudence!

THE COUNT: You will have the goodness to accompany me. *(with assumed amusement)* Madame, my arm. Come.

THE COUNTESS: *(with disdain)* Very well.

THE COUNT: *(pointing to the dressing room)* Susanna will stay here until we return.
(They leave.)

Scena 4

SUSANNA E CHERUBINO.

N° 15 Duettino

SUSANNA: *(uscendo dall'alcova in fretta alla porta del gabinetto)*
Aprite, presto, aprite …
Aprite: è la Susanna.
Sortite, via, sortite …
andate via di qua.
(Cherubino esce dal gabinetto.)

CHERUBINO: *(confuso e senza fiato)*
Ohimè, che scena orribile!
(accostandosi or ad una or ad un'altra porta)
Che gran fatalità!

SUSANNA:
Partite, non tardate …
(accostandosi or ad una or ad un'altra porta)
Di qua, di qua, di là, di là.

SUSANNA, CHERUBINO:
Le porte son serrate …
Che mai, che mai sarà?

CHERUBINO: *(cercando di sciogliersi d'essa)* Qui perdersi non giova.

SUSANNA: V'uccide se vi trova.

CHERUBINO:
M'uccide se mi trova.
(affacciandosi alla finestra che mette in giardino)
Veggiamo un po' qui fuori …
(facendo moto di saltar giù)
Dà proprio nel giardino.

Scene 4

SUSANNA AND CHERUBINO.

Duet

SUSANNA: *(hurrying out of the alcove and goes to the dressing room door)*
Quickly now, open the door!
Open! It's Susanna!
Not a moment more!
I'll get you out of here!
(Cherubino comes out of the dressing room.)

CHERUBINO: *(confused and breathless)*
Oh Lord, I cannot move!
(They try first one door and then the other.)
I am paralyzed with fear!

SUSANNA:
Don't delay, get out of here . . .
(Again they try first one door and then the other.)
Not here . . . not there!

SUSANNA AND CHERUBINO:
The doors are all locked!
We'll never get out of here!

CHERUBINO: *(trying to open them)* No point in losing my head!

SUSANNA: If he finds you, you are dead!

CHERUBINO:
If he finds me, I am dead!
(going to the window, which faces the garden)
Let me just peek outside.
(He makes as if to jump.)
It leads to the garden.

SUSANNA: *(trattenendolo)*
Fermate, Cherubino!
Fermate, per pietà!

CHERUBINO: *(tornando a guardare)*
Un vaso o due di fiori ...
più mal non avverrà.

SUSANNA: *(trattenendolo sempre)*
Tropp'alto per un salto.

CHERUBINO:
Lasciami: *(Si scioglie da Susanna.)*
pria di nuocerle
nel foco volerei.
Abbraccio te per lei.
Addio: *(Salta fuori.)*
così si fa.

SUSANNA:
Ei va a perire, oh dei!
Fermate, per pietà!
(Susanna emette un alto grido, siede un momento, poi va al balcone.)

Recitativo

SUSANNA:
Oh, guarda il demonietto! Come fugge! È già un miglio lontano.
Ma non perdiamci invano: entriam in gabinetto. Venga poi lo
smargiasso: io qui l'aspetto.
(Entra in gabinetto e si chiude dietro la porta.)

SUSANNA: *(stopping him)*
Stop, Cherubino!
Don't, for heaven's sake!

CHERUBINO: *(turning to look down)*
A pot or two of flowers, a rake . . .

SUSANNA: *(holding on to him)*
It is too high for you to jump.
Don't, for heaven's sake!

CHERUBINO:
Let me go! *(freeing himself)*
I would leap into the fire
Rather than harm her!
Give her this embrace!
Farewell! *(He jumps.)*
All for her sake!

SUSANNA:
He'll kill himself! It's dire!
Stop, for heaven's sake!
(She shrieks, sits for a moment, then runs to the window.)

Recitative

SUSANNA: Look at the little devil, look at him run! He's already a mile away! No time to lose, though. Back to the dressing room! I will be waiting for that bully when he returns.
(She goes into the dressing room and locks the door behind her.)

Scena 5

LA CONTESSA, IL CONTE CON MARTELLO E TENAGLIA IN
MANO; AL SUO ARRIVO ESAMINA TUTTE LE PORTE ETC.

Recitativo

IL CONTE:
Tutto è come il lasciai: volete dunque aprir voi stessa, *(in atto di aprir a forza la porta)* o deggio ...

LA CONTESSA: Ahimè, fermate; e ascoltatemi un poco. *(Il Conte getta il martello e la tenaglia sopra una sedia.)* Mi credete capace di mancar al dover?

IL CONTE: Come vi piace. Entro quel gabinetto chi v'è chiuso vedrò.

LA CONTESSA: *(timida e tremante)* Sì, lo vedrete ... ma uditemi tranquillo.

IL CONTE: *(alterato)* Non è dunque Susanna?

LA CONTESSA: *(come sopra)* No, ma invece è un oggetto che ragion di sospetto non vi deve lasciar: per questa sera ... una burla innocente ... di far si disponeva ... ed io vi giuro ... che l'onor ... l'onestà ...

IL CONTE: Chi è dunque? Dite ... *(più alterato)* L'ucciderò.

LA CONTESSA: Sentite ... Ah, non ho cor!

IL CONTE: Parlate.

LA CONTESSA: È un fanciullo ...

Scene 5

THE COUNTESS AND THE COUNT WITH A HAMMER AND
PLIERS. ON HIS ARRIVAL, HE TRIES EVERY DOOR.

Recitative

THE COUNT: Everything is as I left it. Now, will you open this
door, *(He is on the point of forcing it open.)* or must I?

THE COUNTESS: Stop this, please! Listen to me for a moment.
(The Count puts the tools on a chair.) Do you think me capable of
failing in my duty?

THE COUNT: As you please. But I intend to see who is locked
in that room.

THE COUNTESS: *(fearful and trembling)* And see you will, but listen
to me calmly.

THE COUNT: *(angrily)* So it is *not* Susanna!

THE COUNTESS: *(as above)* No, but it is a person whom you would
have no reason to be suspicious of. I was preparing a harmless
. . . entertainment for later this evening . . . I swear on my honor
. . . on my virtue . . .

THE COUNT: Who is it then? Tell me . . . *(even angrier)* I'll kill him!

THE COUNTESS: Listen . . . Ah, my courage fails . . .

THE COUNT: Speak!

THE COUNTESS: He is a child . . .

THE COUNT: *(as above)* A child?

IL CONTE: *(come sopra)* Un fanciul! ...

LA CONTESSA: Sì ... Cherubino ...

IL CONTE: *(da sè)* (E mi farà il destino ritrovar questo paggio in ogni loco!) *(forte)* Come? Non è partito? Scellerati! Ecco i dubbi spiegati: ecco l'imbroglio, ecco il raggiro onde m'avverte il foglio.

Scena 6
IL CONTE, LA CONTESSA E POI SUSANNA IN GABINETTO.

N° 16 Finale
IL CONTE: *(alla porta del gabinetto con impeto)*
Esci omai, garzon malnato,
sciagurato, non tardar.

LA CONTESSA: *(ritirandolo a forza dal gabinetto)*
Ah, signore, quel furore
per lui fammi il cor tremar.

IL CONTE: E d'opporvi ancor osate?

LA CONTESSA: No, sentite ...

IL CONTE: Via, parlate.

LA CONTESSA:
Giuro il ciel ch'ogni sospetto ...
(tremante e sbigottita)
e lo stato in che il trovate ...
sciolto il collo ... nudo il petto ...

IL CONTE: Sciolto il collo! Nudo il petto! ... Seguitate.

THE COUNTESS: Yes, Cherubino.

THE COUNT: *(to himself)* (It seems to be my fate to find this page boy wherever I go!) *(aloud)* What! He hasn't gone? Scoundrels! Now my suspicions are proved true! This is the intrigue, this is the plot the letter warned me of!

Scene 6

THE COUNT, THE COUNTESS, AND THEN SUSANNA IN THE DRESSING ROOM.

Finale

THE COUNT: *(at the dressing room door, in a rage)*
Out at once, you damn brat,
You filthy villain, out of there!

THE COUNTESS: *(trying to restrain him)*
Oh please, my lord, your anger
Gives my heart such a scare.

THE COUNT: You dare still stand in my way?

THE COUNTESS: Only listen . . .

THE COUNT: And what have you to say?

THE COUNTESS:
All of your suspicions, I swear . . .
(trembling and dismayed)
The state in which you find him . . .
His collar undone . . . his chest bare . . .

THE COUNT: Collar undone? . . . Chest bare? . . . And?

LA CONTESSA: Per vestir femminee spoglie …

IL CONTE:
Ah, comprendo, indegna moglie,
(appressandosi al gabinetto)
mi vo' tosto vendicar.

LA CONTESSA: *(con forza)*
Mi fa torto quel trasporto,
m'oltraggiate a dubitar.

IL CONTE: *(tornando indietro)* Qua la chiave!

LA CONTESSA: *(dandogli la chiave)*
Egli è innocente.
Voi sapete …

IL CONTE:
Non so niente.
Va lontan dagl'occhi miei:
un'infida, un'empia sei
e mi cerchi d'infamar.

LA CONTESSA: Vado … sì … ma …

IL CONTE: Non ascolto.

LA CONTESSA: Non son rea.

IL CONTE:
Vel leggo in volto!
Mora, mora e più non sia
ria cagion del mio penar!

THE COUNTESS: It was to dress him as a woman that we . . .

THE COUNT:
Now I understand! Skullduggery!
(He approaches the dressing room.)
Believe me, woman, he will pay!

THE COUNTESS: *(vehemently)*
Your anger does me wrong!
How can you accuse me this way?

THE COUNT: *(turning back)* Give me the key!

THE COUNTESS: *(giving him the key)*
He is innocent!
You know that.

THE COUNT:
I know nothing of the sort!
Out of my sight! Leave me!
You have shamed and deceived me!
You have disgraced my name!

THE COUNTESS: I shall leave . . . yes, but . . .

THE COUNT: I will not listen!

THE COUNTESS: I am not to blame . . .

THE COUNT:
I can read it in your face.
He will die this very minute!
I'll be rid of him and his breed!

LA CONTESSA:
Ah, la cieca gelosia
qualche eccesso gli fa far!
(Il Conte apre il gabinetto.)

Scena 7
LA CONTESSA, SUSANNA CH'ESCE
DAL GABINETTO, IL CONTE.

(Susanna esce sulla porta tutta grave ed ivi si ferma.)

IL CONTE, LA CONTESSA: *(con maraviglia)* Susanna!

SUSANNA:
Signore,
cos'è quel stupore?
(con ironia)
Il brando prendete,
il paggio uccidete,
quel paggio malnato
vedetelo qua.

IL CONTE: *(da sè)*
Che scuola! La testa
girando mi va.

LA CONTESSA: *(da sè)*
Che storia è mai questa?
Susanna v'è là.

SUSANNA: *(da sè)*
Confusa han la testa,
non san come va.

THE COUNTESS:
I fear his blind jealousy
Will lead to some rash deed!
(The Count opens the dressing room.)

Scene 7

THE COUNTESS, SUSANNA EMERGING

FROM THE DRESSING ROOM, AND THE COUNT.

(Susanna solemnly emerges from the door and stops there.)

THE COUNT AND THE COUNTESS: *(astonished)* Susanna!

SUSANNA:
Your servant!
Why this astonishment?
(ironically)
Take your sword!
Kill the page boy!
Here you see him,
The brat himself!

THE COUNT: *(to himself)*
What can this mean?
What is this I see?

THE COUNTESS: *(to herself)*
Susanna in there?
But how can that be?

SUSANNA: *(to herself)*
Confusion all around,
The stuff of comedy!

IL CONTE: Sei sola?

SUSANNA:
Guardate:
qui ascoso sarà.

IL CONTE:
Guardiamo:
qui ascoso sarà.
(Entra nel gabinetto.)

Scena 8

SUSANNA, LA CONTESSA E POI IL CONTE.

LA CONTESSA:
Susanna, son morta:
il fiato mi manca.

SUSANNA: *(allegrissima addita alla Contessa la finestra onde è saltato Cherubino)*
Più lieta, più franca:
in salvo è di già.

IL CONTE: *(esce confuso dal gabinetto)*
Che sbaglio mai presi!
Appena lo credo;
se a torto v'offesi
perdono vi chiedo,
ma far burla simile
è poi crudeltà.

THE COUNT: Are you alone?

SUSANNA:
See for yourself.
Who could be hidden in there?

THE COUNT:
Let's see then, let's just see
Who might be hiding there.
(He enters the dressing room.)

Scene 8

SUSANNA, THE COUNTESS, AND LATER THE COUNT.

THE COUNTESS:
Susanna, I am fainting!
I can't catch my breath!

SUSANNA: *(happily, pointing out to the Countess the window from which Cherubino jumped)*
There's nothing to worry about.
He's escaped the jaws of death!

THE COUNT: *(comes out in confusion)*
How wrong I have been!
I can hardly believe it.
If I have offended you,
I beg your forgiveness.
But to play such a joke
Seems much out of place.

SUSANNA, LA CONTESSA: *(la Contessa col fazzoletto alla bocca per celar il disordine di spirito)*
Le vostre follie
non mertan pietà.

IL CONTE: Io v'amo.

LA CONTESSA: *(rinvenendo dalla confusione a poco a poco)* Nol dite.

IL CONTE: Vel giuro.

LA CONTESSA:
Mentite. *(con forza e collera)*
Son l'empia, l'infida
che ognora v'inganna.

IL CONTE:
Quell'ira, Susanna,
m'aita a calmar.

SUSANNA:
Così si condanna
chi può sospettar.

LA CONTESSA: *(con risentimento)*
Adunque la fede
d'un'anima amante
sì fiera mercede
doveva sperar?

SUSANNA: *(in atto di preghiera)* Signora ...

IL CONTE: *(in atto di preghiera)* Rosina ...

SUSANNA AND THE COUNTESS: *(holding a handkerchief to her mouth to hide her agitation)*
This folly of yours
Is itself a disgrace.

THE COUNT: I love you!

THE COUNTESS: *(gradually regaining her composure)* Don't say that!

THE COUNT: I swear it!

THE COUNTESS:
How can you? *(firmly and angrily)*
You said I had shamed and deceived you.
I had disgraced your name.

THE COUNT:
Help me, Susanna,
I feel so ashamed.

SUSANNA:
Suspicious people
Have themselves to blame.

THE COUNTESS: *(resentfully)*
Does the constancy
Of a loving heart
Deserve contempt,
Deserve such blame?

SUSANNA: *(kneeling)* My lady!

THE COUNT: *(kneeling)* Rosina!

LA CONTESSA: *(al Conte)*
Crudele!
Più quella non sono,
ma il misero oggetto
del vostro abbandono,
che avete diletto
di far disperar.

IL CONTE, SUSANNA:
Confuso, pentito,
son/è troppo punito:
abbiate pietà.

LA CONTESSA:
Soffrir sì gran torto
quest'alma non sa.

IL CONTE: Ma il paggio rinchiuso?

LA CONTESSA: Fu sol per provarvi.

IL CONTE: Ma i tremiti, i palpiti?

LA CONTESSA: Fu sol per burlarvi.

IL CONTE: Ma un foglio sì barbaro? . . .

SUSANNA, LA CONTESSA:
Di Figaro è il foglio,
e a voi per Basilio . . .

IL CONTE: Ah perfidi! Io voglio . . .

THE COUNTESS: *(to the Count)*
How cruel!
I am no longer she,
But the wretched object
Of your callous neglect,
To whom you take pleasure
In causing pain.

THE COUNT AND SUSANNA:
Baffled and contrite,
He has (I have) been punished enough.
Forgive his (my) wrong!

THE COUNTESS:
I have suffered so much.
I have borne it so long.

THE COUNT: But you told me the page was in there . . .

THE COUNTESS: Only a test.

THE COUNT: And all your palpitations . . . ?

THE COUNTESS: Only to jest.

THE COUNT: But that horrid note . . .

SUSANNA AND THE COUNTESS:
It was Figaro who wrote it,
Basilio who brought it . . .

THE COUNT: I will horsewhip those traitors . . . !

SUSANNA, LA CONTESSA:
Perdono non merta
chi agli altri nol dà.

IL CONTE: *(con tenerezza)*
Ebben, se vi piace
comune è la pace;
Rosina inflessibile
con me non sarà.

LA CONTESSA:
Ah, quanto, Susanna,
son dolce di core!
Di donne al furore
chi più crederà?

SUSANNA:
Cogl'uomin, signora,
girate, volgete,
vedrete che ognora
si cade poi là.

IL CONTE: *(con tenerezza)* Guardatemi ...

LA CONTESSA: Ingrato!

IL CONTE: *(bacia e ribacia la mano della Contessa.)* Ho torto e mi
pento.

SUSANNA, LA CONTESSA, IL CONTE:
Da questo momento
quest'alma a conoscerla/mi/vi
apprender potrà.

SUSANNA AND THE COUNTESS:
Who will not forgive his fellow man
Cannot for himself find others who can.

THE COUNT: *(tenderly)*
If it pleases you both,
We'll make peace all around.
Rosina, I know,
Will yield finally to me.

THE COUNTESS:
Susanna, to warmth
My own heart is bound!
Who could ever believe
In a woman's fury?

SUSANNA:
The men, my lady,
Run us up and down,
But it always turns out
That love is the key.

THE COUNT: *(tenderly)* Look at me . . .

THE COUNTESS: Ungrateful man!

THE COUNT: *(He kisses the Countess's hand again and again.)* I was wrong. I apologize.

SUSANNA, THE COUNTESS, AND THE COUNT:
From this moment on,
My (His) heart has learned
Its lesson well.

Scena 9

LA CONTESSA, SUSANNA, IL CONTE, FIGARO.

FIGARO:
Signori, di fuori
son già i suonatori:
le trombe sentite,
i pifferi udite;
tra canti, tra balli
de' nostri vassalli
(prendendo Susanna sotto il braccio)
corriamo, voliamo
le nozze a compir.
(Va per partire.)

IL CONTE: *(trattenendolo)* Pian piano, men fretta.

FIGARO: La turba m'aspetta.

IL CONTE:
Un dubbio toglietemi
in pria di partir.

SUSANNA, LA CONTESSA, FIGARO:
La cosa è scabrosa,
com'ha da finir?

IL CONTE:
Con arte le carte
convien qui scoprir.

IL CONTE: *(a Figaro)*
Conoscete, signor Figaro,
(mostrandogli il foglio ricevuto da Basilio)
questo foglio chi vergò?

Scene 9

THE COUNTESS, SUSANNA, THE COUNT, AND FIGARO.

FIGARO:
My lady, and my lord,
Musicians are at the door!
The trumpets are braying,
The pipers are playing!
There's dancing and singing,
The bells are all ringing!
(taking Susanna's arm)
Hurray and help celebrate
Our wedding day!
(They start to leave.)

THE COUNT: *(stopping him)* Gently, gently, not so fast.

FIGARO: Time is racing and won't last!

THE COUNT:
Answer one question
And you're on your way.

SUSANNA, THE COUNTESS, AND FIGARO:
Things are getting difficult.
How will this play?

THE COUNT:
Who holds the short leash
Makes the dog obey.

THE COUNT: *(to Figaro)*
This letter, Master Figaro,
(showing Figaro the letter)
Who wrote it, do you know?

FIGARO: *(fingendo d'esaminarlo)* Nol conosco …

SUSANNA, LA CONTESSA, IL CONTE: Nol conosci?

FIGARO: *(a tutti e tre, l'un dopo l'altro, con risolutezza)* No, no, no.

SUSANNA: E nol desti a don Basilio …

LA CONTESSA: … per recarlo …

IL CONTE: Tu c'intendi …

FIGARO: Oibò, oibò.

SUSANNA: E non sai del damerino …

LA CONTESSA: … che stasera nel giardino …

IL CONTE: Già capisci …

FIGARO: Io non lo so.

IL CONTE:
Cerchi invan difesa e scusa,
il tuo ceffo già t'accusa:
vedo ben che vuoi mentir.

FIGARO: *(al Conte)* Mente il ceffo, io già non mento.

SUSANNA, LA CONTESSA: *(a Figaro)*
Il talento aguzzi invano,
palesato abbiam l'arcano:
non v'è nulla da ridir.

IL CONTE: Che rispondi?

FIGARO: *(pretending to examine it)* I have no idea.

SUSANNA, THE COUNTESS, AND THE COUNT: You have no idea?

FIGARO: *(to all three, one after the other, resolutely)* None.

SUSANNA: You gave it to Basilio . . . ?

THE COUNTESS: To deliver . . . ?

THE COUNT: Remember now . . . ?

FIGARO: No, no, no.

SUSANNA: But you know about the page . . . ?

THE COUNTESS: In the garden this evening . . . ?

THE COUNT: Remember now . . . ?

FIGARO: Me? No idea.

THE COUNT:
Ignorance is a vain defense.
Your look gives you away.
I can see it is all pretense.

FIGARO: *(to the Count)* Then my face lies, not me.

SUSANNA AND THE COUNTESS: *(to Figaro)*
Why pretend to be so dense?
The secret is out by now.
Come, use your common sense.

THE COUNT: And what have you to say now?

FIGARO: Niente, niente.

IL CONTE: Dunque accordi?

FIGARO: Non accordo.

SUSANNA, LA CONTESSA: *(a Figaro)*
Eh via, chetati, balordo,
la burletta ha da finir.

FIGARO:
Per finirla lietamente,
e all'usanza teatrale,
(prendendo Susanna sotto il braccio)
un'azion matrimoniale
le faremo ora seguir.

LA CONTESSA, SUSANNA, FIGARO: *(al Conte)*
Deh, signor, nol contrastate,
consolate i lor/miei desir.

IL CONTE: *(da sè)*
Marcellina, Marcellina,
quanto tardi a comparir!

Scena 10

LA CONTESSA, SUSANNA, IL CONTE, FIGARO,
ANTONIO GIARDINIERE.

ANTONIO: *(infuriato, con un vaso di garofani schiacciato)* Ah signor
... signor ...

IL CONTE: *(con ansietà)* Cosa è stato? ...

ANTONIO: Che insolenza! Chi'l fece? Chi fu?

FIGARO: Nothing, nothing at all.

THE COUNT: So you admit it?

FIGARO: I admit nothing.

SUSANNA AND THE COUNTESS: *(to Figaro)*
You rogue, no more denials!
The joke is at an end.

FIGARO:
The theater prescribes
It all ends with a smile.
(taking Susanna's arm)
I only hope that wedding bells
Might keep the peace awhile.

THE COUNTESS, SUSANNA, AND FIGARO: *(to the Count)*
Allow, my lord, the bride and groom
To go where they belong.

THE COUNT: *(to himself)*
Marcellina, Marcellina,
Why are you taking so long?

Scene 10

THE COUNTESS, SUSANNA, THE COUNT, FIGARO, AND
ANTONIO THE GARDENER

ANTONIO: *(furious, and carrying a broken flowerpot)* Oh my lord . . .
my lord . . . !

THE COUNT: *(anxiously)* Well, what is it?

ANTONIO: How dare he! Who did it? Who was it?

LA CONTESSA, SUSANNA, IL CONTE, FIGARO: Cosa dici, cos'hai, cosa è nato?

ANTONIO: *(come sopra)* Ascoltate ...

LA CONTESSA, SUSANNA, IL CONTE, FIGARO: Via, parla, di', su.

ANTONIO:
Dal balcone che guarda in giardino
mille cose ogni dì gettar veggio
e poc'anzi—può darsi di peggio? –
vidi un uom, signor mio, gettar giù.

IL CONTE: *(con vivacità)* Dal balcone?

ANTONIO: *(mostrandogli il vaso di fiori schiacciato)* Vedete i garofani.

IL CONTE: In giardino?

ANTONIO: Sì.

LA CONTESSA, SUSANNA: *(piano a Figaro)* Figaro, all'erta.

IL CONTE: Cosa sento!

LA CONTESSA, SUSANNA, FIGARO: *(piano)*
Costui ci sconcerta:
(forte)
quel briaco che viene a far qui?

IL CONTE: *(ad Antonio con foco)* Dunque un uom ... ma dov'è, dov'è gito?

THE COUNTESS, SUSANNA, THE COUNT, AND FIGARO: What is he saying? What is this all about?

ANTONIO: *(as above)* Listen.

THE COUNTESS, SUSANNA, THE COUNT, AND FIGARO: Go on, then, speak.

ANTONIO:
From the balcony over the garden
All sorts of things are thrown.
But today it was a man,
All dressed and fully grown!

THE COUNT: *(alertly)* From the balcony?

ANTONIO: *(showing him the crushed flowerpot)* Just look at my pot!

THE COUNT: Into the garden?

ANTONIO: Yes!

THE COUNTESS AND SUSANNA: *(softly, to Figaro)* Figaro, think quickly!

THE COUNT: Let me put all this together.

THE COUNTESS, SUSANNA, AND FIGARO: *(softly)*
This is not good news.
(loudly)
Who let that drunk in here?

THE COUNT: *(to Antonio, excitedly)* A man, you say! Where did he get to?

ANTONIO:
Ratto ratto il birbone è fuggito
e ad un tratto di vista m'uscì.

SUSANNA: *(piano a Figaro)* Sai che il paggio ...

FIGARO: *(piano a Susanna)*
So tutto, lo vidi.
(Ride forte.)
Ah, ah, ah, ah!

IL CONTE: Taci là.

ANTONIO: *(a Figaro)* Cosa ridi?

FIGARO: *(ad Antonio)* Tu sei cotto dal sorger del dì.

IL CONTE: *(ad Antonio)* Or ripetimi: un uom dal balcone ...

ANTONIO: ... dal balcone ...

IL CONTE: ... in giardino ...

ANTONIO: ... in giardino ...

SUSANNA, LA CONTESSA, FIGARO: Ma signore, se in lui parla il vino!

IL CONTE: *(ad Antonio)* Segui pure: né in volto il vedesti?

ANTONIO: No, nol vidi.

LA CONTESSA, SUSANNA: *(piano a Figaro)* Olà, Figaro, ascolta.

ANTONIO:
The little rat scurried off so fast
I didn't see where he fled to.

SUSANNA: *(softly, to Figaro)* You realize it was the page . . .

FIGARO: *(softly, to Susanna)*
I know. I saw everything.
(laughing out loud)
Ha, *ha*!

THE COUNT: Quiet down!

ANTONIO: *(to Figaro)* Why are you laughing?

FIGARO: *(to Antonio)* Because you are drunk, dawn to dusk.

THE COUNT: *(to Antonio)* Tell me again. A man? From the balcony?

ANTONIO: From the balcony.

THE COUNT: Into the garden?

ANTONIO: Into the garden.

SUSANNA, THE COUNTESS, AND FIGARO: But, my lord, the wine is talking!

THE COUNT: *(to Antonio)* No, go on. Did you see his face?

ANTONIO: No, not his face.

THE COUNTESS AND SUSANNA: *(softly, to Figaro)* Figaro, listen up!

IL CONTE: No?

FIGARO: *(ad Antonio)*
Via, piangione, sta' zitto una volta,
(toccando con disprezzo i garofani)
per tre soldi far tanto tumulto!
Giacché il fatto non può star occulto,
sono io stesso saltato di lì.

IL CONTE: Chi? Voi stesso?

LA CONTESSA, SUSANNA: *(piano)* Che testa! Che ingegno!

FIGARO: *(al Conte)* Che stupor!

ANTONIO: *(a Figaro)* Chi? Voi stesso?

IL CONTE: Già creder nol posso.

ANTONIO: *(a Figaro)*
Come mai diventaste sì grosso?
Dopo il salto non foste così.

FIGARO: A chi salta succede così.

ANTONIO: Chi 'l direbbe?

LA CONTESSA, SUSANNA: *(a Figaro, piano)* Ed insiste quel pazzo!

IL CONTE: *(ad Antonio)* Tu che dici?

ANTONIO: E a me parve il ragazzo.

THE COUNT: No?

FIGARO: *(to Antonio)*
You blubbering old fool, hold your tongue!
(dismissively striking his pot)
Making such a fuss over nothing!
If you really want to hear something,
Yours truly went over the rail!

THE COUNT: What? It was you?

THE COUNTESS AND SUSANNA: *(softly)* Now that was ingenious!

FIGARO: *(to the Count)* You're surprised?

ANTONIO: *(to Figaro)* What? It was you?

THE COUNT: Very hard to believe.

ANTONIO: *(to Figaro)*
Then how have you grown so tall?
When you jumped, you were mighty small.

FIGARO: Jumping can have that effect.

ANTONIO: That's not what you'd expect.

THE COUNTESS AND SUSANNA: *(to Figaro, softly)* This sot is on another spree!

THE COUNT: *(to Antonio)* You were saying?

ANTONIO: It looked like a boy to me.

IL CONTE: *(con foco)* Cherubin!

LA CONTESSA, SUSANNA: *(piano)* Maledetto!

FIGARO:
Esso appunto, *(ironicamente)*
da Siviglia a cavallo qui giunto,
da Siviglia ov'ei forse sarà.

ANTONIO: *(con rozza semplicità)*
Questo no, questo no, ché il cavallo
io non vidi saltare di là.

IL CONTE: Che pazienza! Finiam questo ballo!

LA CONTESSA, SUSANNA: *(piano)* Come mai—giusto ciel!—finirà?

IL CONTE: *(a Figaro con foco)* Dunque tu . . .

FIGARO: *(con disinvoltura)* Saltai giù.

IL CONTE: Ma perché?

FIGARO: Il timor . . .

IL CONTE: Che timor?

FIGARO: *(additando le camere delle serve)*
Là rinchiuso,
aspettando quel caro visetto . . .
tippe tappe un sussurro fuor d'uso . . .
voi gridaste . . . lo scritto biglietto . . .
saltai giù dal terrore confuso . . .
(fingendo d'essersi storpiato il piede)
e stravolto m'ho un nervo del piè.

THE COUNT: *(enraged)* Cherubino!

THE COUNTESS AND SUSANNA: *(softly)* We're ruined!

FIGARO:
You're right, of course! *(sarcastically)*
He arrived here by horse,
Came from Seville just today.

ANTONIO: *(oafishly)*
I'm sure there was no horse.
I would have heard it neigh.

THE COUNT: Give me patience! Enough nonsense now.

THE COUNTESS AND SUSANNA: *(softly)* Merciful heaven, how will this end?

THE COUNT: *(to Figaro, enraged)* So what did you do then?

FIGARO: *(casually)* I jumped.

THE COUNT: But why?

FIGARO: Fear.

THE COUNT: Fear of what?

FIGARO: *(pointing to the servants' quarters)*
Shut up in there
Waiting for Susanna's pretty face . . .
Tap-tappings and odd whispers . . .
You were shouting, that letter . . .
In all the confusion, I jumped . . .
(rubbing his foot as if hurt)
And twisted my foot!

ANTONIO: *(porgendo a Figaro alcune carte chiuse)*
Vostre dunque saran queste carte
che perdeste ...

IL CONTE: *(togliendogliele)* Olà, porgile a me.

FIGARO: *(piano alla Contessa e a Susanna)* Sono in trappola.

LA CONTESSA, SUSANNA: *(piano a Figaro)* Figaro, all'erta.

IL CONTE: *(apre il foglio e lo chiude tosto)* Dite un po', questo foglio
cos'è?

FIGARO: *(cavando di tasca alcune carte per guardare)* Tosto, tosto ...
ne ho tanti ... aspettate.

ANTONIO: Sarà forse il sommario de' debiti.

FIGARO: No, la lista degl'osti.

IL CONTE: *(a Figaro)*
Parlate.
(ad Antonio)
E tu lascialo e parti.

LA CONTESSA, SUSANNA, FIGARO: *(ad Antonio)* Lascialo/mi e
parti.

ANTONIO: Parto, sì, ma se torno a trovarti ... *(Parte.)*

FIGARO: Vanne, vanne, non temo di te.

ANTONIO: *(handing Figaro some folded papers)*
Then these papers you dropped,
Will they be yours?

THE COUNT: *(taking them)* Oh–ho! Give them to me!

FIGARO: *(softly, to the Countess and Susanna)* I'm trapped!

THE COUNTESS AND SUSANNA: *(softly, to Figaro)* Figaro, watch
out!

THE COUNT: *(opening one of the papers and quickly refolding it)* Then
tell me, what does it say here?

FIGARO: *(taking some letters from his pocket and looking through them)*
Of course . . . of course . . . so many here . . . wait . . .

ANTONIO: Probably a list of his creditors.

FIGARO: No, a list of his wineshops.

THE COUNT: *(to Figaro)*
Speak up!
(to Antonio)
And you, let him be.

THE COUNTESS, SUSANNA, AND FIGARO: *(to Antonio)* Let him
(me) alone! Off with you then!

ANTONIO: I'm going, but if I catch you again . . . ! *(He leaves.)*

FIGARO: Out! I'm not afraid of you!

IL CONTE: *(riapre la carta e poi tosto la chiude) (a Figaro)* Dunque …

LA CONTESSA: *(piano a Susanna)* Oh ciel! La patente del paggio!

SUSANNA: *(piano a Figaro)* Giusti dei! La patente!…

IL CONTE: *(a Figaro ironicamente)* Coraggio!

FIGARO: *(fingendo di risovvenirsi della cosa)*
Uh, che testa! Questa è la patente
che poc'anzi il fanciullo mi diè.

IL CONTE: Per che fare?

FIGARO: *(imbrogliato)* Vi manca …

IL CONTE: Vi manca?

LA CONTESSA: *(piano a Susanna)* Il suggello.

SUSANNA: *(piano a Figaro)* Il suggello.

IL CONTE: *(a Figaro)* Rispondi.

FIGARO: *(finge di pensare)* È l'usanza …

IL CONTE: Suvvia, ti confondi?

FIGARO: È l'usanza di porvi il suggello.

THE COUNT: *(opening the letter again and closing it) (to Figaro)* Well, well.

THE COUNTESS: *(softly, to Susanna)* Heavens! The page's commission!

SUSANNA: *(softly, to Figaro)* Oh Lord! The commission!

THE COUNT: *(ironically, to Figaro)* Cheer up!

FIGARO: *(pretending to remember)*
Oh how stupid! It's the commission
The boy left me a while ago.

THE COUNT: What for?

FIGARO *(hesitating)* It lacked . . .

THE COUNT: It lacked . . . ?

THE COUNTESS: *(softly, to Susanna)* The seal.

SUSANNA: *(softly, to Figaro)* The seal.

THE COUNT: Answer me!

FIGARO: *(pretending to ponder)* It is customary . . .

THE COUNT: Go on, stop stalling!

FIGARO: It is customary to seal a document.

IL CONTE: *(guarda e vede che manca il suggello, guasta il foglio e con somma collera lo getta)*
(da sè)
Questo birbo mi toglie il cervello;
tutto, tutto è un mistero per me.

SUSANNA, LA CONTESSA: *(da sè)*
Se mi salvo da questa tempesta,
più non avvi naufragio per me.

FIGARO: *(da sè)*
Sbuffa invano e la terra calpesta;
poverino, ne sa men di me.

Scena 11 ed ultima

SUSANNA, LA CONTESSA, MARCELLINA, BASILIO,
BARTOLO, IL CONTE, FIGARO.

MARCELLINA, BASILIO, BARTOLO: *(al Conte)*
Voi, signor, che giusto siete,
ci dovete or ascoltar.

IL CONTE: *(da sè)*
Son venuti a vendicarmi,
io mi sento consolar.

SUSANNA, LA CONTESSA, FIGARO: *(da sè)*
Son venuti a sconcertarmi,
qual rimedio ritrovar?

FIGARO: *(al Conte)*
Son tre stolidi, tre pazzi,
cosa mai vengono a far?

THE COUNT: *(seeing that the seal is missing, and tearing up the letter in a rage)*
(to himself)
This rascal is driving me mad!
Each way I turn, a dead end!

SUSANNA AND THE COUNTESS: *(to themselves)*
If we can survive this storm,
I'll never fear shipwreck again.

FIGARO: *(to himself)*
He huffs and puffs in vain.
So gullible, these gentlemen!

Scene 11

SUSANNA, THE COUNTESS, MARCELLINA, BASILIO,
BARTOLO, THE COUNT, AND FIGARO

MARCELLINA, BASILIO, AND BARTOLO: *(to the Count)*
Your honor, most noble lord,
We humbly beg a word.

THE COUNT: *(to himself)*
They've come to help vindicate me.
My prayers at last are heard!

SUSANNA, THE COUNTESS, AND FIGARO: *(aside)*
They have come for retribution.
Things are getting absurd!

FIGARO: *(to the Count)*
Three fools, each worse than the last,
What are they doing here?

IL CONTE:
Pian pianin, senza schiamazzi
dica ognun quel che gli par.

MARCELLINA:
Un impegno nuziale
ha costui con me contratto:
e pretendo che il contratto
deva meco effettuar.

SUSANNA, LA CONTESSA, FIGARO: Come! Come!

IL CONTE:
Olà, silenzio:
io son qui per giudicar.

BARTOLO:
Io da lei scelto avvocato
vengo a far le sue difese,
le legittime pretese
io qui vengo a palesar.

SUSANNA, LA CONTESSA, FIGARO: È un birbante! ...

IL CONTE:
Olà, silenzio:
io son qui per giudicar.

BASILIO:
Io com'uom al mondo cognito
vengo qui per testimonio
del promesso matrimonio
con prestanza di danar.

THE COUNT:
I'll have no shouting or bombast!
Let no one interfere!

MARCELLINA:
The man before you once signed
A contract to marry me.
It is time for him to honor it
And not to harry me.

SUSANNA, THE COUNTESS, AND FIGARO: What's this?

THE COUNT:
I will have silence!
This is for me to decide.

BARTOLO:
I appear, sir, for this lady,
To defend her legal rights.
I will argue by my lights
And with justice as my guide.

SUSANNA, THE COUNTESS, AND FIGARO: That charlatan!

THE COUNT:
I will have silence!
This is for me to decide!

BASILIO:
I am a witness for this lady,
To provide firm testimony.
The promise of matrimony
Was made against a loan.

SUSANNA, LA CONTESSA, FIGARO:
Son tre matti.

IL CONTE:
Olà, silenzio! Lo vedremo:
il contratto leggeremo,
tutto in ordin deve andar.

SUSANNA, LA CONTESSA, FIGARO:
Son confusa/confuso, son stordita/stordito,
disperata/disperato, sbalordita/sbalordito!
Certo un diavol dell'inferno
qui li ha fatti capitar.

MARCELLINA, BASILIO, BARTOLO, IL CONTE:
Che bel colpo, che bel caso,
è cresciuto a tutti il naso!
Qualche nume a noi propizio
qui ci/li ha fatti capitar.

Fine dell'atto secondo.

SUSANNA, THE COUNTESS, AND FIGARO:
All of them are mad!

THE COUNT:
Silence, I say! Let me see it.
This contract shall be read.
Its truth will soon be known!

SUSANNA, THE COUNTESS, AND FIGARO:
See them grin, see them gloat!
It is everything I feared!
The very devil himself
Has brought them here!

MARCELLINA, BASILIO, BARTOLO, AND THE COUNT:
A run of luck, a masterstroke!
They have everything to fear!
An angel from on high
Has brought us here!

End of Act II.

Atto terzo

Sala ricca con due troni e preparata a festa nuziale.

Scena 1

IL CONTE SOLO CHE PASSEGGIA.

Recitativo

IL CONTE: Che imbarazzo è mai questo! Un foglio anonimo ...
la cameriera in gabinetto chiusa ... la padrona confusa ... un
uom che salta dal balcone in giardino ... un altro appresso che
dice esser quel desso ... Non so cosa pensar: potrebbe forse
qualcun de' miei vassalli ... A simil razza è comune l'ardir ...
Ma la Contessa ... Ah, che un dubbio l'offende ... Ella rispetta
troppo sé stessa e l'onor mio ... L'onore ... dove diamin l'ha
posto umano errore!

Scena 2

IL SUDDETTO, LA CONTESSA E SUSANNA. S'ARRESTANO IN
FONDO ALLA SCENA, NON VEDUTE DAL CONTE.

LA CONTESSA: *(a Susanna)* Via, fatti core: digli che ti attenda in
giardino.

IL CONTE: Saprò se Cherubino era giunto a Siviglia: a tale
oggetto ho mandato Basilio ...

Act III

A richly decorated hall with two thrones, prepared for a wedding ceremony.

Scene 1

THE COUNT, ALONE AND PACING BACK AND FORTH.

Recitative

THE COUNT: What a predicament! An anonymous letter . . . the maid shut in the closet . . . my wife embarrassed . . . one man jumping from the balcony . . . and another one saying he did it . . . What am I supposed to think? It could be one of the servants . . . a shiftless lot. But the Countess . . . no, to doubt her is an insult . . . She has too much respect for her own dignity and for my honor . . . my *honor* . . . what has human weakness done to that!

Scene 2

THE COUNTESS AND SUSANNA, STANDING IN THE DOORWAY, UNSEEN BY THE COUNT.

THE COUNTESS: *(to Susanna)* Be brave and go tell him to wait for you in the garden.

THE COUNT: I'll soon know if Cherubino really went to Seville. I sent Basilio to find out.

SUSANNA: *(alla Contessa)* Oh cielo! E Figaro?

LA CONTESSA: A lui non dei dir nulla: in vece tua voglio andarci io medesma.

IL CONTE: Avanti sera dovrebbe ritornar ...

SUSANNA: Oddio! ... Non oso! ...

LA CONTESSA: Pensa ch'è in tua mano il mio riposo. *(Si nasconde.)*

IL CONTE: E Susanna? Chi sa ch'ella tradito abbia il secreto mio ... Oh, se ha parlato gli fo sposar la vecchia.

SUSANNA: (Marcellina! ...) Signor ...

IL CONTE: *(serio)* Cosa bramate?

SUSANNA: Mi par che siate in collera!

IL CONTE: Volete qualche cosa?

SUSANNA: Signor ... la vostra sposa ha i soliti vapori e vi chiede il fiaschetto degli odori.

IL CONTE: Prendete.

SUSANNA: Or vel riporto.

IL CONTE: Eh no, potete ritenerlo per voi.

SUSANNA: Per me? Questi non son mali da donne triviali.

SUSANNA: *(to the Countess)* Good heavens! If Figaro . . .

THE COUNTESS: Not a word of this to him. I myself intend to go in your place.

THE COUNT: He will be back before evening.

SUSANNA: I cannot bring myself . . .

THE COUNTESS: Remember, my happiness is in your hands. *(She hides.)*

THE COUNT: And Susanna? Who knows if she has betrayed my secret? If she . . . Oh if she has told anyone, I will make Figaro marry the old woman.

SUSANNA: (Marcellina!) My lord . . .

THE COUNT: *(earnestly)* What is it you want?

SUSANNA: You seem so angry.

THE COUNT: Is there something you wish?

SUSANNA: My lord, your wife is having one of her spells, and begs to borrow your bottle of smelling salts.

THE COUNT: Take it.

SUSANNA: I'll bring it back soon.

THE COUNT: No, no, you may need it yourself.

SUSANNA: Me? Women in my position don't have such ailments.

IL CONTE: Un'amante che perde il caro sposo sul punto d'ottenerlo...

SUSANNA: Pagando Marcellina colla dote che voi mi prometteste...

IL CONTE: Ch'io vi promisi? Quando?

SUSANNA: Credea d'averlo inteso...

IL CONTE: Sì, se voluto aveste intender me voi stessa.

SUSANNA: È mio dovere, e quel di Sua Eccellenza è il mio volere.

N° 17 Duettino

IL CONTE:
Crudel! Perché finora
farmi languir così?

SUSANNA:
Signor, la donna ognora
tempo ha di dir di sì.

IL CONTE: Dunque in giardin verrai?

SUSANNA: Se piace a voi verrò.

IL CONTE: E non mi mancherai?

SUSANNA: No, non vi mancherò.

THE COUNT: Even a girl who loses her bridegroom on the day of her wedding?

SUSANNA: But we can pay off Marcellina with the dowry you promised me . . .

THE COUNT: Promised you? When?

SUSANNA: So I understood . . .

THE COUNT: Well, if you and I could come to an understand-ing . . .

SUSANNA: I know my duty, and your lordship's wish is my command.

Duet

THE COUNT:
Cruel girl! Why do you leave me
In a state of distress?

SUSANNA:
My lord, there is always time
For a woman to say yes.

THE COUNT: Then you will come to the garden?

SUSANNA: If it pleases you, I will come.

THE COUNT: And you will not fail me?

SUSANNA: No, I will not fail you.

IL CONTE: *(con gioia)*
Mi sento dal contento
pieno di gioia il cor.

SUSANNA:
(Scusatemi se mento,
voi che intendete amor.)

Recitativo

IL CONTE: E perché fosti meco stamattina sì austera?

SUSANNA: Col paggio ch'ivi c'era ...

IL CONTE: Ed a Basilio che per me ti parlò? ...

SUSANNA: Ma qual bisogno abbiam noi che un Basilio ...

IL CONTE: È vero, è vero. E mi prometti poi ... Se tu manchi, o cor mio ... Ma la Contessa attenderà il fiaschetto.

SUSANNA: Eh, fu un pretesto: parlato io non avrei senza di questo.

IL CONTE: *(le prende la mano.)* Carissima!

SUSANNA: *(si ritira.)* Vien gente.

IL CONTE: (È mia senz'altro.)

SUSANNA: (Forbitevi la bocca, o signor scaltro.)

THE COUNT: *(happily)*
My heart is bursting with joy!
What more happiness could I buy?

SUSANNA:
(True lovers will surely forgive
My telling this one little lie.)

Recitative

THE COUNT: And why were you so distant to me this morning?

SUSANNA: With the page there . . . ?

THE COUNT: And to Basilio as well, who spoke on my behalf?

SUSANNA: But what need have we of someone like Basilio . . .

THE COUNT: True, true. Promise me again . . . If you fail me, dear heart . . . Ah, the Countess is waiting for her salts.

SUSANNA: Oh, that was just an excuse. I needed one to speak with you.

THE COUNT: *(taking her hand)* My angel!

SUSANNA: *(withdrawing)* Someone is coming.

THE COUNT: (She is mine now for sure.)

SUSANNA: (Don't be so cocksure.)

Scena 3

FIGARO, SUSANNA E SUBITO IL CONTE.

FIGARO: Ehi, Susanna, ove vai?

SUSANNA: Taci: senza avvocato hai già vinta la causa.
(Parte.)

FIGARO: Cos'è nato?
(La segue.)

Scena 4

IL CONTE SOLO.

N° 18 Recitativo accompagnato ed aria

Recitativo

IL CONTE: Hai già vinta la causa! Cosa sento! In qual laccio io cadea! Perfidi! Io voglio di tal modo punirvi! ... A piacer mio la sentenza sarà ... Ma s'ei pagasse la vecchia pretendente? Pagarla! ... In qual maniera? ... E poi v'è Antonio che a un incognito Figaro ricusa di dare una nipote in matrimonio. Coltivando l'orgoglio di questo mentecatto ... Tutto giova a un raggiro ... Il colpo è fatto.

Aria

IL CONTE:
Vedrò, mentre io sospiro,
felice un servo mio?
E un ben che invan desio
ei posseder dovrà?
Vedrò per man d'amore
unita a un vile oggetto

Scene 3

FIGARO AND SUSANNA, AND SUDDENLY THE COUNT.

FIGARO: Susanna! Where are you going?

SUSANNA: Quiet! You have won your case without a lawyer.
(She leaves.)

FIGARO:
What has happened?
(He follows her.)

Scene 4

THE COUNT, ALONE.

Accompanied Recitative and Aria

Recitative

THE COUNT: "Won your case." What do I hear? Have I fallen
into a trap? The traitors! I'll punish them, and have no mercy!
But what if he pays off Marcellina? . . . *Pay* her? How? . . . And
then there's Antonio. He won't give his niece to Figaro, if he's a
mere foundling. If I play on the pride of that half-wit, everything
will go my way. The die is cast.

Aria

THE COUNT:
Why must I be made to languish
While my servant takes his pleasure?
Why must I endure such anguish
And he make off with my treasure?
Shall I see this lowborn knave,
After all the favor I have shown her,

chi in me destò un affetto
che per me poi non ha?
Ah no, lasciarti in pace,
non vo' questo contento;
tu non nascesti, audace,
per dare a me tormento
e forse ancor per ridere
di mia infelicità.
Già la speranza sola
delle vendette mie
quest'anima consola
e giubilar mi fa.
(Vuol partire e s'incontra in Don Curzio.)

Scena 5

IL CONTE, MARCELLINA, DON CURZIO, FIGARO E
BARTOLO; POI SUSANNA.

Recitativo

DON CURZIO: *(tartagliando)* È decisa la lite. O pagarla o sposarla.
Ora ammutite.

MARCELLINA: Io respiro.

FIGARO: Ed io moro.

MARCELLINA: *(da sè)* (Alfin sposa io sarò d'un uom ch'adoro.)

FIGARO: Eccellenza, m'appello ...

IL CONTE: È giusta la sentenza. O pagar o sposar. Bravo, Don
Curzio.

DON CURZIO: Bontà di Sua Eccellenza.

Play lord and master and behave
As if he and he alone now owned her?
Ah no, not a moment's rest!
I will not let you defy me!
You were not born, you pest,
To carry your bride right by me,
Then laugh at my despair
And spit upon my crest.
The hope of my revenge
Alone stirs up my heart.
Oh yes, I will avenge
The wrong I most detest!
(As he turns to leave he runs into Don Curzio.)

Scene 5

THE COUNT, MARCELLINA, DON CURZIO, FIGARO, AND
BARTOLO; LATER SUSANNA.

Recitative

DON CURZIO: *(stuttering)* The case is closed! The verdict is in! He must pay her or marry her.

MARCELLINA: I can breathe again!

FIGARO: I am a dead man!

MARCELLINA: *(to herself)* (At last I shall marry the man I adore.)

FIGARO: Excellency, I appeal . . .

THE COUNT: The ruling seems fair—"Pay up or marry." Bravo, Don Curzio!

DON CURZIO: His excellency is most kind.

BARTOLO: Che superba sentenza!

FIGARO: In che superba?

BARTOLO: Siam tutti vendicati ...

FIGARO: Io non la sposerò.

BARTOLO: La sposerai.

DON CURZIO: O pagarla o sposarla.

MARCELLINA: Io t'ho prestati duemila pezzi duri.

FIGARO: Son gentiluomo e senza l'assenso de' miei nobili parenti ...

IL CONTE: Dove sono? Chi sono?

FIGARO: Lasciate ancor cercarli: dopo dieci anni io spero di trovarli.

BARTOLO: Qualche bambin trovato.

FIGARO: No, perduto, dottor, anzi rubato.

IL CONTE: Come?

MARCELLINA: Cosa?

BARTOLO: La prova?

DON CURZIO: Il testimonio?

BARTOLO: A superb judgment indeed!

FIGARO: And why superb?

BARTOLO: We are all avenged!

FIGARO: I will not marry her.

BARTOLO: You will.

DON CURZIO: Either you pay or you marry.

MARCELLINA: I lent you two thousand crowns.

FIGARO: I am a nobleman, and without the consent of my parents . . .

THE COUNT: Where are they? Who are they?

FIGARO: I'm not yet done looking for them. I hope to find them in about ten years.

BARTOLO: Were you a foundling . . . ?

FIGARO: No, sir, I was lost, or rather, stolen.

THE COUNT: Stolen?

MARCELLINA: What?

BARTOLO: Your proof?

DON CURZIO: Your witness?

FIGARO: L'oro, le gemme e i ricamati panni che ne' più teneri anni mi ritrovaro addosso i masnadieri sono gl'indizi veri di mia nascita illustre, e soprattutto questo al mio braccio impresso geroglifico ...

MARCELLINA: Una spatola impressa al braccio destro ...

FIGARO: E a voi chi 'l disse?

MARCELLINA: Oddio! È egli ...

FIGARO: È ver, son io.

DON CURZIO: Chi?

IL CONTE: Chi?

BARTOLO: Chi?

MARCELLINA: Raffaello.

BARTOLO: E i ladri ti rapir ...

FIGARO: Presso un castello.

BARTOLO: Ecco tua madre.

FIGARO: Balia ...

BARTOLO: No, tua madre.

DON CURZIO, IL CONTE: Sua madre!

FIGARO: Cosa sento!

FIGARO: The gold, the gems, the embroidered clothes which, when I was but an infant, were found on me by the bandits are the proof of my noble birth. That, and this birthmark on my right arm.

MARCELLINA: Birthmark? Your right arm? Shaped like a blade?

FIGARO: Who told you that?

MARCELLINA: Oh my God! It is him . . .

FIGARO: True enough, it's me.

DON CURZIO: Who?

THE COUNT: Who?

BARTOLO: Who?

MARCELLINA: Rafaello.

BARTOLO: And you were stolen by bandits?

FIGARO: Near a castle.

BARTOLO: There stands your mother.

FIGARO: My nursemaid?

BARTOLO: No, your mother.

DON CURZIO AND THE COUNT: His mother!

FIGARO: Come again . . . ?

MARCELLINA: Ecco tuo padre.

N° 19 Sestetto

MARCELLINA: *(abbracciando Figaro)*
Riconosci in questo amplesso
una madre, amato figlio!

FIGARO: *(a Bartolo)*
Padre mio, fate lo stesso,
non mi fate più arrossir.

BARTOLO: *(abbracciando Figaro)*
Resistenza la coscienza
far non lascia al tuo desir.
(Restano così fino al verso "Lascia iniquo.")

DON CURZIO:
Ei suo padre, ella sua madre:
l'imeneo non può seguir.

IL CONTE:
Son smarrito, son stordito:
meglio è assai di qua partir.
(Vuol partire.)

MARCELLINA, BARTOLO: Figlio amato!

FIGARO: Parenti amati!

(Susanna entra con una borsa di danari in mano.)

MARCELLINA: And there stands your father!

Sextet

MARCELLINA: *(embracing Figaro)*
Beloved son, with this embrace
Recognize your mother at last.

FIGARO: *(to Bartolo)*
Father dear, just look at my face.
Where blushes now conspire.

BARTOLO: *(embracing Figaro)*
My conscience now obliges me
To comply with your desire.
(They all stay embraced until the line "Leave me, you wicked man!")

DON CURZIO:
This the father? That the mother?
Then no marriage will transpire.

THE COUNT:
I'm baffled, I'm astonished!
It would be best if I retire.
(He starts to leave.)

MARCELLINA AND BARTOLO: Dearest son!

FIGARO: Beloved parents!

(Susanna enters with a purse of money in her hand.)

SUSANNA: *(arrestando il Conte)*
Alto, alto, signor Conte,
mille doppie son qui pronte:
a pagar vengo per Figaro
ed a porlo in libertà.

DON CURZIO, IL CONTE:
Non sappiam com'è la cosa,
osservate un poco là.

SUSANNA: *(si volge vedendo Figaro che abbraccia Marcellina)*
Già d'accordo ei se la sposa:
giusti dei, che infedeltà!
(Vuol partire.)
Lascia, iniquo.

FIGARO: *(trattenendo Susanna)*
No, t'arresta.
Senti, o cara ...

SUSANNA: *(fa forza, poi dà uno schiaffo a Figaro)* Senti questa.

MARCELLINA, BARTOLO, FIGARO:
È un effetto di bon core,
tutto amore è quel che fa.

IL CONTE, DON CURZIO:
Fremo/Freme, smanio/smania dal furore,
il destino a me la/gliela fa.

SUSANNA:
Fremo, smanio dal furore,
una vecchia a me la fa.

SUSANNA: *(detaining the Count)*
Not so fast, my lord.
I have the money with me
To pay off Figaro's debt
And so to set him free.

DON CURZIO AND THE COUNT:
We know nothing of your business here,
But look at them over there!

SUSANNA: *(turning to see Figaro embracing Marcellina)*
Already warming to his bride?
God in heaven! What faithlessness!
(She starts to leave.)
Leave me, you wicked man!

FIGARO: *(trying to stop her)*
No, wait!
Listen to me, love.

SUSANNA: *(slapping Figaro)* Listen to this!

MARCELLINA, BARTOLO, AND FIGARO:
She fights because her heart is torn.
She fights, but all for love.

THE COUNT AND DON CURZIO:
I am (He is) fuming, frantic, and forlorn.
What is destiny thinking of!

SUSANNA:
I am fuming, frantic, and forlorn.
What is that old crone thinking of!

MARCELLINA: *(corre ad abbracciar Susanna.)*
Lo sdegno calmate,
mia cara figliuola,
sua madre abbracciate
che vostra or sarà.

SUSANNA: *(a Bartolo, al Conte, a Don Curzio, a Marcellina)* Sua madre?

MARCELLINA, DON CURZIO, IL CONTE, BARTOLO: *(a Susanna)*
Sua madre.

SUSANNA: *(a Figaro)* Tua madre?

FIGARO: *(a Susanna)*
E quello è mio padre
che a te lo dirà.

SUSANNA: *(a Bartolo, al Conte, a Don Curzio, a Marcellina)* Suo padre?

MARCELLINA, DON CURZIO, IL CONTE, BARTOLO: *(a Susanna)*
Suo padre.

SUSANNA: *(a Figaro)* Tuo padre?

FIGARO: *(a Susanna)*
E quella è mia madre
che a te lo dirà.
(Corrono tutti e quattro ad abbracciarsi.)

MARCELLINA: *(going to embrace Susanna)*
Calm your anger,
Dearest daughter,
Embrace his mother
As your very own.

SUSANNA: *(to Bartolo, the Count, Don Curzio, and Marcellina)* His mother?

MARCELLINA, DON CURZIO, THE COUNT, AND BARTOLO: *(to Susanna)* His mother.

SUSANNA: *(to Figaro)* Your mother?

FIGARO: *(to Susanna)*
And there stands my father,
Who will tell you he's your own.

SUSANNA: *(to Bartolo, the Count, Don Curzio, and Marcellina)* His father?

MARCELLINA, DON CURZIO, THE COUNT, AND BARTOLO: *(to Susanna)* His father!

SUSANNA: *(to Figaro)* Your father?

FIGARO: *(to Susanna)*
And there stands my mother,
Who has told you she's your own.
(All four rush to embrace one another.)

SUSANNA, MARCELLINA, BARTOLO, FIGARO:
Al dolce contento
di questo momento
quest'anima appena
resister or sa.

DON CURZIO, IL CONTE:
Al fiero tormento
di questo momento
quell'/quest'anima appena
resister or sa.
(Il Conte e Don Curzio partono.)

Scena 6

SUSANNA, MARCELLINA, FIGARO E BARTOLO.

Recitativo

MARCELLINA: *(a Bartolo)* Eccovi, o caro amico, il dolce frutto dell'antico amor nostro ...

BARTOLO: Or non parliamo di fatti sì rimoti; egli è mio figlio, mia consorte voi siete, e le nozze farem quando volete.

MARCELLINA: Oggi, e doppie saranno: *(Dà il biglietto a Figaro.)* prendi, questo è il biglietto del danar che a me devi, ed è tua dote.

SUSANNA: *(getta per terra una borsa di danari.)* Prendi ancor questa borsa.

BARTOLO: *(fa lo stesso.)* E questa ancora.

FIGARO: Bravi, gettate pur ch'io piglio ognora.

SUSANNA, MARCELLINA, BARTOLO, AND FIGARO:
The sweetness
Of this moment
Goes straight
To my heart.

DON CURZIO AND THE COUNT:
The torment
Of this moment
Goes in
Like a dart.
(The Count and Don Curzio leave.)

Scene 6

SUSANNA, MARCELLINA, FIGARO, AND BARTOLO.

Recitative

MARCELLINA: *(to Bartolo)* Here he is, old friend, the sweet fruit of our old love . . .

BARTOLO: Let us not speak now of ancient history. He is my son, you are his mother, so I suppose we must marry as soon as you wish.

MARCELLINA: Today, then, a double wedding! *(She hands Figaro a piece of paper.)* Take this, your promissory note for the money you owe me. It is your dowry now.

SUSANNA: *(throwing down the purse)* Take this purse as well.

BARTOLO: *(doing the same)* And this one as well.

FIGARO: Well done! Whatever you throw at me I will take.

SUSANNA: Voliamo ad informar d'ogni avventura madama e nostro zio. Chi al par di me contenta!

FIGARO: Io.

BARTOLO: Io.

MARCELLINA: Io.

SUSANNA, MARCELLINA, BARTOLO, FIGARO: E schiatti il signor Conte al gusto mio.
(Partono abbracciati.)

Scena 7
BARBARINA, CHERUBINO.

Recitativo

BARBARINA: Andiam, andiam, bel paggio; in casa mia tutte ritroverai le più belle ragazze del castello, di tutte sarai tu certo il più bello.

CHERUBINO: Ah, se il Conte mi trova, misero me! Tu sai che partito ei mi crede per Siviglia.

BARBARINA: Oh, ve' che maraviglia! E se ti trova non sarà cosa nuova … Odi … Vogliamo vestirti come noi: tutte insiem andrem poi a presentar de' fiori a madamina; fidati, o Cherubin, di Barbarina.
(Partono.)

SUSANNA: Let's go tell the Countess and Uncle Antonio what has happened. Who is as happy as I am?

FIGARO: I am!

BARTOLO: I am!

MARCELLINA: I am!

SUSANNA, MARCELLINA, BARTOLO, AND FIGARO: And who cares how jealous the Count is!
(They rush out, arm in arm.)

Scene 7
BARBARINA AND CHERUBINO.

Recitative

BARBARINA: Let's go, my handsome page, off to my house, where you will find all the prettiest girls in the palace—though you, of course, are the . . . prettiest of all.

CHERUBINO: But if the Count should find me, I'm done for! You know he thinks I have left for Seville.

BARBARINA: But how wonderful! If he finds you with a girl, it won't be the first time. Listen! We plan to dress you up like one of us, then we'll all go together to present flowers to her ladyship. Trust me. Oh, Cherubino, trust your Barbarina!
(They leave.)

Scena 8

LA CONTESSA SOLA.

N° 20 Recitativo accompagnato ed aria

Recitativo

LA CONTESSA: E Susanna non vien! Sono ansiosa di saper come il Conte accolse la proposta: alquanto ardito il progetto mi par, e ad uno sposo sì vivace e geloso … Ma che mal c'è? Cangiando i miei vestiti con quelli di Susanna e i suoi co' miei … al favor della notte … Oh cielo, a qual umil stato fatale io son ridotta da un consorte crudel che, dopo avermi con un misto inaudito d'infedeltà, di gelosia, di sdegni prima amata, indi offesa e alfin tradita, fammi or cercar da una mia serva aita!

Aria

LA CONTESSA:
Dove sono i bei momenti
di dolcezza e di piacer,
dove andaro i giuramenti
di quel labbro menzogner?
Perché mai se in pianti e in pene
per me tutto si cangiò,
la memoria di quel bene
dal mio sen non trapassò?
Ah, se almen la mia costanza,
nel languire amando ognor,
mi portasse una speranza
di cangiar l'ingrato cor!
(Parte.)

Scene 8

THE COUNTESS, ALONE.

Accompanied Recitative and Aria

Recitative

THE COUNTESS: Susanna has not come yet! I am longing to know how the Count received her proposal. The plan seems to me too bold, and with a husband so reckless, so jealous . . . But what harm is there in it? To change my clothes with those of Susanna, and hers with mine, and under cover of darkness . . . Good God, to such a humiliating pass have I been brought by a cruel husband. Once he loved me, then he neglected me, and finally deceived me, with his unpredictable mixture of infidelity, jealousy, and contempt. And now he forces me to seek the help of my maid!

Aria

THE COUNTESS:
Where are they now, the vanished days,
The moments of pleasure's afterglow?
Where are the vows, the murmured praise
Spoken by that liar so long ago?
Why, if sweetness turns to regret,
If every hope becomes a grief,
Why is it still I cannot forget
The love that vies with disbelief?
If only my waiting, my long endurance,
The patience that true love imparts,
Could bring the slightest reassurance
Of changing his ungrateful heart!
(She leaves.)

Scena 9

IL CONTE ED ANTONIO CON CAPPELLO IN MANO.

Recitativo

ANTONIO: Io vi dico, signor, che Cherubino è ancora nel castello. E vedete per prova il suo cappello.

IL CONTE: Ma come, se a quest'ora esser giunto a Siviglia egli dovria?

ANTONIO: Scusate, oggi Siviglia è a casa mia. Là vestissi da donna e là lasciati ha gl'altri abiti suoi.

IL CONTE: Perfidi!

ANTONIO: Andiam e li vedrete voi.
(*Partono.*)

Scena 10

LA CONTESSA E SUSANNA.

Recitativo

LA CONTESSA: Cosa mi narri! E che ne disse il Conte?

SUSANNA: Gli si leggeva in fronte il dispetto e la rabbia.

LA CONTESSA: Piano, che meglio or lo porremo in gabbia. Dov'è l'appuntamento che tu gli proponesti?

SUSANNA: In giardino.

Scene 9

THE COUNT AND ANTONIO, HAT IN HAND.

Recitative

ANTONIO: I tell you, sir, that Cherubino is still in the palace. Look, here is his hat to prove it.

THE COUNT: How can that be when by now he ought to be in Seville?

ANTONIO: Forgive me, but today Seville is my house. He has dressed up as a woman and left his clothes there.

THE COUNT: The rogues!

ANTONIO: Come with me, and you can see for yourself.
(They leave.)

Scene 10

THE COUNTESS AND SUSANNA.

Recitative

THE COUNTESS: The things you tell me! Then what did the Count say?

SUSANNA: One could read it on his face—he was all vexation and sputtering rage.

THE COUNTESS: Gently now, if we are to trap him in our cage. Where have you arranged to meet him?

SUSANNA: In the garden.

LA CONTESSA: Fissiamgli un loco. Scrivi.

SUSANNA: Ch'io scriva ... ma signora ...

LA CONTESSA: Eh, scrivi, dico; *(Susanna siede e scrive.)* e tutto io prendo su me stessa. *(dettando)* "Canzonetta sull'aria."

N° 21 Duettino

SUSANNA: *(scrivendo)* "... sull'aria."

LA CONTESSA: *(dettando)* "Che soave zeffiretto ..."

SUSANNA: *(ripete le parole della Contessa.)* "... zeffiretto ..."

LA CONTESSA: "... questa sera spirerà ..."

SUSANNA: "... questa sera spirerà ..."

LA CONTESSA: "... sotto i pini del boschetto."

SUSANNA: *(domandando)* "... sotto i pini ..."

LA CONTESSA: "... sotto i pini del boschetto."

SUSANNA: *(scrivendo)* "... sotto i pini del boschetto."

(Leggono insieme lo scritto.)

LA CONTESSA E SUSANNA:
"Canzonetta sull'aria."
"Che soave zeffiretto
questa sera spirerà
sotto i pini del boschetto."

THE COUNTESS: We must specify a spot. Write this.

SUSANNA: Write to him? . . . But, my lady . . .

THE COUNTESS: Write, I tell you. *(Susanna sits down to write.)* I will take it all on myself. *(The Countess dictates.)* "The Song of the Zephyr."

Duet

SUSANNA: *(writing)* ". . . of the Zephyr."

THE COUNTESS: *(dictating)* "How sweet the zephyr . . ."

SUSANNA: *(repeating the words of the Countess)* ". . . zephyr . . ."

THE COUNTESS: ". . . that will whisper tonight . . ."

SUSANNA: ". . . that will whisper tonight . . ."

THE COUNTESS: "Beneath the pines in the grove."

SUSANNA: *(questioning)* "Beneath the pines . . ."?

THE COUNTESS: "Beneath the pines in the grove."

SUSANNA: *(writing)* "Beneath the pines . . . in the grove."

(They read over together what Susanna has written.)

THE COUNTESS AND SUSANNA:
"The Song of the Zephyr."
"How sweet the zephyr
That will whisper tonight
Beneath the pines in the grove."

LA CONTESSA: Ei già il resto capirà.

SUSANNA: Certo, certo, il capirà.

Recitativo

SUSANNA: *(piega la lettera)* Piegato è il foglio ... Or come si sigilla? ...

LA CONTESSA: *(si cava una spilla e gliela dà)* Ecco ... prendi una spilla: servirà di sigillo. Attendi ... Scrivi sul riverso del foglio: "Rimandate il sigillo."

SUSANNA: È più bizzarro di quel della patente.

LA CONTESSA: Presto, nascondi: io sento venir gente.
(Susanna si mette il biglietto nel seno.)

Scena 11

CHERUBINO VESTITO DA CONTADINELLA, BARBARINA E ALCUNE ALTRE CONTADINELLE VESTITE NEL MEDESIMO MODO CON MAZZETTI DI FIORI.

N° 22 Coro

CORO DI CONTADINELLE:
Ricevete, o padroncina,
queste rose e questi fior
che abbiam colti stamattina
per mostrarvi il nostro amor.
Siamo tante contadine
e siam tutte poverine,
ma quel poco che rechiamo
ve lo diamo di bon cor.

THE COUNTESS: And the rest he will understand.

SUSANNA: He is certain to understand.

Recitative

SUSANNA: *(folding the note)* The note is folded . . . how shall I seal it?

THE COUNTESS: *(taking out a pin and handing it to her)* Here . . . take this pin, it will do as a seal. Wait . . . write on the back of the note, "Return this pin."

SUSANNA: This is odder than the seal on the commission!

THE COUNTESS: Quickly, hide it . . . I hear people coming. *(Susanna tucks the note into her bodice.)*

Scene 11

CHERUBINO DRESSED AS A PEASANT GIRL, BARBARINA
AND OTHER VILLAGE GIRLS SIMILARLY DRESSED,
CARRYING BUNCHES OF FLOWERS, AND THOSE ALREADY
THERE.

Chorus

PEASANT GIRLS:
Pray accept, most noble lady,
These flowers that we strew.
We gathered them at break of day
With hearts devoted and true.
We are simple village peasants
And bring but humble presents,
But these blossoms that we offer
Will show our love for you.

Recitativo

BARBARINA: Queste sono, madama, le ragazze del loco, che il poco ch'han vi vengono ad offrire e vi chiedon perdon del loro ardire.

LA CONTESSA: Oh brave, vi ringrazio.

SUSANNA: Come sono vezzose!

LA CONTESSA: E chi è, narratemi, quell'amabil fanciulla ch'ha l'aria sì modesta?

BARBARINA: Ell'è una mia cugina e per le nozze è venuta ier sera.

LA CONTESSA: Onoriamo la bella forestiera. Venite qui ... *(Prende i fiori di Cherubino e lo bacia in fronte.)* Datemi i vostri fiori. Come arrossì ... Susanna, e non ti pare ... che somigli ad alcuno? ...

SUSANNA: Al naturale.

Scena 12

I DETTI, IL CONTE ED ANTONIO.

(Antonio ha il cappello di Cherubino, entra in Scena pian piano, gli cava la cuffia da donna e gli mette in testa il cappello stesso.)

ANTONIO: Eh! Cospettaccio! È questi l'uffiziale.

LA CONTESSA: (Oh stelle!)

SUSANNA: (Malandrino!)

Recitative

BARBARINA: These, my lady, are the girls from the village, who have come to offer you what little they have, and they beg that you forgive their boldness.

THE COUNTESS: How kind they are. I am grateful.

SUSANNA: How pretty they are!

THE COUNTESS: And tell me, who is that charming girl who seems so shy?

BARBARINA: She is my cousin, and arrived last night for the wedding.

THE COUNTESS: We should single out such a lovely stranger. Come here, give me your flowers . . . *(She takes the flowers from Cherubino's hand and kisses his forehead.)* How she blushes! . . . Susanna, does it seem to you . . . that she resembles someone . . . ?

SUSANNA: To the life!

Scene 12

THOSE BEFORE, THE COUNT, AND ANTONIO.

(Antonio, holding Cherubino's hat, enters very quietly, pulls off Cherubino's bonnet and slaps the hat on him.)

ANTONIO: There he is! There's your officer!

THE COUNTESS: (Heavens!)

SUSANNA: (Naughty boy!)

IL CONTE: Ebben, Madama? ...

LA CONTESSA: Io sono, o signor mio, irritata e sorpresa al par di voi.

IL CONTE: Ma stamane? ...

LA CONTESSA: Stamane ... per l'odierna festa volevam travestirlo al modo stesso che l'han vestito adesso.

IL CONTE: *(a Cherubino)* E perché non partisti?

CHERUBINO: *(cavandosi il cappello bruscamente)* Signor! ...

IL CONTE: Saprò punire la tua disubbedienza.

BARBARINA: Eccellenza, Eccellenza, voi mi dite sì spesso qual volta m'abbracciate e mi baciate: "Barbarina, se m'ami ti darò quel che brami ..."

IL CONTE: Io dissi questo? ...

BARBARINA: Voi. Or datemi, padrone, in sposo Cherubino, e v'amerò com'amo il mio gattino.

LA CONTESSA: *(al Conte)* Ebbene, or tocca a voi.

ANTONIO: Brava, figliuola! Hai buon maestro che ti fa la scuola.

IL CONTE: *(da sè)* (Non so qual uom, qual demone, qual dio rivolga tutto quanto a torto mio.)

THE COUNT: Well, my lady?

THE COUNTESS: I am, my lord, as surprised and annoyed as you are.

THE COUNT: And this morning?

THE COUNTESS: This morning . . . we wanted to dress him up as a girl for this evening's party, just as they have done now.

THE COUNT: *(to Cherubino)* And you! Why did you not leave?

CHERUBINO: *(quickly pulling off his hat)* My lord . . .

THE COUNT: I know just how to punish your disobedience.

BARBARINA: Your excellency, you have so often said to me, when you hug and kiss me, "Barbarina, if you love me, I will give you anything you want."

THE COUNT: I said that?

BARBARINA: You did. Now give me, my lord, Cherubino for my husband, and I will love you as I love my kitten.

THE COUNTESS: *(to the Count)* Well, now it is your turn . . .

ANTONIO: Well said, my child! You have learned from a good master.

THE COUNT: *(to himself)* (What man, what demon, what god is intent on driving me mad!)

Scena 13

I DETTI, FIGARO.

FIGARO: Signor ... se trattenete tutte queste ragazze, addio festa ... addio danza ...

IL CONTE: E che? Vorresti ballar col piè stravolto?

FIGARO: *(finge di drizzarsi la gamba e poi prova a ballare)* Eh, non mi duol più molto. *(Chiama tutte le giovani.)* Andiam, belle fanciulle ... *(Vuol partire, il Conte lo richiama.)*

LA CONTESSA: *(a Susanna)* Come si caverà dall'imbarazzo?

SUSANNA: *(alla Contessa)* Lasciate fare a lui.

IL CONTE: Per buona sorte i vasi eran di creta.

FIGARO:
Senza fallo. *(come sopra)* Andiamo, dunque, andiamo.

ANTONIO: *(lo richiama.)* E intanto a cavallo di galoppo a Siviglia andava il paggio.

FIGARO: Di galoppo o di passo ... buon viaggio. *(come sopra)* Venite, o belle giovani.

IL CONTE: *(torna a ricondurlo in mezzo)* E a te la sua patente era in tasca rimasta ...

FIGARO: Certamente, che razza di domande!

Scene 13

THOSE BEFORE, AND FIGARO.

FIGARO: My lord, if you keep all these girls here, there will be no party, no dancing.

THE COUNT: How's that? You want to dance with an injured foot?

FIGARO: *(pretends to stretch his leg and tries to dance)* Not hurting so much now. *(He calls the girls together.)* Come, my pretty ones . . . *(He starts to leave. The Count calls him back.)*

THE COUNTESS: *(to Susanna)* How will he get out of this one?

SUSANNA: *(to the Countess)* Leave it to him.

THE COUNT: You were lucky the flowerpots were only made of clay.

FIGARO: Right you are, sir. *(as above)* Come along, this way . . .

ANTONIO: *(reminding him)* Meanwhile the page was galloping off to Seville?

FIGARO: Galloping or trotting, off he went! *(as above)* Come along, girls . . .

THE COUNT: *(bringing him back again)* And he left his commission behind, in your pocket . . .

FIGARO: Indeed he did. Why the questions?

ANTONIO: *(a Susanna, che fa de' moti a Figaro)* Via, non gli far più moti, ei non t'intende. *(prende per mano Cherubino e lo presenta a Figaro)* Ed ecco chi pretende che sia un bugiardo il mio signor nipote.

FIGARO: Cherubino?

ANTONIO: Or ci sei.

FIGARO: *(al Conte)* Che diamin canta?

IL CONTE: Non canta, no, ma dice ch'egli saltò stamane in sui garofani ...

FIGARO: Ei lo dice! ... Sarà ... Se ho saltato io si può dare ch'anch'esso abbia fatto lo stesso.

IL CONTE: Anch'esso?

FIGARO: Perché no? ... Io non impugno mai quel che non so.
(S'ode la marcia spagnola da lontano e seguita il recitativo nella marcia.)

N° 23 Finale

FIGARO: Ecco la marcia, andiamo; a' vostri posti, o belle, a' vostri posti. Susanna, dammi il braccio.

SUSANNA: Eccolo.
(Figaro prende per un braccio la Susanna, e partono tutti eccettuati il Conte e la Contessa.)

IL CONTE: Temerari!

LA CONTESSA: Io son di ghiaccio!

ANTONIO: *(to Susanna, who is signaling to Figaro)* No sense in making signals. He can't see them. *(He takes Cherubino by the hand and presents him to Figaro.)* And here is someone who can make my future nephew out to be a liar.

FIGARO: Cherubino!

ANTONIO: The very same!

FIGARO: *(to the Count)* And what story is he telling?

THE COUNT: No story, just that he jumped onto the flowerpots this morning.

FIGARO: He says that! . . . Well, if I jumped, it is possible he did too.

THE COUNT: You both . . . ?

FIGARO: Why not? I would not want to call him a liar.
(A Spanish march is heard in the distance and the recitative follows during the march.)

Finale
FIGARO: There's the march. Let's be off! Take your places, my beauties! Susanna, give me your arm.

SUSANNA: Here it is.
(Figaro takes her arm. They all leave except the Count and Countess.)

THE COUNT: The nerve!

THE COUNTESS: I cannot move.

IL CONTE: Contessa . . .

LA CONTESSA: Or non parliamo. Ecco qui le due nozze, riceverle dobbiam: alfin si tratta d'una vostra protetta. Seggiamo.

IL CONTE: Seggiam (e meditiam vendetta).
(*Siedono. La marcia s'avvicina.*)

Scena 14
I SUDDETTI, CACCIATORI CON FUCILE IN SPALLA,
GENTE DEL FORO, CONTADINI E CONTADINE.

(*Due giovinette che portano il cappello verginale con piume bianche, due altre portano un bianco velo, due altre i guanti e il mazzetto di fiori. Figaro con Marcellina. Due altre giovinette che portano un simile cappello per Susanna etc. Bartolo con Susanna. Due giovinette incominciano il coro che termina in ripieno. Bartolo conduce la Susanna al Conte e s'inginocchia per ricever da lui il cappello etc. Figaro conduce Marcellina alla Contessa e fa la stessa funzione.*)

DUE DONNE:
Amanti costanti,
seguaci d'onor,
cantate, lodate
sì saggio signor.
A un dritto cedendo
che oltraggia, che offende
ei caste vi rende
ai vostri amator.

THE COUNT: Countess . . .

THE COUNTESS: Now is not the time to speak. Here are the two wedding couples. We must receive them. One of the brides is a favorite of yours. Let us be seated.

THE COUNT: Let us be seated (and plan my revenge).
(They sit. The march is closer.)

Scene 14

THOSE BEFORE, HUNTERS WITH RIFLES ON THEIR SHOULDERS, LAWYERS, VILLAGE MEN AND WOMEN.

(Two young girls are carrying a bridal hat with white plumes, two others a white veil, two others gloves and a bouquet. Figaro escorts Marcellina. Two other young girls are carrying a similar headdress for Susanna. Bartolo escorts Susanna. Two young girls begin the anthem which others take up. Bartolo leads Susanna to the Count, and she kneels to receive the headdress, etc. Figaro leads Marcellina to the Countess who performs the same rite.)

TWO YOUNG GIRLS:
Come all happy lovers,
Come praise to the skies
The virtuous honor
Of a lord so just and wise.
He gave up his right
And to lovers restored
That reserved for the lord,
Chastity's stainless prize.

TUTTI:

Cantiamo, lodiamo

sì saggio signor.

(I figuranti ballano.)

(Susanna, essendo in ginocchio durante il duo, tira il Conte per l'abito, gli mostra il bigliettino, dopo passa la mano dal lato degli spettatori alla testa, dove pare che il Conte le aggiusti il cappello, e gli dà il biglietto. Il Conte se lo mette furtivamente in seno. Susanna s'alza, gli fa una riverenza. Figaro viene a riceverla, e si balla il fandango. Marcellina s'alza un po' più tardi. Bartolo viene a riceverla dalle mani della Contessa. I figuranti ballano.)

IL CONTE: *(va da un lato, cava il biglietto e nell'aprirlo si punge il dito, lo scuote, lo preme, lo succhia e, vedendo il biglietto sigillato colla spilla, dice gettando la spilla a terra e intanto che l'orchestra suona pianissimo)* Eh già, solita usanza! Le donne ficcan gli aghi in ogni loco ... Ah ah, capisco il gioco.

FIGARO: *(vede tutto e dice a Susanna)* Un biglietto amoroso che gli diè nel passar qualche galante ed era sigillato d'una spilla ond'ei si punse il dito.

(Il Conte legge, bacia il biglietto, cerca la spilla, la trova e se la mette alla manica del saio.) Il narciso or la cerca: oh, che stordito!

IL CONTE: Andate, amici, e sia per questa sera disposto l'apparato nuziale con la più ricca pompa: io vo' che sia magnifica la festa, e canti e fochi, e gran cena e gran ballo; e ognuno impari com'io tratto color che a me son cari.

(Il coro si ripete, e tutti partono.)

ALL:

Let us sing, let us praise
A lord so wise.
(Dancing ensues.)
(Susanna, while kneeling during the song, tugs on the Count's jacket, shows him the note, then lifts her hand to her head in a way the audience can see, and the Count takes the note while pretending to adjust her hat. He puts it furtively in his breast pocket. Susanna rises and curtsies. Figaro comes to fetch her and a fandango is danced. Marcellina rises a little afterwards. Bartolo comes to take her from the Countess's hands.)

THE COUNT: *(taking out the note and, opening it, pricks his finger; he shakes his finger, squeezes it, sucks it, notices that the note is sealed with a pin, drops the pin on the floor, and as the orchestra plays pianissimo:)* Ouch! Just like a woman to stick pins everywhere! Oh-ho, I get the point!

FIGARO: *(seeing everything, to Susanna)* A billet-doux some admirer slipped into his hand as she passed, and sealed with a pin on which he has pricked his finger.
(The Count reads the note, kisses it, looks for the pin, finds it, and puts it in his sleeve.) Our Narcissus is looking for it—oh, what a pinhead!

THE COUNT: Go now, friends, and let this evening's marriage feast be as lavish as can be! I wish the celebrations to be magnificent—the singing, the fireworks, a sumptuous meal, and a grand ball. Let the world know how well I treat those who are dear to me!

(The chorus is repeated, and everyone leaves.)

CORO:
Amanti costanti,
seguaci d'onor,
cantate, lodate
sì saggio signor.
A un dritto cedendo
che oltraggia, che offende
ei caste vi rende
ai vostri amator.
Cantiamo, lodiamo
sì saggio signor.

Fine dell'atto terzo.

CHORUS:
Come all happy lovers,
Come praise to the skies
The virtuous honor
Of a lord so just and wise.
He gave up his right
And to lovers restored
That reserved for the lord,
Chastity's stainless prize.
Let us sing, let us praise
A lord so wise.

End of Act III.

Atto quarto

Gabinetto.

Scena 1

BARBARINA SOLA.

N° 24 Cavatina

BARBARINA: *(cercando qualche cosa per terra)*
L'ho perduta ... me meschina! ...
Ah, chi sa dove sarà?
Non la trovo ... E mia cugina ...
e il padron ... cosa dirà?

Scena 2

BARBARINA, FIGARO E MARCELLINA.

Recitativo

FIGARO: Barbarina, cos'hai?

BARBARINA: L'ho perduta, cugino.

FIGARO: Cosa?

MARCELLINA: Cosa?

Act IV

An antechamber.

Scene 1

BARBARINA, ALONE.

Cavatina

BARBARINA: *(searching for something on the ground)*
I've lost it . . . My miseries mount!
This is my unlucky day!
I can't find it . . . The Count
And my cousin, what will they say?

Scene 2

BARBARINA, FIGARO, AND MARCELLINA.

Recitative

FIGARO: Barbarina, what is it?

BARBARINA: I've lost it, cousin.

FIGARO: What?

MARCELLINA: What?

BARBARINA: La spilla che a me diede il padrone per recar a Susanna.

FIGARO: A Susanna? ... La spilla? ... *(in collera)* E così tenerella il mestiero già sai ... *(Si calma.)* di far tutto sì ben quel che tu fai?

BARBARINA: Cos'è? Vai meco in collera.

FIGARO: E non vedi ch'io scherzo? Osserva ...
(Cerca un momento per terra, dopo aver destramente cavata una spilla dall'abito o dalla cuffia di Marcellina la dà a Barbarina.)
Questa è la spilla che il Conte da recare ti diede alla Susanna e servia di sigillo a un bigliettino. Vedi s'io sono istrutto.

BARBARINA: E perché il chiedi a me quando sai tutto?

FIGARO: Avea gusto d'udir come il padrone ti diè la commissione.

BARBARINA: Che miracoli! "Tieni fanciulla, reca questa spilla alla bella Susanna e dille: 'questo è il sigillo de' pini.'"

FIGARO: Ah ah! De' pini!

BARBARINA: È ver ch'ei mi soggiunse: "guarda che alcun non veda"; ma tu già tacerai.

FIGARO: Sicuramente.

BARBARINA: A te già niente preme.

FIGARO: Oh niente, niente.

BARBARINA: Addio, mio bel cugino; vo da Susanna e poi da Cherubino.
(Parte saltando.)

BARBARINA: The pin the master gave me to return to Susanna.

FIGARO: To Susanna? The pin? *(angry)* Even at your tender age you already know how . . . *(calmly)* to do everything so well?

BARBARINA: Why are you getting angry with me?

FIGARO: Can't you see I was only joking? Look here . . .
(He searches the ground for a moment and after dexterously taking a pin from Marcellina's dress, gives it to Barbarina.)
This is the pin the Count gave you to take to Susanna. It was used to seal a note. You see, I know everything about it.

BARBARINA: If you know everything already, why ask me questions?

FIGARO: I wanted to know how the master came to send you on such an errand.

BARBARINA: Oh, is that all! "Here, girl, take this pin to the lovely Susanna, and say to her, 'This is the seal of the pines.'"

FIGARO: Yes, yes, the pines!

BARBARINA: Then he warned me, "Take care no one sees you!" But you won't tell.

FIGARO: Trust me.

BARBARINA: Well, there's no harm if you know.

FIGARO: No, none at all.

BARBARINA: Goodbye, cousin dear. I'm off to Susanna, and then Cherubino.
(She skips off.)

Scena 3

MARCELLINA E FIGARO.

FIGARO: *(quasi stupido)* Madre!

MARCELLINA: Figlio!

FIGARO: Son morto.

MARCELLINA: Calmati, figlio mio.

FIGARO: Son morto, dico.

MARCELLINA: Flemma, flemma e poi flemma: il fatto è serio e pensarci convien, ma pensa un poco che ancor non sai di chi si prenda gioco.

FIGARO: Ah, quella spilla, o madre, è quella stessa che poc'anzi ei raccolse.

MARCELLINA: È ver, ma questo al più ti porge un dritto di stare in guardia e vivere in sospetto. Ma non sai se in effetto ...

FIGARO: All'erta dunque: il loco del congresso so dov'è stabilito ...

MARCELLINA: Dove vai, figlio mio?

FIGARO: A vendicar tutti i mariti: addio.
(Parte infuriato.)

Scene 3

MARCELLINA AND FIGARO.

FIGARO: *(in a daze)* Mother!

MARCELLINA: Son!

FIGARO: I'm done for!

MARCELLINA: Calm down, my son.

FIGARO: I tell you, I'm done for.

MARCELLINA: Calm, calm, and more calm. This is a serious matter and must be thought through. To begin with, you still don't know who the victim will be.

FIGARO: Oh, that is the very pin he picked up a little while ago.

MARCELLINA: True, but this only gives you a reason to stay on your guard and be suspicious. You still cannot be certain . . .

FIGARO: I'll be alert all right. In fact, I know where they are planning to meet.

MARCELLINA: Where are you going, son?

FIGARO: To avenge all husbands! Farewell.
(He leaves in a rage.)

Scena 4

MARCELLINA SOLA.

Recitativo

MARCELLINA: Presto, avvertiam Susanna; io la credo innocente: quella faccia, quell'aria di modestia ... E caso ancora ch'ella non fosse? ... Ah, quando il cor non ci arma personale interesse ogni donna è portata alla difesa del suo povero sesso, da questi uomini ingrati a torto oppresso.

N° 25 Aria

MARCELLINA:
Il capro e la capretta
son sempre in amistà,
l'agnello all'agnelletta
la guerra mai non fa.
Le più feroci belve
per selve e per campagne
lascian le lor compagne
in pace e libertà.
Sol noi povere femmine,
che tanto amiam questi uomini,
trattate siam dai perfidi
ognor con crudeltà.
(Parte.)

Scene 4

MARCELLINA, ALONE.

Recitative

MARCELLINA: Quick, I must warn Susanna . . . I am sure she is innocent. That face, that air of modesty . . . But suppose she is not. Ah, when women no longer have to fight in defense of their own hearts, they must fight for each other's. It is ungrateful men who are the real enemy.

Aria

MARCELLINA:
The he-goat and the she-goat
Both live in harmony.
The he-lamb and the she-lamb
Would never disagree.
The most ferocious beast
In the forest or the field
Leaves his mate in peace
And never makes her yield.
Only we poor women
Who love our men so dearly
Are held in mere contempt
And treated so severely.
(She leaves.)

Folto giardino con due nicchie parallele praticabili.

Scena 5

BARBARINA SOLA CON ALCUNI

FRUTTI E CIAMBELLE.

Recitativo

BARBARINA: "Nel padiglione a manca," ei così disse. È questo ... è questo ... E poi se non venisse? Oh, ve' che brava gente! A stento darmi un arancio, una pera e una ciambella. "Per chi madamigella?" "Oh, per qualcun, signori." "Già lo sappiam, ebbene?" "Il padron l'odia ed io gli voglio bene." Però costommi un bacio! E cosa importa? Forse qualcun mel renderà ... Son morta.

(Fugge impaurita ed entra nella nicchia a manca.)

Scena 6

FIGARO SOLO CON MANTELLO E LANTERNINO NOTTURNO,

POI BASILIO, BARTOLO E TRUPPA DI LAVORATORI ETC.

FIGARO: È Barbarina ... Chi va là?

BASILIO: Son quelli che invitasti a venir.

BARTOLO: *(a Figaro)* Che brutto ceffo! Sembri un cospirator: che diamin sono quegli infausti apparati?

FIGARO:
Lo vedrete tra poco.
In questo stesso loco
celebrerem la festa
della mia sposa onesta
e del feudal signor ...

A closely-planted garden with two arbors on either side.

Scene 5

BARBARINA, ALONE, CARRYING SOME
FRUITS AND SWEETMEATS.

Recitative

BARBARINA: In the arbor on the left, he said. This is it! Suppose he does not come! These people are so awful! I could hardly get them to give me an orange, a pear, a pastry. "Who is that for, missy?" For someone, sir. "That we've guessed!" Well, the master hates him, but I love him. All this cost me a kiss, but no matter. Maybe . . . someone . . . will pay it back! Mercy!
(Frightened, she runs into the arbor on the left.)

Scene 6

FIGARO, ALONE, WITH A CLOAK AND LANTERN, THEN
BASILIO, BARTOLO, AND A GROUP OF WORKERS.

FIGARO: That's Barbarina. Who goes there?

BASILIO: Those whom you invited.

BARTOLO: *(to Figaro)* What a scowl! You look like a conspirator. Why all the mystery?

FIGARO:
You'll see very soon.
Under this very moon
Our feudal lord will pursue
With my virtuous bride
What he thinks is his due.

BASILIO: Ah buono, buono! Capisco come ell'è.
(Accordati si son senza di me.)

FIGARO:
Voi da questi contorni
non vi scostate, intanto
io vado a dar certi ordini
e torno in pochi istanti:
a un fischio mio correte tutti quanti.
(Partono tutti eccettuati Bartolo e Basilio.)

Scena 7
BASILIO E BARTOLO.

BASILIO: Ha i diavoli nel corpo.

BARTOLO: Ma cosa nacque?

BASILIO: Nulla: Susanna piace al Conte, ella d'accordo gli diè un appuntamento che a Figaro non piace.

BARTOLO: E che? Dunque dovria soffrirlo in pace?

BASILIO: Quel che soffrono tanti ei soffrir non potrebbe? E poi, sentite, che guadagno può far? Nel mondo, amico, l'accozzarla co' grandi fu pericolo ognora: dan novanta per cento e han vinto ancora.

N° 26 Aria

BASILIO:
In quegl'anni in cui val poco
la mal pratica ragion
ebbi anch'io lo stesso foco,
fui quel pazzo ch'or non son.

BASILIO: My oh my! Now I see.
(They settled things without me.)

FIGARO:
Stay here and wait.
I have to go make
A few more arrangements.
I'll be back, without a doubt.
And when I whistle, you all rush out.
(Everyone leaves except Bartolo and Basilio.)

Scene 7

BASILIO AND BARTOLO.

BASILIO: That man is possessed!

BARTOLO: What is this all about?

BASILIO: Nothing. Susanna has caught the eye of the Count. She has agreed to a rendezvous, and Figaro isn't pleased.

BARTOLO: So? Ought he to suffer that in silence?

BASILIO: Many a man has suffered as much, and why not he? Listen here. What does he have to gain? In this world, my friend, it is a dangerous business to cross swords with the nobility. Nine times out of ten, they win.

Aria

BASILIO:
When I was wet behind the ears,
When reason carried little weight,
I too let nothing interfere
And wanted only to infuriate.

Ché col tempo e coi perigli
donna flemma capitò
e i capricci ed i puntigli
dalla testa mi cavò.
Presso un picciolo abituro
seco lei mi trasse un giorno
e togliendo giù dal muro
del pacifico soggiorno
una pelle di somaro:
"prendi," disse, "o figlio caro!"
Poi disparve e mi lasciò.
Mentre ancor tacito guardo quel dono,
il ciel s'annuvola, rimbomba il tuono,
mista alla grandine scroscia la piova:
ecco le membra coprir mi giova
col manto d'asino che mi donò.
Finisce il turbine, né fo due passi,
che fiera orribile dianzi a me fassi:
già già mi tocca l'ingorda bocca,
già di difendermi speme non ho.
Ma il fiuto ignobile del mio vestito
tolse alla belva sì l'appetito,
che disprezzandomi si rinselvò.
Così conoscere mi fe' la sorte
ch'onte, pericoli, vergogna e morte
col cuoio d'asino fuggir si può.
(Partono.)

But with experience and years,
Dame Discretion came to the fore
And drove away the smirks and sneers.
What once I sought I now deplored.
One day—how long ago it's been!—
She brought me to her dwelling place
And took from the wall an ass's skin
That hung above the fireplace,
And this is what she said.
"Take this, my son," she calmly said,
And into the dark of night she fled.
While I sat and stared at the hide,
A thunderous storm was brewing outside.
The rain was mixed with clattering hail.
It then seemed best, while the tempest prevailed,
To take refuge within the ass's hide.
I had taken two steps—the storm had passed—
When a monstrous beast next reared his mass
And would have eaten me without fail,
There being no help for me to invoke.
But the loathsome smell of my ugly cloak
Suddenly destroyed his appetite.
He crept back to his mountain heights.
So fate has taught me to proclaim
That death and danger, insult or shame
An ass's skin can put to flight.
(They leave.)

Scena 8

FIGARO SOLO.

N° 27 *Recitativo accompagnato ed aria*

Recitativo

FIGARO: Tutto è disposto: l'ora dovrebbe esser vicina, io sento gente ... È dessa ... Non è alcun ... Buia è la notte ... Ed io comincio omai a fare il scimunito mestiero di marito ... Ingrata! Nel momento della mia cerimonia ... Ei godeva leggendo, e nel vederlo io rideva di me senza saperlo. O Susanna, Susanna, quanta pena mi costi! Con quell'ingenua faccia ... con quegli occhi innocenti ... chi creduto l'avria! Ah, che il fidarsi a donna è ognor follia!

Aria

FIGARO:

Aprite un po' quegl'occhi,
uomini incauti e sciocchi,
guardate queste femmine,
guardate cosa son.
Queste chiamate dee
dagli ingannati sensi,
a cui tributa incensi
la debole ragion,
son streghe che incantano
per farci penar,
sirene che cantano
per farci affogar,
civette che allettano
per trarci le piume,
comete che brillano
per toglierci il lume;
son rose spinose,

Scene 8

FIGARO, ALONE.

Accompanied Recitative and Aria

Recitative

FIGARO: Everything is ready. The appointed time must be near.
I hear footsteps. Hers! No, it is no one. The night is dark . . . time
for me to start playing the ridiculous role of being a husband.
That deceiving woman! And on the very day of our wedding! . . .
I watched him read her note, I watched him laugh, and without
realizing it I even laughed at myself. Oh, Susanna, Susanna,
what pain you have caused me! I look at your sweet face, your
innocent eyes . . . Who would have believed it? Trusting a woman
is a great folly.

Aria

FIGARO:

Open wide your eyes,
Avoid a sad surprise,
Look out for women, men,
See them as they are.
Goddesses, so called!
One day you will awaken,
Rudely stunned and shaken
By the whole canard.
Enchantingly they sing
A song that nags and mocks.
A siren song they sing
To drive us onto rocks.
Owls can hypnotize
And mice are easily caught.
Comets tantalize,
Then blind us on the spot.
Roses boast of thorns,

son volpi vezzose,
son orse benigne,
colombe maligne,
maestre d'inganni,
amiche d'affanni,
che fingono, mentono,
amore non senton,
non senton pietà.
No, no, no, no.
Il resto nol dico,
già ognun lo sa.
(Si ritira.)

Scena 9

SUSANNA, LA CONTESSA TRAVESTITE; MARCELLINA.

Recitativo

SUSANNA: Signora, ella mi disse che Figaro verravvi.

MARCELLINA: Anzi è venuto: abbassa un po' la voce.

SUSANNA: Dunque un ci ascolta e l'altro dee venir a cercarmi, incominciam.

MARCELLINA: Io voglio qui celarmi.
(Entra dove entrò Barbarina.)

One hears of vixens who charm,
Smiling cows with horns
And doves who do real harm,
Nymphs of voluptuous deceit,
Angels who hover to cheat,
First sigh to us, then lie,
Have no love left to buy,
Or pity by now to spare.
The rest I need not share.
Every man can testify.
(He withdraws.)

Scene 9

SUSANNA AND THE COUNTESS,
BOTH IN DISGUISE, AND MARCELLINA.

Recitative

SUSANNA: My lady, Marcellina told me Figaro would be coming.

MARCELLINA: He is already here. Keep your voice down.

SUSANNA: So, one of them is eavesdropping on us and the other is prowling for me. Let's begin!

MARCELLINA: I will hide myself in here.
(She enters where Barbarina had gone.)

Scena 10

I SUDDETTI, FIGARO IN DISPARTE.

SUSANNA: Madama, voi tremate: avreste freddo?

LA CONTESSA: Parmi umida la notte ... Io mi ritiro.

FIGARO: (Eccoci della crisi al grande istante.)

SUSANNA: Io sotto queste piante, se madama il permette, resto a prendere il fresco una mezz'ora.

FIGARO: (Il fresco, il fresco!)

LA CONTESSA: Restaci in buon'ora. *(Si nasconde.)*

SUSANNA: *(sottovoce)* Il birbo è in sentinella. Divertiamci anche noi: diamogli la mercé de' dubbi suoi.

N° 28 Recitativo accompagnato ed aria

Recitativo

SUSANNA: Giunse alfin il momento che godrò senz'affanno in braccio all'idol mio. Timide cure, uscite dal mio petto, a turbar non venite il mio diletto. Oh, come par che all'amoroso foco l'amenità del loco, la terra e il ciel risponda! Come la notte i furti miei seconda!

Aria

SUSANNA:
Deh, vieni, non tardar, o gioia bella,
vieni ove amore per goder t'appella,
finché non splende in ciel notturna face,
finché l'aria è ancor bruna e il mondo tace.

Scene 10

THOSE BEFORE, AND FIGARO, IN HIDING.

SUSANNA: Madame, you are trembling. Are you cold?

THE COUNTESS: The night seems damp. I shall go in now.

FIGARO: (At last! The moment it all comes down to!)

SUSANNA: If your ladyship will allow me, I will stay behind here among the pines to take the air for half an hour.

FIGARO: (The pines! The air!)

THE COUNTESS: Stay, take your time. *(She hides.)*

SUSANNA: *(softly)* That rascal is watching. It is time for us to play this game too, and pay him back for his suspicions.

Accompanied Recitative and Aria

Recitative

SUSANNA: At last the moment has come when I can lose myself in the arms of my lover. The moment to banish hesitation from my heart. Let nothing disturb my delight! This place itself—the earth, the sky—is an echo of my love! How the night smiles on my secret!

Aria

SUSANNA:
Come, beloved, no more delay.
Come, the moment will not stay.
The busy moon is not yet bright.
So dark, so still it seems tonight.

Qui mormora il ruscel, qui scherza l'aura
che col dolce sussurro il cor ristaura;
qui ridono i fioretti e l'erba è fresca,
ai piaceri d'amor qui tutto adesca.
Vieni, ben mio, tra queste piante ascose:
ti vo' la fronte incoronar di rose.

Scena 11

I SUDDETTI, POI CHERUBINO.

Recitativo

FIGARO: Perfida! E in quella forma meco mentia? Non so s'io vegli o dorma.

CHERUBINO: *(cantando)* La la la la la la la la lera.

LA CONTESSA: Il picciol paggio!

CHERUBINO: Io sento gente: entriamo ove entrò Barbarina. Oh, vedo qui una donna!

LA CONTESSA: Ahimè meschina!

CHERUBINO: M'inganno? A quel cappello che nell'ombra vegg'io parmi Susanna!

LA CONTESSA: E se il Conte ora vien? Sorte tiranna!

Finale

CHERUBINO:
Pian pianin le andrò più presso,
tempo perso non sarà.

The lilting brook, the playful breeze,
Their whispers gives the soul its ease.
The grass is cool, the flowers smile,
Nature's endearments all beguile.
Come, beloved, our pleasure-ground!
With roses let your head be crowned!

Scene 11

THOSE BEFORE, AND THEN CHERUBINO.

Recitative

FIGARO: Traitor! This is how she has been deceiving me! Am I awake or dreaming?

CHERUBINO: *(singing)* La la la lera . . .

THE COUNTESS: The little page!

CHERUBINO: I hear people. I'll go in here, where Barbarina went. Oh, I see a woman!

THE COUNTESS: Oh, I am betrayed!

CHERUBINO: It cannot be! From that hat of hers, even in the dark I can recognize Susanna.

THE COUNTESS: If the Count should come now! Fate is too cruel!

Finale

CHERUBINO:
I will sneak up on her quietly.
There is no time to lose.

LA CONTESSA:
(Ah, se il Conte arriva adesso
qualche imbroglio accaderà!)

CHERUBINO: *(alla Contessa)*
Susannetta ... Non risponde ...
Colla mano il volto asconde ...
(Le prende la mano e l'accarezza.)
Or la burlo, in verità.

LA CONTESSA: *(cerca di liberarsi alterando la voce a tempo)*
Arditello, sfacciatello,
ite presto via di qua.

CHERUBINO:
Smorfiosa, maliziosa,
io già so perché sei qua.

Scena 12

I SUDDETTI ED IL CONTE.

IL CONTE: *(da lontano, in atteggiamento d'uno che guarda)* Ecco qui la mia Susanna.

SUSANNA, FIGARO: *(da lontano)* Ecco qui l'uccellatore.

CHERUBINO: Non far meco la tiranna.

SUSANNA, IL CONTE, FIGARO: Ah, nel sen mi batte il core! Un altr'uom con lei si sta.

LA CONTESSA: Via, partite o chiamo gente.

THE COUNTESS:
(If the Count sees an impropriety,
He will not be amused.)

CHERUBINO: *(to the Countess)*
Dear Susanna! . . . No reply . . .
She hides her face, but why? . . .
(He takes her hand and caresses it.)
It is time for her to choose!

THE COUNTESS: *(trying to free herself and disguising her voice)*
The impudence! The blasphemy!
How dare you come so near!

CHERUBINO:
You flirt! My secret enemy!
I know just why you're here!

Scene 12
THOSE BEFORE, AND THE COUNT.

THE COUNT: *(watching them from a distance)* There is my Susanna!

SUSANNA AND FIGARO: *(in the distance)* Here comes the bird-catcher!

CHERUBINO: *(to the Countess)* You are so hard on me!

SUSANNA, THE COUNT, AND FIGARO: My heart is racing! Another man is there with her.

THE COUNTESS: Leave at once, or I will call for help.

CHERUBINO: *(sempre tenendola per la mano)* Dammi un bacio o non fai niente.

SUSANNA, IL CONTE, FIGARO: Alla voce è quegli il paggio.

LA CONTESSA: Anche un bacio, che coraggio!

CHERUBINO:
E perché far io non posso
quel che il Conte or or farà?

SUSANNA, LA CONTESSA, IL CONTE, FIGARO: *(tutti da sè)*
Temerario!

CHERUBINO:
Oh, ve' che smorfie!
Sai ch'io fui dietro il sofà.

SUSANNA, LA CONTESSA, IL CONTE, FIGARO: *(come sopra)*
Se il ribaldo ancor sta saldo
la faccenda guasterà.

CHERUBINO: *(volendo dar un bacio alla Contessa)* Prendi intanto ...
(Il Conte mettendosi tra la Contessa ed il paggio riceve il bacio egli stesso.)

LA CONTESSA, CHERUBINO: Oh cielo! Il Conte!
(Il paggio entra da Barbarina.)

FIGARO: *(appressandosi al Conte)* Vo' veder cosa fan là.

CHERUBINO: *(still holding her hand)* Give me a kiss or you'll do nothing at all.

SUSANNA, THE COUNT, AND FIGARO: From his voice, that is the page.

THE COUNTESS: A kiss now? How brazen!

CHERUBINO:
What the Count is about to get,
Can't I have a share?

SUSANNA, THE COUNTESS, THE COUNT, AND FIGARO: *(each aside)* What audacity!

CHERUBINO:
What a tease you are!
You know, I was behind that chair.

SUSANNA, THE COUNTESS, THE COUNT, AND FIGARO: *(as above)*
If he goes on this way,
He will ruin the plan, I fear.

CHERUBINO: *(trying to kiss the Countess)* Just one kiss . . .
(The Count steps between Cherubino and the Countess and receives the kiss himself.)

THE COUNTESS AND CHERUBINO: Oh my God! The Count!
(The page slips into the arbor where Barbarina had gone.)

FIGARO: *(going towards the Count)* I'm going to see what's going on here.

IL CONTE: *(crede di dar uno schiaffo al paggio e lo dà a Figaro.)*
Perché voi nol ripetete,
ricevete questo qua.

FIGARO:
Ah, ci ho fatto un bel guadagno
colla mia curiosità!
(Si ritira.)

SUSANNA, LA CONTESSA, IL CONTE: *(Susanna ch'ode lo schiaffo ride.)*
Ah, ci ha fatto un bel guadagno
colla sua curiosità/temerità!

IL CONTE: *(alla Contessa)*
Partito è alfin l'audace.
Accostati, ben mio.

LA CONTESSA:
Giacché così vi piace,
eccomi qui, signor.

FIGARO:
Che compiacente femmina!
Che sposa di bon cor!

IL CONTE: Porgimi la manina.

LA CONTESSA: Io ve la do.

IL CONTE: Carina!

FIGARO: Carina!

THE COUNT: *(He goes to slap the page but hits Figaro instead.)*
I'll teach you not to try that again!
Take this!

FIGARO:
Ha! So that is what you get
For too much curiosity!
(He withdraws.)

SUSANNA, THE COUNTESS, AND THE COUNT: *(Susanna hearing
the slap and laughing)*
Ah! So that it what you get
For too much effrontery!

THE COUNT: *(to the Countess)*
That scamp has gone at last.
Now let me talk to you.

THE COUNTESS:
As it pleases you, my lord.
What will you have me do?

FIGARO:
Now there's a compliant wife!
She does what she's supposed to.

THE COUNT: Give me your hand.

THE COUNTESS: Here is my hand.

THE COUNT: My darling!

FIGARO: His darling!

IL CONTE:
Che dita tenerelle!
Che delicata pelle!
Mi pizzica, mi stuzzica,
m'empie d'un nuovo ardor.

SUSANNA, LA CONTESSA, FIGARO:
La cieca prevenzione
delude la ragione,
inganna i sensi ognor.

IL CONTE: *(le dà un anello.)*
Oltre la dote, o cara,
ricevi anco un brillante
che a te porge un amante
in pegno del suo amor.

LA CONTESSA:
Tutto Susanna piglia
dal suo benefattor.

SUSANNA, IL CONTE, FIGARO:
Va tutto a maraviglia!
Ma il meglio manca ancor.

LA CONTESSA: *(al Conte)*
Signor, d'accese fiaccole
io veggio il balenar.

IL CONTE:
Entriam, mia bella Venere,
andiamoci a celar.

SUSANNA, FIGARO:
Mariti scimuniti,
venite ad imparar.

THE COUNT:
These fingers are so slender!
Your skin so white and tender!
They thrill me, excite me,
Fill me with a new desire!

SUSANNA, THE COUNTESS, AND FIGARO:
This sudden appreciation
Is merely falsification.
What burns is lust, not fire.

THE COUNT: *(He gives her a ring.)*
To your dowry, my love,
Add this tiny gem.
When you gaze on it,
Think I am with you again.

THE COUNTESS:
Too generous, my lord.
Susanna is all undone.

SUSANNA, THE COUNT, AND FIGARO:
Now to the final reward!
The best is yet to come!

THE COUNTESS: *(to the Count)*
My lord, the light
Of lanterns is drawing near!

THE COUNT:
Come then, my Venus,
Let us conceal ourselves in here!

SUSANNA AND FIGARO:
A lesson for husbands
Who think they have nothing to fear!

LA CONTESSA: Al buio, signor mio?

IL CONTE:
È quello che vogl'io:
tu sai che là per leggere
io non desio d'entrar.

FIGARO:
La perfida lo seguita,
è vano il dubitar.

SUSANNA, LA CONTESSA:
I furbi sono in trappola,
cammina ben l'affar.

IL CONTE: *(Figaro passa, il Conte con voce alterata)* Chi passa?

FIGARO: *(con rabbia)* Passa gente.

LA CONTESSA: È Figaro: men vo.
(Entra a man destra.)

IL CONTE: Andate: io poi verrò.
(Si disperde pel bosco.)

Scena 13
FIGARO E SUSANNA.

FIGARO:
Tutto è tranquillo e placido;
entrò la bella Venere;
col vago Marte prendere,
nuovo Vulcan del secolo,
in rete la potrò.

THE COUNTESS: In the dark, my lord?

THE COUNT:
That is what I wish.
It is not to read a book
I suggest we go there, my dear.

FIGARO:
She is following him!
She's faithless, that is clear.

SUSANNA AND THE COUNTESS:
Both men are in the trap.
It is time to persevere.

THE COUNT: *(his voice disguised, as Figaro passes by)* Who is there?

FIGARO: *(angrily)* No one special.

THE COUNTESS: That's Figaro! I must go.
(She goes to the arbor on the right.)

THE COUNT: Yes, go. I will join you soon.
(He goes off among the trees.)

Scene 13

FIGARO AND SUSANNA.

FIGARO:
Suddenly so peaceful and still.
Fair Venus has gone in,
And Mars has his heroine.
Like Vulcan with his net,
I will catch them at their sport.

SUSANNA: *(cangiando la voce)* Ehi, Figaro, tacete.

FIGARO:
Oh, questa è la Contessa …
A tempo qui giungete …
Vedrete là voi stessa …
il Conte e la mia sposa …
Di propria man la cosa
toccar io vi farò.

SUSANNA: *(si dimentica di alterar la voce.)*
Parlate un po' più basso:
di qua non muovo passo,
ma vendicar mi vo'.

FIGARO: (Susanna!) Vendicarsi?

SUSANNA: Sì.

FIGARO: Come potria farsi?

SUSANNA:
(L'iniquo io vo' sorprendere,
poi so quel che farò.)

FIGARO:
(La volpe vuol sorprendermi
e secondar la vo'.)

FIGARO: *(con comica affettazione)* Ah, se madama il vuole!

SUSANNA: Suvvia, manco parole.

SUSANNA: *(disguising her voice)* Figaro! Quiet, please!

FIGARO:
Ah, that will be the Countess . . .
You are just in time . . .
Here, before your very eyes,
The Count and his prize . . .
You can help me find
A way to pull them up short.

SUSANNA: *(forgetting to disguise her voice)*
Your voice is too loud.
I shall stay where I am
But revenge will be mine.

FIGARO: (Susanna!) Revenge?

SUSANNA: Mine!

FIGARO: How can that be done?

SUSANNA:
(The villain will be taken by surprise.
I know just what to do.)

FIGARO:
(The vixen wants to take me by surprise.
I will help her do it too.)

FIGARO: *(with comic affectation)* Ah, whatever Madame calls for!

SUSANNA: Come now, not a word more.

FIGARO: *(come sopra)*
Eccomi a' vostri piedi ...
Ho pieno il cor di foco ...
Esaminate il loco ...
Pensate al traditor.

SUSANNA:
(Come la man mi pizzica!
Che smania! Che furor!)

FIGARO:
(Come il polmon mi s'altera!
Che smania! Che calor!)

SUSANNA: *(alterando un poco la voce)* E senz'alcun affetto?

FIGARO:
Suppliscavi il rispetto.
Non perdiam tempo invano,
(Si frega le mani.)
datemi un po' la mano ...

SUSANNA: *(parlando in voce naturale, gli dà uno schiaffo)* Servitevi, signor.

FIGARO: Che schiaffo!

SUSANNA: *(Lo schiaffeggia a tempo.)* Che schiaffo! E questo e ancora questo e questo e poi quest'altro.

FIGARO: Non batter così presto.

SUSANNA: E questo, signor scaltro, e questo e qui quest'altro ancor.

FIGARO: *(as above)*
I kneel here at your feet . . .
I burn with the disgrace!
It was in this very place
That you were callously betrayed.

SUSANNA:
(My hand wants only to strike him . . .
The impatience! The anger!)

FIGARO:
(My heart wants only to be hers . . .
The impatience! Oh, hang her!)

SUSANNA: *(altering her voice a little)* But with no show of affection?

FIGARO:
Indignation, on reflection,
Is enough. No time to waste—
(He rubs his hands.)
Your hand, in haste . . .

SUSANNA: *(Speaking in her natural voice, she slaps his face.)* Here it is, sir.

FIGARO: You hit me!

SUSANNA: *(She continues to slap his face.)* And this too! And this! And *this*!

FIGARO: Not so hard! Not so fast!

SUSANNA: And this, Mr. Slyboots! And *this*!

FIGARO:
Oh schiaffi graziosissimi,
oh mio felice amor!

SUSANNA:
Impara, impara, o perfido,
a fare il seduttor.

Scena 14
I SUDDETTI, POI IL CONTE.

FIGARO: *(si mette in ginocchio.)*
Pace, pace, mio dolce tesoro!
Io conobbi la voce che adoro
e che impressa ognor serbo nel cor.

SUSANNA: *(ridendo e con sorpresa)* La mia voce?

FIGARO: La voce che adoro.

SUSANNA, FIGARO:
Pace, pace, mio dolce tesoro,
pace, pace, mio tenero amor!

IL CONTE: Non la trovo e girai tutto il bosco.

SUSANNA, FIGARO: Questi è il Conte, alla voce il conosco.

IL CONTE: *(parlando verso la nicchia dove entrò madama cui apre egli stesso)* Ehi, Susanna … sei sorda … sei muta?

SUSANNA: Bella, bella! Non l'ha conosciuta!

FIGARO:
Oh sweetest, softest of blows!
The delicate raptures of bliss!

SUSANNA:
This will teach you, you two-timer,
How to treat an innocent miss!

Scene 14
THOSE BEFORE, THEN THE COUNT.

FIGARO: *(kneeling)*
Peace, peace, my dearest sweetheart!
Your voice upset the applecart.
I would know and adore it anywhere.

SUSANNA: *(laughing with surprise)* My voice!

FIGARO: The voice I know and adore!

SUSANNA AND FIGARO:
Peace, peace, my dearest sweetheart!
Peace, peace, my tender love!

THE COUNT: I have searched these damn groves and cannot find her anywhere.

SUSANNA AND FIGARO: That's the Count. I know his voice.

THE COUNT: *(calling into the arbor where the Countess had withdrawn)*
Psst! Susanna! . . . Are you deaf? . . . Say something!

SUSANNA: Excellent! He does not recognize her!

FIGARO: Chi?

SUSANNA: Madama.

FIGARO: Madama?

SUSANNA: Madama.

SUSANNA, FIGARO:
La commedia, idol mio, terminiamo,
consoliamo il bizzarro amator.

FIGARO: *(si mette ai piedi di Susanna)* Sì, madama, voi siete il ben mio.

IL CONTE: La mia sposa! ... Ah, senz'arme son io.

FIGARO: Un ristoro al mio cor concedete.

SUSANNA: Io son qui, faccio quel che volete.

IL CONTE: Ah ribaldi!

SUSANNA, FIGARO:
Ah, corriamo, mio bene;
e le pene compensi il piacer.
(Vanno verso la nicchia a man manca. Susanna entra nella nicchia.)

FIGARO: Who?

SUSANNA: My lady.

FIGARO: My lady?

SUSANNA: The Countess!

SUSANNA AND FIGARO:
Time to end this comedy, my dear,
And comfort the deluded lover.

FIGARO: *(throwing himself at Susanna's feet)* It is true, my lady, I want you to be mine!

THE COUNT: My wife? And I have no weapon!

FIGARO: Grant some consolation to my poor heart, I beg you . . .

SUSANNA: I am yours. Do what you will . . .

THE COUNT: Oh, the traitors!

SUSANNA AND FIGARO:
Time to leave, my dear, that's plain.
Let pleasure now make up for pain.
(They go towards the arbor. Susanna enters the arbor.)

Scena ultima

I SUDDETTI, ANTONIO, BASILIO,
SERVITORI CON FIACCOLE ACCESE; POI SUSANNA,
MARCELLINA, CHERUBINO, BARBARINA; INDI LA CONTESSA

IL CONTE: Gente, gente, all'armi, all'armi!

FIGARO: *(finge eccessiva paura)* Il padrone!

IL CONTE: Gente, gente, aiuto, aiuto!

FIGARO: Son perduto!

BASILIO, ANTONIO: Cosa avvenne?

IL CONTE:
Il scellerato!
M'ha tradito, m'ha infamato,
e con chi state a veder.

BASILIO, ANTONIO:
Son stordito, sbalordito,
non mi par che ciò sia ver!

FIGARO:
Son storditi, sbalorditi,
oh, che scena, che piacer!

IL CONTE:
(Tira pel braccio Cherubino, che fa forza per non sortire, nè si vede che per metà.)
Invan resistete,
uscite, madama,
il premio or avrete
di vostra onestà.
Il paggio!

Final Scene

THOSE BEFORE, ANTONIO, BASILIO,
SERVANTS WITH TORCHES; THEN SUSANNA, MARCELLINA,
CHERUBINO, BARBARINA; LATER THE COUNTESS

THE COUNT: Men! You there! Bring your swords!

FIGARO: *(feigning extreme fright)* The master!

THE COUNT: Ho there! Help!

FIGARO: I am ruined!

BASILIO AND ANTONIO: What has happened?

THE COUNT:
The scoundrel!
He has betrayed me, he has shamed me,
And with whom you are about to see.

BASILIO AND ANTONIO:
How shocking! How amazing!
I cannot believe it is true.

FIGARO:
How shocking! How amazing!
What a scene! What derring-do!

THE COUNT:
(He pulls Cherubino by the arm, who struggles not to come out, nor can half of him be seen.)
In vain you resist.
My lady, come forth.
Virtue, I insist,
Will have its reward.
The page!

(Dopo il paggio escono Barbarina, Marcellina, e Susanna vestita cogli abiti della Contessa si tiene il fazzoletto sulla faccia, s'inginocchia ai piedi del Conte.)

ANTONIO: Mia figlia!

FIGARO: Mia madre!

BASILIO, ANTONIO, FIGARO: Madama!

IL CONTE:
Scoperta è la trama,
la perfida è qua.
(Si inginocchiano tutti ad uno ad uno.)

SUSANNA: Perdono, perdono!

IL CONTE: No no, non sperarlo.

FIGARO: Perdono, perdono!

IL CONTE: No no, non vo' darlo.

SUSANNA, BARBARINA, MARCELLINA, CHERUBINO, BASILIO, ANTONIO, FIGARO: Perdono, perdono!

IL CONTE: *(con più forza)* No, no, no, no, no, no, no, no.

LA CONTESSA: *(esce dall'altra nicchia e vuole inginocchiarsi, il Conte nol permette)*
Almeno io per loro
perdono otterrò.

(After the page come Barbarina, Marcellina, and Susanna, dressed in the Countess's clothes; she holds a handkerchief in front of her face and kneels down at the feet of the Count.)

ANTONIO: My daughter!

FIGARO: My mother!

BASILIO, ANTONIO, AND FIGARO: The Countess!

THE COUNT:
The plot is unraveled!
The adulteress is before you!
(One by one they all kneel.)

SUSANNA: Forgive me, forgive me!

THE COUNT: No, never. I will not.

FIGARO: Forgive her, please!

THE COUNT: No, never. I refuse.

SUSANNA, BARBARINA, MARCELLINA, CHERUBINO, BASILIO, ANTONIO, AND FIGARO: Forgive her, we beg you!

THE COUNT: *(more forcefully)* No, no, no, no, *no!*

THE COUNTESS: *(emerging from the other arbor and starts to kneel; the Count prevents her)*
Then for others let me beg instead
A forgiveness that, for me, you will not show.

BASILIO, IL CONTE, ANTONIO:
Oh cielo! Che veggio!
Deliro! Vaneggio!
Che creder non so.

IL CONTE: *(in tono supplichevole)* Contessa, perdono!

LA CONTESSA:
Più docile io sono
e dico di sì.

**SUSANNA, LA CONTESSA, BARBARINA, MARCELLINA, CHERU-
BINO, BASILIO, IL CONTE, ANTONIO, FIGARO:**
Ah, tutti contenti
saremo così.
Questo giorno di tormenti,
di capricci e di follia
in contenti e in allegria
solo amor può terminar.
Sposi, amici, al ballo, al gioco,
alle mine date foco,
ed al suon di lieta marcia
corriam tutti a festeggiar!

Fine dell'opera.

BASILIO, THE COUNT, AND ANTONIO:
Heavens! A delusion!
What utter confusion!
I cannot believe it's so!

THE COUNT: *(in a tone of supplication)* My lady, forgive me.

THE COUNTESS:
I see you in distress.
What can I say but . . . yes.

SUSANNA, THE COUNTESS, BARBARINA, MARCELLINA, CHERUBINO, BASILIO, THE COUNT, ANTONIO, AND FIGARO:
Each and everyone happy again!
A day of madness,
Of folly and sadness
Is now at an end.
In the end there is only love.
Spouses, friends, come join in the dance!
Let us all join now to praise romance.
Night after night of happiness!
In the end there is only love!

End of the Opera.

∶ 4 ∶

The Rake Punished

OR

Don Giovanni

THE RAKE PUNISHED, OR DON GIOVANNI

•

Dramma giocoso, 1787

Libretto by Lorenzo Da Ponte

The Characters

Don Giovanni, a young, licentious nobleman

Leporello, his manservant

Donna Anna, a noblewoman

The Commendatore, her father

Don Ottavio, betrothed to Donna Anna

Donna Elvira, a lady from Burgos, abandoned by Don Giovanni

Zerlina, a peasant girl

Masetto, a peasant betrothed to Zerlina

Chorus, peasants, servants, young women, musicians

Setting: a city in Spain

THE TITLE PAGE ORIGINALLY READ *IL DISSOLUTO*
*punito, ossia il Don Giovanni (The Rake Punished, or Don
Giovanni)*, but from the very beginning it was the Don's character rather than his fate that fascinated audiences, and the opera
has always been known by its hero's name. It is assumed that in
the opening-night audience sat Giacomo Casanova. He had been
summoned to Prague by his friend Da Ponte to help with the
last-minute revisions required before the premiere. He seems
to have had a hand in helping shape Leporello's escape from
Donna Elvira in Act II. Casanova's own memoirs are filled with
wrong doors, inopportune encounters, and breathless escapes,
but what did he think as he sat there and watched the story of
Don Giovanni unfold? After all, the point of this moral fable—
look again at the title—is not the affairs but the punishment.
Don Giovanni isn't given the chance to write his memoirs in
old age, savoring his sensual triumphs though no longer able to
enjoy them. We use both names as almost affectionate or at least
indulgent shorthand for an adventurous lecher—a Don Juan,
a Casanova. But of course our obsession with Don Giovanni
goes far beyond this, even far beyond our settled moral convic-
tions. The Danish philosopher Søren Kierkegaard, in his 1843
Either/Or, contends that the Don is not merely a character but
"an idea, that is to say, energy, life." The Don's life gives the
others theirs: it is "the vital core of their existence, his passion resounds everywhere, lending color and carrying power to

the Commendatore's gravity, Elvira's fury, and Anna's hatred, Ottavio's pompousness, Zerlina's anxiety, Masetto's bitterness, and Leporello's bewilderment . . . Compared with him, all other existence is merely secondary. If one wants uniformity to be the basic rule for an opera, it is easy to see that a more perfect subject . . . than *Don Giovanni* is simply not to be contemplated." That is as much as to say he is beyond judgment; we watch with fascination what we should view with horror. He comes, during the age of Romanticism, to seem more of a Faust than a philanderer. He is the man who takes the full measure of life and death, going fearlessly where others will not, cannot, go. E. T. A. Hoffmann thought that in his fiery fall was revealed his "heavenly nature." Hoffmann's heart was struck, he said, by "a strong, noble body, a carriage emitting sparks of light, igniting the intimations of higher things, possessing a deep spirit and a quick understanding." And of course, during the age of Freud, the Don was seen to be acting out what every man unconsciously yearns for, a polymorphous perversity.

Ironically, though, it is not Don Giovanni's life but his death that is by far the most sensational and dramatically powerful part of this opera, perhaps in all opera. Does this mean that guilt rather than pleasure is the opera's true theme? The appended *scena ultima* implies as much. Operas were expected to conclude with a chorus, and Don Giovanni's death—though stupendous in its theatrical effect—does not provide what was wanted, and so the librettist and composer reassemble the opera's characters to comment on what has happened and draw the appropriate moral. The entrance to hell is closed, the social order reestablished. But the individual lives of the surviving characters suddenly seem diminished, even emptied. Until this moment, each has had an impatience or titillation, a righteous anger or existential loathing caused by the Don. How will the women fare when they return to their own lives? Will Donna Anna ever go through with her wedding? Will Zerlina grow quickly bored with her husband? What will Donna Elvira dream of in her convent cell?

Though Don Giovanni shares the cynicism of Don Alfonso in
Così and the sexual appetite of the Count in *Figaro*, he is of a
different order altogether. He does not just have an eye for the
ladies, he can *smell* them approaching. The sheer number of
women he has seduced and abandoned is not a sign of his heartless charm but of his compulsive personality. When Leporello
begs him to stop, he snorts, "Leave the women alone? Ha! Don't
you realize they mean more to me than the bread I eat, the air I
breathe?" And when his valet asks if he has the heart to deceive
them all, he says, "I do it because I love them. Who is faithful to
one is cruel to the others. I am a man whose heart is so large that
I love all of them." How can such self-knowledge be deceitful?
He is nothing if not driven, but he is not self-centered. In fact,
he has no aria in the entire opera that reflects upon himself. He
is never alone with his thoughts, but constantly on the prowl.
Papageno is in search of a sweetheart, but only willing to go so
far. The Count in *Figaro*, with his aristocratic hauteur, wants
his desires satisfied, but also has an estate to run, a position to
maintain, servants to control. The Don has only his cravings
to sate. Ironically, the Don never beds a woman in the opera.
It is not conquest, but frustration that dominates. Whether in
the aftermath of love (with Donna Anna and Donna Elvira) or
in anticipation (with Zerlina), the Don is kept at the borders
of triumph. And it is desire rather than his technique that is
itself seductive. As Kierkegaard wrote about the Don's power
of seduction, "It is the power of desire, the energy of sensual
desire. He desires in every woman the whole of womanhood, and
therein lies the sensually idealizing power with which he at once
embellishes and overcomes his prey. The reflex of his gigantic
passion beautifies and develops its object, who flushes in the
enhanced beauty by its reflection." In this view, Don Giovanni
is only an instrument, a mirror in which others see their naked,
arching images. Perhaps it is this that finally accounts for the
opera's truly demonic force.

Compared with *Figaro* or *Così*, *Don Giovanni* is more episodic in structure. Scenes reinforce each other but aren't organically related. The exciting opening scene with Donna Anna is as puzzling as it is dramatic. Had, in fact, she been raped? The two women we next meet—the traduced Donna Elvira and the virginal Zerlina—are the contrasting sides of Donna Anna's plight. The three women are like queens on playing cards, snapped off the deck of the Don's interest. Episodic as it is, the opera drives, almost relentlessly, towards death. The plot gets more complicated at the same time it seems to run out of options. Don Giovanni puts himself in death's way. He invites the Commendatore to dine with him, he dismisses Leporello's fears and warnings, he answers the door himself, he takes the statue by the hand. As Albert Camus said, the Don seems to find it natural that he should be punished. "It is the rule of the game. And it is exactly a mark of his generosity, to have entirely accepted the rule of the game. But he knows that he is right, and that there can be no question of punishment. An inevitable end is not the same thing as a penalty."

THE STORY

ACT I

In the garden outside the Commendatore's house, Leporello, Don Giovanni's valet, paces in the dark, complaining of his lot: he stands watch outside while his master is inside, in a lady's bedroom. Suddenly, the lady herself, Donna Anna, the Commendatore's daughter, rushes out, clutching the arm of Don Giovanni, who is trying to conceal his identity. She denounces him as a scoundrel. Her father emerges from the house, sends his daughter back inside, and challenges the Don to a duel. Don Giovanni kills the Commendatore. Leporello jokes, "Well done! Two crimes and no bother. / Rape the daughter and kill the father." The Don threatens him as well, but they both withdraw when Donna Anna returns with her fiancé, Don Ottavio. They find her father's body, call for help, and, as they leave, vow to revenge his murder. Leporello too thinks his master is a scoundrel, but Don Giovanni hushes him. He catches the scent of a woman approaching, another woman he plans to bed. An angry Donna Elvira enters, denouncing the Don for having seduced and abandoned her, and threatening to kill him. Don Giovanni tries to calm her, but she will have none of it—and as he escapes, he tells Leporello to tell her "the whole truth." Leporello then gives her a catalogue of the Don's conquests as a proof of his prowess with women. When the Don saunters off, Donna Elvira's rage boils over.

Villagers are singing and dancing, while two young lovers, Zerlina and Masetto, look forward to their wedding. Don Giovanni and Leporello come by, and the Don looks over the crowd for women he might have, and spots Zerlina. He speaks with the young couple, and tells Leporello to take Masetto and his friends to his palazzo, while he stays behind with Zerlina. Masetto is nervous about the plan, but agrees, knowing that he dare not disobey a nobleman and reminding Zerlina to behave herself. Alone together, Don Giovanni suggests that such a beauty as she shouldn't have anything to do with a rustic. He promises to marry her himself, and takes her hand to serenade her. She is entranced, and they go off together to Don Giovanni's summerhouse. Donna Elvira suddenly appears and interrupts them. She warns Zerlina to flee and avoid the fate that befell her. The two women run off. Annoyed that his plans have come to nothing, Don Giovanni is then approached by Donna Anna and Don Ottavio, seeking his help in finding her father's assassin. Donna Elvira returns and this time warns Donna Anna not to trust the faithless Don, who insists she is lying and demented. He is worried enough, though, to think it better to escape. He takes his leave of Donna Anna, saying that he must follow Donna Elvira to keep her out of harm's way. Donna Anna, feeling faint, recalls to Don Ottavio the scene when a strange man slipped into her bedroom, and how she resisted. Again, they vow to revenge themselves on the assailant, and they leave.

Leporello wonders how he can leave the Don's service. The risks are mounting. He has kept Masetto and his friends busy with food and drink at the palazzo, and managed to lock Donna Elvira out. Don Giovanni looks forward to joining them all for a night of revelry. Back at the party, Zerlina and Masetto are quarreling over her flirtatious behavior, and she pleads for his forgiveness. They hear the Don approach, and Masetto hides himself in a nearby gazebo. Don Giovanni arrives and rouses the group to come dancing, but soon catches sight of Zerlina. He follows her into the gazebo, only to encounter Masetto there, whom he manages to placate with lies, and all three go off to the dance.

Don Ottavio, Donna Anna, and Donna Elvira enter the ballroom in masks, determined now to uncover Don Giovanni's crimes. With all the costumes around them, they recognize his voice. There follows a swirl of dancers, candles, trays with refreshments. Leporello escorts the young men to their seats, while Don Giovanni escorts the young women, whispering in Zerlina's ear while Masetto looks on, fuming. The minuet begins, and Don Ottavio takes Donna Anna onto the dance floor, reminding her to keep up appearances. Don Giovanni takes Zerlina to dance, while Leporello tries to deal with Masetto's impatience. While the dancing continues, suddenly Zerlina runs shouting across the room and condemns Don Giovanni. The Don's enemies rush to protect the girl and confront the villain. He is trapped. His accusers close in on him. Leporello is sure he will escape. Don Giovanni is confident: "Though the powers of hell assail me, / I will live to see another day."

ACT II

Leporello has decided to leave Don Giovanni's service, and tells him so. But the Don gives him money to stay, and he agrees, on the one condition that his master give up chasing women. An utter impossibility, counters the Don, who already plans to rendezvous with Donna Elvira's chambermaid and decides to change clothes with Leporello in order to try a new approach. They pass by Donna Elvira's window, and he addresses her—though it is Leporello, dressed as the Don, who is standing under the window. He flatters her and begs forgiveness, and at once her heart begins to melt. She is torn between her old resentments and her new hopes. Don Giovanni is taking pride in his skill, while Leporello prays that Donna Elvira will resist. She comes outside and embraces the man she thinks is Don Giovanni. Leporello begins to enjoy the attention, and Don Giovanni grows jealous. He pretends he is running someone through with a sword. Leporello and Donna Elvira are startled and flee, leaving the Don free to serenade whichever woman may next appear at the window. Masetto, with a group of villagers, all with pistols, enters in search of Don Giovanni, who from the shadows imitates Leporello's voice, sending the men off in the wrong direction. He takes Masetto's hand and pledges to help him kill the vile seducer, then asks to see his weapons. When Masetto turns them over, Don Giovanni aims them at Masetto and leaves. Zerlina comes in with a lantern, searching for Masetto, whom she finds in distress. She comforts him and they leave together.

In a darkened atrium in Donna Anna's house, Leporello and Donna Elvira are alone. Leporello, trying to escape her affections, exits through the wrong door and, before he can find the right one, Don Ottavio and Donna Anna enter, both dressed in mourning. Again Leporello tries to escape and this time is stopped by Zerlina and Masetto—who, like the others, think Leporello is Don Giovanni. They go to attack him, but Leporello takes off his disguise and falls to his knees to a general consternation. He begs their forgiveness, passes the blame, and escapes through a door. Now the others know for certain that Don Giovanni is the murderer, and Don Ottavio goes to have an arrest warrant issued. Donna Elvira is torn between conflicting emotions of pity and horror.

In a cemetery, where a memorial statue of the Commendatore can be seen, Leporello and Don Giovanni meet up. They exchange clothes once more, while the Don tells of yet another conquest. As if from nowhere, the menacing voice of the Commendatore is heard. Leporello is terrified, but the Don feigns indifference and invites the ghost to dinner that very night. The statue moves and acknowledges the invitation—to Leporello's horror and the Don's disdain. Elsewhere, Don Ottavio gently, if stiffly, presses his suit but Donna Anna will hear of nothing but revenge.

A great banquet has been laid, servants are scurrying and musicians are playing. While Leporello serves him, Don Giovanni savors his supper. Donna Elvira enters in desperation. She is a changed woman, and sympathetic. She begs him to mend his ways, but the Don says he has first to finish his meal. Leporello is moved by Elvira's plea, but the Don pays her no heed. She is hardly out the door when her screams are heard, and Don Giovanni sends his servant to find out the reason. He returns to say that he has seen the statue of the Commendatore without. A loud knocking is heard at the door. Don Giovanni demands that Leporello open it, but he is so scared he hides under the table. The Don takes a light and goes to open the door himself. The stone Commendatore enters, as he said he would, and asks that Don Giovanni return the favor and come dine with him. When the Don gives his hand as a pledge, he is in the unrelenting grip of the statue, who demands that the reprobate beg for forgiveness. The Don refuses. The earth shakes, a fiery pit opens, and Don Giovanni disappears with the Commendatore in the flames with one final scream as he is dragged to hell.

The other characters return and, to their amazement, Leporello explains what has happened. Shakily, they plan their futures—Donna Anna asks that her wedding wait a year, Donna Elvira will enter a convent, Zerlina and Masetto are hungry, and Leporello must find a new master. But all agree that the rake has been properly punished.

THE BACKGROUND

After the enormously successful production of *The Marriage of Figaro* in Prague in 1786, and following soon after the opera's premiere in Vienna, the impresario of the Prague National Theater, Pasquale Bondini, immediately commissioned another opera from Da Ponte and Mozart. Da Ponte was busy writing two other librettos at the time he started *Don Giovanni*, one for Salieri and the other for Martín y Soler, and told in his memoirs of dividing his days and nights among the three projects, "a bottle of *tokai* to my right, a box of Seville snuff to my left, in the middle an inkwell." (The latter composer makes a cameo appearance in *Don Giovanni*'s Act II party scene, only to be trumped when the stage musicians play a bit of *The Marriage of Figaro* for the delighted guests. On the other hand, Da Ponte wrote that the *Arbore di Diana* he wrote for Martín y Soler was "the best of all the operas I ever composed, both as regards the conception and as regards the verse.")

The choice of the legend of Don Juan as the opera's subject was Da Ponte's, and his libretto's immediate source was another libretto, *Don Giovanni, ossia Il Convitato di Pietra* (*Don Giovanni, or The Stone Guest*), written by Giovanni Bertati for Giuseppe Gazzaniga's 1787 opera. Da Ponte expanded, reconfigured, and improved it. The figure of Don Juan has deep roots both in the literature and imagination of Europe. He makes his first appearance in 1630 in *El Burlador de Sevilla y Convidado de Piedra* (*The Trickster of Seville and the Stone Guest*) by the prolific Spanish dramatist Tirso de Molina, and some have thought the play to be based on the life of a four-teenth-century Seville nobleman, Don Juan Tenorio. Since then he has appeared in plays by Molière, Goldoni, Pushkin, Dumas, Rostand, and George Bernard Shaw, as well as in countless poems and novels, operas and ballets. But Da Ponte's version of the luckless libertine is the story's most famous, not least because it is darker, more penetrating and disturbing than most others.

Mozart had worked on the score, on and off, for about ten months and it was considered difficult by both the orchestra and singers. He and Da Ponte had arrived in Prague three weeks before the first performance to supervise rehearsals and add finishing touches—the overture was written just the day before the opening on October 29 at the National Theater. Luigi Bassi, only twenty-two at the time, sang the title role; it is said that, at his insistence, "Là ci darem la mano" was rewritten five times until he was satisfied with it. Teresa Saporiti was Donna Anna. (She lived to 106 and knew Verdi. In the Vienna production, the part was sung by Mozart's sister-in-law and first love, Aloysia Weber Lange.) Saporiti's sister Caterina, married to the impresario Bondini, sang Zerlina. The Donna Elvira was Caterina Micelli (in Vienna the part was taken by Catarina Cavalieri, who was the first Constanza in *The Abduction*). The Leporello was Felice Ponziani (in Vienna it was Francesco Benucci, one of Mozart's favorite singers and the first Figaro). The Commendatore and Masetto were sung by Giuseppe Lolli (in the Vienna production the parts were taken by Francesco Bussani). Don Ottavio was Antonio Baglioni. Mozart conducted. When he first appeared in the pit, and at the end of the opera, he was showered with ecstatic applause. A special edition of the libretto, bound in gold paper, was sold in the lobby.

Joseph II called for performances of the opera in Vienna, and the librettist and composer undertook revisions and additions to the work for the new production, which opened at the Burgtheater on May 7, 1788. The emperor expressed his disappointment delicately: "That opera is divine; I should even venture that it is more beautiful than *Figaro*. But such music is not meat for the teeth of my Viennese!" When Da Ponte reported that remark to Mozart, he says the composer replied, "Give them time to chew on it!" He was not mistaken, thought Da Ponte. "Little by little even Vienna of the dull teeth came to enjoy its savor and appreciate its beauties, and placed *Don Giovanni* among the most beautiful operas that have ever been produced on any stage."

Atto primo

Giardino. Notte.

Scena 1

LEPORELLO CON FERRAIUOLO, CHE PASSEGGIA
DAVANTI LA CASA DI DONN'ANNA; POI DON GIOVANNI,
DONN'ANNA; INDI IL COMMENDATORE.

N° 1 Introduzione

LEPORELLO:

Notte e giorno faticar
per chi nulla sa gradir,
piova e vento sopportar,
mangiar male e mal dormir ...
Voglio far il gentiluomo
e non voglio più servir.
Oh, che caro galantuomo!
Voi star dentro colla bella,
ed io far la sentinella! ...
Voglio far il gentiluomo
e non voglio più servir.
Ma mi par che venga gente,
non mi voglio far sentir.

(S'asconde.)

Act I

A garden at night.

Scene 1

LEPORELLO, IN A CLOAK, IS PACING IN FRONT OF DONNA ANNA'S HOUSE; THEN DON GIOVANNI, DONNA ANNA; LATER THE COMMENDATORE.

Introduction

LEPORELLO:
Always working, night and day,
And not a word of gratitude.
Wind and rain, come what may,
Never a nap, and rotten food.
I want to play the gentleman.
I've had enough with servitude.
Oh, to be a gentleman!
You're in a lady's warm boudoir,
While I'm outside, standing guard.
I want to play the gentleman.
I've had enough with servitude.
But I hear . . . people coming.
To quickly hide myself seems shrewd.
(He hides himself.)

DONN'ANNA: *(tenendo forte pel braccio Don Giovanni, ed egli cercando sempre di celarsi)*
Non sperar, se non m'uccidi,
ch'io ti lasci fuggir mai.

DON GIOVANNI:
Donna folle! Indarno gridi!
Chi son io tu non saprai.

LEPORELLO:
Che tumulto! Oh ciel, che gridi!
Il padron in nuovi guai.

DONN'ANNA: Gente! Servi! Al traditore! ...

DON GIOVANNI: Taci e trema al mio furore!

DONN'ANNA: Scellerato!

DON GIOVANNI: Sconsigliata!

LEPORELLO:
Sta' a veder che il libertino
mi farà precipitar.
Che tumulto! Oh ciel, che gridi!
Sta' a veder che il libertino
mi farà precipitar.

DONN'ANNA:
Come furia disperata
ti saprò perseguitar.

DON GIOVANNI:
Questa furia disperata
mi vuol far precipitar.

DONNA ANNA: *(clutching the arm of Don Giovanni, who is trying to conceal himself)*
Do not think, unless you kill me,
That I will ever let you go!

DON GIOVANNI:
Silly woman! You scream in vain.
Who I am you will never know!

LEPORELLO:
What an uproar! Good God, the noise!
My master's lot is touch-and-go.

DONNA ANNA: Help me! Anyone! Help!

DON GIOVANNI: Quiet or you go to hell!

DONNA ANNA: Wicked man!

DON GIOVANNI: Silly girl!

LEPORELLO:
We'll see if this rake's scheming
Brings about my end.
What an uproar! Good God, the screaming!
We'll see if this rake's scheming
Brings about my end.

DONNA ANNA:
Against his desperate anger,
On whom can I depend?

DON GIOVANNI:
With every ounce of anger
I'll pursue you to the end.

(Donn'Anna sentendo il Commendatore lascia Don Giovanni ed entra in casa.)

IL COMMENDATORE: Lasciala, indegno, battiti meco.

DON GIOVANNI: Va', non mi degno di pugnar teco.

IL COMMENDATORE: Così pretendi da me fuggir?

LEPORELLO: (Potessi almeno di qua partir!)

DON GIOVANNI: Misero, attendi, se vuoi morir.
(Combattono. Don Giovanni ferisce mortalmente il Commendatore.)

IL COMMENDATORE: *(mortalmente ferito)*
Ah soccorso! ... Son tradito! ...
L'assassino ... m'ha ferito ...
e dal seno palpitante
sento l'anima partir. *(Qui il Commendatore more.)*

DON GIOVANNI: *(sottovoce)*
Ah, già cade il sciagurato!
Affannosa e agonizzante
già dal seno palpitante
veggo l'anima partir.

LEPORELLO: *(sottovoce)*
Qual misfatto! Qual eccesso!
Entro il sen dallo spavento
palpitar il cor mi sento;
io non so che far, che dir.

(Hearing the Commendatore, Donna Anna releases Don Giovanni and goes into the house.)

COMMENDATORE: Let her go, coward! Fight with me!

DON GIOVANNI: Fighting an old man is beneath my dignity.

COMMENDATORE: Run from my challenge? Fight, I say!

LEPORELLO: (If only I could sneak away!)

DON GIOVANNI: So be it, wretch, if you wish to die!
(They fight. Don Giovanni mortally woulds the Commendatore.)

COMMENDATORE: *(mortally wounded)*
Help! . . . I am betrayed! . . .
That assassin . . . wounded me! . . .
From my gasping breast
I feel . . . my soul depart. *(He dies.)*

DON GIOVANNI: *(aside)*
Ah . . . the fool is down . . .
In mortal agony he lies.
From his gasping breast
I can see his soul depart.

LEPORELLO: *(aside)*
What a disaster! It's all too much!
My heart is beating away
With terror in my breast.
What should I do? What can I say?

Scena 2

DON GIOVANNI, LEPORELLO.

Recitativo

DON GIOVANNI: *(sottovoce sempre)* Leporello, ove sei?

LEPORELLO: *(sottovoce sempre)* Son qui, per mia disgrazia; e voi?

DON GIOVANNI: Son qui.

LEPORELLO: Chi è morto: voi o il vecchio?

DON GIOVANNI: Che domanda da bestia! Il vecchio.

LEPORELLO:
Bravo: due imprese leggiadre!
Sforzar la figlia ed ammazzar il padre.

DON GIOVANNI: L'ha voluto, suo danno.

LEPORELLO: Ma Donn'Anna cosa ha voluto?

DON GIOVANNI:
Taci. *(in atto di batterlo)*
Non mi seccar, vien meco, se non vuoi
qualche cosa ancor tu!

LEPORELLO: Non vo' nulla, signor, non parlo più.

(Partono.)

Scene 2

DON GIOVANNI AND LEPORELLO.

Recitative

DON GIOVANNI: *(softly throughout)* Leporello, are you there?

LEPORELLO: *(softly throughout)* Unfortunately. And you?

DON GIOVANNI: Here.

LEPORELLO: Who's dead? You or the old man?

DON GIOVANNI: What a dumb question! The old man.

LEPORELLO:
Well done! Two crimes and no bother.
Rape the daughter and murder the father.

DON GIOVANNI: He asked for it. Too bad for him.

LEPORELLO: Was Donna Anna asking for it?

DON GIOVANNI:
Silence! *(about to strike him)*
Or you will provoke me again.
Come with me, if you don't want the same.

LEPORELLO: No, my lord, not a word of blame.

(They leave.)

Scena 3

DON OTTAVIO, DONN'ANNA
CON SERVI CHE PORTANO DIVERSI LUMI.

Recitativo

DONN'ANNA: *(con risolutezza)*
Ah, del padre in periglio
in soccorso voliam!

DON OTTAVIO: *(con ferro ignudo in mano)*
Tutto il mio sangue verserò se bisogna.
Ma dov'è il scellerato?

DONN'ANNA: In questo loco ...
(Vede il cadavere.)

N° 2 Recitativo accompagnato e duetto

Recitativo accompagnato

DONN'ANNA:
Ma qual mai s'offre, oh dei,
spettacolo funesto agli occhi miei!
Il padre ... padre mio ... mio caro padre ...

DON OTTAVIO: Signore ...

DONN'ANNA: Ah, l'assassino mel trucidò! Quel sangue ... quella
piaga ... quel volto ... tinto e coperto dei color di morte ... Ei
non respira più ... fredde ha le membra ... Padre mio ... caro
padre ... padre amato ... Io manco ... io moro ...

Scene 3

DON OTTAVIO AND DONNA ANNA,

WITH SERVANTS CARRYING LIGHTS.

Recitative

DONNA ANNA: *(resolutely)*
My father is in danger.
Quickly! Come help him!

DON OTTAVIO: *(with a drawn sword in hand)*
My lifeblood I will shed, if need be.
The wretched villain, where is he?

DONNA ANNA: Over here . . .
(She sees the body.)

Accompanied Recitative and Duet

Accompanied Recitative

DONNA ANNA:
Oh God! What do I see?
What horrible scene lies before me?
My father . . . my dear father!

DON OTTAVIO: My lord!

DONNA ANNA: Ah, an assassin has murdered him. The blood
. . . the wound . . . his face . . . So pale . . . the color of death itself
. . . He's not breathing . . . his hands are cold . . . Father . . . dear
father . . . beloved father . . . I feel faint . . . I am dying . . .

DON OTTAVIO: Ah, soccorrete, amici, il mio tesoro! Cercatemi, recatemi … qualche odor … qualche spirto … Ah, non tardate … Donn'Anna … sposa … amica … il duolo estremo la meschinella uccide …

DONN'ANNA: Ahi …

DON OTTAVIO: Già rinviene … Datele nuovi aiuti …

DONN'ANNA: Padre mio …

DON OTTAVIO:
Celate, allontanate agli occhi suoi
quell'oggetto d'orrore.
Anima mia … consolati … fa' core …

Duetto

DONN'ANNA: *(disperatamente)*
Fuggi, crudele, fuggi:
lascia ch'io mora anch'io,
ora ch'è morto, oh dio,
chi a me la vita diè.

DON OTTAVIO:
Senti, cor mio, deh, senti,
guardami un solo istante,
ti parla il caro amante
che vive sol per te.

DONN'ANNA:
Tu sei … perdon … mio bene …
l'affanno mio, le pene …
Ah, il padre mio dov'è?

DON OTTAVIO: Help, friends! Help my precious love! Find me some salts, some spirits . . . Quickly! Donna Anna! My bride! My beloved! This terrible grief is killing her.

DONNA ANNA: Ah . . .

DON OTTAVIO: She is coming to . . . Give her another sip . . .

DONNA ANNA: Father . . .

DON OTTAVIO:
Quick now, take that object of horror
Out of her sight.
Dearest, I'm here . . . It will be put right . . .

Duet

DONNA ANNA: *(desperately)*
Leave me, cruel man, leave!
Let me now die as well.
One last farewell
For him who gave me life.

DON OTTAVIO:
Hear me, my love, listen!
Look here, look in the eyes
Of the man you would despise
But who loves you more than life.

DONNA ANNA:
It is you . . . forgive me, love . . .
My anguish . . . my grief . . .
My father, where is he?

DON OTTAVIO:
Il padre … Lascia, o cara,
la rimembranza amara …
hai sposo e padre in me.

DONN'ANNA:
Ah! Vendicar, se il puoi,
giura quel sangue ognor.

DON OTTAVIO:
Lo giuro agl'occhi tuoi,
lo giuro al nostro amor.

DONN'ANNA, DON OTTAVIO:
Che giuramento, oh dei!
Che barbaro momento!
Fra cento affetti e cento
vammi ondeggiando il cor.
(Partono.)

Notte. Strada.

Scena 4

DON GIOVANNI, LEPORELLO, POI DONNA ELVIRA
IN ABITO DA VIAGGIO.

Recitativo
DON GIOVANNI: Orsù, spicciati, presto … cosa vuoi?

LEPORELLO: L'affar di cui si tratta è importante.

DON GIOVANNI: Lo credo.

DON OTTAVIO:
Your father . . . You must let go
Of these memories, this sorrow.
You have a father and husband in me.

DONNA ANNA:
Avenge his blood! Swear!
Swear by heaven above!

DON OTTAVIO:
I swear it by your eyes!
I swear it by our love!

DONNA ANNA AND DON OTTAVIO:
A solemn oath to God!
I swear upon this sword.
My heart is heavy but resolved.
Death will be his just reward.
(They leave.)

Night. A street.

Scene 4

DON GIOVANNI AND LEPORELLO,
THEN DONNA ELVIRA IN TRAVELLING CLOTHES.

Recitative

DON GIOVANNI: Come, out with it. What do you want?

LEPORELLO: A matter of some importance.

DON GIOVANNI: Very well then.

LEPORELLO: È importantissimo.

DON GIOVANNI: Meglio ancora: finiscila.

LEPORELLO: Giurate di non andar in collera.

DON GIOVANNI: Lo giuro sul mio onore, purché non parli del Commendatore.

LEPORELLO: Siam soli.

DON GIOVANNI: Lo vedo.

LEPORELLO. Nessun ci sente.

DON GIOVANNI: Via.

LEPORELLO: Vi posso dire tutto liberamente?

DON GIOVANNI: Sì.

LEPORELLO: Dunque, quando è così, caro signor padrone, la vita che menate *(all'orecchio, ma forte)* è da briccone.

DON GIOVANNI: Temerario! In tal guisa ...

LEPORELLO: E il giuramento! ...

DON GIOVANNI: Non so di giuramenti ... Taci ... o ch'io ...

LEPORELLO: Non parlo più, non fiato, o padron mio.

DON GIOVANNI: Così saremo amici. Or odi un poco, sai tu perché son qui?

LEPORELLO: Of the utmost importance.

DON GIOVANNI: So much the better. Go ahead.

LEPORELLO: Promise you won't get angry.

DON GIOVANNI: I swear on my honor—provided you do not mention the Commendatore.

LEPORELLO: We're alone?

DON GIOVANNI: As you see.

LEPORELLO: No one can hear us?

DON GIOVANNI: Get on with it.

LEPORELLO: Can I speak freely?

DON GIOVANNI: Yes.

LEPORELLO: In that case, my dear master, the life you're leading is that of *(into his ear, loudly)* a scoundrel!

DON GIOVANNI: How dare you! You . . .

LEPORELLO: You gave your word . . .

DON GIOVANNI: I promised nothing . . . Be quiet before I . . .

LEPORELLO: I won't say—even *whisper*—another word, master.

DON GIOVANNI: That way we'll stay friends. Now listen up. Why do you think I'm here?

LEPORELLO: Non ne so nulla, ma essendo l'alba chiara ... non sarebbe qualche nuova conquista? Io lo devo saper per porla in lista.

DON GIOVANNI: Va' là, che se' il grand'uom: sappi chi'io sono innamorato d'una bella dama, e son certo che m'ama. La vidi ... le parlai ... meco al casino questa notte verrà ... Zitto: mi pare sentire odor di femmina ...

LEPORELLO: (Cospetto! Che odorato perfetto!)

DON GIOVANNI: All'aria mi par bella.

LEPORELLO: (E che occhio, dico!)

DON GIOVANNI: Ritiriamoci un poco e scopriamo terren.

LEPORELLO: Già prese foco.

Scena 5

I SUDDETTI IN DISPARTE, DONNA ELVIRA.

N° 3 Aria

DONNA ELVIRA:
Ah, chi mi dice mai
quel barbaro dov'è
che per mio scorno amai,
che mi mancò di fé?
Ah, se ritrovo l'empio,
e a me non torna ancor,
vo' farne orrendo scempio,
gli vo' cavare il cor!

LEPORELLO: I have no idea, but since it's so late . . . could it be some new conquest? I'd need to know—to put her on my list.

DON GIOVANNI:
Well, aren't you the smart one! You should know that I am in love with a beautiful woman, and I am certain she loves me. I have seen her . . . spoken with her . . . and tonight she is coming to my house. Hush! I'm sure that's the scent of a woman.

LEPORELLO: (My, what an *advanced* sense of smell!)

DON GIOVANNI: The aroma of beauty itself!

LEPORELLO: (What an eye he has as well!)

DON GIOVANNI: Let's hide for a while and survey the lay of the land.

LEPORELLO: He's already on fire!

Scene 5
THOSE BEFORE TO ONE SIDE, AND DONNA ELVIRA.

Aria

DONNA ELVIRA:
Who will tell me where, oh where
That filthy monster has run away?
The love I gave him unaware
He has now viciously betrayed.
If I can find the villain, and if
He still will not return to me,
I mean to destroy his miserable life,
To rip out his heart pitilessly.

DON GIOVANNI:
Udisti? Qualche bella dal vago
abbandonata. Poverina!
Cerchiam di consolare il suo tormento.

LEPORELLO: Così ne consolò mille e ottocento.

DON GIOVANNI: Signorina!

Recitativo

DONNA ELVIRA: Chi è là?

DON GIOVANNI: Stelle! Che vedo!

LEPORELLO: Oh bella, Donna Elvira!

DONNA ELVIRA: Don Giovanni! Sei qui mostro, fellon, nido d'inganni.

LEPORELLO: (Che titoli cruscanti! Manco male che lo conosce bene.)

DON GIOVANNI: Via, cara Donna Elvira, calmate questa collera … sentite … lasciatemi parlar …

DONNA ELVIRA: Cosa puoi dire dopo azion sì nera? In casa mia entri furtivamente; a forza d'arte, di giuramenti e di lusinghe arrivi a sedurre il cor mio; m'innamori, o crudele, mi dichiari tua sposa e poi, mancando della terra e del cielo al santo dritto, con enorme delitto dopo tre dì da Burgos t'allontani, m'abbandoni, mi fuggi e lasci in preda al rimorso ed al pianto, per pena forse che t'amai cotanto!

LEPORELLO: (Pare un libro stampato.)

DON GIOVANNI:
Hear that? A lovely lady
Seduced and abandoned. Poor thing!
Let's try to console her distress.

LEPORELLO: Like the thousands before this little princess.

DON GIOVANNI: Signorina!

Recitative

DONNA ELVIRA: Who's there?

DON GIOVANNI: Heavens! What's this!

LEPORELLO: Oh Lord! Donna Elvira!

DONNA ELVIRA: Don Giovanni! You? Here? Monster! Criminal!
Filthy liar!

LEPORELLO: (All of his titles! She must know him well.)

DON GIOVANNI: Come now, dear Donna Elvira, calm your anger
. . . listen . . . let me speak . . .

DONNA ELVIRA: What could you say after what you've done?
You sneaked into my house. With cunning and vows and flattery you seduced my heart and made love to me. You were cruel
enough to promise marriage. Then, defying the holy laws of
heaven and earth with your crime, you fled Burgos. You deceived
me, you ran away, and left me a prey to remorse and weeping,
as my punishment for having loved you so much!

LEPORELLO: (She could write a book.)

DON GIOVANNI: Oh, in quanto a questo ebbi le mie ragioni ... *(a Leporello)* È vero?

LEPORELLO: *(ironicamente)* È vero. E che ragioni forti!

DONNA ELVIRA: E quali sono, se non la tua perfidia, la leggerezza tua? Ma il giusto cielo volle ch'io ti trovassi per far le sue, le mie vendette.

DON GIOVANNI: Eh via, siate più ragionevole ... (Mi pone a cimento costei.) Se non credete al labbro mio, credete a questo galantuomo.

LEPORELLO: (Salvo il vero.)

DON GIOVANNI: *(forte)* Via, dille un poco ...

LEPORELLO: *(piano)* E cosa devo dirle?

DON GIOVANNI: *(forte)* Sì sì, dille pur tutto.

DONNA ELVIRA: *(a Leporello)* Ebben, fa' presto ... *(In questo frattempo Don Giovanni fugge.)*

LEPORELLO: Madama ... veramente ... in questo mondo conciossiacosa quando fosse che il quadro non è tondo ...

DONNA ELVIRA: *(a Leporello)* Sciagurato, così del mio dolor gioco ti prendi? *(verso Don Giovanni che non crede partito)* Ah voi ... Stelle! L'iniquo fuggì! Misera me! Dove, in qual parte ...

LEPORELLO: Eh, lasciate che vada: egli non merta che di lui ci pensiate ...

DON GIOVANNI: As for that, I had my reasons. *(to Leporello)* Didn't I?

LEPORELLO: *(ironically)* Indeed, yes. Valid reasons.

DONNA ELVIRA: What are they, other than lies and infidelity? But a just God wanted me to find you, to carry out His vengeance, and mine.

DON GIOVANNI: Come, be reasonable . . . (My, this woman is a nuisance.) If you won't believe me, believe this honest gentleman.

LEPORELLO: (Anything but the truth.)

DON GIOVANNI: *(loudly)* Go on, tell her . . .

LEPORELLO: *(softly)* What should I say?

DON GIOVANNI: *(loudly)* Yes, yes, the whole truth.

DONNA ELVIRA: *(to Leporello)* Well then . . . be quick about it . . . *(Meanwhile Don Giovanni escapes.)*

LEPORELLO: Madame, truly in this world, as you are no doubt aware, what is called a square cannot be a circle . . .

DONNA ELVIRA: *(to Leporello)* Scoundrel! You use my grief to mock me? *(to Don Giovanni, not realizing he has gone)* And you . . . Heavens! The wretch has run away! God! Where is he! Where has he gone?

LEPORELLO: Oh, let him go. He isn't worth your worry.

DONNA ELVIRA: Il scellerato m'ingannò, mi tradì!

LEPORELLO: Eh, consolatevi: non siete voi, non foste e non sarete né la prima né l'ultima; guardate, questo non picciol libro è tutto pieno dei nomi di sue belle; ogni villa, ogni borgo, ogni paese è testimon di sue donnesche imprese.

N° 4 Aria

LEPORELLO:
Madamina, il catalogo è questo
delle belle che amò il padron mio;
un catalogo egli è che ho fatt'io,
osservate, leggete con me.
In Italia seicento e quaranta,
in Lamagna duecento e trentuna,
cento in Francia, in Turchia novantuna,
ma in Ispagna son già mille e tre.
V'han fra queste contadine,
cameriere e cittadine,
v'han contesse, baronesse,
marchesane, principesse,
e v'han donne d'ogni grado,
d'ogni forma, d'ogni età.
Nella bionda egli ha l'usanza
di lodar la gentilezza,
nella bruna la costanza,
nella bianca la dolcezza.
Vuol d'inverno la grassotta,
vuol d'estate la magrotta;
è la grande maestosa,
la piccina è ognor vezzosa.
Delle vecchie fa conquista
pel piacer di porle in lista,
ma passion predominante

DONNA ELVIRA: That wicked man tricked me, betrayed me . . .

LEPORELLO: Take heart. You weren't the first one, and you won't be the last. Look at this thick book. It's filled with the names of all his sweethearts. Every village, every town, every country offers proof of his prowess with women.

Aria

LEPORELLO:
Dear Madame, here's a little list
Of the beauties my master has won.
I've made some notes, just for fun.
Come over here, read it with me.
In Italy, six hundred and forty.
In Germany, two hundred thirty-one.
In France, a hundred. In Turkey, ninety-one.
But in Spain, it tops a thousand and three.
There are your country girls,
Maidservants and ladies in pearls.
Countesses, baronesses
Princesses, marchionesses.
Women of every rank,
Of any shape, of any age.
With blondes, it is his way
To praise their sweetness.
Dark ones, their bouquet.
Pale ones, their neatness.
In winter he likes them plumper
But then thinner come summer.
Tall ones are "majestic."
Small ones are "domestic."
Older women he can't resist,
Dying to add them to my list.
But his favorite has always been

è la giovin principiante.
Non si picca se sia ricca,
se sia brutta, se sia bella:
purché porti la gonnella
voi sapete quel che fa.

(Parte.)

Scena 6

DONNA ELVIRA SOLA.

Recitativo

DONNA ELVIRA: In questa forma dunque mi tradì il scellerato!
È questo il premio che quel barbaro rende all'amor mio? Ah,
vendicar vogl'io l'ingannato mio cor! Pria ch'ei mi fugga … si
ricorra … si vada … Io sento in petto sol vendetta parlar, rabbia
e dispetto.

(Parte.)

Scena 7

MASETTO, ZERLINA E CORO DI CONTADINI E CONTADINE
CHE SUONANO, BALLANO E CANTANO.

N° 5 Coro

ZERLINA:
Giovinette che fate all'amore,
non lasciate che passi l'età:
se nel seno vi bulica il core,
il rimedio vedetelo qua.
Che piacer, che piacer che sarà!

CORO DI CONTADINE:
Che piacer, che piacer che sarà!
La la la ra la la la la ra la.

The innocent young virgin.
He does not care if they are rich,
Fair or foul is all the same.
If she's in a dress, he's game.
He knows which end is which.
(He leaves.)

Scene 6

DONNA ELVIRA, ALONE.

Recitative

DONNA ELVIRA: This is how that devil betrayed me! Is this the reward that evil man offers for my love? My wounded heart will have its revenge. Before he escapes . . . I'll go after him . . . I hear in my breast only the voice of vengeance, of rage and hate. *(She leaves.)*

Scene 7

MASETTO, ZERLINA, AND A CHORUS OF VILLAGERS WHO
ARE SINGING, PLAYING, AND DANCING.

Chorus

ZERLINA:
Young girls who play at romance,
Don't let time pass you by.
When your heart is in a trance,
Here is why you sigh. Why,
Here is your joy, here your sweet reply.

CHORUS OF VILLAGERS:
Ah . . . Here is your joy, here your sweet reply,
La la ra la, la la ra lie.

MASETTO:
Giovinotti leggeri di testa,
non andate girando qua e là:
poco dura de' matti la festa,
ma per me cominciato non ha.
Che piacer, che piacer che sarà!

CORO DI CONTADINI:
Che piacer, che piacer che sarà!
La la la ra la la la la ra la.

ZERLINA, MASETTO:
Vieni, vieni, carino/carina, e godiamo
e cantiamo e balliamo e saltiamo.
Che piacer, che piacer che sarà!

CORO:
Che piacer, che piacer che sarà!
La la la ra la la ra la la ra la.

Scena 8

MASETTO, ZERLINA, CORO DI CONTADINI E CONTADINE.
DON GIOVANNI E LEPORELLO DA PARTE.

Recitativo

DON GIOVANNI: Manco male è partita: oh, guarda guarda che bella gioventù, che belle donne!

LEPORELLO: Fra tante, per mia fé, vi sarà qualche cosa anche per me.

DON GIOVANNI: Cari amici, buon giorno: seguitate a stare allegramente, seguitate a suonar, o buona gente. C'è qualche sposalizio?

MASETTO:
Young men who are so carefree,
Don't count on your roving eye.
Age will cloud all your revelry
But now it's my turn to try. Why,
Here is my joy, here my sweet reply.

CHORUS OF VILLAGERS:
Ah . . . There is your joy, there your sweet reply.
La la ra la, la la ra lie.

ZERLINA AND MASETTO:
Come, my love, come celebrate.
We must not linger, cannot wait.
Here is our joy, here our sweet reply.

CHORUS OF VILLAGERS:
Ah . . . Here is their joy, here their sweet reply.
La la ra la, la la ra lie.

Scene 8

MASETTO, ZERLINA, AND THE CHORUS OF VILLAGERS. DON
GIOVANNI AND LEPORELLO TO ONE SIDE.

Recitative

DON GIOVANNI: Thank God, she's gone. Oh, look, a crowd of
peasants! And pretty women!

LEPORELLO: Enough of them that he may even leave one for me.

DON GIOVANNI: Dear friends, good day! Please, go on enjoying
yourselves, go on playing. Is there to be a wedding?

ZERLINA: Sì signore, e la sposa son io.

DON GIOVANNI: Me ne consolo. Lo sposo?

MASETTO: Io, per servirla.

DON GIOVANNI: Oh bravo! Per servirmi: questo è vero parlar da galantuomo.

LEPORELLO: Basta che sia marito.

ZERLINA: Oh, il mio Masetto è un uom d'ottimo core!

DON GIOVANNI: Oh, anch'io, vedete! Voglio che siamo amici: il vostro nome?

ZERLINA: Zerlina.

DON GIOVANNI: E il tuo?

MASETTO: Masetto.

DON GIOVANNI: Oh caro il mio Masetto! Cara la mia Zerlina! V'esibisco la mia protezione ... *(a Leporello che fa dei scherzi alle altre contadine)* Leporello ... Cosa fai lì birbone?

LEPORELLO: Anch'io, caro padrone, esibisco la mia protezione.

DON GIOVANNI: Presto, va' con costor: nel mio palazzo conducili sul fatto; ordina ch'abbiano cioccolata, caffè, vini, prosciutti; cerca divertir tutti; mostra loro il giardino, la galleria, le camere; in effetto fa' che resti contento il mio Masetto. Hai capito?

ZERLINA: There is, sir, and I am the bride.

DON GIOVANNI: Happy news! And the groom?

MASETTO: At your service, sir.

DON GIOVANNI: Bravo! "At your service" . . . Spoken like a gentleman.

LEPORELLO: That boy will be lucky to get to the altar.

ZERLINA: Oh, my Masetto is the best of men.

DON GIOVANNI: So am I. I hope we shall be friends. What is your name?

ZERLINA: Zerlina.

DON GIOVANNI: And yours?

MASETTO: Masetto.

DON GIOVANNI: Ah, my dear Masetto! And dearest Zerlina! I want to offer you my protection . . . *(to Leporello who is joking with some of the village girls)* Leporello . . . What are you up to, you rascal?

LEPORELLO: I too, master, am offering these girls my protection.

DON GIOVANNI: Off with you! Take them at once to my palazzo. See that they have cold meats and wine, chocolates and coffee. Keep them amused. Show them the garden, the galleries, each and every room. Be sure my friend Masetto here is well taken care of . . . Understand?

LEPORELLO: Ho capito: andiam.

MASETTO: Signore ...

DON GIOVANNI: Cosa c'è?

MASETTO: La Zerlina senza me non può star.

LEPORELLO: In vostro loco vi sarà Sua Eccellenza ... e saprà bene fare le vostre parti.

DON GIOVANNI: Oh, la Zerlina è in man d'un cavalier! Va' pur, fra poco ella meco verrà.

ZERLINA: Va', non temere! Nelle mani son io d'un cavaliere.

MASETTO: E per questo?

ZERLINA: E per questo non c'è da dubitar.

MASETTO: Ed io, cospetto ...

DON GIOVANNI: Olà, finiam le dispute: se subito senz'altro replicar non te ne vai, *(mostrandogli la spada)* Masetto, guarda ben, ti pentirai.

N° 6 Aria

MASETTO:
Ho capito, signor sì,
chino il capo e me ne vo:
giacché piace a voi così,
altre repliche non fo.
Cavalier voi siete già,
dubitar non posso affé:
me lo dice la bontà

LEPORELLO: Understood. After you . . .

MASETTO: Sir . . .

DON GIOVANNI: What is it?

MASETTO: Zerlina cannot stay here without me.

LEPORELLO: His Excellency will take your place. He'll know exactly what to do.

DON GIOVANNI: Your Zerlina is in the hands of a nobleman. Go along. I'll bring her with me presently.

ZERLINA: Go, don't be afraid. I am in the hands of a nobleman.

MASETTO: And that means?

ZERLINA: That you should have no doubts.

MASETTO: But, by God, I . . .

DON GIOVANNI: No more quarreling. Go immediately, no questions asked. *(putting his hand on his sword)* Watch your step, Masetto, or you'll regret it.

Aria

MASETTO:
Yes, sir, as you wish.
I must bow and slip away.
Your wish is my command.
I dare not disobey.
A nobleman, yes indeed,
That's plain for all to see.
Your kindness, I'll concede,

che volete aver per me.
(da parte a Zerlina)
Bricconaccia, malandrina,
fosti ognor la mia ruina.
(a Leporello che lo vuol condur seco)
Vengo, vengo!
(a Zerlina)
Resta, resta!
È una cosa molto onesta:
faccia il nostro cavaliere
cavaliera ancora te.
(Va via.)

Scena 9

DON GIOVANNI E ZERLINA.

Recitativo

DON GIOVANNI: Alfin siam liberati, Zerlinetta gentil, da quel scioccone. Che ne dite, mio ben, so far pulito?

ZERLINA: Signore, è mio marito ...

DON GIOVANNI: Chi? Colui? Vi par che un onest'uomo, un nobil cavalier, come io mi vanto, possa soffrir che quel visetto d'oro, quel viso inzuccherato, da un bifolcaccio vil sia strapazzato?

ZERLINA: Ma signor, io gli diedi parola di sposarlo.

DON GIOVANNI: Tal parola non vale un zero; voi non siete fatta per essere paesana: un'altra sorte vi procuran quegli occhi bricconcelli, quei labbretti sì belli, quelle dituccia candide e odorose; parmi toccar giuncata e fiutar rose.

Is no cause for rivalry.
(aside to Zerlina)
Little rogue, little flirt,
My downfall lies under your skirt.
(to Leporello who is trying to usher him out)
I'm coming, I'm coming!
(to Zerlina)
Stay here, right here.
Everything's just fine, alas.
Maybe our nobleman
Will make a lady of you at last.
(He goes.)

Scene 9

DON GIOVANNI AND ZERLINA.

Recitative

DON GIOVANNI: Finally we're free, my darling Zerlina, of that buffoon. Tell me, my sweet, didn't I pull that off smoothly?

ZERLINA: Sir, he is my husband . . .

DON GIOVANNI: Who? That boor? Do you think an honest man, indeed a nobleman, could suffer such a lovely face, such a delicious face, to be ill-treated by that ham-fisted peasant?

ZERLINA: But, sir, I am about to exchange vows with him.

DON GIOVANNI: Mere words of no value. You were not made to live like a peasant. Another fate is foretold in your bright eyes, on your delectable lips, in these tiny fingers, so white and tender, whose very touch is like that of roses.

ZERLINA: Ah, non vorrei ...

DON GIOVANNI: Che non vorresti?

ZERLINA: Alfine ingannata restar: io so che raro colle donne voi altri cavalieri siete onesti e sinceri.

DON GIOVANNI: Eh, un'impostura della gente plebea! La nobiltà ha dipinta negl'occhi l'onestà. Orsù, non perdiam tempo: in questo istante io ti voglio sposar.

ZERLINA: Voi?

DON GIOVANNI: Certo, io. Quel casinetto è mio: soli saremo, e là, gioiello mio, ci sposeremo.

N° 7 Duettino

DON GIOVANNI:
Là ci darem la mano,
là mi direte sì;
vedi, non è lontano,
partiam, ben mio, da qui.

ZERLINA:
Vorrei e non vorrei,
mi trema un poco il cor;
felice, è ver, sarei,
ma può burlarmi ancor.

DON GIOVANNI: Vieni, mio bel diletto.

ZERLINA: Mi fa pietà Masetto.

DON GIOVANNI: Io cangerò tua sorte.

ZERLINA: Oh, I couldn't . . .

DON GIOVANNI: Wouldn't you want to?

ZERLINA: And find you'd deceived me? I know that noblemen make empty promises to ladies.

DON GIOVANNI: How the common folk prattle on. You can see the sincerity in a nobleman's eyes. Come, let's not waste our time. I want to marry you at once.

ZERLINA: You?

DON GIOVANNI: Of course. Come to my little summerhouse. We'll be alone. And there, my jewel, we'll be wed.

Duet

DON GIOVANNI:
There you'll give me your hand
And then say, "Yes, I will."
It's near, it's all planned.
God, I can barely stand still.

ZERLINA:
I want to and yet I don't.
My heart is in a knot.
Would I be placed on a throne,
Or would I soon be forgot?

DON GIOVANNI: Come, you are like no other.

ZERLINA: But must Masetto suffer?

DON GIOVANNI: Come, don't wait any longer.

ZERLINA: Presto non son più forte.

DON GIOVANNI: Andiam, andiam.

ZERLINA: Andiam.

ZERLINA, DON GIOVANNI:
Andiam, andiam, mio bene,
a ristorar le pene
d'un innocente amor.

(Vanno verso il casino di Don Giovanni abbracciati etc.)

Scena 10
I SUDDETTI E DONNA ELVIRA CHE FERMA CON ATTI DISPERATISSIMI DON GIOVANNI ETC.

Recitativo

DONNA ELVIRA: Fermati, scellerato! Il ciel mi fece udir le tue perfidie: io sono a tempo di salvar questa misera innocente dal tuo barbaro artiglio.

ZERLINA: Meschina, cosa sento!

DON GIOVANNI: (Amor, consiglio!) *(a Donna Elvira piano)* Idol mio, non vedete ch'io voglio divertirmi ...

DONNA ELVIRA: *(forte)* Divertirti? È vero! Divertirti! Io so, crudele, come tu ti diverti ...

ZERLINA: Ma signor cavaliere ... è ver quel ch'ella dice?

DON GIOVANNI: *(piano a Zerlina)* La povera infelice è di me innamorata, e per pietà deggio fingere amore, ch'io son per mia disgrazia uom di buon core.

ZERLINA: How I wish that I were stronger.

DON GIOVANNI: Come to me, come to me!

ZERLINA: Come to me!

ZERLINA AND DON GIOVANNI:
Come to me now, my beloved.
Only an innocent love can give
Us both the life we want to live.

(They leave for Don Giovanni's summerhouse, arm in arm.)

Scene 10

THOSE BEFORE, AND DONNA ELVIRA, WHO DESPERATELY
INTERCEPTS DON GIOVANNI.

Recitative

DONNA ELVIRA: Stop, you wicked man. Heaven has sent me to catch you in your lies. I am here in time to save this poor girl from your lecherous clutches.

ZERLINA: Poor me! What is she saying?

DON GIOVANNI: (Love itself must inspire me!) *(to Donna Elvira, softly)* But darling, can't you see I'm just amusing myself?

DONNA ELVIRA: *(loudly)* Amusing yourself indeed! I know all too well, you bastard, how you amuse yourself.

ZERLINA: But, my lord, is she telling the truth?

DON GIOVANNI: *(to Zerlina, softly)* This poor unhappy creature is madly in love with me, and out of pity I must pretend to love her in return. A good heart is one of my misfortunes.

N° 8 Aria

DONNA ELVIRA:
Ah, fuggi il traditor,
non lo lasciar più dir!
Il labbro è mentitor,
fallace il ciglio.
Da' miei tormenti impara
a creder a quel cor,
e nasca il tuo timor
dal mio periglio.
(Parte conducendo seco Zerlina.)

Scena 11

DON GIOVANNI SOLO,
POI DON OTTAVIO E DONN'ANNA.

Recitativo

DON GIOVANNI: Mi par ch'oggi il demonio si diverta d'opporsi a miei piacevoli progressi: vanno mal tutti quanti.

DON OTTAVIO: Ah, ch'ora, idolo mio, son vani i pianti! Di vendetta si parli. Ah Don Giovanni!

DON GIOVANNI: (Mancava questo inver!)

DONN'ANNA: Signore, a tempo vi ritroviam: avete core, avete anima generosa?

DON GIOVANNI: (Sta' a vedere che il diavolo gli ha detto qualche cosa.) Che domanda! Perché?

DONN'ANNA: Bisogno abbiamo della vostra amicizia.

Aria

DONNA ELVIRA:
Oh, flee from this traitor!
If you listen to him, you'll die.
His very face is a false one
And every word a lie.
Learn from my suffering
And hear what I have to say.
Look at my broken heart
And leave without delay!
(She leaves, taking Zerlina with her.)

Scene 11

DON GIOVANNI, ALONE,
THEN DON OTTAVIO AND DONNA ANNA.

Recitative

DON GIOVANNI: It's the devil who is amusing himself today, ruining my plans. Everything's gone wrong.

DON OTTAVIO: Since your tears are in vain, my beloved, we must speak of revenge . . . Ah, Don Giovanni!

DON GIOVANNI: (This is all I need!)

DONNA ANNA: Oh sir, we have found you in time. Do you have a heart? A generous soul?

DON GIOVANNI: (Has the devil told her something?) What a question! Why do you ask?

DONNA ANNA: We have need of your friendship.

DON GIOVANNI: (Mi torna il fiato in corpo.) Comandate: *(con molto foco)* i congiunti, i parenti, questa man, questo ferro, i beni, il sangue spenderò per servirvi! Ma voi, bella Donn'Anna, perché così piangete? Il crudele chi fu che osò la calma turbar del viver vostro ...

Scena 12
I SUDDETTI, DONNA ELVIRA.

Recitativo

DONNA ELVIRA:
Ah, ti ritrovo ancor, perfido mostro!

N° 9 Quartetto

DONNA ELVIRA:
Non ti fidar, o misera,
di quel ribaldo cor:
me già tradì quel barbaro,
te vuol tradire ancor.

DONN'ANNA, DON OTTAVIO:
Cieli! Che aspetto nobile!
Che dolce maestà!
Il suo pallor, le lagrime
m'empiono di pietà.

DON GIOVANNI: *(a parte, Donna Elvira ascolta)*
La povera ragazza
è pazza, amici miei:
lasciatemi con lei,
forse si calmerà.

DON GIOVANNI: (I can breathe again.) Say but the word . . . *(ardently)* My household and relations, my own hand and sword, all I own, my heart's blood I place in your service. But why, good Donna Anna, do I see you weeping? Who was the cruel man who dared to trouble your peace of mind . . .

Scene 12

THOSE BEFORE, AND DONNA ELVIRA.

Recitative

DONNA ELVIRA: Ah, I find you once again, faithless monster!

Quartet

DONNA ELVIRA:
Poor woman, do not trust
In that deceitful heart!
Me he cruelly betrayed.
Now you'll play the part.

DONNA ANNA AND DON OTTAVIO:
Heavens! Her noble bearing!
Such wounded dignity!
Her pale face, those tears . . .
What can her story be?

DON GIOVANNI: *(aside; Donna Elvira listens)*
This woman is demented.
That's plain for all to see.
It might just help to calm her
If you leave her here with me.

DONNA ELVIRA: Ah, non credete al perfido!

DON GIOVANNI: È pazza, non badate.

DONNA ELVIRA: Restate ancor, restate!

DONN'ANNA, DON OTTAVIO:
A chi si crederà?
Certo moto d'ignoto tormento
dentro l'alma girare mi sento
che mi dice per quella infelice
cento cose che intender non sa.

DON GIOVANNI:
Certo moto d'ignoto spavento
dentro l'alma girare mi sento
che mi dice per quella infelice
cento cose che intender non sa.

DONNA ELVIRA:
Sdegno, rabbia, dispetto, tormento
dentro l'alma girare mi sento
che mi dice di quel traditore
cento cose che intender non sa.

DON OTTAVIO: *(a parte)*
Io di qua non vado via,
se non scopro questo affar.

DONN'ANNA: *(a parte)*
Non ha l'aria di pazzia
il suo volto, il suo parlar.

DONNA ELVIRA: Do not believe his lies!

DON GIOVANNI: Demented! Just ignore her.

DONNA ELVIRA: Stay here, I beg you.

DONNA ANNA AND DON OTTAVIO:
Which one do we believe?
I have the strangest feeling
Stirring in my breast.
Until I know about her
I will not, cannot rest.

DON GIOVANNI:
I have an eerie feeling
Stirring in my breast.
Until I'm sure about her
I will not, cannot rest.

DONNA ELVIRA:
Scorn, rage, contempt, torment
Storming in my breast.
Until I stop that traitor
I will not, cannot rest.

DON OTTAVIO: *(aside)*
I will not leave this spot
Until I learn the truth.

DONNA ANNA: *(aside)*
There is no sign of madness.
I think she speaks the truth.

DON GIOVANNI: *(a parte)*
Se men vado si potria
qualche cosa sospettar.

DONNA ELVIRA:
Da quel ceffo si dovria
la ner'alma giudicar.

DON OTTAVIO: *(a Don Giovanni)* Dunque quella?

DON GIOVANNI: È pazzarella.

DONN'ANNA: *(a Donna Elvira)* Dunque quegli?

DONNA ELVIRA: È un traditore.

DON GIOVANNI: Infelice!

DONNA ELVIRA: Mentitore!

DONN'ANNA, DON OTTAVIO: Incomincio a dubitar.

DON GIOVANNI: *(piano a Donna Elvira)*
Zitto zitto, che la gente
si raduna a noi d'intorno:
siate un poco più prudente,
vi farete criticar.

DONNA ELVIRA: *(forte a Don Giovanni)*
Non sperarlo, o scellerato,
ho perduta la prudenza:
le tue colpe ed il mio stato
voglio a tutti palesar.

DON GIOVANNI: *(aside)*
If I should try and flee,
They might find out the truth.

DONNA ELVIRA:
See how guilty he looks.
His face betrays the truth.

DON OTTAVIO: *(to Don Giovanni)* So she is . . .

DON GIOVANNI: . . . totally mad.

DONNA ANNA: *(to Donna Elvira)* And he is . . .

DONNA ELVIRA: . . . a traitor.

DON GIOVANNI: Poor woman!

DONNA ELVIRA: Liar! *Liar!*

DONNA ANNA AND DON OTTAVIO: I'm beginning to have doubts.

DON GIOVANNI: *(to Donna Elvira, softly)*
Hush now, can't you see
You're drawing quite a crowd?
If you persist in being loud,
They'll begin to turn on you.

DONNA ELVIRA: *(to Don Giovanni, loudly)*
Have no hope, you wretch,
I have no use for modesty.
Everything you did to me . . .
I'll tell them it was you!

DONN'ANNA, DON OTTAVIO: *(a parte, guardando Don Giovanni)*
Quegli accenti sì sommessi,
quel cangiarsi di colore
son indizi troppo espressi
che mi fan determinar.
(Parte Donna Elvira.)

Recitativo

DON GIOVANNI: Povera sventurata! I passi suoi voglio seguir: non voglio che faccia un precipizio. Perdonate, bellissima Donn'Anna; se servirvi poss'io, in mia casa v'aspetto. Amici, addio.
(Parte.)

Scena 13
DON OTTAVIO E DONN'ANNA.

N° 10 Recitativo accompagnato ed aria

Recitativo accompagnato

DONN'ANNA: Don'Ottavio, son morta!

DON OTTAVIO: Cosa è stato?

DONN'ANNA: Per pietà, soccorretemi.

DON OTTAVIO: Mio bene ... fate coraggio!

DONN'ANNA: Oh dei! Quegli è il carnefice del padre mio.

DON OTTAVIO: Che dite ...

DONNA ANNA AND DON OTTAVIO: *(aside, watching Don Giovanni)*
He's grown so very quiet.
His face has gone quite pale.
These are signs without fail.
Can what she says be true?
(Donna Elvira leaves.)

Recitative

DON GIOVANNI: Poor unfortunate woman! I want to follow her, to keep her from doing anything rash. Forgive me, my dear Donna Anna. If ever I may be of service to you, just send word to me. My friends, farewell.
(He leaves.)

Scene 13

DON OTTAVIO AND DONNA ANNA.

Accompanied Recitative and Aria

Accompanied Recitative

DONNA ANNA: Don Ottavio . . . I am . . . dying!

DON OTTAVIO: What is it?

DONNA ANNA: I beg of you, help me!

DON OTTAVIO: My beloved . . . be strong!

DONNA ANNA: Oh, God! That man . . . is my father's murderer.

DON OTTAVIO: What are you saying?

DONN'ANNA: Non dubitate più: gli ultimi accenti che l'empio proferì, tutta la voce richiamar nel cor mio di quell'indegno che nel mio appartamento ...

DON OTTAVIO: Oh ciel! Possibile che sotto il sacro manto d'amicizia ... Ma come fu? Narratemi lo strano avvenimento.

DONN'ANNA: Era già alquanto avanzata la notte, quando nelle mie stanze, ove soletta mi trovai per sventura, entrar io vidi in un mantello avvolto un uom che al primo istante avea preso per voi, ma riconobbi poi che un inganno era il mio ...

DON OTTAVIO: *(con affanno)* Stelle! Seguite.

DONN'ANNA: Tacito a me s'appressa e mi vuole abbracciar: sciogliermi cerco, ei più mi stringe; grido, non viene alcun. Con una mano cerca d'impedire la voce e coll'altra m'afferra stretta così che già mi credo vinta.

DON OTTAVIO: Perfido! E alfin?

DONN'ANNA: Alfine il duol, l'orrore dell'infame attentato accrebbe sì la lena mia, che a forza di svincolarmi, torcermi e piegarmi da lui mi sciolsi.

DON OTTAVIO: Ohimè, respiro.

DONN'ANNA: Allora rinforzo i stridi miei, chiamo soccorso, fugge il fellon, arditamente il seguo fin nella strada per fermarlo, e sono assalitrice d'assalita; il padre v'accorre, vuol conoscerlo, e l'iniquo, che del povero vecchio era più forte, compie il misfatto suo col dargli morte.

DONNA ANNA: No doubt about it. The parting words of that man, the sound of his voice—brought back to me the horrible scene of him entering my room . . .

DON OTTAVIO: Oh heaven! How could such a man hide behind the sacred bond of friendship . . . But tell me everything that happened.

DONNA ANNA: It was late at night. I was, unhappily, alone in my room. I saw a man enter, wrapped in a cloak. For an instant I thought it was you. Then I realized I was wrong.

DON OTTAVIO: *(anxiously)* Good Lord! What next?

DONNA ANNA: Silently he approached me, tried to embrace me. I went to free myself and he pulled me closer. I cried out, but no one came. With one hand he stifled my cries. With the other he pressed me harder against him. I thought that I was lost.

DON OTTAVIO: Horrible! And then . . .

DONNA ANNA: Finally the horror of his hideous assault so roused me that, by twisting and struggling, I managed to free myself from him.

DON OTTAVIO: Thank God for that!

DONNA ANNA: Then I began to scream even more loudly. The vile creature fled. I ran after him into the street, trying to stop him. I was the assailer of my assailant. My father came running and demanded to know his name. That wicked man, stronger than my old father, then committed the final sin—he murdered him.

Aria

DONN'ANNA:
Or sai chi l'onore
rapire a me volse,
chi fu il traditore
che il padre mi tolse:
vendetta ti chiedo,
la chiede il tuo cor.
Rammenta la piaga
del misero seno,
rimira di sangue
coperto il terreno,
se l'ira in te langue
d'un giusto furor.
(Parte.)

Scena 14

DON OTTAVIO SOLO.

Recitativo

DON OTTAVIO: Come mai creder deggio di sì nero delitto capace
un cavaliero? Ah, di scoprire il vero ogni mezzo si cerchi! Io
sento in petto e di sposo e d'amico il dover che mi parla: disin-
gannar la voglio o vendicarla.

N° 10a Aria

DON OTTAVIO:
Dalla sua pace
la mia dipende,
quel che a lei piace
vita mi rende,
quel che le incresce
morte mi dà.
S'ella sospira,

Aria

DONNA ANNA:

Now you know the man
Who tried to dishonor me
And thereby betray you.
He killed my father as well.
The vengeance that I seek—
Your heart demands it too.
Remember the wound
In the dying man's chest.
Remember the blood
That covered the ground.
Remember, and into your heart
The lust for vengeance will flood.

(She leaves.)

Scene 14

DON OTTAVIO, ALONE.

Recitative

DON OTTAVIO: How could I believe a nobleman capable of so black a crime? I will do everything to uncover the truth. My heart is torn between my duty as a friend and my duty as a lover. I must either set her right or avenge her honor.

Aria

DON OTTAVIO:

My very peace of mind
Depends on hers as well.
What pleasure I may find
Is where we both shall dwell.
When she is unhappy, oh,
Then all is naught.
When she calls with a sigh,

sospiro anch'io;
è mia quell'ira,
quel pianto è mio;
e non ho bene,
s'ella non l'ha.
(Parte.)

Scena 15

LEPORELLO SOLO, POI DON GIOVANNI.

LEPORELLO: Io deggio ad ogni patto per sempre abbandonar questo bel matto! Eccolo qui: guardate con qual indifferenza se ne viene!

DON GIOVANNI: Oh Leporello mio, va tutto bene!

LEPORELLO: Don Giovannino mio, va tutto male!

DON GIOVANNI: Come va tutto male?

LEPORELLO: Vado a casa, come voi l'ordinaste, con tutta quella gente ...

DON GIOVANNI: Bravo!

LEPORELLO: A forza di chiacchiere, di vezzi e di bugie, ch'ho imparato sì bene a star con voi, cerco d'intrattenerli ...

DON GIOVANNI: Bravo!

LEPORELLO: Dico mille cose a Masetto per placarlo, per trargli dal pensier la gelosia ...

I myself feel her pain.
I must stay by her side
Or never see her again.
I cannot be happy, oh,
If she is not.
(He leaves.)

Scene 15

LEPORELLO, ALONE, THEN DON GIOVANNI.

LEPORELLO: Whatever else I do, I must get away from this madman for good. Look at him. He acts with utter indifference.

DON GIOVANNI: Ah, good old Leporello, what a fine day!

LEPORELLO: Good old Don Giovanni, what a fine mess!

DON GIOVANNI: What do you mean, a "mess"?

LEPORELLO: I went home, just as you ordered, with all those
people . . .

DON GIOVANNI: Bravo!

LEPORELLO: By chattering, flattering, and nattering—I've
learned it all from you—I tried to keep them amused . . .

DON GIOVANNI: Bravo!

LEPORELLO: I fed Masetto all manner of folderol to take his
mind off his jealousy . . .

DON GIOVANNI: Bravo, bravo in coscienza mia!

LEPORELLO: Faccio che bevano e gli uomini e le donne: son già mezzo ubriachi, altri canta, altri scherza, altri seguita a ber; in sul più bello chi credete che capiti?

DON GIOVANNI: Zerlina.

LEPORELLO: Bravo! E con lei chi viene?

DON GIOVANNI: Donna Elvira.

LEPORELLO: Bravo! E disse di voi …

DON GIOVANNI: Tutto quel mal che in bocca le venia.

LEPORELLO: Bravo, bravo in coscienza mia!

DON GIOVANNI: E tu cosa facesti?

LEPORELLO: Tacqui.

DON GIOVANNI: Ed ella?

LEPORELLO: Seguì a gridar.

DON GIOVANNI: E tu?

LEPORELLO: Quando mi parve che già fosse sfogata, dolcemente fuor dell'orto la trassi, e con bell'arte chiusa la porta a chiave io mi cavai e sulla via soletta la lasciai.

DON GIOVANNI: On my word, well done indeed!

LEPORELLO: I made sure both men and women had plenty to drink, and before long they were all pretty drunk. Some sang. Others told jokes. The rest just kept drinking. And best of all, who do you think walked in?

DON GIOVANNI: Zerlina!

LEPORELLO: Bravo! And who was with her?

DON GIOVANNI: Donna Elvira!

LEPORELLO: Bravo! And do you know what she said about you?

DON GIOVANNI: Every word in her mouth is vile.

LEPORELLO: On my word, well said indeed!

DON GIOVANNI: And what did you do?

LEPORELLO: I kept quiet.

DON GIOVANNI: And she?

LEPORELLO: She went right on shouting.

DON GIOVANNI: And you?

LEPORELLO: When I thought she was finished, I gently led her out and carefully locked the door behind her. I left her there in the street.

DON GIOVANNI: Bravo, bravo, arcibravo! L'affar non può andar meglio: incominciasti, io saprò terminar. Troppo mi premono queste contadinotte: le voglio divertir finché vien notte.

N° 11 Aria

DON GIOVANNI:
Finch'han dal vino
calda la testa,
una gran festa
fa' preparar.
Se trovi in piazza
qualche ragazza,
teco ancor quella
cerca menar.
Senza alcun ordine
la danza sia:
chi 'l minuetto,
chi la follia,
chi l'alemanna
farai ballar.
Ed io frattanto
dall'altro canto
con questa e quella
vo' amoreggiar.
Ah, la mia lista
doman mattina
d'una decina
devi aumentar!
(Partono.)

DON GIOVANNI: Clever rascal! Well done! I couldn't have managed it better myself. You began it, I'll finish it off. These peasant girls—how can one resist them? I'll tickle their fancies until night falls.

Aria

DON GIOVANNI:
While strong drink
Muddles their heads,
Quick as a wink
We'll ready a feast.
Search every street.
Look for more girls.
Whatever you meet
Just bring to the feast.
Let them whirl,
Let them dance,
A brief minuet
To make them forget
I have taken a girl.
Let them dance!
I'll be here,
I'll go there,
Courting the women
With a practiced flair.
I'll never be missed.
Ten more will be kissed.
By tomorrow,
Ten more for my list!
(They leave.)

Giardino con due porte chiuse a chiave per di fuori.

Scena 16

MASETTO E ZERLINA, CORO DI CONTADINI E
DI CONTADINE SPARSE QUA E LÀ CHE DORMONO
E SIEDONO SOPRA SOFÀ D'ERBE. DUE NICCHIE.

Recitativo

ZERLINA: Masetto, senti un po' ... Masetto, dico.

MASETTO: Non mi toccar.

ZERLINA: Perché?

MASETTO: Perché mi chiedi? Perfida! Il tatto sopportar dovrei d'una man infedele?

ZERLINA: Ah no, taci, crudele: io non merto da te tal trattamento!

MASETTO: Come! Ed hai l'ardimento di scusarti? Star sola con un uom, abbandonarmi il dì delle mie nozze! Porre in fronte a un villano d'onore questa marca d'infamia! Ah, se non fosse, se non fosse lo scandalo! Vorrei ...

ZERLINA: Ma se colpa io non ho! Ma se da lui ingannata rimasi! E poi che temi? Tranquillati, mia vita: non mi toccò la punta delle dita. Non me lo credi? Ingrato! Vien qui, sfogati, ammazzami, fa' tutto di me quel che ti piace, ma poi, Masetto mio, ma poi fa' pace.

A garden with two doors locked from the outside.

Scene 16

MASETTO AND ZERLINA, THE CHORUS OF VILLAGERS
SCATTERED HERE AND THERE, SOME SLEEPING, SOME
SITTING ON GRASSY BANKS, AND TWO GAZEBOS.

Recitative

ZERLINA: Masetto, just a word. Masetto, please!

MASETTO: Don't touch me.

ZERLINA: Why?

MASETTO: You ask me *why?* You wench! Why should I be touched by an unfaithful hand?

ZERLINA: No, that is too cruel! I don't deserve such treatment from you.

MASETTO: What! You dare to tell me you've done nothing? You were alone with a man. You abandoned me on my very wedding day! You disgrace an honest working fellow like this? If it wouldn't cause a scandal, I would . . .

ZERLINA: And if I am not to blame? What if I had been tricked? Would you be so upset then? Calm down, my love. He didn't even touch my fingertips. You don't believe me? You're heartless! Come, unleash you anger, kill me, do whatever you like! But then, Masetto, promise to make peace with me.

N° 12 Aria

ZERLINA:
Batti, batti, o bel Masetto,
la tua povera Zerlina:
starò qui come agnellina
le tue botte ad aspettar.
Lascerò straziarmi il crine,
lascerò cavarmi gli occhi,
e le care tue manine
lieta poi saprò baciar.
Ah, lo vedo, non hai core!
Pace, pace, o vita mia,
in contenti ed allegria
notte e dì vogliam passar.
(Parte.)

Recitativo

MASETTO: Guarda un po' come seppe questa strega sedurmi!
Siamo pure i deboli di testa!

DON GIOVANNI: *(di dentro)* Sia preparato tutto a una gran festa.

ZERLINA: Ah Masetto, Masetto! Odi la voce del monsù cavaliero?

MASETTO: Ebben, che c'è?

ZERLINA: Verrà!

MASETTO: Lascia che venga.

ZERLINA: Ah, se vi fosse un buco da fuggir!

Aria

ZERLINA:
Beat me, beat me, dear Masetto,
Your poor Zerlina awaits.
This innocent little lamb you hate
Is ready for your blows.
Do your worst, pull out my hair,
Then, yes, scratch out my eyes!
Your anger can only purify
The love that counters woes.
I see at last! You haven't the heart!
Let us love and live as one.
Our happiness has just begun,
A light that brightly glows.
(She leaves.)

Recitative

MASETTO: Look how this witch enchants me! Men just go soft in the head.

DON GIOVANNI: *(offstage)* Get everything ready for our grand celebration!

ZERLINA: Masetto, Masetto, that's his lordship's voice!

MASETTO: Well, what of it?

ZERLINA: He's coming!

MASETTO: Let him come, then.

ZERLINA: Oh, if only there were someplace to hide!

MASETTO: Di cosa temi? Perché diventi pallida? Ah, capisco! Capisco, bricconcella! Hai timor ch'io comprenda com'è tra voi passata la faccenda.

N° 13 Finale

MASETTO:
Presto, presto, pria ch'ei venga
por mi vo' da qualche lato:
c'è una nicchia ... qui celato
cheto cheto mi vo' star.

ZERLINA:
Senti senti ... dove vai?
Ah, non t'asconder, o Masetto!
Se ti trova, poveretto,
tu non sai quel che può far.

MASETTO: Faccia, dica quel che vuole.

ZERLINA: Ah, non giovan le parole!

MASETTO: Parla forte e qui t'arresta.

ZERLINA: Che capriccio ha nella testa!

MASETTO: (sottovoce)
Capirò se m'è fedele,
e in qual modo andò l'affar.
(Entra nella nicchia.)

ZERLINA: (sottovoce)
Quell'ingrato, quel crudele
oggi vuol precipitar.

MASETTO: What are you afraid of? Why suddenly so pale? Ah, I understand! You little hussy! You're afraid I'll find out what went on between you two.

Finale

MASETTO:
Quickly, quickly, before he comes.
I'll hide myself over there.
The *ga-bezo* here—this is where
I'll stay quietly out of sight.

ZERLINA:
Listen, listen, where are you going?
There's no point in hiding there.
He's bound to find out where,
And his bark isn't as bad as his bite.

MASETTO: Let him do what he wants!

ZERLINA: Oh, there's no talking to you!

MASETTO: Say it louder—and stay where you are!

ZERLINA: Your head is full of silly ideas!

MASETTO: *(aside)*
Soon I'll know what I can
Of her infidelity to me.
(He enters the alcove.)

ZERLINA: *(aside)*
That rash, ungrateful man,
He acts so stupidly.

Scena 17

ZERLINA, DON GIOVANNI CON
QUATTRO SERVI NOBILMENTE VESTITI.

DON GIOVANNI:
Su, svegliatevi, da bravi,
su, coraggio, o buona gente!
Vogliam stare allegramente,
vogliam rider e scherzar.
(ai servi)
Alla stanza della danza
conducete tutti quanti
ed a tutti in abbondanza
gran rinfreschi fate dar.

CORO DI SERVI:
Su, svegliatevi, da bravi,
su, coraggio, o buona gente!
Vogliam stare allegramente,
vogliam rider e scherzar.
(Partono i servi e i contadini.)

Scena 18

DON GIOVANNI, ZERLINA, MASETTO NELLA NICCHIA.

ZERLINA: *(vuol nascondersi)* Tra quest'arbori celata si può dar che
non mi veda.

DON GIOVANNI:
Zerlinetta mia garbata,
(La prende.)
t'ho già visto, non scappar.

 Scene 17

ZERLINA, AND DON GIOVANNI WITH

FOUR LIVERIED SERVANTS.

DON GIOVANNI:
Up, wake up, good lads!
Up, it's time, my friends!
There's a party to attend
And dancing to be done.
(to the servants)
Lead my honored guests
To the ballroom at once.
And see to all their wants.
Drinks for everyone!

CHORUS OF SERVANTS:
Up, wake up, good lads!
Up, it's time, my friends!
There's a party to attend . . .
And dancing to be done!
(The servants and villagers leave.)

Scene 18

DON GIOVANNI AND ZERLINA,

AND MASETTO IN THE GAZEBO.

ZERLINA: *(trying to hide)* If I hide behind these trees, maybe he won't see me.

DON GIOVANNI:
Zer-*li*-na! My sweetmeat!
(He catches her.)
Now I have you, don't be afraid.

ZERLINA: Ah, lasciatemi andar via …

DON GIOVANNI: No no, resta, gioia mia.

ZERLINA: Se pietade avete in core …

DON GIOVANNI:
Sì, ben mio, son tutto amore.
Vieni un poco in questo loco,
fortunata io ti vo' far.

ZERLINA:
Ah, s'ei vede il sposo mio,
so ben io quel che può far!

DON GIOVANNI: *(nell'aprire la nicchia e vedendo Masetto fa un moto di stupore)* Masetto!

MASETTO: Sì, Masetto.

DON GIOVANNI: *(un poco confuso)*
E chiuso là perché?
(Riprende ardire.)
La bella tua Zerlina
non può, la poverina,
più star senza di te.

MASETTO: *(un poco ironico)* Capisco, sì signore.

DON GIOVANNI: *(a Zerlina)*
Adesso fate core!
(Si sente il preludio della danza.)
I suonatori udite,
venite omai con me.

ZERLINA: Let me go!

DON GIOVANNI: No, no, stay here, my pet.

ZERLINA: Have you no pity in your heart?

DON GIOVANNI:
Yes, my darling, I am made of love.
Come with me for a moment.
You'll be happier than you ever knew.

ZERLINA:
If my bridegroom finds us,
I know very well what he'll do.

DON GIOVANNI: *(as he goes into the gazebo and, seeing Masetto, is struck with astonishment)* Masetto!

MASETTO: Yes, Masetto!

DON GIOVANNI: *(a little confused)*
Why are you hiding in there?
(his swagger restored)
Your beautiful Zerlina,
The poor little darling—ah,
Cannot live without you.

MASETTO: *(a little ironically)* I see what you mean, my lord.

DON GIOVANNI: *(to Zerlina)*
So then, brighten up!
(Dance music starts up.)
Listen to the players.
Come along now with me.

ZERLINA, MASETTO:
Sì sì, facciamo core,
ed a ballar cogli altri
andiamo tutti e tre.
(Partono.)

Scena 19

DON OTTAVIO, DONN'ANNA E DONNA ELVIRA IN MASCHERA;
POI LEPORELLO E DON GIOVANNI ALLA FINESTRA.

DONNA ELVIRA:
Bisogna aver coraggio,
o cari amici miei,
e i suoi misfatti rei
scoprir potremo allor.

DON OTTAVIO:
L'amica dice bene,
coraggio aver conviene:
discaccia, o vita mia,
l'affanno ed il timor.

DONN'ANNA:
Il passo è periglioso,
può nascer qualche imbroglio:
temo pel caro sposo
e per noi temo ancor.

ZERLINA AND MASETTO:
Yes, yes, on to the dance!
Let's join the others,
All of us, all *three*.
(They leave.)

Scene 19

DON OTTAVIO, DONNA ANNA, AND DONNA ELVIRA IN
MASKS; THEN LEPORELLO AND DON GIOVANNI AT THE
WINDOW.

DONNA ELVIRA:
Harden your hearts,
My comrades in grief.
It will be a relief
To uncover his crime.

DON OTTAVIO:
Our friend is right.
We must be brave,
If it's vengeance you crave,
Now is the time.

DONNA ANNA:
The moment of peril.
Everything has led
To what now lies ahead.
I have chills up my spine.

Menuetto

LEPORELLO: *(apre la finestra)*
Signor, guardate un poco
che maschere galanti.

DON GIOVANNI:
Falle passar avanti,
di' che ci fanno onor.

DONN'ANNA, DONNA ELVIRA, DON OTTAVIO: *(piano)*
(Al volto ed alla voce
si scopre il traditore.)

LEPORELLO: Zi zi, signore maschere! Zi zi …

DONN'ANNA, DONNA ELVIRA: *(a Don Ottavio piano)* Via, rispondete.

LEPORELLO: Zi zi, signore maschere!

DON OTTAVIO: Cosa chiedete?

LEPORELLO:
Al ballo, se vi piace,
v'invita il mio signor.

DON OTTAVIO:
Grazie di tanto onore:
andiam, compagne belle.

LEPORELLO:
L'amico anche su quelle
prove farà d'amor.
(Entra e chiude.)

Minuet

LEPORELLO: *(opening the window and looking out)*
My lord, look here.
Fancy masqueraders!

DON GIOVANNI:
Have them come forward.
They can present themselves.

DONNA ANNA, DONNA ELVIRA, AND DON OTTAVIO: *(quietly)*
(By his looks and his voice,
The traitor reveals himself.)

LEPORELLO:
Psst! You there! Masqueraders! Psst!

DONNA ANNA AND DONNA ELVIRA: *(to Don Ottavio, quietly)*
Answer him!

LEPORELLO: Psst! You there! Masqueraders! Psst!

DON OTTAVIO: What do you want?

LEPORELLO:
If you please, my master
Is inviting you to the ball.

DON OTTAVIO:
Thank him for the honor.
Come, ladies, the dancers call!

LEPORELLO:
My master can try his luck.
He has a list, after all.
(He goes in and shuts the window.)

DONN'ANNA, DON OTTAVIO:
Protegga il giusto cielo
il zelo del mio cor.

DONNA ELVIRA:
Vendichi il giusto cielo
il mio tradito amor.
(Partono.)

Sala illuminata e preparata per una gran festa di ballo.

Scena 20

DON GIOVANNI, MASETTO, ZERLINA, LEPORELLO,
CONTADINI E CONTADINE; POI DONN'ANNA,
DONNA ELVIRA E DON OTTAVIO IN
MASCHERA ETC.; SERVI CON RINFRESCHI ETC.

DON GIOVANNI: *(Don Giovanni fa seder le ragazze, e Leporello i ragazzi
che saranno in atto di aver finito un ballo.)*
Riposate, vezzose ragazze.

LEPORELLO: Rinfrescatevi, bei giovinotti.

DON GIOVANNI, LEPORELLO:
Tornerete a far presto le pazze,
tornerete a scherzar e ballar.
(Si portano i rinfreschi.)

DON GIOVANNI: Ehi caffè!

LEPORELLO: Cioccolata!

MASETTO: Ah Zerlina, giudizio!

DONNA ANNA AND DON OTTAVIO:
Just heaven, protect
The fervor of our cause.

DONNA ELVIRA:
Just heaven, now crush
The traitor in your jaws!
(They leave.)

A salon brightly lit and decorated for a festive ball.

Scene 20

DON GIOVANNI, MASETTO, ZERLINA, LEPORELLO, AND THE
VILLAGERS; THEN DONNA ANNA, DONNA ELVIRA, AND DON
OTTAVIO IN MASKS; AND SERVANTS WITH REFRESHMENTS.

DON GIOVANNI: *(A dance has just finished and Don Giovanni is showing some girls to their seats, as Leporello does for the young men.)*
Rest here, my lovely lasses.

LEPORELLO: How about a drink, chums?

DON GIOVANNI AND LEPORELLO:
Soon enough you'll be dancing wildly.
There's time enough for flirting.
(Refreshments are brought in.)

DON GIOVANNI: Coffee here!

LEPORELLO: Hot chocolate!

MASETTO: Oh, Zerlina, be careful!

DON GIOVANNI: Sorbetti!

LEPORELLO: Confetti!

ZERLINA, MASETTO: *(a parte)*
Troppo dolce comincia la scena,
in amaro potria terminar.

DON GIOVANNI: *(fa carezze a Zerlina.)*
Sei pur vaga, brillante Zerlina!

ZERLINA: Sua bontà!

MASETTO: *(guardando e fremendo)* (La briccona fa festa.)

LEPORELLO: *(imita il padrone colle altre ragazze.)* Sei pur cara,
Giannetta, Sandrina!

MASETTO:
Tocca pur, che ti cada la testa.
Ah briccona, mi vuoi disperar!

ZERLINA: *(a parte)*
Quel Masetto mi par stralunato,
brutto brutto si fa quest'affar.

DON GIOVANNI, LEPORELLO:
Quel Masetto mi par stralunato,
qui bisogna cervello adoprar.

MASETTO:
La briccona fa festa.

DON GIOVANNI: Sorbets!

LEPORELLO: Sweets!

ZERLINA AND MASETTO: *(aside)*
The scene begins in glitter
And yet may turn out bitter.

DON GIOVANNI: *(fondling Zerlina)*
You look ravishing, my gorgeous Zerlina!

ZERLINA: You are too kind!

MASETTO: *(fuming)* (That slut is enjoying it all.)

LEPORELLO: *(imitating his master with the other girls)* You look
ravishing, Giannetta. And you, Sandrina!

MASETTO:
Touch her and your head will roll!
The slut is driving me mad.

ZERLINA: *(aside)*
Masetto seems beside himself.
It's going from bad to worse.

DON GIOVANNI AND LEPORELLO:
Masetto seems beside himself.
Time to be truly perverse!

MASETTO:
Just touch her! Just try!
All I have for her is a curse!

(Entrano Don Ottavio, Donn'Anna, Donna Elvira mascherati.)

LEPORELLO:
Venite pur avanti,
vezzose mascherette.

DON GIOVANNI:
È aperto a tutti quanti,
viva la libertà!

DON'ANNA, DONNA ELVIRA, DON OTTAVIO:
Siam grati a tanti segni
di generosità.

DONN'ANNA, DONNA ELVIRA, DON OTTAVIO, DON GIOVANNI,
LEPORELLO: Viva la libertà!

DON GIOVANNI:
Ricominciate il suono.
(a Leporello che porrà in ordine etc.)
Tu accoppia i ballerini.

(Si suona come prima. Don Ottavio balla il minuetto con Donn'Anna.)

LEPORELLO: Da bravi, via, ballate.
(Qui ballano.)

DONNA ELVIRA: *(a Donn'Anna)* (Quella è la contadina.)

DONN'ANNA: Io moro!

(Don Ottavio, Donna Anna, and Donna Elvira enter, masked.)

LEPORELLO:
Come forward, up here,
You charming masqueraders.

DON GIOVANNI:
To all of you, good cheer!
Long live liberty!

DONNA ANNA, DONNA ELVIRA, AND DON OTTAVIO:
How grateful we all are
For your generosity.

DONNA ANNA, DONNA ELVIRA, DON OTTAVIO, DON GIOVANNI, AND LEPORELLO: Long live liberty!

DON GIOVANNI:
Let there be more music!
(to Leporello)
Be sure everyone has a . . . dancing partner.

(Music is played as before. Don Ottavio dances the minuet with Donna Anna.)

LEPORELLO: Come, lads, dance!
(They dance.)

DONNA ELVIRA: *(to Donna Anna)* (There is that peasant girl.)

DONNA ANNA: I can't stand it!

DON OTTAVIO: *(a Donn'Anna)* Simulate.

DON GIOVANNI, LEPORELLO,: Va bene in verità!

MASETTO: *(ironicamente)* Va bene in verità!

DON GIOVANNI: *(a Leporello)* A bada tien Masetto.

LEPORELLO: *(a Masetto)* Non balli, poveretto!

DON GIOVANNI: *(a Zerlina)*
Il tuo compagno io sono:
Zerlina, vien pur qua.
(Si mette a ballar con Zerlina una contradanza.)

LEPORELLO:
Vien qua, Masetto caro:
facciam quel ch'altri fa.

MASETTO: No no, ballar non voglio.

LEPORELLO: *(fa ballar per forza Masetto)* Eh, balla, amico mio!

MASETTO: No.

LEPORELLO: Sì. Caro Masetto, balla!

MASETTO: No no, non voglio.

DONN'ANNA: *(a Donna Elvira)* (Resister non poss'io.)

DON OTTAVIO: *(to Donna Anna)* Keep up appearances!

DON GIOVANNI AND LEPORELLO: Everything is going well!

MASETTO: *(ironically)* Very well, very well indeed!

DON GIOVANNI: *(to Leporello)* Keep Masetto occupied.

LEPORELLO: *(to Masetto)* You're not dancing, poor fellow?

DON GIOVANNI: *(to Zerlina)*
It seems I am your partner.
Zerlina, come to me, do!
(He begins to dance a contredanse with Zerlina.)

LEPORELLO:
Come, dear, *dear* Masetto,
Let's do what others do.

MASETTO: No, no, I don't want to dance.

LEPORELLO: *(forcing Masetto to dance)* Come, dance, my friend!

MASETTO: No!

LEPORELLO: Yes! My dear Masetto, dance!

MASETTO: No, no, I don't want to!

DONNA ANNA: *(to Donna Elvira)* (I can't endure this any longer!)

DONNA ELVIRA, DON OTTAVIO: *(a Donn'Anna)* (Fingete, per pietà.)

LEPORELLO: Balla!

MASETTO: No no, non voglio.

LEPORELLO:
Eh, balla, amico mio:
facciam quel ch'altri fa.
(Balla la Teitsch con Masetto.)

DON GIOVANNI: *(conducendola via quasi per forza)* Vieni con me, mia vita ...

MASETTO: Lasciami! Ah no! Zerlina! ...
(Si cava dalle mani di Leporello e seguita la Zerlina.)

ZERLINA: Oh Numi! Son tradita!

LEPORELLO: Qui nasce una ruina.
(Sorte in fretta.)

DONN'ANNA, DONNA ELVIRA, DON OTTAVIO:
L'iniquo da sé stesso
nel laccio se ne va.

ZERLINA: *(di dentro ad alta voce, strepito di piedi a destra)* Gente, aiuto! Aiuto, gente!

DONN'ANNA, DONNA ELVIRA, DON OTTAVIO: Soccorriamo l'innocente.
(I suonatori e gli altri partono confusi.)

DONNA ELVIRA AND DON OTTAVIO: *(to Donna Anna)* (Please, just play your part!)

LEPORELLO: Dance!

MASETTO: No, no, I don't want to!

LEPORELLO:
Come, my friend, dance!
Do what the others do.
(They dance a German dance.)

DON GIOVANNI: *(leading Zerlina forcibly away)* Come with me, my love, come, come . . .

MASETTO: Let me go! . . . No! . . . Zerlina!
(He frees himself from Leporello and follows after Zerlina.)

ZERLINA: Dear God! I am betrayed!

LEPORELLO: A disaster is what he's made.
(He hurries out.)

DONNA ANNA, DONNA ELVIRA, AND DON OTTAVIO:
That evil man has met a price
That must at last be paid.

ZERLINA: *(screaming from within; footsteps from the right)* Anyone!
. . . Help! . . . Please, help me!

DONNA ANNA, DONNA ELVIRA, AND DON OTTAVIO: We must help that innocent girl!
(The orchestra players and others leave in confusion.)

MASETTO: *(di dentro etc.)* Ah Zerlina! ...

ZERLINA: Scellerato!
(Si sente il grido e lo strepito dalla parte opposta.)

DONN'ANNA, DONNA ELVIRA, DON OTTAVIO:
Ora grida da quel lato:
ah, gittiamo giù la porta!
(Gittano giù la porta.)

ZERLINA: *(esce da un'altra parte)* Soccorretemi, o son morta!

DONN'ANNA, DONNA ELVIRA, DON OTTAVIO, MASETTO: Siam qui noi per tua difesa.

DON GIOVANNI: *(esce con spada in mano. Conduce seco per un braccio Leporello e finge di voler ferirlo, ma la spada non esce dal fodero.)*
Ecco il birbo che t'ha offesa,
ma da me la pena avrà!
Mori, iniquo!

LEPORELLO: Ah, cosa fate!

DON GIOVANNI: Mori, dico!

DON OTTAVIO: *(pistola in mano)* Nol sperate!

DONN'ANNA, DONNA ELVIRA, DON OTTAVIO: *(si cavano la maschera.)* L'empio crede con tal frode di nasconder l'empietà.

DON GIOVANNI: Donna Elvira!

MASETTO: *(from within)* Ah Zerlina! Zerlina!

ZERLINA: Scoundrel!
(A cry and footsteps are heard from the left.)

DONNA ANNA, DONNA ELVIRA, AND DON OTTAVIO:
Her screams are from over there!
Break down the door!
(They force open the door.)

ZERLINA: *(emerging)* Rescue me! I am dying!

DONNA ANNA, DONNA ELVIRA, DON OTTAVIO, AND MASETTO:
We are here to protect you.

DON GIOVANNI: *(He comes out with a sword in his hand. He drags Leporello by the arm and pretends, threatening him, to be unable to draw his sword.)*
Here's the villain who attacked you.
I'll see to it he is punished.
Die, you filthy wretch!

LEPORELLO: What are you doing?

DON GIOVANNI: Die, I tell you!

DON OTTAVIO: *(pistol in hand)* Don't think we aren't on to you!

DONNA ANNA, DONNA ELVIRA, AND DON OTTAVIO: *(removing their masks)* This impious man thinks his fraud can hide his wickedness.

DON GIOVANNI: Donna Elvira!

DONNA ELVIRA: Sì, malvagio!

DON GIOVANNI: Don Ottavio!

DON OTTAVIO: Sì signore!

DON GIOVANNI: *(a Donn'Anna)* Ah, credete!

DONN'ANNA, DONNA ELVIRA, DON OTTAVIO, ZERLINA, MASETTO:
Traditore!
Tutto, tutto già si sa.
Trema, trema, o scellerato!
Saprà tosto il mondo intero
il misfatto orrendo e nero,
la tua fiera crudeltà.
Odi il tuon della vendetta
che ti fischia intorno intorno:
sul tuo capo in questo giorno
il suo fulmine cadrà!

LEPORELLO:
È confusa la sua testa,
non sa più quel ch'ei si faccia,
e un'orribile tempesta
minacciando, oh dio, lo va.
Ma non manca in lui coraggio,
non si perde o si confonde:
se cadesse ancor il mondo,
nulla mai temer lo fa.

DONNA ELVIRA: Yes, you villain!

DON GIOVANNI: Don Ottavio!

DON OTTAVIO: Yes, my lord!

DON GIOVANNI: *(to Donna Anna)* Ah, believe me . . .

DONNA ANNA, DONNA ELVIRA, DON OTTAVIO, ZERLINA, AND MASETTO:
A traitor! Traitor!
All your evil deeds are known!
Tremble for yourself, you vile man!
Hell will end what we now begin.
All your black and hideous sins,
Your cruelty, will now be shown!
Hear the thunder as it circles,
The vengeance you must surely dread.
This very day, upon your head
Will fall the fire and brimstone.

LEPORELLO:
His head must be on fire.
He no longer knows what to do.
The furies have conspired,
Tempests are storming through.
But his courage never fails him,
He will not lose his way.
Though the powers of hell assail him,
He will live to see another day.

DON GIOVANNI, LEPORELLO:
È confusa la mia testa,
non so più quel ch'io mi faccia,
e un'orribile tempesta
minacciando, oh dio, mi va.
Ma non manca in me coraggio,
non mi perdo o mi confondo
se cadesse ancor il mondo,
nulla mai temer mi fa.

Fine dell'atto primo.

DON GIOVANNI:
My head must be on fire.
I no longer know what to do.
The furies have conspired,
Tempests are storming through.
But my courage will not fail me,
I will not lose my way.
Though the powers of hell assail me,
I will live to see another day.

End of Act I.

Atto secondo

Strada.

Scena 1

DON GIOVANNI E LEPORELLO.

N° 14 Duetto

DON GIOVANNI:
Eh via, buffone,
non mi seccar.

LEPORELLO:
No no, padrone,
non vo' restar.

DON GIOVANNI:
Sentimi, amico ...

LEPORELLO:
Vo' andar, vi dico.

DON GIOVANNI:
Ma che ti ho fatto,
che vuoi lasciarmi?

Act II

A street.

Scene 1

DON GIOVANNI AND LEPORELLO.

Duet

DON GIOVANNI:
Don't be a fool.
You'll only annoy me.

LEPORELLO:
Not a chance now
For you to employ me.

DON GIOVANNI:
Listen to me, my friend.

LEPORELLO:
I tell you, this is the end.

DON GIOVANNI:
But what have I done
That you want to leave?

LEPORELLO:
Oh niente affatto!
Quasi ammazzarmi!

DON GIOVANNI:
Va', che sei matto!
Fu per burlar.

LEPORELLO:
Ed io non burlo,
ma voglio andar.
(Va per partire.)

Recitativo

DON GIOVANNI: *(lo richiama)* Leporello.

LEPORELLO: Signore.

DON GIOVANNI: Vien qui, facciamo pace: prendi.
(Gli dà del danaro.)

LEPORELLO: Cosa?

DON GIOVANNI: Quattro doppie.

LEPORELLO: Oh, sentite, per questa volta la cerimonia accetto;
ma non vi ci avvezzate: non credete di sedurre i miei pari, come
le donne, a forza di danari.

DON GIOVANNI: Non parliam più di ciò! Ti basta l'animo di far
quel ch'io ti dico?

LEPORELLO: Purché lasciam le donne.

LEPORELLO:
It's just that you tried
To kill me, I believe.

DON GIOVANNI:
Nonsense, you're crazy.
It was meant to be fun.

LEPORELLO:
The joke was on me.
I've had it. I'm done.
(He starts to leave.)

Recitative

DON GIOVANNI: *(pulling him back)* Leporello.

LEPORELLO: Master.

DON GIOVANNI: Come here. Let's make peace. Take this . . .
(gives him money)

LEPORELLO: What is it?

DON GIOVANNI: Four gold pieces.

LEPORELLO: Well now . . . maybe just this once I'll agree to the arrangement. But don't take advantage of my . . . weakness. Don't think I'm the sort of man you can seduce with money, as you do the women.

DON GIOVANNI: We'll say no more of that. Are you man enough to do as I bid?

LEPORELLO: So long as we leave the women alone.

DON GIOVANNI: Lasciar le donne! Pazzo! Lasciar le donne! Sai ch'elle per me son necessarie più del pan che mangio, più dell'aria che spiro!

LEPORELLO: E avete core d'ingannarle poi tutte?

DON GIOVANNI: È tutto amore. Chi a una sola è fedele verso l'altre è crudele: io, che in me sento sì esteso sentimento, vo' bene a tutte quante; le donne poi, che calcolar non sanno, il mio buon natural chiamano inganno.

LEPORELLO: Non ho veduto mai naturale più vasto e più benigno. Orsù, cosa vorreste?

DON GIOVANNI: Odi, vedesti tu la cameriera di Donna Elvira?

LEPORELLO: Io no.

DON GIOVANNI: Non hai veduto qualche cosa di bello, caro il mio Leporello. Ora io con lei vo' tentar la mia sorte; ed ho pensato, giacché siam verso sera, per aguzzarle meglio l'appetito di presentarmi a lei col tuo vestito.

LEPORELLO: E perché non potreste presentarvi col vostro?

DON GIOVANNI: Han poco credito con gente di tal rango gli abiti signorili.
(Si cava il proprio abito e si mette quello di Leporello.)
Sbrigati ... via ...

LEPORELLO: Signor ... per più ragioni ...

DON GIOVANNI: Leave them alone? You're mad! Leave the women alone? Ha! Don't you realize they mean more to me than the bread I eat, the air I breathe?

LEPORELLO: And do you have the heart to deceive them all?

DON GIOVANNI: I do it because I love them. Who is faithful to one is cruel to the others. I am a man whose heart is so large that I love all of them. Women simply don't understand me. They think that my natural generosity is some sort of deceit.

LEPORELLO: I certainly have never seen a greater or more natural generosity. So what is it you want?

DON GIOVANNI: Listen. Did you notice that chambermaid of Donna Elvira's?

LEPORELLO: Me? No!

DON GIOVANNI: Then, my dear Leporello, you've missed a delicious beauty. I want to try my luck with her now, and since night is coming on, I thought to whet her appetite by presenting myself in *your* clothes.

LEPORELLO: Why not in your own?

DON GIOVANNI: Aristocratic clothing doesn't have much of an effect on girls of her class.
(He quickly takes off his cloak and dons Leporello's.)
Come, come, hurry up now.

LEPORELLO: Sir, there are other reasons . . .

DON GIOVANNI: *(con collera)* Finiscila, non soffro opposizioni.
(Leporello si mette l'abito di Don Giovanni.)

Si fa notte a poco a poco.

Scena 2

DON GIOVANNI, LEPORELLO, DONNA ELVIRA.

N° 15 Terzetto

DONNA ELVIRA: *(alla finestra)*
Ah, taci, ingiusto core,
non palpitarmi in seno!
È un empio, è un traditore,
è colpa aver pietà.

LEPORELLO:
Zitto: di Donna Elvira,
signor, la voce io sento.

DON GIOVANNI:
Cogliere io vo' il momento,
tu fermati un po' là.
(Don Giovanni si mette dietro Leporello e parla a Donna Elvira.)
Elvira, idolo mio …

DONNA ELVIRA: Non è costui l'ingrato?

DON GIOVANNI:
Sì, vita mia, son io,
e chiedo carità.

DON GIOVANNI: *(angrily)* Enough. I won't listen to any arguments against me!

(Leporello puts on Don Giovanni's cloak.)

(It is gradually getting darker.)

Scene 2

DON GIOVANNI, LEPORELLO, AND DONNA ELVIRA.

Trio

DONNA ELVIRA: *(at the window)*
Be still, my unjust heart.
Do not beat so within.
He is a criminal, a traitor.
To pity him is a sin.

LEPORELLO: Quiet, sir! It's Donna Elvira
Whose voice I hear.

DON GIOVANNI:
Time to seize the moment.
You stand right there.
(He stands behind Leporello and addresses Donna Elvira.)
Elvira, I adore you . . .

DONNA ELVIRA: Is that the horrid man himself?

DON GIOVANNI:
Yes, my darling, it is I.
And I beg for your mercy.

DONNA ELVIRA:
(Numi, che strano affetto
mi si risveglia in petto!)

LEPORELLO:
(State a veder la pazza
che ancor gli crederà.)

DON GIOVANNI:
Discendi, o gioia bella:
vedrai che tu sei quella
che adora l'alma mia,
pentito io sono già.

DONNA ELVIRA: No, non ti credo, o barbaro!

DON GIOVANNI: *(con trasporto e quasi piangendo)*
Ah, credimi, o m'uccido!
Idolo mio, vien qua.

LEPORELLO: *(piano a Don Giovanni)* Se seguitate, io rido.

DON GIOVANNI:
(Spero che cada presto!
Che bel colpetto è questo!
Più fertile talento
del mio, no, non si dà.)

LEPORELLO:
(Già quel mendace labbro
torna a sedur costei:
deh, proteggete, o dei,
la sua credulità!)

DONNA ELVIRA:
(God, what a strange passion
Stirs again in my heart.)

LEPORELLO:
(Look at that crazy woman!
She's still willing to believe him.)

DON GIOVANNI:
Oh precious jewel, come down.
You'll see you are the one
My very soul would crown.
My penitence has only begun.

DONNA ELVIRA: No, I don't believe you, cruel man!

DON GIOVANNI: *(passionately, nearly in tears)*
Believe me or I'll kill myself!
My dearest, please come down!

LEPORELLO: *(to Don Giovanni, softly)* If you go on like this, I'll
burst out laughing.

DON GIOVANNI:
(I hope she's soon to be mine.
What a stroke of luck for me!
Who on earth has more talent
Than handsome old yours truly?)

LEPORELLO:
(Lies are ever on his lips.
He'll have her again before long.
Protect and guide her, God.
Make her credulous heart strong.)

DONNA ELVIRA:
(Dei! Che cimento è questo!
Non so s'io vado o resto …
Ah, proteggete voi
la mia credulità!)
(Parte dalla finestra.)

Recitativo
DON GIOVANNI: *(allegrissimo)* Amico, che ti par?

LEPORELLO: Mi par che abbiate un'anima di bronzo.

DON GIOVANNI: Va' là, che sei il gran gonzo! Ascolta bene: quando costei qui viene, tu corri ad abbracciarla, falle quattro carezze, fingi la voce mia; poi con bell'arte cerca teco condurla in altra parte.

LEPORELLO: Ma signore …

DON GIOVANNI: *(mette presso il naso una pistola a Leporello.)* Non più repliche!

LEPORELLO: Ma se poi mi conosce?

DON GIOVANNI: Non ti conoscerà, se tu non vuoi … Zitto, ell'apre: ehi giudizio!
(Va in disparte.)

DONNA ELVIRA:
(God, this terrible dilemma!
I don't know right from wrong.
Protect and guide me, please.
Make my credulous heart strong.)
(She moves away from the window.)

Recitative
DON GIOVANNI: *(exuberantly)* Well, what do you think, my friend?

LEPORELLO: It seems to me you have a heart of stone.

DON GIOVANNI: Go on, you're a simpleton! Listen to me. When she comes down here, run and embrace her, caress her a little, imitate my voice. Then, use a little cunning and lead her off somewhere.

LEPORELLO: But suppose . . .

DON GIOVANNI: *(pointing a pistol at Leporello's nose)* Not another word!

LEPORELLO: But what if she recognizes me?

DON GIOVANNI: She won't recognize you, if you don't allow her to. Hush! She is opening the door. Pay attention.
(He goes to one side.)

Scena 3

I SUDDETTI, DONNA ELVIRA.

Recitativo

DONNA ELVIRA: Eccomi a voi.

DON GIOVANNI: (Veggiamo che farà.)

LEPORELLO: (Che imbroglio!)

DONNA ELVIRA: Dunque creder potrò che i pianti miei abbian vinto quel cor? Dunque pentito l'amato Don Giovanni al suo dovere e all'amor mio ritorna? ...

LEPORELLO: Sì, carina!

DONNA ELVIRA: Crudele! Se sapeste quante lagrime e quanti sospir voi mi costate!

LEPORELLO: Io, vita mia?

DONNA ELVIRA: Voi.

LEPORELLO: Poverina! Quanto mi dispiace!

DONNA ELVIRA: Mi fuggirete più?

LEPORELLO: No, muso bello.

DONNA ELVIRA: Sarete sempre mio?

LEPORELLO: Sempre.

DONNA ELVIRA: Carissimo!

Scene 3

THOSE BEFORE, AND DONNA ELVIRA.

Recitative

DONNA ELVIRA: I am yours!

DON GIOVANNI: (Let's see how he manages.)

LEPORELLO: (What a mess!)

DONNA ELVIRA: Can I believe my tears have conquered your heart? And have you repented? Has my Don Giovanni returned to his duty and to my love?

LEPORELLO: Yes, my darling!

DONNA ELVIRA: You've been so cruel! If only you knew how many tears, how much misery you have cost me.

LEPORELLO: I, beloved?

DONNA ELVIRA: You.

LEPORELLO: Poor dear, I am so sorry.

DONNA ELVIRA: You won't leave me again?

LEPORELLO: No, my beauty.

DONNA ELVIRA: You'll be mine forever?

LEPORELLO: Forever.

DONNA ELVIRA: Dearest of men!

LEPORELLO: Carissima! (La burla mi dà gusto.)

DONNA ELVIRA: Mio tesoro!

LEPORELLO: Mia Venere!

DONNA ELVIRA: Son per voi tutta foco!

LEPORELLO: Io tutto cenere.

DON GIOVANNI: (Il birbo si riscalda.)

DONNA ELVIRA: E non m'ingannerete?

LEPORELLO: No sicuro.

DONNA ELVIRA: Giuratemi.

LEPORELLO: Lo giuro a questa mano che bacio con trasporto … a quei bei lumi …

DON GIOVANNI: *(finge di uccider qualcheduno colla spada alla mano etc.)* Ih eh ih ah, sei morto!

DONNA ELVIRA, LEPORELLO: Oh numi!
(Fuggono.)

DON GIOVANNI: *(inseguendo dalla parte dove fuggirono Donna Elvira e Leporello)* Ih eh ih eh ih ah! Par che la sorte mi secondi. Veggiamo … Le finestre son queste: ora cantiamo.

LEPORELLO: Dearest of women! (I'm beginning to enjoy this.)

DONNA ELVIRA: My Mars!

LEPORELLO: My Venus!

DONNA ELVIRA: I am on fire for you!

LEPORELLO: I am all ashes.

DON GIOVANNI: (The rascal is warming to the task.)

DONNA ELVIRA: And you will not deceive me?

LEPORELLO: No, of course not.

DONNA ELVIRA: Swear to me.

LEPORELLO: I swear it by this hand, which I smother with kisses, by these exquisite eyes . . .

DON GIOVANNI: *(pretending to kill someone with a sword)* Aha! So there! Die, you wretch . . .

DONNA ELVIRA AND LEPORELLO: Good God!
(They flee.)

DON GIOVANNI: *(following in the same direction)* Ha, *ha!* Fate is on my side. Let's see now. These are the windows. Time for a serenade.

N° 16 Canzonetta

DON GIOVANNI:

Deh, vieni alla finestra, o mio tesoro,
deh, vieni a consolar il pianto mio:
se neghi a me di dar qualche ristoro,
davanti agli occhi tuoi morir vogl'io.
Tu ch'hai la bocca dolce più del mele,
tu che il zucchero porti in mezzo al core,
non esser, gioia mia, con me crudele:
lasciati almen veder, mio bell'amore.

Recitativo

DON GIOVANNI: V'è gente alla finestra, sarà dessa: zi zi ...

Scena 4

MASETTO ARMATO D'ARCHIBUSO E PISTOLA,
CONTADINI E SUDDETTO.

MASETTO: Non ci stanchiamo: il cor mi dice che trovar lo dobbiam.

DON GIOVANNI: (Qualcuno parla.)

MASETTO: Fermatevi: mi pare che alcuno qui si muova.

DON GIOVANNI: *(piano)* (Se non fallo è Masetto.)

MASETTO: *(forte)* Chi va là? Non risponde. Animo, schioppo al muso! *(più forte)* Chi va là?

Canzonetta

DON GIOVANNI:
Oh, come to the window, my honeybee.
Come console these tears, this sigh.
If you refuse my tender plea,
Those eyes I worship will see me die.
Your delicate mouth is sweet as honey.
Your swooning heart is sweeter still.
Oh, please, my precious, do not shun me.
Come now to your windowsill.

Recitative

DON GIOVANNI: There's someone at the window! It must be she.
Psst. *Psst.*

Scene 4

MASETTO, ARMED WITH A MUSKET AND PISTOL,
VILLAGERS, AND THOSE BEFORE.

MASETTO: Do not give up now. Something tells me we will find him.

DON GIOVANNI: (Someone's speaking.)

MASETTO: Stop! I think I hear someone moving.

DON GIOVANNI: *(softly)* (Isn't that Masetto?)

MASETTO: *(loudly)* Who goes there? No answer. Keep your weapons cocked. *(louder still)* Who goes there?

DON GIOVANNI: (Non è solo: ci vuol giudizio.) *(Cerca d'imitar la voce di Leporello.)* Amici ... (Non mi voglio scoprir.) *(come sopra)* Sei tu Masetto?

MASETTO: *(in collera)* Appunto quello! E tu?

DON GIOVANNI: Non mi conosci? Il servo son io di Don Giovanni.

MASETTO: *(prendendo per la mano Don Giovanni con furore)* Leporello! Servo di quell'indegno cavaliere!

DON GIOVANNI: Certo, di quel briccone ...

MASETTO: ...di quell'uom senza onore ... Ah, dimmi un poco dove possiam trovarlo: lo cerco con costor per trucidarlo.

DON GIOVANNI: (Bagatelle!) Bravissimo Masetto! Anch'io con voi m'unisco per fargliela a quel birbo di padrone. Or senti un po' qual è la mia intenzione.

N° 17 Aria

DON GIOVANNI: *(accennando a destra)*
Metà di voi qua vadano,
(accennando a sinistra)
e gli altri vadan là,
e pian pianin lo cerchino:
lontan non fia di qua.
Se un uom e una ragazza
passeggian per la piazza,
se sotto a una finestra
fare all'amor sentite,
ferite pur, ferite:
il mio padron sarà.

DON GIOVANNI: (He's not alone. I'd better be careful.) *(He tries to imitate Leporello's voice.)* Friends . . . (I don't want to give myself away.) *(as before)* Is that you, Masetto?

MASETTO: *(angrily)* Yes, it's me. Who are you?

DON GIOVANNI: Don't you recognize me? I'm Don Giovanni's manservant.

MASETTO: *(vehemently taking Don Giovanni's hand)* Leporello! Servant of the craven cavalier!

DON GIOVANNI: Yes, of that scoundrel.

MASETTO: Of a man without honor! Tell me where we can find him. These fellows and I want to murder him.

DON GIOVANNI: (A trifle!) Bravissimo, Masetto! I'll join you. I'd like to kill that miscreant of a master myself. But listen. I have a plan.

Aria

DON GIOVANNI: *(pointing to the right)*
Half of you go this way.
(pointing to the left)
Half of you go that way.
Look for him there, look for him here.
He's bound to be quite near.
If you notice a man
Stroll through the square,
If under a window
You spot a sly pair,
Seize him and strike him!
It's my master for sure.

In testa egli ha un cappello
con candidi pennacchi,
addosso un gran mantello,
e spada al fianco egli ha.
Andate, fate presto ...
(I contadini partono.)
(a Masetto)
Tu sol verrai con me:
noi far dobbiamo il resto,
e già vedrai cos'è.
(Prende seco Masetto e parte.)

Scena 5

DON GIOVANNI E MASETTO.

Recitativo

DON GIOVANNI: *(ritorna in scena conducendo seco per la mano Masetto.)*
Zitto! Lascia ch'io senta ... Ottimamente. Dunque dobbiam
ucciderlo?

MASETTO: Sicuro.

DON GIOVANNI: E non ti basteria rompergli l'ossa ... fracassargli
le spalle ...

MASETTO: No no, voglio ammazzarlo; vo' farlo in cento brani ...

DON GIOVANNI: Hai buon'arme?

MASETTO: Cospetto! Ho pria questo moschetto ... e poi questa
pistola ...
(Dà il moschetto e la pistola a Don Giovanni.)

DON GIOVANNI: E poi?

There's a hat on his head
With fancy white plumes.
A cloak big as a bedspread
And a sword, that's for sure.
Go off quickly, quickly!
(The villagers leave.)
(to Masetto)
You, by yourself, come with me.
We have other things to do.
And what they are you'll soon see.
(He leaves, taking Masetto with him.)

Scene 5

DON GIOVANNI AND MASETTO.

Recitative

DON GIOVANNI: *(returning to the scene leading Masetto by the hand)*
Quiet! Let me listen first. All clear. So the plan is to kill him?

MASETTO: Of course.

DON GIOVANNI: Not just break a few bones? Maybe fracture a shoulder?

MASETTO: No, I want to *kill* him, tear him into a hundred pieces!

DON GIOVANNI: You have good weapons?

MASETTO: The best! I have this musket and this pistol.
(He hands them to Don Giovanni.)

DON GIOVANNI: And?

MASETTO: Non basta?

DON GIOVANNI: Oh, basta certo! Or prendi: *(Batte col rovescio della spada Masetto.)* questa per la pistola ... questa per il moschetto ...

MASETTO: Ahi! Ahi! Soccorso!

DON GIOVANNI: *(minacciandolo colle armi alla mano)* Taci, o sei morto! Questi per ammazzarlo ... questi per farlo in brani ... villano, mascalzon, ceffo da cani.
(Parte.)

Scena 6

MASETTO, POI ZERLINA CON LANTERNA.

Recitativo

MASETTO: *(gridando forte)* Ahi ahi! La testa mia! Ahi ahi! Le spalle e il petto! ...

ZERLINA: Di sentire mi parve la voce di Masetto.

MASETTO: Oddio! Zerlina, Zerlina mia! Soccorso!

ZERLINA: Cosa è stato?

MASETTO: L'iniquo, il scellerato mi ruppe l'ossa e i nervi.

ZERLINA: Oh poveretta me! Chi?

MASETTO: Leporello o qualche diavol che somiglia a lui.

MASETTO: Aren't these enough?

DON GIOVANNI: Oh, certainly they're enough! But now take
. . . *(He beats Masetto with the flat of his sword blade.)* . . . *this*, for
the pistol . . . and *this*, for the musket!

MASETTO: Help! Ay! Help!

DON GIOVANNI: *(threatening him with the weapons)* Quiet, or you're
a dead man! *This*, for killing him. *This*, for tearing him in pieces.
You dog-face peasant! You bastard!
(He leaves.)

Scene 6

MASETTO, THEN ZERLINA WITH A LANTERN.

Recitative

MASETTO: *(groaning loudly)* Ay! Ay! My head! Ay! My shoulder!
My chest!

ZERLINA: Isn't that Masetto's voice?

MASETTO: Oh God! My Zerlina! Help me!

ZERLINA: What's happened?

MASETTO: That villain, that vicious thug, has broken every bone
in my body.

ZERLINA: Oh, dear. Who?

MASETTO: Leporello, or some devil who looks like him.

ZERLINA: Crudel! Non tel diss'io che con questa tua pazza gelosia ti ridurresti a qualche brutto passo? Dove ti duole?`

MASETTO: Qui.

ZERLINA: E poi?

MASETTO: Qui ... e ancora ... qui ...

ZERLINA: E poi non ti duol altro?

MASETTO: Duolmi un poco questo piè, questo braccio e questa mano.

ZERLINA: Via via, non è gran mal, se il resto è sano. Vientene meco a casa. Purché tu mi prometta d'essere men geloso, io, io ti guarirò, caro il mio sposo.

N° 18 Aria

ZERLINA:
Vedrai, carino,
se sei buonino,
che bel rimedio
ti voglio dar.
È naturale,
non dà disgusto,
e lo speziale
non lo sa far.
È un certo balsamo
che porto addosso,
dare tel posso,
se il vuoi provar.
Saper vorresti
dove mi sta?

ZERLINA: That brute! Didn't I warn you that this insane jealousy of yours would get you into trouble? Where does it hurt?

MASETTO: Here.

ZERLINA: And?

MASETTO: Here . . . and also . . . here.

ZERLINA: Nowhere else?

MASETTO: This foot hurts a bit . . . and my arm . . . and my hand.

ZERLINA: Come, come, that's not so bad, if the rest is unhurt. Come home with me. If you promise to control your jealousy, I'll take care of you as a wife should.

Aria

ZERLINA:
You'll soon see,
If you behave,
The remedy I have
Especially for you.
A delicious potion
And so extraordinary
That no apothecary
Knows how to brew.
It's a certain balm
That I carry with me,
And if only you'll agree
I can give it to you.
If you want to know
Where it is on me,

Sentilo battere,
(facendogli toccar il core)
toccami qua.
(Parte con Masetto.)

Atrio terreno oscuro con tre porte in casa di Donn'Anna.

Scena 7

LEPORELLO, DONNA ELVIRA; POI DONN'ANNA, DON
OTTAVIO CON SERVI E LUMI; POI ZERLINA E MASETTO.

Recitativo

LEPORELLO: Di molte faci il lume s'avvicina, o mio ben: stiamci
qui ascosi finché da noi si scosta.

DONNA ELVIRA: Ma che temi, adorato mio sposo?

LEPORELLO: Nulla … nulla … certi riguardi … Io vo' veder se
il lume è già lontano … (Ah come da costei liberarmi?) Rimanti,
anima bella …
(S'allontana.)

DONNA ELVIRA: Ah, non lasciarmi!

N° 19 Sestetto

DONNA ELVIRA:
Sola sola in buio loco
palpitar il cor io sento,
e m'assale un tal pavento
che mi sembra di morir.

It's beating fast and free.
(He lays his hand on her heart.)
Put your hand here. Do.
(She goes off with Masetto.)

A dark atrium with three doors in Donna Anna's house.

Scene 7

LEPORELLO AND DONNA ELVIRA; THEN DONNA ANNA,
DON OTTAVIO WITH SERVANTS AND LIGHTS, AND LATER
ZERLINA AND MASETTO.

Recitative

LEPORELLO: The light of many torches is getting closer, my love.
Let's stay hidden here until they leave.

DONNA ELVIRA: But what are you afraid of, my dearest husband?

LEPORELLO: Nothing, nothing . . . certain precautions . . . I
want to check on those lights. (Oh, how can I free myself of this
woman?) Wait right here, my love.
(He goes off.)

DONNA ELVIRA: Don't leave me!

Sextet

DONNA ELVIRA:
All alone in this dark place,
Fear is pounding in my heart.
Terror stalls and starts.
Any moment Death may grab me.

LEPORELLO: *(andando a tentone etc.)*
Più che cerco, men ritrovo
questa porta sciagurata ...
Piano piano l'ho trovata,
ecco il tempo di fuggir.
(Sbaglia la porta.)

(Entrano vestiti a lutto Don Ottavio e Donn'Anna.)

DON OTTAVIO:
Tergi il ciglio, o vita mia,
e dà calma al tuo dolore;
l'ombra omai del genitore
pena avrà de' tuoi martir.

DONN'ANNA:
Lascia, lascia alla mia pena
questo picciolo ristoro;
sola morte, o mio tesoro,
il mio pianto può finir.

DONNA ELVIRA: *(senza esser vista)* Ah, dov'è lo sposo mio?

LEPORELLO: *(dalla porta senza esser visto)* Se mi trova son perduto!

DONNA ELVIRA, LEPORELLO:
(Una porta là vegg'io,
cheta cheta|cheto cheto vo' partir.)
(Nel sortire s'incontrano in Zerlina e Masetto.)

LEPORELLO: *(groping his way)*
The more I search for the door,
The harder it is to find.
Gently . . . ah, I'm *not* blind.
Here it is. My chance to flee.
(He exits through the wrong door.)

(Don Ottavio and Donna Anna enter, both dressed in mourning.)

DON OTTAVIO:
Dry your eyes, my poor beloved.
Time will ease your grief.
Your anguish will bring no relief
To your dearest father's ghost.

DONNA ANNA:
Leave me to my tears.
There is comfort in my pain.
Death itself, its bloody stain,
Is what I long for most.

DONNA ELVIRA: *(without being seen)* Where is my husband?

LEPORELLO: *(from the door, without being seen)* If she finds me,
I'm done for.

DONNA ELVIRA AND LEPORELLO:
(I see an escape here.
It's through this doorpost.)
(As he leaves, he encounters Zerlina and Masetto.)

Scena 8

I SUDDETTI, ZERLINA, MASETTO.

ZERLINA, MASETTO: Ferma, briccone, dove ten vai?
(Leporello s'asconde la faccia.)

DONN'ANNA, DON OTTAVIO: Ecco il fellone! ... Com'era qua!

DONN'ANNA, ZERLINA, DON OTTAVIO, MASETTO: Ah, mora il perfido che m'ha tradito!

DONNA ELVIRA: È mio marito! Pietà, pietà!

DONN'ANNA, ZERLINA, DON OTTAVIO, MASETTO: *(sottovoce)* È Donna Elvira quella ch'io vedo? Appena il credo!

DONNA ELVIRA: Pietà, pietà!

DONN'ANNA, ZERLINA, DON OTTAVIO, MASETTO: *(in atto di ucciderlo)* No no, morrà!

LEPORELLO: *(Leporello si scopre e si mette in ginocchio davanti gli altri.)* *(quasi piangendo)* Perdon, perdono, signori miei, quello io non sono, sbaglia costei; viver lasciatemi, per carità!

DONN'ANNA, ZERLINA, DONNA ELVIRA, DON OTTAVIO, MASETTO: Dei! Leporello! Che inganno è questo! stupida/stupido resto ... che mai sarà?

Scene 8

THOSE BEFORE, ZERLINA, AND MASETTO.

ZERLINA AND MASETTO: Stop, you rogue! Where do you think *you're* going!
(Leporello hides his face.)

DONNA ANNA AND DON OTTAVIO: Here is the wretch. How did he get here?

DONNA ANNA, ZERLINA, DON OTTAVIO, AND MASETTO: Ah! Let him die, this horrid man who betrayed me!

DONNA ELVIRA: He is my husband . . . Have mercy! Mercy!

DONNA ANNA, ZERLINA, DON OTTAVIO, AND MASETTO: *(softly)* Is that Donna Elvira I see? I can hardly believe this.

DONNA ELVIRA: Have mercy!

DONNA ANNA, ZERLINA, DON OTTAVIO, AND MASETTO: *(Don Ottavio goes to kill him.)* No, he must die!

LEPORELLO: *(Leporello removes his disguise and falls to his knees.)* *(almost in tears)* Pardon, pardon, your lordships . . . I am not the man . . . she's made a mistake . . . Let me live, for pity's sake!

DONNA ANNA, ZERLINA, DONNA ELVIRA, DON OTTAVIO, AND MASETTO: Good God! Leporello! What kind of trick is this? I can't believe it! What's going on?

LEPORELLO:
Mille torbidi pensieri
mi s'aggiran per la testa;
se mi salvo in tal tempesta
è un prodigio in verità!

DONN'ANNA, ZERLINA, DONNA ELVIRA, DON OTTAVIO, MASETTO:
Mille torbidi pensieri
mi s'aggiran per la testa;
che giornata, oh stelle, è questa,
che impensata novità!
(Donn'Anna parte coi servi.)

Scena 9

DONNA ELVIRA, DON OTTAVIO, LEPORELLO,
ZERLINA E MASETTO.

Recitativo

ZERLINA: Dunque quello sei tu che il mio Masetto poco fa crudelmente maltrattasti!

DONNA ELVIRA: Dunque tu m'ingannasti, o scellerato, spacciandoti con me da Don Giovanni!

DON OTTAVIO: Dunque tu in questi panni venisti qui per qualche tradimento!

ZERLINA: A me tocca punirlo!

DONNA ELVIRA: Anzi a me.

DON OTTAVIO: No no, a me.

LEPORELLO:
A thousand troubling thoughts
Are swirling through my head.
If I can save myself from this,
I'll have had a run of luck.

**DONNA ANNA, ZERLINA, DONNA ELVIRA, DON OTTAVIO, AND
MASETTO:**
A thousand troubling thoughts
Are swirling through my head.
What a day, oh stars, is this!
What's next? I'm thunderstruck.
(Donna Anna leaves with her servants.)

Scene 9
DONNA ELVIRA, DON OTTAVIO, LEPORELLO,
ZERLINA, AND MASETTO.

Recitative

ZERLINA: So it was you who just now cruelly attacked my
Masetto?

DONNA ELVIRA: So it was you who deceived me by passing yourself off as Don Giovanni?

DON OTTAVIO: So it was you who came in disguise to commit
some treachery?

ZERLINA: It is for me to punish him.

DONNA ELVIRA: Rather, for *me*.

DON OTTAVIO: No, no, for *me*!

MASETTO: Accoppatelo meco tutti tre.

N° 20 Aria

LEPORELLO: *(a Don Ottavio e Donna Elvira)*
Ah pietà, signori miei,
ah pietà, pietà di me!
Do ragione a voi e lei,
ma il delitto mio non è.
Il padron con prepotenza
l'innocenza mi rubò.
(piano a Donna Elvira)
Donna Elvira, compatite:
già capite come andò.
(a Zerlina)
Di Masetto non so nulla,
(accennando Donna Elvira)
vel dirà questa fanciulla:
è un'oretta circumcirca
che con lei girando vo.
(a Don Ottavio con confusione)
A voi, signore,
non dico niente ...
certo timore ...
certo accidente ...
di fuori chiaro ...
di dentro scuro ...
non c'è riparo ...
la porta ... il muro ...
(additando la porta dov'erasi chiuso per errore)
vo da quel lato ...
poi qui celato ...
l'affar si sa ...
ma s'io sapeva,
fuggia per qua.
(S'avvicina con destrezza alla porta e fugge.)

MASETTO: Let's all three of us set on him.

Aria

LEPORELLO: *(to Don Ottavio and Donna Elvira)*
Ah, take pity on me, my lords!
You are right . . . and so is she.
But the crime was not committed by me.
My master arrogantly
Robbed me of my innocence.
(to Donna Elvira, softly)
Donna Elvira, show mercy!
You know how things went.
(to Zerlina)
Masetto? What's Masetto to me?
(pointing to Donna Elvira)
This young lady will tell you
I've been in her company
For an hour or more. It's true.
(to Don Ottavio, in confusion)
To you, good sir,
I won't say a word . . .
I was afraid, for sure . . .
A misfortune—so absurd . . .
Outside it's clear . . .
Yet so dark within . . .
No shelter near . . .
The door and wall have been . . .
(indicating the door where he concealed himself by mistake)
Well . . . it seemed best . . .
A step to the side . . .
A place to hide . . .
You know the rest . . .
Had I known then
I'd have fled this way fast.
(He nervously nears the door and flees.)

Scena 10

DONNA ELVIRA, DON OTTAVIO, ZERLINA E MASETTO.

Recitativo

DONNA ELVIRA: Ferma, perfido, ferma ...

MASETTO: Il birbo ha l'ali ai piedi ...

ZERLINA: Con qual arte si sottrasse l'iniquo! ...

DON OTTAVIO: Amici miei, dopo eccessi sì enormi dubitar non possiam che Don Giovanni non sia l'empio uccisore del padre di Donn'Anna. In questa casa per poche ore fermatevi ... Un ricorso vo' far a chi si deve, e in pochi istanti vendicarvi prometto. Così vuole dover, pietade, affetto.

N° 21 Aria

DON OTTAVIO:
Il mio tesoro intanto
andate a consolar,
e del bel ciglio il pianto
cercate di asciugar.
Ditele che i suoi torti
a vendicar io vado,
che sol di stragi e morti
nunzio vogl'io tornar.
(Partono.)

Scene 10

DONNA ELVIRA, DON OTTAVIO, ZERLINA, AND MASETTO.

Recitative

DONNA ELVIRA: Stop him! Stop that scoundrel!

MASETTO: That rogue has wings for feet.

ZERLINA: How slyly that wretch escaped!

DON OTTAVIO: My friends, after all these monstrous events we can no longer doubt that Don Giovanni is the infamous murderer of Donna Anna's father. Stay for a while in this house. I am going to ask the authorities to issue a warrant, and very soon you shall have the vengeance you seek. Duty, compassion, and love demand no less.

Aria

DON OTTAVIO:
Meanwhile, please now go.
My treasure must be consoled.
Gently, softy dry
The tears that fill her eyes.
Tell her I am on my way
To avenge an ill-used daughter.
Tell her I will soon return
As a herald of blood and slaughter.
(They leave.)

Scena 10a

DONNA ELVIRA SOLA.

N° 21b Recitativo accompagnato ed aria

Recitativo accompagnato

DONNA ELVIRA: In quali eccessi, oh numi, in quai misfatti orribili tremendi è avvolto il sciagurato! ... Ah no, non puote tardar l'ira del cielo ... la giustizia tardar! Sentir già parmi la fatale saetta che gli piomba sul capo! ... Aperto veggio il baratro mortal ... Misera Elvira, che contrasto d'affetti in sen ti nasce! ... Perché questi sospiri e queste ambasce?

Aria

DONN'ELVIRA:
Mi tradì quell'alma ingrata,
infelice, oddio, mi fa;
ma tradita e abbandonata
provo ancor per lui pietà.
Quando sento il mio tormento,
di vendetta il cor favella;
ma se guardo il suo cimento,
palpitando il cor mi va.
(Parte.)

Loco chiuso. In forma di sepolcreto etc. diverse statue equestri: statua del Commendatore.

Scena 11

DON GIOVANNI ENTRA PEL MURETTO RIDENDO,
INDI LEPORELLO.

Recitativo

DON GIOVANNI: *(ridendo forte)* Ah ah ah, questa è buona! Or lasciala cercar. Che bella notte! È più chiara del giorno: sembra

Scene 10a

DONNA ELVIRA, ALONE.

Accompanied Recitative and Aria

Accompanied Recitative

DONNA ELVIRA: In what huge and horrible crimes, O God, is that wretched man entangled! No, the anger of heaven and justice itself cannot be delayed. I already see the fatal lightning bolt falling on his head! I see the dreadful abyss open . . . Unhappy Elvira! What conflicting emotions tear at your breast? Why these sighs, this torment?

Aria

DONNA ELVIRA:
That ungrateful man seduced me
And made me, God, his prey.
Abandoned me, used me—
Yet there is mercy in my dismay.
When I see my anguished life
It is only revenge I desire.
Then I see him beset with strife
And my pitying heart is afire.
(She leaves.)

An enclosed place in the shape of a cemetery. Several equestrian statues; a statue of the Commendatore.

Scene 11

DON GIOVANNI ENTERS BY JUMPING OVER THE WALL, THEN LEPORELLO.

Recitative

DON GIOVANNI: *(laughing loudly)* Ha, ha! That's a good one! Now let her try and find me! What a beautiful night—brighter than

fatta per gir a zonzo a caccia di ragazze. È tardi? *(Guarda sull'oro-logio.)* Oh ancor non sono due della notte ... Avrei voglia un po' di saper come è finito l'affar tra Leporello e Donna Elvira: s'egli ha avuto giudizio ...

LEPORELLO: *(in strada)* Alfin vuole ch'io faccia un precipizio.

DON GIOVANNI: È desso. Oh Leporello!

LEPORELLO: *(dal muretto)* Chi mi chiama?

DON GIOVANNI: Non conosci il padron?

LEPORELLO: Così nol conoscessi!

DON GIOVANNI: Come? Birbo!

LEPORELLO: *(entra)* Ah, siete voi, scusate.

DON GIOVANNI: Cosa è stato?

LEPORELLO: Per cagion vostra io fui quasi accoppato.

DON GIOVANNI: Ebben, non era questo un onore per te?

LEPORELLO: Signor, vel dono.

DON GIOVANNI: Via via, vien qua, ché belle cose ti deggio dir.

LEPORELLO: Ma cosa fate qui?

DON GIOVANNI:
Vien dentro e lo saprai.
(Leporello entra, si cangiano d'abito.)

day! A night made for lying in wait and feasting on girls. How late is it? *(He looks at the clock.)* Oh, not yet two at night. I'd love to know how that encounter between Leporello and Donna Elvira ended up . . . if he had the wherewithal . . .

LEPORELLO: *(in the street)* He wants to be the end of me!

DON GIOVANNI: The man himself. Hey, Leporello!

LEPORELLO: *(from the wall)* Who's calling?

DON GIOVANNI: You don't recognize your master?

LEPORELLO: If only I didn't!

DON GIOVANNI: What's that, you scamp?

LEPORELLO: *(enters)* Oh, is that you? Beg pardon.

DON GIOVANNI: What happened?

LEPORELLO: Thanks to you, I was nearly killed.

DON GIOVANNI: Well, that would have been quite an honor.

LEPORELLO: An honor I could do without.

DON GIOVANNI: Come, come, listen up. I have a charming tale to tell.

LEPORELLO: But what are you doing here?

DON GIOVANNI: Come over here and you'll know why.
(Leporello enters; they exchange clothes.)

Diverse istorielle che accadute mi son da che partisti ti dirò un'altra volta: or la più bella ti vo' solo narrar.

LEPORELLO: Donnesca al certo.

DON GIOVANNI: C'è dubbio? Una fanciulla bella, giovin, galante per la strada incontrai; le vado appresso, la prendo per la man, fuggir mi vuole, dico poche parole, ella mi piglia ... sai per chi?

LEPORELLO: Non lo so.

DON GIOVANNI: Per Leporello.

LEPORELLO: Per me?

DON GIOVANNI: Per te.

LEPORELLO: Va bene.

DON GIOVANNI: Per la mano essa allora mi prende ...

LEPORELLO: Ancora meglio.

DON GIOVANNI: M'accarezza, mi abbraccia ... "Caro il mio Leporello ... Leporello mio caro ..." Allor m'accorsi ch'era qualche tua bella.

LEPORELLO: Oh maledetto!

DON GIOVANNI: Dell'inganno approfitto. Non so come mi riconosce: grida, sento gente, a fuggire mi metto, e pronto pronto per quel muretto in questo loco io monto.

LEPORELLO: E mi dite la cosa con tale indifferenza?

I'll have to tell you another time about the various adventures that have happened since we parted. But for now I'll tell you about the best one.

LEPORELLO: It's about women certainly.

DON GIOVANNI: Can you doubt it? I met on the street a pretty young girl, a bit of a flirt. I went up to her and took her hand. She tried to break free. I spoke a few words—and do you know who she took me for?

LEPORELLO: No idea.

DON GIOVANNI: Leporello.

LEPORELLO: Me?

DON GIOVANNI: You!

LEPORELLO: Well, well.

DON GIOVANNI: Then she took my hand.

LEPORELLO: Better and better.

DON GIOVANNI: She stroked it, and embraced me. "Oh darling Leporello . . ." That's when I realized she was one of your conquests.

LEPORELLO: Damn him!

DON GIOVANNI: I took advantage of her mistake, but somehow she recognized me, and screamed. I heard people coming, so I ran away. And quickly I climbed over that wall there.

LEPORELLO: And you tell me this as if it were nothing at all?

DON GIOVANNI: Perché no?

LEPORELLO: Ma se fosse costei stata mia moglie!

DON GIOVANNI: Meglio ancora!
(ride molto forte)

IL COMMENDATORE: Di rider finirai pria dell'aurora.

DON GIOVANNI: Chi ha parlato?

LEPORELLO: *(con atti di paura)* Ah, qualche anima sarà dell'altro mondo che vi conosce a fondo!

DON GIOVANNI: Taci, sciocco!
(Mette mano alla spada, cerca qua e là pel seplocreto dando diverse percosse alle staute etc.)
Chi va là? Chi va là?

IL COMMENDATORE: Ribaldo audace, lascia a' morti la pace.

LEPORELLO: Ve l'ho detto.

DON GIOVANNI: *(con indifferenza e sprezzo)* Sarà qualcun di fuori che si burla di noi ... Ehi, del Commendatore non è questa la statua? Leggi un poco quella iscrizion.

LEPORELLO: Scusate ... non ho imparato a leggere a'raggi della luna ...

DON GIOVANNI: Leggi, dico.

LEPORELLO: *(legge)* "Dell'empio che mi trasse al passo estremo qui attendo la vendetta." Udiste? Io tremo!

DON GIOVANNI: Why not?

LEPORELLO: Suppose she had been my wife?

DON GIOVANNI: Even better!
(laughs loudly)

COMMENDATORE: You will laugh your last by dawn.

DON GIOVANNI: Who spoke?

LEPORELLO: *(visibly frightened)* Ah, it must be a spirit from the other world who knows you.

DON GIOVANNI: Quiet, you fool!
(putting his hand on his sword, searching the graveyard, randomly striking statues)
Who goes there! Who is it?

COMMENDATORE: Audacious villain! Leave the dead in peace.

LEPORELLO: I told you so!

DON GIOVANNI: *(with indifference and disdain)* It must be someone out there who's mocking us. Aha! Isn't that the statue of the Commendatore? Read out the inscription.

LEPORELLO: Sorry . . . I never learned to read by moonlight.

DON GIOVANNI: Read it, I say.

LEPORELLO: *(reading)* "Struck down by a traitor, I await here my revenge." Did you hear that? It frightens me.

DON GIOVANNI: Oh vecchio buffonissimo! Digli che questa sera l'attendo a cena meco.

LEPORELLO: Che pazzia! Ma vi par ... Oh dei, mirate che terribili occhiate egli ci dà! Par vivo! Par che senta! E che voglia parlar ...

DON GIOVANNI: Orsù, va' là, o qui t'ammazzo e poi ti seppellisco.

LEPORELLO: *(tremando)* Piano piano, signore, ora ubbidisco.

N° 22 Duetto

LEPORELLO:
O statua gentilissima
del gran Commendatore ...
(a Don Giovanni)
Padron ... mi trema il core,
non posso terminar.

DON GIOVANNI:
Finiscila, o nel petto
ti metto questo acciar.
Che gusto, che spassetto!
Lo voglio far tremar.

LEPORELLO:
Che impiccio, che capriccio!
Io sentomi gelar.

LEPORELLO:
O statua gentilissima,
benché di marmo siate ...
(a Don Giovanni)
Ah padron ... padron mio, mirate
che seguita a guardar.

DON GIOVANNI: The old buffoon! Tell him that tonight I await him at my dinner table!

LEPORELLO: Madness! Do you think . . . Oh God, look how he glares at us, as if he were alive. It's as if he hears you . . . wants to speak . . .

DON GIOVANNI: Do as I say, or I'll kill you and bury you beside him!

LEPORELLO: *(trembling)* Easy, easy there, my lord. I will obey.

Duet

LEPORELLO:
O most noble statue
Of the great Commendatore . . .
(to Don Giovanni)
Master . . . I'm so sorry . . .
I'm simply too afraid.

DON GIOVANNI:
Finish, or my sword
Will end your story.
What fun this is! How nice!
I want to make him afraid.

LEPORELLO:
What a bother! He's capricious!
My blood has turned to ice.

LEPORELLO:
O most noble statue,
Although of stone you're made . . .
(to Don Giovanni)
Ah, master . . . Look! . . .
His gaze . . . it does not fade.

DON GIOVANNI: Mori, mori…

LEPORELLO:
No … No no, attendete …
(alla statua)
Signor, il padron mio,
badate ben, non io,
vorria con voi cenar.
(La statua china la testa.)
Ah ah ah! Che scena è questa?
Oh ciel, chinò la testa!

DON GIOVANNI: Va' là, che se' un buffone…

LEPORELLO: Guardate ancor, padrone.

DON GIOVANNI: E che degg'io guardar?

LEPORELLO:
Colla marmorea testa
(Imita la statua.)
 ei fa così, così.
(La statua china qui la testa.)

DON GIOVANNI:
(Don Giovanni vedendo il capo chino)
Colla marmorea testa
ei fa così, così.

DON GIOVANNI: *(alla statua)*
Parlate, se potete:
verrete a cena?

LA STATUA DEL COMMENDATORE: Sì.

DON GIOVANNI: Then *you* die . . .

LEPORELLO:
No, no . . . wait . . .
(to the statue)
Great sir, my master here . . .
It's his decision . . . not mine . . .
Invites you now to dine . . .
(The statue nods its head.)
Ah, ah! There's a sight to dread,
Heavens! . . . He bowed his head!

DON GIOVANNI: Stop it, you're an idiot. An idiot!

LEPORELLO: Look, look again closely, master!

DON GIOVANNI: And what should I be looking at?

LEPORELLO:
With his marble head
(imitating the statue)
He nods like this.
(The statue nods its head.)

DON GIOVANNI:
(seeing the nod)
With his marble head
He nods like that.

DON GIOVANNI: *(to the statue)*
Speak, if you can.
Will you dine with me?

COMMENDATORE: Yes.

LEPORELLO:
Mover mi posso appena ...
mi manca, oh dei, la lena!
Per carità ... partiamo ...
andiamo via di qui.

DON GIOVANNI:
Bizzarra è inver la scena ...
verrà il buon vecchio a cena ...
A prepararla andiamo ...
partiamo via di qui.
(Partono.)

Camera tetra.

Scena 12
DONN'ANNA E DON OTTAVIO.

Recitativo

DON OTTAVIO: Calmatevi, idol mio: di quel ribaldo vedrem puniti in breve i gravi eccessi. Vendicati sarem.

DONN'ANNA: Ma il padre, oddio!

DON OTTAVIO: Convien chinare il ciglio ai voleri del ciel: respira, o cara! Di tua perdita amara fia domani se vuoi dolce compenso questo cor, questa mano ... che il mio tenero amor ...

DONN'ANNA: Oh dei, che dite? ... In sì tristi momenti ...

DON OTTAVIO: E che? Vorresti con indugi novelli accrescer le mie pene? Crudel!

LEPORELLO:
I don't think . . . I can budge . . .
I feel weak . . . I am not able . . .
For heaven's sake . . . let's leave . . .
Let's go . . . let's get out of here.

DON GIOVANNI:
Bizarre. But who's to judge?
The old man's coming to my table.
There's a meal to prepare, I believe.
It's time to go, that's clear.
(They leave.)

A dark room.

Scene 12

DONNA ANNA AND DON OTTAVIO.

Recitative

DON OTTAVIO: Calm yourself, my love. We will soon see the crimes of that murderer punished. We will have vengeance.

DONNA ANNA: But my father . . . Oh God!

DON OTTAVIO: We must bow to heaven's will. Take comfort, my dearest. I will make up tomorrow for the bitter sorrow you suffer now. To you I devote my heart, my hand, my love.

DONNA ANNA: Oh God, how can you speak to me so at such a sad moment . . .

DON OTTAVIO: What now? Would you increase my grief with new complaints? That's cruel.

N° 23 *Recitativo accompagnato e rondò*

Recitativo accompagnato

DONN'ANNA: Crudele! Ah no, mio bene! Troppo mi spiace allontanarti un ben che lungamente la nostr'alma desia … ma il mondo … oh dio … Non sedur la costanza del sensibil mio core! Abbastanza per te mi parla amore.

Rondò

DONN'ANNA:
Non mi dir, bell'idol mio,
che son io crudel con te;
tu ben sai quant'io t'amai,
tu conosci la mia fé.
Calma, calma il tuo tormento,
se di duol non vuoi ch'io mora;
forse un giorno il cielo ancora
sentirà pietà di me.
(Parte.)

Recitativo

DON OTTAVIO: Ah, si segua il suo passo: io vo' con lei dividere i martiri; saran meco men gravi i suoi sospiri.
(Parte.)

Accompanied Recitative and Rondo

Accompanied Recitative

DONNA ANNA: Cruel? Ah no, beloved! It pains me to postpone that happy hour we have both desired. But what would others think . . . Oh God! . . . Do not test the loyalty of my delicate heart. You know love draws me to you.

Rondo

DONNA ANNA:

Never say, my love, my own,
That I am cruel to you.
You know my heart is always true,
You know my loyalty.
Put aside your silent doubts
Or I will die of grief.
Heaven soon will bring relief.
It must take pity on me.
(She leaves.)

Recitative

DON OTTAVIO: Oh, I must follow her. Her sorrows are my own. With me beside her, her anguish will be eased.
(He leaves.)

Sala, una mensa preparata per mangiare.

N° 24 Finale

Scena 13

DON GIOVANNI, LEPORELLO, ALCUNI SUONATORI.

DON GIOVANNI:
Già la mensa è preparata,
voi suonate, amici cari:
giacché spendo i miei danari,
io mi voglio divertir.
Leporello, presto, in tavola!

LEPORELLO: Son prontissimo a servir.
(I servi portano in tavola mentre Leporello vuol uscire.)

DON GIOVANNI:
Giache spendo i miei danari
io mi voglio divertir.
Voi suonate, amici cari.
(I suonatori cominciano a suonare e Don Giovanni mangia.)

LEPORELLO: Bravi! "Cosa rara"!

DON GIOVANNI: Che ti par del bel concerto?

LEPORELLO: È conforme al vostro merto.

DON GIOVANNI: Ah, che piatto saporito!

A hall; a table prepared for a banquet.

Finale

Scene 13

DON GIOVANNI, LEPORELLO, AND SOME MUSICIANS.

DON GIOVANNI:
Already the table is laid.
Now music, lads in the band.
I've spent as much as I can.
I want to amuse myself.
Leporello, quickly to hand!

LEPORELLO: Ready to serve you, sir.
(Servants bring dishes to the table, while Leporello tries to make off.)

DON GIOVANNI:
I've spent as much as I can.
I want to amuse myself.
More music, you lads in the band!
(He eats; the musicians begin to play)

LEPORELLO: Bravo! It's from *Una Cosa Rara.**

DON GIOVANNI: How does that lovely music strike you?

LEPORELLO: Up to your own high standards, sir.

DON GIOVANNI: Ah, the food is divine!

---

* *Una Cosa Rara* is a 1786 opera by Spanish composer Vicente Martín y Soler, with a libretto by Da Ponte.

LEPORELLO: *(a parte)*
Ah, che barbaro appetito!
Che bocconi da gigante,
mi par proprio di svenir.

DON GIOVANNI: *(a parte)*
Nel veder i miei bocconi
gli par proprio di svenir.

DON GIOVANNI: Piatto!

LEPORELLO:
Servo.
Evvivano i "litiganti"!

DON GIOVANNI:
Versa il vino.
(Leporello versa il vino nel bicchiere. Don Giovanni beve.)
Eccellente marzimino!
(Leporello cangia il piatto a Don Giovanni e mangia in fretta gli avanzi di Don Giovanni.)

LEPORELLO:
(Questo pezzo di fagiano
piano piano vo' inghiottir.)

DON GIOVANNI:
(Sta mangiando, quel marrano;
fingerò di non capir.)

LEPORELLO: Questa poi la conosco purtroppo.

LEPORELLO: *(aside)*
He'd eat anything and everything!
What gigantic mouthfuls!
How he disgusts me.

DON GIOVANNI: *(aside)*
These gigantic mouthfuls
Seem to disgust him!

DON GIOVANNI: Next course!

LEPORELLO:
Coming, sir.
Bravo! That's from *I Litiganti!**

DON GIOVANNI:
Pour the wine.
(Leporello fills his glass with wine.)
A vintage Marzimino!
(Leporello brings Don Giovanni a new plate of food, and hurriedly eats himself.)

LEPORELLO:
(This little breast of pheasant
I'll gulp down in a rush.)

DON GIOVANNI:
(He's eating like a peasant.
Enough to make one blush.)

LEPORELLO: This one I know only too well . . .**

---

* *Fra i Due Litiganti il Terzo Gode* is a 1782 opera by Italian composer Giuseppe Sarti, with a libretto by Carlo Goldoni.
** The stage band is playing "Non più andrai" from Mozart's own *The Marriage of Figaro*, which had premiered the year before.

DON GIOVANNI: *(Lo chiama senza guardarlo.)* Leporello.

LEPORELLO: *(risponde colla bocca piena)* Padron mio ...

DON GIOVANNI: Parla schietto, mascalzone!

LEPORELLO: *(sempre mangiando)* Non mi lascia una flussione le parole proferir.

DON GIOVANNI: Mentre io mangio, fischia un poco.

LEPORELLO: Non so far ...

DON GIOVANNI: *(Lo guarda e s'accorge che mangia.)* Cos'è?

LEPORELLO:
Scusate, scusate.
Sì eccellente è il vostro cuoco,
che lo volli anch'io provar.

DON GIOVANNI:
Sì eccellente è il cuoco mio,
che lo volle anch'ei provar.

Scena 14
I SUDDETTI, DONNA ELVIRA.

DONNA ELVIRA: *(entra disperata.)*
L'ultima prova
dell'amor mio
ancor vogl'io
fare con te.
Più non rammento
gl'inganni tuoi,
pietade io sento ...

DON GIOVANNI: *(calling without looking at him)* Leporello!

LEPORELLO: *(replying with his mouth full)* Yesh, mashter . . .

DON GIOVANNI: Speak clearly, you lout!

LEPORELLO: *(still eating)* It's this cold I've caught . . . too hoarse.

DON GIOVANNI: Then, while I'm eating, whistle a bit.

LEPORELLO: I don't know how.

DON GIOVANNI: *(aware that he is eating)* What's this?

LEPORELLO:
So sorry.
Your cook is so fine
I wanted myself to dine.

DON GIOVANNI:
My cook is so fine,
He wanted himself to dine.

Scene 14
THOSE BEFORE, AND DONNA ELVIRA.

DONNA ELVIRA: *(entering in desperation)*
One last time
I come to you
To prove myself
Eternally true.
Your hurtful lies
No longer wound.
I sympathize . . .

DON GIOVANNI *(sorgendo)*, **LEPORELLO**:
Cos'è? Cos'è?

DONNA ELVIRA: *(s'inginocchia.)*
Da te non chiede
quest'alma oppressa
della sua fede
qualche mercé.

DON GIOVANNI:
Mi maraviglio!
Cosa volete?
Se non sorgete,
non resto in piè.
(S'inginocchia davanti Donna Elvira con affettazione.)

DONNA ELVIRA: Ah, non deridere gli affanni miei!

LEPORELLO: Quasi da piangere mi fa costei.

DON GIOVANNI: *(sorgendo fa sorgere Donna Elvira)*
(sempre con affettata tenerezza)
Io te deridere?
Cieli! Perché?

DON GIOVANNI: Che vuoi, mio bene?

DONNA ELVIRA: Che vita cangi.

DON GIOVANNI: Brava!

LEPORELLO, DONNA ELVIRA: Cor perfido!

DON GIOVANNI *(rising)* **AND LEPORELLO:**
What's going on?

DONNA ELVIRA: *(kneeling)*
My ragged soul is sad,
But begging I refuse.
My ardent loyalty
Is here for you to choose.

DON GIOVANNI:
I am stupefied.
What are you trying to do?
If you will not rise
Then I will kneel with you.
(He kneels.)

DONNA ELVIRA: Do not mock my despair.

LEPORELLO: This is more than I can bear.

DON GIOVANNI: *(rising and making Donna Elvira stand as well)*
(with affected tenderness)
I? Mock you?
Heavens! Whatever for?

DON GIOVANNI: Whatever you want, I am yours.

DONNA ELVIRA: I want you to change your ways.

DON GIOVANNI: Brava!

LEPORELLO AND DONNA ELVIRA: Your heart is cruel.

DON GIOVANNI:
Lascia ch'io mangi;
(Torna a sedere, a mangiare etc.)
e se ti piace, mangia con me.

DONNA ELVIRA:
Restati, barbaro,
nel lezzo immondo,
esempio orribile
d'iniquità!

LEPORELLO:
Se non si muove
nel suo dolore
di sasso ha il core
o cor non ha.

DON GIOVANNI: *(bevendo etc.)*
Vivan le femmine,
viva il buon vino,
sostegno e gloria
d'umanità!

DONNA ELVIRA: *(sorte, poi rientra mettendo un grido orribile e fugge dall'altra parte)* Ah!

DON GIOVANNI, LEPORELLO: Che grido è questo mai!

DON GIOVANNI: Va' a veder che cosa è stato.

LEPORELLO:
(sorte e prima di tornare mette un grido ancora più forte) Ah!
(Entra spaventato e chiude l'uscio.)

DON GIOVANNI:
Let me finish my meal.
(He returns to his seat and eats.)
Join me, if you'd like.

DONNA ELVIRA:
Stay then, you foul man,
Wallow in your crimes,
An example to the world
Of iniquity.

LEPORELLO:
If he's not moved now
By the depth of her sorrow,
His is a heart of stone,
All deformity.

DON GIOVANNI: *(drinking)*
Love live all the ladies!
Here's to fine old wines!
The sustenance and glory
Of humanity!

DONNA ELVIRA: *(She leaves but returns and flees out the other side.)*
Aaah!

DON GIOVANNI AND LEPORELLO: Why did she scream so?

DON GIOVANNI: Go find out what happened.

LEPORELLO:
(Leporello leaves, and before returning lets out a scream.) Aaah!
(He enters, terrified, and slams the door.)

DON GIOVANNI:
Che grido indiavolato!
Leporello, che cos'è?

LEPORELLO:
Ah signor ... per carità! ...
Non andate fuor di qua! ...
L'uom di sasso ... l'uomo bianco ...
Ah padrone! ... Io gelo ... io manco ...
Se vedeste che figura! ...
Se sentiste come fa:
(Si sente il moto de' piedi etc.)
ta ta ta ta ta ta ta ta!

DON GIOVANNI:
Non capisco niente affatto:
tu sei matto in verità!
(Si sente battere fortissimo alla porta che chiuse Leporello.)

LEPORELLO: Ah, sentite!

DON GIOVANNI:
Qualcun batte.
Apri ...
(Seguitano a batter più forte.)

LEPORELLO: *(tremando)* Io tremo ...

DON GIOVANNI: Apri, dico.

LEPORELLO: *(s'allontana impaurito)* Ah ...

DON GIOVANNI:
Matto! Per togliermi d'intrico
ad aprir io stesso andrò.
(Piglia un lume e va per aprire etc.)

DON GIOVANNI:
What a diabolical scream!
Leporello, what is it?

LEPORELLO:
Oh! . . . sir . . . for heaven's sake . . .
Do not leave this room . . .
The man of stone . . . the man all white . . .
Ah, master . . . I'm going . . . to pass out . . .
If you had seen . . . he looks like . . .
If you had heard . . . how . . .
(There is a sound of footsteps.)
He . . . he . . . he . . .

DON GIOVANNI:
I don't understand a word.
You've lost your mind.
(There is a loud knocking at the door Leporello closed.)

LEPORELLO: Listen!

DON GIOVANNI:
Someone is knocking.
Open it.
(The knocking is louder.)

LEPORELLO: *(trembling)* I'm afraid . . .

DON GIOVANNI: Open it, I tell you.

LEPORELLO: *(running away frightened)* Aaah!

DON GIOVANNI:
Idiot! To get to the bottom of all this,
I'll open the door myself.
(He takes a light and goes to open the door.)

LEPORELLO: *(s'asconde sotto la tavola)*
Non vo' più veder l'amico,
pian pianin m'asconderò.
(Don Giovanni apre.)

Scena 15

I SUDDETTI, IL COMMENDATORE.

IL COMMENDATORE:
Don Giovanni, a cenar teco
m'invitasti, e son venuto.

DON GIOVANNI:
Non l'avrei giammai creduto,
ma farò quel che potrò!
Leporello! Un'altra cena
fa' che subito si porti.

LEPORELLO: *(mezzo fuori col capo dalla mensa)* Ah padron! Siam
tutti morti!

DON GIOVANNI: Vanne, dico …
(Leporello con molti atti di paura esce e va per partire.)

IL COMMENDATORE:
Ferma un po'.
Non si pasce di cibo mortale
chi si pasce di cibo celeste:
altre cure più gravi di queste,
altra brama quaggiù mi guidò!

LEPORELLO: *(hiding under the table)*
I'll never see my master again after this.
Best quietly hide myself.
(Don Giovanni opens the door.)

Scene 15

THOSE BEFORE, AND THE COMMENDATORE.

COMMENDATORE:
Don Giovanni! You invited me
To dine and I have come.

DON GIOVANNI:
I never believed you would come,
But I will do whatever I can.
Leporello, set another place
And be quick about it, man.

LEPORELLO: *(sticking his head out from under the table)* Oh, master
. . . this will be the death of us!

DON GIOVANNI: Do as I say!
(With a great show of fear, he comes out from under the table and goes to leave.)

COMMENDATORE:
Stop where you are!
He who dines under heaven's portals
Has no need for the food of mortals.
Other concerns far graver than this
Have driven me here from celestial bliss.

LEPORELLO: *(tremando)*
La terzana d'avere mi sembra,
e le membra fermar più non so.

DON GIOVANNI: Parla, dunque: che chiedi, che vuoi?

IL COMMENDATORE: Parlo, ascolta, più tempo non ho.

DON GIOVANNI: Parla, parla, ascoltando ti sto.

LEPORELLO: Ah, le membra fermar più non so!

IL COMMENDATORE:
Tu m'invitasti a cena,
il tuo dover or sai:
rispondimi, verrai
tu a cenar meco?

LEPORELLO: *(da lontano tremando)* Oibò! Tempo non ha, scusate.

DON GIOVANNI:
A torto di viltate
tacciato mai sarò!

IL COMMENDATORE: Risolvi.

DON GIOVANNI: Ho già risolto.

IL COMMENDATORE: Verrai?

LEPORELLO: *(a Don Giovanni)* Dite di no.

LEPORELLO: *(trembling)*
I feel all feverish and sick . . .
I can't keep myself from shaking.

DON GIOVANNI: Speak then. What is it you want?

COMMENDATORE: Listen to what I say. My time here is brief.

DON GIOVANNI: Speak now. I am listening.

LEPORELLO: I can't keep myself from shaking.

COMMENDATORE:
You invited me here to dine.
But there is a debt you will discern.
Answer me this: will you
Come dine with me in turn?

LEPORELLO: *(from a distance, trembling)* Oh my, no, he hasn't the
time. Sorry, no.

DON GIOVANNI:
No one could ever accuse me, no,
Of being a coward. So . . .

COMMENDATORE: Decide.

DON GIOVANNI: I have already decided.

COMMENDATORE: Then you will come?

LEPORELLO: *(to Don Giovanni)* Say no! Say no!

DON GIOVANNI:
Ho fermo il core in petto:
non ho timor, verrò!

IL COMMENDATORE: Dammi la mano in pegno.

DON GIOVANNI: Eccola.
(Grida forte.)
Ohimè!

IL COMMENDATORE: Cos'hai?

DON GIOVANNI: Che gelo è questo mai?

IL COMMENDATORE:
Pentiti, cangia vita:
è l'ultimo momento!

DON GIOVANNI: *(vuol sciogliersi, ma invano)*
No no, ch'io non mi pento;
vanne lontan da me.

IL COMMENDATORE: Pentiti, scellerato!

DON GIOVANNI: No, vecchio infatuato!

IL COMMENDATORE: Pentiti!

DON GIOVANNI: No!

COMMENDATORE: Pentiti!

DON GIOVANNI: No!

COMMENDATORE: Sì!

DON GIOVANNI:
My heart and hand are steady.
I have no fear. I will go!

COMMENDATORE: Give me your hand as a pledge.

DON GIOVANNI: Here it is.
(He groans loudly.)
Aay!

COMMENDATORE: What is it?

DON GIOVANNI: What is the deadly chill going through me?

COMMENDATORE:
Repent your sins! Change your ways!
You have come to your last hour!

DON GIOVANNI: *(trying to free himself, but in vain)*
No, *no*, I will not repent or change!
Begone! Over me you have no power!

COMMENDATORE: Repent, you foul blasphemer!

DON GIOVANNI: Never, you silly old schemer!

COMMENDATORE: Repent!

DON GIOVANNI: No!

COMMENDATORE: Repent!

DON GIOVANNI: Never!

COMMENDATORE: Yes!

DON GIOVANNI: No!

IL COMMENDATORE, LEPORELLO: Sì!

DON GIOVANNI: No!

IL COMMENDATORE: Ah, tempo più non v'è.
(Parte. Foco da diverse parti, tremuoto etc.)

DON GIOVANNI:
Da qual tremore insolito
sento assalir gli spiriti!
Dond'escono quei vortici
di foco pien d'orror?

CORO: *(di sotterra con voci cupe)*
Tutto a tue colpe è poco,
vieni, c'è un mal peggior.

DON GIOVANNI:
Chi l'anima mi lacera?
Chi m'agita le viscere?
Che strazio, ohimè, che smania!
Che inferno! Che terror!

LEPORELLO:
Che ceffo disperato!
Che gesti da dannato!
Che gridi, che lamenti!
Come mi fa terror!

CORO:
Tutto a tue colpe è poco,
vieni, c'è un mal peggior.
(Il foco cresce. Don Giovanni si sprofonda.)

DON GIOVANNI: No!

COMMENDATORE AND LEPORELLO: Yes!

DON GIOVANNI: No! *No!*

COMMENDATORE: Ah, your time is up.
(He leaves. Flames shoot out in all directions. The earth shakes.)

DON GIOVANNI:
A tremor seizes my body.
I feel . . . my life assailed.
Fiery whirlwinds flail . . .
Where are these horrors from!

CHORUS: *(from under the earth, with hollow voices)*
These are for your sins, and not enough.
There is worse from where these come.

DON GIOVANNI:
Who tears at my soul!
Who lashes my body!
The torment! The pain!
This is hell! This is terror!

LEPORELLO:
The look on his face!
The gestures of the damned!
His screams! His cries of pain!
I cannot bear to watch his terror!

CHORUS:
These are for your sins, and not enough.
There is worse from where these come.
(The fire mounts. Don Giovanni sinks.)

DON GIOVANNI: Ah!

LEPORELLO: Ah!

(Don Giovanni resta inghiottito dalla terra.)

Scena ultima

LEPORELLO, DONN'ANNA, DONNA ELVIRA, DON OTTAVIO,
MASETTO, ZERLINA CON MINISTRI DI GIUSTIZIA.

ZERLINA, DONNA ELVIRA, DON OTTAVIO, MASETTO:
Ah, dove è il perfido,
dov'è l'indegno?
Tutto il mio sdegno
sfogar io vo'.

DONN'ANNA:
Solo mirandolo
stretto in catene
alle mie pene
calma darò.

LEPORELLO:
Più non sperate
di ritrovarlo,
più non cercate:
lontano andò.

DON GIOVANNI: Aah!

LEPORELLO: Aah!

(The earth swallows him up.)

Final Scene

LEPORELLO, DONNA ANNA, DONNA ELVIRA, DON OTTAVIO,

MASETTO, AND ZERLINA, WITH MINISTERS OF JUSTICE.

ZERLINA, DONNA ELVIRA, DON OTTAVIO, AND MASETTO:
Where has the villain gone?
Where is that evil man?
I want to unleash all I can
My indignation.

DONNA ANNA:
Only when I see him
Bound in iron chains . . .
That sight alone could constrain
My agitation.

LEPORELLO:
Do not count on hope . . .
You will not find him now . . .
He's in a place of . . . but how? . . .
His own creation.

DONN'ANNA, ZERLINA, DONNA ELVIRA, DON OTTAVIO, MASETTO: Cos'è? Favella ...

LEPORELLO: Venne un colosso ...

DONN'ANNA, ZERLINA, DONNA ELVIRA, DON OTTAVIO, MASETTO: Via, presto, sbrigati ...

LEPORELLO: Ma se non posso ...

DONN'ANNA, ZERLINA, DONNA ELVIRA, DON OTTAVIO, MASETTO: Via, presto, sbrigati ...

LEPORELLO:
Tra fumo e foco ...
badate un poco ...
l'uomo di sasso ...
fermate il passo ...
giusto là sotto ...
diede il gran botto ...
giusto là il diavolo
se 'l trangugiò.

DONN'ANNA, ZERLINA, DONNA ELVIRA, DON OTTAVIO, MASETTO: Stelle! Che sento!

LEPORELLO: Vero è l'evento.

DONNA ELVIRA:
Ah, certo è l'ombra
che m'incontrò!

DONNA ANNA, ZERLINA, DONNA ELVIRA, DON OTTAVIO, AND MASETTO: What are you saying? Tell us!

LEPORELLO: A giant statue came . . .

DONNA ANNA, ZERLINA, DONNA ELVIRA, DON OTTAVIO, AND MASETTO: Come on, quickly! Hurry!

LEPORELLO: I'm trying to tell you . . .

DONNA ANNA, ZERLINA, DONNA ELVIRA, DON OTTAVIO, AND MASETTO: Quickly! Tell us! Hurry!

LEPORELLO:
Through fire and smoke . . .
This is no joke . . .
A man made of stone . . .
Wait till I've shown . . .
Right there below . . .
He struck a blow . . .
The devil sprang up . . .
Gobbled him up.

DONNA ANNA, ZERLINA, DONNA ELVIRA, DON OTTAVIO, AND MASETTO: Good Lord! What a story!

LEPORELLO: It's a true one.

DONNA ELVIRA:
That is the very ghost!
The very ghost I met!

DONN'ANNA, ZERLINA, DON OTTAVIO, MASETTO:
Ah, certo è l'ombra
che l'incontrò!

DON OTTAVIO:
Or che tutti, o mio tesoro,
vendicati siam dal cielo,
porgi, porgi a me un ristoro,
non mi far languire ancor.

DONN'ANNA:
Lascia, o caro, un anno ancora
allo sfogo del mio cur.

DONN'ANNA, DON OTTAVIO:
Al desio di chi t'adora (m'adora)
ceder deve un fido amor.

DONNA ELVIRA:
Io men vado in un ritiro
a finir la vita mia.

ZERLINA, MASETTO:
Noi, Masetto (Zerlina), a casa andiamo
a cenar in compagnia.

LEPORELLO:
Ed io vado all'osteria
a trovar padron miglior.

DONNA ANNA, ZERLINA, DON OTTAVIO, AND MASETTO:
That is the very ghost!
The very ghost she met!

DON OTTAVIO:
Now, my treasure, that heaven
Has granted us our revenge,
May I at last be given
The reward of vows exchanged?

DONNA ANNA:
Wait one more year, my love.
Let my heart heal and change.

DONNA ANNA AND DON OTTAVIO:
From such injuries there is no appeal.
A faithful love must always yield.

DONNA ELVIRA:
I shall enter the convent
And end my days in prayer.

ZERLINA AND MASETTO:
We'll go off back home.
Dinner awaits us there.

LEPORELLO:
And I'm getting a drink.
And a better master, I swear!

**DONN'ANNA, ZERLINA, DONNA ELVIRA, DON OTTAVIO, LEPO-
RELLO, MASETTO:**
Resti dunque quel birbon
con Proserpina e Pluton;
e noi tutti, o buona gente,
ripetiam allegramente
l'antichissima canzon.

**DONN'ANNA, DONNA ELVIRA, ZERLINA, DON OTTAVIO,
MASETTO, LEPORELLO:**
Questo è il fin di chi fa mal:
e de' perfidi la morte
alla vita è sempre ugual.

Fine dell'opera.

DONNA ANNA, ZERLINA, DONNA ELVIRA, DON OTTAVIO, LEPORELLO, AND MASETTO:
Let the villain rot,
Tied in Pluto's knot!
Good people all agree.
Come sing joyfully
The oldest refrain there is.

DONNA ANNA, DONNA ELVIRA, ZERLINA, DON OTTAVIO, MASETTO, AND LEPORELLO:
Watch out now for what lies ahead.
A sorry fate awaits each sinner.
He suffers life, and ends up dead.

End of the Opera.

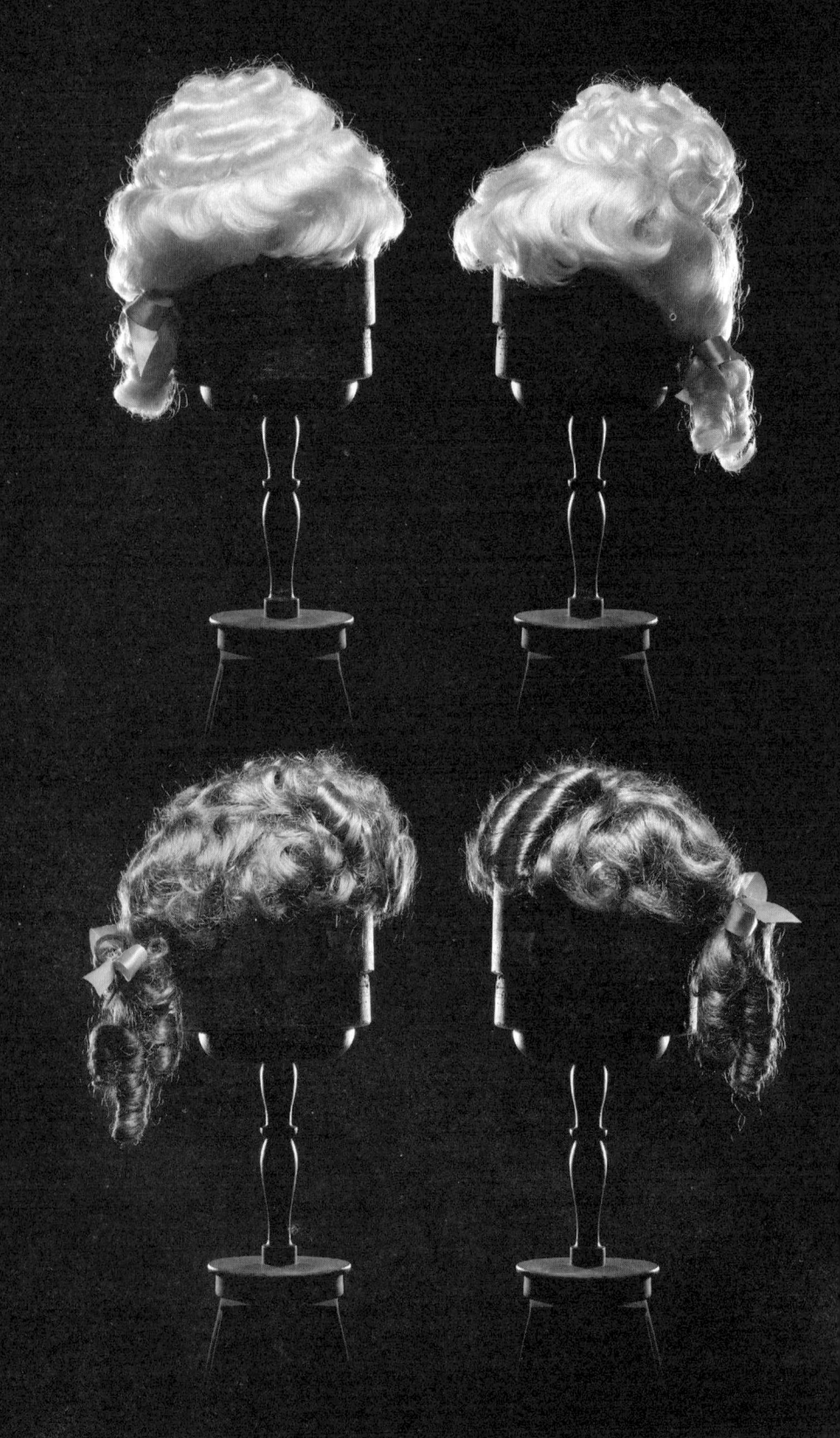

5

Così Fan Tutte

OR

The School for Lovers

COSÌ FAN TUTTE, OR THE SCHOOL FOR LOVERS

•

Dramma giocoso, 1790

Libretto by Lorenzo Da Ponte

The Characters

Fiordiligi, a lady of Ferrara, now living with her sister in Naples

Dorabella, her sister

Guglielmo, the suitor of Fiordiligi

Ferrando, the suitor of Dorabella

Despina, the ladies' chambermaid

Don Alfonso, an old philosopher

Chorus, soldiers, sailors, servants

Setting: Naples

SO PROUD OF *COSÌ*'S SCORE WAS MOZART THAT HE invited his idol, Joseph Haydn, to his apartment while he played through it for the first time. Whatever Haydn may have thought of it—he had a few years earlier told Mozart's father that "your son is the greatest composer whom I know in person or by reputation"—the opera was not a success. To be sure, the premiere was well received, and the score has always been thought ravishing, but the libretto was almost universally scorned— even by Beethoven and Wagner. Mozart's first biographer was puzzled that the composer could "waste his heavenly sweet melodies on such a miserable and clumsy text." The Romantic sensibilities of the nineteenth century thrilled to a demonic sexual predator like Don Giovanni, but found the plot of *Così* degrading, trivial, licentious, and vulgar. Impresarios devised solutions that were thought to improve the opera's morals. The lovers would only court their own girlfriends, for instance, not each other's. Down the years, the opera has even been given an entirely new libretto. In France, the librettists of *Carmen* refit Shakespeare's *Love's Labors Lost* as a libretto for the score, and in Germany, *Dame Kobold*, a version of Calderón de la Barca's *La Dama Duende*, was tried, as recently as 1909. In the end, the opera was most often just ignored, and only in the twentieth century did it earn a proper respect. It is not difficult to understand why. Aside from the score itself—almost symphonic is its composition—the opera's tale of deception and ambivalence had an obvious appeal to audiences in the Age of Psychology.

Clearly, Da Ponte was fascinated with the whole concept of disguises, of switched identities and confused emotions. They are a part of each of his three librettos for Mozart, but in Così the motif is not just an element in the plot but the very story itself. It is not merely a matter of costumes. At the start of the opera, Don Alfonso is trying to convince the young lovers, Guglielmo and Ferrando, that their romantic poses, their inmost feelings, are in a profound sense merely costumes. Don Alfonso, with his "assistant," Despina, is a puppet master here, manipulating the four lovers, if only finally to reveal that it is their own emotions, in fact, that are manipulating them. The piling up of disguised selves is dizzying. The young men dress up first as soldiers in a feigned call to a make-believe war front only to reappear as exotically dressed Albanians, bound to intrigue as much by their mustaches as by their supposedly foreign morals. Despina dresses up twice, first as a doctor and later as a notary. Mozart even has the singer "dress up," since he specifies in the score that she is to "sing through her nose" while in disguise. Fiordiligi dresses up in a soldier's uniform, but the wrong one, so that she resembles not the man she loves but his rival—thereby revealing a good deal about her unconscious. Don Alfonso, of course, has been pretending all along to be a friend and advisor, when in fact his motives are altogether more cynical.

Modern productions of Così have sometimes been played so that the four lovers know from the very beginning what the secret plot is, and go along with it. Presumably the point is to add yet another layer of deception to the story, a play-within-a-play-within-a-play. But that hardly seems necessary. The real drama lies in what the characters don't know about themselves. And the questions asked of them an audience needs to ask itself. Who has never been tempted? Who has never been fooled? Can we really know another's heart? What is fidelity—an erotic exclusivity, an affective loyalty? Fake poisons, fake cures, fake contracts, fake suitors . . . the opera is filled with false fronts and trapdoors. Some may feel that the end of the opera doesn't answer the questions raised earlier. There is a bit of the it-was-all-a-dream treatment at this point. Do people so easily readjust feelings that have been profoundly shaken? Whom did who really love? Some productions simply have the four lovers all hold hands at the end, and no one is paired off except in the lobby after the lights have come up. Other productions have left the four lovers unable to choose, but confused and morose about that fact, and this directorial decision is again meant to reflect an audience's perplexity. More to the point, neither Da Ponte nor Mozart specified how the lovers are to be joined at the end. The moral is formulated, and the trappings of The Happy Ending are on display, but there is no obvious way to interpret what is happening on stage at this crucial moment. This has frustrated commentators, and tantalized stage directors. The libretto has all the characters sing the praises of reason at the end, as if it has been restored:

> Happy is the man who looks
> On the bright side of everything,
> And in all circumstances and trials
> Lets himself be guided by reason.
> What only makes the others weep
> Will be for him a source of joy,
> And amid the storms of this world
> He will find his peace in every season.

Has reason been restored or eviscerated as a guiding principle in human affairs? At the start of things, the women were gazing at miniature portraits of their lovers, the men were joking over cups of coffee, and all was right with the world. By the opera's end, the happy paean to reason can seem the final irony, since what has been released in the interval—in merely a day's time—

has been a drama of unconscious emotions, in one sense artificial, in another sense dark, violent, and unsanctioned. Reason, in other words, may be the final costume.

This is Mozart's most "unreal" opera—confined to a small space that might as well be Don Alfonso's dreaming head. People behave in preposterous, farcical ways that defy logic. Yet, for these same reasons, Così is Mozart's most realistic opera, his most mature, provocative, and demanding. It is an astute study of the mystery of human desire. The dreaming head may as well be a laboratory.

THE STORY

ACT I

In a Naples coffeehouse, two starry-eyed young men, Guglielmo and Ferrando, have just been told that their finacées, Fiordiligi and Dorabella, who are sisters, could be compromised. Making the speculative accusation is an old friend of theirs, the philosopher Don Alfonso, who is cynical about concepts like "fidelity." Their sweethearts are not goddesses, but women. When the romantics angrily protest, the realist challenges them to a wager. If they will unquestioningly follow his directions, he will bet that the women will be revealed as something less than virtuous. Guglielmo and Ferrando agree, certain that all women are pure, that love is true.

In a garden by the seaside, the sisters are each raptly gazing at miniature portraits of their beloveds, to whom they swear eternal devotion. Yet both feel on edge, as if ready to play a joke on their lovers before wedding bells ring. Don Alfonso arrives, with a long face. He tells them that their men have been summoned to the wars and must leave immediately. There is time only for a final farewell. The men come forward, distraught and resigned. The women hear their news fearfully. In asides, they gloat to Don

Alfonso about the faithfulness of their sweethearts. He cautions them to wait and see. As the men make their sad farewells, the drum sounds, their ship awaits, a chorus sings of the joys of the military life. There are further promises of letters to be written and memories to be cherished, and the men leave with the ship. Stunned by their sudden departure, the sisters open themselves to Don Alfonso's consolations and say a prayer for the ship's safe passage, before they retire. Don Alfonso is pleased with himself, convinced that the women will succumb to his ruse.

The ladies' chambermaid, Despina, has brought in a tray of hot chocolate, and wonders why she may only smell it but never taste it. The sisters enter in despair—they want darkness, daggers, poison. Despina mocks them, but Dorabella vows to be a forlorn epitome of tragic love. She and Fiordiligi collapse and, when they tell Despina of their fate, she replies that no woman ever died for love. Men come and go, and there are always others to notice. She urges them to enjoy themselves while their men are gone. When the women all leave, Don Alfonso decides he had better let Despina in on his plans, lest she betray them. She is reluctant, until a bribe is offered. Don Alfonso asks her to introduce two strange men to the ladies. Guglielmo and Ferrando return, now disguised as Albanians. Despina enjoys the charade and leads them in. They fall to their knees before Fiordiligi and Dorabella, who at first are outraged. They call out to Don Alfonso that foreigners have invaded their house, but he assures them that the men are friends of his and asks that they be admitted. Fiordiligi maintains that she and her sister are so steadfast in their devotion to Guglielmo and Ferrando that only death could make them change. Guglielmo begs them to take pity—or at least to admire their fine mustaches. But the ladies leave—and the men burst out laughing, convinced they have won the bet. Don Alfonso laughs too, but says all will end in tears.

Don Alfonso discusses the situation with Despina, who cynically insists her mistresses will yield soon enough. She will push the plan along, and urges him to bring the Albanians back. In the garden, the ladies complain of their misfortune, and the Albanians swear they will die for love's sake. In fact, they take out vials of "poison" and swallow them.

Horrified, the women cry out for help as the men swoon and fall to the ground. Despina rushes in and says she will fetch a doctor. The sisters, meanwhile, have had their pity stirred as they look at the men lying unconscious. The doctor arrives (it is Despina in disguise) and "he" performs a "magnetic cure" on the prostrate Albanians, who revive. They ask for a kiss from the ladies, who are furious. Despina and Don Alfonso know too well that their apparent fury is really a helpless infatuation.

ACT II

The three women are alone, discussing the situation. Despina insists they treat love lightly, that they seize the day: "But we're on earth, not in heaven." The ladies resist, fearing for their reputations. Again, Despina reviews the history of all women, how through the centuries they have had to deceive men. When she leaves, the sisters begin to reason through their dilemma. Dorabella is more interested in having the strangers visit their room than Fiordiligi is, but they both weaken a bit, though each seems attracted to the other's sweetheart.

Again in the garden, a flower-decked barge approaches on the sea; it brings Guglielmo and Ferrando with a band of musicians. The men debark and there is a certain awkwardness among the lovers, none knowing what to do next. So Don Alfonso sends the men away, while he and Despina give ultimatums to the sisters. They are finally persuaded, and a flirtation begins among the lovers—except that, as Fiordiligi and Ferrando pair off, Guglielmo whispers to his friend that his beloved will never yield to his wooing. The two pairs stroll around the garden, the women nervously intrigued, the men worried about the virtue of their fiancées. Guglielmo and Dorabella exchange promises, and when he wants to give her a token of his love, he has first to remove the portrait of Ferrando she wears around her neck. Neither seems to know, in the daze of love, what is happening. They leave arm in arm as Ferrando and Fiordiligi enter, at odds. She will not hear his pleas and, discouraged, he departs. Alone with her thoughts, Fiordiligi contemplates her quandary: he suffers for her, and she scorns him. She begs God's forgiveness for entertaining "evil" thoughts, and accuses herself of weakness in contrast to what she thinks of as her fiancé's purity of heart.

The men, meanwhile, convinced they've won, reveal their romantic adventures to each other, and Ferrando confesses that he did not succeed with Fiordiligi—unlike Guglielmo with Dorabella. Guglielmo shows him the little portrait she gave him. Appalled that within a few short hours Dorabella has betrayed him, Ferrando vows revenge. Guglielmo reasons with him about the fickle nature of a woman's heart. Ferrando is unmoved . . . but how suddenly to banish from his heart the one he loves? Don Alfonso reminds them both that they have until tomorrow to see how things play out.

The two sisters and Despina mull things over. Despina applauds Dorabella's common sense, while Fiordiligi anguishes over her strained feelings, admitting that she is drawn to her new suitor. Dorabella pleads with her that they should both forget their fiancés and marry the Albanians. Love is a devil and one must submit to his urgings. Fiordiligi, astonished by her overnight change of heart, defends her honor (as Guglielmo secretly, and happily, listens). Indeed, she sends Despina to fetch uniforms and swords, so that she and Dorabella can follow their men into battle. Because it fits better, she dons Ferrando's uniform, just as he comes in and, seeing her, begs her to use his own sword to kill him. "Your heart, or my death," he threatens. Overcome, Fiordiligi yields. Guglielmo, who with Don Alfonso has observed all this from their hiding place, is determined to strangle his beloved, and when Ferrando returns the two men are at wit's end. Don Alfonso suggests they be philosophical and marry the ladies, as is. After all, that is what all women are like. *Così fan tutte*—they are all that way.

Despina reports that the ladies are ready to marry their Albanian suitors; a notary is sent for, a wedding celebration prepared. She and Don Alfonso are pleased with their elaborate comedy, and the chorus sings in honor of the marriage couples, who enter joyously. Each couple toasts the other. Despina returns, this time dressed as a notary, to join Fiordiligi with "Sempronio" and Dorabella with "Tizio," when suddenly drums are heard outside and Don Alfonso, at the window, reports that their fiancés have returned. Chaos ensues, the Albanians flee, the sisters are beside themselves with trepidation. Guglielmo and Ferrando return as themselves, Don Alfonso professes surprise. The ladies are dumbfounded. Despina reveals that she was the notary. But the signed marriage contract is discovered. The men pretend indignation, and the sisters confess their guilt . . . until Guglielmo and Ferrando bring out their Albanian costumes. All is now clear. The women turn to blame Don Alfonso, but he says they will now be wiser about love. It is time to turn instead to a chastened love and a real marriage.

THE BACKGROUND

The origins of this third and final collaboration between Mozart and Da Ponte are obscure. There is evidence Da Ponte had first offered his libretto to Salieri, who set a little of it before deciding the text was "unworthy of musical invention." (He was later jealous of Mozart's success with it.) As usual, Mozart insisted on changes, to tighten the structure and set up the ensembles. The libretto itself and its fable of love in disguise has parallels in Greek myth and Renaissance epic, though it does not derive from a single source. It used to be claimed that Joseph II commissioned it because he was amused by the gossipy account of a similar affair afoot in the Vienna of the day. But the story has clear literary antecedents: in the tale of Cephalus and Procris in Book VII of Ovid's *Metamorphoses* and in Cantos 24, 28, and 43 of Ludovico Ariosto's 1532 poem *Orlando Furioso*. In addition, the idea of a wager on fidelity is a part of stories in Boccaccio, Shakespeare, and Cervantes. The libretto's language, in any case, is literary and allusive. Mozart worked on it in the late fall of 1789. He worked so hastily that he several times confused the sisters' names when writing them into the score. He revised heavily, and even in rehearsals was distributing small pieces of paper with changes to the score. The premiere was at the Burgtheater in Vienna, on January 26, 1790, the composer conducting. Fiordiligi was sung by Adriana Ferrarese del Bene, then the mistress of Da Ponte. Dorabella was Louise Villeneuve. Francesco Benucci, who had originated the role of Figaro and was deeply admired by Mozart, sang Guglielmo, and Vincenzo Calvesi sang Ferrando. Francesco Bussani and his wife Dorothea sang the roles of Don Alfonso and Despina, apparently resentful at having been given minor parts (he had played Masetto and the Commendatore in *Don Giovanni*'s Vienna premiere, as well as Bartolo and Antonio in *Figaro*, a night his wife played the first Cherubino). It was performed five times before the death of Joseph II closed all the theaters. It received five more performances that summer, and all of these were successful. (The new emperor, Leopold II, soon enough fired Ferrarese from the company, ignored Mozart, and sacked Da Ponte as the court's theater poet.) Though *Così* made the usual rounds, it was not long before it lagged behind in popularity compared with Mozart's other operas.

Atto primo

Bottega di caffè.

Scena 1

FERRANDO, GUILELMO, DON ALFONSO.

N° 1 Terzetto

FERRANDO:
La mia Dorabella capace non è:
fedel quanto bella il cielo la fe'.

GUILELMO:
La mia Fiordiligi tradirmi non sa:
uguale in lei credo costanza e beltà.

DON ALFONSO:
Ho i crini già grigi, ex cathedra parlo;
ma tali litigi finiscano qua.

FERRANDO, GUILELMO:
No, detto ci avete che infide esser ponno;
provar cel dovete, se avete onestà.

DON ALFONSO:
Tai prove lasciamo …

∴ Act I ∴

A coffeehouse.

Scene 1

FERRANDO, GUGLIELMO, AND DON ALFONSO.

Trio

FERRANDO:
Betray me? Dorabella? Out of your mind!
Her love and her loyalty are sweetly entwined.

GUGLIELMO:
My fair Fiordiligi? Prove herself untrue?
Such candor and beauty the world never knew!

DON ALFONSO:
By my gray hair I know what I know,
But let us not argue. I bid you adieu.

FERRANDO AND GUGLIELMO:
Wait! You basely accuse them and turn to go?
A man of honor is bound to follow through.

DON ALFONSO:
Best forget about proof . . .

FERRANDO, GUILELMO: *(metton mano alla spada)*
No no, le vogliamo;
o, fuori la spada,
rompiam l'amistà.

DON ALFONSO: *(a parte)*
Oh pazzo desire!
Cercar di scoprire
quel mal che trovato
meschini ci fa.

FERRANDO, GUILELMO: *(a parte)*
Sul vivo mi tocca
chi lascia di bocca
sortire un accento
che torto le fa.

Recitativo

GUILELMO: Fuor la spada! Scegliete qual di noi più vi piace.

DON ALFONSO: *(placido)* Io son uomo di pace, e duelli non fo se non a mensa.

FERRANDO: O battervi, o dir subito perché d'infedeltà le nostre amanti sospettate capaci.

DON ALFONSO: Cara semplicità, quanto mi piaci!

FERRANDO: Cessate di scherzar, o giuro al cielo! ...

DON ALFONSO: Ed io, giuro alla terra, non scherzo, amici miei; solo saper vorrei che razza d'animali son queste vostre belle, se han come tutti noi carne, ossa e pelle, se mangian come noi, se veston gonne, alfin se dee, se donne son ...

FERRANDO AND GUGLIELMO: *(reaching for their swords)*
No, show us your proof.
Your sword, sir!
A reckoning is overdue.

DON ALFONSO: *(aside)*
The fatuous lovers!
They want to discover
The very thing
That will bring them shame.

FERRANDO AND GUGLIELMO: *(aside)*
He wounds my pride
Who dares to confide
A single word
That slights her good name.

Recitative

GUGLIELMO: Draw your sword! Choose whichever of us you like.

DON ALFONSO: *(calmly)* I am a peaceful man. The duels I indulge in are at the dinner table.

FERRANDO: Either fight, or tell us at once how you could suspect the faithfulness of our ladies.

DON ALFONSO: Such innocence, how I adore it!

FERRANDO: Stop joking, or I swear by heaven . . .

DON ALFONSO: And I swear by *this* world, I am not joking, my friends. Pray tell me what kind of creatures your beauties are—flesh and blood, skin and bones like the rest of us? Do they eat, wear dresses? In a word, are they goddesses or women?

FERRANDO, GUILELMO: Son donne, ma ... son tali, son tali ...

DON ALFONSO:
E in donne pretendete di trovar fedeltà?
Quanto mi piaci mai, semplicità!

N° 2 Terzetto

DON ALFONSO: *(scherzando)*
È la fede delle femmine
come l'araba fenice:
che vi sia ciascun lo dice,
dove sia nessun lo sa.

FERRANDO: *(con foco)* La fenice è Dorabella!

GUILELMO: *(con foco)* La fenice è Fiordiligi!

DON ALFONSO:
Non è questa, non è quella:
non fu mai, non vi sarà.

Recitativo

FERRANDO: Scioccherie di poeti!

GUILELMO: Scempiaggini di vecchi!

DON ALFONSO: Orbene, udite, ma senza andar in collera: qual prova avete voi che ognor costanti vi sien le vostre amanti, chi vi fe' sicurtà che invariabili sono i lor cori?

FERRANDO: Lunga esperienza ...

GUILELMO: Nobil educazion ...

FERRANDO: Pensar sublime ...

FERRANDO AND GUGLIELMO: Women, but such women . . .

DON ALFONSO:
And honestly, you expect women to be faithful?
Your naiveté is charming!

Trio

DON ALFONSO: *(jokingly)*
The fidelity of women
Is like the Arabian phoenix:
Everyone says its exists
But where it is, no one knows.

FERRANDO: *(ardently)* Dorabella is that phoenix!

GUGLIELMO: *(ardently)* Fiordiligi is that phoenix!

DON ALFONSO:
This one's out, that one I doubt.
It never existed, and it never will!

Recitative

FERRANDO: Poetic gibberish!

GUGLIELMO: An old man's ramblings!

DON ALFONSO: Very well then, listen to me but keep your tempers. What proof do you have that your beloveds are faithful to you? How can you be certain their hearts will not change?

FERRANDO: Our long experience . . .

GUGLIELMO: Their noble upbringing . . .

FERRANDO: Their lofty thoughts . . .

GUILELMO: Analogia d'umor ...

FERRANDO: Disinteresse ...

GUILELMO: Immutabil carattere ...

FERRANDO: Promesse ...

GUILELMO: Proteste ...

FERRANDO: Giuramenti ...

DON ALFONSO:
Pianti, sospir, carezze, svenimenti. Lasciatemi un po' ridere ...

FERRANDO: Cospetto! Finite di deriderci?

DON ALFONSO: Pian piano: e se toccar con mano oggi vi fo che come l'altre sono?

GUILELMO: Non si può dar.

FERRANDO: Non è.

DON ALFONSO: Giochiam?

FERRANDO: Giochiamo.

DON ALFONSO: Cento zecchini?

GUILELMO: E mille, se volete.

DON ALFONSO: Parola?

GUGLIELMO: Our compatibility . . .

FERRANDO: Unselfishness . . .

GUGLIELMO: Strength of character . . .

FERRANDO: Their promises . . .

GUGLIELMO: Their protestations . . .

FERRANDO: Their vows . . .

DON ALFONSO:
Their tears, their sighs, their caresses, their swoons. Pardon me if I laugh a little . . .

FERRANDO: Damn you! Stop making fun of us!

DON ALFONSO: Stay a moment. What if, this very day, I could show you that they are like all the rest?

GUGLIELMO: Not possible.

FERRANDO: Not true.

DON ALFONSO: Then let's make a bet on it.

FERRANDO: Accepted!

DON ALFONSO: A hundred guineas.

GUGLIELMO: A thousand, if you like.

DON ALFONSO: Your word of honor.

FERRANDO: Parolissima.

DON ALFONSO: E un cenno, un motto, un gesto giurate di non far di tutto questo alle vostre Penelopi?

FERRANDO: Giuriamo.

DON ALFONSO: Da soldati d'onore?

GUILELMO: Da soldati d'onore.

DON ALFONSO: E tutto quel farete ch'io vi dirò di far?

FERRANDO: Tutto.

GUILELMO: Tuttissimo.

DON ALFONSO: Bravissimi!

FERRANDO, GUILELMO: Bravissimo, signor Don Alfonsetto!

FERRANDO: A spese vostre or ci divertiremo.

GUILELMO: *(a Ferrando)* E de' cento zecchini che faremo?

N° 3 Terzetto

FERRANDO:
Una bella serenata
far io voglio alla mia dea.

GUILELMO:
In onor di Citerea
un convito io voglio far.

DON ALFONSO: Sarò anch'io de' convitati?

FERRANDO: Our word, absolutely.

DON ALFONSO: And you swear—not a word, not a whisper, not a sign to your Penelopes?

FERRANDO: We swear.

DON ALFONSO: On your honor as soldiers.

GUGLIELMO: On our honor as soldiers.

DON ALFONSO: And you will do everything I tell you?

FERRANDO: Everything.

GUGLIELMO: Everything, absolutely.

DON ALFONSO: Excellent chaps!

FERRANDO AND GUGLIELMO: Don Alfonsetto, your servant!

FERRANDO: The joke will be on him!

GUGLIELMO: *(to Ferrando)* And how shall we spend all his money?

Trio

FERRANDO:
A sweet serenade now
I wish to give my goddess.

GUGLIELMO:
A sumptuous feast now
I shall offer my Venus.

DON ALFONSO: Shall I be invited as well?

FERRANDO, GUILELMO: Ci sarete, sì signor.

FERRANDO, DON ALFONSO, GUILELMO:
E che brindis' replicati
far vogliamo al dio d'amor!
(Partono.)

Giardino sulla spiaggia del mare.

Scena 2

FIORDILIGI E DORABELLA CHE GUARDANO UN RITRATTO CHE LOR PENDE AL FIANCO.

N° 4 Duetto

FIORDILIGI:
Ah, guarda, sorella,
se bocca più bella,
se aspetto più nobile
si può ritrovar!

DORABELLA:
Osserva tu un poco,
che foco ha ne' sguardi,
se fiamma, se dardi
non sembran scoccar!

FIORDILIGI:
Si vede un sembiante
guerriero ed amante.

DORABELLA:
Si vede una faccia
che alletta e minaccia.

FIORDILIGI: Felice son io.

FERRANDO AND GUGLIELMO: Indeed, sir, you shall.

FERRANDO, DON ALFONSO, AND GUGLIELMO:
Again and again, we will raise our glasses
To honor the god of love!
(They all leave.)

A garden by the seaside.

Scene 2

FIORDILIGI AND DORABELLA ARE GAZING AT THE
PORTRAITS IN THEIR LOCKETS.

Duet

FIORDILIGI:
Ah, tell me, sister,
Where could you greet
A sweeter mouth
Or a nobler face?

DORABELLA:
Oh but look here!
His fiery glance!
Flames and arrows
Enhance his grace.

FIORDILIGI:
Mine has a look like no other,
At once the soldier and the lover.

DORABELLA:
Mine has a hundred charms,
So gentle even when it alarms.

FIORDILIGI: I am so happy!

DORABELLA: Io sono felice.

FIORDILIGI, DORABELLA:
Se questo mio core
mai cangia desio,
amore mi faccia
vivendo penar.

Recitativo

FIORDILIGI: Mi par che stamattina volentieri farei la pazzarella: ho un certo foco, un certo pizzicor entro le vene ... Quando Guilelmo viene ... se sapessi che burla gli vo' far!

DORABELLA: Per dirti il vero qualche cosa di nuovo anch'io nell'alma provo: io giurerei che lontane non siam dagli imenei.

FIORDILIGI: Dammi la mano: io voglio astrologarti. Uh, che bell'emme! E questo è un pi! Va bene: matrimonio presto.

DORABELLA: Affé, che ci avrei gusto!

FIORDILIGI: Ed io non ci avrei rabbia.

DORABELLA: Ma che diavol vuol dir che i nostri sposi ritardano a venir? Son già le sei ...

FIORDILIGI: Eccoli.

•

Scena 3
LE SUDDETTE E DON ALFONSO.

DORABELLA: Non son essi: è Don Alfonso, l'amico lor.

FIORDILIGI: Ben venga il signor Don Alfonso!

DORABELLA: How happy I am!

FIORDILIGI AND DORABELLA:
If ever my heart
Should change its affections,
May Love make me feel
Forlorn and abased.

Recitative

FIORDILIGI: I am in the mood to do something quite mad this morning. I feel a sort of fire, a sort of tingling in my blood . . . When Guglielmo arrives . . . If only you knew the joke I might play on him!

DORABELLA: To tell you the truth, I also feel something unusual stirring inside. I could swear that soon we'll hear wedding bells.

FIORDILIGI: Give me your hand. I want to tell your fortune. Oh look! An M! And here's a P. Just what I thought: Marriage Prospect.

DORABELLA: Goodness, that would suit me!

FIORDILIGI: And I would have no objection.

DORABELLA: But why the devil are our "husbands" so late in coming? It's already six . . .

FIORDILIGI: Here they are!

Scene 3

THOSE BEFORE, AND DON ALFONSO.

DORABELLA: No, not them. It is Don Alfonso, their friend.

FIORDILIGI: Welcome, Don Alfonso!

DON ALFONSO: Riverisco.

DORABELLA: Cos'è? Perché qui solo? Voi piangete? Parlate, per pietà! Che cosa è nato? L'amante ...

FIORDILIGI: L'idol mio ...

DON ALFONSO: Barbaro fato!

N° 5 Aria

DON ALFONSO:
Vorrei dir e cor non ho ...
Balbettando il labbro va ...
Fuor la voce uscir non può ...
ma mi resta mezza qua.
Che farete? Che farò?
Oh, che gran fatalità!
Dar di peggio non si può:
ho di voi, di lor pietà.

Recitativo

FIORDILIGI: Stelle! Per carità, signor Alfonso, non ci fate morir.

DON ALFONSO: Convien armarvi, figlie mie, di costanza.

DORABELLA: Oh dei! Qual male è addivenuto mai, qual caso rio? Forse è morto il mio bene?

FIORDILIGI: È morto il mio?

DON ALFONSO: Morti non son, ma poco men che morti.

DORABELLA: Feriti?

DON ALFONSO: My compliments!

DORABELLA: What is it? Why are you here alone? Are you weeping? Speak, for pity's sake. What has happened? My beloved isn't . . .

FIORDILIGI: My darling hasn't . . .

DON ALFONSO: Such a cruel fate!

Aria

DON ALFONSO:
I want to speak, but my courage fails,
My trembling lips can only sputter.
I choke as on a meal of nails—
These words I have no wish to utter.
What will you do? And what will I?
To such a grief are we condemned!
Perhaps it would be easier just to die.
I am sorry for you, and sorry for them!

Recitative

FIORDILIGI: Heavens! We beg you, Don Alfonso, don't kill us with suspense!

DON ALFONSO: Prepare yourselves to be brave, my dear girls.

DORABELLA: Oh God! What terrible thing has happened? My beloved isn't dead, is he?

FIORDILIGI: Mine too? Dead?

DON ALFONSO: No, not dead, but almost worse.

DORABELLA: Wounded?

DON ALFONSO: No.

FIORDILIGI: Ammalati?

DON ALFONSO: Neppur.

FIORDILIGI: Che cosa, dunque?

DON ALFONSO: Al marzial campo ordin regio li chiama.

FIORDILIGI, DORABELLA: Ohimè! Che sento!

FIORDILIGI: E partiran?

DON ALFONSO: Sul fatto.

DORABELLA: E non v'è modo d'impedirlo?

DON ALFONSO: Non v'è.

FIORDILIGI: Né un solo addio? ...

DON ALFONSO: Gl'infelici non hanno coraggio di vedervi; ma se voi lo bramate, son pronti ...

DORABELLA: Dove son?

DON ALFONSO: Amici, entrate.

DON ALFONSO: No.

FIORDILIGI: Sick?

DON ALFONSO: Not that.

FIORDILIGI: What is it then?

DON ALFONSO: A royal command summons them to the field of battle.

FIORDILIGI AND DORABELLA: Oh my! What are you telling us?

FIORDILIGI: And when must they leave?

DON ALFONSO: At once.

DORABELLA: Is there no way to prevent this?

DON ALFONSO: None.

FIORDILIGI: No way to say farewell?

DON ALFONSO: The poor chaps haven't had the nerve to face you. But if you wish, they are ready . . .

DORABELLA: Are they here?

DON ALFONSO: My friends, come in.

Scena 4

N° 6 Quintetto

GUILELMO:
Sento, oddio, che questo piede
è restio nel girle avante.

FERRANDO:
Il mio labbro palpitante
non può detto pronunziar.

DON ALFONSO:
Nei momenti più terribili
sua virtù l'eroe palesa.

FIORDILIGI, DORABELLA:
Or che abbiam la nuova intesa,
a voi resta a fare il meno:
fate core, a entrambe in seno
immergeteci l'acciar!

FERRANDO, GUILELMO:
Idol mio, la sorte incolpa
se ti deggio abbandonar.

DORABELLA: *(a Ferrando)* Ah, no, no, non partirai!

FIORDILIGI: *(a Guilelmo)* No, crudel, non te ne andrai!

DORABELLA: Voglio pria cavarmi il core!

FIORDILIGI: Pria ti vo' morire ai piedi!

Scene 4

THOSE BEFORE; FERRANDO AND GUGLIELMO,
IN TRAVELLING CLOTHES.

Quintet

GUGLIELMO:
God help me, my feet
Refuse to move ahead.

FERRANDO:
My lips seem to dread
Even saying a word.

DON ALFONSO:
In his moment of crisis
The true hero emerges.

FIORDILIGI AND DORABELLA:
Now that we have heard the news,
One thing remains before you depart.
Steel yourselves and plunge your swords
Deep, deep into both our hearts.

FERRANDO AND GUGLIELMO:
My idol, fate itself is to be blamed
That works to keep us sadly apart.

DORABELLA: *(to Ferrando)* Ah, no, no, you must not go!

FIORDILIGI: *(to Guglielmo)* No, cruel man, you will not go!

DORABELLA: I'll tear my heart out first!

FIORDILIGI: I'll die first at your feet!

FERRANDO: *(a Don Alfonso)* (Cosa dici?)

GUILELMO: *(a Don Alfonso)* (Te n'avvedi?)

DON ALFONSO: *(ai due amanti)* (Saldo, amico: finem lauda.)

FIORDILIGI, DORABELLA, FERRANDO, DON ALFONSO, GUILELMO:
Il destin così defrauda
le speranze de' mortali.
Ah, chi mai fra tanti mali,
chi mai può la vita amar?

Recitativo

GUILELMO: Non pianger, idol mio!

FERRANDO: Non disperarti, adorata mia sposa!

DON ALFONSO: Lasciate lor tal sfogo: è troppo giusta la ragion di quel pianto.

(Gli amanti si abbracciano teneramente.)

FIORDILIGI: Chi sa s'io più ti veggio!

DORABELLA: Chi sa se più ritorni!

FIORDILIGI: Lasciami questo ferro: ei mi dia morte, se mai barbara sorte in quel seno a me caro ...

DORABELLA: Morrei di duol, d'uopo non ho d'acciaro.

FERRANDO, GUILELMO: Non farmi, anima mia, quest'infausti presagi! Proteggeran gli dei la pace del tuo cor ne' giorni miei.

FERRANDO: *(to Don Alfonso)* (What do you say to this?)

GUGLIELMO: *(to Don Alfonso)* (Do you see that?)

DON ALFONSO: *(to the two lovers)* (Patience, friends. He who laughs last . . .)

FIORDILIGI, DORABELLA, FERRANDO, DON ALFONSO, AND GUGLIELMO:
Thus harshest destiny, alas,
Mocks all our human hopes.
Amidst dark despair we grope,
And which of us would want to live?

Recitative

GUGLIELMO: Do not weep so, my precious.

FERRANDO: Do not give up, my darling.

DON ALFONSO: Let them weep and wail. They have good reason for their tears.

(The lovers embrace tenderly.)

FIORDILIGI: Who knows if I shall ever see you again!

DORABELLA: Who knows if you will ever return!

FIORDILIGI: Leave me your dagger. Let it grant me death, if a dire fate pierces that heart so dear to mine . . .

DORABELLA: I would die of grief . . . I need no knife for that.

FERRANDO AND GUGLIELMO: Do not dwell, my dearest love, on such grim thoughts. As long as I live, the gods will protect the peace of your heart.

N° 7 Duettino

FERRANDO, GUILELMO:
Al fato dan legge
quegli occhi vezzosi:
Amor li protegge,
né i loro riposi
le barbare stelle
ardiscon turbar.
Il ciglio sereno,
mio bene, a me gira:
felice al tuo seno
io spero tornar.

Recitativo

DON ALFONSO: (La commedia è graziosa, e tutti e due fan ben la loro parte.)

(Si sente un suono di tamburo in distanza.)

FERRANDO: Oh cielo! Questo è il tamburo funesto che a divider mi vien dal mio tesoro.

DON ALFONSO: Ecco, amici, la barca.

FIORDILIGI: Io manco.

DORABELLA: Io moro.

Duet

FERRANDO AND GUGLIELMO:
Those dazzling eyes
Control the fates.
Love protects them.
The cruelest stars
Dare not disturb
Their rest.
Turn, my love, turn
Your gaze to me.
My own heart is forever in
Your breast.

Recitative

DON ALFONSO: (The comedy is delicious, and both are playing their parts well.)

(The sound of a drum is heard.)

FERRANDO: Heavens! That is the dreaded drum that comes to take me from my treasure.

DON ALFONSO: My friends, your ship awaits.

FIORDILIGI: I am fainting!

DORABELLA: I am dying!

Scena 5

I SUDDETTI.

(Marcia militare in qualche distanza, poi il seguente coro.)

N° 8 Coro

CORO:
Bella vita militar!
Ogni dì si cangia loco,
oggi molto, doman poco,
ora in terra ed or sul mar.
Il fragor di trombe e pifferi,
lo sparar di schioppi e bombe
forza accresce al braccio e all'anima,
vaga sol di trionfar.
Bella vita militar!

Recitativo

DON ALFONSO: Non v'è più tempo, amici: andar conviene ove il destino, anzi il dover v'invita.

FIORDILIGI: Mio cor ...

DORABELLA: Idolo mio ...

FERRANDO: Mio ben ...

GUILELMO: Mia vita ...

FIORDILIGI: Ah, per un sol momento ...

DON ALFONSO: Del vostro reggimento già è partita la barca. Raggiungerla convien coi pochi amici che su legno più lieve attendendo vi stanno.

Scene 5

THOSE BEFORE.

(A military march plays in the distance, and a ship arrives.)

Chorus

CHORUS:
The soldier's splendid lot!
Every day a change of scene.
Today is fat, tomorrow lean.
Sea or land, it's all gunshot.
The blare of trumpets and fifes,
The blast of cannons and bombs—
There's what stiffens your spine
And gets you what victory's got.
The soldier's splendid lot!

Recitative

DON ALFONSO: No time left, lads. You must go where destiny, or rather duty, calls you.

FIORDILIGI: My heart . . .

DORABELLA: My idol . . .

FERRANDO: My love . . .

GUGLIELMO: My life . . .

FIORDILIGI: Oh, just a moment more . . .

DON ALFONSO: The regimental ship has already gone. You and a few others can join it by taking a smaller boat.

FERRANDO, GUILELMO: Abbracciami, idol mio.

FIORDILIGI, DORABELLA: Muoio d'affanno.

N° 8a Quintetto

FIORDILIGI: *(piangendo)*
Di … scri … ver … mi o … gni … gior … no …
giu … ra … mi … vita … mi … a …

DORABELLA: *(piangendo)*
Due … vol … te an … co … ra …
tu … scri … vi … mi … se … puo … i …

FERRANDO: Sii … cer … ta … o ca … ra …

GUILELMO: Non … du … bi … tar … mio bene …

DON ALFONSO: (Io crepo se non rido!)

FIORDILIGI: Sii costante a me sol …

DORABELLA: Serbati fido.

FERRANDO: Addio!

GUILELMO: Addio!

FIORDILIGI, DORABELLA: Addio!

FIORDILIGI, DORABELLA, FERRANDO, GUILELMO:
Addio! Addio!
Mi si divide il cor,
bell'idol mio.
Addio! Addio!

FERRANDO AND GUGLIELMO: Embrace me, my beloved.

FIORDILIGI AND DORABELLA: I am dying of sorrow.

Quintet

FIORDILIGI: *(weeping)*
You . . . will . . . write . . . to . . . me . . . ev- . . . ery . . . day . . .
Prom- . . . ise . . . me, . . . my . . . dar- . . . ling . . .

DORABELLA: *(weeping)*
Twice . . . a . . . day . . . you . . . will . . . write . . .
If . . . you . . . can . . .

FERRANDO: Of . . . course . . . I . . . will, . . . my . . . dar- . . . ling . . .

GUGLIELMO: Nev- . . . er . . . doubt . . . me, . . . my . . . dear-
. . . est . . .

DON ALFONSO: (I'll burst if I don't laugh.)

FIORDILIGI: Be faithful to me alone . . .

DORABELLA: Stay true to me only . . .

FERRANDO: Farewell!

GUGLIELMO: Farewell!

FIORDILIGI, DORABELLA: Farewell!

FIORDILIGI, DORABELLA, FERRANDO, AND GUGLIELMO:
Farewell! Farewell!
My heart is breaking,
My fairest love!
Farewell! Farewell!

DON ALFONSO: (Io crepo se non rido!)

N° 9 Coro

CORO:
Bella vita militar!
Ogni dì si cangia loco,
oggi molto, doman poco,
ora in terra ed or sul mar.
Il fragor di trombe e pifferi,
lo sparar di schioppi e bombe
forza accresce al braccio e all'anima,
vaga sol di trionfar.
Bella vita militar!

(Le amanti restano immobili sulla sponda del mare, la barca allontanasi tra suon di tamburi etc.)

Scena 6

LE SUDDETTE E DON ALFONSO.

Recitativo

DORABELLA: *(in atto di chi rinviene da un letargo)* Dove son?

DON ALFONSO: Son partiti.

FIORDILIGI: Oh dipartenza crudelissima, amara!

DON ALFONSO: Fate core, carissime figliuole.
(da lontano facendo moto col fazzoletto)
Guardate, da lontano vi fan cenno con mano i cari sposi.

FIORDILIGI: Buon viaggio, mia vita!

DORABELLA: Buon viaggio!

DON ALFONSO: (I'll burst if I don't laugh.)

Chorus

CHORUS:
The soldier's splendid lot!
Every day a change of scene.
Today is fat, tomorrow lean.
Sea or land, it's all gunshot.
The blare of trumpets and fifes,
The blast of cannons and bombs—
There's what stiffens your spine
And gets you what victory's got.
The soldier's splendid lot!

(The women remain standing on shore, as the ship leaves to the sound of drums, etc.)

Scene 6

FIORDILIGI, DORABELLA, AND DON ALFONSO.

Recitative

DORABELLA: *(as if awakening from a trance)* Where are they?

DON ALFONSO: They've gone.

FIORDILIGI: Oh, most cruel, most bitter parting!

DON ALFONSO: Take heart, dear children.
(from a distance he waves a handkerchief)
Look—in the distance, your lovers are waving to you.

FIORDILIGI: Bon voyage, my love!

DORABELLA: Bon voyage!

FIORDILIGI: Oh dei! Come veloce se ne va quella barca! Già sparisce, già non si vede più. Deh, faccia il cielo ch'abbia prospero corso!

DORABELLA: Faccia che al campo giunga con fortunati auspici!

DON ALFONSO: E a voi salvi gli amanti e a me gli amici.

N° 10 Terzettino

FIORDILIGI, DORABELLA, DON ALFONSO:
Soave sia il vento,
tranquilla sia l'onda,
ed ogni elemento
benigno risponda
ai nostri desir.
(Partono le due donne.)

Scena 7

DON ALFONSO SOLO.

Recitativo

DON ALFONSO: Non son cattivo comico! Va bene ... Al concertato loco i due campioni di Ciprigna e di Marte mi staranno attendendo: or senza indugio raggiungerli conviene ... Quante smorfie, quante buffonerie! ... Tanto meglio per me ... cadran più facilmente: questa razza di gente è la più presta a cangiarsi d'umore. Oh poverini, per femmina giocar cento zecchini!

"Nel mare solca e nell'arena semina
e il vago vento spera in rete accogliere
chi fonda sue speranze in cor di femmina."

FIORDILIGI: Dear God, how swiftly the ship sails away! It's already disappearing! Already out of sight! Oh, may heaven grant it a prosperous voyage.

DORABELLA: May fortune be with it as it reaches the battle!

DON ALFONSO: May your sweethearts and my friends be spared!

Trio

FIORDILIGI, DORABELLA, AND DON ALFONSO:
May the winds be soft
And the waves be calm.
May all the elements aloft
Fall like a gentle balm
On our desires.
(The ladies leave.)

Scene 7

DON ALFONSO, ALONE.

Recitative

DON ALFONSO: I'm not such a bad actor after all! Well then, those two champions of Venus and Mars will be waiting for me at the agreed place. I must go and meet them with no delay . . . Those long faces! That carrying on! So much the better for me. They'll fall into my trap all the more easily. They are the sort of people who change their moods like clothes. Poor fools! A hundred guineas they bet—imagine! On *women!*

"The man who ploughs the sea and plants in the desert sand
And tries to catch the wind as it races through his hands
Is the same who trusts a woman. One day he'll understand!"

Camera gentile con diverse sedie, un tavolino etc.
Tre porte: due laterali, una di mezzo.

Scena 8

DESPINA CHE STA FACENDO IL CIOCCOLATTE.

Recitativo

DESPINA: Che vita maledetta è il far la cameriera! Dal mattino alla sera si fa, si suda, si lavora, e poi di tanto che si fa nulla è per noi. È mezza ora che sbatto, il cioccolatte è fatto, ed a me tocca restar ad odorarlo a secca bocca? Non è forse la mia come la vostra, o garbate signore, che a voi dessi l'essenza e a me l'odore? Perbacco, vo' assaggiarlo ... Com'è buono! Vien gente. *(Si forbe la bocca.)* Oh ciel, son le padrone!

Scena 9

LA SUDDETTA. FIORDILIGI E DORABELLA CH'ENTRANO
DISPERATAMENTE ETC.

DESPINA: *(presenta il cioccolatte sopra una guantiera)* Madame, ecco la vostra colazione. *(Dorabella gitta tutto a terra.)* Diamine! Cosa fate?

FIORDILIGI: Ah!

DORABELLA: Ah!

(Si cavano entrambe tutti gli ornamenti donneschi etc.)

DESPINA: Che cosa è nato?

FIORDILIGI: Ov'è un acciaro? Un veleno dov'è? ...

A pleasant room with several chairs, a small table, etc. Three doors: one on either side, one in the middle.

Scene 8

DESPINA IS PREPARING HOT CHOCOLATE.

Recitative

DESPINA: It's a dog's life, being a lady's maid! Morning to night, in a sweat, hard at work, and after all that, there's nothing in it for us. Half an hour I've been whipping this chocolate. Finally it's ready and—well, must I just smell it and not taste it? Don't I have an appetite like yours? Oh gracious mistresses, why should you get the real thing while I get only the aroma? By Jove, I'm going to take a sip. Oh, how delicious! *(She wipes her mouth.)* Someone's coming. Good Lord, it's my mistresses!

Scene 9

AS BEFORE. FIORDILIGI AND DORABELLA
ENTER IN DESPAIR.

DESPINA: *(serving the chocolate on a tray)* Ladies, here is your breakfast. *(Dorabella knocks it to the floor.)* Good grief, what's the matter?

FIORDILIGI: Ah!

DORABELLA: Ah!

(They both take off all their jewelry.)

DESPINA: What has happened?

FIORDILIGI: Where is a knife? Poison, where is it?

DESPINA: Padrone, dico! ...

DORABELLA: Ah, scostati, paventa il tristo effetto d'un disperato affetto! Chiudi quelle finestre ... Odio la luce, odio l'aria che spiro ... odio me stessa ... chi schernisce il mio duol ... chi mi consola. Deh, fuggi, per pietà, lasciami sola!

N° 11 Aria

DORABELLA:
Smanie implacabili che m'agitate,
dentro quest'anima più non cessate
finché l'angoscia mi fa morir.
Esempio misero d'amor funesto
darò all'Eumenidi, se viva resto,
col suono orribile de' miei sospir.

(Dorabella e Fiordiligi si metton a sedere in disparte da forsennate.)

Recitativo

DESPINA: Signora Dorabella, signora Fiordiligi, ditemi: che cosa è stato?

DORABELLA: Oh terribil disgrazia!

DESPINA: Sbrigatevi, in buonora.

FIORDILIGI: Da Napoli partiti sono gli amanti nostri.

DESPINA: *(ridendo)* Non c'è altro? Ritorneran.

DORABELLA: Chi sa!

DESPINA: *(come sopra)* Come chi sa? Dove son iti?

DESPINA: Ladies, I beg you . . .

DORABELLA: Out of my sight! Beware the sad consequences of a hopeless love! Close the windows . . . I hate the light . . . I hate the air I breathe . . . I hate myself . . . Who mocks my grief, who can console me? Ah, leave, for pity's sake! Out! Out! Leave me alone.

Aria

DORABELLA:
Remorseless longings torment me now.
Let them wring my heart. Let love allow
My anguish to speed my death.
The wretched figure of tragic love,
Let me be torn by the Furies above.
For them is my last breath.

(Dorabella and Fiordiligi collapse onto chairs in their despair.)

Recitative

DESPINA: Signora Dorabella, Signora Fiordiligi, tell me, what's happened?

DORABELLA: Disaster! A terrible disaster!

DESPINA: Tell me, quickly.

FIORDILIGI: Our lovers have left Naples.

DESPINA: *(laughing)* Is that all? They'll be back.

DORABELLA: Who knows?

DESPINA: *(as above)* What do you mean, "Who knows"? Where have they gone?

DORABELLA: Al campo di battaglia.

DESPINA: Tanto meglio per loro: li vedrete tornar carchi d'alloro.

FIORDILIGI: Ma ponno anche perir.

DESPINA: Allora, poi, tanto meglio per voi.

FIORDILIGI: *(Sorge arrabbiata.)* Sciocca, che dici?

DESPINA: La pura verità: due ne perdete, vi restan tutti gli altri.

FIORDILIGI: Ah, perdendo Guilelmo mi pare ch'io morrei!

DORABELLA: Ah, Ferrando perdendo mi par che viva a seppellirmi andrei!

DESPINA: Brave, vi par, ma non è ver: finora non vi fu donna che d'amor sia morta. Per un uomo morir! Altri ve n'hanno che compensano il danno.

DORABELLA: E credi che potria altro uom amar chi s'ebbe per amante un Guilelmo, un Ferrando?

DESPINA: Han gli altri ancora tutto quello ch'han essi. Un uom adesso amate, un altro n'amerete: uno val l'altro, perché nessun val nulla. Ma non parliam di ciò: sono ancor vivi, e vivi torneran; ma son lontani, e, piuttosto che in vani pianti perdere il tempo, pensate a divertirvi.

FIORDILIGI: *(con trasporto di collera)* Divertirci?

DESPINA: Sicuro! E, quel ch'è meglio, far all'amor come assassine e come faranno al campo i vostri cari amanti.

DORABELLA: To the battlefield!

DESPINA: So much the better for them. You'll see them come back loaded with laurels.

FIORDILIGI: But they might be killed.

DESPINA: Well then, so much the better for you.

FIORDILIGI: *(rising angrily)* Stupid girl, what are you saying?

DESPINA: Only the truth. You lose two, but all the rest remain.

FIORDILIGI: Oh, if I lost Guglielmo, I would die.

DORABELLA: Oh, if I lost Ferrando, I would bury myself alive.

DESPINA: Bravo! You might think so, but it's simply not true. There never was a woman who died for love. Die for a man! There are plenty more where he came from!

DORABELLA: And you think a woman could love anyone else after having loved a Guglielmo, a Ferrando?

DESPINA: The others all have what those two have got. You love one man now, another one later on. One's worth as much as the next, because they're all worth nothing. But let's not dwell on that. They're still alive, and they'll come back alive. But they're far away now, and rather than wasting your time in tears, you should think of amusing yourselves.

FIORDILIGI: *(in a fit of rage)* Amuse ourselves?

DESPINA: Why not? And what's even better, make love like the devil—which is just what your lovers are doing at the front.

DORABELLA: Non offender così quelle alme belle, di fedeltà, d'intatto amore esempi.

DESPINA: Via, via! Passaro i tempi da spacciar queste favole ai bambini.

N° 12 Aria

DESPINA:
In uomini, in soldati
sperare fedeltà?
(ridendo)
Non vi fate sentir, per carità!
Di pasta simile son tutti quanti:
le fronde mobili, l'aure incostanti
han più degli uomini stabilità.
Mentite lagrime, fallaci sguardi,
voci ingannevoli, vezzi bugiardi
son le primarie lor qualità.
In noi non amano che il lor diletto;
poi ci dispregiano, neganci affetto,
né val da' barbari chieder pietà.
Paghiam, o femmine, d'ugual moneta
questa malefica razza indiscreta:
amiam per comodo, per vanità!
La ra la la ra la
la ra la la.

(Partono.)

DORABELLA: How dare you insult those noble souls, those paragons of purest love and faithfulness!

DESPINA: Oh, come on now! The days are past when you could tell such tales to children.

Aria

DESPINA:
Men! Soldiers!
You hope to find them true?
(laughing)
Men want nothing new?
Soldiers live only for you?
Don't let anyone hear you make that claim!
Every single one of them—all the same!
The fluttering leaves, the fickle breeze
Are steadier in their course than these!
One lies with his tears, one falsely confesses,
Their two-timing sighs, and treacherous caresses!
These are a man's upstanding qualities!
They only love us while having their fun.
Then they despise us and the game is done.
Why beg for mercy from a barbarian?
O women, we must pay them back in kind,
These cruel, dim-witted masterminds!
Let's flout them and fool them, however we can!
La ra la la ra la
La ra la la.

(They all leave.)

Scena 10

Recitativo

DON ALFONSO: Che silenzio! Che aspetto di tristezza spirano queste stanze! Poverette! Non han già tutto il torto. Bisogna consolarle: infin che vanno i due creduli sposi, com'io loro commisi, a mascherarsi, pensiam cosa può farsi ... Temo un po' per Despina ... Quella furba potrebbe riconoscerli ... potrebbe rovesciarmi le macchine ... Vedremo ... Se mai farà bisogno, un regaletto a tempo, un zecchinetto per una cameriera è un gran scongiuro. Ma per esser sicuro si potria metterla in parte a parte del secreto ... Eccellente è il progetto ... La sua camera è questa ... *(Batte.)* Despinetta!

DESPINA: Chi batte?

DON ALFONSO: Oh!

DESPINA: Ih!

DON ALFONSO: Despina mia, di te bisogno avrei.

DESPINA: Ed io niente di lei.

DON ALFONSO: Ti vo' fare del ben.

DESPINA: A una fanciulla un vecchio come lei non può far nulla.

DON ALFONSO: *(mostrandole una moneta d'oro)* Parla piano ed osserva.

DESPINA: Me la dona?

Scene 10

Recitative

DON ALFONSO: How silent it is! What an air of sadness pervades the room! Poor girls! It's not entirely their fault. They need consoling. While their two credulous lovers are disguising themselves, as I have instructed them, we must think what can be done . . . I'm worried about Despina . . . That little minx might recognize them . . . She could ruin my whole plot. Let's see . . . If a tiny bribe would do the trick, then gold coins work wonders with chambermaids. But just to be sure, I should gradually let her in on the secret. Yes, an excellent plan! This is her room . . . *(He knocks.)* My little Despina!

DESPINA: Who's knocking?

DON ALFONSO: Oh!

DESPINA: Aha!

DON ALFONSO: My dear Despina, I need you.

DESPINA: Well, I don't need you.

DON ALFONSO: I want to do you a favor.

DESPINA: There's nothing an old man like you can do for a young girl.

DON ALFONSO: *(holding up a gold coin)* Keep you voice down, and your eye on this.

DESPINA: Is that for me?

DON ALFONSO: Sì, se meco sei buona.

DESPINA: E che vorrebbe? È l'oro il mio giulebbe.

DON ALFONSO: Ed oro avrai, ma ci vuol fedeltà.

DESPINA: Non c'è altro? Son qua.

DON ALFONSO: Prendi ed ascolta. Sai che le tue padrone han perduti gli amanti ...

DESPINA: Lo so.

DON ALFONSO: Tutti i lor pianti, tutti i deliri loro ancor tu sai ...

DESPINA: So tutto.

DON ALFONSO: Orben, se mai, per consolarle un poco e trar, come diciam, chiodo per chiodo, tu ritrovassi il modo da metter in lor grazia due soggetti di garbo che vorrieno provar, già mi capisci ... C'è una mancia per te di venti scudi, se li fai riuscir.

DESPINA: Non mi dispiace questa proposizione. Ma con quelle buffone ... Basta, udite: son giovani, son belli e soprattutto hanno una buona borsa i vostri concorrenti?

DON ALFONSO: Han tutto quello che piacer può alle donne di giudizio. Li vuoi veder?

DESPINA: E dove son?

DON ALFONSO: Son lì. Li posso far entrar?

DON ALFONSO: Yes, if you're a good girl.

DESPINA: What sort of favor? Gold just happens to be my weakness.

DON ALFONSO: And gold you shall have, but in turn I must have your loyalty.

DESPINA: Is that all? I'm at your service.

DON ALFONSO: Take this, and listen carefully. You know your ladies have lost their lovers.

DESPINA: I know.

DON ALFONSO: You know too all about their weeping and wailing.

DESPINA: I know everything.

DON ALFONSO: Well then, to console them a little and, as it were, to drive one nail out with another, you might find a way of persuading them to receive two charming gentlemen who would like to try . . . but you already understand me . . . There's a bonus of twenty crowns if you help them succeed.

DESPINA: A reasonable proposition. But with these silly creatures . . . Enough. Listen. Are they young? Handsome? And above all, do they have plenty of money, these suitors of yours?

DON ALFONSO: They have everything that could please discerning ladies. Would you like to see them?

DESPINA: Where are they?

DON ALFONSO: Right here. Shall I bring them in?

DESPINA: Direi di sì.

(Don Alfonso fa entrar gli amanti travestiti.)

Scena 11

I SUDDETTI, FERRANDO E GUILELMO;
POI FIORDILIGI E DORABELLA.

N° 13 Sestetto

DON ALFONSO:
Alla bella Despinetta
vi presento, amici miei;
non dipende che da lei
consolar il vostro cor.

FERRANDO, GUILELMO: *(con tenerezza affettata)*
Per la man che lieto io bacio,
per quei rai di grazie pieni,
fa' che volga a me sereni
i begli occhi il mio tesor.

DESPINA: *(da sé, ridendo)*
Che sembianze! Che vestiti!
Che figure! Che mustacchi!
Io non so se son valacchi
o se turchi son costor.

DON ALFONSO: *(piano a Despina)* Che ti par di quell'aspetto?

DESPINA: By all means!

(The lovers enter in disguise.)

Scene 11

THOSE BEFORE, FERRANDO, AND GUGLIELMO,
THEN FIORDILIGI AND DORABELLA.

Sextet

DON ALFONSO:
Friends, let me present you
To lovely Despina the Fair.
Now into her cunning and care
I commend your heart's desire.

FERRANDO AND GUGLIELMO: *(with affected tenderness)*
By this hand I kiss with joy,
By these eyes that brim with grace,
May you help us find a place
Next to the ladies we admire.

DESPINA: *(to herself, laughing)*
What a sight! And those costumes!
Look how odd! And that mustache!
Romanian? Turkish? What a mishmash!
Perhaps it's best not to inquire.

DON ALFONSO: *(softly to Despina)* What do you think of their looks?

DESPINA: *(piano a Don Alfonso)*
Per parlarvi schietto schietto,
hanno un muso fuor dell'uso,
vero antidoto d'amor.

FERRANDO, DON ALFONSO, GUILELMO:
(Or la cosa è appien decisa:
se costei non li/ci ravvisa
non c'è più nessun timor.)

DESPINA: *(ridendo, da sé)*
Che figure! Che mustacchi!
Io non so se son valacchi
o se turchi son costor.

FIORDILIGI, DORABELLA: *(dentro le quinte)* Ehi, Despina! Olà,
Despina!

DESPINA: Le padrone!

DON ALFONSO: *(a Despina)* Ecco l'istante! Fa' con arte, io qui
m'ascondo.
(Si ritira.)

FIORDILIGI, DORABELLA: *(entrano)*
Ragazzaccia tracotante,
che fai lì con simil gente?
Falli uscire immantinente,
o ti fo pentir con lor.

DESPINA, FERRANDO, GUILELMO: *(s'inginocchiano)*
Ah madame, perdonate!
Al bel piè languir mirate
due meschin, di vostro merto
spasimanti adorator.

DESPINA: *(softly to Don Alfonso)*
To be honest,
They have most peculiar mugs,
Enough to douse love's flickering fire.

FERRANDO, DON ALFONSO, AND GUGLIELMO:
(They've fooled her, our disguises.
If she doesn't recognize us,
We are free now to conspire!)

DESPINA: *(to herself, laughing)*
What a sight! And those costumes!
Look how odd! And that mustache!
Romanian? Turkish? What a mishmash!
Perhaps it's best not to inquire.

FIORDILIGI AND DORABELLA: *(offstage)* Despina! Oh, Despina!

DESPINA: My mistresses!

DON ALFONSO: *(to Despina)* Now is the moment! Use your wits.
I'll hide in here.
(He goes off.)

FIORDILIGI AND DORABELLA: *(entering)*
You worthless, impudent girl!
You admitted the likes of them?
Send them away! Never again!
The consequences will be dire!

DESPINA, FERRANDO, AND GUGLIELMO: *(all three on their knees)*
Ladies, we beg your pardon, please!
The wretched men now on their knees
Are swooning in admiration of
The glow your charms inspire.

FIORDILIGI, DORABELLA:
Giusti numi! Cosa sento?
Dell'enorme tradimento
chi fu mai l'indegno autor?

DESPINA, FERRANDO, GUILELMO: Deh, calmate quello sdegno!

FIORDILIGI, DORABELLA:
Ah, che più non ho ritegno!
Tutta piena ho l'alma in petto
di dispetto e di terror.

FERRANDO, GUILELMO: *(da sé)*
Qual diletto è a questo petto
quella rabbia e quel furor!

DESPINA, DON ALFONSO: *(da sé, Don Alfonso dalla porta)*
Mi dà un poco di sospetto
quella rabbia e quel furor.

FIORDILIGI, DORABELLA: *(da sé)*
Ah perdon, mio bel diletto!
Innocente è questo cor.

Recitativo

DON ALFONSO: Che sussurro! Che strepito! Che scompiglio è mai questo! Siete pazze, care le mie ragazze? Volete sollevar il vicinato? Cosa avete? Ch'è nato?

DORABELLA: *(con furore)* Oh ciel! Mirate: uomini in casa nostra!

DON ALFONSO: *(senza guardarli)* Che male c'è?

FIORDILIGI AND DORABELLA:
Good heavens! What do I hear!
What vile traitor has interfered?
How has this outrage transpired?

DESPINA, FERRANDO, AND GUGLIELMO: Oh, calm your anger!

FIORDILIGI AND DORABELLA:
I cannot hold back any longer!
The very soul within my breast
Cries out against such liars!

FERRANDO AND GUGLIELMO: *(to themselves)*
This whole scene is so delicious,
Just what a lover's heart requires.

DESPINA AND DON ALFONSO: *(to themselves, Don Alfonso from the door)*
All this rage seems so suspicious,
As if it were all smoke, not fire.

FIORDILIGI AND DORABELLA: *(to themselves)*
Oh, forgive me, my beloved.
My heart to you alone aspires.

Recitative

DON ALFONSO: All this fuss! Such an uproar! What is all this commotion about? My dear young ladies, are you mad? Do you want to rouse the whole neighborhood? What is it now? What has happened?

DORABELLA: *(furiously)* Heavens! Just look! Men in our house!

DON ALFONSO: *(without looking at the young men)* What's wrong with that?

FIORDILIGI: *(con foco)* Che male? In questo giorno! ... Dopo il caso funesto! ...

DON ALFONSO: Stelle! Sogno o son desto? Amici miei, miei dolcissimi amici! Voi qui? Come? Perché? Quando? In qual modo? Numi! Quanto ne godo! (Secondatemi.)

FERRANDO: Amico Don Alfonso!

GUILELMO: Amico caro!

(Si abbracciano con trasporto.)

DON ALFONSO: Oh bella improvvisata!

DESPINA: Li conoscete voi?

DON ALFONSO: *(come sopra)* Se li conosco! Questi sono i più dolci amici ch'io m'abbia in questo mondo, e vostri ancor saranno.

FIORDILIGI: E in casa mia che fanno?

GUILELMO: Ai vostri piedi due rei, due delinquenti, ecco, madame! Amor ...

DORABELLA: Numi! Che sento?

(Le donne si ritirano, essi le inseguono.)

FERRANDO: Amor, il nume sì possente, per voi qui ci conduce.

GUILELMO: Vista appena la luce di vostre fulgidissime pupille ...

FIORDILIGI: *(excitedly)* What's wrong? On such a day as this? After such a terrible event?

DON ALFONSO: Stars above! Am I dreaming or awake? My *friends!* My dearest friends! You, here? How? Why? When? How did you get—? Goodness, how delighted I am. (Back me up.)

FERRANDO: Don Alfonso, old friend!

GUGLIELMO: My dear friend!

(They embrace him warmly.)

DON ALFONSO: What a wonderful surprise!

DESPINA: You know them?

DON ALFONSO: *(as above)* Know them? They are the friends I love best in the world, and they'll be yours too.

FIORDILIGI: And what are they doing in my house?

GUGLIELMO: You see at your feet, Madame, two guilty men. Love . . .

DORABELLA: Heavens! What is that I hear?

(The women pull back, followed by the men.)

FERRANDO: Love, the all-powerful god, led us to you here.

GUGLIELMO: No sooner had we glimpsed the light in your shining eyes . . .

FERRANDO: ... che alle vive faville ...

GUILELMO: ... farfallette amorose e agonizzanti ...

FERRANDO: ... vi voliamo davanti ...

GUILELMO: ... ed ai lati ed a retro ...

FERRANDO, GUILELMO: ... per implorar pietade in flebil metro!

FIORDILIGI: Stelle, che ardir!

DORABELLA: Sorella, che facciamo?

FIORDILIGI: Temerari, sortite fuori di questo loco!
(Despina sorte impaurita.)
E non profani l'alito infausto degl'infami detti nostro cor, nostro orecchio e nostri affetti. Invan per voi, per gli altri invan si cerca le nostre alme sedur: l'intatta fede che per noi già si diede ai cari amanti saprem loro serbar infino a morte, a dispetto del mondo e della sorte.

N° 14 Aria

FIORDILIGI:
Come scoglio immoto resta
contra i venti e la tempesta,
così ognor quest'alma è forte
nella fede e nell'amor.
Con noi nacque quella face
che ci piace e ci consola,
e potrà la morte sola
far che cangi affetto il cor.
Rispettate, anime ingrate,
questo esempio di costanza,

FERRANDO: . . . than, drawn to the flames . . .

GUGLIELMO: . . . like lovelorn moths . . .

FERRANDO: . . . we fly to be with you . . .

GUGLIELMO: . . . beside you, behind you . . .

FERRANDO AND GUGLIELMO: . . . to beg for pity in plaintive strains.

FIORDILIGI: Heavens above! What arrogance!

DORABELLA: Sister, what shall we do?

FIORDILIGI: How dare you! Leave this place at once!
(Despina runs off, frightened.)
We will not let you poison our hearts, our ears, our affections, with your vile, disgusting words. In vain would you, or any other men, try to seduce our souls. The steadfast faithfulness we have sworn to our dear lovers we shall preserve for them until death, defying the world and Fate itself.

Aria

FIORDILIGI:
Like a rocky fortress I stand,
No wind or wave may command.
My soul can weather any storm
With its loyalty and love.
In our hearts we lit a torch
That shines on pleasure and on peace,
And only Death can now release
Us from our vows to heaven above.
Ruthless creatures, show respect,
My beacon is my constancy.

e una barbara speranza
non vi renda audaci ancor!
(Va per partire. Ferrando la richiama, Guilelmo richiama l'altra.)

Recitativo

FERRANDO: *(a Fiordiligi)* Ah, non partite!

GUILELMO: *(a Dorabella)* Ah barbara, restate!
(a Don Alfonso)
Che vi pare?

DON ALFONSO:
(Aspettate.) *(alle due amanti)* Per carità, ragazze, non mi fate più
far trista figura.

DORABELLA: *(con foco)* E che pretendereste?

DON ALFONSO: Eh, nulla ... ma mi pare ... che un pochin di
dolcezza ... Alfin son galantuomini e sono amici miei.

FIORDILIGI: Come! E udire dovrei ...

GUILELMO: ... le nostre pene e sentirne pietà! La celeste beltà
degl'occhi vostri la piaga aprì nei nostri, cui rimediar può solo
il balsamo d'amore. Un solo istante il core aprite, o belle, a sue
dolci facelle, o a voi davanti spirar vedrete i più fedeli amanti.

N° 15 Aria

GUILELMO:
Non siate ritrosi,
occhietti vezzosi:
due lampi amorosi
vibrate un po' qua.
Felici rendeteci,

Never permit your audacity
To give you hope you dare speak of.
(She starts to leave. Ferrando calls her back. Guglielmo calls back her sister.)

Recitative

FERRANDO: *(to Fiordiligi)* No, don't leave!

GUGLIELMO: *(to Dorabella)* Ah, cruel woman, stay!
(to Don Alfonso)
How do you like that?

DON ALFONSO: (Wait.) *(to the two lovers)* Ladies, for pity's sake, don't make me look like a fool.

DORABELLA: *(angrily)* What do you want from us?

DON ALFONSO: Oh, nothing . . . But it seems to me a little kindness . . . After all, they are gentlemen, and friends of mine.

FIORDILIGI: What? You expect me to listen . . .

GUGLIELMO: . . . to our sufferings and pity them! The heavenly beauty of your eyes has opened a wound in ours which can only be healed by your soothing love. For just a moment, sweetest of ladies, open your hearts to its warmth, or else see, right here, two faithful lovers die at your feet.

Aria

GUGLIELMO:
Now don't be shy!
Let your pretty eyes
Cast a loving glance
On those who idolize.
Come make us happy,

amate con noi;
e noi felicissime
faremo anche voi.
Guardate, toccate,
il tutto osservate:
siam due cari matti,
siam forti e ben fatti;
e come ognun vede,
sia merto, sia caso,
abbiamo bel piede,
bell'occhio, bel naso.
Guardate: bel piede,
osservate: bell'occhio,
toccate: bel naso,
il tutto osservate;
e questi mustacchi
chiamare si possono
trionfi degli uomini,
pennacchi d'amor.
(Qui partono le donne con collera.)
(Guilelmo ridendo)
Trionfi, pennacchi, mustacchi!

Scena 12

DON ALFONSO, GUILELMO, FERRANDO.

N° 16 Terzetto

DON ALFONSO: E voi ridete?

FERRANDO, GUILELMO: *(ridono fortissimo.)* Certo, ridiamo.

DON ALFONSO: Ma cosa avete?

FERRANDO, GUILELMO: *(come sopra)* Già lo sappiamo.

And let us love you.
In return we promise
You'll be happy too.
Just look! Here, touch!
Look at everything!
We're two mad fools,
As strong as mules,
And as you see,
As you'd suppose,
Look at these feet,
These eyes, this nose . . .
Yes, very fine feet,
And beautiful eyes,
And oh, what a nose . . .
Look at everything!
And these mustaches
We're rightly so proud of?
The trophies of manhood,
The plumage of love!
(The ladies leave.)
(laughing)
Trophies, plumage, ah, mustaches!

Scene 12

DON ALFONSO, GUGLIELMO, AND FERRANDO.

Trio

DON ALFONSO: You're laughing?

FERRANDO AND GUGLIELMO: *(laughing heartily)* We're laughing.

DON ALFONSO: But what is all the fun?

FERRANDO AND GUGLIELMO: *(as above)* We know now that we've won.

DON ALFONSO: Ridete piano!

FERRANDO, GUILELMO: Parlate invano.

DON ALFONSO:
Se vi sentissero,
se vi scoprissero,
si guasterebbe
tutto l'affar.

FERRANDO, GUILELMO: *(ridono sottovoce sforzandosi di non ridere.)*
Ah, che dal ridere
l'alma dividere,
ah, che le viscere
sento scoppiar!

DON ALFONSO: *(da sé)*
Mi fa da ridere
questo lor ridere,
ma so che in piangere
dee terminar.

Recitativo

DON ALFONSO: Si può sapere un poco la cagion di quel riso?

GUILELMO: Eh cospettaccio! Non vi pare che abbiam giusta ragione, il mio caro padrone?

FERRANDO: *(scherzando)* Quanto pagar volete, e a monte è la scommessa?

GUILELMO: *(sempre scherzando)* Pagate la metà.

FERRANDO: *(come sopra)* Pagate solo ventiquattro zecchini.

DON ALFONSO: Your laughter is best contained!

FERRANDO AND GUGLIELMO: Your warning's all in vain.

DON ALFONSO:
If they hear you laugh,
If they find out half,
You will ruin
The whole affair.

FERRANDO AND GUGLIELMO: *(laughing quietly while straining not to laugh)*
Your Excellency permitting,
Our very sides are splitting—
Ha, ha!
Our guts will burst! You'll hear!

DON ALFONSO: *(to himself)*
Their laughter, it's true,
Makes me chuckle too—
Ha, ha!
But I know it will end in tears.

Recitative

DON ALFONSO: And may one know the reason for all the hilarity?

GUGLIELMO: Oh, for heaven's sake, good sir, don't you think we have every reason?

FERRANDO: *(playfully)* How much will you pay, now that you're losing the bet?

GUGLIELMO: *(playfully)* Pay half of it.

FERRANDO: *(as above)* Twenty-four guineas will do.

DON ALFONSO: Poveri innocentini! Venite qui: vi voglio porre il ditino in bocca.

GUILELMO: E avete ancora coraggio di fiatar?

DON ALFONSO: Avanti sera ci parlerem.

FERRANDO: Quando volete.

DON ALFONSO: Intanto silenzio e ubbidienza fino a doman mattina.

GUILELMO: Siamo soldati e amiam la disciplina.

DON ALFONSO: Orbene, andate un poco ad attendermi entrambi in giardinetto: colà vi manderò gli ordini miei.

GUILELMO: Ed oggi non si mangia?

FERRANDO: Cosa serve? A battaglia finita fia la cena per noi più saporita.

N° 17 Aria

FERRANDO:
Un'aura amorosa
del nostro tesoro
un dolce ristoro
al cor porgerà,
al cor che nutrito
da speme, da amore
d'un'esca migliore
bisogno non ha.

(Ferrando e Guilelmo partono.)

DON ALFONSO: Poor innocent things! Here, why not suck my thumb!

GUGLIELMO: And you still have the nerve to go on?

DON ALFONSO: We will discuss it before this evening.

FERRANDO: Whenever you like.

DON ALFONSO: Meanwhile, be silent and obey my orders until tomorrow morning.

GUGLIELMO: We are soldiers, and love discipline.

DON ALFONSO: Very well then. Go and wait for me in the garden, both of you. I'll send you my orders there.

GUGLIELMO: Do we get anything to eat today?

FERRANDO: What does that matter? When the battle is over, the feast tastes all the better.

Aria

FERRANDO:
A breath of love
From our sweethearts
Restores our strength
Though we must part.
The heart that feeds
On the hope of love
Has no more need
Of manna from above.

(Ferrando and Guglielmo leave.)

Scena 13

DON ALFONSO SOLO, POI DESPINETTA.

Recitativo

DON ALFONSO: Oh, la saria da ridere: sì poche son le donne costanti in questo mondo, e qui ve ne son due ... Non sarà nulla ...

(Entra Despina.)

Vieni, vieni, fanciulla, e dimmi un poco dove sono e che fan le tue padrone.

DESPINA: Le povere padrone stanno nel giardinetto a lagnarsi coll'aria e colle mosche d'aver perso gli amanti.

DON ALFONSO: E come credi che l'affar finirà? Vogliam sperare che faranno giudizio ...

DESPINA: Io lo farei, e dove piangon esse io riderei. Disperarsi, strozzarsi perché parte un amante? Guardate che pazzia! Se ne pigliano due, s'uno va via.

DON ALFONSO: Brava! Questa è prudenza. (Bisogna impuntigliarla.)

DESPINA: È legge di natura e non prudenza sola. Amor cos'è? Piacer, comodo, gusto, gioia, divertimento, passatempo, allegria: non è più amore se incomodo diventa, se invece di piacer nuoce e tormenta.

DON ALFONSO: Ma intanto quelle pazze ...

DESPINA: Quelle pazze faranno a modo nostro. È buon che sappiano d'esser amate da color.

Scene 13

DON ALFONSO, ALONE, THEN DESPINA.

Recitative

DON ALFONSO: It's enough to make you laugh. I've never yet found a single faithful woman in the whole world, and here we have two of them . . . I don't believe it . . .
(Despina enters.)
Come here, miss, and tell me where your mistresses are and what they're doing.

DESPINA: Those poor fools are in the garden, moaning to the breezes and the flies about the loss of their lovers.

DON ALFONSO: And how do you think this will all end? Is there a chance they will come to their senses?

DESPINA: I would. Instead of weeping, I'd be giggling. To choke yourself with despair because a lover has left? Sheer madness! If you lose one, you can snag two more.

DON ALFONSO: Brava! Very sensible indeed! (Best to flatter her.)

DESPINA: It's not just sensible, it's the law of nature. What's love, after all? Pleasure, convenience, enjoyment, bliss, diversion, pastime, fun. It's no longer love when it's solemn. When it doesn't please, it toments.

DON ALFONSO: Meanwhile, these silly girls . . .

DESPINA: Silly? Oh, they'll fall in with our plan. It would help if they knew those new chaps were in love with them.

DON ALFONSO: Lo sanno.

DESPINA: Dunque riameranno. "Diglielo," si suol dire, "e lascia fare al diavolo."

DON ALFONSO: E come far vuoi perché ritornino, or che partite sono, e che li sentano e tentare si lascino queste due bestioline?

DESPINA: A me lasciate la briga di condur tutta la macchina. Quando Despina macchina una cosa non può mancar d'effetto: ho già menati mill'uomini pel naso, saprò menar due femmine. Son ricchi i due monsieurs mustacchi?

DON ALFONSO: Son ricchissimi.

DESPINA: Dove son?

DON ALFONSO: Sulla strada attendendo mi stanno.

DESPINA: Ite e sul fatto per la picciola porta a me riconduceteli: v'aspetto nella camera mia. Purché tutto facciate quel ch'io v'ordinerò, pria di domani i vostri amici canteran vittoria; ed essi avranno il gusto, ed io la gloria.

(Partono.)

DON ALFONSO: They know it.

DESPINA: Then they'll love them in return. As they say, just start a sentence and the devil will finish it.

DON ALFONSO: And how do you plan to get them back now that they've left? And how do you get your beastly ladies to listen to them and fall in love?

DESPINA: Leave it to me to figure out a way. When Despina puts her mind to something, things never go wrong. I've led thousands of men by the nose in my day, so I should know how to handle a couple of women. Are they rich, your Messieurs Mustaches?

DON ALFONSO: Very rich!

DESPINA: Where are they now?

DON ALFONSO: Waiting for me in the street.

DESPINA: Go and bring them to me at once by the side entrance. I'll wait for you in my room. Provided you do everything I say, before tomorrow your friends will be crowing about their victory. They'll have the pleasure, and I the glory.

(They leave.)

Giardinetto gentile. Due sofà d'erba ai lati.

Scena 14

FIORDILIGI, DORABELLA.

N° 18 Finale

FIORDILIGI, DORABELLA:
Ah, che tutta in un momento
si cangiò la sorte mia!
Ah, che un mar pien di tormento
è la vita omai per me!
Finché meco il caro bene
mi lasciar le ingrate stelle,
non sapea cos'eran pene,
non sapea languir cos'è.
Ah, che tutta in un momento
si cangiò la sorte mia!
Ah, che un mar pien di tormento
è la vita omai per me!

Scena 15

LE SUDDETTE; GUILELMO, FERRANDO E DON ALFONSO
DENTRO LE QUINTE; POI DESPINA.

FERRANDO, GUILELMO: *(dentro le quinte)*
Si mora, sì, si mora
onde appagar le ingrate!

DON ALFONSO: *(dentro le quinte)*
C'è una speranza ancora;
non fate, oh dei, non fate!

FIORDILIGI, DORABELLA: Stelle, che grida orribili!

FERRANDO, GUILELMO: Lasciatemi!

A pleasant little garden with grassy banks on each side.

Scene 14
FIORDILIGI AND DORABELLA.

Finale

FIORDILIGI AND DORABELLA:
Ah, how in a sudden moment
My fate has completely changed!
Ah, what a sea of torment
My life has now become.
As long as the fickle stars
Allowed my love to be mine,
Sorrow never showed its scars,
Nor had I ever felt so numb.
Ah, how in a sudden moment
My fate has completely changed!
Ah, what a sea of torment
My life has now become.

Scene 15
THOSE BEFORE; GUGLIELMO, FERRANDO, AND DON ALFONSO, ALL OFFSTAGE; THEN DESPINA.

FERRANDO AND GUGLIELMO: *(from offstage)*
Let us die, yes, let us die,
To these heartless creatures we must submit.

DON ALFONSO: *(from offstage)*
May hope stifle your cry.
Such a desperate crime you must not commit.

FIORDILIGI AND DORABELLA: Heavens, what terrible screams!

FERRANDO AND GUGLIELMO: Let me go!

DON ALFONSO: Aspettate!

(Ferrando e Guilelmo, portando ciascuno un nappo, entrano seguiti da Don Alfonso.)

FERRANDO, GUILELMO:
L'arsenico mi liberi
di tanta crudeltà!

(Bevono e gittan via il nappo. Nel voltarsi vedono le due donne.)

FIORDILIGI, DORABELLA: Stelle, un velen fu quello?

DON ALFONSO:
Veleno buono e bello
che ad essi in pochi istanti
la vita toglierà.

FIORDILIGI, DORABELLA:
Il tragico spettacolo
gelare il cor mi fa!

FERRANDO, GUILELMO:
Barbare, avvicinatevi!
D'un disperato affetto
mirate il triste effetto
e abbiate almen pietà.

FIORDILIGI, DORABELLA:
Il tragico spettacolo
gelare il cor mi fa!

DON ALFONSO: Wait!

(Ferrando and Guglielmo enter, each carrying a small bottle, and followed by Don Alfonso.)

FERRANDO AND GUGLIELMO:
May arsenic now deliver me
From such cruelty.

(They drink and throw the bottles away; turning around they see the two ladies.)

FIORDILIGI AND DORABELLA: Oh God, was that poison they took?

DON ALFONSO:
Poison good and proper. Look!
In a few seconds now
You will witness their sacrifice.

FIORDILIGI AND DORABELLA:
This tragic spectacle
Turns my heart to ice.

FERRANDO AND GUGLIELMO:
Cruel ones, draw near.
Behold the dire consequence
Of a sad and hopeless romance.
Your pity would be our only paradise.

FIORDILIGI AND DORABELLA:
This tragic spectacle
Turns my heart to ice.

FIORDILIGI, DORABELLA, FERRANDO, DON ALFONSO, GUILELMO:
Ah, che del sole il raggio
fosco per me diventa!
Tremo: le fibre e l'anima
par che mancar si senta,
né può la lingua o il labbro
accenti articolar.

DON ALFONSO:
Giacché a morir vicini
sono quei meschinelli,
pietade almeno a quelli
cercate di mostrar.

FIORDILIGI, DORABELLA:
Gente, accorrete, gente!
Nessuno, oddio, ci sente!
Despina!

DESPINA: *(di dentro)* Chi mi chiama?

FIORDILIGI, DORABELLA: Despina!

DESPINA: *(in scena)*
Cosa vedo!
Morti i meschini io credo,
o prossimi a spirar.

DON ALFONSO:
Ah, che purtroppo è vero!
Furenti, disperati,
si sono avvelenati.
Oh amore singolar!

FIORDILIGI, DORABELLA, FERRANDO, DON ALFONSO, AND GUGLIELMO:

Ah, the rays of the sun
Are turning to darkness for me.
I tremble, I seem to feel
My strength, my soul now flee.
My lips, my very tongue
Cannot form another word.

DON ALFONSO:

Since these wretched men
Are near to death,
Is there not one breath
Of pity to be heard?

FIORDILIGI AND DORABELLA:

Someone! Help! Come quickly!
Good God, no one can hear us!
Despina! Despina!

DESPINA: *(from offstage)* Who is calling me?

FIORDILIGI AND DORABELLA: Despina! Despina!

DESPINA: *(entering)*

What do I see?
I think these poor men are dead,
Or about to draw their last breath. .

DON ALFONSO:

Oh, too true, too true!
Raging and desperate
They poisoned themselves.
They look now for love in death.

DESPINA:
Abbandonar i miseri
saria per voi vergogna:
soccorrerli bisogna.

FIORDILIGI, DORABELLA, DON ALFONSO: Cosa possiam mai far?

DESPINA:
Di vita ancor dan segno:
colle pietose mani
fate un po' lor sostegno.
(a Don Alfonso)
E voi con me correte:
un medico, un antidoto
voliamo a ricercar.
(Parte con Don Alfonso.)

FIORDILIGI, DORABELLA:
Dei, che cimento è questo!
Evento più funesto
non si potea trovar.

FERRANDO, GUILELMO: *(a parte)*
Più bella commediola
non si potea trovar.
Ah!

FIORDILIGI, DORABELLA: *(stando lontano dagli amanti)* Sospiran gli infelici.

FIORDILIGI: Che facciamo?

DORABELLA: Tu che dici?

DESPINA:
To abandon these sorry souls
Would bring both of you shame.
Help them now, in God's name!

FIORDILIGI, DORABELLA, AND DON ALFONSO: Whatever can
we do?

DESPINA:
There is still a sign of life.
Take them up gently
In your merciful arms.
(to Don Alfonso)
You must hurry with me!
A doctor! An antidote!
Quick now! Grab your coat!
(She leaves with Don Alfonso.)

FIORDILIGI AND DORABELLA:
Oh God, what a disaster!
A tragedy worse than this
Would be impossible to find!

FERRANDO AND GUGLIELMO: *(aside)*
A comedy finer than this
Would be impossible to find!
Ahh!

FIORDILIGI AND DORABELLA: *(standing at a distance from the
lovers)* Those poor dears are sighing!

FIORDILIGI: What should we do?

DORABELLA: What would you say?

FIORDILIGI:
In momenti sì dolenti
chi potriali abbandonar?

DORABELLA: *(si accosta un poco)* Che figure interessanti!

FIORDILIGI: *(si accosta un poco)* Possiam farci un poco avanti.

DORABELLA: Ha freddissima la testa.

FIORDILIGI: Fredda fredda è ancora questa.

DORABELLA: Ed il polso?

FIORDILIGI: Io non gliel sento.

DORABELLA: Questo batte lento lento.

FIORDILIGI, DORABELLA:
Ah, se tarda ancor l'aita
speme più non v'è di vita!

FERRANDO, GUILELMO: *(da sé)*
Più domestiche e trattabili
sono entrambe diventate:
sta' a veder che lor pietade
va in amore a terminar.

FIORDILIGI, DORABELLA:
Poverini! La lor morte
mi farebbe lagrimar.

FIORDILIGI:
At such a grievous moment,
Who could abandon them?

DORABELLA: *(coming closer)* What an interesting face!

FIORDILIGI: *(coming closer)* A little closer would be no disgrace.

DORABELLA: His brow is cold, it's true.

FIORDILIGI: Cold, cold, yes, this one too.

DORABELLA: And his pulse?

FIORDILIGI: None. Oh no!

DORABELLA: There is one here, but slow.

FIORDILIGI AND DORABELLA:
Ah, if help does not come soon,
There's no hope they can survive.

FERRANDO AND GUGLIELMO: *(to themselves)*
They seem tamer now,
Much more amenable.
Compassion may turn to love,
But will it keep?

FIORDILIGI AND DORABELLA:
Poor things! Their miserable death
Will surely make me weep.

Scena 16

I SUDDETTI, DESPINA TRAVESTITA
DA MEDICO.

DON ALFONSO: Eccovi il medico, signore belle!

FERRANDO, GUILELMO : (Despina in maschera: che trista pelle!)

DESPINA: Salvete, amabiles bones puelles!

FIORDILIGI, DORABELLA: Parla un linguaggio che non
sappiamo.

DESPINA:
Come comandano, dunque parliamo:
so il greco e l'arabo,
so il turco, il vandalo;
lo svevo e il tartaro
so ancor parlar.

DON ALFONSO:
Tanti linguaggi per sé conservi.
Quei miserabili per ora osservi:
preso hanno il tossico,
che si può far?

FIORDILIGI, DORABELLA: Signor dottore, che si può far?

DESPINA: *(tocca il polso e la fronte ad uno ed all'altro.)*
Saper bisognami pria la cagione
e quinci l'indole della pozione:
se calda o frigida,

Scene 16

THOSE BEFORE, AND DESPINA, DISGUISED
AS A DOCTOR.

DON ALFONSO: Here is the doctor, fair ladies.

FERRANDO AND GUGLIELMO: (Despina in disguise. What a
sorry sight!)

DESPINA: *Salvete, amabiles bones puelles!*

FIORDILIGI AND DORABELLA: He's speaking some language
we can't understand.

DESPINA:
I'll try what tongue you command.
I know Arabic and Greek,
Am fluent in Turkish and Vandal,
Even Swabian I can handle.
Whatever you wish I shall speak.

DON ALFONSO:
We won't ask you that again!
Now what about these poor men?
It's poison they've swallowed,
And what can be done?

FIORDILIGI AND DORABELLA: Yes, doctor, whatever can be
done?

DESPINA: *(feeling the pulse and the brow of each man in turn)*
Before I can diagnose,
I must know their reason and the dose.
Was it hot or cold,

se poca o molta,
se in una volta
ovvero in più.

FIORDILIGI, DORABELLA, DON ALFONSO:
Preso han l'arsenico, signor dottore;
qui dentro il bebbero, la causa è amore,
ed in un sorso sel mandar giù.

DESPINA:
Non vi affannate, non vi turbate:
ecco una prova di mia virtù.

FIORDILIGI, DORABELLA, DON ALFONSO: Egli ha di un ferro
la man fornita ...

DESPINA:
Questo è quel pezzo di calamita
– pietra mesmerica! –
ch'ebbe l'origine nell'Alemagna,
che poi sì celebre
là in Francia fu.

(Tocca con un pezzo di calamita la testa ai finti infermi e striscia dolce-
mente i loro corpi per lungo.)

FIORDILIGI, DORABELLA, DON ALFONSO:
Come si muovono, torcono, scuotono,
in terra il cranio presto percuotono!

DESPINA: Ah, lor la fronte tenete su!

FIORDILIGI, DORABELLA: *(metton la man alla fronte dei due amanti.)*
Eccoci pronte!

A little, a lot?
Did they gulp it,
Or just take a drop?

FIORDILIGI, DORABELLA, AND DON ALFONSO:
Oh doctor, it's arsenic they've taken.
The cause was love, and unless we're mistaken,
They drank—oh horrors!—their fill.

DESPINA:
Don't be upset, don't worry and fret.
Here is the proof of my skill.

FIORDILIGI, DORABELLA, AND DON ALFONSO: There's a strange
metal *thing* in his hand.

DESPINA:
A magnet. Let me expand.
It's the Mesmeric stone.
In Germany it was first known,
But its fame has since grown
Into France.

(Despina applies the magnet to the head of each supposed invalid and gently strokes it along the lengths of their bodies.)

FIORDILIGI, DORABELLA, AND DON ALFONSO:
Look! It's making them move, and writhe, and shake!
They're alive, but oh the backache!

DESPINA: Careful! Hold their heads up!

FIORDILIGI AND DORABELLA: *(placing their hands on the young men's foreheads)* We're ready!

DESPINA:
Tenete forte!
Coraggio! Or liberi siete da morte.

FIORDILIGI, DORABELLA, DON ALFONSO:
Attorno guardano, forze riprendono:
ah, questo medico vale un Perù!

FERRANDO, GUILELMO: *(sorgono in piedi.)*
Dove son? Che loco è questo?
Chi è colui? Color chi sono?
Son di Giove innanzi al trono?
(Ferrando a Fiordiligi, Guilelmo a Dorabella)
Sei tu Palla o Citerea?
No, tu sei l'alma mia Dea:
ti ravviso al dolce viso
e alla man ch'or ben conosco
e che sola è il mio tesor.

(Abbracciano le amanti teneramente e bacian loro la mano etc.)

DESPINA, DON ALFONSO:
Son effetti ancor del tosco:
non abbiate alcun timor.

FIORDILIGI, DORABELLA:
Sarà ver, ma tante smorfie
fanno torto al nostro onor.

FERRANDO, GUILELMO:
(Dalla voglia ch'ho di ridere
il polmon mi scoppia or or.)
(alle amanti)
Per pietà, bell'idol mio,
volgi a me le luci liete!

DESPINA:
Hold tightly! Be brave!
Now you are freed from death.

FIORDILIGI, DORABELLA, AND DON ALFONSO:
They're looking around, they're regaining their strength.
Oh, this doctor is worth his weight in gold.

FERRANDO AND GUGLIELMO: *(getting to their feet)*
Where am I? What place is this?
Who is he? Who are they?
Am I before the throne of Jove?
(Ferrando to Fiordiligi and Guglielmo to Dorabella)
Are you Pallas, or Venus?
No, you are the goddess of my soul!
I recognize your face . . .
And that hand I know so well . . .
My treasure, dearest demoiselle!

(Ferrando and Guglielmo embrace their lovers tenderly and kiss their hands.)

DESPINA AND DON ALFONSO:
This is still the effect of poison.
Do not be alarmed.

FIORDILIGI AND DORABELLA:
True perhaps, but such unseemly conduct
Threatens to blemish our names.

FERRANDO AND GUGLIELMO:
(I have such an urge to laugh,
My lungs will go up in flames!)
(to their sweethearts)
For pity's sake, my dearest one!
Look at me. I insist.

FIORDILIGI, DORABELLA: Più resister non poss'io.

DESPINA, DON ALFONSO:
In poch'ore, lo vedrete,
per virtù del magnetismo
finirà quel parossismo,
torneranno al primo umor.

FERRANDO, GUILELMO:
(Ferrando a Fiordiligi, Guilelmo a Dorabella)
Dammi un bacio, o mio tesoro,
un sol bacio, o qui mi moro.

FIORDILIGI, DORABELLA: Stelle! Un bacio?

DESPINA:
Secondate
per effetto di bontate.

FIORDILIGI, DORABELLA:
Ah, che troppo si richiede
da una fida onesta amante!
Oltraggiata è la mia fede,
oltraggiato è questo cor.
Disperati, attossicati,
ite al diavol quanti siete!
Tardi inver vi pentirete
se più cresce il mio furor.

DESPINA, DON ALFONSO: *(da sé)*
Un quadretto più giocondo
non si vide in tutto il mondo!
Quel che più mi fa da ridere
è quell'ira e quel furor,
ch'io ben so che tanto foco
cangerassi in quel d'amor.

FIORDILIGI AND DORABELLA: I can no longer resist.

DESPINA AND DON ALFONSO:
In a short time you will see
The power of magnetism
Calm all paroxysms.
They will be themselves again.

FERRANDO *(to Fiordiligi)* **AND GUGLIELMO** *(to Dorabella)*:
Give me a kiss, my treasure, my dear,
A single kiss, or I shall die right here!

FIORDILIGI AND DORABELLA: Heavens! A kiss?

DESPINA:
Nothing to it.
A little kindness will do it.

FIORDILIGI AND DORABELLA:
Ah, you are asking too much
Of a pure and faithful lover.
My honor you besmirch.
My heart you have outraged!
Now desperate, now poisoned . . .
Go to the devil, the lot of you!
This is a day you will later rue
If I choose to vent my rage!

DESPINA AND DON ALFONSO: *(to themselves)*
The world could not reveal
A more amusing situation,
This hilarious combination
Of frenzy and of rage.
I know well, with all this fire,
Love could be the next stage.

FERRANDO, GUILELMO: *(da sé)*
Un quadretto più giocondo
non s'è visto in questo il mondo!
Ma non so se finta o vera
sia quell'ira e quel furor,
né vorrei che tanto foco
terminasse in quel d'amor.

Fine dell'atto primo.

FERRANDO AND GUGLIELMO: *(to themselves)*
The world could not reveal
A more amusing situation!
I don't know if it's feigned or real,
All this frenzy and this rage,
Nor would I want, with so much fire,
Love to be its final stage.

End of Act I.

Atto secondo

Camera.

Scena 1

DORABELLA, FIORDILIGI E DESPINA.

Recitativo

DESPINA: Andate là, che siete due bizzarre ragazze!

FIORDILIGI: Oh cospettaccio! Cosa pretenderesti?

DESPINA: Per me nulla.

FIORDILIGI: Per chi dunque?

DESPINA: Per voi.

DORABELLA: Per noi?

DESPINA: Per voi. Siete voi donne o no?

FIORDILIGI: E per questo?

DESPINA: E per questo dovete far da donne.

DORABELLA: Cioè?

— ÷ Act II ÷ —

A room.

Scene 1

DORABELLA, FIORDILIGI, AND DESPINA.

Recitative

DESPINA: Well, I must say, you are a pair of strange girls.

FIORDILIGI: Oh, for heaven's sake, what do you want now?

DESPINA: For myself, nothing.

FIORDILIGI: For whom, then?

DESPINA: For you.

DORABELLA: For us?

DESPINA: For you. Are you women, or not?

FIORDILIGI: What is that supposed to mean?

DESPINA: It means you should act like women.

DORABELLA: How?

DESPINA: Trattar l'amore en bagatelle: le occasioni belle non negliger giammai, cangiar a tempo, a tempo esser costanti, coquettizzar con grazia, prevenir la disgrazia sì comune a chi si fida in uomo, mangiar il fico e non gittare il pomo.

FIORDILIGI: (Che diavolo!) Tai cose falle tu, se n'hai voglia.

DESPINA: Io già le faccio, ma vorrei che anche voi per gloria del bel sesso faceste un po' lo stesso. Per esempio, i vostri ganimedi son andati alla guerra? Infin che tornano fate alla militare: reclutate.

DORABELLA: Il cielo ce ne guardi!

DESPINA: Eh, che noi siamo in terra e non in cielo! Fidatevi al mio zelo: giacché questi forastieri v'adorano, lasciatevi adorar. Son ricchi, belli, nobili, generosi, come fede fece a voi Don Alfonso; avean coraggio di morire per voi: questi son merti che sprezzar non si denno da giovani qual voi belle e galanti, che pon star senza amor, non senza amanti. (Par che ci trovin gusto.)

FIORDILIGI: Perbacco, ci faresti far delle belle cose! Credi tu che vogliamo favola diventar degli oziosi? Ai nostri cari sposi credi tu che vogliam dar tal tormento?

DESPINA: E chi dice che abbiate a far loro alcun torto?

DORABELLA: Non ti pare che sia torto bastante se noto si facesse che trattiamo costor?

DESPINA: Anche per questo c'è un mezzo sicurissimo: io voglio sparger fama che vengono da me.

DESPINA: Treat love like a bauble. Never miss a good opportunity, change your minds or not as necessary, flirt with charm, beware the disgrace of trusting in men, eat the fig but don't toss away the apple.

FIORDILIGI: (What a devil!) *You* behave that way, if that's what you want.

DESPINA: I already do. But I wish you would do the same, for the glory of the fair sex. For example, your Ganymedes have gone off to war. Until they return, do as soldiers do—recruit!

DORABELLA: Heaven forbid!

DESPINA: But we're on earth, not in heaven! Have faith in my devotion. Since these strangers so adore you, let yourselves be worshipped. They are rich, handsome, noble, and generous, just as Don Alfonso pledged. They even had the courage to die for you. These are not virtues to be scorned by beautiful and refined ladies such as you, who may survive without love, but not without lovers. (I think they get my point.)

FIORDILIGI: Goodness, you would have us do all sorts of . . . *things*. Do you think we want to be on the tongues of idle gossips? Do you think we would cause such torment to our dear fiancés?

DESPINA: And who says you would be doing them any harm?

DORABELLA: Don't you think it would be harm enough if they even *heard* we were receiving such men?

DESPINA: There's a perfectly sensible way of dealing with that. I'll spread the rumor that they're courting *me*.

DORABELLA: Chi vuoi che il creda?

DESPINA: Oh bella! Non ha forse merto una cameriera d'aver due cicisbei? Di me fidatevi.

FIORDILIGI: No no, son troppo audaci questi tuoi forastieri. Non ebber la baldanza fin di chieder dei baci?

DESPINA: (Che disgrazia!) Io posso assicurarvi che le cose che han fatto furo effetti del tossico che han preso: convulsioni, deliri, follie, vaneggiamenti. Ma or vedrete come son discreti, manierosi, modesti e mansueti. Lasciateli venir.

DORABELLA: E poi?

DESPINA: E poi … Caspita, fate voi! (L'ho detto che cadrebbero.)

FIORDILIGI: Cosa dobbiamo far?

DESPINA: Quel che volete. Siete d'ossa e di carne, o cosa siete?

N° 19 Aria

DESPINA:
Una donna a quindici anni
dee saper ogni gran moda:
dove il diavolo ha la coda,
cosa è bene e mal cos'è.
Dee saper le maliziette
che innamorano gli amanti,
finger riso, finger pianti,
inventar i bei perché.
Dee in un momento
dar retta a cento;

DORABELLA: Who would ever believe that?

DESPINA: How nice of you! Perhaps a lady's maid doesn't deserve two admirers? Trust me.

FIORDILIGI: No, no. Those foreigners of yours are much too bold. They even had the impudence to ask for a kiss.

DESPINA: (How scandalous!) I can assure you that what they did was merely the effect of the poison they swallowed. Convulsions, delirium, eccentricity, frenzy . . . But now you will see how sensible, polite, modest and gentle they are. Let me come in.

DORABELLA: And then?

DESPINA: And then . . . Confound it! Then it's up to you! (I always said they would give in.)

FIORDILIGI: What should we do?

DESPINA: Whatever you want. Are you flesh and blood, or not?

Aria

DESPINA:
By the age of, say, fifteen
A woman should know what's what—
Where the devil keeps his tail,
What is good and what is not.
She should know the little tricks
To make a lover swoon,
How to feign a smile or tears,
How to blame things on the moon.
She must lend a patient ear
To a hundred men at once,

colle pupille
parlar con mille;
dar speme a tutti,
sien belli o brutti;
saper nascondersi
senza confondersi;
senza arrossire
saper mentire;
e, qual regina
dall'alto soglio,
col "posso e voglio"
farsi ubbidir.
(Par ch'abbian gusto
di tal dottrina:
viva Despina
che sa servir!)
(Parte.)

Scena 2

FIORDILIGI E DORABELLA.

Recitativo

FIORDILIGI: Sorella, cosa dici?

DORABELLA: Io son stordita dallo spirto infernal di tal ragazza.

FIORDILIGI: Ma credimi, è una pazza. Ti par che siamo in caso di seguir suoi consigli?

DORABELLA: Oh certo, se tu pigli pel rovescio il negozio …

And speak with batting eyes
On a thousand other fronts.
Whether with beaux or brutes,
She must give them all some hope,
And conceal the ugly truth
With a laugh as slippery as soap.
She must know how to lie
Without a blush or a pause,
And like a queen on her throne
Issue her commands like laws,
Her "I will" and "Let it be known."
(It seems they agree.
I can tell. I can tell.
Despina was right,
Who has served them well!)
(She leaves.)

Scene 2

FIORDILIGI AND DORABELLA.

Recitative

FIORDILIGI: Sister, what are you thinking?

DORABELLA: I'm appalled by the devilish presumption of that girl.

FIORDILIGI: Believe me, she's crazy. Do you think it's even possible we would take her advice?

DORABELLA: Of course . . . if you turn the whole business upside down.

FIORDILIGI: Anzi, io lo piglio per il suo verso dritto: non credi tu delitto, per due giovani omai promesse spose, il far di queste cose?

DORABELLA: Ella non dice che facciamo alcun mal.

FIORDILIGI: È mal che basta il far parlar di noi.

DORABELLA: Quando si dice che vengon per Despina ...

FIORDILIGI: Oh, tu sei troppo larga di coscienza! E che diranno gli sposi nostri?

DORABELLA: Nulla: o non sapran l'affare, ed è tutto finito; o sapran qualche cosa, e allor diremo che vennero per lei.

FIORDILIGI: Ma i nostri cori?

DORABELLA: Restano quel che sono: per divertirsi un poco e non morire dalla malinconia non si manca di fé, sorella mia.

FIORDILIGI: Questo è ver.

DORABELLA: Dunque?

FIORDILIGI: Dunque fa un po' tu, ma non voglio aver la colpa se poi nasce un imbroglio.

DORABELLA: Che imbroglio nascer deve con tanta precauzion? Per altro ascolta: per intendersi bene qual vuoi sceglier per te de' due narcisi?

FIORDILIGI: No, let's look at it right side up. Don't you think it is scandalous for two young ladies—who are engaged—to do such things?

DORABELLA: She didn't say we would be doing anything wrong.

FIORDILIGI: It would be bad enough if tongues started wagging.

DORABELLA: We can say they came to see Despina!

FIORDILIGI: Your conscience is too accommodating! And what will our finacés say?

DORABELLA: Nothing. Either they'll know nothing about it, and that's that. Or they'll know something, and we say they came to see *her.*

FIORDILIGI: But our hearts?

DORABELLA: They will stay as they are. If we amuse ourselves a little, to keep from dying of melancholy, that is not being unfaithful, dear sister.

FIORDILIGI: That's true.

DORABELLA: So?

FIORDILIGI: So you do as you like, but I don't want to be blamed if it all ends badly.

DORABELLA: How could it end badly, if we act carefully? But one thing more. Just so that we understand each other perfectly, which of these handsome men do you prefer?

FIORDILIGI: Decidi tu, sorella.

DORABELLA: Io già decisi.

N° 20 Duetto

DORABELLA:
Prenderò quel brunettino
che più lepido mi par.

FIORDILIGI:
Ed intanto io col biondino
vo' un po' ridere e burlar.

DORABELLA:
Scherzosetta ai dolci detti
io di quel risponderò.

FIORDILIGI:
Sospirando i sospiretti
io dell'altro imiterò.

DORABELLA: Mi dirà: "ben mio, mi moro."

FIORDILIGI: Mi dirà: "mio bel tesoro."

FIORDILIGI, DORABELLA:
Ed intanto che diletto,
che spassetto io proverò!
(Partono e s'incontrano in Don Alfonso.)

FIORDILIGI: You choose first, sister.

DORABELLA: I've already decided.

Duet

DORABELLA:
I like the little dark one.
He seems wittier to me.

FIORDILIGI:
And with the little blond one
I could be fancy-free.

DORABELLA:
Joking, I'll captivate
My darling's eyes.

FIORDILIGI:
Sighing, I'll imitate
My sweetheart's sighs.

DORABELLA: He'll tell me, "I shall die of my love!"

FIORDILIGI: He'll whisper, "My treasure, my dove!"

FIORDILIGI AND DORABELLA:
And meanwhile what pleasure
What fun I shall have!

(As they start to leave, they encounter Don Alfonso.)

Scena 3

LE SUDDETTE E DON ALFONSO.

Recitativo

DON ALFONSO: Ah, correte al giardino, le mie care ragazze! Che allegria! Che musica! Che canto! Che brillante spettacolo! Che incanto! Fate presto, correte!

DORABELLA: Che diamine esser può?

DON ALFONSO: Tosto vedrete.

(Partono.)

*Giardino alla riva del mare con sedili d'erba
e due tavolini di pietra. Barca ornata di fiori
con banda di stromenti.*

Scena 4

FERRANDO E GUILELMO, DESPINA, SERVI RICCAMENTE
VESTITI. CORO DI MUSICI ETC. POI FIORDILIGI,
DORABELLA E DON ALFONSO.

N° 21 Duetto con coro

FERRANDO, GUILELMO:
Secondate, aurette amiche,
secondate i miei desiri
e portate i miei sospiri
alla dea di questo cor.
Voi che udiste mille volte
il tenor delle mie pene,
ripetete al caro bene
tutto quel che udiste allor.

Scene 3

THOSE BEFORE, AND DON ALFONSO.

Recitative

DON ALFONSO: Ah, hurry to the garden, dear girls! What merriment, what music, what singing, what a brilliant spectacle, what enchantment! Be quick now and run!

DORABELLA: Whatever can it be?

DON ALFONSO: You'll soon see.

(They all leave.)

A garden by the seashore with wicker chairs and two small stone tables. Nearby, a boat decked with flowers and a group of musicians.

Scene 4

FERRANDO AND GUGLIELMO, DESPINA. SERVANTS IN RICH
LIVERIES. A CHORUS, ETC. THEN FIORDILIGI,
DORABELLA AND DON ALFONSO.

Duet with Chorus

FERRANDO AND GUGLIELMO:
Gentle zephyrs, blow this way,
Help fulfill my fond desire.
Carry my sighs and sweetly inspire
The goddess of my heart.
You have heard a thousand times
The story of my sorrow's tears.
Whisper again in my darling's ear,
Take her now the saddest part.

CORO:

Secondate, aurette amiche,
il desir di sì bei cor!

(Nel tempo del ritornello di questo coro Ferrando e Guilelmo scendono con catene di fiori. Don Alfonso e Despina li conducono davanti le due amanti che resteranno ammutite ed attonite.)

Recitativo

DON ALFONSO: *(ai servi che portano un bacile con fiori)* Il tutto deponete sopra quei tavolini, e nella barca ritiratevi, amici.

FIORDILIGI, DORABELLA: Cos'è tal mascherata?

DESPINA: *(a Ferrando e Guilelmo)* Animo, via, coraggio: avete perso l'uso della favella?

FERRANDO: Io tremo e palpito dalla testa alle piante.

GUILELMO: Amor lega le membra a vero amante.

DON ALFONSO: *(alle donne)* Da brave, incoraggiateli.

FIORDILIGI: *(agli amanti)* Parlate.

DORABELLA: *(agli amanti)* Liberi dite pur quel che bramate.

FERRANDO: Madama ...

GUILELMO: Anzi, madame ...

FERRANDO: *(a Guilelmo)* Parla pur tu.

GUILELMO: *(a Ferrando)* No no, parla pur tu.

CHORUS:
Help them, gentle zephyrs, help
Speed the wishes of two brave hearts.

(During the chorus, Ferrando and Guglielmo descend from the boat carrying garlands of flowers; Don Alfonso and Despina lead them to their lovers, who stand there silent and astonished.)

Recitative

DON ALFONSO: *(to the servants bearing bowls of flowers)* My friends, leave everything on these tables and return to the boat.

FIORDILIGI AND DORABELLA: Is this some sort of charade?

DESPINA: *(to Ferrando and Guglielmo)* Come now, cheer up. Has the cat got your tongues?

FERRANDO: I'm trembling, shaking from head to toe.

GUGLIELMO: Love shackles the limbs of a true lover.

DON ALFONSO: *(to the ladies)* Be good girls and encourage them.

FIORDILIGI: *(to the suitors)* Say something.

DORABELLA: *(to the suitors)* Tell us frankly what you want.

FERRANDO: My lady . . .

GUGLIELMO: Or rather, my ladies . . .

FERRANDO: *(to Guglielmo)* You speak.

GUGLIELMO: *(to Ferrando)* No, no, you first.

DON ALFONSO: Oh cospetto del diavolo, lasciate tali smorfie del secolo passato! Despinetta, terminiam questa festa: fa' tu con lei quel ch'io farò con questa.

N° 22 Quartetto

DON ALFONSO:

(prende per mano Dorabella, mentre Despina prende Fiordiligi etc.)

La mano a me date,
movetevi un po'.

(agli amanti)

Se voi non parlate,
per voi parlerò.

(alle donne)

Perdono vi chiede
un schiavo tremante:
v'offese, lo vede,
ma solo un istante.
Or pena, ma tace ...

FERRANDO, GUILELMO: ... tace ...

DON ALFONSO: Or lasciavi in pace ...

FERRANDO, GUILELMO: ... in pace ...

DON ALFONSO:

Non può quel che vuole,
vorrà quel che può.

FERRANDO, GUILELMO: *(con un sospiro)*

Non può quel che vuole,
vorrà quel che può.

DON ALFONSO: Oh, the devil take you both! Enough with these old-fashioned manners. Despinetta, let's end this business. You do with her what I do with this one.

Quartet

DON ALFONSO:
(He takes Dorabella's hand. Despina takes Fiordiligi's.)
Give me your hand.
Bestir yourself a bit.
(to the suitors)
If you will not speak,
I will speak for you.
(to the ladies)
A trembling slave
Begs your pardon.
He acknowledges his offense.
Its pain was merely a moment's.
Now he suffers in silence . . .

FERRANDO AND GUGLIELMO: . . . in silence . . .

DON ALFONSO: Now he will leave you in peace . . .

FERRANDO AND GUGLIELMO: . . . in peace . . .

DON ALFONSO:
He cannot have what he wants,
So he will want only what he can.

FERRANDO AND GUGLIELMO: *(with a sigh)*
He cannot have what he wants,
So he will want only what he can.

DON ALFONSO: *(alle donne)*
Suvvia, rispondete.
Guardate e ridete?

DESPINA: *(si mette davanti le due donne)*
Per voi la risposta
a loro darò.

Recitativo

DESPINA:
Quello ch'è stato è stato.
scordiamci del passato:
(Despina prende la mano di Dorabella, Don Alfonso quella di Fiordiligi:
fan loro rompere i lacci agli amanti e le mettono al braccio dei medesimi.)
rompasi omai quel laccio,
segno di servitù.
A me porgete il braccio,
né sospirate più.

DESPINA, DON ALFONSO: *(a parte sottovoce)*
Per carità, partiamo,
quel che san far veggiamo:
le stimo più del diavolo
s'ora non cascan giù.

(Despina e Don Alfonso partono.)

DON ALFONSO: *(to the ladies)*
Come now, an answer.
You are just staring . . . and giggling.

DESPINA: *(moving in front of the two ladies)*
I will give them
An answer for you.

Recitative

DESPINA:
What's done is done.
Let's forget the past.
*(Despina takes Dorabella's hand, Don Alfonso takes Fiordiligi's; the ladies
undo their garlands and drape them over the arms of their suitors.)*
Its folderol and platitudes
Were symbols of servitude.
Offer me your arm now
And let us change the mood.

DESPINA AND DON ALFONSO: *(softly, aside)*
For heaven's sake, let's leave.
Let's see what they will do.
I'll rank them higher than the devil
If we don't see a small breakthrough.

(Despina and Don Alfonso leave.)

Scena 5

GUILELMO AL BRACCIO DI DORABELLA. FERRANDO E
FIORDILIGI SENZA DARSI IL BRACCIO.

Fanno una piccola scena muta guardandosi, sospirando, ridendo etc.

Recitativo

FIORDILIGI: Oh, che bella giornata!

FERRANDO: Caldetta anzi che no.

DORABELLA: Che vezzosi arboscelli!

GUILELMO: Certo, certo, son belli: han più foglie che frutti.

FIORDILIGI: Quei viali come sono leggiadri! Volete passeggiar?

FERRANDO: Son pronto, o cara, ad ogni vostro cenno.

FIORDILIGI: Troppa grazia!

FERRANDO: *(nel passare, a Guilelmo)* (Eccoci alla gran crisi.)

FIORDILIGI: Cosa gli avete detto?

FERRANDO: Eh, gli raccomandai di divertirla bene.

DORABELLA: *(a Guilelmo)* Passeggiamo anche noi.

GUILELMO: Come vi piace. *(Passeggiano.) (dopo un momento di silenzio)* Ahimè!

DORABELLA: Che cosa avete?

Scene 5

GUGLIELMO ON DORABELLA'S ARM. FERRANDO AND
FIORDILIGI WITHOUT GIVING HIM HER ARM.

(A small pantomime ensues, with gazing, sighing, laughing, etc.)

Recitative

FIORDILIGI: Oh, what a lovely day!

FERRANDO: Warmer than usual.

DORABELLA: What charming little trees!

GUGLIELMO: Yes, very charming indeed. More leaves than fruit.

FIORDILIGI: Very attractive, these paths. Would you care to take
a stroll?

FERRANDO: I am ready, my dearest, to grant your every wish.

FIORDILIGI: You are too kind!

FERRANDO: *(aside, as he passes Guglielmo)* (We've reached the
sticking point.)

FIORDILIGI: What did you just whisper to him?

FERRANDO: Oh, I just told him to amuse the lady.

DORABELLA: *(to Guglielmo)* Let's take a walk ourselves.

GUGLIELMO: *(as they start to go)* As you wish . . . *(after a moment of
silence)* Alas!

DORABELLA: What's the matter?

GUILELMO: Io mi sento sì male, sì male, anima mia, che mi par di morire.

(Gli altri due fanno scena muta in lontananza.)

DORABELLA: (Non otterrà nientissimo.)
Saranno rimasugli del velen che beveste.

GUILELMO: *(con foco)*
Ah, che un veleno assai più forte io bevo in que' crudi e focosi mongibelli amorosi!

(Gli altri due partono in atto di passeggiare.)

DORABELLA: Sarà veleno calido: fatevi un poco fresco.

GUILELMO: Ingrata, voi burlate, ed intanto io mi moro! (Son spariti: dove diamin son iti?)

DORABELLA: Eh via, non fate ...

GUILELMO: Io mi moro, crudele, e voi burlate?

DORABELLA: Io burlo? Io burlo?

GUILELMO: Dunque datemi qualche segno, anima bella, della vostra pietà.

DORABELLA: Due, se volete: dite quel che far deggio e lo vedrete.

GUILELMO: (Scherza o dice davvero?) Questa picciola offerta d'accettare degnatevi.

DORABELLA: Un core?

GUGLIELMO: I feel ill, so awfully ill, my darling, that I think I shall die.

(In the distance, the other pair can be seen in silent conversation.)

DORABELLA: (This will get him nowhere.)
It must be the aftereffects of that poison you swallowed.

GUGLIELMO: *(heatedly)*
Ah, I drink now a stronger poison from your eyes, from those cruel and fiery volcanoes of love!

(The other pair strolls offstage.)

DORABELLA: A heated comparison. You must cool down a bit.

GUGLIELMO: Heartless woman, you can joke while I die! (They've disappeared. Where the devil have they gone?)

DORABELLA: Oh, come now, don't be doing that . . .

GUGLIELMO: I am dying, cruel lady, and still you make fun of me?

DORABELLA: Me? Joking?

GUGLIELMO: Then give me some sign, beloved, of your pity.

DORABELLA: Two, if you like. Just tell me what you'd like, and you'll see.

GUGLIELMO: (A trick, or does she mean it?) I beg you accept this tiny gift.

DORABELLA: A heart?

GUILELMO: Un core: è simbolo di quello ch'arde, languisce e spasima per voi.

DORABELLA: (Che dono prezioso!)

GUILELMO: L'accettate?

DORABELLA: Crudele! Di sedur non tentate un cor fedele.

GUILELMO: (La montagna vacilla. Mi spiace, ma impegnato è l'onor di soldato.) V'adoro!

DORABELLA: Per pietà ...

GUILELMO: Son tutto vostro!

DORABELLA: Oh dei!

GUILELMO: Cedete, o cara ...

DORABELLA: Mi farete morir ...

GUILELMO: Morremo insieme, amorosa mia speme. L'accettate?

DORABELLA: *(dopo breve intervallo con un sospiro)* L'accetto.

GUILELMO: (Infelice Ferrando!) Oh, che diletto!

N° 23 Duetto

GUILELMO:
Il core vi dono,
bell'idolo mio;
ma il vostro vo' anch'io:
via, datelo a me.

GUGLIELMO: A heart. It is a symbol of the one that languishes, burns, and suffers for you.

DORABELLA: (What a precious gift!)

GUGLIELMO: Will you accept it?

DORABELLA: Cruel man, do not try to seduce a faithful heart.

GUGLIELMO: (The mountain is crumbling. I hate doing this, but my honor as a soldier is at stake.) I adore you!

DORABELLA: For pity's sake . . .

GUGLIELMO: I am yours alone!

DORABELLA: Oh, God!

GUGLIELMO: Give in, my darling!

DORABELLA: You are killing me.

GUGLIELMO: Let us die together, my hope of life. Shall we?

DORABELLA: *(after a moment's pause, with a sigh)* We shall!

GUGLIELMO: (Unhappy Ferrando!) Oh, what bliss!

Duet

GUGLIELMO:
I give you my heart,
You for whom I yearn.
But I want yours in return.
Come, give it to me.

DORABELLA:
Mel date, lo prendo;
ma il mio non vi rendo.
Invan mel chiedete,
più meco ei non è.

GUILELMO:
Se teco non l'hai,
perché batte qui?

DORABELLA:
Se a me tu lo dai,
che mai balza lì?

GUILELMO: Perché batte qui?

DORABELLA: Che mai balza lì?

DORABELLA, GUILELMO:
È il mio coricino
che più non è meco:
ei venne a star teco,
ei batte così.

GUILELMO: *(vuol metterle il core dov'ha il ritratto dell'amante.)* Qui
lascia che il metta.

DORABELLA: Ei qui non può star.

GUILELMO: T'intendo, furbetta.

DORABELLA: Che fai?

GUILELMO: Non guardar.

DORABELLA:
You offer and I accept,
But I cannot give you mine.
I must, I will decline.
Alas, it is not free.

GUGLIELMO:
If it is not free,
Why is it beating so?

DORABELLA:
If you gave me yours,
What is fluttering so?

GUGLIELMO: Why is it beating so?

DORABELLA: Why is it fluttering so?

DORABELLA AND GUGLIELMO:
It is my little heart,
And it is mine no more.
From now on it is yours.
That is why it is beating so.

GUGLIELMO: *(trying to put the heart where she keeps the portrait of Ferrando)* Let me put it here.

DORABELLA: It cannot go there.

GUGLIELMO: I understand why, sly one.

DORABELLA: What are you doing?

GUGLIELMO: Don't look.

(Le torce dolcemente la faccia dall'altra parte, le cava il ritratto e vi mette il core.)

DORABELLA:
(Nel petto un Vesuvio
d'avere mi par.)

GUILELMO:
(Ferrando meschino!
Possibil non par.)
L'occhietto a me gira.

DORABELLA: Che brami?

GUILELMO:
Rimira
se meglio può andar.

DORABELLA, GUILELMO:
Oh cambio felice
di cori e d'affetti!
Che nuovi diletti,
che dolce penar!

(Partono abbracciati.)

Scena 6

FERRANDO E FIORDILIGI.

Recitativo

FERRANDO: Barbara! Perché fuggi?

FIORDILIGI: Ho visto un aspide, un'idra, un basilisco!

(He gently turns her face away, and substitutes the heart for the portrait.)

DORABELLA:
(I feel Vesuvius
Erupting in my breast!)

GUGLIELMO:
(Poor Ferrando,
Who would have guessed?)
Now turn your eyes towards me.

DORABELLA: What do you want?

GUGLIELMO:
Tell me, tell me
What could be better.

DORABELLA AND GUGLIELMO:
Oh, happy exchange
Of affections and hearts.
What new delight now starts,
And what sweet new pain!

(Embracing, they leave.)

Scene 6

FERRANDO AND FIORDILIGI.

Recitative

FERRANDO: You defiant girl! Why do you run away?

FIORDILIGI: I have seen a snake, a hydra, a basilisk!

FERRANDO: Ah crudel, ti capisco! L'aspide, l'idra, il basilisco, e quanto i libici deserti han di più fiero, in me solo tu vedi.

FIORDILIGI: È vero, è vero! Tu vuoi tormi la pace.

FERRANDO: Ma per farti felice.

FIORDILIGI: Cessa di molestarmi.

FERRANDO: Non ti chiedo che un guardo.

FIORDILIGI: Partiti.

FERRANDO: Non sperarlo, se pria gli occhi men fieri a me non giri. Oh ciel! Ma tu mi guardi e poi sospiri?

N° 24 Aria

FERRANDO: *(lietissimo)*
Ah, lo veggio, quell'anima bella
al mio pianto resister non sa:
non è fatta per esser rubella
agli affetti di amica pietà.

In quel guardo, in quei cari sospiri
dolce raggio lampeggia al mio cor:
già rispondi a' miei caldi desiri,
già tu cedi al più tenero amor.

Ma tu fuggi, spietata, tu taci
ed invano mi senti languir!
Ah, cessate, speranze fallaci!
La crudel mi condanna a morir.
(Parte.)

FERRANDO: I understand your cruelty at last. The snake, the hydra, the basilisk, and all the wild beasts in the Libyan desert— all these you see in me alone.

FIORDILIGI: True, it's all true. You want to rob me of my peace of mind.

FERRANDO: But only to make you happy . . .

FIORDILIGI: Stop tormenting me!

FERRANDO: I ask for merely a glance.

FIORDILIGI: Go!

FERRANDO: No hope for that until you treat me more kindly. Good God, why do you sigh when you look at me?

Aria

FERRANDO: *(overjoyed)*
Ah, now I see that your sweet soul
Cannot resist my tears.
My tender feelings can control
Your own rebellious fears.

In your glance and in your sigh,
A light comes from above.
Already you respond to my desires,
Already you yield to love.

Yet you are silent, and pitiless you flee.
In vain you hear how I languish.
No more shall I let hope deceive me.
This woman condemns me to vanish.
(He leaves.)

Scena 7

FIORDILIGI SOLA.

Recitativo

FIORDILIGI: Ei parte ... Senti ... Ah no ... partir si lasci, si tolga ai sguardi miei l'infausto oggetto della mia debolezza ... A qual cimento il barbaro mi pose! ... Un premio è questo ben dovuto a mie colpe! ... In tale istante dovea di nuovo amante i sospiri ascoltar? L'altrui querele dovea volger in gioco? Ah, questo core a ragione condanni, o giusto amore! Io ardo, e l'ardor mio non è più effetto di un amor virtuoso: è smania, affanno, rimorso, pentimento, leggerezza, perfidia e tradimento!

N° 25 Rondò

FIORDILIGI:

Per pietà, ben mio, perdona
all'error d'un'alma amante:
fra quest'ombre e queste piante
sempre ascoso, oh dio, sarà!
Svenerà quest'empia voglia
l'ardir mio, la mia costanza;
perderà la rimembranza
che vergogna e orror mi fa.
A chi mai mancò di fede
questo vano, ingrato cor!
Si dovea miglior mercede,
caro bene, al tuo candor.
(Parte.)

Scene 7

FIORDILIGI, ALONE.

Recitative

FIORDILIGI: He's leaving . . . Listen! . . . No! Let him go. At least I will no longer have to look at the unfortunate object of my weakness . . . What danger this horrid man has put me in! . . . This is a well-deserved reward for my sins! . . . How could I think of listening to a new lover's sighs at such a moment? . . . How could I make fun of someone's anguish? How could I worry about his laments? Ah, you justly punish my heart, oh remorseless Love! I burn, but no longer with a virtuous passion. It is madness, suffering, remorse, regret, fickleness, deceit, and betrayal!

Rondo

FIORDILIGI:

Have pity on me, my sweet, and forgive
The wrong my loving heart has wrought.
In the shadows of this grove, distraught,
I will hide it, oh God, forevermore.
My passion and my constancy
Will cure me of this terrible desire,
Will stamp out memory's raging fire
That fills me now with shame to the core.
And whose steadfast faithfulness
Did my ungrateful heart betray?
You deserved a far better reward,
My dearest, for never having strayed.
(*She leaves.*)

Scena 8

FERRANDO, GUILELMO.

Recitativo

FERRANDO: *(lietissimo)* Amico, abbiamo vinto!

GUILELMO: Un ambo o un terno?

FERRANDO: Una cinquina, amico: Fiordiligi è la modestia in carne.

GUILELMO: Niente meno?

FERRANDO: Nientissimo. Sta' attento e ascolta come fu.

GUILELMO: T'ascolto: di' pur, su.

FERRANDO: Pel giardinetto, come eravam d'accordo, a passeggiar mi metto: le do il braccio, si parla di mille cose indifferenti; alfine viensi all'amor.

GUILELMO: Avanti.

FERRANDO: Fingo labbra tremanti, fingo di pianger, fingo di morir al suo piè ...

GUILELMO: Bravo assai, per mia fé! Ed ella?

FERRANDO: Ella da prima ride, scherza, mi burla ...

GUILELMO: E poi?

FERRANDO: E poi finge d'impietosirsi ...

Scene 8

FERRANDO AND GUGLIELMO.

Recitative

FERRANDO: *(overjoyed)* My friend, we have won!

GUGLIELMO: Doubly—or is it triply?

FERRANDO: We've won it all, my boy. Fiordiligi is chastity itself.

GUGLIELMO: Nothing less, eh?

FERRANDO: Not in the slightest. Pay attention now, and I'll tell you what happened.

GUGLIELMO: I'm all yours. Go on.

FERRANDO: As we agreed, I started walking with her in the garden. I gave her my arm. We talked about a thousand things of no importance, when finally we came to the subject of love.

GUGLIELMO: And then?

FERRANDO: I pretended my lips were trembling, I pretended to weep, I pretended to die at her feet . . .

GUGLIELMO: By my faith, well done indeed! And the lady?

FERRANDO: At first she laughed, joked, even mocked me . . .

GUGLIELMO: And then?

FERRANDO: And then she pretended to take pity on me . . .

GUILELMO: Oh cospettaccio!

FERRANDO: Alfin scoppia la bomba: pura come colomba al suo caro Guilelmo ella si serba, mi discaccia superba, mi maltratta, mi fugge, testimonio rendendomi e messaggio che una femmina ell'è senza paraggio.

GUILELMO: Bravo tu, bravo io, brava la mia Penelope! Lascia un po' ch'io ti abbracci per sì felice augurio, o mio fido Mercurio!

(Si abbracciano.)

FERRANDO: E la mia Dorabella? Come s'è diportata? Oh, non ci ho neppur dubbio! *(con trasporto)* Assai conosco quella sensibil alma.

GUILELMO: Eppur un dubbio, parlandoti a quattr'occhi, non saria mal se tu l'avessi!

FERRANDO: Come?

GUILELMO: Dico così per dir! (Avrei piacere d'indorargli la pillola.)

FERRANDO: Stelle! Cesse ella forse alle lusinghe tue? Ah, s'io potessi sospettarlo soltanto!

GUILELMO: È sempre bene il sospettare un poco in questo mondo.

FERRANDO: Eterni dei! Favella, a foco lento non mi far qui morir ... Ma no, tu vuoi prenderti meco spasso: ella non ama, non adora che me.

GUGLIELMO: You devil!

FERRANDO: Finally the bomb exploded. She is "keeping herself as pure as a dove for her dear Guglielmo." Haughtily she gave me what for. She scolded me, ran from me—proof beyond doubt that she is a woman without equal.

GUGLIELMO: Congratulations all round—especially to my Penelope! Here, let me embrace you for this good news. O my trusty messenger.

(They embrace.)

FERRANDO: And my Dorabella? How did she behave? Ah, I have no doubt. *(passionately)* How well I know her sensitive soul.

GUGLIELMO: Well, just between us, it wouldn't hurt to have a doubt or two.

FERRANDO: What?

GUGLIELMO: Just a figure of speech. (I need to sugar the pill.)

FERRANDO: Heavens! Can she have fallen for your flattery? Oh, if I should even suspect that . . . !

GUGLIELMO: In this world, it's always wise to be a little suspicious.

FERRANDO: Good God! Tell me! Don't dangle me over the flames. No, wait, you're just teasing me. She loves—no, *adores* only me.

GUILELMO: Certo! Anzi, in prova di suo amor, di sua fede questo bel ritrattino ella mi diede.

FERRANDO: *(furente)* Il mio ritratto! Ah perfida!

GUILELMO: Ove vai?

FERRANDO: *(come sopra)* A trarle il cor dal scellerato petto e a vendicar il mio tradito affetto.

GUILELMO: Fermati!

FERRANDO: *(risoluto)* No, mi lascia!

GUILELMO: Sei tu pazzo? Vuoi tu precipitarti per una donna che non val due soldi? (Non vorrei che facesse qualche corbelleria!)

FERRANDO: Numi! Tante promesse e lagrime e sospiri e giuramenti in sì pochi momenti come l'empia obliò?

GUILELMO: Perbacco, io non lo so!

FERRANDO: Che fare or deggio? A qual partito, a qual idea m'appiglio? Abbi di me pietà, dammi consiglio!

GUILELMO: Amico, non saprei qual consiglio a te dar.

FERRANDO: Barbara! Ingrata! In un giorno! In poche ore! ...

GUILELMO: Certo un caso quest'è da far stupore!

GUGLIELMO: Of course she does! And as proof of her love and fidelity she gave me this little portrait of you.

FERRANDO: *(angrily)* My portrait! That viper!

GUGLIELMO: Where are you going?

FERRANDO: *(as above)* To tear the heart out of her treacherous breast, and avenge the love she has betrayed.

GUGLIELMO: Stop!

FERRANDO: *(resolved)* No, leave me alone!

GUGLIELMO: Are you mad? Do you want to ruin your life for a worthless woman? (I don't want him to do anything foolish.)

FERRANDO: God, so many promises, so many tears and sighs and vows—how could that wicked woman forget them all in a heartbeat?

GUGLIELMO: By Jove, I don't know.

FERRANDO: What should I do now, how do I face her, how do I act? Have pity on me, give me some advice.

GUGLIELMO: My friend, I don't know what advice to give you.

FERRANDO: Ruthless, heartless woman! In one day! In a few hours!

GUGLIELMO: You're right. An amazing situation!

N° 26 Aria

GUILELMO:
Donne mie, la fate a tanti,
che, se il ver vi deggio dir,
se si lagnano gli amanti
li comincio a compatir.
Io vo' bene al sesso vostro,
lo sapete, ognun lo sa:
ogni giorno ve lo mostro,
vi do marche d'amistà;
ma quel farla a tanti, a tanti,
m'avvilisce in verità.
Mille volte il brando presi
per salvar il vostro onor,
mille volte vi difesi
colla bocca e più col cor;
ma quel farla a tanti, a tanti,
è un vizietto seccator.
Siete vaghe, siete amabili,
più tesori il ciel vi diè,
e le grazie vi circondano
dalla testa fino ai piè;
ma la fate a tanti, a tanti,
che credibile non è;
ma la fate a tanti, a tanti,
che se gridano gli amanti
hanno certo un gran perché.
(Parte.)

Aria

GUGLIELMO:

Dear ladies, you deceive so many men
That, to tell you the honest truth,
If a lover complains of how you offend,
I sympathize with the poor youth.
Mind you, I love the fairest sex—
You know that, everyone knows,
Every day I am more henpecked
And my devotion to you overflows.
But then you deceive so many men,
I'm more depressed than you suppose.
A thousand times I've drawn my sword
To take your sacred honor's part.
A thousand times, with no reward,
With my might and, more, with my heart.
But then you deceive so many men,
You've made it a scandalous art.
Of course you are lovely and charming,
Heaven has given you its every treasure,
Your graces are downright disarming,
From head to toe a delicious pleasure.
But then you deceive so many men,
It's impossible quite to measure.
Mind you, I love the fairest sex,
You know I do.

(He leaves.)

Scena 9

FERRANDO SOLO, POI DON ALFONSO E GUILELMO CHE
PARLANO IN FONDO ETC.

Recitativo

FERRANDO: In qual fiero contrasto, in qual disordine di pensieri
e di affetti io mi ritrovo! Tanto insolito e novo è il caso mio, che
non altri, non io basto per consigliarmi ... Alfonso, Alfonso,
quanto rider vorrai della mia stupidezza! Ma mi vendicherò,
saprò dal seno cancellar quell'iniqua ... saprò cancellarla ...
Cancellarla? Troppo, oh dio, questo cor per lei mi parla!

N° 27 Cavatina

FERRANDO:
Tradito, schernito
dal perfido cor,
io sento che ancora
quest'alma l'adora,
io sento per essa
le voci d'amor.

(Qui capita Don Alfonso con Guilelmo e sta a sentire.)

Recitativo

DON ALFONSO: Bravo, questa è costanza!

FERRANDO: Andate, o barbaro! Per voi misero sono.

DON ALFONSO: Via, se sarete buono vi tornerò l'antica calma.
Udite: Fiordiligi a Guilelmo si conserva fedel, e Dorabella infedel
a voi fu.

FERRANDO: Per mia vergogna.

Scene 9

FERRANDO, ALONE, THEN DON ALFONSO AND GUGLIELMO,
CONVERSING IN THE BACKGROUND, ETC.

Recitative

FERRANDO: What a cruel conflict, what a tumult of thoughts and
feelings rages in me! This situation is so unusual, so new to me
that no one can help me, not even myself . . . Alfonso, Alfonso,
how you'll laugh at my stupidity! But I will be revenged. I will
banish that cruel woman from my heart, banish the very thought
of her! Banish? Oh God, my heart beats only for her.

Cavatina

FERRANDO:
Betrayed and scorned
By her wicked choice,
I feel my soul
Adores only her,
Only hears
Love's beckoning voice.

(Don Alfonso and Guglielmo, walking nearby, overhear him.)

Recitative

DON ALFONSO: Bravo! That's true love indeed!

FERRANDO: Go away, you merciless man. I am miserable because
of you.

DON ALFONSO: Come, come, if you're reasonable, I'll restore
your peace of mind. Listen to me. Fiordiligi has remained faithful
to Guglielmo, and Dorabella has been unfaithful to you.

FERRANDO: To my shame.

GUILELMO: Caro amico, bisogna far delle differenze in ogni cosa. Ti pare che una sposa mancar possa a un Guilelmo? Un picciol calcolo, non parlo per lodarmi, se facciamo tra noi … Tu vedi, amico, che un poco di più merto …

DON ALFONSO: Eh, anch'io lo dico!

GUILELMO: Intanto mi darete cinquanta zecchinetti.

DON ALFONSO: Volentieri. Pria però di pagar, vo' che facciamo qualche altra esperienza.

GUILELMO: Come!

DON ALFONSO: Abbiate pazienza, infin domani siete entrambi miei schiavi: a me voi deste parola da soldati di far quel ch'io dirò. Venite, io spero mostrarvi ben che folle è quel cervello che sulla frasca ancor vende l'uccello.
(Partono.)

Camera con diverse porte, specchio e tavolini.

Scena 10
DORABELLA, DESPINA E POI FIORDILIGI.

Recitativo
DESPINA: Ora vedo che siete una donna di garbo.

DORABELLA: Invan, Despina, di resister tentai: quel demonietto ha un artifizio, un'eloquenza, un tratto che ti fa cader giù se sei di sasso.

GUGLIELMO: My dear friend, one must make distinctions in every case. Do you think a bride-to-be could betray such a man as Guglielmo? Calculate the difference between us—I don't say this to boast—and you'll see that I have a bit more to offer . . .

DON ALFONSO: Ah, you've taken the words out of my mouth!

GUGLIELMO: Meanwhile, you owe me fifty guineas.

DON ALFONSO: Willingly. But before paying up, I want us to make one more experiment.

GUGLIELMO: What?

DON ALFONSO: Be patient. Until tomorrow you are both still my slaves. You gave me your word as soldiers that you would do whatever I ask. So come along now, I hope to show you how foolish it is to count your chickens before they're hatched. *(They leave.)*

A room with several doors, a mirror, and writing desks.

Scene 10
DORABELLA, DESPINA, AND THEN FIORDILIGI.

Recitative
DESPINA: Now I see that you are a woman of the world.

DORABELLA: I tried to resist him, Despina, but in vain. That little devil is so sly, so eloquent and flattering, that he could make a stone melt.

DESPINA: Corpo di satanasso, questo vuol dir saper! Tanto di raro noi povere ragazze abbiamo un po' di bene, che bisogna pigliarlo allorch'ei viene. *(Entra Fiordiligi.)* Ma ecco la sorella. Che ceffo!

FIORDILIGI: Sciagurate! Ecco per colpa vostra in che stato mi trovo!

DESPINA: Cosa è nato, cara madamigella?

DORABELLA: Hai qualche mal, sorella?

FIORDILIGI: Ho il diavolo che porti me, te, lei, Don Alfonso, i forastieri e quanti pazzi ha il mondo.

DORABELLA: Hai perduto il giudizio?

FIORDILIGI: Peggio, peggio … Inorridisci: io amo! E l'amor mio non è sol per Guilelmo.

DESPINA: Meglio, meglio!

DORABELLA: E che sì, che anche tu se' innamorata del galante biondino?

FIORDILIGI: *(sospirando)* Ah, purtroppo per noi!

DESPINA: Ma brava!

DORABELLA: Tieni settantamila baci: tu il biondino, io 'l brunetto, eccoci entrambe spose!

DESPINA: The very devil! Now you've learned a thing or two! It is so rare for us poor girls to be happy at all that we need to seize hold of it when it happens along. *(Fiordiligi enters.)* But here's your sister. What a long face!

FIORDILIGI: Wretched creatures! You are to blame for the state I'm in!

DESPINA: What's happened, dear madam?

DORABELLA: Is something wrong, sister?

FIORDILIGI: The devil take me, you, her, Don Alfonso, the suitors, and every other madman in the world.

DORABELLA: Have you lost your senses?

FIORDILIGI: Worse, worse than that. You'll be horrified. I'm in love. And that love is not only for Guglielmo.

DESPINA: So much the better!

DORABELLA: Have you really fallen in love with the fair-haired gallant?

FIORDILIGI: *(sighing)* Unfortunately for us both!

DESPINA: Congratulations!

DORABELLA: Here—seventy thousand kisses for you! You take the blond one, I'll take the dark one, and we'll both be brides!

FIORDILIGI: Cosa dici? Non pensi agli infelici che stamane partir? Ai loro pianti, alla lor fedeltà tu più non pensi? Così barbari sensi dove, dove apprendesti? Sì diversa da te come ti festi?

DORABELLA: Odimi: sei tu certa che non muoiano in guerra i nostri vecchi amanti? E allora entrambe resterem colle man piene di mosche: fra un ben certo e un incerto c'è sempre gran divario!

FIORDILIGI: E se poi torneranno?

DORABELLA: Se torneran, lor danno! Noi saremo allor mogli, noi saremo lontane mille miglia.

FIORDILIGI: Ma non so come mai si può cangiar in un sol giorno un core.

DORABELLA: Che domanda ridicola! Siam donne! E poi tu com'hai fatto?

FIORDILIGI: Io saprò vincermi.

DESPINA: Voi non saprete nulla.

FIORDILIGI: Farò che tu lo veda.

DORABELLA: Credi, sorella, è meglio che tu ceda.

N° 28 Aria

DORABELLA:
È Amore un ladroncello,
un serpentello è Amor,
che toglie e dà la pace,

FIORDILIGI: What are you saying? Have you no thought for those unhappy men who left this morning? No thought for their tears, their constancy? Wherever did you learn such wicked ways? How did you become so unlike yourself?

DORABELLA: Listen to me. You never know. Our old lovers might very well die in battle. And then we would both be left as helpless as flies. Better to choose the pleasant certainty than the unpleasant uncertainty.

FIORDILIGI: And what if they *do* come back?

DORABELLA: If they come back, so much the worse for them! We'll be married, and a thousand miles away.

FIORDILIGI: I don't understand how you can have had such a change of heart in a single day.

DORABELLA: What a silly question. We're women! And what have you been doing?

FIORDILIGI: I shall be able to control myself.

DESPINA: You'll do nothing of the sort.

FIORDILIGI: I will. You'll see.

DORABELLA: Believe me, dear sister, it would be best if you gave in.

Aria

DORABELLA:
Love is a little thief,
And acts like a little snake.
Oh, he can soothe our hearts

come gli piace, ai cor.
Per gli occhi al seno appena
un varco aprir si fa,
che l'anima incatena
e toglie libertà.
Porta dolcezza e gusto
se tu lo lasci far,
ma t'empie di disgusto
se tenti di pugnar.
Se nel tuo petto ei siede,
s'egli ti becca qui,
fa' tutto quel ch'ei chiede,
che anch'io farò così.
(Parte con Despina.)

Scena 11

FIORDILIGI SOLA; POI GUILELMO, FERRANDO
E DON ALFONSO CHE PASSANO SENZA ESSER VEDUTI;
INDI DESPINA.

Recitativo

FIORDILIGI: Come tutto congiura a sedurre il mio cor! Ma no ...
si mora e non si ceda ... Errai quando alla suora io mi scopersi
ed alla serva mia. Esse a lui diran tutto, ed ei, più audace, fia di
tutto capace ... Agli occhi miei mai più non comparisca ...
(Guilelmo sulla porta)
A tutti i servi minaccerò il congedo, se lo lascian passar ... Veder
nol voglio, quel seduttor.

GUILELMO: *(a Ferrando e Don Alfonso)* (Bravissima! La mia casta
Artemisia! La sentite?)

Or he can make them ache.
He has hardly shown you the way
To the heart through the eyes
Than he takes your freedom away
And has your soul as his prize.
He brings sweetness and delight
If you surrender to his sway.
But he laughs at your plight
If you try to keep him at bay.
If he settles in your breast,
If he takes a bite of you there,
Do everything at his behest.
And I will too, I swear.
(She leaves with Despina.)

Scene 11

FIORDILIGI, ALONE; THEN GUGLIELMO, FERRANDO, AND
DON ALFONSO, WHO PASS BY WITHOUT BEING SEEN;
LATER DESPINA.

Recitative

FIORDILIGI: How everything conspires to tempt my heart! But no . . . I would rather die than yield . . . I was wrong to reveal my feelings to my sister and my maid. They will tell it all to him, and he'll be bolder, capable of anything . . . May I never set eyes on him again . . .
(Guglielmo at the door)
I'll threaten the servants if they dare let him in . . . I do not wish to see that seducer!

GUGLIELMO: *(to Ferrando and Don Alfonso)* (Bravissima, my chaste goddess! Did you hear her?)

FIORDILIGI: Ma potria Dorabella senza saputa mia ... Piano ... un pensiero per la mente mi passa ... In casa mia restar molte uniformi di Guilelmo e Ferrando ... Ardir! ... Despina! Despina!

DESPINA: *(entrando)* Cosa c'è?

FIORDILIGI: Tieni un po' questa chiave, e senza replica, senza replica alcuna, prendi nel guardaroba e qui mi porta due spade, due cappelli e due vestiti de' nostri sposi.

DESPINA: E che volete fare?

FIORDILIGI: Vanne, non replicare!

DESPINA: (Comanda in abrégé, Donna Arroganza!)
(Parte.)

FIORDILIGI: Non c'è altro, ho speranza che Dorabella stessa seguirà il bell'esempio. Al campo, al campo! Altra strada non resta per serbarci innocenti.

DON ALFONSO: *(dalla porta a Despina)* (Ho capito abbastanza: vanne pur, non temer.)

DESPINA: *(ritornando, a Fiordiligi)* Eccomi.

FIORDILIGI: Vanne. Sei cavalli di posta voli un servo a ordinar ... Di' a Dorabella che parlar le vorrei ...

DESPINA: Sarà servita. (Questa donna mi par di senno uscita.)
(Parte.)

FIORDILIGI: But behind my back, Dorabella might even . . . Wait . . . I just had a thought . . . Guglielmo and Ferrando left a couple of their uniforms at my house . . . Courage! Despina! Despina!

DESPINA: *(entering)* What is it?

FIORDILIGI: Just take this key and don't ask any questions, not a single question. In the armoire you'll find two swords, two hats, and two uniforms belonging to our fiancés. Bring them to me.

DESPINA: What are you going to do?

FIORDILIGI: Go now. No questions.

DESPINA: (Lady Arrogance is barking.)
(She leaves.)

FIORDILIGI: There's nothing else for it. I only hope Dorabella will follow my good example. The battle is joined! There is no other way to preserve our innocence.

DON ALFONSO: *(from the door to Despina)* (I understand what she's up to. Go on, don't be scared.)

DESPINA: *(returning, to Fiordiligi)* Here I am.

FIORDILIGI: Go. Send a servant at once to order up six post-horses. And tell Dorabella that I wish to speak with her.

DESPINA: As you wish. (This woman seems out of her mind.)
(She leaves.)

Scena 12

FIORDILIGI, POI FERRANDO; INDI GUILELMO E DON
ALFONSO DALLA CAMERA ETC.

FIORDILIGI: L'abito di Ferrando sarà buono per me, può Dorabella prender quel di Guilelmo: in questi arnesi raggiungerem gli
sposi nostri, al loro fianco pugnar potremo e morir se fa d'uopo.
(Si cava quello che tiene in testa.) Ite in malora, ornamenti fatali! ...
Io vi detesto.

GUILELMO: (Si può dar un amor simile a questo?)

FIORDILIGI: Di tornar non sperate alla mia fronte pria ch'io
qui torni col mio ben. In vostro loco porrò questo cappello ...
Oh, come ei mi trasforma le sembianze e il viso! Come appena
io medesma or mi ravviso!

N° 29 Duetto

FIORDILIGI:
Fra gli amplessi in pochi istanti
giungerò del fido sposo,
sconosciuta a lui davanti
in quest'abito morrò.
Oh, che gioia il suo bel core
proverà nel ravvisarmi!

FERRANDO: *(entrando)*
Ed intanto di dolore
meschinello io mi morrò.

FIORDILIGI:
Cosa veggio! Son tradita!
Deh, partite ...

Scene 12

FIORDILIGI, THEN FERRANDO; LATER GUGLIELMO AND
DON ALFONSO AT THE DOOR, ETC.

FIORDILIGI: Ferrando's uniform will fit me just fine. Dorabella
can have Guglielmo's. In these disguises we can join our sweethearts, fight at their sides, and die if we must. *(She removes her
ornamental veil.)* Off with these stupid frills! I detest you!

GUGLIELMO: (Was there ever a love like this?)

FIORDILIGI: Don't hope to be seen on my head until I return
here with my beloved. In your place I'll put this hat . . . Oh, how
it transforms my face, my whole look! I hardly recognize myself!

Duet

FIORDILIGI:
I will be again, any minute now,
Back in the arms of my dear.
Unrecognized, and yet somehow
Standing before him in this gear.
Oh what joy will flood his heart
When he realizes who it is!

FERRANDO: *(entering)*
And meanwhile, I will die of sorrow,
A wretched creature.

FIORDILIGI:
What do I see? I am betrayed!
Leave me at once!

FERRANDO:

Ah no, mia vita!

(Prende la spada dal tavolino, la sfodera etc.)

Con quel ferro di tua mano

questo cor tu ferirai;

e se forza, oh dio, non hai

io la man ti reggerò.

FIORDILIGI:

Taci ... ahimè! Son abbastanza

tormentata ed infelice!

FIORDILIGI, FERRANDO:

Ah, che omai la mia costanza

a quei sguardi, a quel che dice

incomincia a vacillar!

FIORDILIGI: Sorgi, sorgi ...

FERRANDO: Invan lo credi.

FIORDILIGI:

Per pietà,

da me che chiedi?

FERRANDO: Il tuo cor o la mia morte.

FIORDILIGI: Ah, non son, non son più forte!

FERRANDO: *(le prende la mano e gliela bacia.)* Cedi, cara ...

FIORDILIGI: Dei, consiglio!

FERRANDO:
My love, my life! No, I pray!
(taking up a sword from the table and brandishing it)
Take this sword, and with your hand
Thrust it here, deep into my heart.
Oh God, if you cannot act the part,
I will hold your hand and guide it.

FIORDILIGI:
Enough! Be silent! I am filled
With torment and despair.

FIORDILIGI AND FERRANDO:
Ah, such constancy still
In her (his) glance, in her (his) words . . .
But it begins to falter.

FIORDILIGI: Rise, get up!

FERRANDO: You ask that uselessly.

FIORDILIGI:
For pity's sake,
What do you want of me?

FERRANDO: Your heart, or my death.

FIORDILIGI: Ah, I cannot catch my breath!

FERRANDO: *(taking her hand and kissing it)* Yield to me, my love.

FIORDILIGI: Oh, God help me!

FERRANDO: *(tenerissimamente)*
Volgi a me pietoso il ciglio!
In me sol trovar tu puoi
sposo, amante e più, se vuoi.
Idol mio, più non tardar.

FIORDILIGI: *(tremando)*
Giusto ciel! ... Crudel ... hai vinto:
fa' di me quel che ti par.

(Don Alfonso trattiene Guilelmo che vorria uscire.)

FIORDILIGI, FERRANDO:
Abbracciamci, o caro bene,
e un conforto a tante pene
sia languir di dolce affetto,
di diletto sospirar.
(Partono.)

Scena 13

GUILELMO, DON ALFONSO, POI FERRANDO.

Recitativo

GUILELMO: Oh poveretto me! Cosa ho veduto! Cosa ho sentito mai!

DON ALFONSO: Per carità, silenzio!

GUILELMO: Mi pelerei la barba! Mi graffierei la pelle! E darei colle corna entro le stelle! Fu quella Fiordiligi! La Penelope, l'Artemisia del secolo! Briccona! Assassina ... furfante ... ladra ... cagna ...

DON ALFONSO: Lasciamolo sfogar ...

FERRANDO: *(with great tenderness)*
Let there be pity in your glance.
Only in me will you find
The husband and lover for whom you've pined.
My beloved, why do you hesitate still?

FIORDILIGI: *(trembling)*
Merciful heaven! You are cruel and have conquered . . .
Do with me what you will.

(Don Alfonso restrains Guglielmo from bursting in.)

FIORDILIGI AND FERRANDO:
Embrace me, love, a caress.
Console me for my distress.
Let me languish in your love
And sigh, at last fulfilled.
(They leave.)

Scene 13
GUGLIELMO, DON ALFONSO, THEN FERRANDO.

Recitative

GUGLIELMO: Poor idiot, what have I seen? What have I been listening to?

DON ALFONSO: For goodness' sake, be quiet!

GUGLIELMO: I'll pluck out my beard, tear off my skin, charge at the stars with my cuckold's horns! That was Fiordiligi, the Penelope, the Diana of the age! That cheat, that murderess! Scoundrel! Thief! *Bitch!*

DON ALFONSO: One should let him rant on . . .

FERRANDO: *(entrando lieto)* Ebben?

GUILELMO: Dov'è?

FERRANDO: Chi? La tua Fiordiligi?

GUILELMO: La mia Fior … fior di diavolo che strozzi lei prima e dopo me!

FERRANDO: Tu vedi bene: v'han delle differenze in ogni cosa … *(ironicamente)* "Un poco di più merto … "

GUILELMO: Ah, cessa, cessa di tormentarmi, ed una via piuttosto studiam di castigarle sonoramente.

DON ALFONSO: Io so qual è: sposarle.

GUILELMO: Vorrei sposar piuttosto la barca di Caronte …

FERRANDO: … la grotta di Vulcano …

GUILELMO: … la porta dell'inferno.

DON ALFONSO: Dunque restate celibi in eterno.

FERRANDO: Mancheran forse donne ad uomin come noi?

DON ALFONSO: Non c'è abbondanza d'altro. Ma l'altre che faran, se ciò fer queste? In fondo voi le amate, queste vostre cornacchie spennacchiate.

GUILELMO: Ah purtroppo!

FERRANDO: Purtroppo!

FERRANDO: *(entering happily)* Well, well!

GUGLIELMO: Where is she?

FERRANDO: Who? Your Fiordiligi?

GUGLIELMO: My Fior— Fior-di-devilry! And may the devil strangle her first and then me!

FERRANDO: So you see, one must make distinctions in every case . . . *(ironically)* "A bit more to offer!"

GUGLIELMO: Stop! Stop tormenting me, and let's find a way to punish them for good.

DON ALFONSO: I know a way. Marry them.

GUGLIELMO: I'd rather marry Charon's rowboat.

FERRANDO: Vulcan's forge!

GUGLIELMO: The gate of Hell itself!

DON ALFONSO: Then stay single for eternity.

FERRANDO: Do you think men like us will ever want for women?

DON ALFONSO: There are plenty where they came from. But, if these two have behaved this way, what might the others do? Deep down you love them, these plucked crows of yours.

GUGLIELMO: Unfortunately.

FERRANDO: Sadly.

DON ALFONSO: Ebben pigliatele com'elle son. Natura non potea fare l'eccezione, il privilegio di creare due donne d'altra pasta per i vostri bei musi; in ogni cosa ci vuol filosofia. Venite meco: di combinar le cose studierem la maniera. Vo' che ancor questa sera doppie nozze si facciano. Frattanto un'ottava ascoltate . . . Felicissimi voi, se la imparate!

N° 30

Tutti accusan le donne, ed io le scuso
se mille volte al dì cangiano amore;
altri un vizio lo chiama ed altri un uso,
ed a me par necessità del core.
L'amante che si trova alfin deluso
non condanni l'altrui, ma il proprio errore;
giacché giovani, vecchie, e belle e brutte,
ripetetel con me: "co–sì fan tut–te!"

FERRANDO, DON ALFONSO, GUILELMO: "Co–sì fan tut–te!"

Scena 14
I SUDDETTI E DESPINA.

Recitativo

DESPINA: *(entrando)* Vittoria, padroncini! A sposarvi disposte son le care madame: a nome vostro loro io promisi che in tre giorni circa partiranno con voi; l'ordin mi diero di trovar un notaio che stipuli il contratto; alla lor camera attendendo vi stanno. Siete così contenti?

FERRANDO, DON ALFONSO, GUILELMO: Contentissimi.

DON ALFONSO: Well then, take them as they are. Nature couldn't make an exception or grant a privilege by creating two women of different stuff just to suit the likes of handsome chaps like you. You must be philosophical about everything. Come with me. Let's find a way to work things out. Before the day is done I think a double wedding is in order. Meanwhile, here's a little ditty you would do well to learn by heart.

Andante

Everyone blames women, everyone but me,
If they change their lovers twice a day.
Some call it a vice, others disagree.
I just shrug. Of course the heart will stray.
The lover who is sadly deceived in the end
Can't be surprised or pained or appalled.
Whether fair or foul, foe or friend—
Repeat after me: "Thus are they all!"

FERRANDO, DON ALFONSO, AND GUGLIELMO: Thus are they all!

Scene 14

THOSE BEFORE, AND DESPINA.

Recitative

DESPINA: *(entering)* Victory, my young masters! Your beloved ladies are willing to marry you. In your names I promised them that in three days they will leave with you. They instructed me to find a notary to draw up the marriage contract. They are waiting for you in their room. Are you satisfied?

FERRANDO, DON ALFONSO, AND GUGLIELMO: Perfectly satisfied.

DESPINA: Non è mai senza effetto quand'entra la Despina in un progetto.

(Partono.)

Sala ricchissima illuminata. Orchestra in fondo. Tavola per quattro persone con doppieri d'argento etc. Quattro servi riccamente vestiti.

Scena 15
DESPINA, POI DON ALFONSO. CORO DI SERVI
E DI SUONATORI.

N° 31 Finale

DESPINA:
Fate presto, o cari amici,
alle faci il foco date
e la mensa preparate
con ricchezza e nobiltà!
Delle nostre padroncine
gli imenei son già disposti.
(ai suonatori)
E voi gite ai vostri posti
finché i sposi vengon qua.

CORO DI SERVI E DI SUONATORI:
Facciam presto, o cari amici,
alle faci il foco diamo
e la mensa prepariamo
con ricchezza e nobiltà!

DON ALFONSO: *(entrando)*
Bravi, bravi! Ottimamente!
Che abbondanza, che eleganza!

DESPINA: When Despina puts her hand in things she always gets results.

(They leave.)

A hall richly decorated and illuminated. An orchestra at the back. A table set for four, with silver candelabra, etc. Four servingmen handsomely arrayed.

Scene 15

DESPINA, THEN DON ALFONSO. A CHORUS OF SERVANTS AND MUSICIANS.

Finale

DESPINA:
Be quick about it, my friends.
Make the candles glow,
Set the table just so,
Sumptuous but dignified.
Our dear mistresses—
Their wedding will amaze us.
(to the musicians)
Now take your proper places
Until the grooms have arrived.

CHORUS OF SERVANTS AND MUSICIANS:
Let's be quick about it, my friends.
Let's make the candles glow,
Let's set the table just so,
Sumptuous but dignified.

DON ALFONSO: *(entering)*
Well done! Well done! Excellent indeed!
Such a lavish spread! Such elegance!

(Mentre Don Alfonso canta, i suonatori accordano.)
Una mancia conveniente
l'un e l'altro a voi darà.
Le due coppie omai si avanzano.
Fate plauso al loro arrivo:
lieto canto e suon giulivo
empia il ciel d'ilarità!

DESPINA, DON ALFONSO: *(piano, partendo per diverse porte)*
La più bella commediola
non s'è vista o si vedrà!

Scena 16

I SUDDETTI, DORABELLA, GUILELMO, FIORDILIGI
E FERRANDO. MENTRE S'AVANZANO IL CORO CANTA,
E INCOMINCIA L'ORCHESTRA UNA MARCIA ETC.

CORO:
Benedetti i doppi coniugi
e le amabili sposine!
Splenda lor il ciel benefico,
ed a guisa di galline
sien di figli ognor prolifiche
che le agguaglino in beltà.

FIORDILIGI, DORABELLA, FERRANDO, GUILELMO:
Come par che qui prometta
tutto gioia e tutto amore!
Della cara Despinetta
certo il merito sarà.
Raddoppiate il lieto suono,
replicate il dolce canto,

(While Don Alfonso sings, the musicians play.)
There will be suitable tips
From both gentlemen, I'm sure.
The couples will soon be here.
Let your welcome be loud and long.
Let jubilant music and joyful song
Now fill the air with their gay allure.

DESPINA AND DON ALFONSO: *(softly, as they leave by different doors)*
Here's a comedy you will never forget or
Find one, old or new, that is any better.

Scene 16

THOSE BEFORE, DORABELLA, GUGLIELMO, FIORDILIGI, AND
FERRANDO. WHILE THEY ENTER, THE CHORUS SINGS,
AND THE ORCHESTRA PLAYS A MARCH, ETC.

CHORUS:
Blessed be these grooms
And their lovely brides!
May heaven smile on them,
And like roosters and hens
May they produce a brood
As beautiful as they are!

FIORDILIGI, DORABELLA, FERRANDO, AND GUGLIELMO:
How everything here promises
A perfect joy and love!
Our dear little Despina
Certainly deserves a reward.
Renew the enchanting sounds,
Sing the sweet song again,

e noi qui seggiamo intanto
in maggior giovialità.
(Gli sposi mangiano.)

CORO:
Benedetti i doppi coniugi
e le amabili sposine!
Splenda lor il ciel benefico,
ed a guisa di galline
sien di figli ognor prolifiche
che le agguaglino in beltà.

FERRANDO, GUILELMO:
Tutto, tutto, o vita mia,
al mio foco or ben risponde!

FIORDILIGI, DORABELLA:
Pel mio sangue l'allegria
cresce, cresce e si diffonde!

FERRANDO, GUILELMO: Sei pur bella!

FIORDILIGI, DORABELLA: Sei pur vago!

FERRANDO, GUILELMO: Che bei rai!

FIORDILIGI, DORABELLA: Che bella bocca!

FERRANDO, GUILELMO: *(toccando i bicchieri)* Tocca e bevi!

FIORDILIGI, DORABELLA: *(toccando i bicchieri)* Bevi e tocca!

And while they play we'll sit here
In the happiest of high spirits!
(The two couples eat.)

CHORUS:
Blessed be these grooms
And their lovely brides!
May heaven smile on them,
And like roosters and hens
May they produce a brood
As beautiful as they are!

FERRANDO AND GUGLIELMO:
Everything, everything, oh my beloved,
Now fulfills my desires.

FIORDILIGI AND DORABELLA:
The happiness runs through my blood,
Spreading, spreading like fire.

FERRANDO AND GUGLIELMO: You are so beautiful!

FIORDILIGI AND DORABELLA: You are so handsome!

FERRANDO AND GUGLIELMO: What lovely eyes!

FIORDILIGI AND DORABELLA: What delicious lips!

FERRANDO AND GUGLIELMO: *(raising their glasses)* Clink glasses and drink!

FIORDILIGI AND DORABELLA: *(raising their glasses)* Drink and clink!

FIORDILIGI, DORABELLA, FERRANDO:
E nel tuo, nel mio bicchiero
si sommerga ogni pensiero;
e non resti più memoria
del passato ai nostri cor.

GUILELMO: *(da sè)*
(Ah, bevessero del tossico
queste volpi senza onor!)

(Bevono.)

Scena 17
I SUDDETTI, DON ALFONSO, POI DESPINA
TRASVESTITA DA NOTAIO.

DON ALFONSO: *(entrando)*
Miei signori, tutto è fatto:
col contratto nuziale
il notaio è sulle scale
e ipso facto qui verrà.

FIORDILIGI, DORABELLA, FERRANDO, GUILELMO: Bravo,
bravo! Passi subito.

DON ALFONSO:
Vo' a chiamarlo ...
Eccolo qua.

DESPINA: *(entrando)*
Augurandovi ogni bene
il notaio Beccavivi
coll'usata a voi sen viene
notarile dignità;

FIORDILIGI, DORABELLA, AND FERRANDO:
In your glass and in mine,
Let every care be drowned,
And may no memory of the past
Remain now in our hearts.

GUGLIELMO: *(to himself)*
(Ah, if only it were poison they drank,
Those shameless little tarts!)

(They drink.)

Scene 17

THOSE BEFORE, DON ALFONSO, THEN DESPINA
DRESSED AS A NOTARY.

DON ALFONSO: *(entering)*
Gentlemen, everything is ready.
The notary is on the stairs,
The marriage contract in hand,
And *ipso facto* will be here.

FIORDILIGI, DORABELLA, FERRANDO, AND GUGLIELMO:
Bravo, bravo! Bring him in at once.

DON ALFONSO:
I will go call him.
—Here he is.

DESPINA: *(entering)*
With appropriate good wishes,
Notary Beccavivi
Stands here before you
In all his official dignity.

e il contratto stipulato
colle regole ordinarie
nelle forme giudiziarie,
pria tossendo, poi sedendo,
(pel naso)
clara voce leggerà.

FIORDILIGI, DORABELLA, FERRANDO, GUILELMO, DON ALFONSO: Bravo, bravo, in verità!

DESPINA: *(pel naso)*
Per contratto da me fatto
si congiunge in matrimonio
Fiordiligi con Sempronio,
e con Tizio Dorabella,
sua legittima sorella:
quelle, dame ferraresi;
questi, nobili albanesi;
e per dote e contradote ...

FIORDILIGI, DORABELLA, FERRANDO, GUILELMO, DON ALFONSO:
Cose note, cose note!
Vi crediamo, ci fidiamo,
soscriviam, date pur qua.

(Solamente le due donne sottoscrivono.)

DESPINA, DON ALFONSO: Bravi, bravi, in verità!

(La carta resta in man di Don Alfonso. Si sente gran suono di tamburo e canto.)

And the stipulated contract
With its usual regulations
In proper judicial form—
First coughing, then sitting down—
(in a nasal voice)
He will now read *clara voce.*

FIORDILIGI, DORABELLA, FERRANDO, GUGLIELMO, AND DON ALFONSO: Bravo, bravo indeed!

DESPINA: *(in a nasal voice)*
By this contract, drawn up by myself,
Are joined in matrimony
Fiordiligi with Sempronio
And with Tizio Dorabella,
Her legitimate sister,
The ladies being from Ferrara,
The gentlemen from Albania.
As for dowries and settlements . . .

FIORDILIGI, DORABELLA, FERRANDO, GUGLIELMO, AND DON ALFONSO:
Duly noted, duly noted.
We believe you, we trust you.
Give it here and we will sign.

(Only the two ladies sign.)

DESPINA AND DON ALFONSO: Bravo, bravo indeed!

(The contract remains in Don Alfonso's hand. The sound of a drum is heard.)

CORO: *(lontano)*
Bella vita militar!
Ogni dì si cangia loco,
oggi molto, doman poco,
ora in terra ed or sul mar.

FIORDILIGI, DORABELLA, FERRANDO, GUILELMO: Che romor,
che canto è questo?

DON ALFONSO:
State cheti, io vo a guardar.
(Va alla finestra.)
Misericordia! Numi del cielo!
Che caso orribile! Io tremo, io gelo!
Gli sposi vostri ...

FIORDILIGI, DORABELLA: Lo sposo mio ...

DON ALFONSO:
In questo istante tornano, oh dio ...
ed alla riva sbarcano già!

FIORDILIGI, DORABELLA, FERRANDO, GUILELMO:
Cosa mai sento! Barbare stelle!
In tal momento che si farà?

FIORDILIGI, DORABELLA: *(agli amanti)* Presto, partite!

(I servi portano via la tavola e i suonatori partono in furia.)

FERRANDO, GUILELMO: Ma se ci veggono?

CHORUS: *(offstage)*
The soldier's splendid lot!
Every day a change of scene.
Today is fat, tomorrow lean.
Sea or land, it's all gunshot.

FIORDILIGI, DORABELLA, FERRANDO, AND GUGLIELMO: What
is that commotion, that singing?

DON ALFONSO:
Stay calm. I'll go and see.
(He goes to the window.)
Oh mercy! Gods above!
What a dreadful situation!
I'm trembling, cold with fright!
Your fiancés . . .

FIORDILIGI AND DORABELLA: My fiancé . . .

DON ALFONSO:
. . . are returning this very instant. Oh God!
They are disembarking by the shore.

FIORDILIGI, DORABELLA, FERRANDO, AND GUGLIELMO:
What am I hearing! Cruel fate!
What is to be done at such a moment?

FIORDILIGI AND DORABELLA: *(to the lovers)* Quickly, go!

(The servants remove the table and the musicians hurriedly leave.)

FERRANDO AND GUGLIELMO: But if they see us . . .

DESPINA, DON ALFONSO: Ma se li veggono?

FIORDILIGI, DORABELLA: Presto, fuggite!

FERRANDO, GUILELMO: Ma se ci incontrano?

DESPINA, DON ALFONSO: Ma se li incontrano?

FIORDILIGI, DORABELLA: Là, là celatevi, per carità.

(Fiordiligi e Dorabella conducono i due amanti in una camera. Don Alfonso conduce la Despina in un'altra. Gli amanti escono non veduti e partono.)

FIORDILIGI, DORABELLA: Numi, soccorso!

DON ALFONSO: Rasserenatevi...

FIORDILIGI, DORABELLA: Numi, consiglio!

DON ALFONSO: Ritranquillatevi...

FIORDILIGI, DORABELLA: *(quasi frenetiche)* Chi dal periglio ci salverà? Chi?

DON ALFONSO: In me fidatevi: ben tutto andrà.

FIORDILIGI, DORABELLA:
Mille barbari pensieri
tormentando il cor mi vanno:
se discoprono l'inganno,
ah, di noi che mai sarà!

DESPINA AND DON ALFONSO: But if they see you . . .

FIORDILIGI AND DORABELLA: Quickly, flee!

FERRANDO AND GUGLIELMO: But if they meet us . . .

DESPINA AND DON ALFONSO: But if they meet you . . .

FIORDILIGI AND DORABELLA: There, over there, hide your-selves, for pity's sake!

(Fiordiligi and Dorabella lead their lovers into a room. Don Alfonso leads Despina into another room. The young men slip away unseen and leave.)

FIORDILIGI AND DORABELLA: Heaven help us!

DON ALFONSO: Calm yourselves.

FIORDILIGI AND DORABELLA: Oh God, advise us!

DON ALFONSO: Compose yourselves.

FIORDILIGI AND DORABELLA: *(nearly frantic)* Who will save us from this disaster? Who?

DON ALFONSO: Trust me. All will be well.

FIORDILIGI AND DORABELLA:
A thousand horrible thoughts
Are tormenting my heart.
Ah, what will become of us
If they discover our treachery?

Scena 18

FERRANDO, GUILELMO:
Sani e salvi agli amplessi amorosi
delle nostre fidissime amanti
ritorniamo di gioia esultanti
per dar premio alla lor fedeltà.

DON ALFONSO:
Giusti numi! Guilelmo, Ferrando!
Oh, che giubilo! Qui? Come? E quando?

FERRANDO, GUILELMO:
Richiamati da regio contrordine,
pieni il cor di contento e di gaudio,
ritorniamo alle spose adorabili,
ritorniamo alla vostra amistà.

GUILELMO: *(a Fiordiligi)* Ma cos'è quel pallor, quel silenzio?

FERRANDO: *(a Dorabella)* L'idol mio perché mesto si sta?

DON ALFONSO:
Dal diletto confuse ed attonite,
mute mute si restano là.

FIORDILIGI, DORABELLA:
(Ah, che al labbro le voci mi mancano:
se non moro un prodigio sarà!)

(I servi portano un baule.)

Scene 18

DORABELLA, FIORDILIGI, GUGLIELMO, AND FERRANDO
IN MILITARY UNIFORMS AND HATS. DESPINA IN
AN ADJOINING ROOM, AND DON ALFONSO.

FERRANDO AND GUGLIELMO:
We are home, safe and sound,
Full of joy and eager for the embrace
Of our faithful sweethearts,
To reward their constancy.

DON ALFONSO:
Good God! Guglielmo! Ferrando!
Oh, what joy! Here, but how? And when?

FERRANDO AND GUGLIELMO:
Suddenly recalled by royal orders,
Our hearts full of ease and cheer,
We return to our adorable sweethearts
And to your friendship so dear.

GUGLIELMO: *(to Fiordiligi)* But why so pale, so silent?

FERRANDO: *(to Dorabella)* My darling, why so sad?

DON ALFONSO:
Astonished and confused with delight,
They're tongue-tied . . . yes, struck dumb.

FIORDILIGI AND DORABELLA:
Ah, the words falter on my lips.
It will be a miracle if I'm not overcome.

(The servants bring in a trunk.)

GUILELMO:
Permettete che sia posto
quel baul in quella stanza.
Dei, che veggio! Un uom nascosto?
Un notaio! Qui che fa?

DESPINA: *(esce ma senza cappello.)*
No, signor, non è un notaio:
è Despina mascherata
che dal ballo or è tornata
e a spogliarsi venne qua.

FERRANDO, GUILELMO:
Una furba uguale a questa
dove mai si troverà?

DESPINA:
Una furba che m'agguagli
dove mai si troverà?

(Don Alfonso lascia cadere accortamente il contratto sottoscritto dalle donne.)

FIORDILIGI, DORABELLA:
La Despina! La Despina!
Non capisco come va.

DON ALFONSO: *(piano agli amanti)*
Già cader lasciai le carte:
raccoglietele con arte.

FERRANDO: Ma che carte sono queste?

GUGLIELMO:
Allow me to have this trunk
Placed in the room over there.
Good God, what's this? A man hidden in there?
A notary? What's he doing there?

DESPINA: *(emerging, but without her notary's hat)*
No, sir, it isn't a notary.
It's Despina in fancy dress.
I—I've just returned from a ball
And came in here to change.

FERRANDO AND GUGLIELMO:
Where could one ever find a girl
As clever as this one!

DESPINA:
Where could one ever find a girl
As clever as me!

(Don Alfonso shrewdly drops the marriage contract signed by the ladies.)

FIORDILIGI AND DORABELLA:
It's Despina! *Despina!*
I don't understand what's happening.

DON ALFONSO: *(softly, to the men)*
I've dropped the documents.
Pick them up as if by chance.

FERRANDO: What are these papers?

GUILELMO:
Un contratto nuziale?
Un contratto nuziale?

FERRANDO, GUILELMO: *(alle donne)*
Giusto ciel! Voi qui scriveste:
contraddirci omai non vale!
Tradimento, tradimento!
Ah, si faccia il scoprimento,
e a torrenti, a fiumi, a mari
indi il sangue scorrerà!

(Vanno per entrare nell'altra camera. Le donne li arrestano.)

FIORDILIGI, DORABELLA:
Ah signor, son rea di morte
e la morte io sol vi chiedo.
Il mio fallo tardi vedo:
con quel ferro un sen ferite
che non merita pietà!

FERRANDO, GUILELMO: Cosa fu?

FIORDILIGI: *(addita Despina e Don Alfonso.)*
Per noi favelli
il crudel, la seduttrice.

DON ALFONSO:
Troppo vero è quel che dice,
(Accenna la camera dov'erano entrati prima gli amanti.)
e la prova è chiusa lì.

GUGLIELMO:

A marriage contract?
A marriage contract?

FERRANDO AND GUGLIELMO: *(to the ladies)*

Good heavens! You've signed this.
There is no use in denying it.
Treachery! Treachery!
Now let's get to the bottom of this—
And then torrents, rivers, whole seas
Of blood will flow!

(As they go towards the other room, the ladies stop them.)

FIORDILIGI AND DORABELLA:

Oh sir, I am mortally guilty
And death is all I ask from you.
Too late do I see my error.
Plunge this sword into my breast
Which deserves no pity.

FERRANDO AND GUGLIELMO:

What have you done?

FIORDILIGI: *(pointing to Don Alfonso and Despina)*

Let them speak for us—
That cruel man and that temptress.

DON ALFONSO:

What they say is all too true
(He points to the room the young men had previously entered.)
And the proof is locked in there.

FIORDILIGI, DORABELLA:
Dal timor io gelo, io palpito:
perché mai li discoprì?

(Ferrando e Guilelmo entrano un momento in camera, poi sortono senza cappello, senza mantello e senza mustacchi, ma coll'abito finto etc. e burlano in modo ridicolo le amanti e Despina.)

FERRANDO: *(facendo dei complimenti affettati a Fiordiligi)*
A voi s'inchina, bella damina,
il cavaliere dell'Albania.

GUILELMO: *(a Dorabella)*
Il ritrattino pel coricino
ecco io le rendo, signora mia.

FERRANDO, GUILELMO: *(a Despina)*
Ed al magnetico signor dottore
rendo l'onore che meritò.

FIORDILIGI, DORABELLA, DESPINA: Stelle, che veggo!

FERRANDO, DON ALFONSO, GUILELMO: Son stupefatte!

FIORDILIGI, DORABELLA, DESPINA: Al duol non reggo!

FERRANDO, DON ALFONSO, GUILELMO: Son mezze matte!

FIORDILIGI, DORABELLA: *(accennando Don Alfonso)* Ecco là il barbaro che c'ingannò!

FIORDILIGI AND DORABELLA:
I am frozen with fear, trembling.
Why ever has he betrayed them?

(Ferrando and Guglielmo enter the room, then return without their hats, cloaks, or mustaches, but carrying their Albanian disguises, and joking with their sweethearts and Despina.)

FERRANDO: *(paying affected compliments to Fiordiligi)*
The knight of Albania
Now bows before you, fair lady!

GUGLIELMO: *(to Dorabella)*
A portrait in exchange for a heart,
Behold, I return it, my lady.

FERRANDO AND GUGLIELMO: *(to Despina)*
And to the magnetic doctor
I give the honor he deserves.

FIORDILIGI, DORABELLA, AND DESPINA: Heavens, I'm in disbelief.

FERRANDO, DON ALFONSO, AND GUGLIELMO: They're stupefied!

FIORDILIGI, DORABELLA, AND DESPINA: I cannot bear such grief.

FERRANDO, DON ALFONSO, AND GUGLIELMO: They're nearly wild-eyed . . .

FIORDILIGI AND DORABELLA: *(pointing to Don Alfonso)* There is the villain who deceived us.

DON ALFONSO:

V'ingannai, ma fu l'inganno
disinganno ai vostri amanti,
che più saggi omai saranno,
che faran quel ch'io vorrò.
(*Li unisce e li fa abbracciare.*)
Qua le destre: siete sposi.
Abbracciatevi e tacete.
Tutti quattro ora ridete,
ch'io già risi e riderò.

FIORDILIGI, DORABELLA:

Idol mio, se questo è vero,
colla fede e coll'amore
compensar saprò il tuo core,
adorarti ognor saprò.

FERRANDO, GUILELMO:

Te lo credo, gioia bella,
ma la prova io far non vo'.

DESPINA:

Io non so se veglio o sogno:
mi confondo, mi vergogno.
Manco mal, se a me l'han fatta,
che a molt'altri anch'io la fo.

FIORDILIGI, DORABELLA, DESPINA, FERRANDO, DON
ALFONSO, GUILELMO:

Fortunato l'uom che prende
ogni cosa pel buon verso,
e tra i casi e le vicende
da ragion guidar si fa.

DON ALFONSO:

I deceived you, yes, but the deception
Was meant to undeceive your lovers
And result in a little self-perception
And the impulse to do as I say.
(He brings the couples together and has them embrace.)
Join hands now, as husband and wife.
Embrace each other and silently smile.
The four of you should laugh at my guile,
As I have laughed and will laugh the night away.

FIORDILIGI AND DORABELLA:

My beloved, oh, if this is true,
With faithfulness and with love
I shall study how to ease your heart,
How better to adore you every day.

FERRANDO AND GUGLIELMO:

I believe it, my darling girl,
But don't want to test it straightway.

DESPINA:

I don't know if I am just dreaming.
I am confused, ashamed of my scheming.
At least, if this time they did me in,
With plenty of others I've had my way.

FIORDILIGI, DORABELLA, DESPINA, FERRANDO, DON ALFONSO, AND GUGLIELMO:

Happy is the man who looks
On the bright side of everything,
And in all circumstances and trials
Lets himself be guided by reason.

Quel che suole altrui far piangere
fia per lui cagion di riso,
e del mondo in mezzo ai turbini
bella calma troverà.

Fine dell'opera.

What only makes the others weep
Will be for him a source of joy,
And amid the storms of this world
He will find his peace in every season.

End of the Opera.

6

La Clemenza di Tito

LA CLEMENZA DI TITO

•

Opera seria, 1791

Libretto by Pietro Metastasio, adapted by Caterino Mazzolà

The Characters
Titus, emperor of Rome
Vitellia, daughter of the late emperor Vitellius
Sextus, friend of Titus, in love with Vitellia
Annius, friend of Sextus, in love with Servilia
Servilia, sister of Sextus, in love with Annius
Publius, counselor to Titus, prefect of the Praetorian Guard

Chorus

Setting: Rome

LITERATURE WITH A POLITICAL INTENTION IS A DAN-
gerous thing. The plot can turn into a tract, and characters into
symbols. *The Marriage of Figaro* can be read—and it certainly
has been played—as a political allegory, with the oppressed servant class seen as intelligent and energetic and the jaded upper
class seen as hypocritical and degenerate. But that opera's dramatic complexity and psychological depth blunt any reductive
attempt to turn it into a lecture on class warfare. This is certainly
less true of *La Clemenza di Tito*. It would be fair to say that,
despite its fascinating cast of characters and discerning portrait
of a troubled king, the opera's overt political intentions are clear.
Metastasio said he had conceived of the libretto as a "mirror for
princes," an historical parable offered to a contemporary king
not so that he could see what he was but see what he might
become. Quite deliberately the libretto explores the nature and
uses of royal power and the sources of true authority.

There was good reason to do so again in Prague in 1791. Before
succeeding his brother Joseph II—who, in both senses, patron-
ized Mozart—as Hapsburg monarch, Leopold II had been the
Grand Duke of Tuscany. In some ways, it was a career that paral-
leled that of Titus (which, coincidentally was his brother Joseph's
nickname). As a young man Leopold had been dissolute, but as
Grand Duke he proved to be an enlightened ruler. He instituted
reforms in public works and health, political rights, and taxation;
he also abolished torture and capital punishment. Having the

year before become Holy Roman Emperor, his accession now to the Bohemian throne gave real enthusiasm to those hopeful for a new humanitarianism. Whatever may have happened, it was not to be. Six months after his coronation and Mozart's opera, Leopold died at the age of forty-five.

Those critics who want to read the libretto as merely a chalk-board lesson have complained that its characters are no more than puppets, manipulated to make the point. On closer inspection, the characters are anything but. Vitellia is propelled by an ambition made manifest in its being thwarted. She is the dark shadow of the other noble characters. If Sextus is loyalty itself, she wants betrayal—of his moral bearings, of the Emperor's throne, and of her country's peace and order. Where Publius is cautious, she is reckless. Where Servilia is subservient, she is scheming. And Sextus—what of him? He is a lonely soul. A youth smitten with an older woman, he of course resembles Cherubino in *The Marriage of Figaro*, but without the wise Countess. His love for both Vitellia and Titus, though intense and conflicted, seems blind and passionless. Strangest of all, both submit themselves to imminent death—Sextus as a man of his word, Vitellia as a penitent. Titus cannot make up his mind about Sextus, and argues with himself. He loves Sextus more than he should, and is suspicious more than he need be. Yet he forgives Vitellia rather abruptly, even abstractly, without having explored the true history and dimension of her plot against him. Maybe now that he has decided to marry her—and in effect steal her from Sextus—he realizes instinctively that her treachery had all along been jealousy, her anger had been love. (One suspects, however, that after their wedding he will be forgiving her for other things.)

Far from being stick figures, these characters have an unexpected emotional complexity. The opera opens with Vitellia in haughty mid-accusation. Her jealous rage is apparent at once, and in the stormy duet that concludes the first scene, she is unrelenting, and can see nothing beyond the foreign princess whom Titus has favored. By contrast, in her aria at the end of the opera, she seems filled with a guilty self-knowledge; she imagines herself dragged to her execution before a jeering mob, and when she confesses to the Emperor, her tone is direct and measured, with the kind of natural dignity she seemed earlier to have abjured. And in the course of her changing, of her coming to realize the true consequences of love, there are scenes of extraordinary power. Scenes 10 and 11 of Act I—scenes in Metastasio's libretto that Voltaire particularly admired—are the equal of anything in opera. Vitellia has just dispatched Sextus to kill the Emperor, only to hear—just after he has gone—that the Emperor has chosen her for his bride. The reader can watch the cage close on her. Her mad aria is a wonder. And it is immediately followed by a scene with Sextus alone with his task and his conscience. His monologue is a masterpiece of anguished equivocation. "Unhappy Sextus, you are a traitor! . . . And whom do you betray? The greatest, the most just, the most merciful prince on this earth, to whom you owe all that you do, all that you are." A Freudian would want to make something else of Sextus's passion for an older woman who dominates him, and his betrayal of an older man whom he worships. Metastasio realized the strange tensions, the striking relationships, and didn't bother to pursue them to obvious ends. Instead, he keeps the drama taut with the unspoken.

La Clemenza di Tito was the favorite opera of Mozart's widow and of his first biographer, Franz Xaver Niemetschek. "The last scene or Finale of the first Act," he writes, "is certainly the most perfect of Mozart's works; expression, character, and feeling, all compete with one another to produce the greatest effect. The singing, instrumentation, variety of tone, and echo of distant choruses—at each performance these create an impression and illusion as is seldom apparent at operas." This finale continues to astonish. Rome has been set mysteriously afire. Sextus, who had been charged to set it, runs to save the man he was meant to kill. Annius, Servilia, and Publius are transfixed by the horror. Vitellia, terrified her plot will be revealed, rushes in to find

Sextus. Titus is missing. The screams of the citizenry are heard in the background. Suddenly Sextus returns to say he has seen Titus murdered—and is about to say why, when Vitellia silences him, and a final chorus sings of a world plunged into chaos. By contrast, for the end of Act II the same forces are arrayed— except this time Titus is among them, and changes everything. The scene opens just outside the grand arena where prisoners are about to be thrown to wild beasts—the kind of "justice" that Titus abhors. He forgives Sextus for a crime he did not commit, when Vitellia enters and makes her dramatic confession—only to be forgiven as well. Everyone's confusion now is the result, not of chaos and rumors in the city, but of munificence and social order. The chorus sings not of betrayal but of peace.

Forgiveness can be seen as the single most recurring theme in all of Mozart's operas, and it pulses through *Clemenza* from its very title to its final scene. Titus, of course, is its embodiment. His character combines self-sacrifice (giving up two brides— Berenice, whom he loved, and Servilia, whom he thought better for Rome) with farsightedness. He sees into the hearts of his friends and of his empire with a rare balance. He tolerates betrayal—though he is not unhurt by it—because he values friendship more than pride. He values the social fabric more than the individual, and thereby redeems both. Titus has been tried, but mastered himself, and it is that drama that is slowly, almost ritualistically, enacted, while around that slow transfor- mation passions swirl, bonds are broken, anarchy threatens. It is, finally, the sweet grandeur of music that mends, restores, and triumphs.

THE STORY

The story takes place during the reign of Titus Flavius Sabi- nus Vespanianus (40–81), who became Roman emperor in 79, following the death of his father, the popular Vespasian. As a young commander he had served in Britain and Germany, and continued his father's siege of Jerusalem until the city fell in 70. He lost favor because of his liaison with the Judean princess Berenice, sister of Herod Agrippa, whom he had moved into the royal palace. He finally sent her back, and on assuming the throne showed himself a peaceful and tolerant ruler. He ended the prosecutions for treason, banished informers, and was lenient to plotters. While he was visiting Pompeii when it was destroyed in 79, a great fire ravaged Rome for three days and he returned to bring relief. As Suetonius wrote in his *Lives of the Caesars*,

> With a degree of virtuous resolution unexampled in history, he had no sooner taken into his hands the entire reins of government, than he renounced every vicious attachment. Instead of wallowing in luxury, as before, he became a model of temperance; instead of cruelty, he displayed the strongest proofs of humanity and benevolence; and in the room of lewdness, he exhibited a transition to the most unblemished chastity and virtue. In a word, so sudden and great a change was never known in the character of mortal; and he had the peculiar glory to receive the appellation of "the darling and delight of mankind."

It is the year 79.

ACT I

Vitellia, the daughter of the hated Emperor Vitellius, who was deposed a decade earlier by the new emperor's father, Vespasian, is pacing back and forth in her room. She is with the Emperor's loyal friend Sextus, and is heatedly discussing the plot she has hatched. Enraged that Titus has decided to ignore her claims on his love and marry a foreign princess, Berenice, thereby defiling the imperial throne, she has persuaded Sextus and Lentulus to set fire to the Capitol. The ensuing riot, she is certain, will topple the new Emperor. Sextus pleads on Titus's behalf, singling out his nobility. When Vitellia angrily dismisses him as a coward, Sextus capitulates and agrees to carry out her plan. Even as he agrees, he is troubled. Annius, a trusted friend of Sextus, enters to report that Berenice has been sent away. Titus has bowed to the wishes of his people, and has summoned Sextus. Vitellia's hopes are secretly revived, and Sextus's faith in Titus is renewed. She insists that Sextus postpone the plot, and leaves. Alone, Annius begs Sextus to petition the Emperor for the hand of Servilia, Sextus's own sister and long the beloved of Annius, and Sextus agrees.

In a magnificent hall in the Roman Forum, the court has gathered, and the people sing a hymn in praise of the Emperor. Publius, Titus's counselor, announces that the Senate has designated the Emperor "The Father of Our Country" and lays its tribute at his feet. Graciously, Titus declares that he will use the treasure to help the citizens of Pompeii, recently devastated by the eruption of Vesuvius. The court is dismissed, and Titus asks Sextus and Annius to stay behind. He confides in them that he has decided it is proper that he marry a Roman, and he has chosen Servilia to be his bride. Annius and Sextus are overwhelmed with surprise. Seeing his friend speechless, Annius comes forward and praises Titus for his choice. The Emperor is pleased and tells him to take the news to Servilia himself, and pledges that he will do everything he can for Sextus, now that he is a part of the imperial family. Both men depart. Annius is left alone, battling with his feelings, when Servilia suddenly appears. She is astonished by the news he can barely bring himself to impart. Her new station cannot make them forget their old love.

Publius is presenting Titus with a document listing those who have been disloyal, but the Emperor refuses to bother with it. Servilia enters, and privately tells Titus of her love for Annius and her desire to obey the Emperor. Titus understands at once, and praises her honesty. When he leaves, Vitellia enters, ostensibly to offer her congratulations to Servilia. When Servilia has gone without revealing the truth, Vitellia rails against Titus for preferring any woman to her. Sextus comes in and she demands that he carry out her vengeful plot at once, and vows to give her hand to him if he succeeds. Still, he hesitates, and she scorns him. Finally, he decides to obey her, and rushes off. Publius enters to tell Vitellia that Titus is searching for her. She is torn. The Emperor is asking for her . . . and she has sent Sextus to instigate Titus's death. The scene shifts to the Capitol, where Sextus is battling with his conscience. His devotion to Vitellia is not as strong as his loyalty to Titus. But suddenly a fire breaks out. He hurries to save the Emperor's life, when Annius and Servilia enter and describe the chaos in the city, as the far-off screams of the people are heard. Vitellia next enters, searching for Sextus, wanting to stop him. Confusion mounts. Sextus returns to say he has witnessed Titus being slain, and is about to confess his role in the tragedy when Vitellia stops him. A great funeral dirge is taken up by everyone.

ACT II

At the imperial residence on the Palatine Hill Annius reassures Sextus that Titus was not killed after all. What he saw was someone dressed in the royal robes. Disconcerted but relieved, Sextus tells his friend that he was behind the whole plot, and he vows to go into exile. Instead, Annius urges him to redeem his standing and show his loyalty by going to Titus and confessing everything. Vitellia interrupts to insist he flee: if his secret is known, then her own guilt will be revealed. He swears he will die with the secret, but Vitellia is anxious that Titus's mercy will be worse than wrath and that Sextus will tell him too much. Flanked by the palace guards, Publius enters and demands Sextus surrender his sword. The man who was killed, he tells Sextus, was in fact the conspirator Lentulus, who told the truth. The Senate will put Sextus on trial. Vitellia is only worried about herself, and Sextus leaves for prison feeling betrayed by and yet still devoted to her.

At the palace, grateful citizens are hailing Titus and his miraculous escape from death. Publius insists he appear at the festival games to show the people of Rome that he is safe, but Titus, certain of Sextus's innocence, wants only to hear of the trial's outcome. Publius promises to fetch news, but is convinced the suspect will be found guilty. Annius brings word that Sextus has confessed his treachery to the Senate and been condemned to die. The Emperor is disheartened, and Annius begs that he show mercy. Left alone, Titus is at his desk, ready to sign the death warrant. He is torn between his sense of justice and his old friendship, and decides that he must let Sextus speak for himself. He sends for the prisoner, and broods on the weight of cares put upon a ruler. Sextus is brought in under guard and fearfully approaches the Emperor. Titus bids everyone withdraw, then asks Sextus how he could betray a friend. Sextus begs for death, but his tears move Titus, who questions him further. Sextus cannot bring himself to reveal Vitellia's plot, despite the Emperor's pleas, and he begs Titus to be his judge, not his friend. After he is taken away, Titus ponders why Sextus has scorned his clemency, and signs the death warrant. Immediately, he is wracked with his own guilt at shedding blood and tears up the document, saying, "Let my friend live, even though he is disloyal. If the world wishes to accuse me of mistakes, let it accuse me of mercy, not severity." He instructs Publius to have Sextus brought to the public arena. He leaves, and Vitellia runs in, calling Publius back, questioning him about what Sextus may have told Titus. She is certain Sextus has betrayed her. Servilia and Annius enter to beg her to plead with Titus for Sextus's life. And Annius tells her that the Emperor has decided to marry her—meaning that Sextus could not have betrayed her. Caught now in the maze of her own machinations, Vitellia realizes she must go to Titus herself and confess everything.

The scene changes to the entrance of the vast arena, where the conspirators can be seen, soon to have wild beasts fall upon them. The chorus praises Titus, who commands the criminal be brought before him, proclaiming that his fate has been decided. He is about to reveal it when Vitellia throws herself at his feet, saying that she has brought him the real perpetrator of the evil conspiracy. When Titus asks for his name, she says, "I am the guiltiest of all. I hatched the plot. I seduced your most loyal friend. I took advantage of his blind love in order to strike at you." Titus notes how the stars seem determined to make him cruel, but he forgives everyone, and all the characters are left to wonder at and to praise the extraordinary clemency of Titus.

THE BACKGROUND

Pietro Metastasio (1698–1782) was one of the greatest librettists in operatic history. He was born Pietro Antonio Domenico Trapassi in Rome. As a child he drew crowds by improvising verses, and attracted the attention of a rich jurist, Giovanni Vincenza Gravina, who eventually adopted him and changed his name to Metastasio. The word itself means "change," and it was just the right name for the man who changed opera by creating librettos with a dramatic urgency and poetic power unknown until his day. By the time he was twenty he was famous and rich, and began writing for the leading composers in Italy. In 1729, he was made the court poet in Vienna, where he remained for forty years. The librettos he wrote during this period achieved an incomparable fame. His 1734 libretto, *La Clemenza di Tito*, was first set by Antonio Caldara, and premiered in Vienna; it was later set over forty times by various composers. It has sources both in ancient writing, notably in Cassius Deo and Suetonius, and in French tragedy, especially Pierre Corneille (his 1641 *Cinna* and his 1670 *Tite et Bérénice*) and Jean Racine (his 1670 *Bérénice* and his 1667 *Andromaque*). Metastasio wrote it to be part of the name-day celebrations of Emperor Charles VI in 1734, and its account of political intrigue and imperial wisdom made it an appropriate choice when Mozart was commissioned in 1791 to write an opera to celebrate the coronation in Prague of the Hapsburg Emperor Leopold II as King of Bohemia. (He was, by the way, the grandson of Charles VI.) The impresario Domenico Guardasoni, who was charged to provide an *opera seria* for the occasion and had chosen Metastasio's libretto, first approached Antonio Salieri, who declined. He then went to Mozart, who was eager both to take advantage of Leopold's patronage and to write a form of opera he admired. Whether it was Guardasoni or Mozart who wanted the libretto revised we do not know, but Mozart himself wrote that he wanted it "reduced to a proper opera," and librettist Caterino Mazzolà (1745–1806) set about the task. He reduced the text by a third, changed it from three acts to two, and added lines of his own. Some commentators think that, in doing so, he distorted Metastasio's carefully calibrated dramaturgy and grave lyricism, yet it was he who arranged the stunning finale of Act I. Mozart wrote the opera in two months, over the summer of 1791, and finished it barely in time for its premiere on September 6. When he and his wife arrived in Prague on August 28 for rehearsals, he was still composing, and writing so quickly that he did not have time to devise the simple recitatives, which he left to his pupil Franz Xaver Süssmayr. The title role was sung by Antonio Baglioni, who had earlier created the role of Don Ottavio in *Don Giovanni*. An important singer in Italian houses, Maria Marchetti Fantozzi, sang Vitellia, and the castrato Domenico Bedini was Sextus. Carolina Perini was Annius, Gaetano Campi was Publius, and one Signora Antonini was Servilia. The premiere took place in the presence of the Emperor and his court at the elegant National Theater, where *Figaro* and *Don Giovanni* had triumphed. The next day, the Empress wrote to her daughter: "In the evening to the theater. The grand opera is not so grand, and the music very bad, so that almost all of us went to sleep. The coronation went marvelously." By the time of the last performance on September 30—ironically, the opening night of *The Magic Flute* in Vienna—audiences were enthusiastic. The opera fell out of favor in the nineteenth century, and has only returned to the active repertory in the last several decades.

Atto primo

Appartamenti di Vitellia.

Scena 1

VITELLIA E SESTO.

Recitativo

VITELLIA: Ma che? Sempre l'istesso, Sesto, a dir mi verrai? So che sedotto fu Lentulo da te, che i suoi seguaci son pronti già, che il Campidoglio acceso darà moto a un tumulto. Io tutto questo già mille volte udii, la mia vendetta mai non veggo però. S'aspetta forse che Tito a Berenice in faccia mia offra d'amor insano l'usurpato mio soglio e la sua mano? Parla, di': che s'attende?

SESTO: Oh dio!

VITELLIA: Sospiri?

SESTO: Pensaci meglio, o cara, pensaci meglio. Ah, non togliamo in Tito la sua delizia al mondo, il padre a Roma, l'amico a noi. Fra le memorie antiche trova l'egual, se puoi. Fingiti in mente eroe più generoso e più clemente. Parlagli di premiar: poveri a lui sembran gli erari suoi. Parlagli di punir: scuse al delitto cerca in ognun. Chi all'inesperta ei dona, chi alla canuta età. Risparmia in uno l'onor del sangue illustre, il basso stato compatisce

∴ Act I ∴

Vitellia's apartments.

Scene 1

VITELLIA AND SEXTUS.

Recitative

VITELLIA: What's this? Will you always be telling me the same thing, Sextus? I know that you have won over Lentulus, that his followers are ready, that setting the Capitol on fire will cause a riot. I have heard all this a thousand times, but I have yet to see my revenge. Perhaps you are waiting for Titus, besotted with love for Berenice, to offer her—before my very eyes—my usurped throne and his hand? Tell me, is that what you are waiting for?

SEXTUS: Oh God!

VITELLIA: You sigh?

SEXTUS: Think clearly, my love, think carefully. If we do away with Titus, we deprive the world of its favorite, Rome of its father, and ourselves of a friend. History cannot disclose a hero more generous or clement. If you speak to him of a reward, his treasury is not large enough. If you speak to him of punishment, he finds excuses for criminals. Some he forgives for their youth, others for their old age. One man is spared because of his noble

nell'altro. Inutil chiama, perduto il giorno ei dice in cui fatto non ha qualcun felice.

VITELLIA: Dunque a vantarmi in faccia venisti il mio nemico? E più non pensi che questo eroe clemente un soglio usurpa dal suo tolto al mio padre? Che mi ingannò, che mi sedusse—e questo è il suo fallo maggior—quasi ad amarlo? E poi—perfido! —, e poi di nuovo al Tebro richiamar Berenice! Una rivale avesse scelta almeno degna di me fra le beltà di Roma. Ma una barbara, Sesto, un'esule antepormi, una regina!

SESTO: Sai pur che Berenice volontaria tornò.

VITELLIA: Narra a' fanciulli codeste fole. Io so gli antichi amori, so le lacrime sparse allorché quindi l'altra volta partì, so come adesso l'accolse e l'onorò. Chi non lo vede? Il perfido l'adora.

SESTO: Ah principessa, tu sei gelosa!

VITELLIA: Io?

SESTO: Sì.

VITELLIA: Gelosa io sono, se non soffro un disprezzo?

SESTO: Eppur ...

VITELLIA: Eppure non hai cor d'acquistarmi.

SESTO: Io son ...

VITELLIA: Tu sei sciolto d'ogni promessa. A me non manca più degno esecutor dell'odio mio.

lineage, another for his lowly circumstances. He calls that day useless and lost if he has not made someone happy.

VITELLIA: So you have come to praise my enemy to my face? Have you forgotten that clement hero of yours sits on the throne he stole from my father? Deceived me, seduced me—oh, this is the worst thing—into almost loving him? And then—the traitor!—be brought Berenice back to the Tiber! At least he could have chosen a rival worthy of me from among the beauties of Rome. But a barbarian, Sextus . . . to prefer an exile, a queen, to *me*!

SEXTUS: But you know that Berenice returned of her own free will.

VITELLIA: Tell such nonsense to children. I know all about their old love. I know all about his tears when she left before. And I know that now he has received her again and honored her. Who has not seen it? That faithless man adores her.

SEXTUS: Ah! Princess, you are jealous.

VITELLIA: I?

SEXTUS: Yes.

VITELLIA: Am I jealous if I will not endure his contempt?

SEXTUS: And yet . . .

VITELLIA: And yet you do not have the heart to win me.

SEXTUS: I am . . .

VITELLIA: You are released from all your promises. I can find others who will carry out my hatred.

SESTO: Sentimi…

VITELLIA: Intesi assai.

SESTO: Fermati…

VITELLIA: Addio.

SESTO: Ah Vitellia, ah mio nume, non partir! Dove vai? Perdonami, ti credo, io m'ingannai.

N° 1 Duetto

SESTO:
Come ti piace imponi,
regola i moti miei:
il mio destin tu sei,
tutto farò per te.

VITELLIA:
Prima che il sol tramonti
estinto io vo' l'indegno:
sai ch'egli usurpa un regno
che in sorte il ciel mi diè.

SESTO: Già il tuo furor m'accende.

VITELLIA: Ebben, che più s'attende?

SESTO:
Un dolce sguardo almeno
sia premio alla mia fé.

VITELLIA, SESTO:
Fan mille affetti insieme
battaglia in me spietata:

SEXTUS: Listen to me!

VITELLIA: I have listened enough.

SEXTUS: Wait!

VITELLIA: Farewell.

SEXTUS: Ah, Vitellia, my goddess! Do not leave! Where are you going? Forgive me, I believe you. I was mistaken.

Duet

SEXTUS:
Command me as you please.
Control my every move.
My very fate you prove.
I will do anything for you.

VITELLIA:
Before the sun has set
I want that wretched man dead.
A kingdom that heaven said
Was mine, he stole to subdue.

SEXTUS: Already your rage has me aflame.

VITELLIA: And yet you delay, to your shame.

SEXTUS:
Give me, at least, one glance.
My faith will be renewed.

VITELLIA AND SEXTUS:
A thousand emotions
Are ruthlessly at war within me.

un'alma lacerata
più della mia non v'è.

Scena 2

ANNIO E DETTI.

Recitativo

ANNIO: Amico, il passo affretta: Cesare a sé ti chiama.

VITELLIA: Ah, non perdete questi brevi momenti! A Berenice
Tito li usurpa.

ANNIO: Ingiustamente oltraggi, Vitellia, il nostro eroe. Tito ha
l'impero e del mondo e di sé. Già per suo cenno Berenice partì.

SESTO: Come?

VITELLIA: Che dici?

ANNIO: Voi stupite a ragion. Roma ne piange di meraviglia e di
piacere. Io stesso quasi nol credo; ed io fui presente, o Vitellia,
al grande addio.

VITELLIA: (Oh speranze!)

SESTO: Oh virtù!

VITELLIA: Quella superba, oh, come volentieri udita avrei escla-
mar contro Tito!

ANNIO: Anzi, giammai più tenera non fu: partì, ma vide che
adorata partiva e che al suo caro men che a lei non costava il
colpo amaro.

A more conflicted soul you will never see,
Wounded through and through.

Scene 2

ANNIUS, AND THOSE BEFORE.

Recitative

ANNIUS: Hurry, my friend. Caesar summons you.

VITELLIA: Ah! Do not waste the few moments Titus is stealing from Berenice.

ANNIUS: Vitellia, you insult our hero unjustly. Titus is emperor both of the world and of himself. At his command Berenice has already gone.

SEXTUS: What!

VITELLIA: What are you saying?

ANNIUS: You are surprised at the news with good reason. Rome weeps at it with astonishment and pleasure. I can hardly believe it myself, and I was there, Vitellia, at their solemn leave-taking.

VITELLIA: (My hopes return!)

SEXTUS: What virtue!

VITELLIA: Oh, how gladly I would have liked to listen to that haughty woman berate Titus!

ANNIUS: But never was she more tender. True, she departed, but she saw that she was adored. She saw that their bitter parting cost her beloved no less than it did her.

VITELLIA: Ognun può lusingarsi.

ANNIO: Eh, si conobbe che bisognava a Tito tutto l'eroe per superar l'amante. Vinse, ma combatté; non era oppresso, ma tranquillo non era; ed in quel volto—dicasi per sua gloria—si vedea la battaglia e la vittoria.

VITELLIA: (Eppur forse con me, quanto credei, Tito ingrato non è.) Sesto, sospendi d'eseguire i miei cenni: il colpo ancora non è maturo.

SESTO: E tu non vuoi ch'io vegga ... ch'io mi lagni, o crudele! ...

VITELLIA: Or che vedesti? Di che ti puoi lagnar?

SESTO: Di nulla. (Oh dio! Chi provò mai tormento eguale al mio?)

N° 2 Aria

VITELLIA:
Deh, se piacer mi vuoi,
lascia i sospetti tuoi:
non mi stancar con questo
molesto dubitar.
Chi ciecamente crede
impegna a serbar fede,
chi sempre inganni aspetta
alletta ad ingannar.
(Parte.)

VITELLIA: Anyone can be mistaken.

ANNIUS: But everyone understood the necessity that Titus let the hero in him conquer the lover in him. Conquer he did, but not without a struggle. He was not overwhelmed, but neither was he at peace. On his face—be it said to his credit—were signs of both the battle and the victory.

VITELLIA:(Perhaps Titus is not so unmindful of me as I had thought.) Sextus, put off carrying out my order. The time is not yet ripe.

SEXTUS: You do not want me to see . . . or to complain, cruel woman!

VITELLIA: And what did you see? Of what can you complain?

SEXTUS: Nothing. (Oh God! Who has ever endured such torments as mine?)

Aria

VITELLIA:
You have no wish to please me.
You are suspicious just to tease me.
Give up your tiresome doubts
About me, now, at once.
He who blindly believes
Can never be deceived.
He who expects to be betrayed
Every day finds what he wants.
(She leaves.)

Scena 3

SESTO ED ANNIO.

Recitativo

ANNIO: Amico, ecco il momento di rendermi felice. All'amor mio
Servilia promettesti. Altro non manca che d'Augusto l'assenso.
Ora da lui impetrarlo potresti.

SESTO: Ogni tua brama, Annio, m'è legge. Impaziente anch'io
questo nuovo legame, Annio, desio.

N° 3 Duettino

SESTO, ANNIO:
Deh, prendi un dolce amplesso,
amico mio fedel,
e ognor per me lo stesso
ti serbi amico il ciel.
(*Partono.*)

*Parte del Foro Romano magnificamente adornato d'archi,
obelischi e trofei; in faccia aspetto esteriore del Campidoglio
e magnifica strada per cui vi si ascende.*

Scena 4

PUBLIO, SENATORI ROMANI E I LEGATI DELLE PROVINCIE
SOGGETTE, DESTINATI A PRESENTARE AL SENATO GLI
ANNUI IMPOSTI TRIBUTI. MENTRE TITO PRECEDUTO DA
LITTORI, SEGUITO DA PRETORIANI E CIRCONDATO DA
NUMEROSO POPOLO SCENDE DAL CAMPIDOGLIO, CANTASI
IL SEGUENTE CORO.

Scene 3

SEXTUS AND ANNIUS.

Recitative

ANNIUS: My friend, this is the time you can make me a happy man. You promised Servilia to me. Only the Emperor's consent remains. Now you could ask him for it.

SEXTUS: Your wish, Annius, is my command. I, too, am impatient for this new bond.

Brief Duet

SEXTUS AND ANNIUS:
Pray, accept this warm embrace,
My dear and ever faithful friend
And may it be, by heaven's grace,
That we be one, until the end.
(They leave.)

A part of the Roman Forum, magnificently adorned with arches, obelisks, and trophies; in the foreground the exterior of the Capitol and a grand street leading up to it.

Scene 4

PUBLIUS, ROMAN SENATORS, AND THE LEGATES OF SUBJUGATED PROVINCES WHO ARE TO PRESENT TO THE SENATE THEIR ANNUAL TRIBUTES. AS TITUS DESCENDS FROM THE CAPITOL, PRECEDED BY LICTORS, FOLLOWED BY PRAETORION GUARDS, AND SURROUNDED BY A LARGE CROWD, THE FOLLOWING IS SUNG.

N° 4 Marcia

N° 5 Coro

CORO:
Serbate, o dei custodi
della romana sorte,
in Tito il giusto, il forte,
l'onor di nostra età.

(Nel fine del coro suddetto Annio e Sesto da diverse parti.)

PUBLIO, ANNIO E TITO.

Recitativo

PUBLIO: *(a Tito)* Te della patria il padre oggi appella il senato, e mai più giusto non fu ne' suoi decreti, o invitto Augusto.

ANNIO: Né padre sol, ma sei suo nume tutelar. Più che mortale giacché altrui ti dimostri, a' voti altrui comincia ad avvezzarti. Eccelso tempio ti destina il senato, e là si vuole che fra divini onori anche il nume di Tito il Tebro adori.

PUBLIO: Quei tesori che vedi, delle serve province annui tributi, all'opra consagriam. Tito non sdegni questi del nostro amor pubblici segni.

TITO: Romani, unico oggetto è de' voti di Tito il vostro amore, ma il vostro amor non passi tanto i confini suoi che debbano arrossirne e Tito e voi. Quegli offerti tesori non ricuso però. Cambiarne solo l'uso pretendo. Udite. Oltre l'usato terribile il Vesevo ardenti fiumi dalle fauci eruttò, scosse le rupi, riempié di ruine i campi intorno e le città vicine. Le desolate genti fug-

March

Chorus

CHORUS:
O gods on high who guard
Our empire's destiny,
Preserve Rome's ancestry
In Titus, the just and strong.

(At the end of the chorus, Annius and Sextus enter from opposite sides.)

PUBLIUS, ANNIUS, AND TITUS.

Recitative

PUBLIUS: *(to Titus)* "The Father of Our Country" the Senate designates you today. Never has it been so just in its decrees, O invincible Emperor.

ANNIUS: Not only Father, but its tutelary deity as well. Because you prove yourself more than merely mortal, you must accustom yourself to the people's prayers. The Senate has dedicated a lofty temple to you, and wishes that Rome may worship you there among the other gods.

PUBLIUS: The treasures you see, the annual tribute of the subjugated provinces, are sanctioned for this work. Do not scorn, Titus, these signs of a city's love.

TITUS: Romans, the sole object of Titus's prayers is your love. But let not your love become so excessive that it embarrasses both Titus and yourselves. Still, I will not refuse the treasures you offer. But I shall put them to another use. Attend. Vesuvius has spewed up rivers of fire, with more than its usual fury, shaking the rocks and ruining the surrounding fields and towns. Desolated, the citizens have fled, but poverty oppresses those

gendo van, ma la miseria opprime quei che al foco avanzar. Serva quell'oro di tanti afflitti a riparar lo scempio. Questo, o romani, è fabbricarmi il tempio.

ANNIO: Oh vero eroe!

PUBLIO: Quanto di te minori tutti i premi son mai, tutte le lodi!

TITO: Basta, basta, o miei fidi. Sesto a me s'avvicini, Annio non parta. Ogn'altro s'allontani.

(Si ritirano tutti fuori dell'atrio, e vi rimangono Tito, Sesto ed Annio.)

N° 4 Marcia
ANNIO, SESTO E TITO.

Recitativo
ANNIO: (Adesso, o Sesto, parla per me.)

SESTO: Come, signor, potesti la tua bella regina …

TITO: Ah Sesto, amico, che terribil momento! Io non credei … Basta, ho vinto: partì. Tolgasi adesso a Roma ogni sospetto di vederla mia sposa. Una sua figlia vuol veder sul mio soglio, e appagarla convien. Giacché l'amore scelse invano i miei lacci, io vo' che almeno l'amicizia li scelga. Al tuo s'unisca, Sesto, il cesareo sangue. Oggi mia sposa sarà la tua germana.

SESTO: Servilia!

TITO: Appunto.

ANNIO: (Oh me infelice!)

spared by the flames. Let this gold serve to alleviate the suffering of so many afflicted people. This, Romans, is how to build a temple for me.

ANNIUS: Our true hero!

PUBLIUS: How much greater you are than any reward or praise!

TITUS: Enough, enough, my loyal subjects. Let Sextus approach. Annius, do not leave. All the others may withdraw.

(Everyone departs from the atrium, while Titus, Sextus, and Annius remain.)

March
ANNIUS, SEXTUS, AND TITUS.

Recitative
ANNIUS: (Now, Sextus, speak for me.)

SEXTUS: How, my lord, could you allow your lovely queen . . .

TITUS: Ah, Sextus, dear friend, what a terrible moment! I never thought . . . Enough! I conquered my desires, and she's gone. Now let Rome have no suspicion that she will be my wife. I want only one of Rome's own daughters to share my throne. That is my duty. Love chose my bond in vain, now friendship must choose it. My royal blood shall be joined with yours, Sextus. Today your sister shall be my wife.

SEXTUS: Servilia!

TITUS: Precisely.

ANNIUS: (Oh my unhappy fate!)

SESTO: (Oh dei! Annio è perduto.)

TITO: Udisti? Che dici? Non rispondi?

SESTO: E chi potrebbe risponderti, signor? M'opprime a segno la tua bontà che non ho cor ... Vorrei ...

ANNIO: (Sesto è in pena per me.)

TITO: Spiegati. Io tutto farò per tuo vantaggio.

SESTO: (Ah, si serva l'amico!)

ANNIO: (Annio, coraggio!)

SESTO: Tito ...

ANNIO: Augusto, conosco di Sesto il cor. Fin dalla cuna insieme tenero amor ne strinse. Ei, di sé stesso modesto estimator, teme che sembri sproporzionato il dono e non s'avvede ch'ogni distanza eguaglia d'un Cesare il favor. Ma tu consiglio da lui prender non dei. Come potresti sposa elegger più degna dell'impero e di te? Virtù, bellezza, tutto è in Servilia. Io le conobbi in volto ch'era nata a regnar. De' miei presagi l'adempimento è questo.

SESTO: (Annio parla così! Sogno o son desto?)

TITO: Ebben recane a lei, Annio, tu la novella. E tu mi segui, amato Sesto, e queste tue dubbiezze deponi. Avrai tal parte tu ancor nel soglio, e tanto t'innalzerò che resterà ben poco dello spazio infinito che frapposer gli dei fra Sesto e Tito.

SEXTUS: (Oh gods! Annius is lost!)

TITUS: Did you hear me? What do you have to say? Have you no reply?

SEXTUS: Who could answer you, my lord? Your goodness so overwhelms me that I do not have the heart to . . . I would like . . .

ANNIUS: (Sextus is tormented for my sake.)

TITUS: Explain yourself. I will do everything for your advantage.

SEXTUS: (Ah! I must help my friend.)

ANNIUS: (Courage, Annius.)

SEXTUS: Titus . . .

ANNIUS: Sire, I know Sextus's heart. Since the cradle, we have been bound together by a tender love. He has always underestimated himself, and now fears your generosity may seem too great. He does not see that the Emperor's favor levels all distinctions. But you must not listen to him. You could not have chosen a wife more worthy of the empire or yourself. Virtue, beauty, Servilia is blessed with everything. I could see in her face she was born to rule. This only confirms what I had foreseen.

SEXTUS: (Annius, what are you saying? Am I dreaming or awake?)

TITUS: Well then, you take her the news, Annius. And you, beloved Sextus, follow me. Put your doubts aside. You shall have a share in the throne yourself. I shall raise you so high that almost nothing will remain of the small space the gods have put between Sextus and Titus.

SESTO: Questo è troppo, o signor. Modera almeno, se ingrati non ci vuoi, modera, Augusto, i benefici tuoi.

TITO: Ma che, se mi negate che benefico io sia, che mi lasciate?

N° 6 Aria

TITO:
Del più sublime soglio
l'unico frutto è questo:
tutto è tormento il resto
e tutto è servitù.

Che avrei, se ancor perdessi
le sole ore felici
che ho nel giovar gli oppressi,
nel sollevar gli amici,
nel dispensar tesori
al merto e alla virtù?
(Parte con Sesto.)

Scena 5
ANNIO E POI SERVILIA.

Recitativo

ANNIO: Non ci pentiam. D'un generoso amante era questo il dover. Mio cor, deponi le tenerezze antiche. È tua sovrana chi fu l'idolo tuo. Cambiar conviene in rispetto l'amore. Eccola. Oh dei! Mai non parve sì bella agli occhi miei.

SERVILIA: Mio ben ...

ANNIO: Taci, Servilia. Ora è delitto il chiamarmi così.

SERVILIA: Perché?

SEXTUS: Too kind, my lord. If you do not wish us to be ungrateful, sire, at least modify your beneficence.

TITUS: What! If you deny me my generosity, what have I left?

Aria

TITUS:
From the most sublime of thrones
My single pleasure is this.
All the rest is an abyss,
All is slavery and pain.

What would I have if I lost
These, my only happy hours
In helping those star-crossed,
In using wisely my powers,
In passing out my riches
To those whom virtue has restrained?
(He leaves with Sextus.)

Scene 5
ANNIUS, THEN SERVILIA.

Recitative

ANNIUS: I must not have regrets. This was the duty of a generous lover. Put aside, my heart, your former love. She is now your Empress who was once your idol. Love must become respect. Here she is. Oh gods! She has never seemed so beautiful to my eyes.

SERVILIA: My love . . .

ANNIUS: Silence, Servilia. It is now a crime to call me that.

SERVILIA: Why?

ANNIO: Ti scelse Cesare (che martir!) per sua consorte. A te (morir mi sento), a te m'impose di recarne l'avviso (oh pena!), ed io ... io fui ... (parlar non posso ...) Augusta, addio!

SERVILIA: Come! Fermati. Io sposa di Cesare! E perché?

ANNIO: Perché non trova beltà, virtù che sia più degna d'un impero, anima ... Oh stelle! Che dirò? Lascia, Augusta, deh, lasciami partir.

SERVILIA: Così confusa abbandonar mi vuoi? Spiegati, dimmi: come fu? Per qual via? ...

ANNIO: Mi perdo, s'io non parto, anima mia.

N° 7 Duetto

ANNIO:
Ah, perdona al primo affetto
questo accento sconsigliato!
Colpa fu del labbro usato
a così chiamarti ognor.

SERVILIA:
Ah, tu fosti il primo oggetto
che finor fedel amai,
e tu l'ultimo sarai
ch'abbia nido in questo cor!

ANNIO: Cari accenti del mio bene!

SERVILIA: Oh mia dolce, cara speme!

ANNIUS: The Emperor has chosen you (this kills me!) as his consort. He has commanded me (I feel I am dying!) to bring you this news (oh grief!) and I . . . I was . . . (I cannot speak) . . . Empress, farewell!

SERVILIA: What! Stop! I the Emperor's wife? And why?

ANNIUS: Because he could not find elsewhere the beauty or virtue worthy of an empire, my dearest . . . Oh heavens! What can I say? Please, my Empress, allow me to leave.

SERVILIA: You cannot leave me in such confusion. Explain things, tell me—what happened? How did this . . .

ANNIUS: I am lost unless I leave, beloved.

Duet

ANNIUS:
Ah, forgive my former love
For the ill-chosen word.
My thoughtless lips have erred,
Accustomed to call you this.

SERVILIA:
Ah, you were sent from above,
The one I could adore.
There is only you, evermore,
Whom my heart would miss.

ANNIUS: Your words, my heartbeat.

SERVILIA: Oh, dear hope, my sweet.

SERVILIA, ANNIO:
Più che ascolto i sensi tuoi,
in me cresce più l'ardor.
Quando un alma è all'altra unita
qual piacere un cor risente!
Ah, si tronchi dalla vita
tutto quel che non è amor!
(Partono.)

Ritiro delizioso nel soggiorno imperiale sul Colle Palatino.

Scena 6

TITO E PUBLIO CON UN FOGLIO.

Recitativo

TITO: Che mi rechi in quel foglio?

PUBLIO: I nomi ei chiude de' rei che osar con temerari accenti de' Cesari già spenti la memoria oltraggiar.

TITO: Barbara inchiesta che agli estinti non giova e somministra mille strade alla frode d'insidiar gl'innocenti.

PUBLIO: Ma v'è, signor, chi lacerare ardisce anche il tuo nome.

TITO: E che perciò? Se 'l mosse leggerezza, nol curo; se follia, lo compiango; se ragion, gli son grato; e se in lui sono impeti di malizia, io gli perdono.

PUBLIO: Almen ...

ANNIUS AND SERVILIA:
The more I listen to you,
The more my ardor grows.
When souls are united so,
How the heart is thrilled!
All of life I would forgo,
Save for one lingering kiss.
(They leave.)

*A pleasant retreat in the imperial residence
on the Palatine Hill.*

Scene 6

TITUS AND PUBLIUS WITH A SHEET OF PAPER.

Recitative

TITUS: What is that document you have?

PUBLIUS: It lists the names of those guilty of having recklessly insulted the memory of former emperors.

TITUS: A barbarous inquiry which is useless to the dead and opens a thousand avenues for fraud to set a trap for the innocent.

PUBLIUS: But there is one, my lord, who has dared to insult even your name.

TITUS: What does that matter? If it causes laughter, I am indifferent. If foolishness, I pity him. If he is right, I am grateful. And if there are episodes of malice, I forgive him.

PUBLIUS: At least . . .

Scena 7

SERVILIA E DETTI.

Recitativo

SERVILIA: Di Tito al piè …

TITO: Servilia! Augusta!

SERVILIA: Ah signor, sì gran nome non darmi ancora! Odimi prima: io deggio palesarti un arcan.

TITO: Publio, ti scosta; ma non partir.

(Publio si ritira.)

SERVILIA: Che del cesareo alloro me fra tante più degne, generoso monarca, inviti a parte, è dono tal che desteria tumulto nel più stupido cor. Ma …

TITO: Parla.

SERVILIA: Il core, signor, non è più mio. Già da gran tempo Annio me lo rapì. Valor che basti non ho per obliarlo. Anche dal trono il solito sentiero farebbe a mio dispetto il mio pensiero. So che oppormi è delitto d'un Cesare al voler, ma tutto almeno sia noto al mio sovrano; poi, se mi vuol sua sposa, ecco la mano.

TITO: Grazie, o numi del ciel. Pur si ritrova chi s'avventuri a dispiacer col vero. Alla grandezza tua la propria pace Annio pospone! Tu ricusi un trono per essergli fedele! Ed io dovrei turbar fiamme sì belle? Ah, non produce sentimenti sì rei di Tito

Scene 7

SERVILIA, AND THOSE BEFORE.

Recitative

SERVILIA: At Titus's feet . . .

TITUS: Servilia! My Empress!

SERVILIA: Ah, my lord, do not bestow on me such a lofty title yet. First hear what I say. I must reveal a secret to you.

TITUS: Publius, stand back, but do not leave.

(Publius withdraws.)

SERVILIA: Most generous monarch, your choice of me from so many others more worthy of the imperial laurels is a gift that would waken trepidation in the most foolish of hearts . . .

TITUS: Speak.

SERVILIA: My lord, my heart is no longer mine. Annius stole it long ago. I have not the strength to forget him. Even on the throne my mind would wander back in spite of myself. I know it is a crime for me to oppose the Emperor's will, but at least now everything is known to my sovereign. If he still wants me as his wife, here is my hand.

TITUS: Heavenly gods be thanked! At last there is one who risks displeasing me with the truth. Annius has put your greatness before his own happiness, and you refuse a throne to remain faithful to him! Should I disrupt these noble passions? Ah! Titus's heart cannot entertain such unworthy sentiments. Banish

il core! Sgombra ogni tema. Io voglio stringer nodo sì degno, e n'abbia poi cittadini la patria eguali a voi.

SERVILIA: Oh Tito! Oh Augusto! Oh vera delizia de' mortali! Io non saprei come il grato mio cor ...

TITO: Se grata appieno esser mi vuoi, Servilia, agli altri inspira il tuo candor. Di pubblicar procura che grato a me si rende, più del falso che piace, il ver che offende.

N° 8 Aria

TITO:
Ah, se fosse intorno al trono
ogni cor così sincero,
non tormento un vasto impero,
ma saria felicità!

Non dovrebbero i regnanti
tollerar sì grave affanno
per distinguer dall'inganno
l'insidiata verità.
(Parte.)

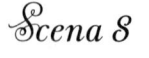Scena 8

SERVILIA, POI VITELLIA.

Recitativo

SERVILIA: Felice me!

VITELLIA: Posso alla mia sovrana offrir del mio rispetto i primi omaggi? Posso adorar quel volto per cui d'amor ferito ha perduto il riposo il cor di Tito?

your fears. I wish to tie a worthy knot. May our country always
have such citizens as you.

SERVILIA: O Titus! Emperor! True delight of mankind! I do not
know how my grateful heart . . .

TITUS: If you truly want to show me your gratitude, Servilia,
let your honesty inspire others. Let them know that I am more
grateful for the offensive truth than for the pleasing lie.

Aria

TITUS:
Ah, if round about a lofty throne,
Every heart were so sincere,
A vast empire would then appear
Not a torment but a delight.

Rulers should not have to suffer
The anxious moments they must
To distinguish those they can trust
From those who only seem right.
(He leaves.)

Scene 8

SERVILIA, THEN VITELLIA.

Recitative

SERVILIA: How happy I am!

VITELLIA: May I be the first to offer my sovereign my respects?
May I worship the face that has caused Titus's heart, wounded
with love, such restlessness?

SERVILIA: Non esser meco irata: forse la regia destra è a te serbata.

(Parte.)

Scena 9

VITELLIA, POI SESTO.

Recitativo

VITELLIA: Ancora mi schernisce? Questo soffrir degg'io vergognoso disprezzo? Ah, con qual fasto qui mi lascia costei! Barbaro Tito, ti parea dunque poco Berenice antepormi? Io dunque sono l'ultima de' viventi. Ah, trema, ingrato, trema d'avermi offesa! Oggi 'l tuo sangue ...

SESTO: Mia vita.

VITELLIA: Ebben, che rechi? Il Campidoglio è acceso? È incenerito? Lentulo dove sta? Tito è punito?

SESTO: Nulla intrapresi ancor.

VITELLIA: Nulla! E sì franco mi torni innanzi? E con qual merto ardisci di chiamarmi tua vita?

SESTO: È tuo comando il sospendere il colpo.

VITELLIA: E non udisti i miei novelli oltraggi? Un altro cenno aspetti ancor? Ma ch'io ti creda amante, dimmi, come pretendi, se così poco i miei pensieri intendi?

SESTO: Se una ragion potesse almen giustificarmi ...

SERVILIA: Do not be angry with me. Perhaps the imperial hand is destined for you.

(She leaves.)

Scene 9

VITELLIA, THEN SEXTUS.

Recitative

VITELLIA: Still she mocks me? Must I suffer her shameful contempt? With such pretense she left me here! Cruel Titus, was I merely a trifle for you to prefer Berenice to me? Am I the meanest of mortals? Ah, tremble, ungrateful man! Tremble for having insulted me! Today your blood . . .

SEXTUS: Dearest . . .

VITELLIA: And what is your news? Is the Capitol in flames? In ashes? Where is Lentulus? Has Titus been punished?

SEXTUS: I have undertaken nothing yet.

VITELLIA: Nothing! And you return to me so coolly? What right have you to call me your dearest?

SEXTUS: It was your command to defer the strike.

VITELLIA: Have you not heard of the latest outrages against me? Are you waiting for a second order? Tell me, how can you expect me to think of you as a lover when you cannot understand my thoughts?

SEXTUS: If one reason at least could justify my taking action . . .

VITELLIA: Una ragione! Mille n'avrai, qualunque sia l'affetto da cui prenda il tuo cor regola e moto. È la gloria il tuo voto? Io ti propongo la patria a liberar. Sei d'un illustre ambizion capace? Eccoti aperta una strada all'impero. Renderti fortunato può la mia mano? Corri, mi vendica, e son tua. D'altri stimoli hai d'uopo? Sappi che Tito amai, che del mio cor l'acquisto ei t'impedì, che se rimane in vita si può pentir, ch'io ritornar potrei—non mi fido di me—forse ad amarlo. Or va', se non ti move desio di gloria, ambizione, amore. Se tolleri un rivale che usurpò, che contrasta, che involarti potrà gli affetti miei, degli uomini 'l più vil dirò che sei.

SESTO: Quante vie d'assalirmi! Basta, basta, non più, già m'inspirasti, Vitellia, il tuo furore. Arder vedrai fra poco il Campidoglio, e quest'acciaro nel sen di Tito ... (Ah sommi dei! Qual gelo mi ricerca le vene ...)

VITELLIA: Ed or che pensi?

SESTO: Ah Vitellia!

VITELLIA: Il previdi che tu pentito già sei.

SESTO: Non son pentito, ma ...

VITELLIA: Non stancarmi più. Conosco, ingrato, che amor non hai per me. Folle ch'io fui! Già ti credea, già mi piacevi, e quasi cominciavo ad amarti. Agli occhi miei involati per sempre e scordati di me.

SESTO: Fermati! Io cedo, io già volo a servirti.

VITELLIA: One reason! You shall have a thousand, whatever emotions govern and drive your heart. Is it glory you seek? I bid you liberate your country. Are you capable of great ambition? I open before you a way to the throne. Can my hand in marriage make you happy? Hurry, avenge me, and I am yours. Do you need other incentives? Know that I loved Titus, that he prevented you from winning my heart, that if he remains alive I may relent and—I do not trust myself—come to love him again. Now go. If you are not spurred by a desire for glory, ambition, and love, if you can abide a rival who stole my affections, now opposes them, and will steal them again, then I say you are the most cowardly of men.

SEXTUS: You assail me from every side! Enough, no more! Your fury, Vitellia, has already inspired me. You will soon see the Capitol in flames, and this sword in Titus's breast . . . (Oh great gods! What a chill runs through my heart . . .)

VITELLIA: Now what are you brooding about?

SEXTUS: Ah, Vitellia!

VITELLIA: I expected this. You are already wavering.

SEXTUS: I am not wavering, but . . .

VITELLIA: Vex me no longer. I know, you ungrateful man, that you no longer love me. What a fool I was! I already believed you, already admired you, was even beginning to love you. Leave my sight forever. Forget me.

SEXTUS: Stop! I yield. I stand ready to serve you.

VITELLIA: Eh, non ti credo: m'ingannerai di nuovo. In mezzo all'opra ricorderai ...

SESTO: No, mi punisca Amore se penso ad ingannarti.

VITELLIA: Dunque corri! Che fai? Perché non parti?

N° 9 Aria

SESTO:
Parto; ma tu, ben mio,
meco ritorna in pace:
sarò qual più ti piace,
quel che vorrai farò.

Guardami, e tutto oblio
e a vendicarti io volo:
a questo sguardo solo
da me si penserà.
(Ah, qual poter—oh dei! –
donaste alla beltà.)
(Parte.)

Scena 10
VITELLIA, POI PUBLIO ED ANNIO.

Recitativo

VITELLIA: Vedrai, Tito, vedrai che alfin sì vile questo volto non è. Basta a sedurti gli amici almen, se ad invaghirti è poco. Ti pentirai ...

PUBLIO: Tu qui, Vitellia? Ah, corri! Va Tito alle tue stanze.

VITELLIA: I do not believe you. You will only deceive me again. In the midst of your mission you will remember . . .

SEXTUS: No. May Love punish me if I think of deceiving you.

VITELLIA: Hurry then! What are you doing? Why are you not leaving?

Aria

SEXTUS:
I go, but, my beloved, please
Make peace with me again.
I shall be entirely yours, then.
I will do what you desire.

One look, and all memories flee.
I will rush to revenge your wrongs,
And your glance, knowing it belongs
To me alone, is all I will require.
Oh, what power, dear gods,
Have you given beauty to inspire!
(He leaves.)

Scene 10

VITELLIA, THEN PUBLIUS AND ANNIUS.

Recitative

VITELLIA: One day, Titus, you will see that my face is not so distasteful. If it cannot charm you, at least it can seduce your friends. You will regret . . .

PUBLIUS: You here, Vitellia? Ah, hurry now, Titus is on his way to your apartments.

ANNIO: Vitellia, il passo affretta. Cesare di te cerca.

VITELLIA: Cesare!

PUBLIO: Ancor nol sai? Sua consorte t'elesse.

ANNIO: Tu sei la nostra Augusta, ed il primo omaggio già da noi ti si rende.

PUBLIO: Ah principessa, andiam: Cesare attende.

N° 10 Terzetto

VITELLIA:
Vengo ... aspettate ... Sesto ...
Ahimè! ... Sesto! ... È partito? ...
Oh sdegno mio funesto!
Oh insano mio furor!
Che angustia! Che tormento!
lo gelo—oh dio!—d'orror.

ANNIO, PUBLIO:
Oh, come un gran contento,
come confonde un cor!

(Partono.)

ANNIUS: Vitellia, do not delay. The Emperor is looking for you.

VITELLIA: The Emperor!

PUBLIUS: Do you not know? He has chosen you as his consort.

ANNIUS: You are our Empress, and we are the first to pay you homage.

PUBLIUS: Ah, Princess, let us go. The Emperor is waiting.

Trio

VITELLIA:
I am coming . . . Wait . . . Sextus! . . .
Alas! . . . Sextus! . . . Has he gone? . . .
Oh, what will my fatal anger foment!
Oh, my fury was a terror!
What anguish! What torment!
Oh God! I freeze with horror.

ANNIUS AND PUBLIUS:
Oh, how a great happiness
Can lead a heart into error!

(They leave.)

Campidoglio come prima.

Scena 11

SESTO SOLO, INDI ANNIO, POI SERVILIA, PUBLIO,
VITELLIA DA DIVERSE PARTI.

N° 11 Recitativo accompagnato

SESTO: Oh Dei, che smania è questa! Che tumulto ho nel cor!
Palpito, agghiaccio, m'incammino, m'arresto; ogn'aura, ogn'ombra mi fa tremare. Io non credea che fosse sì difficile impresa
esser malvagio. Ma compierla convien. Almen si vada con valore
a perir. Valore! E come può averne un traditor? Sesto infelice!
Tu traditor! Che orribil nome! Eppure t'affretti a meritarlo. E
chi tradisci? Il più grande, il più giusto, il più clemente principe
della terra, a cui tu devi quanto puoi, quanto sei. Bella mercede
gli rendi invero! Ei t'innalzò per farti il carnefice suo. M'inghiotta il suolo prima ch'io tal divenga. Ah, non ho core, Vitellia, a secondar gli sdegni tuoi! Morrei prima del colpo in faccia a
lui. S'impedisca … *(Si desta nel Campidoglio un incendio che a poco
a poco va crescendo.)* Ma come, arde già il Campidoglio? Un gran
tumulto io sento d'armi e d'armati: ahi, tardo è il pentimento!

N° 12 Quintetto con coro

SESTO:
Deh, conservate, o dei,
a Roma il suo splendor,
o almeno i giorni miei
coi suoi troncate ancor.

ANNIO: Amico, dove vai?

The Capitol, as before.

Scene 11

SEXTUS, ALONE, THEN ANNIUS AND LATER SERVILIA,
PUBLIUS, AND VITELLIA FROM DIFFERENT DIRECTIONS.

Accompanied Recitative

SEXTUS: O gods, what is the frenzy? What is this turmoil in my heart? I tremble. I freeze. I make a start, then stop. Every breeze, every shadow, makes me quiver. I never realized how difficult it would be to commit an evil act. But it must be done. Let me at least die courageously. Courage? How can a traitor have that? Unhappy Sextus, you are a traitor! What a horrible word! Yet you plunge into deserving it. And whom do you betray? The greatest, the most just, the most merciful prince on this earth, to whom you owe all that you do, all that you are. And you repay him like this! He has raised you up so that you may be his executioner. May the ground swallow me before I become that. Oh, Vitellia, I do not have the heart to carry out your wrath. I would rather die than strike a blow at him. *(A fire breaks out in the Capitol and slowly spreads.)* It must be stopped . . . what? The Capitol is on fire. I can hear a great din of soldiers and weapons. Alas, regret comes too late.

Quintet with Chorus

SEXTUS:
Gods on high, preserve
His glory and Rome's,
Or at least, as I deserve,
Let his last day be my own.

ANNIUS: Friend, where are you going now?

SESTO: Io vado ... Lo saprai
– oh dio!—per mio rossor.
(Ascende frettoloso nel Campidoglio.)

Scena 12

ANNIO:
Io Sesto non intendo ...
Ma qui Servilia viene.

SERVILIA: Ah, che tumulto orrendo!

ANNIO: Fuggi di qua, mio bene.

SERVILIA:
Si teme che l'incendio
non sia dal caso nato,
ma con peggior disegno
ad arte suscitato.

CORO IN DISTANZA: Ah! ...

PUBLIO:
V'è in Roma una congiura;
per Tito, ahimè, pavento.
Di questo tradimento
chi mai sarà l'autor?

CORO: Ah! ...

SERVILIA, ANNIO, PUBLIO: Le grida, ahimè, ch'io sento ...

CORO: Ah! ...

SEXTUS: I am going . . . you soon will know,
Oh God, by the shame I bemoan.
(Rapidly he enters the Capitol.)

Scene 12

ANNIUS:
What is this he is trying to say?
But now my dear Servilia is near.

SERVILIA: The horrid uproar of this fray!

ANNIUS: Beloved, fly at once from here.

SERVILIA:
It is feared that this fire
Did not start by accident.
Who wants Rome to be a pyre
Did so with evil intent.

CHORUS *(in the distance)*: Ah . . .

PUBLIUS:
There is a conspiracy afoot.
It is for Titus that I fear.
Someone, it will appear,
Is behind this traitorous plot.

CHORUS: Ah! . . .

SERVILIA, ANNIUS, AND PUBLIUS: Alas, the awful screams I hear . . .

CHORUS: Ah! . . .

SERVILIA, ANNIO, PUBLIO: ... mi fan gelar d'orror.

(Vitellia entra.)

CORO: Ah! ...

Scena 13

VITELLIA:
Chi per pietade—oh dio! –
m'addita dov'è Sesto?
(In odio a me son io
ed ho di me terror.)

SERVILIA, ANNIO, PUBLIO:
Di questo tradimento
chi mai sarà l'autor?

CORO: Ah! ... Ah! ...

SERVILIA, ANNIO, PUBLIO, VITELLIA: Le grida, ahimè, ch'io
sento ...

CORO: Ah! ... Ah! ...

SERVILIA, ANNIO, PUBLIO, VITELLIA: ... mi fan gelar d'orror.

CORO: Ah! ... Ah! ...

SERVILIA, ANNIUS, AND PUBLIUS: . . . freeze me in horror to this spot.

(Vitellia enters.)

CHORUS: Ah! . . .

Scene 13

VITELLIA:
Good God! Who will pity me
And say where Sextus is?
(I hate myself unmercifully
And am tied in terror's knot.)

SERVILIA, ANNIUS, AND PUBLIUS:
Someone, it will appear,
Is behind this traitorous plot.

CHORUS: Ah! . . . Ah! . . .

SERVILIA, ANNIUS, PUBLIUS, AND VITELLIA: Alas, the awful screams I hear . . .

CHORUS: Ah! . . . Ah! . . .

SERVILIA, ANNIUS, PUBLIUS, AND VITELLIA: . . . freeze me in horror to this spot.

CHORUS: Ah! . . . Ah! . . .

Scena 14

SESTO: *(scende dal Campidoglio)*
(Ah, dove mai m'ascondo?
Apriti, o terra, inghiottimi,
e nel tuo sen profondo
rinserra un traditor.)

VITELLIA: Sesto! ...

SESTO: Da me che vuoi?

VITELLIA: Quai sguardi vibri intorno? ...

SESTO: Mi fa terror il giorno.

VITELLIA: Tito? ...

SESTO:
La nobil alma
versò dal sen trafitto.

SERVILIA, ANNIO, PUBLIO:
Qual destra rea macchiarsi
poté d'un tal delitto?

SESTO:
Fu l'uom più scellerato,
l'orror della natura,
fu ...

VITELLIA:
Taci, forsennato:
ah, non ti palesar!

Scene 14

SEXTUS: *(coming from the Capitol)*
(Wherever now can I hide?
Open, O earth, and swallow me!
In your depths let this parricide
Sink in sorrow and rot.)

VITELLIA: Sextus!

SEXTUS: What do you want of me?

VITELLIA: Why that frantic look in your eyes?

SEXTUS: It is the day's horror I recognize.

VITELLIA: Titus? . . .

SEXTUS:
His noble soul
Fled from his wounded breast.

SERVILIA, ANNIUS, AND PUBLIUS:
What guilty hand now is stained
With the gore of such criminal excess?

SEXTUS:
It was the most villainous of men,
The horror of nature has slain . . .
It was . . . it was . . .

VITELLIA:
Silence, madman.
Do not give yourself away.

VITELLIA E SERVILIA, SESTO ED ANNIO, PUBLIO:
Ah, dunque l'astro è spento
di pace apportator!

VITELLIA E SERVILIA, SESTO ED ANNIO, PUBLIO, CORO IN LONTANANZA:
Oh nero tradimento,
oh giorno di dolor!

Fine dell'atto primo.

VITELLIA, SERVILIA, SEXTUS, ANNIUS, AND PUBLIUS:
Oh, extinguished is the light
That brought the world its peace.

**VITELLIA, SERVILIA, SEXTUS, ANNIUS, PUBLIUS, AND
CHORUS IN THE DISTANCE:**
The betrayal plunges us into night,
Into sorrow without cease.

End of Act I.

Atto secondo

*Ritiro delizioso nel soggiorno imperiale
sul Colle Palatino.*

Scena 1

ANNIO E SESTO.

Recitativo

ANNIO: Sesto, come tu credi, Augusto non perì. Calma il tuo duolo: in questo punto ei torna illeso dal tumulto.

SESTO: Eh, tu m'inganni. Io stesso lo mirai cader trafitto da scellerato acciaro.

ANNIO: Dove?

SESTO: Nel varco angusto onde si ascende quinci presso al Tarpeo.

ANNIO: No, travedesti tra il fumo e tra il tumulto. Altri Tito ti parve.

SESTO: Altri! E chi mai delle cesaree vesti ardirebbe adornarsi? Il sacro alloro, l'augusto ammanto ...

Act II

A pleasant retreat in the imperial residence on the Palatine Hill.

Scene 1

ANNIUS AND SEXTUS.

Recitative

ANNIUS: Sextus, the Emperor did not die, as you believed. Calm your grief. He has just now returned unharmed from the turmoil.

SEXTUS: Ah, you are deceiving me. I myself saw him fall wounded by the treacherous sword.

ANNIUS: Where?

SEXTUS: In the narrow passage that leads from here to the Tarpeian Rock.

ANNIUS: No, you were mistaken. In all the smoke and confusion, you thought someone else was Titus.

SEXTUS: Someone else? What other man would dare to wear the imperial robes? The sacred laurel, the royal mantle . . .

ANNIO: Ogni argomento è vano. Vive Tito ed è illeso. In questo istante io da lui mi divido.

SESTO: Oh dei pietosi! Oh caro prence! Oh dolce amico! Ah, lascia che a questo sen ... Ma non m'inganni? ...

ANNIO: Io merto sì poca fé? Dunque tu stesso a lui corri e 'l vedrai.

SESTO: Ch'io mi presenti a Tito dopo averlo tradito?

ANNIO: Tu lo tradisti?

SESTO: Io del tumulto, io sono il primo autor.

ANNIO: Come! Perché?

SESTO: Non posso dirti di più.

ANNIO: Sesto è infedele!

SESTO: Amico, m'ha perduto un istante. Addio. M'involo alla patria per sempre. Ricordati di me. Tito difendi da nuove insidie. Io vo ramingo, afflitto a pianger fra le selve il mio delitto.

ANNIO: Fermati. Oh dei! Pensiamo ... Incolpan molti di questo incendio il caso, e la congiura non è certa finora ...

SESTO: Ebben, che vuoi?

ANNIO: Che tu non parta ancora.

ANNIUS: You argue in vain. Titus is alive and unharmed. I left him only a moment ago.

SEXTUS: Oh merciful gods! Oh dear prince! Oh sweet friend! Oh, let me embrace you . . . You are not deceiving me?

ANNIUS: Do I deserve so little faith? Hurry to him and see for yourself.

SEXTUS: Can I appear before Titus after having betrayed him?

ANNIUS: You betrayed him?

SEXTUS: I . . . I was the instigator of all the chaos.

ANNIUS: What! Why?

SEXTUS: I cannot tell you any more.

ANNIUS: Sextus . . . disloyal!

SEXTUS: My friend, in an instant I was lost. Farewell! I am leaving my country forever. Remember me. Defend Titus from fresh intrigues. I will wander the forests, cursed and lamenting my crime.

ANNIUS: Wait! Oh gods! Let us think . . . Many people think the fire was an accident, and no conspiracy has yet been proved . . .

SEXTUS: What are you suggesting?

ANNIUS: That you not leave yet.

N° 13 Aria

ANNIO:
Torna di Tito a lato:
torna e l'error passato
con replicate emenda
prove di fedeltà.

L'acerbo tuo dolore
è segno manifesto
che di virtù nel core
l'immagine ti sta.
(Parte.)

Scena 2

SESTO, POI VITELLIA.

Recitativo

SESTO: Partir deggio o restar? Io non ho mente per distinguer consigli.

VITELLIA: Sesto, fuggi, conserva la tua vita e 'l mio onor. Tu sei perduto, se alcun ti scopre; e se scoperto sei, pubblico è il mio segreto.

SESTO: In questo seno sepolto resterà. Nessuno il seppe. Tacendolo morrò.

VITELLIA: Mi fiderei, se minor tenerezza per Tito in te vedessi. Il suo rigore non temo già, la sua clemenza io temo: questa ti vincerà.

Aria

ANNIUS:
Stand again at Titus's side.
Put aside your grieving pride.
If you show your loyalty,
Your honor is redeemed.

Your sorrow's bitter pain
Is far the clearest of signs
That virtue still remains
In your heart's esteem.
(He leaves.)

Scene 2

SEXTUS, THEN VITELLIA.

Recitative

SEXTUS: Should I go or stay? My mind is torn.

VITELLIA: Flee, Sextus, save your life and my honor. You are lost if anyone discovers you, and if you are discovered, my secret is known.

SEXTUS: It is buried in my breast. No one has known about it, and I will die concealing it.

VITELLIA: I would trust you if I saw less affection for Titus in you. I no longer fear his wrath. I fear his mercy. That is what will defeat you.

Scena 3

PUBLIO CON GUARDIE, E DETTI.

Recitativo

PUBLIO: Sesto.

SESTO: Che chiedi?

PUBLIO: La tua spada.

SESTO: E perché?

PUBLIO: Colui che cinto delle spoglie regali agli occhi tuoi cadde trafitto al suolo, ed ingannato dall'apparenza tu credesti Tito, era Lentulo: il colpo la vita a lui non tolse. Il resto intendi. Vieni.

VITELLIA: (Oh colpo fatale!)

SESTO: *(dà la spada)* Alfin, tiranna . . .

PUBLIO: Sesto, partir conviene. È già raccolto per udirti il senato, e non poss'io differir di condurti.

SESTO: Ingrata, addio.

Scene 3

PUBLIUS WITH GUARDS, AND THOSE BEFORE.

Recitative

PUBLIUS: Sextus!

SEXTUS: What do you want?

PUBLIUS: Your sword.

SEXTUS: And why?

PUBLIUS: The man you saw dressed in royal robes, who fell to the ground and who, misled by his appearance, you thought was Titus, was in fact Lentulus. He survived the attack. You know the rest. Come.

VITELLIA: (Oh fatal blow!)

SEXTUS: *(giving up his sword)* At last, you heartless woman . . .

PUBLIUS: Sextus, we must go. The Senate has already convened to hear your case, and I can brook no delay in escorting you there.

SEXTUS: Ungrateful woman, farewell!

Scena 4

DETTI.

N° 14 Terzetto

SESTO:
Se al volto mai ti senti
lieve aura che s'aggiri,
gli estremi miei sospiri
quell'alito sarà.

VITELLIA:
(Per me vien tratto a morte.
Ah, dove mai m'ascondo?
Fra poco noto al mondo
il fallo mio sarà.)

PUBLIO: Vieni ...

SESTO: *(a Publio)* Ti seguo ... *(a Vitellia)* Addio.

VITELLIA: *(a Sesto)* Senti ... Mi perdo, oh dio!
(a Publio) Che crudeltà!

SESTO: *(a Vitellia, in atto di partire)*
Rammenta chi t'adora
in questo stato ancora.
Mercede al mio dolore
sia almen la tua pietà.

VITELLIA:
(Mi laceran il core
rimorso, orror, spavento!
Quel che nell'alma io sento
di duol morir mi fa.)

Scene 4

THOSE BEFORE.

Trio

SEXTUS:

If you ever feel a breeze
Play around your face,
My breath is in that embrace,
The last sigh of my life.

VITELLIA:

(For me he is led to death.
Wherever can I hide?
Too soon, and far and wide,
Word of my crime will be rife.)

PUBLIUS: Come . . .

SEXTUS: *(to Publius)* I follow . . . *(to Vitellia)* Until we meet.

VITELLIA: *(to Sextus)* Listen . . . I am lost . . . Oh bittersweet . . .
(to Publius) In my heart this knife!

SEXTUS: *(to Vitellia, in the act of leaving)*
Remember who adores you still,
Even in this dreadful plight.
At least let your pity requite
And be recompense for my grief.

VITELLIA:

(My heart is cruelly torn
By remorse and horror and fear!
With all this suffering so near,
My soul finds no relief.)

PUBLIO:

(L'acerbo amaro pianto,
che da suoi lumi piove,
l'anima mi commove,
ma vana è la pietà.)

(Publio e Sesto partono con le guardie, e Vitellia dalla parte opposta.)

*Gran sala destinata alle pubbliche udienze.
Trono, sedia e tavolino.*

Scena 5

TITO, PUBLIO, PATRIZI, PRETORIANI E POPOLO.

N° 15 Coro

CORO:

Ah, grazie si rendano
al sommo fattor
che in Tito del trono
salvò lo splendor.

TITO:

Ah no, sventurato
non sono cotanto,
se in Roma il mio fato
si trova compianto,
se voti per Tito
si formano ancor.

CORO:

Ah, grazie si rendano
al sommo fattor

PUBLIUS:

(The hot and harrowing tears
That fall so from his eyes
Strike my spirit with no surprise,
But pity now is like disbelief.)

(Publius and Sextus depart with the guards, while Vitellia leaves in the
opposite direction.)

A great hall used for public audiences. Throne, chair, and writing desk.

Scene 5
TITUS, PUBLIUS, PATRICIANS,
PRAETORIAN GUARDS, AND CITIZENS.

Chorus

CHORUS:

To the Almighty Creator
Let our gratitude be known.
He has kept safe, in Titus,
The glory of the Roman throne.

TITUS:

Ah no, I am not
So unfortunate
If my earthly lot
In Rome's estimate
Finds some favor.
On high your prayers have flown.

CHORUS:

To the Almighty Creator
Let our gratitude be known.

che in Tito del trono
salvò lo splendor.

PUBLIO, TITO.

Recitativo

PUBLIO: Già de' pubblici giochi, signor, l'ora trascorre. Il dì solenne sai che non soffre il trascurarli. È tutto colà d'intorno alla festiva arena il popolo raccolto, e non s'attende che la presenza tua. Ciascun sospira dopo il noto periglio di rivederti salvo. Alla tua Roma non differir sì bel contento.

TITO: Andremo, Publio, fra poco. Io non avrei riposo, se di Sesto il destino pria non sapessi. Avrà il senato omai le sue discolpe udite; avrà scoperto, vedrai, ch'egli è innocente; e non dovrebbe tardar molto l'avviso.

PUBLIO: Ah, troppo chiaro Lentulo favellò!

TITO: Lentulo forse cerca al fallo un compagno per averlo al perdono. Ei non ignora quanto Sesto m'è caro. Arte comune questa è de' rei. Pur dal senato ancora non torna alcun. Che mai sarà? Va', chiedi: che si fa, che si attende? Io voglio tutto saper pria di partir.

PUBLIO: Vado, ma temo di non tornar nunzio felice.

TITO: E puoi creder Sesto infedele? Io dal mio core il suo misuro, e un impossibil parmi ch'egli m'abbia tradito.

PUBLIO: Ma signor, non han tutti il cor di Tito.

He has kept safe, in Titus,
The glory of the Roman throne.

PUBLIUS AND TITUS.

Recitative

PUBLIUS: The hour for the public games, sire, is fast approaching. You know this solemn day must not be neglected. The people have gathered in the festival arena, and only your presence is missing. Everyone longs to see that you are safe, now that they know that your life was in danger. Do not deny Rome that satisfaction.

TITUS: We shall go soon, Publius. But I will not rest until I first know the fate of Sextus. By now the Senate will have heard his defense, and be certain—as I am—of his innocence. The verdict cannot be delayed much longer.

PUBLIUS: Ah, Lentulus spoke all too directly.

TITUS: Lentulus perhaps seeks to name an accomplice in the crime in order to secure his own pardon. He is not unaware of how dear Sextus is to me. Still, no one has yet returned from the Senate. What can this mean? Go, ask what is happening, what they are waiting for. I want to know everything before I set off.

PUBLIUS: I go, but I fear I will not return with happy news.

TITUS: Do you believe Sextus is disloyal? I take the measure of his heart by my own. It seems impossible to me that he has betrayed me.

PUBLIUS: But, my lord, not everyone has the heart of a Titus.

N° 16 Aria

PUBLIO:
Tardi s'avvede
d'un tradimento
chi mai di fede
mancar non sa.

Un cor verace,
pieno d'onore,
non è portento,
se ogn'altro core
crede incapace
d'infedeltà.
(Parte.)

Scena 6
TITO, POI ANNIO.

Recitativo

TITO: No, così scellerato il mio Sesto non credo. Io l'ho veduto non sol fido ed amico, ma tenero per me. Tanto cambiarsi un'alma non potrebbe. Annio, che rechi? L'innocenza di Sesto? Consolami.

ANNIO: Signor, pietà per lui ad implorar io vengo.

Scena 7
DETTI, PUBLIO CON FOGLIO.

Recitativo

PUBLIO: Cesare, nol diss'io? Sesto è l'autore della trama crudel.

TITO: Publio, ed è vero?

Aria

PUBLIUS:
Too late, alas, is betrayal
Known to that man
Who has never been disloyal,
Nor failed in his largesse.

No one is surprised
If a true heart,
Full of piety,
Believes all men start
With hearts also prized
For faithfulness.
(He leaves.)

Scene 6

TITUS, THEN ANNIUS.

Recitative

TITUS: No, I refuse to believe Sextus is a wicked man. I have seen in him not only loyalty and friendship but also affection for me. No soul could change overnight. Annius, what news? Sextus has been found innocent? Bring me some comfort.

ANNIUS: My lord, I come to beg pity for him.

Scene 7

THOSE BEFORE, PUBLIUS WITH A DOCUMENT.

Recitative

PUBLIUS: Sire, did I not say so? Sextus is the instigator of this vile plot.

TITUS: Publius, is it true?

PUBLIO: Purtroppo. Ei di sua bocca tutto affermò. Co' complici il senato alle fiere il condanna. Ecco il decreto terribile, ma giusto; *(Dà il foglio a Tito.)* né vi manca, o signor, che il nome Augusto.

TITO: *(si getta a sedere.)* Onnipossenti dei!

ANNIO: *(inginocchiandosi)* Ah pietoso monarca ...

TITO: Annio, per ora lasciami in pace.

PUBLIO: Alla gran pompa unite sai che le genti omai ...

TITO: Lo so. Partite.

ANNIO: Deh, perdona s'io parlo in favor d'un insano. Della mia cara sposa egli è germano.

N° 17 Aria

ANNIO:
Tu fosti tradito,
ei degno è di morte;
ma il core di Tito
pur lascia sperar.

Deh, prendi consiglio,
signor, dal tuo core;
il nostro dolore
ti degna mirar.

(Publio ed Annio partono.)

PUBLIUS: Sadly, words from his own mouth confirmed everything. The Senate has condemned him and his accomplices to be thrown to the wild beasts. Here is the harsh but just decree. *(He hands the document to Titus.)* It lacks only the royal signature, sire.

TITUS: *(throwing himself into a chair)* All-powerful gods!

ANNIUS: *(kneeling)* Ah, merciful monarch . . .

TITUS: Annius, leave me in peace for now.

PUBLIUS: As you know the people are gathered for the solemnities . . .

TITUS: I know. Leave me.

ANNIUS: Forgive me in I speak in a madman's favor. He is the brother of my dear bride.

Aria

ANNIUS:
Sire, you have been betrayed,
And he is worthy of death.
But in your heart there may
Still be hope's faint gleam.

Look inward, my lord.
Consult your generous heart.
Deign to consider the part.
Mercy may play in the scheme.

(Publius and Annius leave.)

Scena 8

TITO SOLO A SEDERE.

Recitativo accompagnato

TITO: Che orror! Che tradimento! Che nera infedeltà! Fingersi amico, essermi sempre al fianco, ogni momento esiger dal mio core qualche prova d'amore, e starmi intanto preparando la morte! Ed io sospendo ancor la pena? E la sentenza ancora non segno? ... Ah sì, lo scellerato mora. *(Prende la penna per sottoscrivere e poi s'arresta.)* Mora ... Ma senza udirlo mando Sesto a morir? Sì, già l'intese abbastanza il senato. E s'egli avesse qualche arcano a svelarmi? *(Depone la penna, intanto esce una guardia.)* (Olà.) S'ascolti, e poi vada al supplicio. (A me si guidi Sesto.) *(La guardia parte.)* È pur di chi regna infelice il destino! A noi si nega ciò che a' più bassi è dato. In mezzo al bosco quel villanel mendico, a cui circonda ruvida lana il rozzo fianco, a cui è mal fido riparo dall'ingiurie del ciel tugurio informe, placido i sonni dorme, passa tranquillo i dì. Molto non brama; sa chi l'odia e chi l'ama; unito o solo torna sicuro alla foresta, al monte; e vede il core a ciascheduno in fronte. Noi fra tante ricchezze sempre incerti viviam, ché in faccia a noi la speranza o il timore sulla fronte d'ognun trasforma il core. Chi dall'infido amico *(chiamando verso il fondo)* (olà), chi mai questo temer dovea?

Scena 9

TITO E PUBLIO.

Recitativo

TITO: Ma Publio, ancora Sesto non viene?

PUBLIO: Ad eseguire il cenno già volaro i custodi.

Scene 8

TITUS, ALONE AND SEATED.

Accompanied Recitative

TITUS: What horror! What treachery! What black infidelity! To pretend to be my friend, always at my side, always asking my heart for tokens of its love, and the whole time plotting my murder! And still I have delayed the punishment? Still not signed the sentence? *(He takes up the quill to sign, but then stops.)* Yes, let the evil man die! Die . . . Send Sextus to his death without hearing his side? Well, the Senate has already heard enough. Yet what if he should have a secret to divulge only to me? *(He puts down the quill as a guard appears.)* (You there!) I shall hear him, and then let him go to his death. (Bring Sextus to me.) *(The guard leaves.)* How unhappy is the lot of those who rule! We are denied what is given to the lowliest of men. In the midst of the forest any wretched peasant, his scabby body clad in coarse wool, his squalid hut a shaky shelter from the ravages of the heavens, sleeps soundly and peacefully, and passes his days without fear. He has few desires, knows who loves and who hates him. In company or alone, he walks in safety to his forest or mountain, and sees each man's heart mirrored in his face. We, amid all this splendor, live in uncertainty. In our presence, hope or fear changes a man's face. Why from a faithless friend . . . *(He calls out behind him.)* (Ho!) . . . have I now to fear this?

Scene 9

TITUS AND PUBLIUS.

Recitative

TITUS: But Publius, Sextus has still not come.

PUBLIUS: The guards are hurrying to carry out your order.

TITO: Io non comprendo un sì lungo tardar.

PUBLIO: Pochi momenti sono scorsi, o signor.

TITO: Vanne tu stesso, affrettalo.

PUBLIO: Ubbidisco ... I tuoi littori veggonsi comparir. Sesto dovrebbe non molto esser lontano. Eccolo.

TITO: Ingrato! All'udir che s'appressa già mi parla a suo pro l'affetto antico. Ma no, trovi il suo prence e non l'amico.

Scena 10

TITO, PUBLIO, SESTO E CUSTODI. SESTO,
ENTRATO APPENA, SI FERMA.

N° 18 Terzetto

SESTO:
(Quello di Tito è il volto! ...
Ah, dove—oh stelle!—è andata
la sua dolcezza usata?
Or ei mi fa tremar.)

TITO:
(Eterni dei! Di Sesto
dunque il sembiante è questo!
Oh come può un delitto
un volto trasformar!)

PUBLIO:
(Mille diversi affetti
in Tito guerra fanno:
s'ei prova un tale affanno,
lo seguita ad amar.)

TITUS: I do not understand the long delay.

PUBLIUS: Only a little time has passed, my lord.

TITUS: Go yourself. Hasten things along.

PUBLIUS: I obey . . . I see your lictors coming. Sextus must be near. Here he is.

TITUS: The ungrateful man! Just hearing that he approaches, my old affection for him speaks up in his favor. But no. He will find here his prince, not his friend.

Scene 10

TITUS, PUBLIUS, SEXTUS, AND GUARDS. SEXTUS HAS BARELY ENTERED BEFORE HE STOPS.

Trio

SEXTUS:
(Behold the Emperor's face!
Ah, where, in heaven's name,
Is the sweetness once acclaimed!
Now it makes me afraid!)

TITUS:
(Eternal gods! Is this now
How Sextus looks somehow?
A man's face, I see, his crime
Can sadly change and degrade.)

PUBLIUS:
(So many conflicting emotions
Are warring in Titus's breast.
If his heart in sorrow is pressed,
The love will soon be repaid.)

TITO: Avvicinati!

SESTO: (Oh voce che piombami sul core!)

TITO: Non odi?

SESTO: (Di sudore mi sento—oh dio!—bagnar.)

SESTO: (Non può chi more di più penar.)

TITO, PUBLIO: (Palpita il traditore, né gli occhi ardisce alzar.)

Recitativo

TITO: (Eppur mi fa pietà.) Publio, custodi, lasciatemi con lui.

(Publio e le guardie partono.)

SESTO: (No, di quel volto non ho costanza a sostener l'impero.)

TITO: *(depone l'aria maestosa.)* Ah Sesto, è dunque vero? Dunque vuoi la mia morte? In che t'offese il tuo prence, il tuo padre, il tuo benefattor? Se Tito Augusto hai potuto obliar, di Tito amico come non ti sovvenne? Il premio è questo della tenera cura ch'ebbi sempre di te? Di chi fidarmi in avvenir potrò, se giunse—oh dei!—anche Sesto a tradirmi? E lo potesti? E 'l cor te lo sofferse?

SESTO: *(s'inginocchia.)* Ah Tito, ah mio clementissimo prence, non più, non più! Se tu veder potessi questo misero cor, spergiuro, ingrato pur ti farei pietà. Tutte ho sugli occhi tutte le colpe mie, tutti rammento i benefici tuoi; soffrir non posso né l'idea di me stesso né la presenza tua. Quel sacro volto, la voce tua, la tua

TITUS: Approach!

SEXTUS: (That voice weighs so heavily on my heart.)

TITUS: Do you not hear me?

SEXTUS: (Oh God, I feel drenched in sweat.)

SEXTUS: (Oh God! No dying man could be more agonized.)

TITUS AND PUBLIUS: (The traitor is trembling, and dares not raise his eyes.)

Recitative

TITUS: (And yet he rouses my pity.) Publius, guards, leave him with me.

(Publius and the guards withdraw.)

SEXTUS: (No, I have not the courage to bear the majesty of that face.)

TITUS: *(putting aside his imperial manner)* Ah, Sextus, is it true then? Did you wish for my death? How did your prince, your father, your benefactor offend you? If you were able to forget the Emperor Titus, how could you not remember your friend? Is this how you repay the tender care I have taken of you? Whom can I trust in future if even, dear God, Sextus has betrayed me? How could you? How could your heart allow it?

SEXTUS: *(kneeling)* O Titus, most merciful Prince, no more, no more. If you could see into this miserable heart, perjured and ungrateful, it might yet move you to pity. I have it all before my eyes, all my guilt. I cannot bear either the thought of myself or your presence. That sacred countenance, your voice, your

clemenza istessa diventò mio supplicio. Affretta almeno, affretta il mio morir. Toglimi presto questa vita infedel: lascia ch'io versi, se pietoso esser vuoi, questo perfido sangue ai piedi tuoi.

TITO: Sorgi, infelice. *(Sesto si leva.)* (Il contenersi è pena a quel tenero pianto.) Or vedi a quale lacrimevole stato un delitto riduce, una sfrenata avidità d'impero! E che sperasti di trovar mai nel trono? Il sommo forse d'ogni contento? Ah sconsigliato! Osserva quai frutti io ne raccolgo; e bramalo, se puoi.

SESTO: No, questa brama non fu che mi sedusse.

TITO: Dunque che fu?

SESTO: La debolezza mia, la mia fatalità.

TITO: Più chiaro almeno spiegati.

SESTO: Oh dio! Non posso.

TITO: Odimi, Sesto. Siam soli, il tuo sovrano non è presente. Apri il tuo core a Tito, confidati all'amico. Io ti prometto che Augusto nol saprà. Del tuo delitto di' la prima cagion. Cerchiamo insieme una via di scusarti. Io ne sarei forse di te più lieto.

SESTO: Ah, la mia colpa non ha difesa!

TITO: In contraccambio almeno d'amicizia lo chiedo. Io non celai alla tua fede i più gelosi arcani: merito ben che Sesto mi fidi un suo segreto.

SESTO: (Ecco una nuova specie di pena! O dispiacere a Tito o Vitellia accusar.)

clemency itself have become my punishment. At least hasten my death. Take my sorry life, quickly. If you would truly be merciful, let me shed this perfidious blood at your feet.

TITUS: Rise, unhappy man. *(Sextus rises.)* (It is difficult to control myself when I see his tender tears.) Now you see to what a pitiable state a crime, an unchecked greed for power, can reduce a man. And what did you hope for in a throne? The summit perhaps of every contentment? Rash man, just look at the fruits I gather from it, and desire if you can . . .

SEXTUS: No, it was not this desire that seduced me.

TITUS: What was it then?

SEXTUS: My weakness. My destiny!

TITUS: Explain yourself more clearly.

SEXTUS: Oh God! I cannot.

TITUS: Listen, Sextus. We are alone. Your sovereign is not present. Open your heart to Titus, confide in your friend. I promise you the Emperor will not know of it. Tell me the true reason for your crime. Let us, together, find a way to pardon you. I would probably be happier to find a way than you would.

SEXTUS: But my guilt is indefensible.

TITUS: I ask you out of friendship. I have never hidden from your trust my most jealous secrets. It behooves Sextus to trust me with one of his.

SEXTUS: (Here is a new kind of punishment! Either displease Titus or accuse Vitellia.)

TITO: *(incomincia a turbarsi.)* Dubiti ancora? Ma Sesto, mi ferisci nel più vivo del cor. Vedi che troppo tu l'amicizia oltraggi con questo diffidar. Pensaci. *(con impazienza)* Appaga il mio giusto desio.

SESTO: *(con disperazione)* (Ma qual astro splendeva al nascer mio!)

TITO: E taci? E non rispondi? Ah, giacché puoi tanto abusar di mia pietà ...

SESTO: Signore ... Sappi dunque ... (Che fo?)

TITO: Segui.

SESTO: (Ma quando finirò di penar?)

TITO: Parla una volta: che mi volevi dir?

SESTO: Ch'io son l'oggetto dell'ira degli dei; che la mia sorte non ho più forza a tollerar; ch'io stesso traditor mi confesso, empio mi chiamo; ch'io merito la morte e ch'io la bramo.

TITO: Sconoscente! E l'avrai *(alle guardie che saranno uscite)* Custodi, il reo toglietemi d'innanzi.

SESTO: Il bacio estremo su quella invitta man ...

TITO: *(senza guardarlo)* Parti: non è più tempo, or tuo giudice sono.

SESTO: Ah, sia questo, signor, l'ultimo dono.

TITUS: *(beginning to grow agitated)* You still doubt me? Sextus, you hurt me to the quick. This lack of confidence offends our friendship. Reflect on this. *(impatiently)* Grant a reasonable request.

SEXTUS: *(desperately)* (What an unlucky star presided over my birth!)

TITUS: Silent? No answer? Ah, since you abuse my sympathy . . .

SEXTUS: Sire . . . You should know . . . (What am I doing?)

TITUS: Continue.

SEXTUS: (When will my torture be done?)

TITUS: Speak, then. What is it you started to say?

SEXTUS: That I am the object of the wrath of the gods. That I no longer have the strength to bear my fate. That I confess I am a traitor, and call myself a villain. That I deserve death and long for it.

TITUS: Then you shall have it, wretched man! *(to the guards, who had withdrawn)* Guards, remove the culprit from my sight.

SEXTUS: Let me one last time kiss that invincible hand.

TITUS: *(without looking at him)* Leave. I have no more time. I am now your judge.

SEXTUS: Ah, sire, let this be your final gift to me.

N° 19 Rondò

SESTO:

Deh, per questo istante solo
ti ricorda il primo amor,
ché morir mi fa di duolo
il tuo sdegno, il tuo rigor.
Di pietade indegno, è vero,
sol spirar io deggio orror;
pur saresti men severo,
se vedessi questo cor.
Disperato vado a morte,
ma il morir non mi spaventa;
il pensiero mi tormenta
che fui teco un traditor.
Tanto affanno soffre un core,
né si more di dolor!
(Parte.)

Scena 11

TITO SOLO.

Recitativo

TITO: Ove s'intese mai più contumace infedeltà? Deggio alla mia negletta disprezzata clemenza una vendetta. Vendetta! ... Il cor di Tito tali sensi produce? ... Eh, viva ... Invano parlar dunque le leggi? Io lor custode l'eseguisco così? Di Sesto amico non sa Tito scordarsi? ... Ogn'altro affetto d'amicizia e pietà taccia per ora. *(Siede.)* Sesto è reo: Sesto mora. *(Sottoscrive e s'alza.)* Eccoci aspersi di cittadino sangue, e s'incomincia dal sangue d'un amico. Or che diranno i posteri di noi? Diran che in Tito si stancò la clemenza, come in Silla e in Augusto la crudeltà; che Tito era l'offeso e che le proprie offese, senza ingiuria del

Rondo

SEXTUS:

Ah, for just this single moment,
Recall your former love to mind.
Your mood, so harsh and arrogant,
Leaves me in a wretched grief confined.
Unworthy of pity, it is true,
I am a horror now to mankind.
You would take less severe a view
If to search my heart you now inclined.
Desperate, I go now to my death,
But to die does not frighten me.
What distresses me constantly
Is that to my loyalties I was blind.
One may seem to draw his last breath
And still not be undermined.

(He is taken away.)

Scene 11

TITUS, ALONE.

Recitative

TITUS: Who has ever heard of such obstinate disloyalty? He
scorns and mocks my clemency, which I must avenge. Vengeance!
. . . Can the heart of Titus shelter such a sentiment? . . . Well then,
let him live . . . Does the law then mean nothing? Can I, its custo-
dian, enforce it like this? Can Titus forget Sextus is his friend? For
now let every impulse towards friendship and mercy be silent. *(He
sits.)* Sextus is guilty. Sextus will die. *(He signs the document.)* Now I
am spattered with the blood of citizens, and first by the blood of
a friend. What will posterity say of us? It will say that Titus wearied of clemency, even as Sulla and Augustus wearied of cruelty.
That Titus was the offended one, and could have forgiven those
offenses without injury to the law. So shall I do violence against

giusto, ben poteva obliar. Ma dunque faccio sì gran forza al mio cor? Né almen sicuro sarò ch'altri l'approvi? Ah, non si lasci il solito cammin … *(Lacera il foglio.)* Viva l'amico! Benché infedele. E se accusarmi il mondo vuol pur di qualche errore, m'accusi di pietà, non di rigore. *(Getta il foglio lacerato.)*

Scena 12

DETTO E PUBLIO.

Recitativo

TITO: Publio.

PUBLIO: Cesare.

TITO: Andiamo al popolo che attende.

PUBLIO: E Sesto?

TITO: E Sesto venga all'arena ancor.

PUBLIO: Dunque il suo fato? …

TITO: Sì, Publio, è già deciso.

PUBLIO: (Oh sventurato!)

N° 20 Aria

TITO:
Se all'impero, amici dei,
necessario è un cor severo,
o togliete a me l'impero
o a me date un altro cor.

my own heart, and never be certain that the future will commend me? Oh, let us not stray from our usual path . . . *(He tears up the paper.)* Let my friend live, even though he is disloyal. If the world wishes to accuse me of mistakes, let it accuse me of mercy, not severity. *(He throws away the torn-up document.)*

Scene 12

TITUS AND PUBLIUS.

Recitative

TITUS: Publius.

PUBLIUS: Sire.

TITUS: Let us proceed to the people who are waiting.

PUBLIUS: And Sextus?

TITUS: Have Sextus brought to the arena as well.

PUBLIUS: Then his fate . . .

TITUS: Yes, Publius, it has been sealed.

PUBLIUS: (Oh poor soul!)

Aria

TITUS:
Ye benevolent gods, if a heart
Of stone is required for an empire,
Either take the realm I desire
Or give another heart to me.

Se la fé de' regni miei
coll'amor non assicuro,
d'una fede non mi curo
che sia frutto del timor.
(Parte.)

Scena 13

VITELLIA USCENDO DALLA PORTA OPPOSTA
RICHIAMA PUBLIO CHE SEGUITA TITO.

Recitativo

VITELLIA: Publio, ascolta.

PUBLIO: *(in atto di partire)* Perdona: deggio a Cesare appresso andar ...

VITELLIA: Dove?

PUBLIO: All'arena.

VITELLIA: E Sesto?

PUBLIO: Anch'esso.

VITELLIA: Dunque morrà?

PUBLIO: Purtroppo.

VITELLIA: (Ohimè!) Con Tito Sesto ha parlato?

PUBLIO: E lungamente.

VITELLIA: E sai quel ch'ei dicesse?

If loyalty stands apart,
In any kingdom, from love,
Then what is it to rule from above
A people who cower fearfully?
(He leaves.)

Scene 13

VITELLIA, COMING FROM THE OPPOSITE DOOR, CALLING
BACK PUBLIUS WHO HAS FOLLOWED TITUS.

Recitative

VITELLIA: Publius, listen!

PUBLIUS: *(about to leave)* Pardon me, but I must attend the
Emperor.

VITELLIA: Where is he going?

PUBLIUS: To the arena.

VITELLIA: And Sextus?

PUBLIUS: He too.

VITELLIA: He is to die then?

PUBLIUS: Unfortunately.

VITELLIA: (Alas!) Has Sextus spoken with Titus?

PUBLIUS: At length.

VITELLIA: Do you know what he said?

PUBLIO: No, solo con lui restar Cesare volle: escluso io fui.
(Parte.)

Scena 14

VITELLIA, E POI ANNIO E SERVILIA DA DIVERSE PARTI.

Recitativo

VITELLIA: Non giova lusingarsi: Sesto già mi scoperse. A Publio istesso si conosce sul volto. Ei non fu mai con me sì ritenuto. Ei fugge: ei teme di restar meco. Ah, secondato avessi gl'impulsi del mio cor! Per tempo a Tito dovea svelarmi e confessar l'errore. Sempre in bocca d'un reo, che la detesta, scema d'orror la colpa. Or questo ancora tardi saria. Seppe il delitto Augusto, e non da me. Questa ragione istessa fa più grave ...

SERVILIA: Ah Vitellia!

ANNIO: Ah principessa!

SERVILIA: Il misero germano ...

ANNIO: Il caro amico ...

SERVILIA: È condotto a morir.

ANNIO: Fra poco in faccia di Roma spettatrice delle fere sarà pasto infelice.

VITELLIA: Ma che posso per lui?

SERVILIA: Tutto. A' tuoi prieghi Tito lo donerà.

PUBLIUS: No. The Emperor wished to be alone with him. I was excluded.

(He leaves.)

Scene 14

VITELLIA, AND THEN ANNIUS AND SERVILIA FROM OPPOSITE SIDES.

Recitative

VITELLIA: It is useless to deceive myself. Sextus has already exposed me. I could see that in Publius's face. He has never been so reserved with me. He left too quickly, afraid to be seen with me. Ah, if only I had followed my heart. I should long ago have gone to Titus and confessed my sin. When a crime is admitted and detested by the guilty party, the horror of it is lessened. Now it is too late. The Emperor knows of my crime, but not from me. And this makes it even more serious . . .

SERVILIA: Ah, Vitellia!

ANNIUS: Ah, princess!

SERVILIA: My poor brother . . .

ANNIUS: My dear friend . . .

SERVILIA: . . . is condemned to death.

ANNIUS: Soon, before the eyes of Rome, the wretched man will be thrown to the wild beasts.

VITELLIA: But what can I do for him?

SERVILIA: Everything. Titus will listen to your plea.

ANNIO: Non può negarlo alla novella Augusta.

VITELLIA: Annio, non sono Augusta ancor.

ANNIO: Pria che tramonti il sole Tito sarà tuo sposo. Or, me presente, per le pompe festive il cenno ei diede.

VITELLIA: (Dunque Sesto ha taciuto! Oh amore! Oh fede!) Annio, Servilia, andiam. (Ma dove corro così senza pensar?) Partite, amici: vi seguirò.

ANNIO: Ma se d'un tardo aiuto Sesto fidar si dee, Sesto è perduto. *(Parte.)*

SERVILIA: Andiam. Quell'infelice t'amò più di sé stesso: avea fra labbri sempre il tuo nome, impallidia qualora si parlava di te. Tu piangi!

VITELLIA: Ah, parti!

SERVILIA: Ma tu perché restar? Vitellia, ah, parmi. ...

VITELLIA: Oh dei! Parti: verrò, non tormentarmi.

N° 21 Aria

SERVILIA:
S'altro che lagrime
per lui non tenti,
tutto il tuo piangere
non gioverà.

ANNIUS: He would deny nothing to his new Empress.

VITELLIA: Annius, I am not the Empress yet.

ANNIUS: Before the sun sets, Titus will be your husband. Just now, in my presence, he gave the order for the solemn festivities.

VITELLIA: (Then Sextus has remained silent! What love! What faithfulness!) Annius, Servilia, let us go. (But where am I running without first thinking?) You go on, friends, I will follow.

ANNIUS: But if Sextus must rely on help that arrives too late, he is lost.
(He leaves.)

SERVILIA: Let us hurry. My poor brother loves you more than life itself. Your name was always on his lips. He grew pale whenever your name was mentioned. You are weeping!

VITELLIA: Ah, leave me!

SERVILIA: But why are you staying here? Vitellia, it seems to me . . .

VITELLIA: Oh gods! Leave, I shall come. Stop tormenting me!

Aria

SERVILIA:
If all you think to do
Is sadly weep for him,
Your tears, however true,
Will be of no avail.

A questa inutile
pietà che senti,
oh, quanto è simile
la crudeltà!
(Parte.)

Scena 15

VITELLIA SOLA.

N° 22 Recitativo accompagnato

VITELLIA: Ecco il punto, o Vitellia, d'esaminar la tua costanza.
Avrai valor che basti a rimirar esangue il Sesto tuo fedel? Sesto
che t'ama più della vita sua? Che per tua colpa divenne reo? Che
t'ubbidì crudele? Che ingiusta t'adorò? Che in faccia a morte sì
gran fede ti serba? E tu frattanto, non ignota a te stessa, andrai
tranquilla al talamo d'Augusto? Ah, mi vedrei sempre Sesto
d'intorno, l'aure e i sassi temerei che loquaci mi scoprissero a
Tito! A' piedi suoi vadasi il tutto a palesar; si scemi il delitto di
Sesto, se scusar non si può, col fallo mio. D'impero e d'imenei,
speranze, addio.

N° 23 Rondò

VITELLIA:
Non più di fiori
vaghe catene
discenda Imene
ad intrecciar.

Stretta fra barbare
aspre ritorte
veggo la morte
ver me avanzar.

The pity that you feel,
So useless now to him,
How similar the ordeal
To cruelty's betrayal!
(She leaves.)

Scene 15

VITELLIA, ALONE.

Accompanied Recitative

VITELLIA: Now is the moment, Vitellia, to test your steadfastness. Will you have the courage to look on the corpse of your faithful Sextus? Sextus, who loves you more than life itself? Who was found guilty of your crime? Who obeyed even when you were cruel? Who adored you even when you were unjust? Who in the face of death stays so true to you? And you, aware of all this, you would go calmly to the Emperor's marriage bed? Oh, Sextus would always be in my mind's eye. I would fear that every breeze, every stone would tell my secret to Titus. Let me throw myself at his feet and tell him everything. Let my guilt lessen Sextus's crime, even if it can't be forgiven. All my hopes of marriage and the throne, farewell.

Rondo

VITELLIA:
No longer will Hymen
Descend to braid
His garlands made
Of flowers so sweet.

Bound in an iron
And barbarous chain,
I see Death strain
To seize me by the feet.

Infelice! Qual orrore!
Ah, di me che si dirà?
Chi vedesse il mio dolore
pur avria di me pietà.
(Parte.)

*Luogo magnifico che introduce a vasto anfiteatro
di cui per diversi archi scopresi la parte interna.
Si vedranno già nell'arena i complici della
congiura condannati alle fiere.*

Scena 16

NEL TEMPO CHE SI CANTA IL CORO, PRECEDUTO DA'
LITTORI, CIRCONDATO DA' SENATORI E PATRIZI ROMANI
E SEGUITO DA' PRETORIANI ESCE TITO, E DOPO ANNIO E
SERVILIA DA DIVERSE PARTI.

N° 24 Coro

CORO:
Che del ciel, che degli dei
tu il pensier, l'amor tu sei,
grand'eroe, nel giro angusto
si mostrò di questo dì.
Ma cagion di maraviglia
non è già, felice Augusto,
che gli dei chi lor somiglia
custodiscano così.

TITO, ANNIO, SERVILIA

Recitativo

TITO: Pria che principio a' lieti spettacoli si dia, custodi, innanzi
conducetemi il reo. (Più di perdono speme non ha. Quanto
aspettato meno più caro esser gli dee).

Oh, the horror! Woe is me!
How will the people jeer?
If they could only see,
Their censure would disappear.
(She leaves.)

*The magnificent entrance to a vast amphitheater,
its interiors glimpsed through several arches. The
conspirators, condemned to the wild beasts, can be
seen already in the arena.*

Scene 16

WHILE THE CHORUS IS SINGING, TITUS ENTERS,
PRECEDED BY LICTORS, SURROUNDED BY SENATORS
AND ROMAN PATRICIANS, AND FOLLOWED BY THE
PRAETORIAN GUARD, THEN ANNIUS AND SERVILIA
FROM DIFFERENT SIDES.

Chorus

CHORUS:
In the brief course of this day,
It is clear the gods have displayed,
Great hero, the love and care
They have reserved for you.
There is no cause to be amazed
By this favor beyond compare.
The gods have always upraised
Those whose own divinity shines through.

TITUS, ANNIUS, AND SERVILIA.

Recitative

TITUS: Before the signal to begin these joyous celebrations, let
the guards bring the criminal before me. (He has no hope of
pardon. The less looked for, the dearer it will be to him.)

ANNIO: Pietà, signore!

SERVILIA: Signor, pietà!

TITO: Se a chiederla venite per Sesto, è tardi. È il suo destin deciso.

ANNIO: E sì tranquillo in viso lo condanni a morir?

SERVILIA: Di Tito il core come il dolce perdé costume antico?

TITO: Ei si appressa: tacete.

SERVILIA: Oh Sesto!

ANNIO: Oh amico!

Scena 17

TITO, PUBLIO E SESTO FRA LITTORI, POI VITELLIA E DETTI.

Recitativo

TITO: Sesto, de' tuoi delitti tu sai la serie e sai qual pena ti si dee. Roma sconvolta, l'offesa maestà, le leggi offese, l'amicizia tradita, il mondo, il cielo voglion la morte tua. De' tradimenti sai pur ch'io son l'unico oggetto. Or senti.

VITELLIA: Eccoti, eccelso Augusto, eccoti al piè la più confusa ... *(s'inginocchia)*

TITO: Ah, sorgi, che fai? Che brami?

ANNIUS: Take pity, my lord!

SERVILIA: My lord, take pity!

TITUS: If you come to beg for Sextus, you come too late. His fate has been decided.

ANNIUS: And you can condemn him to death so calmly?

SERVILIA: How can Titus's heart have forgotten its customary generosity?

TITUS: He is approaching. Be silent.

SERVILIA: Oh Sextus!

ANNIUS: Dear friend!

Scene 17

TITUS, PUBLIUS, AND SEXTUS BETWEEN LICTORS, THEN
VITELLIA, AND THOSE BEFORE.

Recitative

TITUS: Sextus, you know your many crimes, and you know what punishment is due. Rome turned upside down, offended majesty, offended laws, friendship betrayed. Earth and heaven both demand your death. You know too that I was the sole object of your treachery. Now listen.

VITELLIA: Behold, mighty Emperor. Here at your feet is the most ashamed . . .
(She kneels.)

TITUS: Ah! Rise. What are you doing? What do you wish?

VITELLIA: Io ti conduco innanzi l'autor dell'empia trama.

TITO: Ov'è? Chi mai preparò tante insidie al viver mio?

VITELLIA: Nol crederai.

TITO: Perché?

VITELLIA: Perché son io.

TITO: Tu ancora?

SESTO, SERVILIA: Oh stelle!

ANNIO, PUBLIO: Oh numi!

TITO: E quanti mai, quanti siete a tradirmi?

VITELLIA: Io la più rea son di ciascuro! Io meditai la trama, il più fedele amico io ti sedussi, io del suo cieco amore a tuo danno abusai.

TITO: Ma del tuo sdegno chi fu cagion?

VITELLIA: La tua bontà. Credei che questa fosse amor. La destra e 'l trono da te sperava in dono, e poi negletta restai due volte e procurai vendetta.

VITELLIA: I bring you the perpetrator of the evil conspiracy.

TITUS: Where is he? How many plots against me can there be?

VITELLIA: You will not believe it.

TITUS: Why?

VITELLIA: Because it is I.

TITUS: Even you?

SEXTUS AND SERVILIA: Oh heavens!

ANNIUS AND PUBLIUS: Oh gods!

TITUS: How many are there? How many would betray me?

VITELLIA: I am the guiltiest of all. I hatched the plot. I seduced your most loyal friend. I took advantage of his blind love in order to strike at you.

TITUS: Why did you hate me so?

VITELLIA: Your goodness. I mistook it for love. I hoped you would give me both your hand and your throne. Then I was twice passed over, and sought my revenge.

N° 25 Recitativo accompagnato

TITO: Ma che giorno è mai questo? Al punto stesso che assolvo un reo ne scopro un altro! E quando troverò, giusti numi, un'anima fedel? Congiuran gli astri, cred'io, per obbligarmi a mio dispetto a diventar crudel. No, non avranno questo trionfo. A sostener la gara già m'impegnò la mia virtù. Vediamo se più costante sia l'altrui perfidia o la clemenza mia. Olà, Sesto si sciolga; abbian di nuovo Lentulo e i suoi seguaci e vita e libertà; sia noto a Roma ch'io son lo stesso e ch'io tutto so, tutti assolvo e tutto oblio.

N° 26 Sestetto con coro

SESTO:

Tu, è ver, m'assolvi, Augusto;
ma non m'assolve il core
che piangerà l'errore
finché memoria avrà.

TITO:

Il vero pentimento
di cui tu sei capace
val più d'una verace
costante fedeltà.

VITELLIA, SERVILIA, ANNIO:

Oh generoso! Oh grande!
E chi mai giunse a tanto?
Mi trae dagli occhi il pianto
l'eccelsa sua bontà.

Accompanied Recitative

TITUS: What kind of day is this? At the very moment I pardon one criminal, I discover another. When, just gods, shall I find a loyal soul? I feel the stars are conspiring to force me, against my will, to turn cruel. No, they will not have their way. My virtue has pledged itself to continue the struggle. We shall see which prevails, the treachery of others or my clemency. Ho there! Release Sextus. Let Lentulus and his accomplices again enjoy life and liberty. Let it be known in Rome that I am the same, that I know all, that I pardon everyone and forget everything.

Sextet with Chorus

SEXTUS:
Sire, it is true you pardon me
But in my heart I am guilty still.
My error will cause a mortal chill
As long as my memories last.

TITUS:
The true repentance you now show,
The knowledge you are capable of,
Is to be valued far above
Any loyalty to me held fast.

VITELLIA, SERVILIA, AND ANNIUS:
Oh generous ruler! Oh noble sire!
Who has ever attained such heights?
His sublime goodness and insight
Bring tears for a model unsurpassed.

VITELLIA, SERVILIA, ANNIO, SESTO, PUBLIO, CORO:
Eterni dei, vegliate
sui sacri giorni suoi:
a Roma in lui serbate
la sua felicità.

TITO:
Troncate, eterni dei,
troncate i giorni miei
quel dì che il ben di Roma
mia cura non sarà.

Fine dell'opera.

VITELLIA, SERVILIA, ANNIUS, SEXTUS, PUBLIUS, AND CHORUS:

Eternal gods, watch and guard
All the sacred days of his life.
Preserve in Titus from afar
Rome's greatness, present and past.

TITUS:

Eternal gods, think to cut short,
Cut short my life and all my efforts
On that day the good of Rome
Is not my duty, strong and steadfast.

End of the Opera.

7

The Magic Flute

THE MAGIC FLUTE

•

Singspiel, 1791

Libretto by Emanuel Schikaneder

The Characters
Tamino, a Javanese Prince
The Queen of the Night
The Three Ladies, attendants to the Queen
Pamina, the Queen's daughter
Sarastro, High Priest of the Sun
First Priest, a member of Sarastro's Brotherhood
Second Priest
Third Priest
Speaker, an elderly priest
Monostatos, a Moor, and overseer at the temple
Papageno, a birdcatcher for the Queen
Papagena, eventually Papageno's sweetheart
The Three Boys
Two Men in Armor
Three Slaves of Monostatos

Chorus, priests, slaves, attendants

ALL OF MOZART'S EARLIER OPERAS HAD BEEN WRIT-ten for gilded court theaters filled with polite, bewigged aristocrats. *The Magic Flute*, on the other hand, was written for a commercial theater accustomed to staging farces and operettas, rigged with stage machinery to make spectacular effects, and thronged with the common people. And that has been its home ever since, around the world. For more than two centuries, its unique combination of the sublime and the ridiculous has worked its theatrical magic. Farce and symbolism, fairy-tale adventures and obscure Masonic lore succeed one another in a dizzying sequence that never fails to convince and captivate. As it has from the start, the opera enchants both the novice and the sophisticate, the child and the connoisseur.

One of the first children to see the opera was Mozart's seven-year-old son, Carl, who went with his father to one of the early performances. Mozart wrote to his wife that the boy was "absolutely delighted." Three years later, no less a figure than Goethe, enthralled by the music's sublimity and compassion, had the opera performed at the court theater in Weimar and began a sequel to it. Even the dour and lofty Beethoven later claimed that "Mozart's greatest work remains *The Magic Flute*." It can truly be said that no opera has a more universal appeal.

Both Mozart and his librettist, Emanuel Schikaneder, were Masons. The confraternity of Freemasonry was an important part of the eighteenth-century Enlightenment, its members promoting the cause of rationality and reform. Mozart must have approved of the group's hatred of hierarchy, its idealistic teachings based on equality and tolerance, its espousal of salvation through reason and brotherly love. In Vienna, he was admitted to the "Beneficence" Lodge in December, 1784. The speaker at his induction ceremony addressed him in these words: "Favorite of a guardian angel. Friend of the sweetest muse. Chosen by benevolent Nature to move our hearts through rare magical powers and to pour consolation and comfort into our souls. You shall be embraced by all the warm feelings of mankind, which you so wonderfully express through your fingers, through which stream all the magnificent works of your ardent imagination!" Shortly afterwards, Mozart was promoted to the highest rank, that of Master Mason, and he was a loyal and active member until his death. Masonic rites—the padlock, the silence, the priesthood, the initiatory rites of passage—must have appealed to the composer, who was fascinated all his life by codes and tests. The secret rituals are part of *The Magic Flute*'s structure, and the Masonic vision—embodied in Sarastro, the ideal, benevolent Father, the Great Architect of the common good—is at the opera's heart.

Some years after Mozart's death, his sister, Nannerl, wrote down her memories of their childhood together. His rich fantasy life was apparent from the start:

> He would think out a kingdom for himself as we traveled from one place to another, and this he called the Kingdom of Back—why this name, I can no longer recall. This kingdom and its inhabitants were endowed with everything that could make them good and happy children. He was the king of this land—and this notion became so rooted within him, and he carried it so far, that our servant, who could draw a little, had to make a chart of it, and he would dictate the names of the cities, market towns, and villages to him.

This is the Mozart whose imagination was fired by Schikaneder's plot, the Mozart who never lost his sense of play and wonder. There are readers who will see in Tamino's search for and submission to the mighty Sarastro a wish-fulfillment fantasy of Mozart's own troubled relationship with his father, Leopold. Or view Papageno's happily fallen humanity as a version of Mozart's darker, lustful impulses. Other commentators have wanted historical allegory, with the Queen of the Night a satiric picture of the autocratic Austrian empress Maria Theresa, and Sarastro an homage to her successor, the tolerant Joseph II. The three couples in the opera can also be seen as aspects of human love: the romantic in Tamino and Pamina; the erotic in Papageno and Papagena; and the rational in Sarastro and the Queen. But the opera's triumph has less to do with psychobiography or history than with the universal story of a hero's quest for his true home, a home made up of both memory and desire.

Schikaneder's libretto has often been derided. Some have disliked its mix of high and low, or criticized the story as a muddle that switches its emphasis halfway through. Yet no audience has trouble following the story or fails to be moved by it. Beyond the high jinks and stock characters, there exists a deeper drama. There are aspects of Schikaneder's pastiche that merit special notice. No woman would ever have been admitted to the inner sanctum, much less the membership, of any Masonic lodge the way Pamina is accepted along with Tamino into Sarastro's temple. In fact, it is Pamina who leads the way through the trials by fire and water; her unquestioning devotion and bravery—like that of later operatic heroines, from Beethoven's Leonora to Wagner's Brünnhilde—are as much the portrait of perfection in action as the picture of her first given to Tamino is the portrait of beauty itself. The portrait of Pamina that so moves Tamino cannot speak, nor is Tamino allowed to speak, as part of his initiation. It is ironic that silence is used so expressively in a work overflowing with musical genius. It is music that finally speaks of the pair's love, of their victory over darkness and deceit.

Undercurrents of myth continually swirl through the opera's folkloric charm. The magic flute itself, with its ability to render wild beasts spellbound, is a version of Orpheus's lyre. And like Orpheus, Tamino and his creators are rescuers. In the end, music rescues and reconciles: all tricks and reversals are undone, all true desires are brought to light in the opera's final, resplendent chorus. And all along, Mozart finds in the exotic and farcical the outlines of the ideal and the haunts of the heart.

THE STORY

ACT I

A handsome young prince, Tamino, is fleeing a monstrous serpent. He calls out in vain for help, then falls into a terrified faint. Three Ladies, attendants to the fabled Queen of the Night, come to his rescue and kill the serpent. While they gaze on the unconscious youth, they admire his beauty, each wanting him for herself. They withdraw, and a gaily feathered birdcatcher, Papageno, strolls in. Tamino awakens and questions him. Papageno tells him that he catches birds for the Queen of the Night in exchange for food and drink, which the Three Ladies bring him each day. He then boasts of having slain the serpent in order the save the prince. The Ladies emerge and offer Papageno water instead of wine, a stone instead of sweet cake, and instead of figs a golden padlock, which they fasten to his mouth while scolding him for lying. To Tamino they give a portrait of the Queen's daughter, Pamina, the sight of which fills him with rapture. The Ladies explain that the girl has been kidnapped by an evil wizard named Sarastro.

There is a sudden burst of thunder, and the mountain parts to reveal the Queen of the Night herself. She describes her embittered sorrow at the loss of her daughter and promises Tamino the girl's hand in marriage if only he can rescue her. The mountains close over her again. The Ladies remove Papageno's padlock, once he promises never to lie again. At the Queen's bidding, they give Tamino a magic flute and Papageno a set of magic bells as protection on their journey to Sarastro's palace. They also explain that Three Spirit–Boys will lead them on their way.

In a room of Sarastro's palace, the Moorish slave Monostatos is threatening Pamina and attempts to seduce her despite her anguished pleas. Papageno happens by and peers in the window. When Monostatos and Papageno notice one another, both are frightened and they run away in opposite directions. But Papageno returns and promises Pamina that she will soon be rescued by a prince who has fallen in love with her. Meanwhile, the Three Spirit–Boys have led Tamino to a grove where stand three temples, to Wisdom, to Reason, and to Nature. Awed by the grandeur of the temples, Tamino tries to gain entrance to each but is denied, and an old priest he questions, the Speaker, explains that he has been deceived by the Queen: Sarastro is not a monster but the wise leader of the sacred Brotherhood within the Temple of Wisdom. Tamino is also told that Pamina is still alive. Overjoyed, he plays upon his magic flute, and animals of all kinds approach to listen. Papageno's pipe is heard as if in response to Tamino's flute, but the two cannot find each other, and Tamino rushes off in search of Pamina.

Papageno and Pamina, fleeing from the evil Monostatos and his slaves, are meanwhile searching for Tamino. When Monostatos is about to seize the pair, Papageno plays upon his magic bells, so that the slaves fall under the music's spell and dance away, allowing Papageno and Pamina to escape again. A solemn fanfare sounds, and Sarastro enters with his priests. Pamina kneels before him and asks to be forgiven for having tried to escape, explaining Monostatos' villainy and her mother's grief. Monostatos now leads in the captive Tamino. Sarastro unexpectedly punishes Monostatos and turns beneficently to the lovers to tell them they must undergo an ordeal of purification before they can be united.

ACT II

Sarastro tells the assembled Brotherhood that he wants Tamino to become a member of their sacred band after undergoing the necessary trials. It was for Tamino, he explains, that he separated Pamina—destined by the gods to marry the young prince—from her wicked mother. The priests signify their agreement, and Sarastro prays to the gods Isis and Osiris that the lovers be granted wisdom and strength during their ordeal.

Tamino and Papageno are told by the Two Priests of the trials awaiting them and are promised that if they pledge themselves to silence each will be granted his desire—Pamina for Tamino, and Papagena for Papageno. The Three Ladies return and, predicting disaster, try to tempt the two men to break their vow. Tamino has difficulty restraining Papageno from speaking.

In a garden where she is sleeping, Monostatos again sneaks up on Pamina. This time, the Queen of the Night intervenes to save her. When Pamina tells her that Tamino has decided to join the Brotherhood, the angry Queen swears her revenge and gives her daughter a dagger, demanding that she kill Sarastro. The Queen vanishes, and Monostatos snatches the dagger from Pamina and is about to kill her when Sarastro arrives to save her.

Tamino and Papageno are led by priests into a great hall, where again they are enjoined to silence. Papagena, disguised as a crone, enters and teasingly banters with Papageno before hobbling away. The Three Spirit-Boys appear next and present Tamino and Papageno with their magic instruments, the flute and the bells. When Tamino begins to play, Pamina at last appears. True to his vow, Tamino remains silent, puzzling his beloved. In a great vault, Sarastro bids Tamino to undergo one more grievous trial. He must bid Pamina a last farewell. The lovers part sadly.

Papageno, enjoying a glass of wine that has mysteriously appeared, is asked by one of the priests what he most desires. A little wife, he replies. The crone comes in and asks Papageno to marry her. With a reluctant cheerfulness, he decides a crone is better than nothing, and agrees—at which point Papagena's disguise disappears. As he rushes to embrace her, a priest keeps them apart, and Papageno sinks to the ground.

In a garden, the Three Spirit-Boys watch as Pamina, in her despair, is about to turn the dagger on herself. To stop her, they reassure her of Tamino's love. In a mountain ravine, two Men in Armor lead Tamino to the start of his trials by fire and water. Pamina is reunited with him and allowed to accompany him on the perilous path. She pledges her devotion and leads the way.

Papageno, alone again, calls and calls for his Papagena, but there is only silence all around. He decides he will hang himself to end his sorrows. The Three Spirit-Boys prevent this and urge him to play his magic bells. When he does, Papagena appears for a joyful reunion.

In her mountain fortress, the Queen plots with Monostatos and her Three Ladies to storm Sarastro's palace and have their bloody revenge. When, amid thunder and lightning, the forces of darkness attack, they are destroyed and plunged into endless night. Sunlight bursts out in glory. Sarastro and his priests, Tamino, and Pamina are seen assembled. Sarastro pronounces his blessing, and a final chorus praises the gods and the young lovers.

THE BACKGROUND

Emanuel Schikaneder (1751–1812) was a true man of the theater—a dancer, a singer, an actor (he played Hamlet at the court theater in Munich), a composer, a dramatist, and, finally, the director of his own troupe that travelled around Germany and Austria giving performances of plays and operas. He wrote more than fifty librettos for operas and *Singspiels*. He is said to have approached Mozart, whom he had worked with before, in early March, 1791. It is also said that he sought out Mozart to ensure a box-office success that would save his theater from bankruptcy. The libretto's exotic Egyptian setting and Masonic allegory were very much a part of the Enlightenment ethos. The libretto's more serious Masonic aspect derives from Abbé Jean Terrason's utopian *Séthos* (1731); its fairy-tale quest draws on A. J. Liebeskind's story "Lulu, oder Die Zauberflöte," collected in Christoph Martin Wieland's *Dschinnistan* (1789). Schikaneder—a Masonic lodge brother of Mozart's—is said to have lent Mozart a small wooden summerhouse in the garden adjoining the theater so that he could compose in peace. Mozart began composing the opera in May; most of the work was done in June, and by mid-July, when the commission for *La Clemenza di Tito* arrived, he was nearly finished. Even so, the March of the Priests and the overture were finished only two days before the premiere on September 30, 1791. The first performances were given at the Theater auf der Wieden in suburban Vienna, where Schikaneder had for a couple of years already been presenting popular "magic-comedies." Mozart himself conducted the first two performances from the harpsichord, and attended later ones. During one of them, when Schikaneder, who was playing Papageno, was on stage pretending to play the glockenspiel that was used for Papageno's magic bells, Mozart was in the wings and took the backstage glockenspiel and improvised extravagantly, leaving Schikaneder scrambling on stage, pretending to keep up. The singer playing Tamino, Benedikt Schack, on the other hand, played his character's flute solos; he was a friend of Mozart's and a composer himself. The Queen of the Night was undertaken by Mozart's sister-in-law Josepha Hofer. Franz Xaver Gerl was Sarastro, and his wife Barbara Gerl played Papagena. Anna Gottlieb, who had sung the first Barbarina in *Figaro* five years earlier, was Pamina. Monostatos was Johann Joseph Nouseul. The opera was an immediate success, and there were twenty performances in the first month; within a year there had been nearly a hundred. It was soon being performed all over Germany, and as far away as St. Petersburg. Translations followed in many languages, and English versions were playing in London and New York by 1833. The first printed edition of the libretto appeared in time for the premiere in Vienna.

Erster Aufzug

Das Theater ist eine felsichte Gegend, hie und da mit Bäumen überwachsen; auf beiden Seiten sind gangbare Berge nebst einem runden Tempel.

Erster Auftritt

TAMINO KOMMT IN EINEM PRÄCHTIGEN JAPONISCHEN JAGDKLEIDE RECHTS VON EINEM FELSEN HERUNTER MIT EINEM BOGEN, ABER OHNE PFEIL; EINE SCHLANGE VERFOLGT IHN

N° 1 Introduktion

TAMINO:
Zu Hilfe! zu Hilfe! sonst bin ich verloren
Der listigen Schlange zum Opfer erkoren, –
Barmherzige Götter! schon nahet sie sich.
Ach rettet mich! Ach schützet mich!
(Er fällt in Ohnmacht. Sogleich öffnet sich die Pforte des Tempels; drei verschleierte Damen kommen heraus, jede mit einem silbernen Wurfspieß.)

DIE DREI DAMEN:
Stirb, Ungeheuer, durch unsre Macht!
Triumph! Triumph! sie ist vollbracht
Die Heldentat. Er ist befreit
Durch unsers Armes Tapferkeit.

Act I

The scene is a rocky landscape, with trees here and there; on both sides are mountains; also a round temple.

First Scene

TAMINO, IN A MAGNIFICENT ORIENTAL HUNTING OUTFIT,
RUNS IN FROM THE ROCKS ON THE RIGHT,
CARRYING A BOW BUT NO ARROWS;
A MONSTROUS SERPENT PURSUES HIM.

Introduction

TAMINO:
Help me! Help! Or else I'm lost,
Crushed between this monster's jaws!
Have mercy, gods! It's almost here!
Oh, save me from my darkest fear!
(He faints. At once the door of the temple opens. Three veiled Ladies emerge, each with a silver spear.)

THE THREE LADIES:
Die, foul monster, by our power!
The final triumph now is ours!
At last your helpless victim's free,
Thanks to our swift bravery!

989

ERSTE DAME: *(ihn betrachtend)* Ein holder Jüngling, sanft und schön,

ZWEITE DAME: So schön, als ich noch nie gesehn!

DRITTE DAME: Ja, ja! gewiss zum Malen schön.

DIE DREI DAMEN:
Würd ich mein Herz der Liebe weihn,
So müsst es dieser Jüngling sein.
Lasst uns zu unsrer Fürstin eilen,
Ihr diese Nachricht zu erteilen.
Vielleicht, dass dieser schöne Mann
Die vor'ge Ruh ihr geben kann.

ERSTE DAME:
So geht und sagt es ihr!
Ich bleib indessen hier.

ZWEITE DAME:
Nein, nein! geht ihr nur hin,
Ich wache hier für ihn!

DRITTE DAME:
Nein, nein! das kann nicht sein,
Ich schütze ihn allein.

ERSTE DAME: Ich bleib indessen hier.

ZWEITE DAME: Ich wache hier für ihn!

DRITTE DAME: Ich schütze ihn allein.

ERSTE DAME: Ich bleibe,

FIRST LADY: *(gazing at Tamino)* A handsome youth. How sweet, how fair!

SECOND LADY: The handsomest I've ever seen!

THIRD LADY: Yes, like a picture, lying there!

THE THREE LADIES:
If ever love could sway my heart
This youth alone would have the art.
Come, let's hasten to our Queen
To tell her all that we have seen.
Perhaps this lad himself may find
Some way to give her peace of mind.

FIRST LADY:
You go on. We may be late.
I'll remain with him and wait.

SECOND LADY:
No! Your urgent task is great.
I'll watch out for him and wait.

THIRD LADY:
Why this wrangling and debate?
I'll protect him while I wait.

FIRST LADY: I'll remain with him and wait!

SECOND LADY: I'll watch out for him and wait!

THIRD LADY: I'll protect him while I wait!

FIRST LADY: I'll remain!

ZWEITE DAME: Ich wache,

DRITTE DAME: Ich schütze,

DIE DREI DAMEN:
Ich, ich, ich!
(für sich)
Ich sollte fort! Ei, ei! wie fein!
Sie wären gern bei ihm allein,
Nein, nein, das kann nicht sein!
(eine nach der andern, dann alle drei zugleich)
Was wollte ich darum nicht geben,
Könnt ich mit diesem Jüngling leben!
Hätt ich ihn doch so ganz allein!
Doch keine geht, es kann nicht sein.
Am besten ist es nun, ich geh.
Du, Jüngling, schön und liebevoll,
Du, trauter Jüngling, lebe wohl,
Bis ich dich wiederseh.
(Sie gehen alle drei zur Pforte des Tempels ab, die sich selbst öffnet und schließt.)

Dialog

TAMINO: *(erwacht, sieht furchtsam umher)* Wo bin ich! Ist's Fantasie, dass ich noch lebe? oder hat eine höhere Macht mich gerettet? *(steht auf, sieht umher)* Wie? – Die bösartige Schlange liegt tot zu meinen Füßen? – *(Man hört von fern ein Waldflötchen, worunter das Orchester piano akkompagniert. Tamino spricht unter dem Ritornell.)* Was hör ich? Wo bin ich? Welch unbekannter Ort! – Ha, eine männliche Figur nähert sich dem Tal. *(versteckt sich hinter einem Baume)*

SECOND LADY: I'll watch out!

THIRD LADY: I'll protect!

THE THREE LADIES:
I—! I—! I—!
(each to herself)
They stay behind? And I go home?
Each one wants him for her own!
This is no time to leave them alone!
(one after the other, then all three together)
The longer I stay, the more I yearn.
One secret glance and my heart burns.
Is there a way we two might flee?
But no one moves. It's not to be.
It's best if I myself depart.
O noble youth, you have my heart!
O sweet stranger, farewell then!
Farewell! Until we meet again!
(The Ladies depart through the temple door, which opens and closes by itself.)

Spoken Dialogue

TAMINO: *(waking, looking fearfully around, speaking)* Where am I? Is this just a dream that I am alive? Or has some higher power come to save me? *(He stands, looks around.)* What's this! The monstrous serpent dead at my feet? *(From the distance comes the sound of panpipes. The orchestra softly accompanies it and Tamino speaks over it.)* What am I hearing? Where am I? What an odd place this is.—Aha, a stranger's approaching the valley. *(Tamino hides himself behind a tree.)*

Zweiter Auftritt

(PAPAGENO KOMMT DEN FUSSSTEIG HERUNTER, HAT AUF
DEM RÜCKEN EINE GROSSE VOGELSTEIGE, DIE HOCH ÜBER
DEN KOPF GEHT, WORIN VERSCHIEDENE VÖGEL SIND; AUCH
HÄLT ER MIT BEIDEN HÄNDEN EIN FAUNEN-FLÖTCHEN, –
PFEIFT UND SINGT.)

N° 2 Aria

PAPAGENO: *(pfeift von ferne, kommt heraus)*
Der Vogelfänger bin ich ja, –
Stets lustig, heißa hopsasa!
Ich Vogelfänger bin bekannt
Bei Alt und Jung im ganzen Land.
Weiß mit dem Locken umzugehn
Und mich aufs Pfeifen zu verstehn. *(pfeift)*
Drum kann ich froh und lustig sein,
Denn alle Vögel sind ja mein. *(pfeift)*

Der Vogelfänger bin ich ja,
Stets lustig, heißa hopsasa!
Ich Vogelfänger bin bekannt
Bei Alt und Jung im ganzen Land.
Ein Netz für Mädchen möchte ich,
Ich fing sie dutzendweis für mich.
Dann sperrte ich sie bei mir ein,
Und alle Mädchen wären mein.

[Wenn alle Mädchen wären mein,
So tauschte ich brav Zucker ein:
Die, welche mir am liebsten wär',
Der gäb' ich gleich den Zucker her.
Und küßte sie mich zärtlich dann,
Wär sie mein Weib und ich ihr Mann.
Sie schlief' an meiner Seite ein,
Ich wiegte wie ein Kind sie ein]
(pfeift, will nach der Arie nach der Pforte gehen)

Second Scene

PAPAGENO COMES DOWN A FOOTPATH, A LARGE BIRDCAGE
ON HIS BACK THAT STRETCHES OVER HIS HEAD AND
CONTAINS ALL SORTS OF BIRDS. WITH BOTH HANDS HE
HOLDS PANPIPES, ON WHICH HE PLAYS AS HE SINGS.

Aria

PAPAGENO: *(plays at a distance, then appears)*
A jolly trapper of birds am I
And tra-la-la is what I cry.
The Birdcatcher is how I'm known,
In every corner, by child or crone.
My snares are laid. My sights are set.
Then I whistle them into my net. *(He pipes.)*
Mine's the life, so gay and free,
For all the birds belong to me! *(He pipes.)*

A jolly trapper of birds am I
And tra-la-la is what I cry.
The Birdcatcher is how I'm known,
In every corner, by child or crone.
If only there were traps for girls,
I'd catch a dozen by their curls.
I'd keep them in a cage, you'd see,
For all would then belong to me!

When I'd got them nice and plump,
I'd trade some for a sugar lump,
Then give it to my favorite one
And woo her till her heart was won.
And if she'd kiss me tenderly
I'd ask her next to marry me.
Then snuggled in my nest we'd lie
And rock and rock to a lullaby.
(He pipes, and after he sings goes towards the doors.)

Dialog

TAMINO: *(nimmt ihn bei der Hand)* He da!

PAPAGENO: Was da!

TAMINO: Sag mir, du lustiger Freund, wer du seist?

PAPAGENO: Wer ich bin? *(für sich)* Dumme Frage! *(laut)* Ein Mensch, wie du. – Wenn ich dich nun fragte, wer du bist? –

TAMINO: So würde ich dir antworten, dass ich aus fürstlichem Geblüte bin.

PAPAGENO: Das ist mir zu hoch. – Musst dich deutlicher erklären, wenn ich dich verstehen soll!

TAMINO: Mein Vater ist Fürst, der über viele Länder und Menschen herrscht; darum nennt man mich Prinz.

PAPAGENO: Länder? – Menschen? – Prinz? –

TAMINO: Daher frag ich dich! –

PAPAGENO: Langsam! Lass mich fragen. – Sag du mir zuvor: Gibt's außer diesen Bergen auch noch Länder und Menschen?

TAMINO: Viele Tausende!

PAPAGENO: Da ließ sich eine Spekulation mit meinen Vögeln machen.

TAMINO: Nun sag du mir, in welcher Gegend wir sind. –

PAPAGENO: In welcher Gegend? *(sieht sich um)* Zwischen Tälern und Bergen.

Spoken Dialogue

TAMINO: *(taking him by the hand)* Hey there!

PAPAGENO: What's going on?

TAMINO: Tell me, my jolly friend, who are you?

PAPAGENO: Who am I? *(to himself)* A stupid question. *(aloud)* I'm a man like you. Now may I ask, sir, who are you?

TAMINO: Since you ask, I am born of royal blood.

PAPAGENO: That's over my head. Could you put it so I can understand?

TAMINO: My father is a king who rules over many lands and peoples. So I am—a prince.

PAPAGENO: Lands? Peoples? Prince?

TAMINO: My question is—

PAPAGENO: Hold on! Let me do the asking. First tell me this—are there other lands and people beyond these mountains?

TAMINO: Many thousands!

PAPAGENO: That would add some business for my trade in birds.

TAMINO: Now tell me, what is this country called?

PAPAGENO: Country called . . . ? *(looking around)* Well, it's between the valleys and the mountains.

TAMINO: Schon recht! Aber wie nennt man eigentlich diese Gegend? – Wer beherrscht sie? –

PAPAGENO: Das kann ich dir ebenso wenig beantworten, als ich weiß, wie ich auf die Welt gekommen bin.

TAMINO: *(lacht)* Wie? Du wüsstest nicht, wo du geboren oder wer deine Eltern waren? – –

PAPAGENO: Kein Wort! – Ich weiß nicht mehr und nicht weniger, als dass mich ein alter, aber sehr lustiger Mann auferzogen und ernährt hat.

TAMINO: Das war vermutlich dein Vater? –

PAPAGENO: Das weiß ich nicht.

TAMINO: Hattest du denn deine Mutter nicht gekannt?

PAPAGENO: Gekannt hab ich sie nicht. Erzählen ließ ich mir's einige Mal, dass meine Mutter einst da in diesem verschlossenen Gebäude bei der nächtlich sternflammenden Königin gedient hätte. – Ob sie noch lebt oder was aus ihr geworden ist, weiß ich nicht. – Ich weiß nur so viel, dass nicht weit von hier meine Strohhütte steht, die mich vor Regen und Kälte schützt.

TAMINO: Aber wie lebst du?

PAPAGENO: Von Essen und Trinken wie alle Menschen.

TAMINO: Wodurch erhältst du das?

PAPAGENO: Durch Tausch. – Ich fange für die sternflammende Königin und ihre Jungfrauen verschiedene Vögel; dafür erhalt ich täglich Speis und Trank von ihr.

TAMINO: Yes, all right. But what exactly is it called? Who is your ruler?

PAPAGENO: If I could answer that, I could tell you too how I came into the world.

TAMINO: *(laughing)* You mean you don't know where you were born or who your parents are?

PAPAGENO: No idea! All I know is that I was brought up and cared for by an old man—a very cheery old man.

TAMINO: Probably your father?

PAPAGENO: Don't know.

TAMINO: Did you know your mother?

PAPAGENO: No, but I was once told she worked for the star-shimmering Queen of the Night . . . in the locked-up building over there. But alive or dead—I don't know. All I know is that my little straw hut is nearby, and it shelters me from rain and cold.

TAMINO: But how do you live?

PAPAGENO: On food and drink, like other men.

TAMINO: And how do you come by that?

PAPAGENO: By trading. I catch pretty birds for the star-shimmering Queen and her Ladies, and get in return from them my daily food and drink.

TAMINO: *(für sich)* Sternflammende Königin! – Wenn es etwa gar die mächtige Herrscherin der Nacht wäre! – *[zu Papageno]* Sag mir, guter Freund! warst du schon so glücklich, diese Göttin der Nacht zu sehen?

PAPAGENO: *(der bisher öfters auf seiner Flöte geblasen)* Deine letzte alberne Frage überzeugt mich, dass du aus einem fremden Lande geboren bist. –

TAMINO: Sei darüber nicht ungehalten, lieber Freund! Ich dachte nur –

PAPAGENO: Sehen? – Die sternflammende Königin sehen? – Wenn du noch mit einer solchen albernen Frage an mich kommst, so sperr ich dich, so wahr ich Papageno heiße, wie einen Gimpel in mein Vogelhaus, verhandle dich dann mit meinen übrigen Vögeln an die nächtliche Königin und ihre Jungfrauen. Dann mögen sie dich meinetwegen sieden oder braten.

TAMINO: *(für sich)* Ein wunderlicher Mann!

PAPAGENO: Sehen? – Die sternflammende Königin sehen? – Welcher Sterbliche kann sich rühmen, sie je gesehen zu haben? – Welches Menschen Auge würde durch ihren schwarz durchwebten Schleier blicken können?

TAMINO: *(für sich)* Nun ist's klar; es ist eben diese nächtliche Königin, von der mein Vater mir so oft erzählte. – Aber zu fassen, wie ich mich hierher verirrte, ist außer meiner Macht. – Unfehlbar ist auch dieser Mann kein gewöhnlicher Mensch. – Vielleicht einer ihrer dienstbaren Geister.

PAPAGENO: *(für sich)* Wie er mich so starr anblickt! Bald fang ich an, mich vor ihm zu fürchten. – *(zu Tamino)* Warum siehst du so verdächtig und schelmisch nach mir?

TAMINO: *(to himself)* The star-shimmering Queen! Could this be the fabled Queen of the Night? *(to Papageno)* Tell me, my friend, have you been lucky enough then to see her?

PAPAGENO: *(who until now has been playing his panpipes more and more frequently)* That silly question proves you're not from around here.

TAMINO: I meant no offense . . .

PAPAGENO: Seen her? Seen the star-shimmering Queen? If you ask another dumb question, as sure as my name's Papageno, I'll slap you in my cage and sell you, fool, to the Queen and her Ladies, who can boil or roast you for all I care.

TAMINO: *(to himself)* What a strange chap!

PAPAGENO: Seen her? Seen the star-shimmering Queen? What mere mortal can claim to have seen her? What human eye could see through her inky veil of darkness?

TAMINO: *(to himself)* So it's true. This is the Queen of the Night my father told me about so often. But I can't explain how I came to be here. And this chap is no ordinary human being. Maybe he is a spirit who serves her.

PAPAGENO: *(to himself)* How he stares at me! He makes me nervous. *(to Tamino)* Why do you look at me so suspiciously?

TAMINO: Weil – weil ich zweifle, ob du Mensch bist. –

PAPAGENO: Wie war das?

TAMINO: Nach deinen Federn, die dich bedecken, halt ich dich – *(geht auf ihn zu)*

PAPAGENO: Doch für keinen Vogel? - Bleib zurück, sag ich, und traue mir nicht; – denn ich habe Riesenkraft, wenn ich jemand packe. – *(für sich)* Wenn er sich nicht bald von mir schrecken lässt, so lauf ich davon.

TAMINO: Riesenkraft? *(Er sieht auf die Schlange.)* Also warst du wohl gar mein Erretter, der diese giftige Schlange bekämpfte?

PAPAGENO: Schlange! *(sieht sich um, weicht zitternd einige Schritte zurück)* Was da! Ist sie tot oder lebendig?

TAMINO: Du willst durch deine bescheidene Frage meinen Dank ablehnen, – aber ich muss dir sagen, dass ich ewig für deine so tapfere Handlung dankbar sein werde.

PAPAGENO: Schweigen wir davon still. – Freuen wir uns, dass sie glücklich überwunden ist.

TAMINO: Aber um alles in der Welt, Freund! wie hast du dieses Ungeheuer bekämpft? – Du bist ohne Waffen.

PAPAGENO: Brauch keine! - Bei mir ist ein starker Druck mit der Hand mehr als Waffen.

TAMINO: Du hast sie also erdrosselt?

PAPAGENO: Erdrosselt! *(für sich)* Bin in meinem Leben nicht so stark gewesen als heute.

TAMINO: Because I'm beginning to wonder if you are a human being.

PAPAGENO: What are you talking about?

TAMINO: By the look of the feathers on you, I'd take you for . . . *(He goes closer.)*

PAPAGENO: . . . for a bird? Back off! Don't play games with me. When I grab someone, I have the strength of a giant! *(to himself)* If he doesn't scare soon, I'm getting out of here.

TAMINO: The strength of a giant? *(looking down at the dead serpent)* Then are you my savior? You killed this venomous serpent and rescued me?

PAPAGENO: Serpent? *(He looks around, and retreats in fear.)* What's that? Is it dead or alive?

TAMINO: You're refusing my thanks, and being too modest. I must tell you, I'll be forever grateful.

PAPAGENO: Say no more. Let's be glad it's all over.

TAMINO: For all the world, my friend, how did you slay this monster? And without a weapon?

PAPAGENO: Never need them. The force of my grip is stronger than any weapon.

TAMINO: So you strangled it?

PAPAGENO: Strangled it! *(to himself)* I've never felt so strong in all my life.

Dritter Auftritt

DIE DREI DAMEN, VORIGE.

DIE DREI DAMEN: *(drohen und rufen zugleich)* Papageno!

PAPAGENO: Aha! das geht mich an. – Sieh dich um, Freund!

TAMINO: Wer sind diese Damen?

PAPAGENO: Wer sie eigentlich sind, weiß ich selbst nicht. – Ich weiß nur so viel, dass sie mir täglich meine Vögel abnehmen und mir dafür Wein, Zuckerbrot und süße Feigen bringen.

TAMINO: Sie sind vermutlich sehr schön?

PAPAGENO: Ich denke nicht! – Denn wenn sie schön wären, würden sie ihre Gesichter nicht bedecken.

DIE DREI DAMEN: *(drohend)* Papageno! –

PAPAGENO: Sei still! Sie drohen mir schon. – Du fragst, ob sie schön sind, und ich kann dir darauf nichts antworten, als dass ich in meinem Leben nichts Reizenders sah. – *(für sich)* Jetzt werden sie bald wieder gut werden. – –

DIE DREI DAMEN: *(drohend)* Papageno!

PAPAGENO: Was muss ich denn heute verbrochen haben, dass sie gar so aufgebracht wider mich sind? – Hier, meine Schönen, übergeb ich meine Vögel.

ERSTE DAME: *(reicht ihm eine schöne Bouteille Wasser)* Dafür schickt dir unsre Fürstin heute zum ersten Mal statt Wein reines helles Wasser.

Third Scene

THE THREE LADIES, AND THOSE BEFORE.

THE THREE LADIES: *(threatening and calling at the same time)* Papageno!

PAPAGENO: Ah, that's for me!—Look behind you, friend!

TAMINO: Who are these ladies?

PAPAGENO: Who exactly, I don't know myself. All I know is that every day they take my birds and bring me wine, a sugarloaf, and sweet figs in exchange.

TAMINO: I suppose they are very beautiful?

PAPAGENO: Probably not. If they were beautiful, after all, they wouldn't need to cover their faces so.

THE THREE LADIES: *(menacingly)* Papageno!

PAPAGENO: Shh! They're threatening me!—You asked if they are beautiful, and I must say I've never seen anyone more lovely. *(to himself)* That should put them in a good mood.

THE THREE LADIES: *(menacingly)* Papageno!

PAPAGENO: What can I have done today to make them so angry? Here, fair Ladies, I have brought you my birds.

FIRST LADY: *(giving him a flask of water)* For those, Her Majesty sends you today, instead of wine, this pure, clear water.

ZWEITE DAME: Und mir befahl sie, dass ich statt Zuckerbrot diesen Stein dir überbringen soll. – Ich wünsche, dass er dir wohl bekommen möge.

PAPAGENO: Was? Steine soll ich fressen?

DRITTE DAME: Und statt der süßen Feigen hab ich die Ehre, dir dies goldene Schloss vor den Mund zu schlagen. *(Sie schlägt ihm das Schloss vor.)*

(Papageno hat seinen Scherz durch Gebärden.)

ERSTE DAME: Du willst vermutlich wissen, warum die Fürstin dich heute so wunderbar bestraft?

(Papageno bejaht es.)

ZWEITE DAME: Damit du künftig nie mehr Fremde belügst.

DRITTE DAME: Und dass du nie dich der Heldentaten rühmst, die andre vollzogen. –

ERSTE DAME: Sag an! Hast du diese Schlange bekämpft?

(Papageno deutet nein.)

ZWEITE DAME: Wer denn also?

(Papageno deutet, er wisse es nicht.)

SECOND LADY: And instead of a sugarloaf, this stone. I hope it's to your liking.

PAPAGENO: I'm meant to eat a stone?

THIRD LADY: And instead of sweet figs, I give you this golden padlock for your mouth. *(She fastens the padlock.)*

(Papageno gestures his frustration.)

FIRST LADY: Do you wish to know why Her Majesty punishes you so strangely today?

(Papageno nods his head.)

SECOND LADY: So you will never lie to strangers again!

THIRD LADY: And not boast of brave deeds that others have dared.

FIRST LADY: Tell us now—did you slay this serpent?

(Papageno shakes his head.)

SECOND LADY: Who did then?

(Papageno shrugs.)

DRITTE DAME: *(zu Tamino)* Wir waren's, Jüngling, die dich befreiten. – Zittre nicht! Dich erwartet Freude und Entzücken. – Hier, dies Gemälde schickt dir die große Fürstin; es ist das Bildnis ihrer Tochter. "Findest du", sagte sie, "dass diese Züge dir nicht gleichgültig sind, dann ist Glück, Ehr und Ruhm dein Los." – Auf Wiedersehen.

(geht ab)

ZWEITE DAME: Adieu, Monsieur Papageno!

(geht ab)

ERSTE DAME:

Fein nicht zu hastig getrunken!

(geht lachend ab)

(Papageno hat immer sein stummes Spiel gehabt. Tamino ist gleich bei Empfang des Bildnisses aufmerksam geworden. Seine Liebe nimmt zu, ob er gleich für alle diese Reden taub schien.)

Vierter Auftritt
TAMINO, PAPAGENO

N° 3 Aria

TAMINO:
Dies Bildnis ist bezaubernd schön,
Wie noch kein Auge je gesehn.
Ich fühl es, wie dies Götterbild
Mein Herz mit neuer Regung füllt.
Dies Etwas kann ich zwar nicht nennen,
Doch fühl ich's hier wie Feuer brennen.
Soll die Empfindung Liebe sein? –
Ja, ja, die Liebe ist's allein.
O wenn ich sie nur finden könnte!
O wenn sie doch schon vor mir stünde!
Ich würde – würde – warm und rein –

THIRD LADY: *(to Tamino)* It was we, young man, who set you free. Fear nothing. Only joy and enchantment await you. Here, our great Queen sends you a likeness of her daughter. If you find yourself not unmoved by her features . . . then you are destined for happiness, honor, and glory!—Farewell! Until we meet again! *(She goes off.)*

SECOND LADY: Adieu, Monsieur Papageno! *(She goes off.)*

FIRST LADY: Don't gulp down your water! *(She goes off, laughing.)*

(Papageno continues gesticulating. Tamino, since receiving the portrait, has stared at it, ignoring the speeches around him, his love mounting.)

•

Fourth Scene
TAMINO AND PAPAGENO.

Aria

TAMINO:
This portrait's beauty I adore!
Who has seen its like before?
I feel it now, this heaven-sent art
Bewitches me and fills my heart.
I cannot name this new desire,
Burning, freezing, with one fire.
Can these be pangs of love I feel?
If so, it is to love I yield!
If only I could find her here!
If only she were somewhere near!
I would—I want—tell me,

Was würde ich? - Ich würde sie voll Entzücken
An diesen heißen Busen drücken,
Und ewig wäre sie dann mein.
(will ab)

Fünfter Auftritt
DIE DREI DAMEN, VORIGE.

Dialog

ERSTE DAME: Rüste dich mit Mut und Standhaftigkeit, schöner Jüngling! - Die Fürstin -

ZWEITE DAME: Hat mir aufgetragen, dir zu sagen -

DRITTE DAME: Dass der Weg zu deinem künftgen Glücke nunmehr gebahnt sei.

ERSTE DAME: Sie hat jedes deiner Worte gehört, so du sprachst; - sie hat -

ZWEITE DAME: Jeden Zug in deinem Gesichte gelesen. - Ja noch mehr, ihr mütterliches Herz -

DRITTE DAME: Hat beschlossen, dich ganz glücklich zu machen. - "Hat dieser Jüngling", sprach sie, "auch so viel Mut und Tapferkeit, als er zärtlich ist, o so ist meine Tochter ganz gewiss gerettet."

TAMINO: Gerettet? O ewige Dunkelheit! was hör ich? - Das Original? -

ERSTE DAME: Hat ein mächtiger, böser Dämon ihr entrissen.

TAMINO: Entrissen? - O ihr Götter! - sagt, wie konnte das geschehen?

Image, what to do?
Gently first I would caress her,
And to my ardent heart I'd press her.
Forever then would I be true.
(He is about to leave.)

Fifth Scene
THE THREE LADIES, AND THOSE BEFORE.

Spoken Dialogue

FIRST LADY: Arm yourself with courage and steadfastness, noble youth! The Queen . . .

SECOND LADY: . . . has commanded us to say . . .

THIRD LADY: . . . the path to your future happiness now lies open before you.

FIRST LADY: She has heard every word you have spoken; she has . . .

SECOND LADY: . . . read every feature in your face. Moreover, her motherly heart . . .

THIRD LADY: . . . has decided to grant your happiness. If this young man's courage, she said, is equal to his tenderness, then my daughter will be saved.

TAMINO: Saved? O eternal darkness! What are they saying?— You mean, the maiden in this picture . . . ?

FIRST LADY: Has been kidnapped by an evil wizard.

TAMINO: Kidnapped!—Oh God!—How did it happen?

ERSTE DAME: Sie saß an einem schönen Maientage ganz allein in dem alles belebenden Zypressenwäldchen, welches immer ihr Lieblingsaufenthalt war. – Der Bösewicht schlich unbemerkt hinein –

ZWEITE DAME: Belauschte sie, und –

DRITTE DAME: Er hat nebst seinem bösen Herzen auch noch die Macht, sich in jede erdenkliche Gestalt zu verwandeln. Auf solche Weise hat er auch Pamina –

ERSTE DAME: Dies ist der Name der königlichen Tochter, so ihr anbetet.

TAMINO: O Pamina! du mir entrissen – du in der Gewalt eines üppigen Bösewichts! – bist vielleicht in diesem Augenblicke – schrecklicher Gedanke!

DIE DREI DAMEN: Schweig, Jüngling! – –

ERSTE DAME: Lästere der holden Schönheit Tugend nicht! – Trotz aller Pein, so die Unschuld duldet, ist sie sich immer gleich. – Weder Zwang, noch Schmeichelei ist vermögend, sie zum Wege des Lasters zu verführen. – –

TAMINO: O sagt, Mädchen! sagt, wo ist des Tyrannen Aufenthalt?

ZWEITE DAME: Sehr nahe an unsern Bergen lebt er in einem angenehmen und reizenden Tale. – Seine Burg ist prachtvoll und sorgsam bewacht.

TAMINO: Kommt, Mädchen! führt mich! – Pamina sei gerettet! – Der Bösewicht falle von meinem Arm; das schwör ich bei meiner Liebe, bei meinem Herzen! *(Sogleich wird ein heftig erschütternder Akkord mit Musik gehört.)* Ihr Götter! Was ist das?

FIRST LADY: On a sunny day in May, she was sitting alone in the cypress grove that is her favorite spot . . . The evil creature slipped in unseen . . .

SECOND LADY: Saw her there . . .

THIRD LADY: Besides his evil heart he also has the power to change into any shape. And so it was he approached Pamina . . .

FIRST LADY: That is the name of the Queen's daughter whom you adore.

TAMINO: Pamina! Torn from me! In the clutches of a hateful fiend! Perhaps at this very moment you are—ghastly thought!

THE THREE LADIES: Silence, young man!

FIRST LADY: Do not besmirch the honor of that precious maiden! Despite her ordeal, her innocence is untouched. Neither force nor flattery could lead her down the path of vice.

TAMINO: Tell me, Ladies, where this tyrant lives.

SECOND LADY: He lives near our mountains in a quiet valley. His castle is grand, and vigilantly guarded.

TAMINO: Come, Ladies, show me the way! Pamina will be saved! The villain will fall by my hand. I swear it by my love, by my heart! *(A thunderous chord of music is heard.)* Good Lord, what's that?

DIE DREI DAMEN: Fasse dich!

ERSTE DAME: Es verkündigt die Ankunft unserer Königin.
(Donner)

DIE DREI DAMEN: Sie kommt! – *(Donner)* Sie kommt! – *(Donner)*
Sie kommt! –

Die Berge teilen sich auseinander und das Theater
verwandelt sich in ein prächtiges Gemach.
Die Königin sitzt auf einem Thron, welcher
mit transparenten Sternen geziert ist.

Sechster Auftritt

N° 4 Recitativo ed Aria

Recitativo

KÖNIGIN DER NACHT:
O zittre nicht, mein lieber Sohn,
Du bist unschuldig, weise, fromm, –
Ein Jüngling so wie du vermag am besten,
Das tief betrübte Mutterherz zu trösten. –

Aria

Zum Leiden bin ich auserkoren,
Denn meine Tochter fehlet mir.
Durch sie ging all mein Glück verloren,
Ein Bösewicht entfloh mit ihr.
Noch seh ich ihr Zittern
Mit bangem Erschüttern,
Ihr ängstliches Beben,
Ihr schüchternes Streben.
Ich musste sie mir rauben sehen.

THE THREE LADIES: Be brave!

FIRST LADY: It heralds the arrival of our Queen.
(Thunder.)

THE THREE LADIES: She comes! *(Thunder.)* She comes! *(Thunder.)*
She comes!

*The mountains part and the stage is transformed into
a splendid room. The Queen is seated on a throne which
is blazoned with transparent stars.*

Sixth Scene

Recitative and Aria

Recitative

QUEEN OF THE NIGHT:
O tremble not, my son, arise,
For you are innocent, pure, and wise.
Such a youth alone may heal
The wound these robes and crown conceal.

Aria

Grievous Fate's decree has stung me.
My daughter has been stolen from me.
My happiness all vanished the day
That evil fiend stole my darling away.
I see it still before my eyes,
Her torment and her fear.
Still I hear her frightened cries
And see her anguished tears.
Helpless I watched, as if in a dream.

"Ach helft!" war alles, was sie sprach, –
Allein vergebens war ihr Flehen,
Denn meine Hilfe war zu schwach.
Du wirst sie zu befreien gehen,
Du wirst der Tochter Retter sein!
Und werd ich dich als Sieger sehen,
So sei sie dann auf ewig dein.
(mit den drei Damen ab)

Das Theater verwandelt sich wieder so, wie es vorher war.

Siebenter Auftritt
TAMINO, PAPAGENO.

TAMINO: *(nach einer Pause)* Ist's denn auch Wirklichkeit, was ich
sah? oder betäubten mich meine Sinnen? – O ihr guten Götter,
täuscht mich nicht! oder ich unterliege eurer Prüfung. – Schützet
meinen Arm, stählt meinen Mut, und Taminos Herz wird ewigen
Dank euch entgegenschlagen.
(Er will gehen, Papageno tritt ihm in den Weg.)

N° 5 Quintetto
PAPAGENO: *(mit dem Schlosse vor dem Maul, winkt traurig darauf)* Hm!
Hm! Hm! Hm! Hm! Hm! Hm! Hm!

TAMINO:
Der Arme kann von Strafe sagen, –
Denn seine Sprache ist dahin!

PAPAGENO: Hm! Hm! Hm! Hm! Hm! Hm! Hm! Hm!

"Help me" was all that she could scream.
It faded. I followed. I tore and shrieked.
But all my struggling was far too weak.
Now you shall go to set her free
Now you can life and love restore.
And when you've won your victory
She will be yours forevermore!
(She leaves with the Ladies.)

The scene changes back to what it was before.

Seventh Scene
TAMINO AND PAPAGENO.

TAMINO: *(after a pause, speaking)* Can it be true, what I've just seen? Or have my senses been tricked? Gracious gods, pray don't deceive me, or I shall fail the task you set me! Strengthen my arm, steel my courage, and Tamino's heart will beat for you with gratitude.
(He is about to leave. Papageno steps in his way.)

Quintet

PAPAGENO: *(pointing sadly to the padlock on his mouth)* Hm! Hm! Hm! Hm! Hm! Hm! Hm! Hm!

TAMINO:
The poor man's punishment is plain.
His tongue is under lock and key.

PAPAGENO: Hm! Hm! Hm! Hm! Hm! Hm! Hm! Hm!

TAMINO:
Ich kann nichts tun, als dich beklagen,
Weil ich zu schwach zu helfen bin!

PAPAGENO: Hm! Hm! Hm! Hm! Hm! Hm!

Achter Auftritt
DIE DREI DAMEN, VORIGE.

ERSTE DAME:
Die Königin begnadigt dich,
Entlässt die Strafe dir durch mich.
(nimmt ihm das Schloss vom Maul weg)

PAPAGENO: Nun plaudert Papageno wieder!

ZWEITE DAME: Ja plaudre! – lüge nur nicht wieder!

PAPAGENO: Ich lüge nimmermehr! Nein, nein!

DIE DREI DAMEN: Dies Schloss soll deine Warnung sein!

PAPAGENO: Dies Schloss soll meine Warnung sein!

DIE DREI DAMEN, PAPAGENO:
Bekämen doch die Lügner alle
Ein solches Schloss vor ihren Mund;
Statt Hass, Verleumdung, schwarzer Galle
Bestünde Lieb und Bruderbund!

ERSTE DAME:
O Prinz! nimm dies Geschenk von mir,
Dies sendet unsre Fürstin dir.
(gibt ihm eine goldene Flöte)

TAMINO:
I sympathize but can't explain,
And have no power to set you free.

PAPAGENO: Hm! Hm! Hm! Hm! Hm! Hm! Hm! Hm!

Eighth Scene
THE THREE LADIES RETURN, AND THOSE BEFORE.

FIRST LADY:
The Queen has heard your mumbled plea
And bids us lift her stern decree.
(She removes the padlock.)

PAPAGENO: At last! Again! A chatterbox!

SECOND LADY: Another lie, and double locks!

PAPAGENO: I'll never tell another lie!

THE THREE LADIES: This lock should warn you not to try!

PAPAGENO: That lock sure warns me not to try!

THE THREE LADIES AND PAPAGENO:
If lies and envy could be banished
And truth alone were understood,
Then hatred, slander, all would vanish
And mankind live in brotherhood.

FIRST LADY:
Young Prince, our mighty Queen has sent
A gift to honor your consent.
(gives Tamino a golden flute)

Die Zauberflöte wird dich schützen,
Im größten Unglück unterstützen.

DIE DREI DAMEN:
Hiemit kannst du allmächtig handeln,
Der Menschen Leidenschaft verwandeln,
Der Traurige wird freudig sein,
Den Hagestolz nimmt Liebe ein.

DIE DREI DAMEN, PAPAGENO:
O so eine Flöte ist
Mehr als Gold und Kronen wert,
Denn durch sie wird Menschenglück
Und Zufriedenheit vermehrt.

PAPAGENO:
Nun, ihr schönen Frauenzimmer, –
Darf ich? so empfehl ich mich.

DIE DREI DAMEN:
Dich empfehlen kannst du immer,
Doch bestimmt die Fürstin dich,
Mit dem Prinzen ohn Verweilen
Nach Sarastros Burg zu eilen.

PAPAGENO:
Nein, dafür bedank ich mich!
Von euch selbsten hörte ich,
Dass er wie ein Tigertier
Sicher ließ ohn alle Gnaden
Mich Sarastro rupfen, braten,
Setzte mich den Hunden für.

This flute has strong and magic powers
To guide you through the dangerous hours.

THE THREE LADIES:
With this you can do anything.
Beasts will come and rocks will sing,
The grieving heart forget its pain
And sour hearts turn sweet again.

THE THREE LADIES AND PAPAGENO:
The spell this magic flute can cast
More than gold is worth.
It calms the soul and brings at last
Happiness on earth.

PAPAGENO:
And now, fair Ladies, there's work to do,
So may I take my leave of you?

THE THREE LADIES:
But listen first. You should know
The Queen's expressly chosen you.
You must stand by the Prince and go
To fight the villainous Sarastro.

PAPAGENO:
That's not for me—I'm grateful, though.
You've told me he's a tiger, no?
He's sure to run me to the ground,
Then have me plucked and roasted
And feed me to his snarling hounds.

DIE DREI DAMEN:
Dich schützt der Prinz, trau ihm allein!
Dafür sollst du sein Diener sein.

PAPAGENO: *(für sich)*
Dass doch der Prinz beim Teufel wäre,
Mein Leben ist mir lieb;
Am Ende schleicht, bei meiner Ehre,
Er von mir wie ein Dieb.

ERSTE DAME: *(gibt ihm ein stählernes Gelächter)* Hier nimm dies Kleinod, es ist dein.

PAPAGENO: Ei, ei! was mag drinnen sein?

DIE DREI DAMEN: Darinnen hörst du Glöckchen tönen.

PAPAGENO: Werd ich sie auch wohl spielen können?

DIE DREI DAMEN: O ganz gewiss! Ja, ja gewiss!

DIE DREI DAMEN, PAPAGENO:
Silber-Glöckchen, Zauber-Flöten
Sind zu eurem|unserm Schutz vonnöten!
Lebet wohl! Wir wollen gehn!
Lebet wohl! Auf Wiedersehn!
(Alle wollen gehen.)

TAMINO: Doch schöne Damen saget an,

PAPAGENO: Wo man die Burg wohl finden kann? –

TAMINO, PAPAGENO: Wo man die Burg wohl finden kann? –

THE THREE LADIES:
Stay by the Prince and have no fear.
You will be safe while he is near.

PAPAGENO: *(to himself)*
The devil take this valiant Prince.
My life means more to me.
I'll bet that when the fight begins
He'd be the first to flee.

FIRST LADY: *(handing him a box with chimes inside)* This precious
case is meant for you.

PAPAGENO: Aha! And may I open it too?

THE THREE LADIES: The bells inside sound bright and true.

PAPAGENO: How can I—do I strike or squeeze?

THE THREE LADIES: Oh, you can play it as you please.

THE THREE LADIES AND PAPAGENO:
With magic flute and silver bells
A lad can cast enchanted spells.
So now farewell! All's been explained.
Farewell, until we meet again!
(All are about to go.)

TAMINO: One moment, Ladies. Tell me, pray—

PAPAGENO: How are we to find our way!

TAMINO AND PAPAGENO: Yes, how are we to find our way?

DIE DREI DAMEN:
Drei Knäbchen, jung, schön, hold und weise,
Umschweben euch auf eurer Reise.
Sie werden eure Führer sein,
Folgt ihrem Rate ganz allein.

TAMINO, PAPAGENO:
Drei Knäbchen, jung, schön, hold und weise,
Umschweben uns auf unsrer Reise?

DIE DREI DAMEN, TAMINO, PAPAGENO:
So lebet wohl! wir wollen gehn;
Lebt wohl, lebt wohl, auf Wiedersehn.
(alle ab)

Neunter Auftritt

ZWEI SKLAVEN TRAGEN, SOBALD DAS THEATER IN EIN
PRÄCHTIGES ÄGYPTISCHES ZIMMER VERWANDELT IST,
SCHÖNE PÖLSTER NEBST EINEM PRÄCHTIGEN TÜRKISCHEN
TISCH HERAUS, BREITEN TEPPICHE AUF; SODANN KOMMT
DER DRITTE SKLAVE.

Dialog

DRITTER SKLAVE: Ha, ha, ha!

ERSTER SKLAVE: Pst, Pst!

ZWEITER SKLAVE: Was soll denn das Lachen? –

DRITTER SKLAVE: Unser Peiniger, der alles belauschende Mohr,
wird morgen sicherlich gehangen oder gespießt. – Pamina! – Ha,
ha, ha!

THE THREE LADIES:
Three Spirit-Boys are now to guide you.
Along the way they'll stay beside you.
If you faithfully obey,
They'll be sure you never stray.

TAMINO AND PAPAGENO:
Three Spirit-Boys are now to guide us.
Along the way they'll stay beside us.

THE THREE LADIES, TAMINO, AND PAPAGENO:
So now farewell! All's been explained.
Farewell, until we meet again!
(They all leave.)

Ninth Scene

ONCE THE SCENE HAS BEEN TRANSFORMED INTO A
RESPLENDENT EGYPTIAN ROOM, TWO SLAVES
CARRY IN BEAUTIFUL CUSHIONS AND AN INLAID TURKISH
TABLE, AND SPREAD OUT CARPETS; THEN THE
THIRD SLAVE ENTERS.

Spoken Dialogue

THIRD SLAVE: Ha, ha, ha!

FIRST SLAVE: Shh! Shh!

SECOND SLAVE: Why are you laughing?

THIRD SLAVE: Our tormentor, the all-seeing Moor, is surely
going to be hanged and run through with a spit tomorrow . . .
Pamina! . . . Ha, ha, ha!

ERSTER SKLAVE: Nun?

DRITTER SKLAVE: Das reizende Mädchen! – Ha, ha, ha!

ZWEITER SKLAVE: Nun?

DRITTER SKLAVE: Ist entsprungen.

ERSTER SKLAVE, ZWEITER SKLAVE: Entsprungen? – –

ERSTER SKLAVE: Und sie entkam?

DRITTER SKLAVE: Unfehlbar! – Wenigstens ist's mein wahrer Wunsch.

ERSTER SKLAVE: O Dank euch ihr guten Götter! Ihr habt meine Bitte erhört.

DRITTER SKLAVE: Sagt ich euch nicht immer, es wird doch ein Tag für uns scheinen, wo wir gerochen und der schwarze Manostatos bestraft werden wird.

ZWEITER SKLAVE: Was spricht nun der Mohr zu der Geschichte?

ERSTER SKLAVE: Er weiß doch davon?

DRITTER SKLAVE: Natürlich! Sie entlief vor seinen Augen. – Wie mir einige Brüder erzählten, die im Garten arbeiteten und von Weitem sahen und hörten, so ist der Mohr nicht mehr zu retten, auch wenn Pamina von Sarastros Gefolge wieder eingebracht würde.

ERSTER SKLAVE, ZWEITER SKLAVE: Wieso?

FIRST SLAVE: So?

THIRD SLAVE: The charming maiden!—Ha, ha, ha!

SECOND SLAVE: Yes?

THIRD SLAVE: She's escaped.

FIRST AND SECOND SLAVES: Escaped?

FIRST SLAVE: She got away?

THIRD SLAVE: Gone! At least I certainly hope she is.

FIRST SLAVE: Oh, thank you, good gods! You have heard my prayer.

THIRD SLAVE: Didn't I always say, the day will come when all of us will be avenged, and the black Monostatos will be punished!

SECOND SLAVE: What does the Moor have to say about it all?

FIRST SLAVE: Does he even know about it?

THIRD SLAVE: Naturally! She ran away right under his nose. Some of our brothers, working in the garden, saw and heard everything from a distance, and told me about it. Nothing can save the Moor now, even if Sarastro's men bring her back.

FIRST AND SECOND SLAVES: How so?

DRITTER SKLAVE: Du kennst ja den üppigen Wanst und seine Weise; das Mädchen aber war klüger, als ich dachte. – In dem Augenblicke, da er zu siegen glaubte, rief sie Sarastros Namen: Das erschütterte den Mohren, er blieb stumm und unbeweglich stehen. – Indes lief Pamina nach dem Kanal und schiffte von selbst in einer Gondel dem Palmwäldchen zu.

ERSTER SKLAVE: O wie wird das schüchterne Reh mit Todes-angst dem Palaste ihrer zärtlichen Mutter zueilen.

Zehnter Auftritt
VORIGE, MANOSTATOS (VON INNEN).

MANOSTATOS: He Sklaven!

ERSTER SKLAVE: Manostatos Stimme!

MANOSTATOS: He, Sklaven! schafft Fesseln herbei. –

DIE DREI SKLAVEN: Fesseln?

ERSTER SKLAVE: *(läuft zur Seitentüre)* Doch nicht für Pamina? O ihr Götter! Da seht Brüder, das Mädchen ist gefangen.

ZWEITER SKLAVE, DRITTER SKLAVE: Pamina? – Schrecklicher Anblick!

ERSTER SKLAVE: Seht, wie der unbarmherzige Teufel sie bei ihren zarten Händchen fasst. – Das halt ich nicht aus.
(geht auf die andere Seite ab)

ZWEITER SKLAVE: Ich noch weniger.
(auch dort ab)

THIRD SLAVE: You know that fat-headed fleshpot and his ways. But the girl was cleverer than I thought. At the very moment he was certain she was his, she called out Sarastro's name. The Moor was stunned. He just stood there slack-jawed and motionless, while Pamina ran off to the canal and rowed a gondola all by herself towards the palm grove.

FIRST SLAVE: How that timid fawn, her heart aflutter with fear, must be hurrying to her tender mother's palace!

Tenth Scene
THOSE BEFORE, AND MONOSTATOS (FROM WITHIN).

MONOSTATOS: Hey there, slaves!

FIRST SLAVE: Monostatos's voice!

MONOSTATOS: Hey, slaves! Fetch me some chains!

THE THREE SLAVES: Chains?

FIRST SLAVE: *(peering out the side door)* Not for Pamina! Oh ye gods! Look, brothers, the maiden has been captured.

SECOND AND THIRD SLAVES: Pamina! What a terrible sight!

FIRST SLAVE: Look at the way that filthy devil grabs her tender little hand. I cannot bear it.
(He goes out the other side.)

SECOND SLAVE: I can't either.
(He also runs out.)

DRITTER SKLAVE: So was sehen zu müssen, ist Höllenmarter.
(ab)

Elfter Auftritt
MANOSTATOS, PAMINA
(DIE VON SKLAVEN HEREINGEFÜHRT WIRD).

N° 6 Terzetto

MANOSTATOS: *(sehr schnell)* Du, feines Täubchen, nur herein.

PAMINA: O welche Marter, welche Pein!

MANOSTATOS: Verloren ist dein Leben.

PAMINA:
Der Tod macht mich nicht beben;
Nur meine Mutter dauert mich,
Sie stirbt vor Gram ganz sicherlich.

MANOSTATOS:
He, Sklaven, legt ihr Fesseln an;
Mein Hass soll dich verderben!
(Sie legen ihr Fesseln an.)

PAMINA:
O lass mich lieber sterben,
Weil nichts, Barbar, dich rühren kann.
(sinkt in Ohnmacht auf ein Sofa)

MANOSTATOS:
Nun fort, lasst mich bei ihr allein.
(Die Sklaven gehen ab.)

THIRD SLAVE: To have to watch this is hell on earth.
(He leaves.)

Eleventh Scene

MONOSTATOS AND PAMINA, LED IN BY SLAVES.

Trio

MONOSTATOS: *(very quickly)* Come, my fawn, in here!

PAMINA: Nothing but torment, nothing but pain!

MONOSTATOS: Submit or you will surely die!

PAMINA:
Mere death is simple to defy!
But spare me for my mother's sake.
With word of this her heart would break.

MONOSTATOS:
Slaves, bring chains! Their effect's well known!
I'll force you to obey me!
(They put the chains on Pamina.)

PAMINA:
I'd rather that you slay me!
Can nothing move a heart of stone?
(She falls onto a couch in a swoon.)

MONOSTATOS:
Get out! Leave me with her alone.
(The slaves leave.)

Zwölfter Auftritt
PAPAGENO (AM FENSTER AUSSEN, OHNE GLEICH GESEHEN ZU WERDEN), VORIGE.

PAPAGENO:
Wo bin ich wohl! Wo mag ich sein?
Aha, da find ich Leute;
Gewagt, ich geh herein.
(geht herein)
Schön Mädchen, jung und rein,
Viel weißer noch als Kreide…

(Manostatos und Papageno sehen sich, – erschrickt einer über den andern)

MANOSTATOS, PAPAGENO:
Hu – – – das ist – der Teu – – fel sicherlich.
Hab Mitleid – verschone mich. –
Hu – Hu – Hu – Hu –
(laufen beide ab)

Dreizehnter Auftritt
PAMINA ALLEIN.

Dialog
PAMINA: *(spricht wie im Traum)* Mutter – Mutter – Mutter! – *(Sie erholt sich, sieht sich um.)* Wie? – Noch schlägt dieses Herz? – Noch nicht vernichtet? – Zu neuen Qualen erwacht? – O das ist hart, sehr hart! – mir bitterer als der Tod.

Twelfth Scene

PAPAGENO (OUTSIDE THE WINDOW, UNSEEN AT FIRST),

AND THOSE BEFORE.

PAPAGENO:

Where am I now? Where can this be?

Aha! There's someone there inside.

I'll take a chance and try to see . . .

(He goes inside.)

A maiden, fair as soft moonlight,

With skin like snow, so white!

(Monostatos and Papageno are terrified by the sight of each other.)

MONOSTATOS AND PAPAGENO:

The very devil, certainly!

Have mercy! Please! Oh, pity me!

Shoo! Shoo! Shoo!

(They both run off.)

Thirteenth Scene

PAMINA, ALONE.

Spoken Dialogue

PAMINA: *(speaking as if in a dream)* Mother . . . Mother . . . Mother!
(She wakes up and looks around.) What . . . My heart is still beating!
I'm not dead after all! But have I woken to new agonies? Oh, this
is so hard, so cruel! More bitter than death itself!

Vierzehnter Auftritt

PAPAGENO, PAMINA.

PAPAGENO: Bin ich nicht ein Narr, dass ich mich schrecken ließ? – Es gibt ja schwarze Vögel in der Welt; warum denn nicht auch schwarze Menschen? – Ah, sieh da! hier ist das schöne Fräulenbild noch. – Du Tochter der nächtlichen Königin!

PAMINA: Nächtliche Königin? – Wer bist du?

PAPAGENO: Ein Abgesandter der sternflammenden Königin.

PAMINA: *(freudig)* Meiner Mutter? – O Wonne! – Dein Name!

PAPAGENO: Papageno!

PAMINA: Papageno? – Papageno – Ich erinnere mich, den Namen oft gehört zu haben, dich selbst aber sah ich nie. –

PAPAGENO: Ich dich ebenso wenig.

PAMINA: Du kennst also meine gute, zärtliche Mutter?

PAPAGENO: Wenn du die Tochter der nächtlichen Königin bist – ja!

PAMINA: O ich bin es.

PAPAGENO: Das will ich gleich erkennen. *(Er sieht das Porträt an, welches der Prinz zuvor empfangen und Papageno nun an einem Bande am Halse trägt.)* Die Augen schwarz – richtig, schwarz. – Die Lippen rot – richtig, rot. – Blonde Haare – Blonde Haare. – Alles trifft ein, bis auf Händ und Füße. – – – Nach dem Gemälde zu schlüssen, sollst du weder Hände noch Füße haben; denn hier sind auch keine angezeigt.

Fourteenth Scene

PAPAGENO AND PAMINA.

PAPAGENO: What a fool I am to be so frightened! There are black birds in the world—so why not black men?—Ah, the pretty girl's still here! You must be the daughter of the Queen of the Night . . .

PAMINA: The Queen of the Night! And who are you?

PAPAGENO: A messenger from the star-shimmering Queen.

PAMINA: *(joyfully)* From my mother? Oh joy! What is your name?

PAPAGENO: Papageno.

PAMINA: Papageno? Papa . . . geno . . . I have often heard that name before, but you yourself I've never seen.

PAPAGENO: I can't remember you either.

PAMINA: But you know my good, gentle mother?

PAPAGENO: If you are the daughter of the Queen of the Night— then, yes!

PAMINA: Yes, I am her daughter!

PAPAGENO: I can verify that! *(He looks at the portrait the Prince had been given, which he now wears on a ribbon around his neck.)* Eyes, black.—Right, black. Lips, red.—Right, red. Hair, blonde.— Blonde hair. Everything's right . . . except your hands and feet. According to this picture, you shouldn't have hands or feet. There aren't any here.

PAMINA: Erlaube mir. – Ja, ich bin's. – Wie kam es in deine Hände?

PAPAGENO: Dir das zu erzählen, wäre zu weitläufig. Es kam von Hand zu Hand.

PAMINA: Wie kam es in die deinige?

PAPAGENO: Auf eine wunderbare Art. – Ich habe es gefangen.

PAMINA: Gefangen?

PAPAGENO: Ich muss dir das umständlicher erzählen. – Ich kam heute früh wie gewöhnlich zu deiner Mutter Palast mit meiner Lieferung. –

PAMINA: Lieferung?

PAPAGENO: Ja, ich liefere deiner Mutter und ihren Jungfrauen schon seit vielen Jahren alle die schönen Vögel in den Palast. – Eben als ich im Begriff war, meine Vögel abzugeben, sah ich einen Menschen vor mir, der sich Prinz nennen lässt. – Dieser Prinz hat deine Mutter so eingenommen, dass sie ihm dein Bildnis schenkte und ihm befahl, dich zu befreien. – Sein Entschluss war so schnell als seine Liebe zu dir.

PAMINA: Liebe? *(freudig)* Er liebt mich also? O sage mir das noch einmal. Ich höre das Wort Liebe gar zu gerne.

PAPAGENO: Das glaube ich dir, ohne zu schwören; bist ja ein Fräulenbild. – Wo blieb ich denn?

PAMINA: Bei der Liebe.

PAMINA: May I?—Yes, that's me.—How did it come into your hands?

PAPAGENO: That story would take forever. Let's just say it passed from hand to hand.

PAMINA: But how did it get into yours?

PAPAGENO: In a most peculiar manner. I captured it.

PAMINA: Captured it?

PAPAGENO: Let me tell you how. This morning, I came around to your mother's palace as usual, with my delivery . . .

PAMINA: Delivery?

PAPAGENO: For years I've caught all sorts of pretty birds and brought them to the palace for your mother. Today I was making my delivery when suddenly someone was standing before me who called himself a "Prince." Your mother was so taken with him that she gave him a portrait of you and commanded him to rescue you. He obeyed at once because he had fallen in love with you.

PAMINA: Love? *(joyfully)* He loves me? Oh, say that again! I love to hear the word "love"!

PAPAGENO: I believe you. After all, you're a woman, aren't you? Anyway . . . where was I?

PAMINA: You were talking about love.

PAPAGENO: Richtig, bei der Liebe! – Das nenn ich Gedächtnis haben. – Kurz also, diese große Liebe zu dir war der Peitschenstreich, um unsre Füße in schnellen Gang zu bringen. Nun sind wir hier, dir tausend schöne und angenehme Sachen zu sagen, dich in unsre Arme zu nehmen und, wenn es möglich ist, ebenso schnell, wo nicht schneller als hierher, in den Palast deiner Mutter zu eilen.

PAMINA: Das ist alles sehr schön gesagt. Aber lieber Freund! wenn der unbekannte Jüngling oder Prinz, wie er sich nennt, Liebe für mich fühlt, warum säumt er so lange, mich von meinen Fesseln zu befreien? –

PAPAGENO: Da steckt eben der Haken. – Wie wir von den Jungfrauen Abschied nahmen, so sagten sie uns, drei holde Knaben würden unsre Wegweiser sein, sie würden uns belehren, wie und auf was Art wir handeln sollen.

PAMINA: Sie lehrten euch?

PAPAGENO: Nichts lehrten sie uns, denn wir haben keinen gesehen. – Zur Sicherheit also war der Prinz so fein, mich vorauszuschicken, um dir unsre Ankunft anzukündigen. –

PAMINA: Freund, du hast viel gewagt! – Wenn Sarastro dich hier erblicken sollte. – –

PAPAGENO: So wird mir meine Rückreise erspart. – Das kann ich mir denken.

PAMINA: Dein martervoller Tod würde ohne Grenzen sein.

PAPAGENO: Um diesem auszuweichen, so gehen wir lieber beizeiten.

PAPAGENO: Right, about love. You sure have a good memory. In a word, this love of his whipped him into action. Off we went, and now we're here, to coo a thousand sweet words in your ear, to take you in our arms, and, if we can, quick as a wink, whisk you off to your mother's palace.

PAMINA: Very prettily said. But, dear friend, if this young man— or Prince, as he calls himself—really loves me, why is it taking him so long to free me from my chains?

PAPAGENO: That's the problem. As we were saying farewell to your mother's Ladies, they told us three sweet Boys would guide us and give us instruction on what to do and how.

PAMINA: Did they?

PAPAGENO: We haven't seen them, so they've told us nothing. But just to be safe, the Prince sent me on ahead to announce our arrival.

PAMINA: Friend, you have been so brave! If Sarastro sees you here . . .

PAPAGENO: Then I guess we won't have to worry about the return trip.

PAMINA: You would be executed—after being tortured.

PAPAGENO: Let's avoid that—and leave at once!

PAMINA: Wie hoch mag wohl die Sonne sein?

PAPAGENO: Bald gegen Mittag.

PAMINA: So haben wir keine Minute zu versäumen. – Um diese Zeit kommt Sarastro gewöhnlich von der Jagd zurück.

PAPAGENO: Sarastro ist also nicht zu Hause? – Pah! da haben wir gewonnenes Spiel! – Komm, schönes Fräulenbild! du wirst Augen machen, wenn du den schönen Jüngling erblickst.

PAMINA: Wohl denn! Es sei gewagt! *(Sie gehen, Pamina kehrt um.)* Aber wenn dies ein Fallstrick wäre, – wenn dieser nun ein böser Geist von Sarastros Gefolge wäre? – *(sieht ihn bedenklich an)*

PAPAGENO: Ich ein böser Geist? – Wo denkt ihr hin Fräulenbild? – Ich bin der beste Geist von der Welt.

PAMINA: Doch nein; das Bild hier überzeugt mich, dass ich nicht getäuscht bin. Es kommt von den Händen meiner zärtlichsten Mutter.

PAPAGENO: Schön's Fräulenbild, wenn dir wieder ein so böser Verdacht aufsteigen sollte, dass ich dich betrügen wollte, so denke nur fleißig an die Liebe, und jeder böse Argwohn wird schwinden.

PAMINA: Freund, vergib! vergib! wenn ich dich beleidigte. Du hast ein gefühlvolles Herz; das sehe ich in jedem deiner Züge.

PAPAGENO: Ach freilich hab ich ein gefühlvolles Herz. – Aber was nützt mich das alles? – Ich möchte mir oft alle meine Federn ausrupfen, wenn ich bedenke, dass Papageno noch keine Papagena hat.

PAMINA: What time is it?

PAPAGENO: Near noon, I think.

PAMINA: Not a moment to lose. Sarastro usually returns from the hunt about this time.

PAPAGENO: So Sarastro's not home now? Ha! Then let's not worry. Come, pretty maiden. You'll be dazzled by the sight of the handsome young man who's come for you.

PAMINA: Let's take our chances! *(They start to leave, but Pamina turns back.)* But what if this is all a trick? What if this fellow is an evil spirit in Sarastro's gang? *(She looks at him suspiciously.)*

PAPAGENO: Me? An evil spirit? What can you be thinking, young lady? Why, I'm the best spirit in the whole world.

PAMINA: I'm sure you're right! After all, this picture is proof that I'm not being deceived. It comes from my dear mother herself.

PAPAGENO: Dear lady, if such a foul suspicion ever strikes you again—that I would ever deceive you—then just think about love and every doubt will disappear.

PAMINA: Forgive me, friend. I hope I haven't offended you. You have a tender heart. That I can see.

PAPAGENO: Well . . . yes . . . a tender heart. Though what good does it do me? I'd as soon pull out all my feathers, when I think that Papageno has no Papagena!

PAMINA: Armer Mann! Du hast also noch kein Weib?

PAPAGENO: Nicht einmal ein Mädchen, viel weniger ein Weib! – Ja das ist betrübt! – Und unsereiner hat doch auch bisweilen seine lustigen Stunden, wo man gern gesellschaftliche Unterhaltung haben möcht. –

PAMINA: Geduld Freund! Der Himmel wird auch für dich sorgen; er wird dir eine Freundin schicken, ehe du dir's vermutest. –

PAPAGENO: Wenn er's nur bald schickte.

N° 7 Duetto

PAMINA:
Bei Männern, welche Liebe fühlen,
Fehlt auch ein gutes Herze nicht.

PAPAGENO:
Die süßen Triebe mitzufühlen,
Ist dann der Weiber erste Pflicht.

PAMINA, PAPAGENO:
Wir wollen uns der Liebe freun,
Wir leben durch die Lieb allein.

PAMINA:
Die Lieb versüßet jede Plage,
Ihr opfert jede Kreatur.

PAPAGENO:
Sie würzet unsre Lebenstage,
Sie wirkt im Kreise der Natur.

PAMINA, PAPAGENO:
Ihr hoher Zweck zeigt deutlich an:
Nichts Edlers sei als Weib und Mann.

PAMINA: Poor man! You have no wife?

PAPAGENO: Not even a sweetheart, much less a wife! That is my sorry state! A man like me wants to be happy every now and then, and have a little company . . .

PAMINA: Patience, friend! Heaven will send her sooner than you think.

PAPAGENO: If only she'd come soon!

Duet

PAMINA:
A man who's touched by love's emotion
Surely has a tender heart.

PAPAGENO:
To share a man's sincere devotion—
That should be the woman's part.

PAMINA AND PAPAGENO:
The greatest joy that each may own—
To live by love, by love alone.

PAMINA:
Love can lighten every sorrow.
Every creature pays her due.

PAPAGENO:
Love today and love tomorrow
Keep Nature's circle turning true.

PAMINA AND PAPAGENO:
The noblest aim of human life
Is to be joined as man and wife.

Mann und Weib und Weib und Mann
Reichen an die Gottheit an.

(beide ab)

*Das Theater verwandelt sich in einen Hain. Ganz im Grunde
der Bühne ist ein schöner Tempel, worauf diese Worte
stehen: "Tempel der Weisheit". Dieser Tempel führt mit
Säulen zu zwei andern Tempeln. Rechts auf den einen steht:
"Tempel der Vernunft". Links steht: "Tempel der Natur".*

Fünfzehnter Auftritt

DREI KNABEN FÜHREN DEN TAMINO HEREIN, JEDER
HAT EINEN SILBERNEN PALMZWEIG IN DER HAND.

N° 8 Finale

DREI KNABEN:
Zum Ziele führt dich diese Bahn,
Doch musst du, Jüngling, männlich siegen;
Drum höre unsre Lehre an:
Sei standhaft, duldsam und verschwiegen!

TAMINO:
Ihr holden Kleinen sagt mir an,
Ob ich Paminen retten kann? –

DREI KNABEN:
Dies kundzutun, steht uns nicht an;
Sei standhaft, duldsam und verschwiegen!
Bedenke dies, kurz: Sei ein Mann, –
Dann, Jüngling, wirst du männlich siegen.

(gehen ab)

Man and wife, and wife and man,
Both are parts of heaven's plan.
(They both go off.)

*The scene changes to a grove. At the back of the stage is
a beautiful temple upon which is inscribed "Temple of
Wisdom." Colonnades join this temple to two others. The one
on the right says "Temple of Reason," and the one on the left,
"Temple of Nature."*

Fifteenth Scene

THE THREE BOYS LEAD TAMINO IN. EACH OF THEM HAS
A SILVER PALM FROND IN HIS HAND.

Finale

THE THREE BOYS:
This path will lead you on your way.
A manly spirit will not stray.
To these three virtues now hold fast—
Be silent, patient, and steadfast!

TAMINO:
But, blessed spirits, first tell me—
May I set Pamina free?

THE THREE BOYS:
The answer is not ours to tell.
Be silent, patient, and steadfast!
A manly courage most excels.
Who bravely dares will win at last!
(They leave.)

TAMINO:

Die Weisheitslehre dieser Knaben
Sei ewig mir ins Herz gegraben.
Wo bin ich nun? – Was wird mit mir?
Ist dies der Sitz der Götter hier? –
Doch zeigen die Pforten, – es zeigen die Säulen,
Dass Klugheit und Arbeit und Künste hier weilen.
Wo Tätigkeit thronet und Müßiggang weicht,
Erhält seine Herrschaft das Laster nicht leicht.
Ich wage mich mutig zur Pforte hinein,
Die Absicht ist edel und lauter und rein.
Erzittre feiger Bösewicht!
Paminen retten, ist mir Pflicht.
(geht an die Pforte rechts, macht sie auf, und als er hinein will, hört man
von fern eine Stimme)

EINE STIMME: Zurück!

TAMINO: Zurück? So wag ich hier mein Glück!
(geht an die Pforte links)

EINE STIMME: *(von innen)* Zurück!

TAMINO:

Auch hier ruft man zurück?
(sieht sich um)
Da seh ich noch eine Tür,
Vielleicht find ich den Eingang hier!
(Er klopft, ein alter Priester erscheint.)

PRIESTER:

Wo willst du, kühner Fremdling, hin?
Was suchst du hier im Heiligtum? –

TAMINO:

May the truths these Boys impart
Be carved forever on my heart!
Where am I now! And what's inside?
Can this be where the gods abide?
It's here, these portals seem to tell,
That Skill and Work and Wisdom dwell.
Where all men strive and vigor's crowned,
No vice or baseness will be found.
All danger mocked, and death defied,
My purpose noble, my courage high,
Evil wizard, beware my scorn!
To save Pamina I have sworn!
(As he rushes towards the temple on the right, a distant voice is heard.)

A VOICE: Go back!

TAMINO: Go back? I'll try my fortune here!
(He goes to the temple on the left.)

A VOICE: *(from within)* Go back!

TAMINO:

"Go back, go back" is all I hear.
(He looks around.)
One last door remains. I'll dare
Once more to find an entrance there.
(He knocks. An old Priest appears.)

PRIEST:

Who is it comes? Bold stranger, speak!
Why have you sought this sacred place?

TAMINO: Der Lieb und Tugend Eigentum.

PRIESTER:
Die Worte sind von hohem Sinn, –
Allein, wie willst du diese finden?
Dich leitet Lieb und Tugend nicht,
Weil Tod und Rache dich entzünden.

TAMINO: Nur Rache für den Bösewicht.

PRIESTER: Den wirst du wohl bei uns nicht finden.

TAMINO: *(schnell)* Sarastro herrscht in diesen Gründen?

PRIESTER: Ja, ja, Sarastro herrschet hier

TAMINO: *(schnell)* Doch in der Weisheit Tempel nicht? –

PRIESTER: *(langsam)* Er herrscht im Weisheit-Tempel hier. –

TAMINO: So ist denn alles Heuchelei!
(will gehen)

PRIESTER: Willst du schon wieder gehn?

TAMINO:
Ja, ich will gehen, froh und frei, –
Nie euren Tempel sehn! –

PRIESTER:
Erklär dich näher mir,
Dich täuschet ein Betrug! –

TAMINO: Love and Virtue are what I seek.

PRIEST:
Your words bespeak a noble mind,
But success is honor's counterpart.
Love and Virtue you will never find
While death and vengeance rule your heart.

TAMINO: Upon a fiend, revenge in kind!

PRIEST: Within this temple, all's benign.

TAMINO: *(quickly)* It's here the great Sarastro rules?

PRIEST: Indeed, it's here Sarastro rules.

TAMINO: *(quickly)* But not in Wisdom's sacred shrine?

PRIEST: *(slowly)* He rules in Wisdom's sacred shrine!

TAMINO: So everything's hypocrisy!
(He starts to leave.)

PRIEST: You wish, I gather, now to go?

TAMINO:
Yes, I'll go, relieved and free—
The wisdom here is just a show.

PRIEST:
Explain yourself to me.
I fear you've been misled.

TAMINO:

Sarastro wohnet hier,

Das ist mir schon genug! –

PRIESTER:

Wenn du dein Leben liebst,

So rede, bleibe da! –

Sarastro hassest du?

TAMINO: Ich hass ihn ewig, ja! –

PRIESTER: Nun gib mir deine Gründe an! –

TAMINO: Er ist ein Unmensch, ein Tyrann! –

PRIESTER: Ist das, was du gesagt, erwiesen?

TAMINO:

Durch ein unglücklich Weib bewiesen.

Die Gram und Jammer niederdrückt!

PRIESTER:

Ein Weib hat also dich berückt? –

Ein Weib tut wenig, plaudert viel;

Du, Jüngling, glaubst dem Zungenspiel.

O legte doch Sarastro dir

Die Absicht seiner Handlung für. –

TAMINO:

Die Absicht ist nur allzu klar!

Riss nicht der Räuber ohn Erbarmen

Paminen aus der Mutter Armen? –

PRIESTER: Ja, Jüngling, was du sagst, ist wahr! –

TAMINO:

If Sarastro is your head,
That's quite enough for me.

PRIEST:

Listen, boy, as your life is dear.
I command you not to move from here!
It is Sarastro you hate so?

TAMINO: I hate him, and the reason's clear.

PRIEST: And can you tell me how you know?

TAMINO: He is a tyrant, a monstrous foe!

PRIEST: And can you prove what you now say?

TAMINO:

A woman can, who day by day
Suffers grief and endless woe.

PRIEST:

A woman told you it was so?
Foolish youth, to so believe
The webs that chattering women weave.
Would Sarastro himself were here
At last to make his motives clear!

TAMINO:

His motives from the first I knew!
Did not that villain connive and tear
A daughter from her mother's care?

PRIEST: Young stranger, what you say is true.

TAMINO:
Wo ist sie, die er uns geraubt?
Man opferte vielleicht sie schon? –

PRIESTER:
Dir dies zu sagen, teurer Sohn,
Ist itzund mir noch nicht erlaubt. –

TAMINO: Erklär dies Rätsel, täusch mich nicht!

PRIESTER: Die Zunge bindet Eid und Pflicht!

TAMINO: Wann also wird die Decke schwinden? –

PRIESTER:
Sobald dich führt der Freundschaft Hand
Ins Heiligtum zum ew'gen Band.
(geht ab)

TAMINO: *(allein)*
O ew'ge Nacht! wann wirst du schwinden? –
Wann wird das Licht mein Auge finden? –

EINIGE STIMMEN: *(von innen)* Bald, Jüngling, oder nie!

TAMINO:
Bald, sagt ihr, oder nie? –
Ihr Unsichtbaren saget mir:
Lebt denn Pamina noch?

EINIGE STIMMEN: *(von innen)* Pamina lebet noch!

TAMINO: *(freudig)*
Sie lebt, sie lebt! Ich danke euch dafür.
(nimmt seine Flöte heraus)

TAMINO:
Where is she now? What is her plight?
Who could survive this cruel ordeal?

PRIEST:
The secrets of the temple's rites
I am forbidden to reveal.

TAMINO: Explain your riddle! Tell me now!

PRIEST: I am bound to silence by my vow.

TAMINO: When are Light and Truth allowed?

PRIEST:
When you are led by friendship's hand
To join this temple's sacred band.
(He withdraws.)

TAMINO: *(alone)*
Oh starless night! Oh endless sorrow!
Will the answers come tomorrow?

SEVERAL VOICES: *(from within)* Soon, fair youth, or nevermore.

TAMINO:
Soon, they say, or nevermore?
Unseen powers, answer me—
Is Pamina still alive?

SEVERAL VOICES: *(from within)* Yes, Pamina's still alive!

TAMINO: *(joyfully)*
Alive! For that one word my thanks!
(He takes up his flute.)

O wenn ich doch nur imstande wäre,
Allmächtige, zu eurer Ehre,
Mit jedem Tone meinen Dank
Zu schildern, *(aufs Herz deutend)* wie er hier entsprang.
(Er spielt. Es kommen wilde Tiere von allen Arten hervor, ihm zuzuhören.
Er hört auf und sie fliehen. Die Vögel pfeifen dazu.)
Wie stark ist nicht dein Zauberton, *(spielt)*
Weil, holde Flöte, durch dein Spielen
Selbst wilde Tiere Freude fühlen. *(spielt)*
Doch nur Pamina bleibt davon,
(spielt)
Pamina! höre, höre mich! *(spielt)*
Umsonst! – *(spielt)* Wo? *(spielt)* ach! wo find ich dich! – *(spielt)*
(Papageno antwortet von innen mit seinem Flötchen.)
Ha, das ist Papagenos Ton! – *(spielt. Papageno antwortet.)*
(spielt. Papageno antwortet.)
Vielleicht sah er Paminen schon! –
Vielleicht eilt sie mit ihm zu mir! –
Vielleicht führt mich der Ton zu ihr!
(eilt ab)

Sechzehnter Auftritt
PAPAGENO, PAMINA (OHNE FESSELN)

PAMINA, PAPAGENO:
Schnelle Füße, rascher Mut
Schützt vor Feindes List und Wut.
Fänden wir Tamino doch!
Sonst erwischen sie uns noch!

PAMINA: Holder Jüngling! –

If only I could find the phrases,
Mighty forces, to sing your praises.
This song comes *(points to his heart)* from a heart in love.
Let it be heard in heaven above!
(He plays. The beasts of the forest come out to hear him. When he stops,
they flee. Birds sing to his playing.)
How this magic flute enchants! *(He plays)*
In its music spells hold sway.
The birds will sing, the beasts will dance. *(He plays)*
But only Pamina stays away!
(He plays.)
Pamina! Can you hear me call?: *(He plays.)*
How *(He plays)* will I ever *(He plays)* find you at all? *(He plays.)*
(From afar, Papageno answers on his panpipe.)
That is Papageno's sound! *(He plays. Again, Papageno answers.)*
(He plays. Papageno answers once more.)
Perhaps it means Pamina's found.
Perhaps Pamina's by his side!
This magic flute must be my guide!
(He runs off.)

Sixteenth Scene

PAPAGENO AND PAMINA (WITHOUT HER CHAINS).

PAMINA AND PAPAGENO:
Swift of foot and bold of heart
Can still outrun, and still outsmart.
Unless we find Tamino, though,
We can't just scramble to-and-fro.

PAMINA: Ta-mi-no!

PAPAGENO: Stille, stille, ich kann's besser!
(pfeift)
(Tamino antwortet von innen mit seiner Flöte.)

PAMINA, PAPAGENO:
Welche Freude ist wohl größer,
Freund Tamino hört uns schon,
Hieher kam der Flöte Ton.
Welch ein Glück, wenn ich ihn finde!
Nur geschwinde, nur geschwinde!
(wollen hineingehen)

Siebzehnter Auftritt
VORIGE, MANOSTATOS.

MANOSTATOS: *(ihrer spottend)*
Nur geschwinde, nur geschwinde, nur geschwinde.
Ha! – hab ich euch noch erwischt!
Nur herbei mit Stahl und Eisen;
Wart, man wird euch Mores weisen!
Den Manostatos berücken! –
Nur herbei mit Band und Stricken,
He, ihr Sklaven, kommt herbei! –

PAMINA, PAPAGENO: Ach, nun ist's mit uns vorbei.

MANOSTATOS: He, ihr Sklaven, kommt herbei! –

(Die Sklaven kommen mit Fesseln.)

PAPAGENO: Shh! I know a better way!
(He plays.)
(Tamino, from within, answers on his flute.)

PAMINA AND PAPAGENO:
It's closer! Yes, it does not fade!
At last Tamino hears our cry.
His magic flute's his sweet reply.
We'll tell all we've seen and done!
Hurry now! Run! Let's run!
(They are about to enter.)

Seventeenth Scene

THOSE BEFORE, AND MONOSTATOS.

MONOSTATOS: *(mocking her)*
"Hurry now! Run! Let's run!"
Ha! Now I have you both again!
Bring the heavy iron chains!
They will teach you to obey.
You both were foolish to betray!
Monostatos has won the day!
Bring the chains to bind them with!

PAMINA AND PAPAGENO: Now all, I fear, is over with!

MONOSTATOS: Bring the chains to bind them with!

(Slaves come with chains.)

PAPAGENO:

Wer viel wagt, gewinnt oft viel,
Komm du schönes Glockenspiel!
Lass die Glöckchen klingen, klingen,
Dass die Ohren ihnen singen.
(schlägt auf seinem Instrument)

MANOSTATOS UND SKLAVEN:

Das klinget so herrlich, das klinget so schön!
La ra la la la la ra la la la la ra la.
Nie hab ich so etwas gehört und gesehn!
La ra la la la la ra la la la la ra la.
(gehen marschmäßig ab)

PAMINA, PAPAGENO: *(lachen)*

Könnte jeder brave Mann
Solche Glöckchen finden,
Seine Feinde würden dann
Ohne Mühe schwinden.
Und er lebte ohne sie
In der besten Harmonie!
Nur der Freundschaft Harmonie
Mildert die Beschwerden,
Ohne diese Sympathie
Ist kein Glück auf Erden.

(Ein starker Marsch mit Trompeten und Pauken fällt ein.)

CHOR: *(von innen)* Es lebe Sarastro! Sarastro lebe! –

PAPAGENO: Was soll dies bedeuten? Ich zittre, ich bebe! –

PAPAGENO:
He who dares has all to gain!
Come, my chimes, let bells begin!
Let the precious silver ring!
Let the bells sound out and sing!
(He plays his chimes.)

MONOSTATOS AND HIS SLAVES:
It sounds so happy, sounds so gay!
La ra la la la la ra la!
Let's sing and dance our time away!
La ra la la la la ra la!
(They dance out.)

PAMINA AND PAPAGENO: *(both laughing)*
If every man had silver bells,
And played them to deceive,
Charmed at once by music's spells,
His enemies would leave.
Music gladdens every soul
In perfect harmony!
Life on earth's again made whole
By friendship's sympathy.
Sorrow first will yield to laughter,
Then joy forever follows after!

(A sturdy march with trumpets and timpani starts up.)

CHORUS: *(from within)* Long live Sarastro! Sarastro all hail!

PAPAGENO:
What's that noise those men are making?
And why are my feathery knees so shaking?

PAMINA:

O Freund! Nun ist's um uns getan!
Dies kündigt den Sarastro an!

PAPAGENO:

O wär ich eine Maus,
Wie wollt ich mich verstecken;
Wär ich so klein wie Schnecken,
So kröch ich in mein Haus! –
Mein Kind, was werden wir nun sprechen? –

PAMINA:

Die Wahrheit! sei sie auch Verbrechen! –

Achtzehnter Auftritt

EIN ZUG VON GEFOLGE, ZULETZT FÄHRT SARASTRO
AUF EINEM TRIUMPHWAGEN HERAUS, DER VON SECHS
LÖWEN GEZOGEN WIRD. VORIGE.

CHOR:

Es lebe Sarastro! Sarastro soll leben!
Er ist es, dem wir uns mit Freuden ergeben!
Stets mög' er des Lebens als Weiser sich freun, –
Er ist unser Abgott, dem alle sich weihn.
(Dieser Chor wird gesungen, bis Sarastro aus dem Wagen ist.)

PAMINA: *(kniet)*

Herr, ich bin zwar Verbrecherin! –
Ich wollte deiner Macht entfliehn. –
Allein die Schuld ist nicht an mir!
Der böse Mohr verlangte Liebe,
Darum, o Herr, entfloh ich Dir!

PAMINA:

Dear friend, the day is lost, I fear.

Those shouts must mean Sarastro's near!

PAPAGENO:

Oh, I wish I were a mouse

And so could quickly hide!

Or had a snail's shell house

To slip at once inside!

What now are we supposed to say?

PAMINA: The truth! The truth! Let come what may.

Eighteenth Scene

A PROCESSION OF ATTENDANTS, AT THE END OF WHICH
COMES SARASTRO IN A TRIUMPHAL CHARIOT DRAWN BY
SIX LIONS, AND THOSE BEFORE.

CHORUS:

Long live Sarastro! Sarastro all hail!

Long may his tolerant vision prevail!

Long may he guide us to wisdom and light!

Sarastro's our leader, ordaining the right!

(The chorus sings until Sarastro descends from his chariot.)

PAMINA: *(kneeling)*

My lord, I here confess my crime.

I broke your law and tried to flee.

Yet in the end the guilt's not mine.

That wicked Moor demanded love.

What choice, my lord, was left to me?

SARASTRO:

Steh auf, erheitre dich, o Liebe;
Denn ohne erst in dich zu dringen,
Weiß ich von deinem Herzen mehr.
Du liebest einen andern sehr,
Zur Liebe will ich dich nicht zwingen,
Doch geb ich dir die Freiheit nicht.

PAMINA:

Mich rufet ja die Kindespflicht,
Denn meine Mutter – –

SARASTRO:

Steht in meiner Macht,
Du würdest um dein Glück gebracht,
Wenn ich dich ihren Händen ließe. –

PAMINA:

Mir klingt der Mutter Namen süße.
Sie ist es –

SARASTRO:

– Und ein stolzes Weib. –
Ein Mann muss eure Herzen leiten,
Denn ohne ihn pflegt jedes Weib,
Aus ihrem Wirkungskreis zu schreiten.

Neunzehnter Auftritt

MANOSTATOS, TAMINO, VORIGE.

MANOSTATOS:

Na, stolzer Jüngling, nur hieher!
Hier ist Sarastro, unser Herr!

SARASTRO:

Arise, my child, and dry that tear.
Your story's meaning is quite clear.
And with no question on my part,
I discern the secrets of your heart.
Your true love's name is known to me,
But still I may not set you free.

PAMINA:

It's not just for myself I plead.
My mother is . . .

SARASTRO:

. . . under my command.
All is lost—the happiness foretold—
If I return you to your mother.

PAMINA:

Her love is truer than all others.
My mother is . . .

SARASTRO:

. . . too swollen with pride.
A man must show your heart its way.
Without a man to stand beside,
A woman's bearings go astray.

Nineteenth Scene
MONOSTATOS, TAMINO, AND THOSE BEFORE.

MONOSTATOS:

Now, proud Princeling, if you please . . .
The great Sarastro! On your knees!

PAMINA: Er ist's,

TAMINO: Sie ist's,

PAMINA: Ich glaub es kaum.

TAMINO: Sie ist's,

PAMINA: Er ist's,

TAMINO: Es ist kein Traum!

PAMINA, TAMINO:
Es schling mein Arm sich um ihn/sie her,
Und wenn es auch mein Ende wär!

CHOR: Was soll das heißen?

MANOSTATOS:
Welch eine Dreistigkeit!
Gleich auseinander, das geht zu weit!
(trennt sie, kniet)
Dein Sklave liegt zu deinen Füßen,
Lass den verwegnen Frevler büßen.
Bedenk, wie frech der Knabe ist!
Durch dieses seltnen Vogels List
Wollt er Paminen dir entführen.
Allein, ich wusst ihn aufzuspüren.
Du kennst mich! – Meine Wachsamkeit –

SARASTRO:
Verdient, dass man ihr Lorbeer streut.
He! gebt dem Ehrenmann sogleich –

MANOSTATOS: Schon deine Gnade macht mich reich!

PAMINA: It's he!

TAMINO: It's she!

PAMINA: Are things what they seem?

TAMINO: It's she!

PAMINA: It's he!

TAMINO: Surely this is no dream!

PAMINA AND TAMINO:
To hold him (her) once is all I ask!
Though this one kiss may be the last!

CHORUS: Are they mad!

MONOSTATOS:
Stop them! What impertinence!
Will you add a fresh offense?
(He parts them and kneels.)
Your slave is prostrate at your feet.
This upstart's punishment I seek.
Just think what brazen schemes he dared!
Helped by this . . . bird, he was prepared
To find the fair Pamina and steal her.
But in the end could he conceal her?
You know me . . . my loyalty . . .

SARASTRO:
. . . is plain for every eye to see.
Your sort of vigilance deserves . . .

MONOSTATOS: What a generous lord I serve!

SARASTRO: Nur siebenundsiebenzig Sohlenstreich!

MANOSTATOS: *(kniet)* Ach Herr, den Lohn verhofft ich nicht.

SARASTRO: Nicht Dank! Es ist ja meine Fflicht!
(Manostatos wird fortgeführt.)

CHOR:
Es lebe Sarastro, der göttliche Weise,
Er lohnet und strafet in ähnlichem Kreise.

SARASTRO:
Führt diese beiden Fremdlinge
In unsern Prüfungstempel ein,
Bedecket ihre Häupter dann –
Sie müssen erst gereinigt sein.
(Zwei bringen eine Art Sack und bedecken die Häupter der beiden Fremden.)

CHOR:
Wenn Tugend und Gerechtigkeit
Den großen Pfad mit Ruhm bestreut,
Dann ist die Erd ein Himmelreich
Und Sterbliche den Göttern gleich.

Ende des ersten Aufzugs.

SARASTRO: . . . a hundred lashes for your nerve.

MONOSTATOS: *(kneeling)*
Oh, how can you treat a servant so?

SARASTRO: No need for thanks. It's what I owe.
(Monostatos is led away.)

CHORUS:
Hail Sarastro! His wisdom combines
Both mercy and justice in our shrine!

SARASTRO:
Bring both strangers reverently
Into our temple to be tried.
Cover their heads. They may not see.
First they must be purified.
(Two men bring in a kind of sack and cover the heads of the two outsiders.)

CHORUS:
When Justice is a certainty,
And Virtue triumphs over Vice,
Then mankind will be truly free
And earth become a paradise!

End of Act I.

Zweiter Aufzug

Das Theater ist ein Palmwald; alle Bäume sind silberartig, die Blätter von Gold. 18 Sitze von Blättern; auf einem jeden Sitze steht eine Pyramide und ein großes schwarzes Horn mit Gold gefasst. In der Mitte ist die größte Pyramide, auch die größten Bäume. Sarastro nebst andern Priestern kommen in feierlichen Schritten, jeder mit einem Palmzweige in der Hand. Ein Marsch mit blasenden Instrumenten begleitet den Zug.

Erster Auftritt

N° 9 Marcia

Dialog

SARASTRO: *(nach einer Pause)* Ihr, in dem Weisheitstempel eingeweihten Diener der großen Göttin Osiris und Isis! – Mit reiner Seele erklär ich euch, dass unsre heutige Versammlung eine der wichtigsten unsrer Zeit ist. – Tamino, ein Königssohn, 20 Jahre seines Alters, wandelt an der nördlichen Pforte unsers Tempels und seufzt mit tugendvollem Herzen nach einem Gegenstande, den wir alle mit Mühe und Fleiß erringen müssen. – Kurz, dieser Jüngling will seinen nächtlichen Schleier von sich reißen und ins Heiligtum des größten Lichtes blicken. – Diesen Tugendhaften zu bewachen, ihm freundschaftlich die Hand zu bieten, sei heute eine unsrer wichtigsten Pflichten.

Act II

The scene is a palm grove, the trees made of silver, their leaves of gold. Eighteen seats made of fronds; on each stands a pyramid and a large black horn festooned with gold. In the center is the largest pyramid and also the largest tree. Sarastro and Priests with palm fronds in hand enter in a solemn procession. A march with wind instruments accompanies them.

First Scene

March of the Priests

Spoken Dialogue

SARASTRO: *(after a pause)* You here in the Temple of Wisdom, consecrated servants of the great gods Isis and Osiris! With a pure soul I declare that our gathering today is one of the weightiest of our time. Tamino, the son of a king, just twenty years of age, waits at the northern gate of our temple, his virtuous heart sighing, hoping to attain what we all must win with hard work and diligence. In a word, this youth wants to tear the dark veil from his eyes and gaze on the holiness of the sacred light. It is a solemn duty now to watch over this high-minded youth and extend to him the hand of friendship.

ERSTER PRIESTER: *(steht auf)* Er besitzt Tugend?

SARASTRO: Tugend!

ZWEITER PRIESTER: Auch Verschwiegenheit?

SARASTRO: Verschwiegenheit!

DRITTER PRIESTER: Ist wohltätig?

SARASTRO: Wohltätig! – Haltet ihr ihn für würdig, so folgt meinem Beispiele.
(Sie blasen dreimal in die Hörner.)
Gerührt über die Einigkeit eurer Herzen, dankt Sarastro euch im Namen der Menschheit. – Mag immer das Vorurteil seinen Tadel über uns Eingeweihte auslassen! – Weisheit und Vernunft zerstückt es gleich dem Spinnengewebe. – Unsere Säulen erschüttern sie nie. Jedoch das böse Vorurteil soll schwinden; und es wird schwinden, sobald Tamino selbst die Größe unserer schweren Kunst besitzen wird. – Pamina, das sanfte, tugendhafte Mädchen haben die Götter dem holden Jünglinge bestimmt. Dies ist der Grundstein, warum ich sie der stolzen Mutter entriss. – Das Weib dünkt sich, groß zu sein, hofft, durch Blendwerk und Aberglauben das Volk zu berücken und unsern festen Tempelbau zu zerstören. Allein, das soll sie nicht. Tamino, der holde Jüngling selbst soll ihn mit uns befestigen und als Eingeweihter der Tugend Lohn, dem Laster aber Strafe sein.

(Der dreimalige Akkord in den Hörnern wird von allen wiederholt.)

SPRECHER: *(steht auf)* Großer Sarastro, deine weisheitsvollen Reden erkennen und bewundern wir; allein, wird Tamino auch die harten Prüfungen, so seiner warten, bekämpfen? – Verzeih, dass ich so frei bin, dir meinen Zweifel zu eröffnen! Mich bangt es um den Jüngling. Wenn nun im Schmerz dahin gesunken

FIRST PRIEST: *(standing)* Is he virtuous?

SARASTRO: He is.

SECOND PRIEST: Can he keep silent?

SARASTRO: He can.

THIRD PRIEST: Is he good-hearted?

SARASTRO: Indeed. If you find him worthy, then follow my example.
(Three trumpet fanfares sound.)
Moved by the unanimity of your hearts, Sarastro thanks you in the name of humanity. Prejudice will forever heap its scorn on the Brotherhood, but wisdom and reason will brush evil aside like a cobweb. The pillars of righteousness will not be shaken, and evil prejudice will itself vanish when Tamino comes to possess the majesty of our noble purposes. Pamina, a pure and gentle maiden, has been designated by the gods for this young man. This was the reason I separated her from her arrogant mother. That woman thinks she is great, and hopes by superstition and delusion to bewitch people and undermine the very foundations of our temple. She shall not succeed! To strengthen our case, Tamino himself will become one of us. As a Brother among us, he will be the champion of Virtue and the scourge of Evil.

(The brass chords of assent are sounded three times.)

SPEAKER: *(standing)* Great Sarastro, we hear and heed your words of wisdom. But can Tamino survive the ordeals that lie before him? Forgive my doubts. I am troubled by his youth. What if,

sein Geist ihn verließe und er dem harten Kampfe unterläge. – Er ist Prinz!

SARASTRO: Noch mehr – – Er ist Mensch!

SPRECHER: Wenn er nun aber in seiner frühen Jugend leblos erblasste?

SARASTRO: Dann ist er Osiris und Isis gegeben und wird der Götter Freuden früher fühlen als wir.
(Der dreimalige Akkord wird wiederholt.)
Man führe Tamino mit seinem Reisegefährten in den Vorhof des Tempels ein.
(zum Sprecher, der vor ihm niederkniet)
Und du, Freund! den die Götter durch uns zum Verteidiger der Wahrheit bestimmten, – vollziehe dein heiliges Amt und lehre durch deine Weisheit beide, was Pflicht der Menschheit sei; lehre sie, die Macht der Götter erkennen.

(Sprecher geht mit einem Priester ab, alle Priester stellen sich mit ihren Palmzweigen zusammen.)

N° 10 Aria con coro

SARASTRO:
O Isis und Osiris schenket
Der Weisheit Geist dem neuen Paar!
Die ihr der Wandrer Schritte lenket,
Stärkt mit Geduld sie in Gefahr.

TUTTI: Stärkt mit Geduld sie in Gefahr.

overcome by suffering, his spirit fails him and he is defeated in the difficult struggle? After all he is merely a prince.

SARASTRO: No, he is more than that. He is a man!

SPEAKER: What if, in the flower of his youth, he were to die?

SARASTRO:
He would be given to Osiris and Isis and would know the heavenly delights sooner than we.
(The threefold chord is repeated.)
Let Tamino and his companion be led into the forecourt of the temple.
(to the Speaker, who kneels before him)
And you, friend, whom the gods through us appointed as spokesman of the truth, perform your holy office, and through your wisdom teach them both what the duty of mankind is. Teach them to acknowledge the power of the gods.

(The Speaker and a Priest leave; the other priests, with their fronds, gather together.)

Aria with Chorus

SARASTRO:
Grant, Osiris and great Isis,
This noble pair your wisdom's power.
Grant your strength for every crisis,
Your light in danger's darkest hour.

CHORUS: Your light in danger's darkest hour.

SARASTRO:

Lasst sie der Prüfung Früchte sehen;
Doch sollten sie zu Grabe gehen,
Nehmt sie in euren Wohnsitz auf!
So lohnt der Tugend kühnen Lauf,

TUTTI: Nehmt sie in euren Wohnsitz auf!
(Sarastro geht voraus, dann alle ihm nach ab.)

*Nacht, der Donner rollt von Weitem. Das Theater verwandelt
sich in einen kurzen Vorhof des Tempels, wo man Rudera
von eingefallenen Säulen und Pyramiden sieht nebst einigen
Dornbüschen. An beiden Seiten stehen praktikable hohe
altägyptische Türen, welche mehr Seitengebäude vorstellen.*

Zweiter Auftritt

TAMINO UND PAPAGENO WERDEN VOM SPRECHER UND DEM
ANDERN PRIESTER HEREINGEFÜHRT, SIE LÖSEN IHNEN
DIE SÄCKE AB. DIE PRIESTER GEHEN DANN AB.

Dialog

TAMINO: Eine schreckliche Nacht! – Papageno, bist du noch
bei mir?

PAPAGENO: I, freilich!

TAMINO: Wo denkst du, dass wir uns nun befinden?

PAPAGENO: Wo? Ja wenn's nicht finster wäre, wollt ich dir's
schon sagen, – aber so *(Donnerschlag)* O weh! –

TAMINO: Was ist's?

SARASTRO:
Grant they may yet conquer death,
But if they fail the final test,
Find for them in heaven's breadth
A final peace, eternal rest.

CHORUS: A final peace, eternal rest.
(Sarastro leaves first, then the others follow.)

*Night. Thunder rolls in the distance. The stage changes
to reveal the small forecourt of the temple, where fallen
columns and pyramids appear, and thorn bushes. On both
sides are tall ancient Egyptian doors through which can be
seen other outbuildings.*

Second Scene

TAMINO AND PAPAGENO ARE LED IN BY THE SPEAKER AND
THE OTHER PRIEST, WHO REMOVE THE COVERINGS FROM
THEIR HEADS, THEN LEAVE.

Spoken Dialogue

TAMINO: What a terrible night! Papageno, are you still with me?

PAPAGENO: Sure, I'm with you!

TAMINO: Where do you think we are?

PAPAGENO: Where? If it weren't so dark, I could tell you. But as
it is . . . *(thunderclap)* Oh my!

TAMINO: What's that?

PAPAGENO: Mir wird nicht wohl bei der Sache!

TAMINO: Du hast Furcht, wie ich höre.

PAPAGENO: Furcht eben nicht, nur eiskalt läuft's mir über den Rücken. *(starker Donnerschlag)* O weh!

TAMINO: Was soll's?

PAPAGENO: Ich glaube, ich bekomme ein kleines Fieber.

TAMINO: Pfui, Papageno! sei ein Mann!

PAPAGENO: Ich wollt, ich wär ein Mädchen! *(ein sehr starker Donnerschlag)* O! O! O! Das ist mein letzter Augenblick.

Dritter Auftritt
SPRECHER UND DER ANDERE PRIESTER
(MIT FACKELN), VORIGE

SPRECHER: Ihr Fremdlinge, was sucht oder fordert ihr von uns? Was treibt euch an, in unsre Mauern zu dringen?

TAMINO: Freundschaft und Liebe.

SPRECHER: Bist du bereit, es mit deinem Leben zu erkämpfen?

TAMINO: Ja!

SPRECHER: Auch wenn Tod dein Los wäre?

TAMINO: Ja!

PAPAGENO: This sort of affair is not for me!

TAMINO: You're afraid, I hear in your voice.

PAPAGENO: It's not my voice. There are icy shivers up and down my back. *(louder thunder)* Oh dear!

TAMINO: What is it now?

PAPAGENO: I think I'm coming down with a fever.

TAMINO: Shame on you, Papageno. Be a man!

PAPAGENO: I wish I was a girl! *(Very loud thunderclap.)* Oh! Oh! This is my last moment on earth!

Third Scene

SPEAKER AND THE OTHER PRIEST (WITH TORCHES),
AND THOSE BEFORE.

SPEAKER: Strangers, what do you seek? What do you wish of us? What drives you to enter within our walls?

TAMINO: Friendship and love.

SPEAKER: Are you prepared to strive for them at the cost of your life?

TAMINO: Yes!

SPEAKER: Even if death is your fate?

TAMINO: Yes!

SPRECHER: Prinz, noch ist's Zeit zu weichen. Einen Schritt weiter und es ist zu spät. –

TAMINO: Weisheitslehre sei mein Sieg; Pamina, das holde Mädchen, mein Lohn.

SPRECHER: Du unterziehst jeder Prüfung dich?

TAMINO: Jeder!

SPRECHER: Reiche deine Hand mir! *(Sie reichen sich die Hände.)* So!

ZWEITER PRIESTER: Ehe du weitersprichst, erlaube mir, ein paar Worte mit diesem Fremdlinge zu sprechen. – – Willst auch du dir Weisheitsliebe erkämpfen?

PAPAGENO: Kämpfen ist meine Sache nicht. – Ich verlang auch im Grunde gar keine Weisheit. Ich bin so ein Naturmensch, der sich mit Schlaf, Speise und Trank begnügt; und wenn es ja sein könnte, dass ich mir einmal ein schönes Weibchen fange.

ZWEITER PRIESTER: Die wirst du nie erhalten, wenn du dich nicht unsern Prüfungen unterziehst.

PAPAGENO: Worin besteht diese Prüfung? –

ZWEITER PRIESTER: Dich allen unsern Gesetzen unterwerfen, selbst den Tod nicht scheuen.

PAPAGENO: Ich bleibe ledig!

SPRECHER: Aber wenn du dir ein tugendhaftes, schönes Mädchen erwerben könntest?

SPEAKER: Prince, there is still time to withdraw. One more step and it will be too late.

TAMINO: Wisdom is my goal. The fair maid Pamina, my reward.

SPEAKER: You will undergo each trial?

TAMINO: Every one!

SPEAKER: Then give me your hand! *(They clasp hands.)* Onward!

SECOND PRIEST: Before you continue, let me say a word to this other one.—Will you also strive for the love of wisdom?

PAPAGENO: Striving's not for me. To tell the truth, I don't much care for wisdom. I'm a simple man. A little sleep, a little food and drink—that's enough for me. And if only I could catch myself a pretty little wife . . .

SECOND PRIEST: That you shall never do, unless you undergo these ordeals.

PAPAGENO: What are they exactly?

SECOND PRIEST: To submit to all our commands and not to shrink even from death itself.

PAPAGENO: I'll stay single!

SPEAKER: But what if you could win a beautiful and virtuous young maiden?

PAPAGENO: Ich bleibe ledig!

ZWEITER PRIESTER: Wenn nun aber Sarastro dir ein Mädchen aufbewahrt hätte, das an Farbe und Kleidung dir ganz gleich wäre? –

PAPAGENO: Mir gleich! Ist sie jung?

ZWEITER PRIESTER: Jung und schön!

PAPAGENO: Und heißt?

ZWEITER PRIESTER: Papagena.

PAPAGENO: Wie? – Pa? –

ZWEITER PRIESTER: Papagena!

PAPAGENO: Papagena? – Die möcht ich aus bloßer Neugierde sehen.

ZWEITER PRIESTER: Sehen kannst du sie! – –

PAPAGENO: Aber wenn ich sie gesehen habe, hernach muss ich sterben? *(Zweiter Priester macht eine zweideutige Pantomime.)* Ja? – Ich bleibe ledig!

ZWEITER PRIESTER:
Sehen kannst du sie, aber bis zur verlaufenen Zeit kein Wort mit ihr sprechen. Wird dein Geist so viel Standhaftigkeit besitzen, deine Zunge in Schranken zu halten?

PAPAGENO: O ja!

PAPAGENO: I'll stay single!

SECOND PRIEST: And what if Sarastro has already destined a bride for you, a maiden who looks just like you, down to the last feather?

PAPAGENO: Just like me? Is she young?

SECOND PRIEST: Young and beautiful!

PAPAGENO: What's her name?

SECOND PRIEST: Papagena.

PAPAGENO: What's that? Pa . . . Pa . . .

SECOND PRIEST: Papagena!

PAPAGENO: Papagena? I'd at least like to see her—just out of curiosity.

SECOND PRIEST: You may see her.

PAPAGENO: But after I've seen her I have to die? *(The Second Priest gives an ambiguous shrug.)*—I'll stay single!

SECOND PRIEST: You may see her, but until you are allowed you may not speak with her. Do you possess the steadfastness to keep your mouth shut?

PAPAGENO: Oh yes!

ZWEITER PRIESTER: Deine Hand! Du sollst sie sehen.

SPRECHER: Auch dir, Prinz, legen die Götter ein heilsames Stillschweigen auf; ohne dieses seid ihr beide verloren. – Du wirst Pamina sehen, aber nie sie sprechen dürfen; dies ist der Anfang eurer Prüfungszeit. –

N° 11 Duetto

ERSTER PRIESTER, ZWEITER PRIESTER:
Bewahret euch vor Weiber Tücken,
Dies ist des Bundes erste Pflicht.
Manch weiser Mann ließ sich berücken,
Er fehlte und versah sich's nicht.
Verlassen sah er sich am Ende,
Vergolten seine Treu mit Hohn! –
Vergebens rang er seine Hände,
Tod und Verzweiflung war sein Lohn.
(beide Priester ab)

Vierter Auftritt
TAMINO, PAPAGENO.

Dialog

PAPAGENO: He, Lichter her! Lichter her! – Das ist doch wunderlich, sooft einen die Herrn verlassen, so sieht man mit offenen Augen nichts.

TAMINO: Ertrag es mit Geduld und denke, es ist der Götter Wille.

SECOND PRIEST: Then give me your hand! You shall see her.

SPEAKER: On you as well, Prince, the gods impose a vow of silence. Unless you keep it, you both are lost. You will see Pamina, but you must not speak with her. Now begins the first of your trials.

Duet

SPEAKER AND SECOND PRIEST:
Beware the wiles of womankind,
The temple's first command insists.
Wiser men have been made blind
And yielded where they should resist.
Too late they see they've been mistaken,
Their loyalty repaid with scorn.
By all but death are they forsaken,
Betrayed, abandoned, and forlorn.
(Both priests leave.)

Fourth Scene
TAMINO AND PAPAGENO.

Spoken Dialogue

PAPAGENO: Hey! Some light here! Light! It's strange—every time those men leave you can't see a thing, even with your eyes wide open!

TAMINO: Bear it with patience, and remember it is the will of the gods.

Fünfter Auftritt

DIE DREI DAMEN AUS DER VERSENKUNG,
VORIGE.

N° 12 Quintetto

DIE DREI DAMEN:
Wie? Wie? Wie?
Ihr an diesem Schreckensort?
Nie! Nie! Nie!
Kommt ihr wieder glücklich fort!
Tamino! dir ist Tod geschworen!
Du, Papageno! bist verloren.

PAPAGENO: Nein, nein, nein, das wär zu viel.

TAMINO:
Papageno schweige still!
Willst du dein Gelübde brechen,
Nichts mit Weibern hier zu sprechen.

PAPAGENO: Du hörst ja, wir sind beide hin!

TAMINO: Stille sag ich, - schweige still!

PAPAGENO: Immer still und immer still!

DIE DREI DAMEN:
Ganz nah ist euch die Königin!
Sie drang in Tempel heimlich ein! -

PAPAGENO: Wie? Was? Sie soll im Tempel sein?

Fifth Scene

THE THREE LADIES, EMERGING FROM A TRAPDOOR,

AND THOSE BEFORE.

Quintet

THE THREE LADIES:

Why? Why? Why
Stay amid such dark and gloom?
Fly! Fly! Fly
For fear you meet a gruesome doom!
Tamino, you are now death's pawn!
For Papageno, all hope's gone!

PAPAGENO: No, no, no! This is all too much!

TAMINO:

Papageno, hold your tongue!
Have you so soon forgotten your vow?
Words with women are not allowed.

PAPAGENO: Haven't you heard? We're both done for!

TAMINO: Silence, I said! Not one word more!

PAPAGENO: Agreed, agreed. Not one word more.

THE THREE LADIES:

But now the Queen herself is near!
In secrecy she has come here!

PAPAGENO: What? The Queen herself's appeared?

TAMINO:

Stille sag ich, - schweige still! -
Wirst du immer so vermessen,
Deiner Eides Pflicht vergessen? -

DIE DREI DAMEN:

Tamino, hör, du bist verloren,
Gedenke an die Königin!
Man zischelt viel sich in die Ohren
Von dieser Priester falschem Sinn!

TAMINO: *(für sich)*

Ein Weiser prüft und achtet nicht,
Was der gemeine Pöbel spricht.

DIE DREI DAMEN:

Man sagt, wer ihrem Bunde schwört,
Der fährt zur Höll mit Haut und Haar.

PAPAGENO:

Das wär der Teufel! Unerhört!
Sag an, Tamino, ist das wahr?

TAMINO:

Geschwätz von Weibern nachgesagt,
Von Heuchlern aber ausgedacht.

PAPAGENO: Doch sagt es auch die Königin!

TAMINO:

Sie ist ein Weib, hat Weibersinn!
Sei still, mein Wort sei dir genug,
Denk deiner Pflicht und handle klug.

TAMINO:
Silence, I said! Not one word more!
I've scolded your impudence before.
Remember the solemn oath you swore.

THE THREE LADIES:
Tamino, listen! You are doomed!
Think now only of the Queen!
People whisper. They assume
That nothing here is what it seems.

TAMINO: *(to himself)*
A truly wise man's not deceived
By gossip only fools believe.

THE THREE LADIES:
Join this Brotherhood, they say,
And hell is where you're sent to stay.

PAPAGENO:
Now what the devil am I to do?
Tell me, Tamino, is it true?

TAMINO:
The idle tales old wives repeat
Are filled with drivel and deceit.

PAPAGENO: The Queen herself has said it's true.

TAMINO:
She thinks as other women do.
Stay silent now, and trust my word.
Your vow comes first, not what you've heard.

DIE DREI DAMEN: *(zu Tamino)*
Warum bist du mit uns so spröde?
(Tamino deutet bescheiden, dass er nicht sprechen darf.)
Auch Papageno schweigt, – so rede! –

PAPAGENO: *(zu den Damen heimlich)* Ich möchte gerne, – woll – –

TAMINO: Still!

PAPAGENO: Ihr seht, dass ich nicht soll! – –

TAMINO: Still!

PAPAGENO:
Dass ich nicht kann das Plaudern lassen,
Ist wahrlich eine Schand für mich.

TAMINO:
Dass du nicht kannst das Plaudern lassen,
Ist wahrlich eine Schand für dich.

DIE DREI DAMEN:
Wir müssen sie mit Scham verlassen,
Es plaudert keiner sicherlich!

TAMINO, PAPAGENO:
Sie müssen uns mit Scham verlassen,
Es plaudert keiner sicherlich!

DIE DREI DAMEN, TAMINO, PAPAGENO:
Von festem Geiste ist ein Mann,
Er denket, was er sprechen kann!
(Die Damen wollen gehen.)

THE THREE LADIES: *(to Tamino)*
Is prudishness a frank reply?
(He indicates he dare not speak.)
And Papageno silent. Why?

PAPAGENO: *(under his breath, to the Ladies)* I'd gladly speak . . . I wish . . .

TAMINO: Hush!

PAPAGENO: As you see, I'm not . . .

TAMINO: Hush!

PAPAGENO:
My blithering, babbling tongue's to blame,
And I should truly be ashamed.

TAMINO:
Your blithering, babbling tongue's to blame.
Yes, you should truly be ashamed!

THE THREE LADIES:
In shame we must depart at last.
Their vow of silence holds steadfast.

TAMINO AND PAPAGENO:
In shame they must depart at last.
Our vow of silence holds steadfast!

THE THREE LADIES, TAMINO, AND PAPAGENO:
This proves the ways of women weak.
Men will think before they speak.
(The Ladies turn to leave.)

DIE EINGEWEIHTEN: *(von innen)*
Entweiht ist die heilige Schwelle!
Hinab mit den Weibern zur Hölle!

(Ein schrecklicher Akkord mit allen Instrumenten, Donner, Blitz und Schlag; zugleich zwei starke Donner.)

DIE DREI DAMEN:
O weh! O weh! O weh!
(Die Damen stürzen in die Versenkung.)

PAPAGENO: *(fällt vor Schrecken zu Boden)* O weh! O weh! O weh!

(Dann fängt der dreimalige Akkord an.)

Sechster Auftritt

TAMINO, PAPAGENO, SPRECHER, ZWEITER PRIESTER
(MIT FACKELN).

Dialog

SPRECHER: Heil dir, Jüngling! Dein standhaft männliches Betragen hat gesiegt. Zwar hast du noch manch rauen und gefährlichen Weg zu wandern, den du aber durch Hülfe der Götter glücklich endigen wirst. – Wir wollen also mit reinem Herzen unsere Wanderschaft weiter fortsetzen. – *(Er gibt ihm den Sack um.)* So! nun komm.
(ab)

ZWEITER PRIESTER: Was seh ich! Freund, stehe auf! wie ist dir?

PAPAGENO: Ich lieg in einer Ohnmacht!

ZWEITER PRIESTER: Auf! Sammle dich und sei ein Mann!

THE BROTHERHOOD: *(from within)*
These women are to be reviled!
Our sacred temple is defiled!

(A terrifying chord with all instruments, thunder, lightning, a crash. Two loud thunderclaps strike at the same time.)

THE THREE LADIES:
Alas! Alas! Away!
(The Three Ladies plunge through the trapdoor.)

PAPAGENO: *(falling frightened to the ground)* Alas! Alas, I say . . .

(The threefold chord begins.)

Sixth Scene
TAMINO AND PAPAGENO; THE SPEAKER AND THE SECOND
PRIEST (WITH TORCHES).

Spoken Dialogue
SPEAKER: Hail, young man! Your steadfast, manly bearing has won the day. But many perilous paths still lie ahead! With the help of the gods, they will end in joy. With hearts pure, let us continue on our way! *(He places a sack over Tamino's head.)* So now, come!
(They leave.)

SECOND PRIEST: What's this? Up, friend, stand up! What's wrong with you?

PAPAGENO: I fainted dead away!

SECOND PRIEST: Up! Pull yourself together and be a man!

PAPAGENO: *(steht auf)* Aber sagt mir nur meine lieben Herren, warum muss ich denn alle die Qualen und Schrecken empfinden? – Wenn mir ja die Götter eine Papagena bestimmten, warum denn mit so vielen Gefahren sie erringen?

ZWEITER PRIESTER: Diese neugierige Frage mag deine Vernunft dir beantworten. Komm! Meine Pflicht heischt, dich weiterzuführen. *(Er gibt ihm den Sack um.)*

PAPAGENO: Bei so einer ewigen Wanderschaft möcht einem wohl die Liebe auf immer vergehen.
(ab)

Das Theater verwandelt sich in einen angenehmen Garten; Bäume, die nach Art eines Hufeisens gesetzt sind; in der Mitte steht eine Laube von Blumen und Rosen, worin Pamina schläft. Der Mond beleuchtet ihr Gesicht. Ganz vorn steht eine Rasenbank.

Siebenter Auftritt
MANOSTATOS KOMMT, SETZT SICH NACH EINER PAUSE.

MANOSTATOS: Ha, da find ich ja die spröde Schöne! – – Und um so einer geringen Pflanze wegen wollte man meine Fußsohlen behämmern? – Also bloß dem heutigen Tage hab ich's zu verdanken, dass ich noch mit heiler Haut auf die Erde trete. – Hm! – Was war denn eigentlich mein Verbrechen? – dass ich mich in eine Blume vergaffte, die auf fremdem Boden versetzt war? – Und welcher Mensch, wenn er auch von gelinderm Himmelsstrich daher wanderte, würde bei so einem Anblick kalt und unempfindlich bleiben? – Bei allen Sternen! Das Mädchen wird noch um meinen Verstand mich bringen. – Das Feuer, das in mir glimmt, wird mich noch verzehren. *(Er sieht sich allenthalben um.)* Wenn ich wüsste – dass ich so ganz allein und unbelauscht wäre,

PAPAGENO: *(standing up)* But tell me, good sir, why all these ordeals? If the gods have already promised me a Papagena, why do I have to go through so many dangers to find her?

SECOND PRIEST: Reason out your own answers to such questions. Come! My duty is to lead you further on. *(He puts a sack on Papageno's head.)*

PAPAGENO: In all this endless wandering, a man could fall out of love forever.
(He leaves.)

•

The scene is transformed into a charming garden. Trees are arranged in a horseshoe pattern; in the middle is a bed of flowers where Pamina is sleeping. Moonlight plays about her face. Downstage is a grassy bank.

Seventh Scene

MONOSTATOS COMES IN AND, AFTER A PAUSE, SITS DOWN.

MONOSTATOS: *(speaking)* Aha! So here's my elusive beauty! And for such a common blossom as this they wanted to whip the soles of my feet? I'm told I should count myself lucky just to be left alive with my skin still on me! Hmm! What exactly did I do wrong? Falling in love with a transplanted flower? Find me the man, even a traveller from tropic climes, who could remain cold and unfeeling at the sight of her. My stars, this girl will drive me mad! The fire in me will consume me. *(He looks carefully around.)* If I could be sure I was completely alone . . . and could not be

– ich wagte es noch einmal. *(Er macht sich Wind mit beiden Händen.)*
Es ist doch eine verdammte närrische Sache um die Liebe! – Ein
Küsschen, dächte ich, ließe sich entschuldigen. –

N° 13 Aria

*(Alles wird so piano gesungen und gespielt, als wenn die Musik in weiter
Entfernung wäre.)*

MANOSTATOS:
Alles fühlt der Liebe Freuden,
Schnäbelt, tändelt, herzet, küsst, –
Und ich soll die Liebe meiden,
Weil ein Schwarzer hässlich ist.
Ist mir denn kein Herz gegeben,
Bin ich nicht von Fleisch und Blut? –
Immer ohne Weibchen leben,
Wäre wahrlich Höllenglut.
Drum so will ich, weil ich lebe,
Schnäbeln, küssen, zärtlich sein! –
Lieber, guter Mond vergebe
Eine Weiße nahm mich ein!
Weiß ist schön, – ich muss sie küssen.
Mond! verstecke dich dazu! –
Sollt es dich zu sehr verdrießen,
O so mach die Augen zu.
(Er schleicht langsam und leise hin.)

overheard, I would dare to . . . *(He fans himself with both hands.)* What a damn silly thing love is! One little kiss . . . who would hold it against me . . .

Aria

(Everything is sung and played softly, as if the music were coming from a distance.)

MONOSTATOS:
All men feel love's sweet attack,
Billing, cooing, caress, and kiss,
But because my skin is black,
All these joys are mine to miss.
Doesn't my heart beat like theirs?
I have flesh and blood as well!
Without a woman's tender airs,
I'd sooner spend my life in hell!
Why me? Why won't life allow
Billing, cooing, caress, and kiss?
Pale moon above, forgive me now
If I just touch this pearly wrist.
So white! Too fair a chance to miss!
If, pale moon, you feel disgrace
While I steal one silvery kiss,
Then turn away and hide your face.
(Slowly, silently, he steals closer.)

Achter Auftritt

DIE KÖNIGIN KOMMT UNTER DONNER AUS DER MITTLERN VERSENKUNG UND SO, DASS SIE GERADE VOR PAMINA ZU STEHEN KOMMT.

Dialog

KÖNIGIN: Zurücke!

PAMINA: *(erwacht)* Ihr Götter!

MANOSTATOS: *(prallt zurück)* O weh! – Das ist, wo ich nicht irre, die Göttin der Nacht. *(steht ganz still)*

PAMINA: Mutter! Mutter! Meine Mutter! – *(Sie fällt ihr in die Arme.)*

MANOSTATOS: Mutter? Hm! Das muss man von Weitem belauschen. *(schleicht ab)*

KÖNIGIN: Verdank es der Gewalt, mit der man dich mir entriss, dass ich noch deine Mutter mich nenne. – Wo ist der Jüngling, den ich an dich sandte?

PAMINA: Ach Mutter, der ist der Welt und den Menschen auf ewig entzogen. – Er hat sich den Eingeweihten gewidmet.

KÖNIGIN: Den Eingeweihten? – Unglückliche Tochter, nun bist du auf ewig mir entrissen. –

PAMINA: Entrissen? – O fliehen wir, liebe Mutter! Unter deinem Schutz trotz ich jeder Gefahr.

KÖNIGIN: Schutz? Liebes Kind, deine Mutter kann dich nicht mehr schützen. – Mit deines Vaters Tod ging meine Macht zu Grabe.

Eighth Scene

AMID THUNDER, THE QUEEN EMERGES FROM THE
CENTRAL TRAPDOOR SO THAT SHE IS STANDING
RIGHT BEFORE PAMINA.

Spoken Dialogue

QUEEN OF THE NIGHT: Stand back!

PAMINA: *(awaking)* Heavens!

MONOSTATOS: *(recoiling)* Alas! That is . . . if I'm not mistaken . . . the Goddess of the Night! *(He stands stock-still.)*

PAMINA: Mother! Mother! My mother! *(She falls into her arms.)*

MONOSTATOS: Mother? Hmm. This I should watch from afar. *(He steals away.)*

QUEEN OF THE NIGHT: You should be grateful I still call myself your mother, after you were torn from me. Where is the young man I sent to you?

PAMINA: Oh, Mother, he is lost to the world and to men forever. He has sworn himself to the Brotherhood.

QUEEN OF THE NIGHT: The Brotherhood? Unhappy daughter, now you have been torn from me forever.

PAMINA: Torn from you? Oh, dearest Mother, let us flee from here together. With your protection, I will defy every danger.

QUEEN OF THE NIGHT: My protection? Dear child, your mother can no longer protect you. When your father died, my power ended.

PAMINA: Mein Vater –

KÖNIGIN: Übergab freiwillig den siebenfachen Sonnenkreis den Eingeweihten. Diesen mächtigen Sonnenkreis trägt Sarastro auf seiner Brust. – Als ich ihn darüber beredete, so sprach er mit gefalteter Stirne: "Weib! Meine letzte Stunde ist da; alle Schätze, so ich allein besaß, sind dein und deiner Tochter." – "Der alles verzehrende Sonnenkreis", fiel ich hastig ihm in die Rede, – "ist den Geweihten bestimmt", antwortete er: – "Sarastro wird ihn so männlich verwalten wie ich bisher. – Und nun kein Wort weiter. Forsche nicht nach Wesen, die dem weiblichen Geiste unbegreiflich sind. – Deine Pflicht ist, dich und deine Tochter der Führung weiser Männer zu überlassen."

PAMINA: Liebe Mutter, nach allem dem zu schließen, ist wohl auch der Jüngling auf immer für mich verloren.

KÖNIGIN: Verloren, wenn du nicht, eh die Sonne die Erde färbt, ihn durch diese unterirdischen Gewölbe zu fliehen beredest. – Der erste Schimmer des Tages entscheidet, ob er ganz dir oder den Eingeweihten gegeben sei.

PAMINA: Liebe Mutter, dürft ich den Jüngling als Eingeweihten denn nicht auch ebenso zärtlich lieben, wie ich ihn jetzt liebe? – Mein Vater selbst war ja mit diesen weisen Männern verbunden; er sprach jederzeit mit Entzücken von ihnen, preiste ihre Güte – ihren Verstand – ihre Tugend. – Sarastro ist nicht weniger tugendhaft. – –

KÖNIGIN: Was hör ich! – Du meine Tochter könntest die schändlichen Gründe dieser Barbaren verteidigen? – So einen Mann lieben, der mit meinem Todfeinde verbunden, mit jedem Augenblick mir meinen Sturz bereiten würde? – Siehst du hier diesen Stahl? – Er ist für Sarastro geschliffen. – Du wirst ihn töten und den mächtigen Sonnenkreis mir überliefern.

PAMINA: My father—

QUEEN OF THE NIGHT: He freely surrendered the sevenfold Circle of the Sun to the Brotherhood. Sarastro now wears the great Circle around his neck. When I asked your father about this, his brow furrowed, "Wife, my last hour is at hand—all my treasure belongs now to you and our daughter." I interrupted him, "And the all-consuming Circle of the Sun?" "It is meant for the Brotherhood," he replied. "Sarastro will now bravely hold it in trust, as I have. Not another word on the subject! Do not try to understand a matter not meant for a woman's mind. It is your duty to place yourself and your daughter under the leadership of wise men."

PAMINA: Dear Mother, is the young man lost to me forever?

QUEEN OF THE NIGHT: Lost, unless before dawn you can persuade him to flee these underground vaults. The first ray of daylight decides whether he is to be yours or the Brotherhood's.

PAMINA: Dear Mother, could I not love him just as tenderly if he were part of the Brotherhood? My own father had dealings with them. He always spoke warmly of them, praised their benevolence—their wisdom—their virtue. Sarastro is surely no less virtuous.

QUEEN OF THE NIGHT: How dare you! You, my daughter, defend the shameful ways of those barbarians! Love a man allied to my mortal enemy, a man preparing at this very moment to crush me! Do you see this dagger? It has been sharpened for Sarastro. You will kill him, and return to me the great Circle of the Sun.

PAMINA: Aber liebste Mutter! –

KÖNIGIN: Kein Wort!

N° 14 Aria

KÖNIGIN:
Der Hölle Rache kocht in meinem Herzen,
Tod und Verzweiflung flammet um mich her!
Fühlt nicht durch dich Sarastro Todesschmerzen,
So bist du meine Tochter nimmermehr:
Verstoßen sei auf ewig,
Zertrümmert sei'n auf ewig alle Bande der Natur,
Wenn nicht durch dich Sarastro wird erblassen! –
Hört, Rachegötter! – Hört! der Mutter Schwur! –
(Sie versinkt.)

Neunter Auftritt
PAMINA (MIT DEM DOLCH IN DER HAND).

Dialog
PAMINA: Morden soll ich? – Götter! Das kann ich nicht. – Das kann ich nicht!
(steht in Gedanken)

Zehnter Auftritt
VORIGE, MANOSTATOS.

MANOSTATOS: *(kommt schnell, heimlich und sehr freudig)* Sarastros Sonnenkreis hat also auch seine Wirkung? – Und diesen zu erhalten, soll das schöne Mädchen ihn morden? – Das ist Salz in meine Suppe!

PAMINA: Aber schwur sie nicht bei allen Göttern, mich zu verstoßen, wenn ich den Dolch nicht gegen Sarastro kehre? – Götter! – Was soll ich nun?

PAMINA: But Mother—!

QUEEN OF THE NIGHT: Not a word!

Aria

QUEEN OF THE NIGHT:
Hell's blood surges through my breast,
Despair and death now blind my eyes!
You'll plunge this knife into his chest
Or forever after agonize.
No more my daughter! Outcast! Alone!
Unless Sarastro dies, the worst
Will harrow you. You'll be disowned!
Hear, vengeful gods, a mother's curse!
(She sinks down.)

Ninth Scene
PAMINA (WITH THE DAGGER IN HER HAND).

Spoken Dialogue
PAMINA: Murder him?—Oh God, I cannot do it! I cannot . . .
(She stands lost in thought.)

Tenth Scene
THE ABOVE, AND MONOSTATOS.

MONOSTATOS: *(entering swiftly, stealthily, joyfully)* So, Sarastro's Circle of the Sun has a certain power! And to obtain it, the lovely maiden is meant to murder him? That's salt in my soup!

PAMINA: She swore by all the gods to disown me unless I turned this dagger on Sarastro. Gods! What am I to do now?

MANOSTATOS: Dich mir anvertrauen! *(nimmt ihr den Dolch)*

PAMINA: *(erschrickt und schreit)* Ha!

MANOSTATOS: Warum zitterst du? vor meiner schwarzen Farbe oder vor dem ausgedachten Mord?

PAMINA: *(schüchtern)* Du weißt also? –

MANOSTATOS: Alles. – Ich weiß sogar, dass nicht nur dein, sondern auch deiner Mutter Leben in meiner Hand steht. – Ein einziges Wort sprech ich zu Sarastro, und deine Mutter wird in diesem Gewölbe in eben dem Wasser, das die Eingeweihten reinigen soll, wie man sagt, ersäuft. – Aus diesem Gewölbe kommt sie nun sicher nicht mehr mit heiler Haut, wenn ich es will. – Du hast also nur einen Weg, dich und deine Mutter zu retten.

PAMINA: Der wäre?

MANOSTATOS: Mich zu lieben.

PAMINA: *(zitternd für sich)* Götter!

MANOSTATOS: *(freudig)* Das junge Bäumchen jagt der Sturm auf meine Seite. – Nun Mädchen! – Ja oder nein!

PAMINA: *(entschlossen)* Nein!

MANOSTATOS: *(voll Zorn)* Nein? Und warum? Weil ich die Farbe eines schwarzen Gespensts trage? – Nicht? – Ha, so stirb! *(Er ergreift sie bei der Hand.)*

PAMINA: Manostatos, sieh mich hier auf meinen Knien, – schone meiner!

MONOSTATOS: Trust yourself to me! *(He takes the dagger from her.)*

PAMINA: *(startled)* Ah!

MONOSTATOS: What makes you tremble so? Is it my black skin, or is it the murder you're planning?

PAMINA: *(timidly)* So you know?

MONOSTATOS: Everything. I know too that both your life and your mother's are in my hands. If I say the word to Sarastro, your mother drowns in this vault, in the very water where new members of the Brotherhood are purified. She will never get out of here alive, if that is my choice. So you have only one way to save yourself and your mother.

PAMINA: What way?

MONOSTATOS: By loving me!

PAMINA: *(shuddering, to herself)* Gods!

MONOSTATOS: *(gloating)* The storm bends the sapling towards me. Which is it then, young lady, yes or no?

PAMINA: *(determined)* No!

MONOSTATOS: *(angrily)* No? And why not? Because I look like a black devil? Is that it? Ha! Then die! *(He grabs her hand.)*

PAMINA: Monostatos, look! I am on my knees before you! Spare me!

MANOSTATOS: Liebe oder Tod! – Sprich! dein Leben steht auf der Spitze.

PAMINA: Mein Herz hab ich dem Jüngling geopfert.

MANOSTATOS: Was kümmert mich dein Opfer. – Sprich! –

PAMINA: *(entschlossen)* Nie!

Elfter Auftritt
VORIGE, SARASTRO.

MANOSTATOS: So fahr denn hin!
(Sarastro hält ihn schnell ab.)
Herr, mein Unternehmen ist nicht strafbar; man hat deinen Tod geschworen, darum wollt ich dich rächen.

SARASTRO: Ich weiß nur allzu viel. – Weiß, dass deine Seele eben so schwarz als dein Gesicht ist. – Auch würde ich dies schwarze Unternehmen mit höchster Strenge an dir bestrafen, wenn nicht ein böses Weib, das zwar eine sehr gute Tochter hat, den Dolch dazu geschmiedet hätte. – Verdank es der bösen Handlung des Weibes, dass du ungestraft davon ziehst. – Geh! –

MANOSTATOS: *(im Abgehen)* Jetzt such ich die Mutter auf, weil die Tochter mir nicht beschieden ist.
(ab)

MONOSTATOS: Love me or die! Speak! Your life rests on the point of this dagger.

PAMINA: I have promised my heart to the young man.

MONOSTATOS: What do I care about your promise—speak!

PAMINA: *(resolute)* Never!

Eleventh Scene

THOSE BEFORE, AND SARASTRO.

MONOSTATOS: Then die!
(Sarastro quickly restrains him.)
My lord, I am innocent! They wanted to murder you! I wanted only to avenge you!

SARASTRO: I know, I know all too well. I know that your soul is as black as your face. I would punish you for this foul deed as harshly as I could, were it not that the dagger was forged by an evil woman, who has a virtuous daughter. Thanks to the wicked conniving of that woman you get away unpunished. Go!

MONOSTATOS: *(as he leaves)* Since I cannot have the daughter, I'll go in search of the mother!
(He goes.)

Zwölfter Auftritt

VORIGE, OHNE MANOSTATOS.

PAMINA: Herr, strafe meine Mutter nicht, der Schmerz über meine Abwesenheit. –

SARASTRO: Ich weiß alles. – Weiß, dass sie in unterirdischen Gemächern des Tempels herumirrt und Rache über mich und die Menschheit kocht. – Allein, du sollst sehen, wie ich mich an deiner Mutter räche. – Der Himmel schenke nur dem holden Jüngling Mut und Standhaftigkeit in seinem frommen Vorsatz, denn bist du mit ihm glücklich, und deine Mutter soll beschämt nach ihrer Burg zurückekehren.

N° 15 Aria

SARASTRO:

In diesen heil'gen Hallen
Kennt man die Rache nicht!
Und ist ein Mensch gefallen,
Führt Liebe ihn zur Pflicht.
Dann wandelt er an Freundes Hand
Vergnügt und froh ins bessre Land.
In diesen heil'gen Mauern,
Wo Mensch den Menschen liebt, –
Kann kein Verräter lauern,
Weil man dem Feind vergibt.
Wen solche Lehren nicht erfreun,
Verdienet nicht, ein Mensch zu sein.

(gehen beide ab)

Twelfth Scene
THOSE BEFORE, WITHOUT MONOSTATOS.

PAMINA: Lord, do not punish my mother! Her grief at losing me . . .

SARASTRO: I know all. I know that she skulks around the caverns under the temple, plotting revenge on me and all of mankind. But you will see how I take my revenge on her. If heaven grants to the noble youth the courage and steadfastness he needs for his pious task, then you will find happiness with him, and your mother will grovel back to her castle in shame.

Aria

SARASTRO:
Within these sacred halls
Revenge remains unknown.
And if a man should fall,
His way by love is shown.
Gently led by friendship's hand,
He's guided to a better land.
Within these sacred walls
By love do all men live,
No treachery befalls.
Our enemies we forgive.
Those who scorn our noble plan
Do not deserve the name of man.
(They depart.)

*Das Theater verwandelt sich in eine Halle, wo das Flugwerk
gehen kann. Das Flugwerk ist mit Rosen und Blumen
umgeben, wo sich sodann eine Türe öffnet. Tamino und
Papageno werden ohne Säcke von den zwei Priestern
hereingeführt. Ganz vorne sind zwei Rasenbänke.*

Dreizehnter Auftritt
TAMINO UND PAPAGENO WERDEN OHNE SÄCKE VON DEN
ZWEI PRIESTERN HEREINGEFÜHRT.

Dialog

SPRECHER: Hier seid ihr euch beide allein überlassen. – Sobald
die röchelnde Posaune tönt, dann nehmt ihr euren Weg dahin.
– Prinz, lebt wohl! Wir sehen uns, eh ihr ganz am Ziele seid. –
Noch einmal, vergesst das Wort nicht: Schweigen. –
(ab)

ZWEITER PRIESTER: Papageno, wer an diesem Ort sein Stillschweigen bricht, den strafen die Götter durch Donner und Blitz.
Leb wohl!
(ab)

Vierzehnter Auftritt
TAMINO, PAPAGENO.

(Tamino setzt sich auf eine Rasenbank.)

PAPAGENO: *(nach einer Pause)* Tamino!

TAMINO: *(verweisend)* St!

PAPAGENO: Das ist ein lustiges Leben! – Wär ich lieber in meiner
Strohhütte oder im Walde, so hört ich doch manchmal einen
Vogel pfeifen.

TAMINO: *(verweisend)* St!

The stage is transformed into a hall, where a flying-machine, decked with roses and flowers, can be seen. It has a door that opens. Downstage are two grassy banks.

Thirteenth Scene

TAMINO AND PAPAGENO, WITHOUT THE SACKS ON THEIR HEADS, ARE LED IN BY TWO PRIESTS.

Spoken Dialogue

SPEAKER: Here you shall both be left alone. When you hear the trumpets sound, make your way at once towards them. Prince, farewell! We shall meet again before you reach your goal. Be mindful of one word: silence!

(He leaves.)

SECOND PRIEST: Papageno, he who breaks the vow of silence in this place shall be punished with thunder and lightning. Farewell.

(He leaves.)

•

Fourteenth Scene

TAMINO AND PAPAGENO.

(Tamino sits on a grassy bank.)

PAPAGENO: *(after a pause)* Tamino!

TAMINO: *(silencing him)* Shh!

PAPAGENO: Isn't this the life! If I were back in my straw hut, or in the forest, at least I'd hear a bird sing once in a while.

TAMINO: *(silencing him)* Shh!

PAPAGENO: Mit mir selbst werd ich wohl sprechen dürfen; und auch wir zwei können zusammen sprechen, wir sind ja Männer.

TAMINO: *(verweisend)* St!

PAPAGENO: *(singt)* La la la – la la la! – Nicht einmal einen Tropfen Wasser bekommt man bei diesen Leuten, viel weniger sonst was. –

Fünfzehnter Auftritt

EIN ALTES HÄSSLICHES WEIB KOMMT AUS DER VERSENKUNG, HÄLT AUF EINER TASSE EINEN GROSSEN BECHER MIT WASSER.

PAPAGENO: *(sieht sie lang an)* Ist das für mich?

WEIB: Ja, mein Engel!

PAPAGENO: *(sieht sie wieder an, trinkt)* Nicht mehr und nicht weniger als Wasser. – Sag du mir, du unbekannte Schöne! werden alle fremden Gäste auf diese Art bewirtet?

WEIB: Freilich, mein Engel!

PAPAGENO: So, so! – Auf die Art werden die Fremden auch nicht gar zu häufig kommen. – –

WEIB: Sehr wenig.

PAPAGENO: Kann mir's denken. – Geh Alte, setze dich her zu mir, mir ist die Zeit verdammt lange. – Sag du mir, wie alt bist du denn?

WEIB: Wie alt?

PAPAGENO: Surely I'm allowed to talk to myself. And why can't we speak just to each other, man to man?

TAMINO: *(silencing him)* Shh!

PAPAGENO: *(singing)* La la la—la la la! These people won't even give us a drop of water, much less anything else.

Fifteenth Scene

THOSE BEFORE. AN UGLY OLD WOMAN COMES UP THROUGH THE TRAPDOOR, HOLDING A TRAY WITH A LARGE GOBLET OF WATER.

PAPAGENO: *(staring at her for a long time)* Is that for me?

OLD WOMAN: It is, my angel!

PAPAGENO: *(looking at her again and drinking)* It's only water! Tell me, my mysterious beauty, is this how you entertain all your visitors?

OLD WOMAN: It is indeed, my angel!

PAPAGENO: I see. In that case, you must not get many.

OLD WOMAN: Not many.

PAPAGENO: I can imagine. Come, Granny, sit here by me. The time passes so slowly. Tell me, how old are you?

OLD WOMAN: How old?

PAPAGENO: Ja!

WEIB: 18 Jahr und 2 Minuten.

PAPAGENO: 18 Jahr und 2 Minuten?

WEIB: Ja!

PAPAGENO: Ha ha ha! – Ei du junger Engel! Hast du auch einen Geliebten?

WEIB: I, freilich!

PAPAGENO: Ist er auch so jung wie du?

WEIB: Nicht gar, er ist um 10 Jahre älter. –

PAPAGENO: Um 10 Jahr ist er älter als du? – Das muss eine Liebe sein! – – Wie nennt sich denn dein Liebhaber?

WEIB: Papageno!

PAPAGENO: *(erschrickt, Pause)* Papageno? – Wo ist er denn dieser Papageno?

WEIB: Da sitzt er, mein Engel!

PAPAGENO: Ich wär dein Geliebter?

WEIB: Ja, mein Engel!

PAPAGENO: *(nimmt schnell das Wasser und spritzt sie ins Gesicht)* Sag du mir, wie heißt du denn?

PAPAGENO: Yes.

OLD WOMAN: Eighteen years and two minutes.

PAPAGENO: Eighteen years and two minutes!

OLD WOMAN: Yes.

PAPAGENO: Ha, ha! My little angel! And have you a sweetheart?

OLD WOMAN: Me? Indeed I do!

PAPAGENO: And is he as young as you?

OLD WOMAN: Not quite. He is ten years older.

PAPAGENO: Ten years older than you? Now, that must be a real romance! And what is your sweetheart's name?

OLD WOMAN: Papageno!

PAPAGENO: *(startled, hesitant)* Papageno? Where is he then, this Papageno?

OLD WOMAN: Sitting beside me, my angel!

PAPAGENO: What, me your sweetheart?

OLD WOMAN: You, my angel!

PAPAGENO: *(taking the cup and flicking water on her face)* Tell me, what is your name!

WEIB: Ich heiße –

(starker Donner, die Alte hinkt schnell ab)

PAPAGENO: O weh! *(Tamino steht auf, droht ihm mit dem Finger.)* Nun sprech ich kein Wort mehr!

Sechzehnter Auftritt

DIE DREI KNABEN KOMMEN IN EINEM MIT ROSEN BEDECKTEN FLUGWERK. IN DER MITTE STEHT EIN SCHÖNER GEDECKTER TISCH. DER EINE HAT DIE FLÖTE, DER ANDERE DAS KÄSTCHEN MIT GLÖCKCHEN. VORIGE.

N° 16 Terzetto

DREI KNABEN:
Seid uns zum zweiten Mal willkommen,
Ihr Männer, in Sarastros Reich! –
Er schickt, was man euch abgenommen,
Die Flöte und die Glöckchen euch.
Wollt ihr die Speisen nicht verschmähen,
So esset, trinket froh davon! –
Wenn wir zum dritten Mal uns sehen,
Ist Freude eures Mutes Lohn!
Tamino, Mut! – nah ist das Ziel,
Du, Papageno! schweige still!
(Unter dem Terzett setzen sie den Tisch in die Mitte und fliegen auf.)

OLD WOMAN: My name is . . .

(Thunder. The old woman hobbles quickly away.)

PAPAGENO: Uh-oh! *(Tamino stands up and wags his finger.)* Not another word!

Sixteenth Scene

THE THREE BOYS ARRIVE IN THE FLYING MACHINE
COVERED IN ROSES. IN THE MIDST OF IT IS A BEAUTIFULLY
SET TABLE. ONE OF THE BOYS CARRIES THE MAGIC FLUTE,
ANOTHER THE BOX OF CHIMES. THOSE BEFORE.

Trio

THE THREE BOYS:
Welcome, strangers, a second time.
It's here that great Sarastro dwells.
At his command, you now will find
Your magic flute, your magic bells.
This tasty feast we now provide you.
So eat and drink, and have no fear.
When next we three shall stand beside you,
You both will find rewards are near.
Close by, Tamino, is she you seek.
And Papageno—do not speak!
(During the trio they place the table in the middle of the stage, and then withdraw.)

Siebzehnter Auftritt
TAMINO, PAPAGENO.

Dialog

PAPAGENO: Tamino, wollen wir nicht speisen? – – *(Tamino bläst auf seiner Flöte.)* Blase du nur fort auf deiner Flöte, ich will meine Brocken blasen. – Herr Sarastro führt eine gute Küche. – Auf die Art, ja da will ich schon schweigen, wenn ich immer solche gute Bissen bekomme. *(Er trinkt.)* Nun will ich sehen, ob auch der Keller so gut bestellt ist. – Ha! – Das ist Götterwein! –

(Die Flöte schweigt.)

Achtzehnter Auftritt
PAMINA, VORIGE.

PAMINA: *(freudig)* Du hier? – Gütige Götter! Dank euch, dass ihr mich diesen Weg führtet. – Ich hörte deine Flöte, und so lief ich pfeilschnell dem Tone nach. – Aber du bist traurig? – Sprichst nicht eine Silbe mit deiner Pamina?

TAMINO: *(seufzt)* Ah! *(winkt ihr fortzugehen)*

PAMINA: Wie? Ich soll dich meiden? Liebst du mich nicht mehr?

TAMINO: *(seufzt)* Ah! *(winkt wieder fort)*

PAMINA: Ich soll fliehen, ohne zu wissen, warum. – Tamino, holder Jüngling! hab ich dich beleidigt? – O kränke mein Herz nicht noch mehr. – Bei dir such ich Trost, – Hülfe, – und du kannst mein liebevolles Herz noch mehr kränken? – Liebst du mich nicht mehr?
(Tamino seufzt.)

PAMINA: Papageno, sage du mir, sag, was ist meinem Freund?

Seventeenth Scene

TAMINO AND PAPAGENO.

Spoken Dialogue

PAPAGENO: Tamino, shouldn't we eat something? *(Tamino plays his flute.)* So tootle on that flute of yours, I'm going to play with my food! Mmm, Sarastro sure has sent us a feast. I'd happily stay silent if there were always such things to eat. Let's see if his cellar is as good as his kitchen. *(He drinks.)* Ahh!—what heavenly wine!

(The flute stops playing.)

Eighteenth Scene

PAMINA, AND THOSE BEFORE.

PAMINA: *(joyfully)* You're here! Thanks to the gods I've found you. I heard your flute and, swift as an arrow, I flew towards the sound. But . . . you look sad. Not even a word for your Pamina?

TAMINO: *(sighing)* Ah! *(He motions to her to go away.)*

PAMINA: What? Leave you? Do you no longer love me?

TAMINO: *(sighing)* Ah! *(He repeats his gesture.)*

PAMINA: I must just leave without knowing why? Tamino, love of my life, what have I done wrong? Oh, do not hurt my heart even more. I've come to you for comfort—for help—and still you would wound my sad heart? Do you no longer love me? *(Tamino sighs.)*

PAMINA: Papageno, tell me, what is troubling him?

(Papageno hat einen Brocken in dem Mund, hält mit beiden Händen die Speisen zu, winkt fortzugehen.)

PAMINA: Wie? auch du? – Erkläre mir wenigstens die Ursache eures Stillschweigens. – –

PAPAGENO: St! *(Er deutet ihr fortzugehen.)*

PAMINA: O das ist mehr als Kränkung – mehr als Tod! *(Pause)* Liebster, einziger Tamino! –

N° 17 Aria

PAMINA:
Ach ich fühl's, es ist verschwunden!
Ewig hin der Liebe Glück! –
Nimmer kömmt ihr Wonnestunden
Meinem Herzen mehr zurück!
Sieh Tamino! diese Tränen
Fließen, Trauter, dir allein.
Fühlst du nicht der Liebe Sehnen,
So wird Ruh im Tode sein!
(ab)

Neunzehnter Auftritt

TAMINO, PAPAGENO.

Dialog

PAPAGENO: *(isst hastig)* Nicht wahr, Tamino, ich kann auch schweigen, wenn's sein muss. – Ja, bei so einem Unternehmen da bin ich Mann. – *(Er trinkt.)* Der Herr Koch und der Herr Kellermeister sollen leben. –

(dreimaliger Posaunenton)

(Tamino winkt Papageno, dass er gehen soll.)

(Papageno, his mouth full of food, covers the table with both hands and he too motions her to go away.)

PAMINA: What? You too? At least tell me why you are silent.

PAPAGENO: Shh! *(He gestures that she should leave.)*

PAMINA: Oh, this is worse than any wound—worse than death itself! *(pause)* Oh, Tamino, my beloved!

Aria

PAMINA:
I feel it now! The empty sadness!
Gone forever love's delight!
Gone forever joy and gladness!
Every brightness turned to night!
Look, Tamino, see these tears
Shed in grief for you, my own!
If your love were to disappear,
The friend who's left is Death alone.
(She leaves.)

Nineteenth Scene
TAMINO AND PAPAGENO.

Spoken Dialogue

PAPAGENO: *(eating hurriedly)* You see, Tamino, I can be silent when I have to. Yes, in a treacherous situation I'm as brave as any man. *(He drinks.)* Here's to the cook! Long live the master of the wine cellar!

(The trumpet sounds three times.)

(Tamino gestures to Papageno that it is time to go.)

PAPAGENO: Gehe du nur voraus, ich komm schon nach.
(Tamino will ihn mit Gewalt fortführen.)

PAPAGENO: Der Stärkere bleibt da! *(Tamino droht ihm und geht rechts ab, ist aber links gekommen.)*

PAPAGENO: Jetzt will ich mir's erst recht wohl sein lassen. – Da ich in meinem besten Appetit bin, soll ich gehen. – Das lass ich wohl bleiben. – Ich ging jetzt nicht fort, und wenn Herr Sarastro seine sechs Löwen an mich spannte. *(Die Löwen kommen heraus, er erschrickt.)* O Barmherzigkeit, ihr gütigen Götter! – Tamino, rette mich! Die Herrn Löwen machen eine Mahlzeit aus mir. – –

(Tamino bläst seine Flöte, kommt schnell zurück; die Löwen gehen hinein.) *(Tamino winkt ihm.)*

PAPAGENO: Ich gehe schon! Heiß du mich einen Schelmen, wenn ich dir nicht in allem folge.
(dreimaliger Posaunenton)
Das geht uns an. – Wir kommen schon. – Aber hör einmal, Tamino, was wird denn noch alles mit uns werden?
(Tamino deutet gen Himmel.)

PAPAGENO: Die Götter soll ich fragen?
(Tamino deutet ja.)

PAPAGENO: Ja, die könnten uns freilich mehr sagen, als wir wissen!
(dreimaliger Posaunenton)

(Tamino reißt ihn mit Gewalt fort.)

PAPAGENO: Eile nur nicht so, wir kommen noch immer zeitlich genug, um uns braten zu lassen.
(ab)

PAPAGENO: You go on ahead. I'll be along soon.
(Tamino tries to force him to go with him.)

PAPAGENO: The stronger of us—that's me!—stays right here.
(Tamino threatens him, then leaves to the right, even though he came on from the left.)

PAPAGENO: Now at last I can enjoy myself. Should I have to go just when my appetite is all worked up? No sirree! I wouldn't leave now even if Master Sarastro unleashed his six lions on me. *(The lions appear, terrifying him.)* Lord have mercy! Tamino, save me! These lordly lions will have me for their supper!

(Tamino plays his flute, and comes quickly back; the lions retreat. Tamino gestures to Papageno.)

PAPAGENO: I'm coming, I'm coming! Just call me a fool, but I'd follow you anywhere.
(The chord sounds three times.)
That's for us. Let's get going. But tell me, Tamino, what's going to happen to us now?
(Tamino points to heaven.)

PAPAGENO: You mean, I should ask the gods?
(Tamino nods.)

PAPAGENO: Yes, they sure know more than we do!
(The chord sounds three times.)

(Tamino drags him along by force.)

PAPAGENO: Why the big hurry? We'll only get there in time to be roasted.
(They leave.)

Das Theater verwandelt sich in das Gewölbe von Pyramiden.

Zwanzigster Auftritt

SPRECHER, UND EINIGE PRIESTER.

(Zwei Priester tragen eine beleuchtete Pyramide auf den Schultern; jeder Priester hat eine transparente Pyramide in der Größe einer Laterne in der Hand.)

N° 18 Chor der Priester

CHOR DER PRIESTER:
O Isis und Osiris, welche Wonne!
Die düstre Nacht verscheucht der Glanz der Sonne! –
Bald fühlt der edle Jüngling neues Leben,
Bald ist er unserm Dienste ganz gegeben.
Sein Geist ist kühn, sein Herz ist rein.
Bald wird er unser würdig sein.

Einundzwanzigster Auftritt

SARASTRO, TAMINO (DER HEREINGEFÜHRT WIRD),
VORIGE, SPÄTER PAMINA.

Dialog

SARASTRO: Prinz, dein Betragen war bis hieher männlich und gelassen. Nun hast du noch zwei gefährliche Wege zu wandern. – Schlägt dein Herz noch eben so warm für Pamina – und wünschest du, einst als ein weiser Fürst zu regieren, so mögen die Götter dich ferner begleiten. – – Deine Hand – Man bringe Paminen!

(Eine Stille herrscht bei allen Priestern, Pamina wird mit eben diesem Sack, welcher die Eingeweihten bedeckt, hereingeführt; Sarastro löst die Bande am Sacke auf.)

PAMINA: Wo bin ich? – Welch eine fürchterliche Stille! – Saget, wo ist mein Jüngling? –

The stage is transformed into the vaults of pyramids.

Twentieth Scene

THE SPEAKER AND SOME PRIESTS.

(Two Priests carry an illuminated pyramid on their shoulders; each Priest has a transparent pyramid in his hand, the size of a lantern.)

Chorus of Priests

CHORUS OF PRIESTS:
O Isis and Osiris! The light!
The sun has banished darkest night!
Soon this youth will know the good,
Soon be part of our Brotherhood.
His spirit is bold, his heart is pure.
Soon his worthiness is assured.

Twenty-first Scene

SARASTRO, TAMINO (WHO IS LED IN), AND THOSE BEFORE; LATER PAMINA.

Spoken Dialogue

SARASTRO: Prince, your conduct so far has been manly and patient. Now you have two perilous paths still to go. If your heart still yearns for Pamina and you wish to rule as a wise leader, then may the gods be with you. Your hand—Bring Pamina forward!

(A silence falls over the assembled Priests. Pamina is led in, wearing the same head-covering. Sarastro loosens the sack.)

PAMINA: Where am I? Everything so silent! Where is my Tamino?

SARASTRO: Er wartet deiner, um dir das letzte Lebewohl zu sagen.

PAMINA: Das letzte Lebewohl! – Wo ist er? – Führe mich zu ihm! –

SARASTRO: Hier! –

PAMINA: Tamino!

TAMINO: Zurück!

N° 19 Terzetto

PAMINA: Soll ich dich, Teurer! nicht mehr sehn?

SARASTRO: Ihr werdet froh euch wiedersehn!

PAMINA: Dein warten tödliche Gefahren!

TAMINO: Die Götter mögen mich bewahren!

SARASTRO: Die Götter mögen ihn bewahren!

PAMINA:
Du wirst dem Tode nicht entgehen,
Mir flüstert dieses Ahndung ein!

TAMINO, SARASTRO:
Der Götter Wille mag geschehen,
Ihr Wink soll mir Gesetze sein.

PAMINA:
O liebtest du, wie ich dich liebe,
Du würdest nicht so ruhig sein.

SARASTRO: He awaits you . . . to bid a last farewell.

PAMINA: A last farewell? Oh, where is he? Take me to him!

SARASTRO: Here!

PAMINA: Tamino!

TAMINO: Stay back!

Trio

PAMINA: Why now, beloved, must we part?

SARASTRO: To meet again with joyful hearts.

PAMINA: But deadly dangers lie ahead!

TAMINO: The gods will protect me from every dread.

SARASTRO: The gods will protect him from every dread!

PAMINA:
Something whispers inside my heart
That certain death awaits you there.

TAMINO AND SARASTRO:
A hidden destiny will play its part.
What fate decrees, we all must bear.

PAMINA:
If only you loved as I love you!
You have the feelings of a stone!

TAMINO:
Glaub mir, ich fühle gleiche Triebe,
Werd ewig dein Getreuer sein.

SARASTRO:
Glaub mir, er fühlet gleiche Triebe,
Wird ewig dein Getreuer sein.
Die Stunde schlägt, nun müsst ihr scheiden!

PAMINA, TAMINO: Wie bitter sind der Trennung Leiden!

SARASTRO: Tamino muss nun wieder fort!

PAMINA: Tamino muss nun wirklich fort!

TAMINO: Pamina, ich muss wirklich fort!

SARASTRO: Nun muss er fort!

TAMINO: Nun muss ich fort!

PAMINA: Tamino! So musst du fort!

TAMINO: Pamina! Lebe wohl!

PAMINA: Tamino! Lebe wohl!

TAMINO:
Believe me, I feel the ache like you.
My heart is yours and yours alone!

SARASTRO:
Believe me, he feels the ache like you.
His heart is yours and yours alone.
The hour has come, you must now part.

PAMINA AND TAMINO: This bitter moment pierces my heart.

SARASTRO: Tamino, it is time to go.

PAMINA: Tamino, oh must you go?

TAMINO: Pamina, it is time I go!

SARASTRO: Now you must go.

TAMINO: Now I must go!

PAMINA: Oh must you go?

TAMINO: Pamina, farewell!

PAMINA: Tamino, farewell!

SARASTRO:
Nun eile fort!
Dich ruft dein Wort!

TAMINO, SARASTRO: Die Stunde schlägt! Wir sehn uns wieder!

PAMINA: O goldne Ruhe kehre wieder!

(entfernen sich)

Zweiundzwanzigster Auftritt
PAPAGENO.

Dialog

PAPAGENO: *(von außen)* Tamino! Tamino! willst du mich denn
gänzlich verlassen? *(Er sucht herein.)* Wenn ich nur wenigstens
wüsste, wo ich wäre – Tamino! – Tamino! – So lang ich lebe,
bleib ich nicht mehr von dir, – – nur diesmal verlass mich armen
Reisgefährten nicht!
(Er kommt an die Türe, wo Tamino abgeführt worden ist.)

EINE STIMME: *(ruft)* Zurück!
*(dann ein Donnerschlag, das Feuer schlägt zur Türe heraus; starker
Akkord)*

PAPAGENO: Barmherzige Götter! – Wo wend ich mich hin? –
Wenn ich nur wüsste, wo ich hereinkam. *(Er kommt an die Türe,
wo er hereinkam.)*

DIE STIMME: Zurück!
(Donner, Feuer und Akkord wie oben)

PAPAGENO: Nun kann ich weder zurück noch vorwärts! *(weint)*
Muss vielleicht am Ende gar verhungern. – Schon recht! –
Warum bin ich mitgereist.

SARASTRO:
On your way!
Your vow summons you.

TAMINO AND SARASTRO: The hour strikes. We will meet again.

PAMINA: Danger and death our love transcends!

(They go off.)

Twenty-second Scene
PAPAGENO.

Spoken Dialogue

PAPAGENO: *(from offstage)* Tamino! Tamino! Are you leaving me all alone? *(searching)* If I only knew where I was. Tamino! Ta-mi-no! As long as I live, I'll never leave your side again. Oh, just this once, please don't abandon me!
(He comes to the door through which Tamino has just been led away.)

A VOICE: *(calling out)* Stand back!
(A thunderclap. Fire flashes through the door. A loud chord.)

PAPAGENO: Merciful gods! If only I could remember which door it was I came in. *(He goes up to the door through which he first entered.)*

THE VOICE: Stand back!
(Thunder, fire, and the chord as before.)

PAPAGENO: I can't go one way or the other. *(He bursts into tears.)* Perhaps I'm just meant to starve to death . . . That's it! Oh, why did I ever come along?

Dreiundzwanzigster Auftritt
SPRECHER (MIT SEINER PYRAMIDE), VORIGE.

Dialog

SPRECHER: Mensch! du hättest verdient, auf immer in finstern Klüften der Erde zu wandern. – Die gütigen Götter aber entlassen der Strafe dich. – Dafür aber wirst du das himmlische Vergnügen der Eingeweihten nie fühlen.

PAPAGENO: Je nun, es gibt ja noch mehr Leute meinesgleichen. – Mir wäre jetzt ein gut Glas Wein das größte Vergnügen.

SPRECHER: Sonst hast du keinen Wunsch in dieser Welt?

PAPAGENO: Bis jetzt nicht.

SPRECHER: Man wird dich damit bedienen! –
(ab. Sogleich kommt ein großer Becher mit rotem Wein angefüllt aus der Erde.)

PAPAGENO: Juchhe! Da ist er ja schon! *(trinkt)* Herrlich! – Himmlisch! – Göttlich! – Ha! ich bin jetzt so vergnügt, dass ich bis zur Sonne fliegen wollte, wenn ich Flügel hätte – Ha! – mir wird ganz wunderlich ums Herz. – Ich möchte, – ich wünschte, – ja was denn?

N° 20 Aria

PAPAGENO: *(Er schlägt dazu.)*
Ein Mädchen oder Weibchen
Wünscht Papageno sich!
O so ein sanftes Täubchen
Wär Seligkeit für mich!
Dann schmeckte mir Trinken und Essen,

Twenty-third Scene

THE SPEAKER (WITH HIS PYRAMID) AND PAPAGENO.

Spoken Dialogue

SPEAKER: Mortal! You have deserved to wander forever in the gloomy abysses of the earth. But the gentle gods have remitted that punishment. However, you shall never experience the exalted pleasure of the Brotherhood.

PAPAGENO: Well, there are plenty of chaps like me. For me, a glass of wine right now would be exalted enough.

SPEAKER: Have you no other earthly desire?

PAPAGENO: Not at the moment.

SPEAKER: Then your wish is granted.
(He leaves; at the same time a large glass of red wine appears from underground.)

PAPAGENO: Whew! That was sure quick! *(He drinks.)* Delicious!—Splendid!—Heavenly! I feel so good now I could fly up to the sun if only I had wings! Ha! My heart suddenly feels a little strange. I want . . . I'd like to . . . Now what could it have been?

Aria

PAPAGENO: *(playing his chimes)*
A sweetheart or a bride
Is Papageno's wish.
A cute and curvy, moon-eyed
Turtledove's his dish!
With food to sate and wine to rinse,

Dann könnt ich mit Fürsten mich messen,
Des Lebens als Weiser mich freun
Und wie im Elysium sein.

Ein Mädchen oder Weibchen
Wünscht Papageno sich!
O so ein sanftes Täubchen
Wär Seligkeit für mich!
Ach kann ich denn keiner von allen
Den reizenden Mädchen gefallen?
Helf eine mir nur aus der Not,
Sonst gräm ich mich wahrlich zu Tod.

Ein Mädchen oder Weibchen
Wünscht Papageno sich!
O so ein sanftes Täubchen
Wär Seligkeit für mich!
Wird keine mir Liebe gewähren,
So muss mich die Flamme verzehren;
Doch küsst mich ein weiblicher Mund,
So bin ich schon wieder gesund.

Vierundzwanzigster Auftritt

DIE ALTE (TANZEND UND AUF IHREN STOCK
DABEI SICH STÜTZEND), VORIGE.

Dialog

WEIB: Da bin ich schon, mein Engel!

PAPAGENO: Du hast dich meiner erbarmt?

WEIB: Ja, mein Engel!

I'd be the equal of any prince.
That's all the wisdom I'd ever need.
There's my heaven, yes indeed!

A sweetheart or a bride
Is Papageno's wish.
A cute and curvy, moon-eyed
Turtledove's his dish!
So many girls flutter around me.
Not a single one as yet has found me.
With no one to love me, no one to care,
I'm driven into the arms of despair!

A sweetheart or a bride
Is Papageno's wish.
A cute and curvy, moon-eyed
Turtledove's his dish!
If just one kiss is longer denied,
I'll die of this burning fever inside!
All I need is just that kiss
To put me in a twittering bliss.

Twenty-fourth Scene

THE OLD WOMAN (DANCING AND LEANING
ON HER STICK) AND PAPAGENO.

Spoken Dialogue

OLD WOMAN: Here I am, my angel!

PAPAGENO: So you've taken pity on me?

OLD WOMAN: I have, my angel!

PAPAGENO: Das ist ein Glück!

WEIB: Und wenn du mir versprichst, mir ewig treu zu bleiben, dann sollst du sehen, wie zärtlich dein Weibchen dich lieben wird.

PAPAGENO: Ei du zärtliches Närrchen!

WEIB: O wie will ich dich umarmen, dich liebkosen, dich an mein Herz drücken!

PAPAGENO: Auch ans Herz drücken?

WEIB: Komm, reiche mir zum Pfand unsers Bundes deine Hand.

PAPAGENO: Nur nicht so hastig, lieber Engel! – So ein Bündnis braucht doch auch seine Überlegung.

WEIB: Papageno, ich rate dir, zaudre nicht. – Deine Hand oder du bist auf immer hier eingekerkert.

PAPAGENO: Eingekerkert?

WEIB: Wasser und Brot wird deine tägliche Kost sein. – Ohne Freund, ohne Freundin musst du leben und der Welt auf immer entsagen. –

PAPAGENO: Wasser trinken? – Der Welt entsagen? – Nein, da will ich doch lieber eine Alte nehmen als gar keine. – Nun, da hast du meine Hand, mit der Versicherung, dass ich dir immer getreu bleibe, *(für sich)* so lang ich keine Schönere sehe.

WEIB: Das schwörst du?

PAPAGENO: That's lucky!

OLD WOMAN: And if you promise to be true to me forever, you will see how tenderly your little wife will love you.

PAPAGENO: Oh, you little goose, you!

OLD WOMAN: I will hold you and kiss you and press you to my heart!

PAPAGENO: Press me to your heart?

OLD WOMAN: Here, give me your hand, and we will plight our troth.

PAPAGENO: Not so fast, dear heart. With marriage, a man needs time to think things over.

OLD WOMAN: Papageno, I'd advise you not to hesitate. Give me your hand, or you'll be imprisoned here forever.

PAPAGENO: Imprisoned?

OLD WOMAN: Bread and water once a day. You'll have to live without a friend or a sweetheart and renounce the world forever.

PAPAGENO: Drink water? Renounce the world? No, better an old wife than no wife. So here is my hand on it. I will always be true to you . . . *(to himself)* until I see a prettier bird!

OLD WOMAN: Do you swear it?

PAPAGENO: Ja, das schwör ich!

(Weib verwandelt sich in ein junges Weib, welches ebenso gekleidet ist wie Papageno.)

PAPAGENO: Pa – Pa – Papagena! –

(Er will sie umarmen.)

Fünfundzwanzigster Auftritt
SPRECHER, VORIGE.

SPRECHER: *(nimmt sie hastig bei der Hand)* Fort mit dir, junges Weib! Er ist deiner noch nicht würdig. *(Er schleppt sie hinein, Papageno will nach.)* Zurück, sag ich! oder zittre.

PAPAGENO: Eh ich mich zurückziehe, soll die Erde mich verschlingen. *(Er sinkt hinab.)* O ihr Götter!

Das Theater verwandelt sich in einen kurzen Garten.

Sechsundzwanzigster Auftritt
DIE DREI KNABEN FAHREN HERUNTER.

N° 21 Finale

DREI KNABEN:
Bald prangt, den Morgen zu verkünden,
Die Sonn auf goldner Bahn.
Bald soll der Aberglaube schwinden,
Bald siegt der weise Mann! –
O holde Ruhe steig hernieder,
Kehr in der Menschen Herzen wieder,
Dann ist die Erd ein Himmelreich
Und Sterbliche den Göttern gleich. –

PAPAGENO: Yes, I swear it!

(The Old Woman turns into a young woman dressed exactly like Papageno.)

PAPAGENO: Pa-Pa-Papagena!

(He rushes forward to embrace her.)

Twenty-fifth Scene
THE SPEAKER, AND THOSE BEFORE.

SPEAKER: *(taking her quickly by the hand)* Away with you, young woman! He is not yet worthy of you. *(He drags her off; Papapeno goes to follow.)* Stand back, or you will pay!

PAPAGENO: The earth would have to open its jaws and swallow me, before I'd ever stand back. *(He sinks to the ground.)* Oh gods!

The stage changes into a small garden.

Twenty-sixth Scene
THE THREE BOYS DESCEND.

Finale

THE THREE BOYS:
Soon the glorious sun will take
Its golden course across the sky!
The foes of superstition wake
And wisdom is enthroned on high.
Soon peace will bring its remedies.
Enlightenment will bless the wise.
Then mankind will be truly free
And earth become a paradise!

ERSTER KNABE: Doch seht, Verzweiflung quält Paminen! –

ZWEITER KNABE, DRITTER KNABE: Wo ist sie denn?

ERSTER KNABE: Sie ist von Sinnen!

DREI KNABEN:
Sie quält verschmähter Liebe Leiden,
Lasst uns der Armen Trost bereiten! –
Fürwahr ihr Schicksal geht uns nah,
O wäre nur ihr Jüngling da! –
Sie kömmt, lasst uns beiseite gehn,
Damit wir, was sie mache, sehn.
(gehen beiseite)

Siebenundzwanzigster Auftritt
PAMINA, VORIGE

PAMINA: *(halb wahnwitzig, mit einem Dolch; zum Dolch)*
Du also bist mein Bräutigam? –
Durch dich vollend ich meinen Gram! –

DREI KNABEN: *(beiseite)*
Welch dunkle Worte sprach sie da! –
Die Arme ist dem Wahnsinn nah!

PAMINA:
Geduld! mein Trauter! ich bin dein,
Bald werden wir vermählet sein!

DREI KNABEN: *(beiseite)*
Wahnsinn tobt ihr im Gehirne, –
Selbstmord steht auf ihrer Stirne! –
(zu Pamina)
Holdes Mädchen, sieh uns an!

FIRST BOY: But see, despair torments Pamina.

SECOND BOY AND THIRD BOY: How is she then?

FIRST BOY: Her mind wanders . . .

THE THREE BOYS:
She feels the pang of love's rejection,
So let us grant her our protection.
To her fortunes we all feel near—
If only her young Prince were here!
She comes, so let us stay unseen
And wait to learn what this may mean.
(They withdraw.)

Twenty-seventh Scene
PAMINA, AND THOSE BEFORE.

PAMINA: *(half crazed, with a dagger in her hand)*
This blade's the groom I now must wed.
The grave will be my marriage bed.

THE THREE BOYS: *(aside)*
What gloomy words to overhear.
The poor girl's madness must be near.

PAMINA:
Be calm, beloved, I belong to you.
What grief your kiss will now undo!

THE THREE BOYS: *(aside)*
Surely madness clouds her brain.
How would suicide end her pain?
(to Pamina)
Dearest maiden, look!—over here!

PAMINA:
Sterben will ich, - weil der Mann,
Den ich nimmermehr kann hassen,
Seine Traute kann verlassen! -
(auf den Dolch zeigend)
Dies gab meine Mutter mir - -

DREI KNABEN: Selbstmord strafet Gott an dir! -

PAMINA:
Lieber durch dies Eisen sterben,
Als durch Liebesgram verderben. -
Mutter! durch dich leide ich,
Und dein Fluch verfolget mich! -

DREI KNABEN: Mädchen! willst du mit uns gehn?

PAMINA:
Ja, des Jammers Maß ist voll!
Falscher Jüngling, lebe wohl!
Sieh, Pamina stirbt durch dich!
Dieses Eisen töte mich! -
(will sich erstechen)

DREI KNABEN: *(halten ihr den Arm)*
Ha Unglückliche! halt ein!
Sollte dies dein Jüngling sehen,
Würde er für Gram vergehen,
Denn er liebet dich allein. -

PAMINA: *(erholt sich)*
Was? Er fühlte Gegenliebe
Und verbarg mir seine Triebe, -
Wandte sein Gesicht von mir?
Warum sprach er nicht mit mir?

PAMINA:
Death is certain. Now all is clear.
The husband who could never hurt me
Has cruelly chosen to desert me.
(pointing to the dagger)
This friend my mother gave to me.

THE THREE BOYS: The gods forbid this by decree!

PAMINA:
Better by this blade to die
Than live a loveless lie.
Mother, Mother, it is your curse
That forces me to do the worst.

THE THREE BOYS: Maiden, come away with us!

PAMINA:
My grief is now too much to tell.
False Tamino, farewell, farewell!
See how for you Pamina dies.
This dagger stops the tears and sighs.
(She starts to stab herself.)

THE THREE BOYS: *(staying her hand)*
Stop! Poor girl, so sad and lonely!
If Tamino could be near you,
He would surely weep to hear you.
The Prince loves you and you only.

PAMINA: *(recovering her senses)*
You say he loved me in return
Pretending so to scoff and spurn?
Is it one's beloved one betrays?
For me alone he could not stay?

DREI KNABEN:
Dieses müssen wir verschweigen,
Doch wir wollen dir ihn zeigen,
Und du wirst mit Staunen sehn,
Dass er dir sein Herz geweiht
Und den Tod für dich nicht scheut!

PAMINA: Führt mich hin, ich möcht ihn sehn.

DREI KNABEN: Komm, wir wollen zu ihm gehn.

PAMINA, DREI KNABEN:
Zwei Herzen, die von Liebe brennen,
Kann Menschenohnmacht niemals trennen, –
Verloren ist der Feinde Müh,
Die Götter selbsten schützen sie.

(gehen ab)

*Das Theater verwandelt sich in zwei große Berge; in
dem einen ist ein Wasserfall, worin man Sausen und
Brausen hört; der andre speit Feuer aus; jeder Berg hat ein
durchbrochenes Gegitter, worin man Feuer und Wasser sieht.
Da, wo das Feuer brennt, muss der Horizont hellrot sein, und
wo das Wasser ist, liegt schwarzer Nebel. Die Szenen sind
Felsen, jede Szene schließt sich mit einer eisernen Türe.*

Achtundzwanzigster Auftritt

TAMINO IST LEICHT ANGEZOGEN OHNE SANDALEN. ZWEI
SCHWARZ GEHARNISCHTE MÄNNER FÜHREN TAMINO
HEREIN. AUF IHREN HELMEN BRENNT FEUER, SIE LESEN
IHM DIE TRANSPARENTE SCHRIFT VOR, WELCHE AUF
EINER PYRAMIDE GESCHRIEBEN STEHT. DIESE
PYRAMIDE STEHT IN DER MITTE, GANZ IN
DER HÖHE NAHE AM GEGITTER.

THE THREE BOYS:
To answer you is not allowed,
Though we may lead you to him now.
Follow us and you will see
His devotion and his bravery.
Death itself he dares somehow!

PAMINA: Lead me to him! I long to see!

THE THREE BOYS: Follow us and you will see.

PAMINA AND THE THREE BOYS:
Two hearts that beat as one forever
Not even doubt and weakness sever.
Their enemies may plot elsewhere,
But the gods protect this noble pair.
(They leave.)

*The scene changes to two towering mountains; inside one
is a waterfall whose roaring can be heard; the other
spits out fire. Each mountain has a grating through which
the water and fire can be seen. Where the fire blazes, the
horizon must glow bright red, and where the water is,
there is a black mist. Two pieces of scenery are rocks,
each inset with iron doors.*

Twenty-eighth Scene

TAMINO IS LIGHTLY DRESSED, WITHOUT SANDALS. TWO
MEN IN BLACK ARMOR LEAD HIM IN. FIRE BURNS IN
THEIR HELMETS. THEY READ TO HIM THE TRANSPARENT
WRITING INSCRIBED ON THE PYRAMID. THIS PYRAMID
LOOMS IN THE MIDDLE, HIGH UP NEAR THE GRATING.

ERSTER UND ZWEITER GEHARNISCHTER MANN:
Der, welcher wandert diese Straße voll Beschwerden,
Wird rein durch Feuer, Wasser, Luft und Erden.
Wenn er des Todes Schrecken überwinden kann,
Schwingt er sich aus der Erde himmelan!
Erleuchtet wird er dann imstande sein,
Sich den Mysterien der Isis ganz zu weihn. –

TAMINO:
Mich schreckt kein Tod, als Mann zu handeln,
Den Weg der Tugend fortzuwandeln! –
Schließt mir des Schreckens Pforten auf –
Ich wage froh den kühnen Lauf. –
(will gehen)

PAMINA: *(von innen)* Tamino, halt! ich muss dich sehn!

TAMINO: Was hör ich? Paminens Stimme? –

ERSTER UND ZWEITER GEHARNISCHTER MANN: Ja, ja, das ist
Paminens Stimme! –

TAMINO:
Wohl mir, nun kann sie mit mir gehen!
Nun trennet uns kein Schicksal mehr,
Wenn auch der Tod beschieden wär.

ERSTER UND ZWEITER GEHARNISCHTER MANN:
Wohl dir, nun kann sie mit dir gehen!
Nun trennet euch kein Schicksal mehr,
Wenn auch der Tod beschieden wär.

TAMINO: Ist mir erlaubt, mit ihr zu sprechen? –

FIRST AND SECOND MEN IN ARMOR:
He who walks this path to the trials' crest,
By fire, water, air, and earth is tested.
If he can but conquer fear of death,
He soon will rise to heaven from earth.
Enlightened, he will at last understand
All of those mysteries of Isis he can.

TAMINO:
Death I defy, and like a man
Keep on the journey I began.
Unlock the fatal gates of fear—
Virtue leads me, the way is clear.
(He is about to enter.)

PAMINA: *(from afar)* Tamino, wait! I must see you!

TAMINO: What was that? Pamina's voice!

FIRST AND SECOND MEN IN ARMOR: Yes, that was Pamina's voice.

TAMINO:
What joy if she is at my side!
No destiny can separate us,
Though death itself at last awaits us!

FIRST AND SECOND MEN IN ARMOR:
What joy if she is at his side!
No destiny can separate them,
Though death itself at last awaits them!

TAMINO: Am I allowed to break my silence?

ERSTER UND ZWEITER GEHARNISCHTER MANN: Es ist erlaubt, mit ihr zu sprechen!

TAMINO: Welch Glück, wenn wir uns wiedersehn.

ERSTER UND ZWEITER GEHARNISCHTER MANN: Welch Glück, wenn wir euch wiedersehn.

TAMINO, ERSTER UND ZWEITER GEHARNISCHTER MANN:
Froh Hand in Hand in Tempel gehn.
Ein Weib, das Nacht und Tod nicht scheut,
Ist würdig und wird eingeweiht.

(Die Türe wird aufgemacht. Pamina und Tamino umarmen sich. Pause.)

PAMINA: Tamino mein! O welch ein Glück!

TAMINO:
Pamina mein! O welch ein Glück!
Hier sind die Schreckenspforten,
Die Not und Tod mir dräun.

PAMINA:
Ich werde aller Orten
An deiner Seite sein. –
Ich selbsten führe dich, –
Die Liebe leite mich! –
(nimmt ihn bei der Hand)
Sie mag den Weg mit Rosen streun,
Weil Rosen stets bei Dornen sein.
Spiel du die Zauberflöte an,
Sie schütze uns auf unsrer Bahn.
Es schnitt in einer Zauberstunde
Mein Vater sie aus tiefstem Grunde

FIRST AND SECOND MEN IN ARMOR: You are allowed to break your silence.

TAMINO: What joy when we can meet again!

FIRST AND SECOND MEN IN ARMOR: What joy when they can meet again!

TAMINO AND FIRST AND SECOND MEN IN ARMOR:
To enter the temple hand in hand!
The woman who braves the deadly night
Is worthy to receive the light.

(The gates are opened. Tamino and Pamina embrace.)

PAMINA: Oh Tamino! My love! My joy!

TAMINO:
Oh Pamina! My love! My joy!
Behold the gates of terror
Where death and destiny loom.

PAMINA:
Whatever we walk through
When I am by your side,
I myself will lead you
And Love will be my guide.
(She takes him by the hand.)
With roses we'll the path adorn,
For roses always bloom with thorns.
So take your magic flute and play.
It will protect us on our way.
It was carved at the witching hour,
Releasing ancient wondrous powers

Der tausendjähr'gen Eiche aus,
Bei Blitz und Donner – Sturm und Braus. –
Nun komm und spiel die Flöte an!
Sie leite uns auf grauser Bahn.

PAMINA, TAMINO:
Wir wandeln durch des Tones Macht
Froh durch des Todes düstre Nacht.

ERSTER UND ZWEITER GEHARNISCHTER MANN:
Ihr wandelt durch des Tones Macht
Froh durch des Todes düstre Nacht.

(Die Türen werden nach ihnen zugeschlagen. Man sieht Tamino und Pamina wandern. Man hört Feuergeprassel und Windesgeheul, manchmal den Ton eines dumpfen Donners und Wassergeräuschs. Tamino bläst seine Flöte; gedämpfte Pauken akkompagnieren manchmal darunter. Sobald sie vom Feuer herauskommen, umarmen sie sich und bleiben in der Mitte.)

Marcia

PAMINA, TAMINO:
Wir wandelten durch Feuergluten,
Bekämpften mutig die Gefahr.
Dein Ton sei Schutz in Wasserfluten,
So wie er es im Feuer war.

(Tamino bläst; man sieht sie hinuntersteigen und nach einiger Zeit wieder heraufkommen. Sogleich öffnet sich eine Türe; man sieht einen Eingang in einen Tempel, welcher hell beleuchtet ist. Eine feierliche Stille. Dieser Anblick muss den vollkommensten Glanz darstellen. Sogleich fällt der Chor unter Trompeten und Pauken ein. Zuvor aber:)

PAMINA, TAMINO:
Ihr Götter, welch ein Augenblick!
Gewähret ist uns Isis' Glück!

From deep within the oak's strong wood
Where no storm reached, but my father could.
The magic flute! It's time you played,
To guard us on our ominous way.

PAMINA AND TAMINO:
Encircled with sweet music's might
We enter now death's darkest night.

FIRST AND SECOND MEN IN ARMOR:
Encircled with sweet music's might
They enter now death's darkest night.

(The doors are closed behind them. We see Tamino and Pamina walking on. We hear the fire crackle, the wind howl; at times, too, thunder booms and water roars. Tamino plays his flute. As soon as they emerge from the fire, they embrace, standing in the middle of the stage.)

March

PAMINA AND TAMINO:
We've travelled through the blazing furnace,
And withstood its fiery grave.
Now to try the watery menace,
Hoping the flute will keep us safe.

(Tamino plays; we see them descending and later ascending; suddenly a door is opened; we see the entrance of a glorious temple. A solemn silence. This sight should represent the utmost resplendence. At once, the chorus enters, accompanied by trumpets and drums. But before this:)

PAMINA AND TAMINO:
Our triumph the all-wise gods allow!
The mighty Isis stands by us now!

CHOR:
Triumph, Triumph, du edles Paar!
Besieget hast du die Gefahr!
Der Isis Weihe ist nun dein!
Kommt, tretet in den Tempel ein!
(alle ab)

Das Theater verwandelt sich wieder in vorigen Garten.

Neunundzwanzigster Auftritt
PAPAGENO, SPÄTER DIE DREI KNABEN UND PAPAGENA

PAPAGENO: *(pfeift)*
Papagena! Papagena! Papagena! *(pfeift)*
Weibchen! Täubchen! Meine Schöne! –
Vergebens! Ach! Sie ist verloren!
Ich bin zum Unglück schon geboren! –
Ich plauderte, und das war schlecht,
Und drum geschieht es mir schon recht! –
Seit ich gekostet diesen Wein,
Seit ich das schöne Weibchen sah,
So brennt's im Herzenskämmerlein,
So zwicket's hier, so zwicket's da!
Papagena! Herzensweibchen!
Papagena! liebes Täubchen!
S' ist umsonst! Es ist vergebens,
Müde bin ich meines Lebens!
Sterben macht der Lieb ein End,
Wenn's im Herzen noch so brennt.
(nimmt einen Strick von seiner Mitte)
Diesen Baum da will ich zieren,
Mir an ihm den Hals zuschnüren,
Weil das Leben mir missfällt.
Gute Nacht, du schwarze Welt! –

CHORUS:
Rejoice! Rejoice! You valiant pair!
You have emerged from danger's lair.
Isis has smiled on your noble minds.
Come, enter now our temple's shrine.
(They all leave.)

The scene is changed back into the earlier garden.

Twenty-ninth Scene

PAPAGENO. LATER THE THREE BOYS AND PAPAGENA.

PAPAGENO: *(playing his panpipe)*
Papagena, Papagena, Papagena! *(plays)*
Sweetheart! Dearest! My beloved!
Useless! She is lost forever!
I was never meant to have her.
By chattering I missed my chance.
Here's the end to my romance.
Ever since I sipped that wine
And saw the girl that should be mine,
The fire in my heart's severe.
It warms me there, and scorches here!
Papagena! My dove! My darling!
Papagena! My pretty starling!
She doesn't know the way to find me.
It's time to leave the world behind me.
Since my love was all in vain,
It's time to end a life of pain.
(He takes a rope from his waist.)
I'd decorate this sturdy tree
With the hanging body of . . . me.
My wretched life has been misspent.
Goodbye, world. You won't lament.

Weil du böse an mir handelst,
Mir kein schönes Kind zubandelst,
So ist's aus, so sterbe ich,
Schöne Mädchen, denkt an mich! –
Will sich eine um mich Armen,
Eh ich hänge, noch erbarmen;
Wohl, so lass ich's diesmal sein!
Rufet nur, ja oder nein! –
Keine hört mich!

(sieht sich um)

Alles stille!
Also ist es euer Wille!
Papageno frisch hinauf,
Ende deinen Lebenslauf!

(sieht sich um)

Nun! Ich warte noch! Es sei –
Bis man zählet: Eins, zwei, drei!

(pfeift)

Eins!

(sieht sich um; pfeift)

Zwei!

(sieht sich um; pfeift)

Drei!

(sieht sich um)

Nun wohlan! Es bleibt dabei!
Weil mich nichts zurückehält,
Gute Nacht, du falsche Welt!

(will sich hängen)

DREI KNABEN: *(fahren herunter)*
Halt ein! o Papageno, und sei klug!
Man lebt nur einmal, dies sei dir genug!

All you did was to mistreat me,
And now—no little wife to greet me.
So this is it. It's time to die.
Pretty maidens, goodbye! Goodbye!
If there were just someone to care,
Take pity on me, want to spare—
Yes! this once I might relent!
Speak up! Have I your consent?
(He looks around.)
No one hears me. No reply.
Well, I guess I'll have to die.
Come on, Papageno, the rope—
Can't you see there is no hope.
(He looks around.)
Wait! One more chance. Let's see.
Suppose I count from one to three . . .
(He plays his pipe.)
One!
(He looks around and pipes.)
Two!
(He looks around and pipes.)
Three.
(He looks around.)
Not a sound. The die is cast!
This moment then is to be my last.
No sympathy? No help? All right!
You unlucky world of pain, goodnight!
(He starts to hang himself.)

THE THREE BOYS: *(flying down)*
Papageno! Wait! Take our advice.
You live just once. Let that suffice.

PAPAGENO:
Ihr habt gut reden, gut zu scherzen;
Doch brennt' es euch wie mich im Herzen,
Ihr würdet auch nach Mädchen gehn.

DREI KNABEN:
So lasse deine Glöckchen klingen,
Dies wird dein Weibchen zu dir bringen.

PAPAGENO:
Ich Narr vergaß der Zauberdinge! –
(nimmt sein Instrument heraus)
Erklinge, Glockenspiel, erklinge,
Ich muss mein liebes Mädchen sehn!
(Die drei Knaben laufen zu ihrem Flugwerk und bringen das Weib heraus.)
Klinget, Glöckchen, klinget,
Schafft mein Mädchen her! –
Klinget, Glöckchen, klinget,
Bringt mein Weibchen her! –

DREI KNABEN: *(im Auffahren)* Nun, Papageno, sieh dich um!

*(Papageno sieht sich um. Papagena, Papageno sehen sich; beide haben
unter dem Ritornell komisches Spiel.)*

PAPAGENO: Pa–Pa–Pa–Pa–Pa–Pa–Papagena!

PAPAGENA: Pa–Pa–Pa–Pa–Pa–Pa–Papageno!

PAPAGENO: Pa–Pa–Pa–Pa–Pa–Pa–Papagena!

PAPAGENA: Pa–Pa–Pa–Pa–Pa–Pa–Papageno!

PAPAGENO: Bist du mir nun ganz gegeben? –

PAPAGENO:
Wise advice. Go on, mock me!
If, like mine, your hearts were aswirl,
You too would be pursuing girls.

THE THREE BOYS:
Take up your magic bells and play.
Your sweetheart will soon enough obey.

PAPAGENO:
What a fool! I forgot the bells!
(He takes out his instrument.)
My pretty chimes, come cast your spell!
You'll bring her back as nothing will.
(The Three Boys run back to their flying machine and bring a woman out of it.)
Ring, little bells, ring out,
Bring my sweetheart here!
Ring, little bells, ring out,
Bring my sweetheart dear!

THE THREE BOYS: *(flying up)* Now, Papageno, look around!

(Papageno looks around. During the introduction, there is some comic business between the two.)

PAPAGENO: Pa-Pa-Pa-Pa-Pa-Pa-Papagena!

PAPAGENA: Pa-Pa-Pa-Pa-Pa-Pa-Papageno!

PAPAGENO: Pa-Pa-Pa-Pa-Pa-Pa-Papagena!

PAPAGENA: Pa-Pa-Pa-Pa-Pa-Pa-Papageno!

PAPAGENO: Now will you be mine forever?

PAPAGENA: Nun bin ich dir ganz gegeben. –

PAPAGENO: Nun so sei mein liebes Weibchen!

PAPAGENA: Nun so sei mein Herzenstäubchen!

PAPAGENA, PAPAGENO:
Welche Freude wird das sein,
Wenn die Götter uns bedenken,
Unsrer Liebe Kinder schenken,
So liebe kleine Kinderlein!

PAPAGENO: Erst einen kleinen Papageno!

PAPAGENA: Dann eine kleine Papagena!

PAPAGENO: Dann wieder einen Papageno!

PAPAGENA: Dann wieder eine Papagena!

PAPAGENO, PAPAGENA:
Papageno! Papagena!
Es ist das höchste der Gefühle,
Wenn viele
Pa–Pa–Papageno
Pa–Pa–Pa–Pa–Pa–Pa–Papagena
Der Eltern Segen werden sein.
(beide ab)

PAPAGENA: Now I will be yours forever!

PAPAGENO: Now you'll be my little love!

PAPAGENA: Now you'll be my turtledove!

PAPAGENO AND PAPAGENA:
Oh, what bliss! Oh, what joy!
May the gods bless us
And crown our caresses
With many a little girl and boy!

PAPAGENO: First a little Papageno!

PAPAGENA: Then a little Papagena!

PAPAGENO: Then another Papageno!

PAPAGENA: Then another Papagena!

PAPAGENO AND PAPAGENA:
Papagenas! Papagenos!
The greatest joy of any
Is many, many
Pa-Pa-Pa-Papagenos,
Pa-Pa-Pa-Papagenas.
To bless their parents' nest!
(They both rush off.)

Dreißigster Auftritt

DER MOHR, DIE KÖNIGIN MIT ALLEN IHREN DAMEN
KOMMEN VON BEIDEN VERSENKUNGEN. SIE TRAGEN
SCHWARZE FACKELN IN DER HAND.

MANOSTATOS:
Nur stille! stille! stille! stille!
Bald dringen wir in Tempel ein!

DIE DREI DAMEN:
Nur stille! stille! stille! stille!
Bald dringen wir in Tempel ein.

MANOSTATOS:
Doch Fürstin! halte Wort! erfülle!
Dein Kind muss meine Gattin sein!

KÖNIGIN:
Ich halte Wort! Es ist mein Wille.
Mein Kind soll deine Gattin sein!

DIE DREI DAMEN: Ihr Kind soll deine Gattin sein!

(Man hört dumpfen Donner und Wassergeräusch.)

MANOSTATOS:
Doch still, ich höre schrecklich Rauschen
Wie Donnerton und Wasserfall. –

KÖNIGIN, DIE DREI DAMEN:
Ja, fürchterlich ist dieses Rauschen
Wie fernen Donners Wiederhall!

MANOSTATOS: Nun sind sie in des Tempels Hallen!

Thirtieth Scene

THE MOOR, THE QUEEN, AND ALL HER LADIES ENTER
FROM BOTH TRAPDOORS. THEY CARRY BLACK TORCHES
IN THEIR HANDS.

MONOSTATOS:
Softly, softly, one step more!
We'll soon be at the temple door.

THE THREE LADIES:
Softly, softly, one step more!
We'll soon be at the temple door.

MONOSTATOS:
Your Highness, I pray you keep your word—
You promised your child as my bride.

QUEEN OF THE NIGHT:
That is my will. I'll keep my word.
I promised my child as your bride.

THE THREE LADIES: She promised her child as his bride.

(Thunder and rushing water are heard.)

MONOSTATOS:
Silence! I hear a roaring sound
Like thunder, or a waterfall.

THE QUEEN AND THE THREE LADIES:
Yes, that roaring is a frightful sound,
Like distant thunder's threatening call.

MONOSTATOS: Now they are in the temple's hall.

KÖNIGIN, DIE DREI DAMEN, MANOSTATOS:

Dort wollen wir sie überfallen, –
Die Frömmler tilgen von der Erd
Mit Feuers Glut und mächt'gem Schwert!

DIE DREI DAMEN, MANOSTATOS:

Dir, große Königin der Nacht,
Sei unsrer Rache Opfer gebracht!

(Donner, Blitz, Sturm)

KÖNIGIN, DIE DREI DAMEN, MANOSTATOS:

Zerschmettert, zernichtet ist unsere Macht,
Wir alle gestürzet in ewige Nacht! –
(versinken)

(Sogleich verwandelt sich das ganze Theater in eine Sonne. Sarastro steht erhöht; Tamino, Pamina, beide in priesterlicher Kleidung. Neben ihnen die ägyptischen Priester auf beiden Seiten. Die drei Knaben halten Blumen.)

SARASTRO:

Die Strahlen der Sonne vertreiben die Nacht,
Zernichten der Heuchler erschlichene Macht!

CHOR:

Heil sei euch Geweihten! ihr dranget durch Nacht!
Dank sei dir, Osiris, Dank dir, Isis, gebracht!
Es siegte die Stärke und krönet zum Lohn
Die Schönheit und Weisheit mit ewiger Kron!

Ende

THE QUEEN, THE THREE LADIES, AND MONOSTATOS:
And now is when the lightning falls!
Our flaming swords for the enemy!
We will destroy their blasphemy!

THE THREE LADIES AND MONOSTATOS:
Glorious Queen, accept this fight
As your last sacrificial rite!

(Thunder, lightning, storm.)

THE QUEEN, THE THREE LADIES, AND MONOSTATOS:
Shattered, ruined is our might,
All plunged into endless night!
(They sink down.)

(Suddenly the whole scene is transformed into a blaze of sunlight. Sarastro stands on high. Tamino, Pamina, both in priestly garments. Beside them on both sides, the Egyptian Priests. The Three Boys are holding flowers.)

SARASTRO:
The sun's golden splendor has banished the night,
The forces of evil are vanquished by right.

CHORUS:
Hail to those who have passed through the night!
By Osiris and Isis brought to the light!
Brave hearts have won the glorious crown!
May Beauty to Wisdom forever be bound!

End of the Opera.

A Biographical Note
÷ on Mozart ÷

HE WAS BORN IN SALZBURG ON JANUARY 27, 1756, AND
baptized Johannes Chrysostomus Wolfgangus Theophilus
Mozart. He was called "Wolferl" by his family; he signed his
letters "Wolfgang Amadè Mozart." He and his older sister, Maria
Anna (1751–1829), known as Nannerl, were the only ones of the
seven children born to the family to survive. His father, Leopold
(1719–1787), was descended from a line of artisans, and was a
violinist and pedagogue who served as the deputy Kapellmeister
to the court orchestra of the Archbishop of Salzburg. Mozart's
mother, Anna Maria Pertl (1720–1778), came from a humble family and made a good marriage. Leopold was the children's only
teacher, and by the time Mozart was five his father had copied
down his first compositions. A year later, Leopold took his son
and his eleven-year-old daughter on tour, first to perform for
the Elector Maximilian III Joseph of Bavaria in Munich, and then
on to Linz and Vienna, a trip that set the pattern for much of
Mozart's childhood. As child prodigies, Mozart and his sister
were paraded around the capitals of Europe, and the arduous
travelling conditions at times endangered the boy's health. But
by the age of seven the wunderkind had played before the royal
courts of Paris, London, and Vienna, and written his fledgling
sonatas and symphonies. By thirteen, he had been appointed as
a violinist in the court orchestra at Salzburg.

During the winter of 1769, Leopold took Mozart on the first of three extended trips to Italy, where he was admired and loved everywhere he went. He met the famous musicians of the day, was decorated by the Pope, awarded diplomas and certificates, and wrote his first two *opera seria*, one for the Teatro Regio Ducal in Milan, *Mitridate, Rè di Ponte*, and the other for the marriage of Archduke Ferdinand of Austria, *Ascanio in Alba*. In 1772, he wrote two more, *Il Sogno di Scipione* and *Lucio Silla*, the first of them in honor of the new Prince Archbishop of Salzburg, Count Hieronymus Colloredo, who appointed Mozart concertmaster of his court orchestra. His compositions, hitherto joyous and conventional, started to take on more complexity and brilliance.

The next few years in Salzburg were a productive time for Mozart. Violin and piano concertos, new symphonies and sonatas, divertimenti and serenades, church music and two more operas, *La Finta Giardiniera* and *Il Rè Pastore*, were written, and in 1777 he undertook a sixteen-month tour the first without his father. Restive with the restrictions of court life and eager for more independence at the age of twenty-one, he set out this time accompanied by his mother and stopped in Munich, Augsburg, and Paris. None of his hopes for employment worked out, but two crucial emotional crises occurred. While in Mannheim he met and fell in love with the singer Aloysia Weber, one of four daughters in a musical family (her first cousin was composer Carl Maria von Weber). And in Paris, on July 3, 1778, his mother died of typhus. On his way back to Salzburg he stopped in Mannheim and then Munich to see Aloysia Weber again, who to his consternation rejected his advances. He returned home, defeated and depressed, and in 1779 reluctantly accepted the position of organist and composer at Archbishop Colloredo's court.

The next year, however, following an invitation from the Bavarian court to compose a new opera, he left for Munich, not knowing that he would never return to Salzburg. The opera he then composed, *Idomeneo*, was a turning point in his career: a bold advance in his mastery, a brilliant success, and the start of his extraordinary opera career. A few months later, though, Archbishop Colloredo, in Vienna to attend the coronation of Hapsburg Emperor Joseph II, summoned Mozart to join his retinue there. Flush with his triumph and resentful of being treated like a servant, Mozart obeyed but began to make demands on the archbishop and after three months—to his father's dismay and the archbishop's anger—resigned his post. He resolved to stay in Vienna, and quickly established himself as the capital's finest keyboard player. It was then too that a neighbor caught his eye, Constanze Weber (1762–1842), Aloysia's younger sister, whom he married in 1782, the year of his success with the *Singspiel, Die Entführung aus dem Serail*, which helped spread his fame as the preeminent German composer. He capitalized on that fame with many other rich compositions during this period.

Mozart and his wife had six children, only two of whom survived infancy, Carl Thomas (1784–1858) and Franz Xaver Wolfgang (1791–1844). By now he was the toast of the Viennese music world. Audiences received each new work rapturously. If the Emperor was in attendance he would wave his hat and shout "Bravo Mozart!" One of Mozart's idols, Joseph Haydn, called him "the greatest composer whom I know in person and by reputation." Even Mozart's stern father relished his son's triumph. Success did not keep him from debt and only prompted more work, but he longed most to write operas. He had met Lorenzo Da Ponte in 1783 and two years later came to him with the idea of *Le Nozze di Figaro*, which premiered the next year in Vienna. In 1784, following the example of his liberal friends, be became a Freemason and was eventually promoted to "master."

In 1787, *Le Nozze di Figaro* was performed in Prague to such acclaim that the theater there commissioned a new opera from Mozart and Da Ponte, *Don Giovanni*, during the composition of which Leopold Mozart died. The opera triumphed in both Prague and Vienna, but Mozart—who every year performed new piano concertos that enthralled his public—remained short of cash and struggled, all the while creating masterpieces, with hackwork and loans. He longed for patronage and a permanent position. Emperor Joseph II appointed him court composer, but Mozart felt the stipend was "too much for what I do, too little for what I could do." The sixteen-year-old Beethoven came to study with him, but left after two weeks because his mother was ill. Mozart and his wife moved to less expensive living quarters and both suffered from health problems. Though troubled by what he called "black thoughts," he continued composing, and wrote his three last and greatest symphonies with no commission. In search of work, he travelled to Dresden, Leipzig, Potsdam, and Berlin. During the winter of 1789–90, he wrote *Così Fan Tutte*, his third and last collaboration with Da Ponte. The opera premiered in Vienna in January but performances were soon halted because of the death of the Emperor, with whose successor, Leopold of Austria, Mozart hoped to gain favor. An old friend, the impresario Emanuel Schikaneder, commissioned a new *Singspiel* from Mozart, *Die Zauberflöte*, but work on it was interrupted by two other commissions, one brought by a mysterious messenger for a requiem and the other for a new opera, *La Clemenza di Tito*, to celebrate the coronation in Prague of Leopold II as King of Bohemia. *La Clemenza* premiered on September 6, 1791, and *Die Zauberflöte* premiered on September 30. Mozart had felt ill while in Prague and by the end of November his condition had worsened. He was wracked by swelling, fever, and vomiting, and died in the early hours of December 5, his wife at his bedside. He was thirty-five years old. Speculation says the cause was either kidney failure or rheumatic fever. In accordance with the custom of the era, he was buried the next day in an unmarked communal grave, with no mourners in attendance.

About the
Translator

J. D. McCLATCHY IS THE AUTHOR OF SIX COLLECTIONS
of poems, most recently *Mercury Dressing* (Knopf). He has also
written three books of prose, and edited dozens of other books,
including *The Whole Difference: Selected Writings of Hugo von
Hofmannsthal* (Princeton University Press). *Opera News* has
called him "arguably the most important librettist on the current
American opera scene." The many librettos he has written for
leading composers of the day, as well as his singing translations,
have been performed at the Metropolitan Opera, Covent Garden,
La Scala, the Los Angeles Opera, the New York City Opera, and
other opera houses around the world. In 1999 he was elected to
the American Academy of Arts and Letters, and currently serves
as its president. He teaches at Yale University, is editor of *The
Yale Review*, and lives in Stonington, Connecticut.